W9-CCM-771

ENCYCLOPEDIA OF EDUCATION

SECOND EDITION

EDITORIAL BOARD

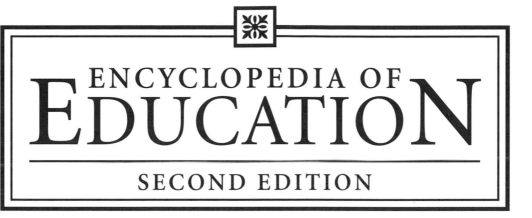

ENCYCLOPEDIA OF EDUCATION

SECOND EDITION

James W. Guthrie, Editor in Chief

VOLUME

7

States–Zirbes

**MACMILLAN
REFERENCE
USA™**

THOMSON

GALE

New York • Detroit • San Diego • San Francisco • Cleveland • New Haven, Conn. • Waterville, Maine • London • Munich

Encyclopedia of Education, Second Edition

James W. Guthrie, Editor in Chief

For permission to use material from this product, submit your request via Web at http://www.gale-edit.com/permissions, or you may download our Permissions Request form and submit your request by fax or mail to:

Permissions Department
The Gale Group, Inc.
27500 Drake Road
Farmington Hills, MI 48331-3535
Permissions Hotline: 248-699-8006 or
800-877-4253 ext. 8006
Fax: 248-699-8074 or 800-762-4058

While every effort has been made to ensure the reliability of the information presented in this publication, The Gale Group, Inc. does not guarantee the accuracy of the data contained herein. The Gale Group, Inc. accepts no payment for listing; and inclusion in the publication of any organization, agency, institution, publication, service, or individual does not imply endorsement of the editors or publisher. Errors brought to the attention of the publisher and verified to the satisfaction of the publisher will be corrected in future editions.

LIBRARY OF CONGRESS CATALOGING-IN-PUBLICATION DATA

Encyclopedia of education / edited by James W. Guthrie.—2nd ed.
   p. cm.
Includes bibliographical references and index.
   ISBN 0-02-865594-X (hardcover : set : alk. paper)
   1. Education—Encyclopedias. I. Guthrie, James W.
   LB15 .E47 2003
   370'.3—dc21
                                      2002008205

ISBNs
Volume 1: 0-02-865595-8
Volume 2: 0-02-865596-6
Volume 3: 0-02-865597-4
Volume 4: 0-02-865598-2
Volume 5: 0-02-865599-0
Volume 6: 0-02-865600-8
Volume 7: 0-02-865601-6
Volume 8: 0-02-865602-4

Printed in the United States of America
10 9 8 7 6 5 4 3 2 1

S

CONTINUED

STATES AND EDUCATION

LEGAL BASIS OF STATE RELATIONS TO NONPUBLIC SCHOOLS

In the United States' federal system, states carry out the function of providing for the education of their citizens. The U.S. Constitution does not specifically identify education as a federal obligation and the Tenth Amendment to the Constitution reserves to the states those areas not specifically delegated to the federal government. Historically, since the early nineteenth century, towns and villages provided education and this practice continues in the early twenty-first century with local governance by school boards and similar entities.

In the early twenty-first century, states provide for compulsory education of children, typically through age sixteen. State governing boards make policy and promulgate regulations for public and nonpublic schools within a framework established by state law and state and federal constitutional requirements.

State Regulation and Parental Choice

Although states gradually assumed more responsibility for providing public education, nonpublic schools also formed in order to carry out the particular areas of emphasis. In the twentieth century, as the country strove to assimilate diverse populations, states sought to impose restrictions upon nonpublic schools. A series of court decisions provided the legal framework for the right of parents to choose schools appropriate for their own children.

Robert Meyer, a teacher in a nonpublic parochial school challenged his conviction in 1920 under a Nebraska statute that prohibited the teaching of German to elementary school age children until they had passed the eighth grade. The purpose of the statute was to "Americanize" Nebraska's increasingly diverse population. In *Meyer v. State of Nebraska* (1923), the United States Supreme Court ruled the statute unconstitutional since it effectively deprived the parents of a liberty right—the right to chose their children's school—in violation of the U.S. Constitution Fourteenth Amendment due process clause. The Court affirmed the right of states to regulate education even to the point of requiring that the instruction be carried on in English: "The power of the state to compel attendance at some school and to make reasonable regulations for all schools, including a requirement that they shall give instructions in English, is not questioned." The Court also ruled, however, that there was no adequate foundation for the statute: "No emergency has arisen which renders knowledge by a child of some language other than English so clearly harmful as to justify its inhibition with the consequent infringement of rights long freely enjoyed. We are constrained to conclude that the statute as applied is arbitrary and without reasonable relation to any end within the competency of the state." The Court opinion was grounded on the constitutionally protected liberty interests of the parents and the teacher. "His right thus to teach and the right of parents to engage him so to instruct their children, we think, are within the liberty of the amendment."

When the state of Oregon enforced a statute compelling every child between the ages of eight to sixteen years of age to attend public schools, the U.S. Supreme Court affirmed the right of parents to chose nonpublic schools. In 1924 in *Pierce v. Society of Sisters,* the court upheld the right of the Society of Sisters and another private school challenger to operate their schools and affirmed the right of the state to regulate nonpublic schools. The court again reaffirmed the right of the state to regulate private schools.

> No question is raised concerning the power of the State reasonably to regulate all schools, to inspect, supervise, and examine them, their teachers and pupils; to require that all children of proper age attend some school, that teachers shall be of good moral character and patriotic disposition, that certain studies plainly essential to good citizenship must be taught, and that nothing be taught which is manifestly inimical to the public welfare.

Parents, however, have rights.

> The fundamental theory of liberty upon which all governments in this Union repose excludes any general power of the State to standardize its children by forcing them to accept instruction from public teachers only. The child is not the mere creature of the State; those who nurture him and direct his destiny have the right, coupled with the high duty, to recognize and prepare him for additional obligations.

Several years later, parents challenged a Hawaiian statute that prohibited attendance at foreign language schools until after the second grade and limited attendance to such schools to six hours per week and specified the curriculum. The schools were regulated in order that the Americanism of the pupils may be promoted. In *Farrington v. Tokushige,* 1927, the U.S. Supreme Court held the law was unconstitutional because its enforcement according to the court "would deprive parents of fair opportunity to procure for their children instruction which they think important and we cannot say is harmful."

Types of Nonpublic Schools

Most states recognize three types of nonpublic schools: private schools without religious affiliation, religiously affiliated private schools, and home schools. According to the U.S. Department of Education, the total nonpublic school student population in 1999 was about 5.2 million and represented about 10 percent of the total U.S. elementary and secondary school population, a percentage that had not changed significantly in the preceding years. Religious schools represented about 80 percent of the total nonpublic schools. Home schools represented a new and rapidly growing option although they did not educate a significant percent of the total school population. Estimates suggest that the home school population is growing about 10 percent to 15 percent per year.

State Regulation

States can regulate nonpublic schools under their police powers relating to health and safety. Further, because education is compulsory, states possess the authority to promulgate requirements concerning areas such as teacher qualifications, time spent in class, and curriculum. A balance is involved. States may encounter legal challenges if their regulatory activities are determined to be so intrusive as to obliterate the mission of the nonpublic schools, if the regulation is found to be arbitrary, or if the regulation represents an unconstitutional intrusion into religion. Challenges to state regulation of nonpublic schools are typically based on the principles of parental choice, free speech, or religious freedom.

Wisconsin v. Yoder (1972) is a classic case in which Amish parents objected to a state requirement that their children must attend school until they were sixteen, a requirement in conflict with Amish parents' tradition of training their own children after the eighth grade. The U.S. Supreme Court ruled that given the particular nature of the Amish religion and its documented record of beliefs, this regulation violated the free exercise rights of the Amish. The Court, however, again reaffirmed the right of the states to regulate education: "There is no doubt as to the power of a State, having a high responsibility for education of its citizens, to impose reasonable regulations for the control and duration of basic education."

In *State v. Whisner* (1976), Tabernacle Christian School, a school affiliated with a fundamentalist

Christian church, objected to certain minimum standards required for Ohio schools that included, as the Ohio Supreme Court found, "the content of the curriculum, the manner in which it is taught, the persons who teach it, the physical layout of the buildings, the hours of instruction, and the educational policies intended to be achieved." The Court particularly examined the rule requiring that four-fifths of the total instructional time per week must be devoted to language arts, mathematics, social studies, health, citizenship, and optional foreign language, and one fifth to physical education, music, art, special activities and optional applied arts. The school argued that these requirements precluded the teaching of other subjects such as additional instruction in religion.

The court reasoned that First Amendment free exercise protections and that parental rights placed a burden on the state that only could be met if the state could demonstrate a compelling need for the regulation. The state must demonstrate that the regulation is the only way the state could achieve its objective of providing a "general education of high quality."

The court ruled Ohio failed to meet this burden when it concluded that the standards were "so pervasive and all-encompassing that total compliance with each and every standard by a non-public school would effectively eradicate the distinction between public and non-public education," and therefore would deprive the parents of their "traditional interest as parents to direct the upbringing and education of their children."

States have broad jurisdiction in regulating nonpublic schools, leading to a wide variation in regulation and therefore the regulations of these schools varies among the states. States may not prohibit teaching certain subjects but they may prescribe a core curriculum. States often require instruction in the U.S. Constitution and the history of the United States. Some states require that nonpublic schools teach "patriotism" or "good citizenship."

State regulation of nonpublic schools can cover the following areas: record keeping, length of school year and day, teacher certification, curriculum, health, evidence of immunization, and safety, including fire prevention, guns prohibition, and child abuse reporting.

During the early years of the country's history most schooling occurred in the home. Over time, many states adopted legislation prohibiting home schooling. Since there is not any federal constitutional basis for claiming a right to home school a child, parents' efforts focused on obtaining enabling legislation at the state level. Currently, states permit home schools and state regulation is minimal, generally covering such areas as training of parents, hours and days of attendance, and required tests. There have been legal challenges to state regulation such as requirements that home-school teachers be certified, requirements that home-schooled students take nationally standardized achievement tests, and regulations regarding fire and health codes. An area of continuing litigation relates to efforts by home-schooled children to select certain benefits from the public school system such as participating in extracurricular activities, like athletics and music programs. Few state courts have sustained claims by home-schooled children to a right to participate in extracurricular activities.

Public Funding of Nonpublic Schools

Although many nonpublic schools eschew state regulation, some seek federal or state financing of certain educational components of their schools. The controversies arise when the aid is available to a sectarian school, or students in that school, raising issues related to the First Amendment establishment clause prohibition against government aid of religion and similar state constitutional prohibitions.

The U.S. Supreme Court approved public support of school bus transportation for both public and nonpublic students as early as 1947. Subsequently, the Court developed a three-part test to measure the constitutionality of public funding. In *Lemon v. Kurtzman* (1971), the court ruled that government action must satisfy the following requirements: (1) have a secular legislative purpose; (2) have a primary effect that neither advances nor impedes religion; and (3) avoid excessive government entanglement with religion. The decision led to a series of conflicting decisions that prohibited use of public school teachers in parochial schools to teach remedial education, sustained tax deductions from the state income tax for school expenses paid to a public or a nonpublic school, and allowed regular textbooks to be loaned to students who attended a nonpublic school.

Eventually, the U.S. Supreme Court moved away from the Lemon test and toward a "neutrality" principle that appears to sanction more government accommodation toward religion. The result is reflected in the overruling of some precedents and permitting a closer connection between public funds and religious schools and their activities. The court, in 1993, sanctioned public funds to employ a public school teacher to interpret for a hearing impaired student in a parochial school. In 1997, the court sustained use of public funds to pay for public school teachers to provide remedial education to disadvantaged children on the premises of parochial schools.

The constitutional battles will continue since the stakes are high for nonpublic schools and for the states as they try to steer through the constitutional maze of what is and what is not permissible under the religion clauses proscriptions.

The Public Nature of Nonpublic Schools

Although some nonpublic schools seek funding for various programs, others voluntarily submit to minimum state regulation in order to have their programs approved by the state. Benefits from such approval include the acceptance of courses and credits when students transfer to a public school, and teacher accrual of teaching experience for purposes of placement on the public school salary scale if they become employed by a public school. Such voluntary state regulation must not be intrusive or arbitrary and must be accomplished within constitutional proscriptions.

New challenges to state regulation may arise as states increase their accountability efforts by developing "high-stakes" end-of-course tests that students must pass in order to graduate. If states require nonpublic students to take these tests, challengers may argue that the state is effectively establishing curriculum and is intruding on the right of the nonpublic school to certify its graduates.

Other new areas of government policy will contribute to a further blurring of the line between public and nonpublic schools. For example, public models similar to some nonpublic schools may be established through choice programs that permit the establishment of public charter schools with more latitude in decision-making and resource allocation. If state voucher programs expand, recipients of voucher funds may be required to comply with additional state requirements that could contribute to a blurring of the distinction between public and nonpublic schools.

Through the litigation and legislative initiatives, states seem to have developed accommodations in regulating nonpublic schools by balancing the need to ensure that children receive adequate educational opportunities with the need to recognize legitimate religious claims and parental rights.

See also: CONSTITUTIONAL REQUIREMENTS GOVERNING AMERICAN EDUCATION; HOME SCHOOLING; PRIVATE SCHOOLING.

BIBLIOGRAPHY

BJORKLUN, EUGENE C. 1996. "Home Schooled Students: Access to Public School Extracurricular Activities," *Education Law Reporter* 109(1), June 27.

NATIONAL CENTER FOR EDUCATION STATISTICS, U.S. DEPARTMENT OF EDUCATION. 2000. *Education Statistics Quarterly* 2:124.

KENT M. WEEKS

STATE ADMINISTRATIVE SERVICES IN EDUCATION

Power to administer school and college programs is shared among state bodies and the governing boards of school districts, community colleges, public universities, and private entities. Since the U.S. Constitution does not refer to education, jurisdiction over education is left to the states and the people, although states may not, in their actions, violate the Constitution. Forty-nine of the fifty state constitutions call for "uniform," "thorough," or "efficient" educational systems that make schooling available to all. In accord of these constitutions and court rulings, states have enacted legislative statutes to establish school districts, colleges, universities, and separate schools for special purposes. To each has been given a significant degree of autonomy to make many of the crucial decisions by which education is shaped. Chief responsibility for operating education has been placed on their shoulders, while both external accrediting bodies and state agencies hold them accountable for their performance. In the mid-twentieth century, education could fairly have been termed a local matter, since state frameworks established early in the century made it so; that era has passed. Hawaii has been the exception as it entered the Union without local school districts for elementary and secondary education.

Elements of state governments—including state boards of education, state superintendents, state departments and boards for higher educational institutions—perform a number of crucial roles in each state's education system. Constitutions and statutes assign them significant powers as overseers, as formulators, and as enforcement officers to propose, draft, and carry out legislation. They serve as auditors of local unit performance and as reporters on what is transpiring, or what should transpire, with respect to education in the state. In addition, each state has at least one state-level agency charged with providing services—as distinguished form regulatory actions—to local units in order to assist them in developing the capacity to deliver effective educational services.

Thus, the people of the states have established and are continuously modifying a statutory division of power and accountability between local units and state government administrative agencies. In this system, a state administrative agency is not directly in charge of educational performance in the state (with the exception of Hawaii). It usually discharges its administrative function by influencing local units that use a variety financial and regulatory means. In many states, this influence has grown dramatically since the mid-1960s when the federal government took on as a goal the strengthening of state educational agencies. Reflecting this growth in the state role, by 2001 twenty-three states had adopted legislation allowing direct administrative control of local unit by the state in order to address unresolved fiscal and educational problems, including "academic bankruptcy," that is, chronically poor performance by students. Also, between 1991 and 1999 thirty-six states passed legislation allowing the creation of new local units—charter schools—to offer publicly funded competition to existing local school districts.

State Administrative Agencies

Most states have multiple administrative agencies for education. All have a state educational agency, typically titled the *state department of education* or *state department of public instruction,* that handles administrative concerns for early childhood, elementary, secondary, and vocational programs. In some states this same agency also is responsible for adult education, vocational rehabilitation, and higher education. The majority of states, however, have a separate agency that provides administrative coordination for state-supported colleges and universities.

It would be misleading to imply that state administrative services to local units are always so neatly packaged. These two types of agencies usually have duties and powers extending beyond the confines of their primary concerns. State education agencies may preside over the state's program for vocational rehabilitation or operate certain colleges, special schools, or custodial institutions. Most are involved in higher education through their power to approve college programs for the preparation of teachers. Similarly, coordinating state agencies for higher education may serve as administrators of student loan programs or may affect high school programs by establishing uniform entrance requirements for all state-supported colleges. As an added complication, voluntary accrediting associations of schools, colleges, and professional programs have concurrent jurisdiction over many of the same matters as the state agencies.

In addition, state government structure is typically pluralistic in designating agencies to perform state-level administration of education-related matters. For example, a separate state building authority may administer a large program of capital outlay for building construction; as well, the purchase and equipment of school buses may be under the jurisdiction of a state purchasing authority. Assessment of K–12 students, required by forty-eight states in 2001, is often the responsibility of a distinctive unit or agency.

In nearly all states, the requests for legislative appropriations by public institutions of higher education are screened by at least one state budgeting agency in addition to the coordinating agency established for higher education. The power to audit and report publicly on expenditures, a significant administrative control, typically resides in a state auditor's office, which acts independently of the education agencies. Surplus agricultural commodities, crucial to school lunch programs, are often handled by a separate administrative agency, as are state building codes for school and college structures. The total list of such dispersed responsibilities has increased as units linked to federal categorical grants have developed their own identity and serve to link the federal government to the management of specific local programs. Although the dispersal of authority may not constitute a negative factor affecting the ability to provide good government, they do compound the complexity of state administrative services to local education units.

Also complicating administrative services is their commingling with leadership services. For example, the state education agency usually has the power to promulgate a set of curriculum standards for all schools of the state. This administrative service, however, is used as a vehicle to promote and develop local unit capacity and willingness to provide good instruction—a leadership service. For example, if "authentic assessment" is used as a part of standards-based testing of students, the state will typically offer professional development programs to inform teachers how to instruct students to perform effectively. Although state education agency functions normally are classified either as regulatory (administrative) or leadership (developmental), the line between these functions is largely obscured in practice.

Revenue Services

Revenue available to local units is largely controlled by state law and legislative appropriations rather than by state administrative agencies (which often act more as lobbies than disinterested civil agencies). A common feature of state law is the requirement that local school districts make an effort to derive revenues from local taxes, usually the property tax, before they can become eligible for state transfer payments. In many states, a state administrative agency (usually not the state education agency) determines the valuation of property upon which a district's require effort should be based.

Distribution of state-collected taxes to local school districts is preponderantly by formula; the state agency applies the formula, verifying the base figures, and processes the distribution with few judgmental actions. Some state education agencies, however, are influential with legislatures in changing the amounts of revenue to be distributed from state-collected taxes and in establishing the statutory formulas for distributing state aid. All states distribute some state-level revenue among local districts on an approved-program or approved-need basis, with a state agency as the approving authority. For example, special aid for special needs students is frequently allotted only after a state agency has determined the need and has been satisfied that the agency's criteria for an adequate program has been met. This type of judgmental revenue distribution is typical for vocational education and new categorically funded programs that address particular issues. Reflecting concern that too much is spent "outside the classroom," restrictions on the proportion of funds that may be spent on noninstructional purposes have become common, as have expenditure and tax rate limitations, the latter dating back to California's Proposition 13 and the "property tax revolt" of the late 1970s.

Revenue for capital outlay purposes is preponderantly within the jurisdiction of local units. In a few states, however, a state building authority may issue bonds against the credit of the whole state and use the proceeds to finance construction within local units. This device, adopted for example in Arizona as the result of a court case that found local funding of school buildings to be unconstitutional, results in considerable state agency control of most facets of school housing even as it benefits those districts that could not afford adequate school accommodations on their own. In other states an annual distribution of current state revenue is made on a formula basis to local units, which are accorded the privilege of issuing debentures against future receipts for the construction of their physical plant. This approach is closely regulated by the state. State agencies in several states have a variety of approval functions with respect to local bond issues to ensure that excessive debt is not undertaken or that debt is incurred for spurious purposes. Also significant is the availability of advisory and consultative services in state education agencies for use by local units—chiefly small ones—in handling bond issues and sales. In higher education state agencies are active in determining what revenue shall be available for construction at individual colleges and universities as the "echo" to the baby boom enters its postsecondary phase.

State-supported colleges and universities depend heavily upon legislative appropriations for operating revenue, although in the early twenty-first century tuition, federal, and private funding make up more than half the revenue of many nominally public institutions. In some states, state-collected taxes are a significant revenue source for the private sector of higher education as well. A state's coordinating board for higher education typically exercises considerable authority in determining the distribution of appropriations among eligible institutions. Usually that agency develops distribution formulas; sometimes it sits in judgment on each institution's request before the legislature acts. At least one other state agency conducts similar reviews in states with coordinating boards, and all states have at least one agency, such as the executive department budget office, empowered to advise the legislature on higher education appropriations.

In states that authorize state contracts with private institutions for educational services, an administrative agency usually has considerable ministerial power in awarding contracts. In the late 1990s, actual appropriations to individual state-supported institutions were largely determined in the majority of states by transactions between the legislature and the state's higher education governing board (twenty-two states), coordinating body (twenty-one states) or planning agency and individual institutional boards. Consolidated governing boards exercise the most authority, including that for personnel, programs and budgets; coordinating bodies typically control programs and/or budgets or are advisory; planning agencies are advisory only. During the 1990s, there was a decisive shift toward the provision of greater power to oversight bodies, with an increase in the number of governing boards and in coordinating bodies, which exercised authority over both program and budgets.

With the advent of large federal government supports for education in the 1960s, state administrative agencies assumed expanded roles in the allocation of revenues to local units. Grants to school districts, private institutions, and state-supported colleges and universities are usually made in response to applications filed by those units. Under several pieces of federal legislation, a state agency reviews those applications and, in practical effects, makes or withholds awards. For example, the No Child Left Behind Act of 2001 is the most recent reauthorization of the Elementary and Secondary Education Act (ESEA), an act originally adopted in 1965 as part of President Lyndon Johnson's "Great Society" initiative. The current act includes nine sections or "titles" that detail numerous programs for areas such as technology, improvement of teaching, English language learning, and dropout prevention that are administered by the states, generally require formal application for funds, and may entail competition among applicants. In some cases consortia including higher education institutions are required. Currently, most federal funds assisting higher educational institutions do so by aiding students or research. State higher education agencies may be involved in administration with these programs as with the 529 college savings plans created under Sec. 529—Qualified State Tuition Programs of federal income tax legislation.

Accompanying the allocation of funds may be state-provided advisory services to enhance the capacity of local units in developing and operating projects. Agencies may develop master plans for developing program areas targeted by the federal government. State agencies have been actively involved in the administration of federal programs for more than a century, dating from the first vocational education legislation. The federal government tries to balance its own role, which now emphasizes accountability, with support for state agencies and local units. The No Child Left Behind Act requires all states to conduct annual academic assessments for grades three through eight and produce annual report cards describing school and statewide progress. Statewide reports must disaggregate data according to race, gender, and other criteria to provide evidence of closing the achievement gap between disadvantaged students and other groups of students. At the same time, to reduce federal red tape and enhance local control, it cuts the overall number of ESEA programs from fifty-five to forty-five and for the first time offers most local school districts the freedom to transfer up to 50 percent of the federal dollars that they receive among several education programs without separate approval.

Permanent state administrative agencies influence operating revenues of local units in a number of ways. State agencies usually accredit elementary and secondary schools. To meet accreditation standards, local taxing units may have to increase the funds they make available. Or, by offering state funds to support part of a given program and thereby reducing the tax price of education, they may stimulate the local taxpayers to provide additional support. As of January 2002, of the twenty-three states that were implementing high school graduate exit exams, twelve provided state funds for remediation. The reports and recommendations of state-level administrative agencies affect the state's allocation of general revenue for education, as have numerous court decisions concerned with the equity and adequacy of funds for both operating and capital expenses. As with the federal government, states have adopted competitive bidding for grants requiring applications, sometime termed *challenge grants,* thereby extending the influence of the funds allocated. The permanent state administrative agencies for education, however, have been relatively unsuccessful in securing revenue to support their own activities, particularly those directed toward capacity building in local units. In 1992 to 1993, states averaged $46 per pupil in state-level K–12 administration funding, with a ratio of 1,496 students per state staff member. Approximately 27 percent of the funding of $2 billion for came from the federal government and the number of staff ranged from 25 in Wyoming to 2,565 in New York and averaged about 575.

In the majority of states, the most dramatic influences upon educational revenue since the 1960s have come from outside the permanent administrative agency structure. Political influence has been brought to bear through both through all branches of government—executive, legislative and judicial. One mechanism has been the use education commissions and committees: temporary quasi-agencies created to appraise current provisions for and effectiveness of K–12 or higher education. The 1983 report of the National Commission on Excellence in Education, titled *A Nation at Risk,* stimulated the creation of more than 300 commissions and committees across the United States. Usually chartered by legislatures and/or governors, composed of lay citizens as well as legislators and educators and financed by government funds, these committees marshaled public opinion and legislative action to support large-scale school reform initiatives affecting programs (e.g., state curriculum and assessment), administrative arrangements (e.g., charter schools and mayoralty appointment of school boards in large cities), and state revenue structures (e.g., new standards of adequacy and a shift from the local property tax to earmarked state funds). Free to use resources of talent and publicity typically denied to administrative agencies, these committees often effectively supplement established government structures for supervising education. During the 1980s and 1990s, governors came to play an unprecedented role in educational policy as did the courts, which overturned dozens of state funding mechanisms as being inconsistent with state constitutions.

Expenditure Services

State control of the monies expended by local units for education is provided chiefly by two devices: legislative earmarking of funds to restrict the purposes for which they shall be spent and the requirement that local agencies submit annual operating budget. Increasingly, the latter task is accomplished over the Internet, with forms downloaded and uploaded using state-agency-designed forms or spreadsheets that conform to state-mandated codes of account.

Legislative Earmarking

State administrative agencies are usually charged with presiding over the sanctity of statutory or appropriation directives regarding the purposes for which state funds shall be spent. This responsibility involves educating local officials on the intricacies of the law and establishing guidelines and interpretations regarding legal stipulations. It also entails auditing local unit performance and may require withholding funds or other sanctions, including state takeover, to secure compliance. A large number of states have statutory stipulations that a certain portion of state funds shall be expended only for teaching salaries and that a state-adopted minimum teaching salary schedules shall be met. A state administrative agency administers this requirement, defining who is a teacher, checking on salaries actually paid, and preventing application of teaching-salary money to other objects of expenditure. Some states, concerned about the deterioration of buildings, increasing class sizes, or other shortcomings, have put restrictions of the amount of funds that may be used for functions such as administration.

When stipulations are programmatic (e.g., that state funds that should be used to improve literacy) the state administrative agency may function in advisory and developmental capacities more than in a regulatory capacity. Few state education agencies are staffed sufficiently to provide such services statewide, however. As a result, they tend to concentrate their efforts on smaller, weaker local units or those that have been identified as failing to meet state standards. Some state agencies actively collaborate with urban school districts to improve results from activities funded through earmarked state and federal funds. Greater federal accountability threatens the removal or reallocation of funds if improvements cannot be demonstrated.

Budgets

The Progressive movement of the early part of the twentieth century helped to establish a formal state role in funding education more equitably. At the same time, the state assumed a key role in establishing annual budgets for local units, a practice that has become universally taken for granted. As a result of the property tax revolt of the 1970s and 80s, commencing with California's Proposition 13, and court cases calling for more equitable funding, a number of states have moved to effectively fund education at the state level, implying that local budgets are set by these states. State education agencies advise local school districts on budget planning and may disseminate comparative data on budgeted items as a service to local school officials. In the typical state, state agencies lack the authority to modify local budgets when regulations are followed, but some states with strong agencies influence budgets through advice, persuasion, comparative reports, accrediting regulations, and public promotion. Sanctions adopted in the 1990s, such as state takeovers of fiscally and academically troubled districts, help to ensure that the agency's voice is heard.

The expenditure-control power of the state agency is also considerable in federally financed programs administered by the state. Reports on expenditures submitted to the state by local units are generally made public, sometimes on the Internet as a part of school and school district "report cards," ensuring that local units and the public at large has access to norms and averages. Records of expenditures also provide information that is useful for planning and for undertaking cost-effectiveness studies, although a tradition of local control has often undermined their use for systematic planning. "Every-student" databases that are being developed in a number of states, in part to ensure that students are not counted multiple times for state aid purposes, along with state and federal assessment data, are beginning to change this situation. The National Center for Educational Statistics (NCES), a federal agency that is part of the Department of Education, plays a central role in developing uniform methods of collecting and reporting fiscal, enrollment, program, and other data. It also helps to build the capacity of state agencies to mount more sophisticated information systems.

Local Unit Reorganization

Local unit reorganization affects both higher education and local school districts.

Higher education. The exponential postwar expansion in postsecondary education, much of it in state-supported state colleges and universities, slowed in the early 1970s as the "baby bust" replaced the "baby boom." Still, with higher rates of participation in higher education, especially for women, enrollment in degree-granting postsecondary institutions (including two-year colleges) increased by 16 percent between 1978 and 1988. From 1988 to 1998, enrollment increased another 11 percent from 13.1 million to 14.5 million, about three-quarters of which was

in public institutions. In 1998 to 1999 there were 613 public degree-granting institutions with four-year programs and 1,730 degree-granting private institutions with four-year programs; total enrollment in these institutions with four-year programs was 9,034,062 of which one-third was private. Of those students in private institutions, according to the National Center for Education Statistics, about 10 percent were enrolled in for-profit institutions (Table 171). Each state legislature has the final authority for establishing new four-year colleges, universities, and professional schools. In a majority of states, governing or coordinating bodies have key responsibilities and powers, including making public recommendations as to the establishment of new institutions or campuses. Indeed, legislatures often will not act without such a recommendation, although such a recommendation does not guarantee action. Governing and coordinating bodies also define the role and scope of each institution, provide the legislature with a master plan for higher education, and sometimes establish enrollment limits for existing institutions.

Community colleges, formerly referred to as junior colleges, absorbed much of the growth in higher education during the boom years and experienced an expansion of their mission when the decline in the age-cohort for transfer programs made the provision of career and vocationally oriented programs advantageous. According to the National Center for Education Statistics, in 1998 to 1999 there were 1075 two-year public institutions and 652 two-year private colleges (Table 246). Total enrollment was 5,687,742, of which only 5 percent was private. More than 70 percent of the students in private institutions were enrolled in for-profit colleges. Local initiative is still the dominant force in the creation and expansion of community colleges and technical institutes; although in most cases state administrative agencies or coordinating bodies approve new plans and serve to link the institutions into a statewide network. Increasingly, at the behest of legislatures, governing boards and coordinating bodies for state colleges and universities have worked closely with their peer group for community colleges to improve the articulation between the two levels of high education. In some states, community college courses used for transfer purposes are specified explicitly and must be accepted by state universities so that students can plan their academic careers.

Local school districts. Reorganization of local school district structures, long a preoccupation of states, shifted direction in the 1990s from a focus on consolidation to the creation of a new a new form of local unit, the charter school. Looking back, between 1946 and 1966, thirty-eight states carried out major consolidation of school districts, a number made more impressive by noting that most Southern states have always operated on a county or parish basis. Between 1961 and 1968 alone, the number of districts declined from 37,000 to 22,860, the latter figure including 15,824 districts that enrolled fewer than 1800 pupils. The rate of decline has slowed: between 1989 to 1990 and 1997 to 1998, the number of districts declined from 15,367 to 14,805 including 10,508 with fewer than 2,500 enrollees. Although the number of districts with fewer than 2,500 decreased during the decade, the number of districts with more than 2500 students increased. Those having more than 25,000 students climbed in number from 179 to 230, according to National Center for Education Statistics (Table 88). Rapid urbanization brought structural problems at both ends of the scale: metropolitan areas outgrew the traditional districting principle—a sophisticated urban center surrounded by more traditional rural areas—as suburban district enrollment grew and both rural and urban centers declined, with the latter districts often inheriting the responsibility for a minority population that has never enjoyed adequate educational opportunities.

The creation of charter schools as an alternative to traditional local educational units began in Minnesota in 1991. California followed suit in 1992. By 1999 thirty-six states, Puerto Rico, and the District of Columbia had passed charter legislation. Since 1994 the federal Department of Education has provided grants to support states' charter school efforts, from $6 million in fiscal year 1995, to $100 million in fiscal year 1999, when more than 1,700 charter schools were in operation. Of these, 58 percent were elementary schools, 20 percent secondary schools, and 22 percent included grades at both levels. Arizona, with more than 300, has the largest number of charters, followed by California (234), Michigan (more than 175), Texas (more than 150), and Florida (112).

Charter schools vary from state to state and are significantly influenced by legislation.

The laws cover seven areas: charter development—who may propose a charter, how charters are granted, the number of charter schools allowed, and related issues; school status—how the school is legally defined and related governance, operations, and liability issues; fiscal—the level and types of funding provided and the amount of fiscal independence and autonomy; students—how schools are to address admissions, non-discrimination, special education, etc.; staffing and labor relations—whether the school may act as an employer, which labor relations laws apply, and other staff rights and privileges; instruction—the degree of control a school has over the development of its instructional goals and practices; accountability—whether the charter serves as a performance-based contract, how assessment methods are selected, and charter revocation and renewal issues (uscharterschools.org).

In spite of quite radical actions by the states in the 1990s embodied in charter schools and district takeover legislation, state education agencies are not executive agents for reforming local district structures. The United States has held strongly to a tradition of local determination. When mandates are issued, they flow chiefly from legislative enactments. Laws fostering consolidation usually offer incentives to districts. On occasion, independent state commissions have been created to propose redistricting in a given territory but then accept locally originated counterproposals. Charter school laws typically require local initiatives to launch a school, thus reflecting the American tradition of local determination.

Redistricting is, in short, a political process and state education agencies move within limitations imposed by this fact, particularly because they represent the state while existing districts represent local control. Nevertheless, state education agencies exert influence over district structure, the amount of such influence varying between states. In many states, the agencies are supported by statutory discretionary power in applying those criteria. On occasion, they must enforce (that is, work out) new legislative mandates or are instructed, in effect, to promote the inducements to consolidate. State agencies may take the initiative and foster local action by using consultation and public advocacy or turn to de facto sanctions by strict application of state accreditation standards that are difficult for very small units to satisfy. A few state education agencies may undertake, usually upon request, surveys of district structure in a given territory and make recommendations based on these surveys to local authorities or interested citizens' groups. The greatest source of state agency influence lies in the reports and recommendations provided to state legislatures, study commissions, and other groups.

Curriculum and Instruction

State administrative agency influence on curriculum and instruction, including vocational education, is substantial at the elementary and secondary level and notable in some program areas in higher education.

Elementary, secondary, and vocational. In elementary and secondary education, including vocational education, state education agencies have statutory power to significantly influence what is taught in local school districts. Typically, the agencies are empowered to prescribe minimal course offerings and outline course content. They also establish standards for accrediting schools; many of these standards deal with the quality of curriculum and the results of teaching as measured by state-administered criterion-referenced tests. In 2000 to 2001, all but three states (Iowa, Montana, and Wisconsin) used such assessments aligned to state standards in English/language arts and mathematics; about half of the states also examined science and social studies/history. Although no state limits the offerings of local schools to those approved by the state education agency, prevailing practice is to await state outlines for new high school courses before they are introduced widely. Experiments with online education by private and public suppliers to public school student, charter school students, and those being home schooled are challenging agencies to develop new guidelines about what constitutes instruction for both academic and financial purposes.

In vocational education, state practices usually require state agency approval of the details of each offering before it becomes eligible for reimbursement from state and federal funds. In some cases, the state education agency may prescribe or approve uniform tests linked to certification, which can have an important influence on curricula. Through its administration of federal programs, the state agency becomes involved in program control. State education agencies also may have statutory authority over the adoption of textbooks, content of instructional broadcasts, and the selection of audiovisual and technological resources, including software, pur-chased with state funds. Upgrading school and school district communication and computing capacity both for administrative and instructional purposes is a focal point in most states.

The milieu in which state education agencies operate exerts pressure to reduce regulatory implementation of statutes to a minimal level. Constructive influence arises chiefly from their advisory, leadership, and developmental services for curriculum, instruction, and assessment. The extent and quality of these services distinguish strong from weak education agencies. In the 1960s, before the Great Society initiative, state education agencies were primarily concerned with assisting small and high-need districts. Between 1965 and the *Nation at Risk* report in 1983, state agencies created developmental services to build local capacity across their states. Since 1983, pushed by governors, state legislatures, and the federal government, they have assumed a central role in translating national aspirations into effective programs at the local level.

Capacity building services include in-service education for teachers, statewide curriculum improvement studies and implementation, demonstration projects, and the compilation and provision of curriculum and methodological guides. Some agencies undertake vigorous promotion of certain curriculum reforms, enlisting the services of colleges, universities, and private providers. The power of the agency to specify curriculum may be used to create committees of expert teachers to formulate course guides. Several states have initiated Internet-based curriculum guides with linked resources and are experimenting with online testing in the classroom using central databanks of test items. Major information system and textbook companies play an active role in both testing programs and development of online capabilities.

These examples illustrate an important generalization: the role of the state education agency in the instructional realm is primarily that of persuader. The local school district, in most cases, is the final arbiter of the quality of instruction. In only exceptional cases will the state agency turn from persuading its way into the local district toward dictating to a district that which will be done. For assessments, however, they have been given the authority by both state and federal law to insist that districts measure and report on the progress of students.

Higher education. For institutions of higher education, no state administrative agencies carry out curriculum and instruction functions comparable to those that state education agencies perform for K–12 schooling. Some coordinating agencies have the authority to approve or disapprove specializations offered for degrees and have veto powers over new courses. These powers are aimed primarily at diminishing the proliferation of courses and the overlap of programs among institutions rather than developing course content, although in attempts to increase articulation between community colleges and universities some states have become quite directive. Statutes in coordinating-board (vs. governing board) states normally allow persuasive approaches including setting criteria and insisting on accountability. Indeed, state legislatures during the 1990s bolstered their power to do so.

Local Unit Personnel

Selection, retention, advancement, and dismissal of personnel are jealously guarded prerogatives of the local units. Yet these crucial decisions are constrained by statutory prescriptions and by ministerial actions of state administrative agencies. Statutes and legislative appropriations have much to do with the salaries that local units can offer and hence with these units' ability to attract recruits. Statutes frequently govern the contract provisions regarding teachers: conditions of tenure, fringe benefits including pensions, and the status of collective bargaining between employee organizations and governing boards particularly as they relate to working conditions (i.e., class size, hours of instruction, etc.). Statutes and court rulings limit the pupil-disciplinary actions of school officials, sometimes leading to employee dissatisfaction. Inadequate district revenue, sometimes caused by state funding regulations, and difficult social environments can result in school conditions that make it almost impossible to staff particular schools with certificated professionals. All states require state-issued licenses for teachers and other professional workers in the school systems. To implement and enforce these statutes, all states delegate some authority to state education agencies; some states delegate this authority to commissions that maintain records and adjudicate problems related to licensure.

State licensure is rare in higher education, applicable in a few instances to community college personnel. Tenure is seldom a subject of specific state statutes, although administrative law and court rulings sustain the necessity for due process in dismiss-

als. A state-coordinating agency for higher education may suggest uniform guarantees of academic freedom and tenure. In some cases, state labor legislation may facilitate collective bargaining by faculty in public postsecondary institutions. Coordinating agencies may also specify average salary levels in state-supported institutions and earned-degree status expected of faculty members. Most personnel matters, however, are within the jurisdiction of institutional (or multiunit system) governing boards.

Licensure Requirements

State education agencies exercise the greatest influence over local school district personnel through licensure of professional workers. States vary widely in the amount of discretionary leeway that is accorded to state education agencies. Some are very specific and others merely authorize the state education agency to design and implement a suitable certification framework. Most states fall between these two extremes although the trend during the 1990s was toward greater specification and concern about quality. The NASDTEC Manual on the Preparation and Certification of Educational Personnel for the Year 2000, published by the National Association of State Directors of Teacher Education and Certification, classifies state requirements in seven areas: broad academic study; assessment; ancillary and special education; general education; professional preparation; student teaching; and subject matter endorsement. All states mandate a bachelor's degree, subject matter study, and pedagogical study for entry-level teachers. Most states require examinations of basic skills, subject matter knowledge, and teaching knowledge examination for initial licensure. About one-third also require and assessment of teaching performance. All states have emergency routes through which districts can employ persons not qualified for standard certification and alternative preparation programs to expedite the entry of new teachers to the profession. State officials have considerable autonomy in establishing standard patterns for educational qualifications, but they also interpret whether standards are actually met. To local unit officials, some state agencies appear bound to the letter of the regulations while others are quite liberal in their interpretations, focusing on the broad intent of the regulations. In most cases, what is being licensed is a college transcript, not an individual; licensure is a mass-production enterprise. An alternative approach, developed by the National Board for

Professional Teaching Standards, certifies individual teachers; the board reports that forty-seven states offer inducements for individual teachers who already hold state licensure to gain National Board Certification.

State education agencies' licensure of teachers requires effective working relationships with the state colleges and universities that provide teacher education programs. The universal approach taken is the approval of institutions by a state agency based on one or more sets of standards. The state education agency establishes criteria for the approval of institutions offering programs for educators and for the approval of each program designed to qualify students for a given type of certificate or license. Advisory groups of nonagency personnel often formulate criteria. More than two-thirds of the states have formally or informally adopted one or more of regional accrediting standards or standards promulgated by the National Council for Accreditation of Teacher Education (NCATE) or by NASDTEC. Standards have become increasingly performance based. NCATE standards emphasize six areas: candidate knowledge, skills, and dispositions; assessment system and unit evaluation; field experiences and clinical practice; diversity; faculty qualifications, performance, and development; and unit governance and resources. Once an institution and its curricula are approved—typically for a five-year period—the institution merely certifies to the state agency that a given individual has satisfactorily completed an approved program and is recommended by the institution for licensure. The legal credential is then issued by the state education agency, usually for a given term subject to recertification requirements such as the completion of additional approved professional development courses.

The institutional approval process places the state education agency in at least a semi-accreditation role with respect to colleges and universities, private as well as public, and make for a degree of uniformity among teacher preparation programs. In the past, critics contended this approach placed too much faith in the integrity of individual colleges to prepare teachers properly, by making higher education institutions—not school systems and professional practitioners—the arbiters of personnel qualifications for teachers. Overreliance on course work was also faulted. The emergence of performance testing as part of the qualification process and more formal standards managed by national bodies, often with the support of federal funds, reflect credence given to these critics. Although there is growing accountability for teaching certification to and the direction to agencies outside of state education agencies, state agencies nevertheless maintain a legal monopoly on the function.

Administration in Local Units

Decisions and executive actions made within local units form the administrative core of American education, despite the steady trend toward nationalization of the educational endeavor. States direct local units to make many decisions through statutory law and traditions and yet influence those decisions and actions through the behavior of their state administrative agencies. Federal funding regulations, court decisions, and collective agreements similarly affect local choices by proscribing and prescribing available options. Although waivers may be available to promote or permit local experimentation and charter schools allow an alternative to traditional public schools, these initiatives operate at the margin.

Within institutions of higher education, state administrative agencies offer minimal levels of consultation and personal advice to influence decisions or executive actions of administrators. Nevertheless, recommendations made by such agencies may have considerable influence, as in the case of the prescribed form and content for fiscal appropriation requests that can affect policies on teaching loads or the emphasis accorded research activities. Reports, especially comparative ones, also influence local policies and procedures. Comparative analyses of institutions across a state or of comparable institutions in other states are standard instruments to argue for the need of additional resources, new programs, and the like. Concern about a potential shortage of qualified teachers between 2000 and 2010 as teachers from the baby boom generation retire and as enrollments increase has encouraged states to advise their colleges and universities to respond accordingly.

State agency regulations also influence administrative decisions by local school districts. As well, the agencies operate an array of consultative and instructional services in such areas as school transportation, fiscal accounting, school law, purchasing procedures, school–plant planning and construction, and information system development and operation. When new issues arise or new programs are introduced, agencies will often initiate systematic dissemination projects, often in partnership with professional associations or postsecondary institutions, to assist local units in responding appropriately. Management services and policy advice, however, are in most cases minimal.

Appeals of administrative decisions within local school districts may be made to the commissioner of education in most states. Quasi-judicial hearings are conducted on such matters as the dismissal of an employee, boundaries of school attendance areas, and allegations of impropriety in the award of contracts. Aggrieved parties also have access to the courts, although until established routes of appeal within the educational system have been exhausted, courts generally will not accept pleas. They may also turn to the state attorney general on debatable points of law, although they must first seek resolution through the office of the commissioner of education. In a number of states, issues related to collective bargaining legislation for teachers are the responsibility of a special agency that may invoke various means of dispute resolution.

Informing and Planning

State education agencies and coordinating bodies for higher education can be treated together as far as informing and planning is concerned. Statutes typically empower these agencies to collect and interpret data to monitor the operations of the total state educational system. Data are used to inform the public, school officials, and governmental authorities about a variety of inputs, processes and outputs. According to statutes, information collected should be used to appraise the results of education, the effectiveness of present arrangements, and the effects of legislative and educational strategies. Simultaneously, research conducted or commissioned by the agencies is used to suggest alternative educational means and to identify emerging demands upon and new challenges to the state's system. Ultimately, agencies propose recommendations for immediate and long-term plans to improved educational arrangements throughout the state.

Measured against such expectations, few state agencies perform adequately, in part because of scarce resources and political complexity. Data collection and statistical reporting, rather than elaborate master plans substantiated by sound research, are their forte. More often, a government commission or task force operating with adequate funds and substantial political capital will fill the breach, although federal planning grants also stimulate development of strategic initiatives.

Private Institutions

Some state administrative agencies charter privately incorporated institutions for education although the requirements to receive a charter vary widely in prescriptiveness. Private institutions need not seek accreditation, but most secondary and postsecondary institutions do so, thereby subjecting themselves to the same state agency influences as public institutions. The same situation pertains to approvals for teacher education and certification. State agencies also subject private institutions to enforcement of fire and other safety statutes. To benefit from many federal programs, private institutions accept the influence of those agencies with respect to fiscal accountability and program performance.

As private elementary and secondary institutions enter into agreements for cooperative instruction with public schools, state education agencies become more important in their affairs. The provision of vouchers that allow students in low-performing public schools to transfer to private schools may also bring involvement of a state agency. A number of states have statutes and appropriations permitting the state to purchase educational services from private colleges and universities; the state agency administering such provisions quite naturally exerts considerable influence upon the recipients. State-provided scholarships to students attending private institutions can also result in a state monitoring, if not supervising. Thus, private institutions are rarely as independent of the state as popularly believed.

Intermediate Units

Between the state and the individual school district are administrative units, which incorporate a number of school districts. Although county boards of education have provided this function in some states, in others regional services agencies have been created. During the late 1960s and early 1970s, for example, Texas created Educational Service Centers for each of twenty regions, Pennsylvania created Intermediate Units, and New York formed Boards of Cooperative Educational Services (BOCES). These entities have as their primary purpose the support of local school districts and the reduction of service redundancy to take advantage of economies of scale. Intermediate unit employees are simultaneously vendors, service providers, grant writers, financial and management specialists, researchers, advisers, advocates, and facilitators. Typical programs and service offered include adult education, cooperative projects, curriculum services, educational technology and media, psychological services, and the operation of regional special education and vocational schools.

These units are not, strictly speaking, branches of the state education agencies, but neither are they agents of local districts. Typically, they stand as district-controlled but state-allied agencies for connecting local districts with changing approaches to education. As an alternative to school district consolidation, they appear to have become established as a permanent fixture in many states. Although some speculated that they might evolve into the major planning units for educational services and gain strong financial support and ministerial authority, this has not been the case.

Context of State Agency Actions

To understand state administrative agency influence upon educational practice, at least four features of the context in which they operate should be noted.

First, in most states, state education agencies do not establish policy or develop procedures to be followed. Both of these critical functions come about through extensive participation of non-agency persons—local district employees, college and university personnel, citizen panels, outside consultants, and political staff in the executive and legislative branches. Non-agency committees frequently possess almost autonomous jurisdiction over certain matters—selection of state-approved textbooks or approval of new school construction, for example. Committees, sometimes including several hundred individuals, write state curriculum guides. Until the 1980s and 1990s, with the push to align state standards with assessment and teacher preparation, there were few administrative regulations that did not bear the imprint of local unit administrators serving as advisers.

Moreover, vast networks of influential groups and individuals surround state administrative agencies, just as they do state legislatures. Professional organizations, parent associations, special-interest groups, combinations of local units seeking fair treatment, legislators speaking on behalf of constituents, and private enterprises with a stake in decisions and regulations all lobby to obtain their goals. To conclude that the involvement of so many viewpoints and competing influences weakens the quality of state administrative agency decisions would be erroneous, however. Simply put, state agencies are not clusters of individuals concocting directives and plans in Olympian fashion to be imposed on the state educational system.

Second, state statutes reflect, to a marked degree, the principle of plaguing power with power. In very few domains is there a clear distinction between the authority of state agencies and the authority of local units. Statutory delegations are typically broad and vague; often, both parties can justly claims primary jurisdiction. For example, the question might arise as to whether the state agency has the right to determine who can serve as a counselor in a high school. The local unit can cite jurisdiction over student affairs; the state agency can say its power to accredit implies the power to specify who does what in a school. Or, the power of the governing board of a postsecondary institution to adopt an operating budget and the power of a state agency for higher education to approve budgets can conflict over an attempt to expand a local department of engineering to include optical engineering if the state agency does not think this content should be offered by that institution. It is a truism of administrative science that any agency tends to increase its field of jurisdiction and, in so doing, comes into conflict with the jurisdictions claimed by other agencies. Evaluating the work of state administrative agencies for education must take this constant tension into account.

Third, state administrative agencies develop reputations over long periods of time. Prevailing images of them vary tremendously from state to state. One agency may be viewed as competent, judicious, flexible, and the source of constructive influence; another may be seen as a regulatory body interested only in bureaucratic formalities; and a third as a minor bureau concerned with minutiae and processing paper. Deserved or not, these images persist and largely determine whether the state's political actions will be favorable toward the education agency, thereby affecting the roles of state agencies in relation to local units. Although history indicates that image transformations tend to occur very slowly, on occasion some states have dramatically transformed state education agencies almost overnight, reorganizing them and changing mandates in order to pursue state goals more effectively.

Fourth, the size and quality of staff in state administrative agencies have more to do with the agencies' influence than perhaps any other factor. Highly qualified staff with significant professional attainment, if placed in strategic positions to formulate policy, plan, and help to build local capacity, succeed where others would fail. With few exceptions, states do not provide attractive positions with the appropriate remuneration required to attract the best educational talent. Local units provide higher salaries, better fringe benefits, and the like, making it possible for them to lure promising individuals away from state agencies. State civil service classification systems often thwart efforts to obtain specialists and limit opportunities for advancement. Although federal funds and the increased attention paid to education by governors and legislatures have infused new talent into state education agencies, this talent often is clustered in special units dedicated to a particular programmatic activity, fragmenting rather than unifying the agency. Nevertheless, because of their role in assessment and quality improvement initiatives, most state education agencies are far more central to the unfolding drama of public education in 2002 than they were in 1965, in large part due to national aspirations fostered by federal initiatives.

See also: FINANCIAL SUPPORT OF SCHOOLS, *subentry on* STATE SUPPORT; SCHOOL BOARDS; STATE DEPARTMENTS OF EDUCATION; STATE EDUCATIONAL SYSTEMS; TESTING, *subentry on* STATEWIDE TESTING PROGRAMS.

BIBLIOGRAPHY

EDUCATION COMMISSION OF THE STATES. 1999. *Governing America's Schools: Changing the Rules. Report of the National Commission on Governing America's Schools.* Denver, CO: Education Commission of the States.

NATIONAL BOARD FOR PROFESSIONAL TEACHING STANDARDS. 2002. *Backgrounder.* Arlington, VA: National Board for Professional Teaching Standards.

NATIONAL CENTER FOR EDUCATION STATISTICS. 2002. *The Digest of Education Statistics: 2000.* Washington, DC: National Center for Education Statistics.

NATIONAL COMMISSION ON EXCELLENCE IN EDUCATION. 1983. *A Nation at Risk: The Imperative for Educational Reform.* Washington, DC: National Commission on Excellence in Education.

NATIONAL COUNCIL FOR ACCREDITATION OF TEACHER EDUCATION. 2002. *Professional Standards for the Accreditation of Schools, Colleges, and Departments of Education.* Washington, DC: National Council for Accreditation of Teacher Education.

TIMAR, THOMAS, and TYACK, DAVID. 1999. *The Invisible Hand of Ideology: Perspectives from the History of School Governance.* Denver, CO: Education Commission of the States.

INTERNET RESOURCES

EDUCATION COMMISSION OF THE STATES. 2002. "ECS Tools and Resources: K–12 Governance Structures Database." <www.ecs.org/clearinghouse/27/29/2729.htm>.

INTERNAL REVENUE SERVICE. 2002. "Internal Revenue Code, Title 26, Subtitle A, Chapter 1, Subchapter F, Part VIII, Sec. 529: Qualified State Tuition Programs." <www4.law.cornell.edu/uscode/26/index.html>.

KNOTT, JACK H., and PAYNE, A. ABIGAIL. 2001. "The Impact of State Governance Structures on Higher Education Resources and Research Activity." <www.igpa.uiuc.edu/publications/html/abstracts.html#stateGovt>.

NATIONAL ASSOCIATION OF STATE DIRECTORS OF TEACHER EDUCATION AND CERTIFICATION. 2001. "The NASDTEC Manual on the Preparation and Certification of Educational Personnel for the Year 2000," 5th edition. <www.gapsc.com/tom/>.

USCHARTERSCHOOLS.ORG. 2002. "Overview of Charter Schools." <www.uscharterschools.org/pub/uscs_docs/gi/overview.htm>.

STEPHEN B. LAWTON

STATE BOARDS OF EDUCATION

Education is legally a responsibility of state government in the United States. The Tenth Amendment to the U.S. Constitution states that "the powers not delegated to the United States by the Constitution nor prohibited by it to the states are reserved to the states respectively or to the people." Because the Constitution does not specifically mention education, this amendment serves as the legal basis for the historical evolution of education as a state function.

The New Context

For most of the nation's history, the states have exercised these responsibilities gingerly and have been a weak link in the federal system. It was not until the late twentieth century that the states have begun to proactively exercise their powerful legal responsibilities and great reservoir of unused power in the field of education. Most states, in congruence with the historical norms of local control of education, have traditionally delegated much of the operational responsibility for schools to local boards of education.

This pattern of unaggressive state leadership changed dramatically in the last quarter of the twentieth century. Public education without question has become the nation's most salient domestic public policy issue. The country's influential business and political leadership (on a bipartisan basis) have become engaged in unprecedented ways in implementing their commitment to improved public education. Presidents, governors, corporate CEOs, and state and federal legislators all proclaim the need for high standards and academic achievement for all children. This laser-like concern for and focus upon education has elicited escalating public demands and political pressure for the states to focus and discharge their legal responsibilities to improve the quality of education.

The Role of State Boards

State boards of education along with governors, legislatures, and state education agencies are integral components of the state policy system. State boards, which exist in all but two states (Minnesota and Wisconsin are the exceptions), are agencies with major general responsibilities for the development and management of public education within each state. Typically, the state board of education governs the state education department or agency. Although state boards have only recently become influential entities in a number of states, the aforementioned pressures to improve education will inevitably make them more visible and significant players in all jurisdictions.

Membership

There is enormous variety among the forty-eight states that have approximately 500 citizens serving on state boards of education. As Table 1 indicates, the states have numerous and wide variations in the manner in which members are selected, the size of their boards, and the length of terms of office.

Thirty state boards are appointed by governors subject to legislative approval in six states. Ten states elect their state boards: six on partisan and four on nonpartisan ballots. State boards are appointed by the legislature in three states (New York, Pennsylvania, and South Carolina). In four states (Louisiana, Mississippi, New Mexico, and Ohio) the state boards comprise both elected and appointed members. In Washington State, the state board consists of nine members elected by local school board members and one member elected by private schools.

The number of voting state board members also varies from a low of seven (in nine states) to twenty-one in Pennsylvania. There are thirty-eight states with seven to eleven members serving. Twelve states have a nine-member board, ten states have an eleven-member board, and nine states have seven member boards. These seven-, nine-, and eleven-member boards are the most prevalent in the nation.

The length of term of office for state board members likewise varies across the country. The term of office ranges from three years to nine years, the most common term by far being four years (in twenty-two states) and six years (in eleven states). The overwhelming number of states have statutes that require overlapping terms. Special provisions or unique features of state boards abound from state to state with infinite variety. For example, in Alabama the governor presides as president of the board. In Delaware, two of the seven state board members must have experience as local board members. In Indiana, four of the eleven members must be professional educators. In New Jersey, three of the thirteen members must be women. In Washington State, the chief state school officer can vote only to break ties. More generic or common provisions mandate residency requirements for board members and the exclusion of educators from board service in a number of states.

In the late twentieth century there was a trend toward more student participation on state boards. As Table 1 reflects, five states have students as voting members of the board and an additional five states have students as nonvoting members. This reflects the growing voice of students as testing and related policy issues come to the forefront. Table 1 also reinforces the wide structural and operational diversity that characterizes state boards with forty-eight boards having "unique features" and thirty-eight earning "special notes" to distinguish them from their counterparts.

TABLE 1

State education governance, 2001

State	Method of selection of state board members	Number of voting state board members	Length of term (years)	Method of selection of chief state school officer (CSSO)	Official role of chief state school officer on state board	Unique feature of state board	Special notes
Alabama	Partisan ballot	8 elected and governor	4	Appointed by state board of education	Secretary and executive officer	Governor sits as president of board	Four members elected in 1998 received two-year terms so that four members will run for election every other year
Alaska	Appointed by governor	7	5	Appointed by state board of education with approval by governor	Executive officer	Board appoints one non-voting student adviser and one non-voting military adviser	CSSO must have five years experience in education; three in administration
Arizona	Appointed by governor; confirmed by senate	9	4	Partisan ballot	Executive officer	Sits as vocational and technical education board	Requires three lay members
Arkansas	Appointed by governor	10	6	Appointed by state board of education	Agent ex officio	The CSSO serves at the pleasure of the governor	CSSO must have ten years experience as a teacher, including five in administration or supervision, and hold Arkansas teacher's certificate
California	Appointed by governor	11 including student member	4 (1 year for student)	Non-partisan ballot	Secretary and executive officer	Voting student member who has full participation rights	
Colorado	Partisan ballot	7	6	Appointed by state board of education	Secretary		
Connecticut	Appointed by governor, approved by house and senate	9	4	Appointed by state board of education	Secretary	The commissioner of higher education serves as an ex officio, non-voting member of the board	Beginning in 1998, two student members (non-voting) serve one-year terms on the board
Delaware	Appointed by governor, approved by senate. President serves at the pleasure of the governor	7	6	Appointed by governor	Executive secretary	Two state board of education members must have local board experience; must be a resident for five years in order to sit on board	Change from state board-appointed CSSO to governor-appointed CSSO occurred in 1997
Florida	Partisan ballot	7	4	Elected statewide	Secretary and executive officer	State board of education consists of seven elected cabinet members: governor, CSSO, secretary of state, treasurer/insurance commissioner, comptroller, attorney general, commissioner of agriculture	Has jurisdiction over the board of regents of the state university system and state board of community colleges

[continued]

TABLE 1 [CONTINUED]

State education governance, 2001

State	Method of selection of state board members	Number of voting state board members	Length of term (years)	Method of selection of chief state school officer (CSSO)	Official role of chief state school officer on state board	Unique feature of state board	Special notes
Georgia	Appointed by governor	11	7	Elected statewide	Executive secretary	Must be a resident for five years to sit on board	CSSO must have three years teaching experience
Hawaii	Non-partisan ballot	13	4	Appointed by state board of education	Executive officer	Non-voting student member selected by the state student council	
Idaho	Appointed by governor	8	5	Non-partisan ballot	Executive secretary and voting ex officio member of the board	Must be a resident for three years in order to sit on board; members are also regents of the University of Idaho	
Illinois	Appointed by governor	9	6	Appointed by state board of education	Chief executive officer	Requirements for regional and political balance on board	Chair is appointed by governor
Indiana	Ten appointed by governor and elected chief	11	4	Partisan ballot	Chairman and voting member	Four members must be educators; political balance is required	$2,000 per year for state board members
Iowa	Appointed by governor	9	6	Appointed by governor	Executive officer		
Kansas	Partisan ballot	10	4	Appointed by state board of education	Executive officer		
Kentucky	Appointed by governor	11	4	Appointed by state board of education	Executive secretary, executive administrator	President of council on postsecondary education is non-voting ex officio member; board members must be resident for three years, be at least thirty years old, and hold a two-year associate degree	Governor appoints secretary of education, arts, and humanities
Louisiana	Eight elected, three appointed by governor	11	4	Appointed by state board of education	Ex officio secretary		
Maine	Appointed by governor	9	5	Appointed by governor	None		
Maryland	Appointed by governor	12 including student member	4	Appointed by state board of education	Chief executive/ secretary treasurer	Voting high school student, which is a one-year appointment by the governor	CSSO must have seven years teaching experience and administration experience
Massachusetts	Appointed by governor	9 including student member	5	Appointed by state board of education	Board secretary and chief executive officer	Chancellor of higher education board is voting member; voting student elected by the state student advisory council	Board reduced from 15 to 9 members in August, 1996; current terms vary in length to provide transition period
Michigan	Partisan ballot	8	8	Appointed by state board of education	Chairman	Constitutional board with defined responsibility for K-12 education and more limited role in postsecondary	

[continued]

TABLE 1 [CONTINUED]

State education governance, 2001

State	Method of selection of state board members	Number of voting state board members	Length of term (years)	Method of selection of chief state school officer (CSSO)	Official role of chief state school officer on state board	Unique feature of state board	Special notes
Minnesota	None			Appointed by governor			State board ended operations as of December 31, 1999; most board authority was transferred to the commissioner of children, families, and learning
Mississippi	Five appointed by governor; four appointed by legislature	9	9	Appointed by state board of education	Executive secretary	Lieutenant governor and speaker of the house each appoint two members	CSSO must have five years administrative experience
Missouri	Appointed by governor with consent of senate	8	8	Appointed by state board of education	Chief administrative officer	Authority over university and community college system teacher education programs	
Montana	Appointed by governor	7	7	Partisan ballot	Ex officio member	Non-voting sudent member; governor is ex officio member	
Nebraska	Non-partisan ballot	8	4	Appointed by state board of education	Executive officer	Constitutional board	Teachers, state officials or candidates, and nonresidents are not eligible for board membership
Nevada	Non-partisan ballot	11	4	Appointed by state board of education	Secretary	Non-voting student member	
New Hampshire	Appointed by governor	7	5	Appointed by state board of education	None	Governor and council appoint state board of education	
New Jersey	Appointed by governor	13	6	Appointed by governor	Secretary	Three members of state board of education must be women	Resident for five years to sit on board
New Mexico	Ten elected/five appointed by governor	15	4	Appointed by state board of education	Chief administrative officer	Three appointed members are of same affiliation as governor who appointed them	
New York	Appointed by legislature	16	5	Appointed by state board of education	Chief executive officer	Responsible for higher education, cultural institutions, and licensed professions	
North Carolina	Appointed by governor	11	8	Partisan ballot	Secretary and chief administrative officer	Two teacher of the year advisers; two student advisers	
North Dakota	Appointed by governor	7	6	Non-partisan ballot	Executive director and secretary		Separate higher education board, separate community colleges board

[continued]

TABLE 1 [CONTINUED]

State education governance, 2001

State	Method of selection of state board members	Number of voting state board members	Length of term (years)	Method of selection of chief state school officer (CSSO)	Official role of chief state school officer on state board	Unique feature of state board	Special notes
Ohio	Eleven elected by non-partisan ballot; eight appointed by governor	19	4	Appointed by state board of education	Secretary and administrative officer	Separate board for higher education	Two ex officio members (non-voting)
Oklahoma	Appointed by governor	7	6	Partisan ballot	Chairperson of both state board and state board of vocational and technical education	State board members are ex officio voting members of the state board of vocational and technical education	New board member must take new board member training established by the state department during the first year of membership to remain on board
Oregon	Appointed by governor	7	4	Non-partisan ballot	Administrative officer	K–12 and community college authority	
Pennsylvania	Appointed by governor, confirmed by Senate	21	6	Appointed by governor	Chief executive officer	Statutory responsibility for postsecondary education	Also sits as state board for vocational education; four ex officio legislative members
Rhode Island	Appointed by governor	11	3	Appointed by state board of education	Chief executive officer	One member is appointed from house; one member is appointed from senate	Separate higher education board
South Carolina	Appointed by legislature	17	4	Partisan ballot	Secretary and administrative officer	Legislative delegations elect sixteen state board education members; governor appoints one state board of education member	
South Dakota	Appointed by governor	9	4	Appointed by governor	Executive officer		
Tennessee	Appointed by governor, confirmed by general assembly	10 including student member	9	Appointed by governor	Required to be present at state board of education meetings	Voting student member (one-year term), board selects executive director; serves as state board for vocational education	The board maintains its own staff apart from the department of education; executive director of higher education commission is ex officio, non-voting member of state board of education
Texas	Partisan ballot	15	4	Appointed by governor	Executive secretary	The state board of education is also the state board for vocational education	
Utah	Non-partisan ballot	15	4	Appointed by state board of education	Executive officer	The state board of education is also the state board for career and technology education	$3,000 per year for state board of education members

[continued]

TABLE 1 [CONTINUED]

State education governance, 2001

State	Method of selection of state board members	Number of voting state board members	Length of term (years)	Method of selection of chief state school officer (CSSO)	Official role of chief state school officer on state board	Unique feature of state board	Special notes
Vermont	Appointed by governor and approved by senate	9 including student member	6	Appointed by state board of education and approved by governor	Chief executive officer and secretary	Chair is elected by the board for two-year term	Two student members: one is appointed each year for a two-year term; student does not vote during first year of term, has full voting rights during second
Virginia	Appointed by governor	9	4	Appointed by governor	Secretary		Secretary of education is a cabinet member
Washington	Nine elected by local school board members, one elected by private schools	11	4	Non-partisan statewide ballot	Chief executive officer and ex officio member	CSSO votes only to break ties; private school representative votes only on issues affecting private schools; non-voting students and governor's representatives	
West Virginia	Appointed by governor	9	9	Appointed by state board of education	Chief executive officer		
Wisconsin	None			Non-partisan ballot			
Wyoming	Appointed by governor	11	6	Partisan ballot	Ex officio member	Meets quarterly; reviews all school accreditation compliance for approval or disapproval	Deputy CSSO is ex officio member and parliamentarian
District of Columbia	Five by non-partisan ballot; four appointed by mayor	9	4	Appointed by state board of education	Ex officio member	Board president elected at-large	Newly reconfigured board took office in January 2001
Guam	No central board; four district boards elected by voters in each district			Appointed by governor, confirmed by legislature	Chief executive officer		The CSSO (director of education) has policymaking authority for state-level functions
Northern Marianas	Elected	5	4			Serves as both the state and local school board	
Puerto Rico	Appointed by governor	7	5	Appointed by governor	None	General council on education is a state agency for licensing and accreditation of public and private schools from pre-school to postsecondary—not university level	

SOURCE: National Association of State Boards of Education website.

Basic Responsibilities

Although state legislatures have the ultimate legal authority for determining educational policy, a number of specific legal responsibilities have been delegated to state boards and are commonly shared. State boards generally serve as representatives of the larger public in conceptualizing and formulating the mission of the schools, and exercising overall leadership responsibility in the following areas:

- Standards setting
- Accreditation of state education programs
- Teacher and administrator certification
- Review of state education department budgets
- Promulgation of graduation requirements
- Development and implementation of state testing and assessment programs

The historical role of most state boards had been the articulation of rules and regulations that mandated only minimum standards with regard to matters such as subjects to be included in the curriculum, school construction, and school bus safety. This relatively passive role of state boards has changed with the advent of the standards movement.

The power state boards have to appoint the chief state school officers in twenty-five states (gubernatorial approval is required in two jurisdictions) may represent their most important responsibility. It is the state education agency that customarily staffs state boards. The chief thus is in a pivotal position to control the staff, agenda setting, and information flow through his or her authority as the line leader of the state education agency. As a full-time educator with the requisite professional standing and expertise, the chief is in the best position to determine whether state board policies are successfully designed and implemented.

State Boards and the New Politics of Education

As the nation's influential business and political leaders have asserted leadership in the education reform movement, the former, relatively closed, system of decision-making dominated by education groups has been opened to new players at all governmental levels. At the state level, governors, corporate leaders, legislators and governors' education aides, for example, frequently have become the drivers of policy changes preempting the traditional prerogatives of chief state school officers, and state education agencies as well as state boards.

This "new politics of education" and its attendant focus upon education reform have made state boards somewhat more visible or (at least) less invisible. As education has become a more significant policy concern at the state level, more attention is being paid to the caliber and influence of state board members. A governor appointing a state board member in the current environment is less likely to view the selection process as a midlevel patronage matter. The trend is toward designating influential higher status appointees who can move the governor's substantive agenda on increasingly visible and politically important education issues such as testing and accountability. In the past, governors would rarely interfere with the deliberations of their appointees and commonly took a "hands-off" posture on the relatively mundane issues that were on the agendas of the state board. This has changed dramatically at the start of the twenty-first century as the political stakes have escalated on education issues and growing numbers of state board members have moved into the mainstream of state politics.

These developments have been a mixed blessing for appointed state board members. The visibility and increased status of board members has certainly been a very positive development; on the other hand, board members are often less politically independent and not infrequently are viewed as being not civic leaders promoting education improvement but political agents of the governor.

As the standards movement has emerged as the often-controversial cornerstone of education reform, state board members have become much more publicly visible and engaged in highly volatile and complex issues such as testing and accountability. They have been far less insulated from state politics and in many cases have become influential participants in the ongoing policy debates about standards, assessments, and accountability. Many state board members likewise have become less parochial and currently are involved in national discussions as well as issues in their own states. There is, for example, keen interest among state board members in the possible fiscal and political implications of President George W. Bush's federal educational program on state powers and responsibilities.

In jurisdictions that elect their state board members the political dynamics are, of course, quite different. Elected officials understandably depend upon various special interest groups whose political power and financial resources can swing elections. State board elections, like their counterparts at the local level, do not customarily attract large voter turnouts. Indeed, candidates for state boards commonly are little known to the public. This provides organized interest groups with inordinate influence in state board elections. In other words, small core groups readily can control the composition of boards in elective states that provide very fertile ground for organized special interest groups to dominate the election process.

Changing Dynamics

The changing state politics of education has caused new sets of relationships among the several components of the state policy system. The new transcendency of education and the opening up of the once relatively closed policymaking system to business and political leaders has changed the relationship of state board members to other participants in the state policysetting process in significant ways. As school issues have become more embroiled in the political mainstream, chief state school officers, for example, have become more pleased to have influential state board members serve as buffers. In essence, many politically well-connected board members currently are positioned to provide valuable political cover for pressured appointed chiefs. On the other hand, in states in which chiefs are elected and have their own independent political base they can be more dismissive of their boards and in some cases even totally ignore them.

The recent visibility and political involvement of state board members have created new forms of pressure upon these formerly relatively obscure state officials. Early-twenty-first-century appointees are more likely to be very busy high-powered successful business and civic leaders who do not have the time to serve extended terms on state boards. As a result of growing turnover, the National Association of State Boards of Education (NASBE) estimates that the average tenure of its members has decreased from twelve to six years. Highly volatile struggles over the testing issue in states like Virginia and Massachusetts and the bitter struggle over evolution in Kansas reflect only a few examples of the conflicts that have engulfed board members in states where members are both appointed and elected. These highly controversial issues, not surprisingly, have attracted escalating media interest. The saliency of school issues at the state level has triggered the growth of coverage of state boards by a much more sophisticated and knowledgeable media corps.

Pivotal Role of Governors

The nation's governors see education as a "hot" issue, and as a result, all want to be viewed as "Education Governors." Whether they are Republican or Democrat or liberal or conservative, all governors are cognizant of the political rewards of being viewed as a proponent or supporter of education reform and improvement. These chief executives, of course, are the pivotal players in determining education policy in the states. State boards have not only been profoundly affected by the quality of gubernatorial appointments but they also have been influenced in states (where board members are elected as well as appointed) by more vigorous efforts of their governors to consolidate their power to determine and shape educational policy.

In their efforts to build a more diverse base of support for their policies, governors in many states have appointed broadly based influential commissions, roundtables, and/or advisory bodies to make recommendations about complex, controversial state-policy issues such as finance, teacher quality, standards, governance, and accountability. Issues such as these logically should be within the purview of the policysetting responsibilities of state boards. In essence, these gubernatorial or, on occasion, legislatively appointed entities are making recommendations that legally should be promulgated under the aegis of state boards. This not uncommon utilization of commissions and analogous groups certainly clouds and dilutes the authority of state boards. Governors, of course, view such entities as a means through which they can not only broaden support for desired policies but also buffer themselves from state boards that because of overlapping terms or turnover may not be politically responsive to their programs and not as controllable as time-limited commissions.

The recent increase in gubernatorial authority has been paralleled quite logically by the escalating influence of governors' aides in the state education policymaking process. These aides, while often young and not particularly experienced in education issues, usually are politically savvy and well-connected. Many have served as campaign aides to their governors and "have their ear" in special or unique ways. Their influence, while often unacknowledged, can hardly be underestimated as loyal and trusted confidants to the chief executives.

The Future

In the early twenty-first century, one can predict with much confidence that state boards will continue their climb out of obscurity in the years ahead. State board members will be increasingly visible and more influential public figures. Governors and the electorate will seek to have more business or private sector types serve on these bodies because they bring different and needed knowledge and understanding of budgets, management, and the changing demographics that are so profoundly reshaping U.S. society. The demographic revolution increasingly will reconfigure the composition of state boards with the inevitable designation of many more Hispanic Americans and citizens of color to serve.

State boards will continue to be under pressure to assume a more aggressive leadership role. They will be expected to provide guidance and advocacy in this enlarged leadership role. They must be more effective and "out front" mobilizers of public and community support for the school enterprise. They also must reach out as lay leaders in the mobilization of the coalitions that will be essential in the more participatory and complicated state educational politics of the future.

See also: School Boards; States and Education, *subentry on* State Governments in Higher Education; State Departments of Education; State Educational Systems.

Michael D. Usdan

STATE GOVERNMENTS IN HIGHER EDUCATION

As Paul E. Peterson states, studying higher education as an organization is challenging because the locus of control has changed. Higher education institutions have for most of their histories been governed by a sense of internal control with authority largely falling to the faculty and administration of the single institution. These institutions represent professional bureaucracies in which faculty seek control of their work and also solicit a voice in the decisions affecting their lives. In comparison to the more common machine bureaucracy form of business and industry, these professional networks are based upon mutual respect and dedication to the community. This rare form of organizational structure and control causes particular stress to elected officials accustomed to looking to profits for measures of success.

History of Local Control

Defining autonomy as "the power to govern without outside controls" and accountability as "the requirement to demonstrate responsible actions," Robert Berdahl posits that each side should realize that a balance is ideal (p. 38). Paula Sabloff characterizes the struggle between autonomy and accountability as inevitable and as a future force in higher education concerns. She argues that the relationship between state government and the institutions has always been involved in a debate between autonomy versus accountability. Throughout the last half of the twentieth century, regulations increased that inevitably stripped away institutional rights to govern themselves. Legislative members have increased their staff numbers and devoted themselves to much more of a year-round schedule of activities. The establishment of legislative standing committees has combined with governing and coordinating boards to create a constant regulatory environment for the individual campuses. Though higher education may not get caught up in partisan politics to the extent that other areas of government have, it is constantly part of a political process.

Higher Education and the Economy

In the 1980s economic development strategies shifted from the issues of labor, land, and taxes to a focus on investments in human resources and research. Economic and social viability is increasingly linked to "what you know" as much as they are to "what you do." In a 1998 report released by the American Association of State Colleges and Universities, the national job market was predicted to grow by 18.6 million positions between 1996 and 2006. Service industries were predicted to outpace the growth of goods-producing industries as a more knowledge-based economy replaces a skill dependent system. For the early twenty-first century, the report forecasts that jobs in professional specialties, such as business and health care, will supplant manufacturing and production in driving economic growth. Because of this new focus on human capital, public and private spending on education and training must be viewed as investments rather than consumptive costs, and a premium must be placed on lifelong learning.

Social scientists, such as Manuel Justiz in 1994, have pointed out that the radical demographic shifts being faced in America are prompting change more dramatically than government policy has ever done.

The importance of access to and diversity of participation in higher education is acknowledged because of the rapid developments in technology and changing workforce needs. In a report developed by the Institute for Higher Education Policy, the public and private benefits of going to college were distilled into four categories: (1) individual economic benefits; (2) public economic benefits; (3) individual social benefits; and (4) public social benefits.

State legislatures are much more specialized and informed at the beginning of the twenty-first century than they have been in the past and they continue to increase their involvement in higher education planning. Because of the myriad of benefits to be gained through a high quality higher education system, the stakes have been raised regarding cooperation between business interests, state government, and campus expertise. The public and private benefits associated with an increase in educational participation and attainment support the argument that a greater emphasis must be placed on an educated citizenry. As the global economy has put a premium on knowledge capital rather than manufacturing skills, employers and government officials are demanding a higher education of the work force than ever before.

Shift in Control

The postwar baby boom and explosion of higher education the 1960s led to the increased desire of state leaders to acquire more control of higher education matters. During that time of growth, states created many of the coordinating and governing boards that exist in the early twenty-first century. Although originally created to bring order and accountability to higher education, in some instances the boards have been allowed by the states to "become the centerpiece of top-level patronage politics and public score settling" (Graham, p. 93). Modeled primarily after the boards of trustees that have traditionally led private institutions, governing and coordinating boards have become permanent fixtures on the higher education map. Approximately 65 percent of students attend postsecondary schools that are a part of a multicampus system. As of 2000, state higher education structures basically fell into three categories: consolidated governing board systems, coordinating board systems, and planning agency systems. Under consolidated governing board systems, governance is centralized in one or two governing boards. Twenty-four states operate under this model. Coordinat-

ing board systems are also found in twenty-four states and provide for a liaison board between state government and the governing boards of individual institutions. Planning agency structures are only found in Delaware and Michigan. These agencies coordinate communication and planning with little direct authority over the institutions or their governing boards.

According to Peterson, around the mid-1970s institutions became much more aware of the growing external forces that were less controlled and much less understood by the general campus community. It was at this time that governing boards and publicly elected officials began exercising greater authority in the name of accountability. In the 1980s governors and legislators began seeking even more control over institutions through quality initiatives. Governors and legislators began expecting these higher education boards to exercise firm control of the institutions rather than working as advocates for them. As a result of giving new responsibilities and authority to the governing and coordinating boards, more opportunities for friction with the campus were created. Until this shift, faculty had a much more successful role in academic governance because local leadership largely shaped the control and mission of campuses. In order for shared governance to exist on a campus, it must be based on some level of commitment to coordination between faculty desires, campus interests and state-level concerns.

Higher education is one of many sectors of state government vying for increased funding during a time when more is expected of many areas of government. As far back as the early 1970s, higher education was predicted to fall in line with other divisions of state government in having to fight for their piece of dwindling state resources. Governing and coordinating boards grew out of state government's desire for a rational system of postsecondary education delivery. Set up to deal with the interests of the day, those interests have shifted over time, and the struggle between centralization and decentralization has grown.

Increases in demand for public services fueled the growth in state expenditures in the last quarter of the twentieth century. Charles Bonser, Eugene McGregor, and Clinton Oster stated in 1996 that some of the reasons for the increase in demands on state coffers are demographic changes, growing populations, income growth, income redistribution, and risk aversion. Michael Mills pointed to rapid pace of change faced by higher education in such areas as information technology, restricted funding, expansions in the economy, and multiple stakeholders as the driving forces behind challenges facing higher education and other public sectors.

State Finance

State governments currently fund higher education through combinations of three principal budget tools—incremental funding, formula funding, and performance funding. Incremental funding assumes that services in one year will continue to the next year and as a result a previous year's budget will be used for the following year. Currently, forty of the fifty states and the District of Columbia use incremental funding as their primary method of funding. Formula funding uses quantitative factors to determine the needs of each institution. Currently ten states use formula funding as their principle model. Incidentally, sixteen of the forty states using incremental models rely upon some version of formula funding to inform their budget decisions. Performance funding relies upon incentives to tie accountability and performance to state allocations.

During the 1980s and 1990s there was a shift nationwide in the sources of support for higher education. According to the National Center for Education Statistics, the public higher education revenue attributed to state government funds increased by 125 percent from 1980 to 1996. During this time period tuition and fees increased by 318 percent. Increasing at three times the rate of state appropriations, tuition and fees have become the primary mechanism for meeting higher education's need for improvement dollars. Between 1980 and 1996, institutions looked to private sources and endowment returns for budget balancing mechanisms. Revenue attributed to private sources increased 363 percent from 1980 to 1996, and endowment income increased by 236 percent.

The Illinois State University's Grapevine Database of state higher educational funding data stated that higher education was given nearly $61 billion by state governments in fiscal year 2000 through 2001. The state with the largest appropriation was California at just over $9 billion; the lowest was Vermont at just under $68 million. Of course adjustments must be made for population in comparing the effort of each state toward higher education expenses. On a per capita basis, Mississippi ranked first in appropriations of tax funds to higher education ($313

per capita) and New Hampshire ranked fiftieth ($81 per capita).

As mentioned earlier, states increasingly relied upon tuition and fees to provide necessary improvement dollars to universities and colleges in the 1990s. Nationally, states increased resident undergraduate tuition and required fees by 19 percent between the years of 1997 and 2001 alone, according to the Washington State Higher Education Board. States vary in terms of total required fees per resident participating in higher education. For flagship universities, New Hampshire charged the highest of any state in 2000 ($7,395) and Nevada charged the lowest ($2,220). For comprehensive colleges and universities, New Jersey led the nation ($5,328) and California charged the least ($1,859). Community colleges also vary in terms of fees as New Hampshire charged almost double that of any other state ($4,114) while California charged the least ($330).

The large increases in tuition and fees during the 1990s have been tempered with sizable commitments to state-level grant and aid programs. Annual need- and merit-based aid increased from a national average of $45 million in 1992 though 1993 to $67 million in 1998 through 1999, according to the National Association of State Student Grant and Aid Programs. Nationally, aid dollars per resident aged 18 to 24 stood at $118 and aid per undergraduate full-time equivalency (FTE) stood at $397.

Governance Issues

As noted earlier, higher education governance has undergone a dynamic shift in its locus of control since the mid-twentieth century. Once governed locally by faculty and ceremonially by governing boards, many campuses now find themselves subject to heightened scrutiny at the state-level and in many cases under direct control by state government bodies. Governing and coordinating boards are now found in all fifty states, as governments have found it necessary to establish professional bodies to direct and shape the growing systems of higher education. The relationships between these boards and the institutions have been further strained by the increasing involvement of elected officials in daily activities of the campuses. Elected officials have looked to the boards as a vehicle for delegated powers with intervention always an option if lawmakers deem it necessary. The pressure has then fallen to the campuses as presidents feel torn between the business perspective of board members and the established faculty culture, and the educational planning process is continually influenced by partisan politics.

An Association of Governing Boards study revealed in 1999 that most political leaders wanted strong and effective boards, but felt that intervention was needed. Most governing board members take their responsibilities seriously, but too many political obstacles stand in their way. Among legislative leaders there is strong support for governance by lay board members, but concerns abound for the current performance of these groups. Key findings noted by the Association of Governing Boards were placed into three categories: serving public interest, negotiation of the political environment, and increasing board responsiveness. In another study of governance developments, Frank Bowen and colleagues found that state boards that are both part of higher education and part of state government are more successful at balancing public interests and institutional concerns than solely institutional governing boards.

Aims McGuinness spoke further in 1997 of this critical role between postsecondary structures and overall governmental and economic system demands. He cited instability of state leadership, ambiguous missions, and growing political controls as the factors hindering optimum effectiveness. With massive turnover in federal and state government elections in 1994, the instability of leadership in state government had a great impact on the turnover of commission members and trustees in the late 1990s. Sabloff also discussed the political transformation that state governments have gone through since the 1980s. She pointed to year-round activities, increased staff, career politicians, increasing education levels of officials, and standing committees as evidence of a changing system of governance over all state programs and services. State government is experiencing what has been called at the federal level *a professionalization of the legislative body*. Higher education officials and scholars have been forced to adjust to the increasing activities and involvement. As noted in Lawrence Marcus's 1997 study of higher education governance restructuring, when relationships between government and higher education systems become more strained, the likelihood of government becoming more involved increases.

A proliferation of state-level advisory commissions established to study the issue of higher education governance and policy reform has occurred in the last decade. Since 1990 an estimated twenty-one states have established state-level governmental advisory groups with similar charges of improving higher education. Whether as a sensible policy development tool or as the latest fad in government, these commissions—drawn primarily from elected leaders, top higher education officials, and politically-connected citizens—shaped much of the public policy debate surrounding higher education in the 1990s.

Though executive advisory councils or "blue-ribbon commissions" are nothing new to state higher education policymaking, the 1990s saw an unusually high number of such bodies. In his descriptive study of the activities of twenty-one states, Mills defines these higher education policy entities as "specially constituted groups with a majority of its members from outside the higher education system and a broad charge allowing them to take a comprehensive look at the structure and operation of all public higher education in the state" (p. 3). Though these entities are not the only planning mechanisms in higher education, they do "claim an atmosphere where independent citizens can work along with higher education and government representatives to deal with problems and policy issues" (p. 3).

Mills found concerns about higher education's role in the state economy and desires for more accountability to be the dominant problems addressed in the reports of twenty-one states' executive advisory commissions. It is no surprise to find that the concerns revolve around structural and economic recommendations, since competitiveness, efficiency, and specialization are dominant themes of the corporate and rational models of planning used by most elected officials and business leaders. In nearly every report Mills found recommendations concerning overhaul or strengthening of coordination and governance of higher education systems.

McGuinness charged that the most perplexing issue facing lawmakers is how to position the higher education system to take on the changes brought by a more market-driven economy. Wrestling with concerns for issues such as mission clarity, technology infrastructure, and increasing political control is becoming commonplace in state-level higher education planning across the country. In their seminal piece on the campus and state policy environment, Malcolm Moos and Francis Rourke stated in 1959 that properly positioning the public higher education system within the overall system of government has always been a problem. Roger Benjamin and Stephen Carroll conducted a survey in 1996 that found that governance structures commonly were not able to tie resource allocation to the mission. Instead of being able to focus scarce resources to areas of weakness or strengths, funding was spread uniformly to all disciplines, programs, and institutions within a system.

In the last quarter of the twentieth century, nearly every state reevaluated its higher education system in terms of quality, accountability, and efficiency. Conflicting desires surface as elected officials expect governing boards to meet public interests and set direction for higher education while the institutions desire the governing boards to be advocates for funding and keep the politics at a minimum.

See also: AMERICAN ASSOCIATION OF STATE COLLEGES AND UNIVERSITIES; FINANCE, HIGHER EDUCATION; GOVERNANCE AND DECISION-MAKING IN COLLEGES AND UNIVERSITIES; STATES AND EDUCATION, *subentry on* STATE BOARDS OF EDUCATION.

BIBLIOGRAPHY

AMERICAN ASSOCIATION OF STATE COLLEGES AND UNIVERSITIES. 1998. *Higher Education and the Labor Market.* Washington, DC: American Association of State Colleges and Universities.

ASSOCIATION OF GOVERNING BOARDS. 1999. *Bridging the Gap Between State Government and Higher Education.* Washington, DC: Association of Governing Boards.

BENJAMIN, ROGER, and CARROLL, STEPHEN J. 1996. "Impediments and Imperatives in Restructuring Higher Education." *Education Administration Quarterly* 32:705–720.

BERDAHL, ROBERT O. 1990. "Public Universities and State Governments: Is the Tension Benign?" *Educational Record* 71(1):38–42.

BONSER, CHARLES F.; MCGREGOR, EUGENE B., JR.; and OSTER, CLINTON V., JR. 1996. *Policy Choices and Public Action.* Upper Saddle River, NJ: Prentice-Hall.

BOWEN, FRANK M., et al. 1997. *State Structures for the Governance of Higher Education: A Comparative Study.* Sacramento: California Higher Education Policy Center.

GOVE, SAMUEL K. 1971. "The Politics of Higher Education." In *New Perspectives in State and Local Politics,* ed. James A. Reidel. Waltham, MA: Xerox College Publishing.

GRAHAM, HUGH DAVIS. 1989. "Structure and Governance in American Higher Education: Historical and Comparative Analysis in State Policy." *Journal of Policy History* 1(1):80–107

GREER, DARRYL G. 1986. "Politics and Higher Education: The Strategy of State-Level Coordination and Policy Implementation." In *Policy Controversies in Higher Education,* ed. Samuel K. Gove and Thomas M. Stauffer. Westbrook, CT: Greenwood.

INSTITUTE FOR HIGHER EDUCATION POLICY. 1998. *The New Millenium Project on Higher Education Costs, Pricing, and Productivity: Reaping the Benefits.* Washington DC: Institute for Higher Education Policy.

JONES, DENNIS; EWELL, PETER; and MCGUINNESS, AIMS. 1998. *The Challenges and Opportunities Facing Higher Education: An Agenda for Policy Research.* San Jose, CA: National Center for Public Policy and Higher Education.

JUSTIZ, MANUEL. 1994. "Demographic Trends and the Challenges to American Higher Education." In *Minorities in Higher Education,* ed. Manuel Justiz, Reginald Wilson, and Lars G. Bjork. Phoenix, AZ: Oryx Press.

MARYLAND HIGHER EDUCATION COMMISSION. 1996. *Higher Education Funding Study, Part 1: Methods for Funding Higher Education in Other States.* Annapolis: Maryland Higher Education Commission.

MARCUS, LAURENCE R. 1997. "Restructuring State Higher Education Governance Patterns." *The Review of Higher Education* 20, 4:399–418.

MELVILLE, J. G., and CHMURA, THOMAS J. 1991. "Strategic Alignment of Community Colleges and State Economic Policy." In *New Directions for Community Colleges: Economic and Workforce Development,* ed. Geneva W. Waddell. San Francisco: Jossey-Bass.

MILLS, MICHAEL. 1999. "Stories of Excellence and Enterprise in Higher Education Policy Making: A Narrative Analysis of the Reports of the Blue Ribbon Commissions on Higher Education." Paper presented at the Annual Meeting for the Study of Higher Education (ASHE), San Antonio, TX, November 21–23.

MOOS, MALCOLM, and ROURKE, FRANCIS E. 1959. *The Campus and the State.* Baltimore: The Johns Hopkins Press.

NATIONAL CENTER FOR EDUCATION STATISTICS. 1999. *The Condition of Education.* Washington DC: National Center for Education Statistics.

NORTH CAROLINA CENTER FOR PUBLIC POLICY RESEARCH. 2000. *Governance and Coordination of Public Higher Education in All Fifty States.* Raleigh: North Carolina Center for Public Policy Research.

PETERSON, PAUL E. 1985. "Did the Education Commissions Say Anything?" *Education and Urban Society* 17(2):126–144.

SABLOFF, PAULA L. 1997. "Another Reason Why State Legislatures Will Continue to Restrict Public University Autonomy." *The Review of Higher Education* 20(2):141–162.

WASHINGTON STATE HIGHER EDUCATION BOARD. 2001. *Tuition and Fee Rates: A National Comparison.* Olympia: Washington State Higher Education Board.

INTERNET RESOURCES

BALILES, GERALD L. 1997. "Partisan Political Battles: Governing Boards and University Presidents are Plagued by Divided Loyalties." *National CrossTalk* 5(3). <www.highereducation.org/crosstalk/ct1097/voices1097-partisan.shtml>.

ILLINOIS STATE UNIVERSITY. 2001. "Grapevine: A National Database of Tax Support for Higher Education." <www.coe.ilstu.edu/grapevine>.

McGUINNESS, AIMS C., JR. 1997. "A Complex Relationship: State Coordination and Governance of Higher Education." *National CrossTalk* 5(3). <www.highereducation.org/crosstalk/ct1097/voices1097-complex.shtml>.

NATIONAL ASSOCIATION OF STATE STUDENT GRANT AND AID PROGRAMS. 2002. *1998–1999 Financial Aid Survey.* National Association of State Student Grant and Aid Programs. <www.nassgap.org/researchsurveys/30thsurrep.pdf>.

HOUSTON D. DAVIS

STATEWIDE TESTING

See: TESTING, *subentry on* STATEWIDE TESTING PROGRAMS.

STATISTICS

See: INTERNATIONAL EDUCATION STATISTICS; NATIONAL CENTER FOR EDUCATION STATISTICS.

STEINER, RUDOLF (1861–1925)

Educator, philosopher, artist, and scientist, Rudolf Steiner founded the Freie Waldorfschule (Independent Waldorf School) in Stuttgart, Germany, in 1919; its establishment led to the Waldorf educational movement with more than 800 schools worldwide in the early twenty-first century. Steiner's spiritual–scientific research is known as anthroposophy.

Rudolf Steiner was born in Kraljevec, Austria-Hungary (now Croatia). His father was stationmaster on the Southern Austrian Railroad. Rudolf Steiner first attended the Volksschule, then the scientific Realschule in Wiener Neustadt, and graduated from the Technical University in Vienna in 1884. In 1882 he was offered the editorship of Goethe's natural scientific writings for the Kürschner edition of German national literature. Steiner was called to Weimar, Germany, as collaborator at the Goethe-Schiller Archives in 1890, and remained there until 1897. His principal publications during the Weimar period were *Wahrheit und Wissenschaft* (Truth and science) in 1892; *Philosophie der Freiheit* (Philosophy of freedom) in 1894; and *Goethes Weltanschauung* (Goethe's world conception) in 1897. Moving to Berlin in 1897, Steiner became the editor of the weekly *Magazin für Literatur.* He taught history at the Berlin Workers' School from 1899 to 1905.

In 1900 he was asked by leaders of the Theosophical Society to speak on his own spiritual–scientific research. This led, in 1902, to his being asked to head the newly established German section of the International Theosophical Society. By 1912 it had become clear that the insights derived from Steiner's spiritual–scientific research led in a different direction than those represented by the Theosophical Society. Early in 1913, those members who wished to follow the path described by Rudolf Steiner established the Anthroposophical Society. Steiner served as the new society's adviser and mentor. His principal publications during this period were *Theosophie* (Theosophy) in 1904; *Wie erlangt man Erkenntnisse der höheren Welten* (How to attain knowledge of higher worlds) in 1904/1905; and *Die Geheimwissenschaft im Umriss* (An outline of occult science) in 1909.

During the years from 1910 to 1913, Steiner wrote and directed four dramas portraying the destinies of a community of spiritually seeking individuals. Plans developed for a festival center in Munich that, in fact, led to construction of a festival and study/research/teaching center in Dornach, Switzerland. The original building, designed by Steiner, came to be known as the *Goetheanum*. Under construction from 1913 to 1920; the *Goetheanum* burned to the ground on New Year's Eve 1922/1923. It was replaced by the present building of reinforced concrete, according to Steiner's sculptured model, created in 1924.

In 1917 Steiner completed thirty years of research on the threefold nature of the human being. These findings became the basis for his later work in education, medicine, social science, and the arts and sciences. Rudolf Steiner died in Dornach, Switzerland. His written and published works total more than thirty volumes and some 6,000 lectures, many published in book form.

Steiner's Pedagogical Approach

The distinguishing feature in Steiner's educational philosophy is that it is based on a perception of the human being as threefold, comprising body, soul, and spirit. In Steiner's view, the human bodily organism, in the mature adult, is built up of four interactive members, of which only the physical/mineral body is directly perceptible to the physical senses. The three supersensible members manifest in and through the physical organism and are directly perceptible to spiritual perception and cognition. Sustaining the life and growth of the physical body is the human "etheric" or "life" body, a characteristic held in common with the plant kingdom. Penetrating the physical and etheric bodies is the "astral" body, instrument of consciousness and emotion, which is shared with the animal kingdom. Penetrating physical, etheric, and astral organisms is the human ego, unique to the human species. The human soul, which mediates between the human spirit and the bodily organism, is endowed with the capacities of thinking, feeling, and will. It is the task of education, from birth to adulthood, to exercise and nurture the human bodily instruments and the soul, to become as responsive, as flexible, and as readily available to the individual human ego as possible. The true fruits of education in childhood come to full expression in the later years of human life.

The developmental process underlying Steiner's education is the result of the unfolding of the three supersensible members from birth to the "coming of age" at twenty-one. This process proceeds in three stages of approximately seven years each. During the first phase, from birth to about the seventh year, the etheric or life body gradually penetrates the physical organism, culminating in the change of teeth. The astral, or "soul" body, penetrates the physical/ etheric organism approximately from seven to fourteen years, culminating in the reproductive, sexual changes at puberty. And the ego gradually penetrates the physical, etheric, and astral organisms at about twenty-one. Psychologically, this latter culmination manifests in the individual's ability, not only to know, but to know that she/he knows. Consciousness is transformed into self-consciousness.

The educational insights arising through this developmental process are characterized in Steiner's pedagogy in the following way: During the first phase (0–7) the child's basic cognitive faculty is imitation. With the change of teeth, a significant portion of the etheric-formative forces that have shaped the child's organism are released and become available to the child as the awakening faculty of imagination. With the physical changes at puberty, a significant portion of the astral forces is freed from the organism and is now available as intellectual cognition and emotional response. During adolescence, the "personality" gradually yields to the "individuality." Language reflects this. *Per-sonare* means to "sound through." As in Greek drama, in which the god speaks through the mask, personality is the "mask" through which the individual sounds. The individuality is that in the human being which cannot be further divided, is "indivisible."

This developmental picture gives rise to Steiner's pedagogical approach in practice. The key to preschool education is imitation, not intellectualization. In these years it is primarily through the imitative will that education occurs. The key to elementary education is learning through imagination—through story, myth, art, narrative, and biography—and doing. In these years, human feeling is the primary focus. And the time to exercise and challenge the intellectual intelligence, human thinking, is primarily in adolescence.

The original Waldorf School in Stuttgart began with 253 children in eight grades. It soon grew to be the largest private school in Germany, with more than 1,000 students, through high school. When Hitler came to power in 1933, there were seven Waldorf Schools in Germany, all of which were closed by the National-Socialist government. The Stuttgart school reopened in 1945 under the auspices of the American Occupation Forces in southern Germany. In the early twenty-first century, there are more than 180 Waldorf schools in Germany. The first school in the English-speaking world opened in England in 1925. In 1928, the Rudolf Steiner School opened in New York City. There are 152 Waldorf schools in the United States, Canada, and Mexico, and there are 11 Waldorf teacher training centers. They are represented by the Association of Waldorf Schools of North America (AWSNA).

See also: INTERNATIONAL EDUCATION; PHILOSOPHY OF EDUCATION.

BIBLIOGRAPHY

Barnes, Henry. 1980."Waldorf Education: An Introduction." *Teachers College Record* 81(3):323–336.

BARNES, HENRY. 1991. "Learning That Grows with the Learner." *Educational Leadership: Journal of the Association for Supervision and Curriculum Development* 49(2):52–54.

BARNES, HENRY. 1997. *A Life for the Spirit: Rudolf Steiner in the Crosscurrents of Our Time.* New York: Anthroposophic Press.

HARWOOD, A. CECIL. 1982. *The Recovery of Man in Childhood.* New York: Anthroposophic Press.

STEINER, RUDOLF. 1971. *Human Values in Education.* London: Rudolf Steiner.

STEINER, RUDOLF. 1986. *Soul Economy and Waldorf Education.* New York: Anthroposophic Press.

STEINER, RUDOLF. 1988a. *Kingdom of Childhood.* New York: Anthroposophic Press.

STEINER, RUDOLF. 1988b. *The Child's Changing Consciousness and Waldorf Education.* New York: Anthroposophic Press.

HENRY BARNES

ST. JOHN'S COLLEGE

St. John's College, with campus sites in Annapolis, Maryland, and Santa Fe, New Mexico, is the most enduring example of the Great Books program of study in American liberal education. The four-year program at St. John's is aimed at producing "liberally educated human beings" who acquire "a lifelong commitment to the pursuit of fundamental knowledge and to the search for unifying ideas" (St. John's College, p. 6). Approximately 450 students on each campus attend seminars, tutorials, laboratory sessions, and lectures, which support their reading and discussion of ancient and modern classical texts in science, mathematics, literature, philosophy, history, economics, psychology, political science, theology, languages, and music.

Founded as King William's School in 1696, the St. John's Annapolis campus is among the oldest continuing American institutions of higher education. It was chartered as St. John's, a nondenominational school, in 1784. The buildings on the thirty-six-acre site in downtown Annapolis include a number of eighteenth-century homes now used as classroom and office space. The school was nearly bankrupt in 1937 when the trustees invited noted educators Stringfellow Barr and Scott Buchanan to come from the University of Chicago and oversee a wholly new curriculum at St. John's. Buchanan had earlier pioneered a Great Books lecture series at the People's Institute outreach program in New York City. He and Barr first met when both were Rhodes scholars at Oxford University and renewed their friendship as faculty colleagues at the University of Virginia. There they tried unsuccessfully to spark interest in a liberal arts curriculum based on classical texts, and in 1935 they joined University of Chicago President Robert Maynard Hutchins in his determination to design an undergraduate liberal education program around the classical texts of Western literature.

With Barr as president and Buchanan as dean, St. John's quickly became widely known for its commitment to the liberal arts, to student-faculty community, and to classical texts featuring Greek and Roman philosophers. Proponents of its curriculum inspired debate about the nature of the liberal arts at a time of expanding vocational and professional higher education and about the place of lockstep course requirements at a time of widespread regard for individuality in subject selection and learning pace. Other college experiments of the time (e.g., Black Mountain, Bennington, and Bard) garnered attention for the progressive nature of curriculums that encouraged students to design customized courses of study. St. John's, however, held fast to the notion that the essence of liberal education occurred when community-wide dialogue, largely supported by Socratic teaching, inspired diverse individual meanings from the enduring ideas offered in classical texts.

Committed to the idea of a community of scholars, St. John's administrators decided to create a second campus rather than expand the Annapolis campus beyond 450 students. The New Mexico campus opened in 1964 with new buildings erected on 250 acres just outside downtown Santa Fe. Although student athletics, newspapers, literary magazines, concerts, and other extracurricular activities vary on the two campuses, the academic program remains the same. The two campuses share a common curriculum and a single governing board. The required readings of the freshman and sophomore year emphasize classical texts from those of the Greek poet Homer and the Greek playwright Sophocles to the English dramatist and poet William Shakespeare and the French mathematician and philosopher René Descartes, as well as the musical works of notable composers. By the senior year, required reading includes works by the American authors William Faulkner, Flannery O'Connor, Booker T. Washington, W. E. B. DuBois, and William James. All students study ancient Greek, French, and English composition, and graduates earn a bachelor of arts in liberal education. Seniors write a final essay and successfully complete an oral examination before graduating.

The liberal arts curriculum and community of dialogue inherent in the St. John's approach to undergraduate education is, according to the 2000 *Statement of the St. John's Program,* aimed at encouraging students to examine assumptions they hold and to "acquire a new perspective which enables them to recognize both the sameness of a recurrent problem and the variety of its historical manifestations." The long-term objective is "to help the students make reasonable decisions in whatever circumstances they face" (St. John's College, p. 7).

See also: GENERAL EDUCATION IN HIGHER EDUCATION; HIGHER EDUCATION IN THE UNITED STATES, *subentry on* HISTORICAL DEVELOPMENT.

BIBLIOGRAPHY

GRANT, GERALD, and RIESMAN, DAVID. 1978. *The Perpetual Dream: Reform and Experiment in the American College.* Chicago: University of Chicago Press.

NELSON, CHARLES A., ed. 1995. *Scott Buchanan: A Centennial Appreciation of His Life and Work.* Annapolis, MD: St. John's College Press.

ST. JOHN'S COLLEGE. 2000. *Statement of the St. John's Program.* Annapolis, MD: St. John's College Press.

WOFFORD, HARRIS, JR., ed. 1969. *Embers of the World: Scott Buchanan's Conversations with Harris Wofford Jr.* Santa Barbara, CA: Center for the Study of Democratic Institutions.

KATHERINE C. REYNOLDS

STRATEGIC AND LONG-RANGE PLANNING IN HIGHER EDUCATION

The major test of a modern U.S. university, according to Clark Kerr, President Emeritus and former Chancellor at the University of California, is how wisely and how quickly it is able to adjust to important new possibilities. As its popularity and presence has grown on college campuses, planning has become the process-oriented means to pass the test of change referred to by Kerr. Planning has been defined by Marvin Peterson as the "conscious process by which an institution assesses its current state and the likely future condition of its environment, identifies possible future states for itself, and then develops organizational strategies, policies and procedures for selecting and getting to one or more of them" (Peterson, p. 12).

Planning became a necessary component of higher-education administration after World War II, due to the rapid expansion and growth of federal policies regarding access to, and financial support of, higher education. Soon thereafter came the surge of baby boomers into colleges, and in the 1990s institutions prepared for and responded to the echo boom of college-age students on campuses across the United States. In addition, colleges have become increasingly heterogeneous as more diverse populations have been admitted, resulting in the need for planning regarding financial aid, student services, remedial education, vocational education, and more.

Furthermore, various types of postsecondary knowledge providers have emerged, such as private companies offering degrees via the Internet, corporations providing their own internal education and training, and traditional institutions collaborating with industry. Simultaneously, the knowledge industry has become quite consumer driven. The convenience and affordability of postsecondary education has caused students, employers, and institutions themselves to rethink the very core of the institutional mission, and to plan for the future much differently than ever before. Globalization has broadened the institutional view of the regions served, as well as placement of students in internships, exchange programs, and careers. All these factors have produced an approach to planning that includes much more than simple short-term budgeting. Rather, planning encompasses short- and long-range plans connecting budget, capital outlay, programming, enrollment, and every element of a college or university.

Long-Range Planning

Following World War II and through the 1960s, the purpose of long-range planning was to justify resources. Use of long-range planning presupposes that the environment is fairly stable and predictable, and that resources are certain. This use of long-range terminology has been trivialized because it often was, in effect, the university budgeting process. The idea that planning was tied to a dollar amount meant that the planning process actually represented how to spend resources. The popularity of this method declined in the latter part of the 1970s, because it did not account for certain environmental aspects that became critical.

Strategic Planning

As long-range planning began to seem limited, *strategic planning* became the buzz phrase in both business and in higher education. Frequently advocated in the late 1970s and 1980s, strategic planning's primary purpose is to cultivate adaptation in a rapidly changing environment by designing a plan and corresponding strategies for the future. The institutional situation is assessed for opportunities and threats via scanning the regional, national, and global external environments, the most distinctive feature of this form of planning. Also, internal strengths and weaknesses are defined for needed strategies for survival and enhancements. Strategy implies that the approach is more short-term, and possibly reactive to a current situation. This process assumes that some aspects of the organization do not require intervention and seeks to find the problem areas that need improvement. Often this occurs when the environment is unstable and relatively unpredictable.

Contextual Planning

Whereas long-range planning is typically responsive in nature, and strategic planning is adaptive, contextual planning is proactive. Particularly in the 1990s, planning progressively became connected to fundraising as federal and state financial subsidies declined. Needing to compensate for the loss of funding, institutions were forced to seek funding support from private sources. Combined with the impact of technology, globalization, and the increasing presence of nontraditional-age learners to the collegiate environment, institutions have sought new and different ways to plan for the realities of uncertainty.

Emergent virtual universities have caused leaders to move away from thinking about planning at a traditional physical campus and toward being more perceptive about planning for other possibilities. Existing as part of an increasingly complex organization with little stability, new and different planning models are constantly implemented, based on political demands, business models, or internal leadership. This method of planning assumes uncertain financial resources, an ever more competitive environment, and a critical public.

Cooperation and Leadership in Planning

The higher-education mantra since the 1990s has called for improved access for students, increased quality, enhanced accountability of expenditures, and more and better use of technology. While these promote positive change, the irony is that there is no easy solution to achieve change, and the solution is different for each institution. In order to progress toward goals, it has become necessary for strategic planning to be linked to major programs, such as institutional research, institutional advancement (also known as development or fundraising), and data management (also known as data warehousing).

Planning has spurred more and different kinds of analytic studies in order to make internal and external comparisons, both historical and contemporary. These studies are used not only to plan for programmatic and curricular transformation, but also to identify competing institutions and potential students and donors. This information is critical to raising the private funds that have become necessary for many institutions.

Due to the constantly changing environment of higher education, research has shown that planning should be an ongoing, rather than occasional, process, done in collaboration with institutional research and assessment. There already exists a massive amount of data related to planning. As higher education continues to search for ways to manage this information, data support and knowledge-management systems will become increasingly crucial to effective planning.

The thoughtful and effective leaders of change have resisted the idea of planning as a formal process. An effective planning process should be a broad-based balance of deliberate and emergent strategies, and should involve the participation of middle managers. Fundamental to this idea is that planning should not be bogged down in specific strategy; but should create broad visions. Additionally, a positive relationship between managers and planners or administration is critical to successful implementation of plans. This requires strong leadership that will include hands-on contributions by frontline managers and faculty. A pragmatic consideration that can assist in bolstering internal political relationships at institutions is frequent and thorough information dissemination. These considerations will allow for participation at many levels, and will make good communication a cornerstone of the process. Essentially, planning at the institutional level is connected to planning at the division level, which is integrated with individual plans and includes leadership and vision at every echelon.

Conclusion

As the paradigm of higher education continues to shift, it is clear that the institutions that resist change are predestined to decline, and possibly fail. Effective leaders realize that reasonable risks must be taken in order to attend to the demands of a changing and competitive environment. "A lack of thoughtful change could lead to inept adaptation and undermine the quality of our universities" (Rowley et al., p. 19). While the approach and methods vary, it is clear that planning is a vital component of successful contemporary higher education.

See also: INSTITUTIONAL ADVANCEMENT IN HIGHER EDUCATION; RESOURCE ALLOCATION IN HIGHER EDUCATION.

BIBLIOGRAPHY

KERR, CLARK. 2001. *The Uses of the University,* 5th edition. Cambridge, MA: Harvard University Press.

PETERSON, MARVIN. 1999a. "Analyzing Alternative Approaches to Planning." In *ASHE Reader on Planning and Institutional Research,* ed. Marvin Peterson. Needham Heights, MA: Pearson Custom Publishing.

PETERSON, MARVIN. 1999b. "Using Contextual Planning to Transform Institutions." In *ASHE Reader on Planning and Institutional Research,* ed. Marvin Peterson. Needham Heights, MA: Pearson Custom Publishing.

ROWLEY, DANIEL JAMES; LUJAN, HERMAN D.; and DOLENCE, MICHAEL G., eds. 1997. *Strategic Change in Colleges and Universities.* San Francisco: Jossey-Bass.

ALTON L. TAYLOR
LEANNA BLEVINS RUSSELL

STRATEMEYER, FLORENCE (1900–1980)

Faculty member at Teachers College, Columbia University, from 1930 through 1965, Florence Barbara Stratemeyer was a founding figure in the field of teacher education and curriculum.

Stratemeyer was born in Detroit and from 1917 through 1919 attended the Western State Teachers College in Kalamazoo, Michigan, where she earned a diploma and license in elementary teaching. She spent 1920 through 1921 teaching at the Detroit Teachers College. In 1921 to 1922 she taught in the Brady Elementary School in Detroit. She then came to Teachers College, Columbia University, and in 1923 earned a bachelor of science degree; in 1927 she completed the master of arts degree and the Ph.D in 1931. Her dissertation title was "The Effective Use of Curriculum Materials: A Study of Units Relating to the Curriculum to Be Included in the Professional Preparation of Elementary Teachers." This was a compendium of the curriculum and the critical questions future elementary teachers should deal with in their programs of teacher preparation. From 1929 to 1930 she was an associate in the Teachers College teacher education program, and from 1924 to 1929 she served as a research associate in the

Teachers College Bureau of Curriculum Research. Stratemeyer became assistant professor in Curriculum and Teaching at Teachers College in 1930, was promoted to associate professor in 1936, and to full professor in 1942. In the early 1930s she was part of a group of faculty who developed a nontraditional approach to teacher education based on direct experience and more active forms of learning. This model was called New College.

The idea was that if future teachers participated in active problem solving during their teacher preparation, this would ensure that they would be likely to pursue this method with children in their future teaching. The students in New College therefore did not simply read about problems and issues but sought to become directly involved. If they were studying strikes they went to Pittsburgh and interviewed management and labor. They did not simply read about communism but traveled to Russia to observe and experience it. In 1934 Stratemeyer spent the summer in Nazi Germany with students from New College.

From these early efforts it is possible to see how Stratemeyer was beginning to evolve in her approach to curriculum study and teacher preparation. The method used was the project method and the learning approach was based on connecting the interests of the learner with direct experiences. The curriculum was organized around the basic life functions performed by all individuals in any form of social order.

Stratemeyer contributed several important books to the field of curriculum. With H. B. Brunner she coauthored *Rating Elementary School Courses of Study* (1926). There can be no question that her major book was *Developing a Curriculum for Modern Living* (1947), with coauthors Hamden L. Forkner and Margaret McKim. In 1948 she wrote *School and Community Laboratory Experiences in Teacher Education*.

Stratemeyer's influence in teacher education far exceeded that of anyone in the United States during her service as a faculty member in the Department of Curriculum and Teaching at Teachers College, Columbia University. There were essentially three reasons for her great influence. First was the power of her theory of persistent life problems faced by all learners of all ages in all societies. Stratemeyer believed that the subjects and disciplines taught in schools and universities were not there because of

intrinsic validity but because the learner needed this basic knowledge as an cornerstone for trying to deal with persistent life problems effectively.

In *Developing a Curriculum for Modern Living*, she argued that the persistent problems of living were related to health, intellectual power, moral choices, aesthetics, interpersonal relations, group relations, dealing with the physical world, technology, and economic and political structures. In this scheme the subject matters (e.g. mathematics, science, art, and so forth) are regarded as instrumentalities that provide students at all levels with a way to deal with the essential problems of living that they will face at all stages of their development. This theory resonated with professional teacher educators, who knew that future teachers needed more than the discrete required courses, but were unsure of just why future teachers should study these things and how such knowledge might apply to the curriculum being offered children and youth.

Stratemeyer's work legitimized the offering of general education and specialization (i.e., college majors) to future teachers. Although few colleges of liberal arts have used her theory and still generally offer future teachers only a list of required courses and the compilation of such coursework into traditional majors or areas of specialization, her theory of persistent life problems became a fundamental part of all doctoral students' preparation for becoming teacher educators. Various abbreviated versions of persistent life problems have been widely adopted in elementary schools.

The second reason for her great influence over the field of curriculum in teacher education were the number and quality of her doctoral students, who were scattered across America and became well-known teacher educators and school of education deans. One of her earliest doctoral students was Margaret Lindsey, who then joined her in the Department of Curriculum and Teaching at Teachers College. Together Stratemeyer and Lindsey turned out several hundred doctoral students who had an impact on teacher education that is hard to overestimate.

Stratemeyer helped to create a specialized audience for her work. From 1940 to 1965 schools of education were either expanding rapidly or starting up. Stratemeyer's influence over these institutions resulted from her being able to stock them with teacher education faculty who were generalists rather than specialized teacher educators, limited by narrow definitions of content (e.g., teacher educator of secondary science, teacher educator in reading, and so forth). Stratemeyer's work then influenced curriculum in teacher education on three levels: (1) as a way of conceiving teacher education for grander purposes than the mastery of traditional college courses; (2) as a way of placing doctoral students who shared her views into critically important positions; and (3) as a way for helping deans and leaders of teacher education explain why there should be schools of education and what people needed to learn and do with children that could best be taught in such places.

See also: TEACHER EDUCATION, *subentry on* HISTORICAL OVERVIEW.

BIBLIOGRAPHY

STRATEMEYER, FLORENCE B. 1931. *The Effective Use of Curriculum Material: A Study of Units Relating to the Curriculum to Be Included in the Professorial Preparation of Elementary Teachers.* Ph.D. diss., Columbia University.

STRATEMEYER, FLORENCE B., and BRUNER, HERBERT B. 1926. *Rating Elementary School Courses of Study,* New York: Teachers College, Columbia University, Bureau of Publications.

STRATEMEYER, FLORENCE B.; FORKNER, HAMDEN L.; and McKIM, MARGARET M. 1947. *Developing a Curriculum for Modern Living.* New York: Teachers College, Columbia University, Bureau of Publications.

STRATEMEYER, FLORENCE B., and LINDSEY, MARGARET. 1958. *Working with Student Teachers.* New York: Teachers College, Columbia University, Bureau of Publications.

MARTIN HABERMAN

STRESS AND DEPRESSION

Children's success in their educational endeavors and their general socioemotional adjustment are influenced by a variety of personal characteristics and environmental experiences. One of the most powerful determinants of children's developmental course is the social context in which they live. In particular, experiencing a stable and supportive environment during childhood is likely to foster healthy cognitive, social, and emotional development, whereas experiencing a disruptive or stressful environment has been linked to a wide range of adverse mental health outcomes, including depression. Stress and the accompanying emotional distress may then interfere with some of the major tasks of childhood, such as academic achievement and fulfillment of educational goals.

The Role of Stress in Depression

Theory and empirical research have implicated stress as a critical risk factor for depression during childhood and adolescence. Stress may take the form of an accumulation of minor daily hassles, more severe chronic strains, or specific negative life events. Each of these types of stress has been linked to depression. Stress also may arise from normative developmental transitions, such as entrance into middle school or moving away from home for the first time. For example, research has shown that school transitions, which often are characterized by many social and academic stressors, have negative effects on academic motivation, performance, and school engagement, as well as on emotional well-being. In particular, Karen Rudolph and colleagues demonstrated in 2001 that the experience of school-related stress (such as poor academic performance, negative feedback from parents and teachers about school work, and daily hassles in the school environment) leads to increases in depression in the context of a transition into middle school.

An important question that has not yet been fully answered concerns how stressful life events and circumstances heighten vulnerability to depression. Stress may contribute to depression through many different pathways. Unpredictable or disruptive environments may undermine children's sense of control and mastery, leading to a sense of helplessness or hopelessness that acts as a precursor to depression. For example, Rudolph and colleagues demonstrated in 2001 that family disruption, as well as exposure to chronic stressful circumstances within the family, peer, and school settings, predicted decreases in perceptions of control and increases in helpless behavior in academic and social situations. These maladaptive beliefs and behavior were in turn associated with depression. Exposure to stress and failure also are likely to influence adversely children's perceptions of their competence. For instance, David Cole and colleagues suggested in 1991 that negative environmental feedback is internalized by children in the form of negative self-perceptions and low self-esteem, which then heighten depressive symptoms. Stress within the school environment may exert specific influences on children's academic-related beliefs, self-perceptions, and goals, and, consequently, on emotional well-being at school. As reviewed by Robert Roeser and Jacquelynne Eccles in 2000, classroom-level and school-level stressors involving instructional practices, emotional climate, and teachers' goals and behavior influence children's subjective perceptions of school, which then determine academic and emotional adjustment.

The Impact on Academic Functioning and Educational Progress

Stressful life experiences as well as acute or chronic periods of depression may interrupt the normative progression of developmental milestones. Given the prominent role that schools play in children's lives, the school setting represents a salient context for development and mental health. Stressful experiences and emotional difficulties are therefore likely to undermine a variety of school-related competencies, including academic motivation and school engagement, goal orientation, scholastic performance, and school conduct.

Educational Implications of Stress

Stressful life circumstances may influence school adjustment in many ways. First, dealing with stress in other areas of their lives may interfere directly with children's performance at school by depleting the amount of time, energy, and focused attention available for academic tasks and school involvement, such as completing homework or engaging in after-school activities. Second, exposure to high levels of stress may divert coping resources away from efforts to deal with the challenges of school. This lack of resources may lead adolescents to feel overwhelmed, and create a sense of helplessness that results in disengagement from school. Third, stressful circumstances outside of school may lead children to place less of a priority on educational goals, thereby undermining school investment. Finally, if stress originates within the family setting, it is likely that family members have less availability and lower levels of school involvement, which would diminish emotional and instrumental support necessary for educational success.

Educational Implications of Depression

Depression has been linked to a range of negative school-related outcomes, including poor grades, a lack of persistence in the face of academic challenges, and decreased classroom participation. These effects may range from short-term declines in academic performance to long-term problematic school outcomes. For example, depressive symptoms as early as first grade predict school difficulties many years later, including increased use of special education services, grade retention, and poor grades.

Less is known, however, about how and why depression interferes with school adjustment. The symptoms and accompanying features of depression themselves may have a negative impact on academic achievement and motivation. For example, concentration difficulties, a lack of interest and energy, and withdrawal are likely to undermine performance and engagement at school. Depressive behaviors also may elicit negative reactions from teachers and peers, leading to social isolation and alienation from the school setting. In fact, teachers may feel overwhelmed by the emotional difficulties of their students, leading to low levels of perceived self-efficacy and less than optimal teaching performance. Finally, depression may induce negative beliefs about one's competence and a sense of helplessness, leading to a lack of persistence in academic tasks. Indeed, Carol Dweck and colleagues described in 1988 a profile of "learned helplessness" in achievement contexts, characterized by an avoidance of challenge, lack of persistence in the face of failure, excessive concerns about competence, ineffective learning strategies, maladaptive attributions about failure, and negative emotions. Additional research is needed to determine if in fact this profile characterizes depressed children in the school context.

Remaining Issues

Whether it is most common for academic difficulties to precede depression or for depression to precede academic difficulties has not yet been clearly determined. It also is possible, of course, that the presence of significant academic difficulties in depressed children reflects a common third influence. For example, both depression and academic impairment are linked to behavior problems and attentional deficits. In fact, research has suggested that depression may be most strongly associated with academic stress, failure, and school conduct problems when it co-occurs with acting-out behavior or attentional deficits.

Another important question is why some children who experience high levels of stress or depression show resilience in their school adjustment: A subgroup of high-risk children does show academic success and educational investment in the face of adversity. Many factors may promote such resilience, including personal characteristics of children as well as positive school climates, but additional research is needed to examine this process in more depth.

School-Based Prevention and Intervention Programs

In light of theory and research linking stress and depression with school-related impairment, there has been a call for a new generation of school-based prevention and intervention programs that address the joint issues of academic difficulties and mental health problems. Such programs may range from child-level approaches implemented within the school setting to schoolwide or districtwide approaches directed at systems-level changes.

Several child-level programs have been created to address issues of stress and depression within the school setting. One representative program, developed by Martin Seligman and colleagues, was designed to prevent severe depression in at-risk children—that is, children with elevated levels of depressive symptoms and exposure to family stress—as well as to remediate performance deficits in these children, such as lowered academic achievement and behavior problems. The program emphasized teaching children strategies to cope with stressful events and negative emotions, enhancing children's sense of mastery and competence, and modifying distortions in the ways that children viewed themselves and their surroundings. An extensive evaluation revealed that the program successfully decreased children's level of depressive symptoms and behavior problems. Several similar programs have targeted coping with stress and depression in the school context. These programs tend to yield positive results in terms of decreasing levels of depression, although assessments have not always been conducted to determine why these improvements occur. Less commonly used have been systems-level school-based mental health programs. Such programs focus on promoting change in more distal environmental influences, such as the classroom climate or broader school ecology. Undoubtedly, effectively addressing the complex links among stress, depression, and school adjustment will require an integrated approach that considers both personal resources of children as well as the broader contexts in which they live.

See also: AFFECT AND EMOTIONAL DEVELOPMENT; AGGRESSIVE BEHAVIOR GUIDANCE AND COUNSELING, SCHOOL; MENTAL HEALTH SERVICES AND CHILDREN.

BIBLIOGRAPHY

CLARKE, GREGORY N.; HAWKINS, WESLEY; MURPHY, MARY; SHEEBER, LISA B.; LEWINSOHN, PETER M.; and SEELEY, JOHN R. 1995. "Targeted Prevention of Unipolar Depressive Disorder in an At-Risk Sample of High School Adolescents: A Randomized Trial of a Group Cognitive Intervention." *Journal of the American Academy of Child and Adolescent Psychiatry* 34:312–321.

COLE, DAVID A. 1991. "Preliminary Support for a Competency-Based Model of Depression in Children." *Journal of Abnormal Psychology* 100:181–190.

DWECK, CAROL S., and LEGGETT, ELLEN L. 1988. "A Social-Cognitive Approach to Motivation and Personality." *Psychological Review* 95:256–273.

ECCLES, JACQUELYNNE S.; WIGFIELD, ALLAN; and SCHIEFELE, ULRICH. 1998. "Motivation to Succeed." In *Handbook of Child Psychology*, Vol. 4, ed. Nancy Eisenberg. New York: Wiley.

GARBER, JUDY, and HILSMAN, RUTH. 1992. "Cognitions, Stress, and Depression in Children and Adolescents." In *Child and Adolescent Clinics of North America*, Vol. 1: *Mood Disorders*, ed. Dennis P. Cantwell. Philadelphia: Saunders.

IALONGO, NICHOLAS S.; EDELSOHN, GAIL; and KELLAM, SHEPPHARD G. 2001. "A Further Look at the Prognostic Power of Young Children's Reports of Depressed Mood and Feelings." *Child Development* 72:736–747.

JAYCOX, LISA H.; REIVICH, KAREN J.; GILLHAM, JANE; and SELIGMAN, MARTIN E. P. 1994. "Prevention of Depressive Symptoms in School Children." *Behavior Research and Therapy* 32:801–816.

REYNOLDS, WILLIAM M., and COATS, KEVIN I. 1986. "A Comparison of Cognitive-Behavioral Therapy and Relaxation Training for the Treatment of Depression in Adolescents." *Journal of Consulting and Clinical Psychology* 54:653–660.

ROESER, ROBERT W., and ECCLES, JACQUELYNNE S. 2000. "Schooling and Mental Health." In *Handbook of Developmental Psychopathology,* ed. Arnold J. Sameroff, Michael Lewis, and Suzanne M. Miller. New York: Plenum.

ROSE, DONNA T., and ABRAMSON, LYN Y. 1992. "Developmental Predictors of Depressive Cognitive Style: Research and Theory." In *Rochester Symposium on Developmental Psychopathology,* Vol. 4, ed. Dante Cicchetti and Sherre L. Toth. Rochester, NY: University of Rochester Press.

RUDOLPH, KAREN D.; HAMMEN, CONSTANCE; BURGE, DORLI; LINDBERG, NAGEL; HERZBERG, DAVID; and DALEY, SHANNON E. 2000. "Toward an Interpersonal Life-Stress Model of Depression: The Developmental Context of Stress Generation." *Development and Psychopathology* 12:215–234.

RUDOLPH, KAREN D.; KURLAKOWSKY, KATHRYN D.; and CONLEY, COLLEN S. 2001. "Developmental and Social-Contextual Origins of Depressive Control-Related Beliefs and Behavior." *Cognitive Therapy and Research* 25:447–475.

RUDOLPH, KAREN D.; LAMBERT, SHARON M.; CLARK, ALYSSA G.; and KURLAKOWSKY, KATHRYN D. 2001. "Negotiating the Transition to Middle School: The Role of Self-Regulatory Processes." *Child Development* 72:929–946.

KAREN D. RUDOLPH

STUDENT ACTIVITIES

OVERVIEW

Student activities are an integral part of the school program. Qualified students must be able to participate in any activity without regard to race, religion, national origin, disability, or sex. Generally approved by the principal and under the direct supervision of the staff, activities should contribute to the educational objectives of the school and should avoid interrupting the instructional program.

Purpose

One purpose of student activities is to provide opportunities for students to be involved in the life of the school. Students experience leadership opportunities that help them grow into well-rounded adults. Activities expand interactions among students, who are likely to interact with others who are different from them. Thus, opportunities to experience diversity are enhanced.

Schools organize student activities in different ways. Some principals believe that student activities should be an integral part of the school day and that all students should participate in one or more activities. As a result, meetings occur during the school day at a prescribed time. For example, club day may be the first and third Tuesday of every month from 9 A.M. to 10 A.M. All students are expected to participate in at least one activity. Other principals believe that activities should be extracurricular and should meet outside of the instructional day.

Types of Student Activities

Common activities include student government, honor societies, service clubs, arts organizations (band, choral, theater), academic (forensics, debate, academic competition), and literary publications (newspaper, yearbook, literary magazine). Most schools will have a variety of clubs. Some clubs will be similar among schools, for example, foreign language clubs, science clubs, and art clubs, and others will be affiliated with national organizations such as Vocational Industrial Clubs of America (VICA), Future Business Leaders of America (FBLA), and Future Farmers of America (FFA). Some clubs will be unique to an individual school.

Student government is an integral part of most secondary schools. It may have different names (student council association or student government association), but the purpose is to involve all students in the life of the school. Each student is considered a member of the organization with a right to vote for its officers and representatives. Developing leadership and citizenship are fundamental goals of most student government organizations.

Most schools have honor societies, although such societies may differ from school to school. The purpose of most honor societies is to promote and encourage scholarship, service, leadership, and character. The two largest honor societies with a national reputation are the National Honor Society (NHS) and the National Beta Club. In both organizations, membership is by selection and invitation. Thus, honor societies are set apart from other activities. These national groups are governed by a national constitution so they are similar nationwide. Some schools will develop their own local honor societies to promote excellence in specific areas. For example, one school may have a mathematics honors club while another may have a vocational honors club. In all honor societies, there will be established criteria for selection and invitation.

Service clubs are found in most secondary schools. These clubs have open membership. Some are affiliated with national organizations. For example, the Key Club is supported by the Kiwanis Club, and the Rotary Interact Club is supported by Rotary International. Some service clubs are school specific. Service clubs are generally involved in community service projects, such as canned food drives, working with Special Olympics, peer counseling, or tutoring.

Activities associated with the arts are found in most secondary schools. Concert or symphonic band is generally offered as a class for academic credit, but marching band is generally an extracurricular activity. Marching bands play at football games and generally participate in competition during the year. Other band opportunities may include a jazz band or a pep band. Most secondary schools have choral groups. These groups often perform in the community as well as compete in state and/or national competitions. Many schools have an orchestra. Theater activities are important in most high schools. While theater or drama may be a high school course, most theater productions require open auditions. The number of theater performances offered annually differs from school to school.

Academic activities include a range of experiences; for example, many schools participate in academic competitions. These may include quiz bowls and academic decathlons. Forensics, or public speaking, offers students a variety of experiences, including extemporaneous speaking, original oratory, spelling, and prose and poetry reading. Students are often involved in local and state competitions. Debate activities can take many forms, including Four-Person, Switch-Side, and Lincoln-Douglas. Students participate in local and state debate tournaments.

Most schools have one or more literary activities. The most popular are the yearbook, newspaper, and literary magazine. In some cases, students may be enrolled in an academic class and get academic credit to work on these activities. In other cases, the work is done outside regular school hours.

Clubs are an important part of student activities. As noted earlier, some clubs are tied to national organizations, such as FFA, VICA, and FBLA. These clubs must follow national constitutions and bylaws. Some school clubs are connected to the curriculum, such as Spanish club, French club, and science club. Other clubs may have no direct relationship to the curriculum and are driven by student interest. These clubs will vary from school to school. For example, various high schools around the country support the following clubs: the martial arts club (Killingly, Connecticut), Asian-American club (Carlmont, California), and the Native American student union (Ken Valley, California). In Hall, Arkansas, there is a Political Animals club, garden club, and Teachers of Tomorrow club.

Some student activities are governed by the state high school league. In most cases, the high school league is an organization of high schools that join together with the approval of their local school boards. The leagues encourage student participation in school activities by supporting interscholastic programs. They establish eligibility criteria for activities. Students participating in league activities should be familiar with the league handbook. Extracurricular activities involving athletics and some literary, dramatic, and forensic activities must follow eligibility requirements established by the appropriate high school league.

Some student-initiated clubs may fall under the Equal Access Act. This act, passed by Congress in 1984, prohibits secondary schools that receive federal funds from preventing voluntary student groups, including religious ones, from using school facilities for meetings if the school allows any noncurriculum-related activities to meet on school grounds. Secondary public schools must treat all student-initiated clubs equally, regardless of the religious, political, or philosophical orientation of the club. The act includes the following guidelines.

• The club must be voluntary and student-initiated.

• There is no sponsorship by the school or its employees.

• School employees are present only in a nonparticipatory manner. (The principal can require the club to find a faculty member to be present during the meetings even though the faculty member should not participate.)

- The club does not interfere with the orderly conduct of educational activities within the school.

- Meetings cannot be directly conducted, controlled, or regularly attended by nonschool persons.

Student activities serve an important role in helping secondary schools develop well-rounded students.

See also: CLUBS; SPORTS, SCHOOL.

INTERNET RESOURCES

FUTURE BUSINESS LEADERS OF AMERICA–PHI BETA LAMDA. 2002. <www.fbla-pbl.org>.

FUTURE FARMERS OF AMERICA. 2002. <www.ffa.org>.

KEY CLUB INTERNATIONAL. 2002. <www.keyclub.org/index.htm>.

NATIONAL BETA CLUB. 2002. <www.betaclub.org>.

NATIONAL HONOR SOCIETY and NATIONAL JUNIOR HONOR SOCIETY. 2002. <http://dsa.principals.org/nhs>.

ROTARY INTERNATIONAL: INTERACT. 2002. <www.rotary.org/programs/interact/>.

ROGER E. JONES

FINANCING

Student body funds do not represent a significant portion of the school district budget, and they are not available for discretionary spending by the administration or board of education. Student body funds do represent one of the most visible and likely areas for breaches of internal control.

Depending on the size and location of the school, student body funds can range in size from hundreds of dollars to hundreds of thousands of dollars. Laws and rules govern how student body funds can be used and accounted for; these vary from state to state, but most contain detailed rules and procedures that are to be followed for collecting, accounting, and distributing student body funds. Although student body funds are for the purpose of conducting activities on behalf of students, they are still considered school district funds under the su-

pervision of the local board of education. Student body organizations acquire their purpose, power, and privileges from the rights conferred upon them by the local governing board and the applicable state law.

To avert potential problems regarding the handling of funds, certain principles—a type of "student Bill of Rights"—are suggested here. Students have a right to expect that these principles will be respected in the handling of their funds.

Student Bill of Rights

Student funds shall be segregated from district and other appropriated funds, and shall be accounted for separately. This is an important element of internal control that is easily lost if funds are comingled. Many schools take advantage of the laws that govern student body funds by incorporating their implementation into a learning experience for their students. For instance, a formal constitution that states the name and purpose of the organization is usually required. The constitution presents the framework within which the organization will operate. Students and advisors are heavily involved in creating and maintaining their constitution. The constitution outlines the titles and duties of officers, election of officers, terms of office, and the requirements for eligibility to hold office. At a minimum, the elected officers include a president and treasurer. The constitution also includes rules governing financial activities including budgets, reporting requirements, and authorization of disbursements.

For most secondary schools detailed minutes of meetings are also kept. The minutes contain details of proceedings, including financial matters pertaining to the budget, approval of fund-raising venture, and expenditure authorizations. These study body functions of fund governance often are incorporated into the schools' leadership classes as a learning tool for public governance.

Accountability

There are occurrences of "disappearing" student money that can adversely effect a school's reputation or the reputation of its employees. Most disappearances involve cash where proper internal controls were not in place. Stories of missing game gate receipts or student store money are not uncommon.

To maintain the public's trust and safeguard the student funds, it is important that the funds be accounted for in a responsible manner. Uniform systems to insure adequate accounting procedures, supervision, segregation of duties, and auditing are necessary. As part of the annual audit of a school district, auditors routinely audit a sample of student body funds within the district. The auditors review for proper accounting procedures, compliance with the law, and for solvency. In addition, unlike many other types of audits, they check to see that reserves are not excessive—the reason being that typically, funds raised in a school year should be spent on those students doing the fundraising and not for future students.

Student body funds also have to comply with state and federal regulations that affect all types of businesses. As an example, student body payments often are made to independent contractors to perform services such as catering, concessions, performances, and so forth. Like everyone else, they have to comply with the Internal Revenue Service's guidelines. Amounts exceeding $600 in one calendar year must be reported on form 1099MISC. This task can be overwhelming and complex. As a result, many school districts require that contractor payments be made through the centralized business office.

Sometimes employees are funded through student body funds to provide help for extracurricular activities. Because student bodies typically do not have the expertise or technology to be employers, most districts run student-body-funded salary payments through their district payroll office. There are several other issues such as use tax and sales tax that also apply to student body funds. Using existing payroll and human resource systems for positions funded by student body funds is a good idea because it allows all of the applicable taxes, employee deductions, and fringe benefits processing to be automated and compliant with the law.

Fund-raising

Fund-raisers involving students and parents are the biggest source of income for student body funds. Car washes, candy sales, and carnivals bring in millions of dollars to student body funds each year. This money pays for computers, playground equipment, field trips, and many other athletic and enrichment programs.

To best ascertain which fund-raisers are the most profitable or worthwhile, revenue and cost projections need to be done prior to conducting

fund-raising activity. For example if the cost of the item being sold is $1 and the selling price is $3, and the plan is to sell 1,000 of the items, the projected costs should be $1,000 and projected revenues should be $3,000 for a profit of $2,000. At the conclusion of the fund-raiser, a reconciliation should be completed to account for actual monies raised as compared to the projection. Any differences should be reviewed and accounted for with remaining items not sold. Since many students and parents often have an emotional investment in the fund-raiser, being able to account for the profitability is critical.

The tenets above represent a minimum level of care in the handling of student body funds and are meant to serve as a guide. The fiduciary duty school personnel have with regard to student funds is clear. The standards and practices observed by schools and school districts set the tone for trust levels held by the community.

RON BENNETT
JOHN GRAY

STUDENT AID
See: COLLEGE FINANCIAL AID.

STUDENT ASSEMBLIES
See: ASSEMBLIES, STUDENT.

STUDENT ENROLLMENT, HIGHER EDUCATION
See: ENROLLMENT MANAGEMENT IN HIGHER EDUCATION.

STUDENT LOANS IN AN INTERNATIONAL CONTEXT

Student loans are increasingly used to provide financial assistance for students in higher education, in both industrialized and developing countries. The need for financial assistance to enable students from low-income families to meet direct and indirect costs of education (tuition fees, books, and living expenses) is widely recognized, and the case for student support programs to ensure equality of opportunity, equity, and social justice is rarely questioned. What is a matter of dispute however, is whether financial support should be provided by governments, private agencies, employers, or institutions, and whether it should be in the form of scholarships, bursaries, grants—either available to all students or means-tested (i.e., targeted by financial need)—or repayable loans. Fierce controversy has surrounded the idea of student loan programs since their inception.

National student loan programs were first established in the 1950s in countries as diverse as Colombia, Denmark, Norway, Sweden, Japan, and the United States. The following decades saw a steady expansion of student loan programs, through the introduction of student loans in new countries and expansion in the number of loans available and their average size. In response to higher education expansion, combined with increasing financial stringency and concern for equity, there was a surge of interest in student loans in the late 1980s and 1990s, with new programs introduced in Australia, New Zealand, and the United Kingdom; several countries in eastern Europe and the former Soviet Union, including Hungary and Russia, considering introducing student loans for the first time; and some developing countries in Asia, Africa, and Latin America establishing or expanding student loan programs. Yet student loans remain controversial, and advantages and disadvantages of loans continue to be widely debated. Debate also surrounds the question of how student loans should be administered: in particular, eligibility and terms of repayment of loans, appropriate rates of interest, and mechanisms to target disadvantaged students while minimizing default. This entry summarizes the recent growth of student loan programs, reviews the literature analyzing the international experience of student loans, both in developed and developing countries, and examines some implications of the growth of student loans for student and labor mobility.

Development of Student Loan Programs

Early examples of national student loan programs included the National Defense Student Loan (NDSL) program, introduced in the United States in 1958; state loan funds for students established in Denmark, Norway, and Sweden in the early 1950s; and a small-scale program introduced in Colombia in 1953, the *Instituto Colombiano de Credito Educativo y Estudios Tecnicos en el Exterior* (ICETEX). During the 1960s and 1970s student loan programs

were set up in many countries, including Canada (the Canada Student Loan Program began in 1964), several Latin American countries (by 1980 student loan programs existed in at least fifteen countries in Latin America and the Caribbean), and a few developing countries in Africa and Asia (including Ghana and India). But many programs were either small-scale, as in many Latin American countries, or short-lived—the loan program in Ghana lasted only a few years.

During the 1980s there was continued growth in student loan programs and many countries, including Japan, Scandinavian countries, and the United States, began to rely increasingly on loans as a means of student support. Many countries, particularly in Europe, still offer student support through a combination of grants and loans, but there has been a marked shift towards greater use of loans. In the United States, the College Board noted in 1999 that "Over the past quarter century, federal student aid has drifted from a grant-based to a loan-based system, producing a sea change in the way many students and families finance post-secondary education" (p. 4). In the United Kingdom the first student loan program was set up in 1989 to provide "top-up" loans to supplement maintenance grants for students' living expenses. However, since the introduction of tuition fees in 1998, loans have been the main form of student support, with the abolition of grants for all but a minority of financially needy students in England and Wales; a different scheme has operated in Scotland since 2000. In Australia, the Higher Education Contribution Scheme (HECS) was introduced in 1989, with students able to opt for deferred payment through income-contingent loans with payments collected by the tax authorities, and support for living expenses in Australia is now also in the form of income-contingent loans.

There has also been renewed interest in student loans in developing countries, partly due to growing recognition of the need to increase cost recovery in secondary and higher education. The World Bank's 1994 policy paper on higher education recommended: "Cost-sharing coupled with student financial assistance is an efficient strategy for achieving expanded coverage and better quality in higher education . . . while protecting equity of access. . . . Given that in every developing country students attending higher education represent an elite group, with income-earning potential significantly higher than that of their peers, it is appropriate that the major form of student financial assistance offered be government-guaranteed student loans rather than grants" (p. 50). In the 1990s new student loan programs were set up in several African countries, including Kenya, Nigeria, and South Africa, and in the Asian countries of China, Malaysia, Thailand, and Vietnam.

Characteristics of Student Loans

The basic characteristic of all student loan schemes is that students are offered the chance to borrow money to help them finance tuition costs or living expenses. After completing their studies, graduates must repay the amount borrowed, with or without interest. Although all loan schemes share this basic characteristic, there are important differences in the way different programs are administered, particularly in terms of (1) whether loan programs are operated by the government, independent agencies, banks, or higher education institutions; (2) the level of interest charged, and whether this is subsidized (i.e., lower than commercial or market interest rates); and (3) the way in which repayments are collected—in particular whether loan repayments are fixed over a specific time period (often described as *mortgage-type* loans), or whether graduates must repay a fixed proportion of their income each year until the loan is repaid (usually described as *income-contingent* loans).

Evaluation of International Experience

Increased popularity of student loans since the 1960s has stimulated research on both theoretical and empirical issues. As wide variations exist between programs, comparative studies of international experience—which highlight significant differences, examine economic or social effects of alternative systems, and identify strengths and weaknesses—can be particularly valuable. A 1986 comparative study of student support in the United States and four European countries (France, Germany, Sweden, and the United Kingdom) by Bruce Johnstone argued that "it was a major premise of this study, borne out by the research, that these and other countries must balance very similar public policy goals in apportioning the costs [of higher education] . . . and that each country can benefit . . . by understanding what countries with similar higher educational systems and public policy objectives are doing" (p. 1).

Since this and a few other comparative studies were published in the 1980s there has been growing interest in learning from international experience. Reforms of student aid policies and systems taking place between 1989 and 1999 in Australia, Sweden, and the United Kingdom drew upon lessons from experience in other countries. In Sweden, the government changed the national system in 1989 by reducing the level of interest subsidy offered on student loans, but introducing income-contingent repayment, linking the amount of graduates' loan repayments with their level of income. This reflected Johnstone's comparative analysis of student loan schemes that showed that under the previous scheme Swedish students enjoyed far higher "implicit grants" because of the interest subsidy than American students. A major policy shift also occurred in the United Kingdom with the introduction of student loans in 1989, and the British government drew heavily on international experience in justifying loans as a means of student support. More recently the experience of Australia and Sweden in introducing and implementing income-contingent loans has been widely quoted as offering important lessons for the design of student loan schemes. Nicholas Barr described income-contingent student loans as "an idea whose time has come" (1991, p. 155), and praised Australia for having introduced a "highly effective income-contingent loan scheme" (1998, p. 186).

Other reviews of international experience have focused on developing countries, where the effectiveness of student loans has often proved disappointing. In the early 1990s a series of international forums on student loans organized by the International Institute for Educational Planning (IIEP) analyzed experiences in the United States, Europe, and in developing countries. An evaluation of student loan experience in developing countries was summarized with the conclusion that "student loans can make a contribution to relieving the financial pressures facing higher education, provided that loan programmes are properly designed, effectively managed and a high rate of recovery is achieved" (Woodhall 1992, p. 355). Requirements for success include:

- sound financial management, including appropriate interest rates to maintain the capital value of the loan fund and cover administrative costs;

- a sound legal framework to ensure that loan recovery is legally enforceable;

- effective machinery for targeting financial support and selecting recipients of subsidies on grounds of financial need or manpower priorities;

- effective machinery for loan recovery, to minimize default;

- publicity campaigns to ensure widespread understanding and acceptance of the principles of student loans and the importance of the obligation to repay.

These broad conclusions on feasibility and scope for use of student loans in developing countries were echoed in a 1995 comparative study for the World Bank by Adrian Ziderman and Douglas Albrecht, who concluded that: "student loans have received much attention both in the literature and in practice. While they have not always worked well . . . suitably reformed, they can constitute a productive, though limited mechanism for cost recovery" (p. 371).

International Issues

The first student loan schemes were mainly concerned with enhancing higher education participation in a domestic context, but implications for international student mobility were quickly recognized. An important feature of student loan schemes is that they provide financial assistance and subsidies to individual students, rather than to institutions. In principle, loans should be portable from one institution to another, and even across national boundaries. The first student loan program in Latin America, ICETEX in Colombia, was initially set up to provide financial assistance for students intending to study abroad. This remains one of the main purposes of ICETEX, although growing cost differentials between higher education in Colombia and in the United States or other developed countries mean that it now provides loans for many more students who study in Colombia than for students studying abroad. Some other national schemes offer loans for study abroad as well as for those studying in national higher education institutions, but a number of issues limit the use of student loans to finance study abroad. These include the cost differentials already mentioned, and the difficulties of enforcing loan repayments if graduates choose to work abroad after completing their studies.

Programs designed to increase student mobility, such as the Erasmus and Tempus programs set up to promote student exchange and mobility in the European Union (EU), are mainly concerned with facilitating student mobility between member countries (for example by harmonizing entry requirements for study programs in different countries and establishing credit transfer arrangements) rather than with setting up a system of financial support transportable across national boundaries. Students' own governments are generally expected to finance the costs of study abroad—whether by grants, student loans, or other means—but the need for greater harmonization of rules determining levels of tuition fees and student support in different countries is increasingly emphasized, as student mobility and opportunities for study abroad increase.

Another important issue now recognized in several countries, as skilled labor becomes increasingly mobile, is the need to design mechanisms for collecting loan repayments from graduates working abroad. Implications for student loans of what is variously described as international labor mobility or "brain drain" have received limited attention, although potential losses from graduates who choose to work abroad and then default on loan repayments have been emphasized by critics of student loans. Barr argues that income-contingent loans could be collected by the tax authorities in any country where a graduate subsequently works, and the revenue transferred to the country that originally provided a student loan: "With such an arrangement loan repayments are transparent with respect to international boundaries" (2001, p. 234). Barr further proposes that that "it would be possible for the EU or the World Bank to establish an International Learning Bank from which students in poor countries would borrow to finance their tertiary education—both those who subsequently stay at home and those who emigrate" (2001, p. 234). Such possibilities, and their implications for the finance of higher education and for labor mobility, remain to be explored.

See also: COLLEGE FINANCIAL AID; HIGHER EDUCATION, INTERNATIONAL ISSUES.

BIBLIOGRAPHY

BARR, NICHOLAS. 1991. "Income-Contingent Student Loans: An Idea Whose Time Has Come." In *Economics, Culture and Education: Essays in Honour of Mark Blaug,* ed. Graham K. Shaw. Aldershot: Edward Elgar.

BARR, NICHOLAS. 1998. "Higher Education in Australia and Britain: What Lessons?" *The Australian Economic Review* 31(2):179–188.

BARR, NICHOLAS. 2001. *The Welfare State as Piggy Bank: Information, Risk, Uncertainty, and the Role of the State.* Oxford: Oxford University Press.

COLLEGE BOARD. 1999. *Trends in Student Aid.* Washington, DC: The College Board.

JOHNSTONE, D. BRUCE. 1986. *Sharing the Costs of Higher Education: Student Financial Assistance in the United Kingdom, the Federal Republic of Germany, France, Sweden, and the United States.* New York: The College Board.

WOODHALL, MAUREEN, ed. 1989. *Financial Support for Students: Grants, Loans or Graduate Tax?* London: Kogan Page, in association with the Institute of Education, University of London.

WOODHALL, MAUREEN. 1990. *Student Loans in Higher Education (1) Western Europe and the U.S.* Paris: International Institute for Educational Planning.

WOODHALL, MAUREEN. 1991. *Student Loans in Higher Education (2) Asia.* Paris: International Institute for Educational Planning.

WOODHALL, MAUREEN. 1991. *Student Loans in Higher Education (3) English-Speaking Africa.* Paris: International Institute for Educational Planning.

WOODHALL, MAUREEN. 1992. "Student Loans in Developing Countries: Feasibility, Experience and Prospects for Reform." *Higher Education* 23(4):347–356.

WOODHALL, MAUREEN. 1993. *Student Loans in Higher Education (4) Latin America and the Caribbean.* Paris: International Institute for Higher Educational Planning.

WORLD BANK. 1994. *Higher Education: The Lessons of Experience.* Washington, DC: The World Bank.

ZIDERMAN, ADRIAN, and ALBRECHT, DOUGLAS. 1995. *Financing Universities in Developing Countries.* London and Washington, DC: The Falmer Press.

MAUREEN WOODHALL

STUDENT MOBILITY

Student mobility is the practice of students changing schools other than when they are promoted from one school level to the other, such as when students are promoted from elementary school to middle school or middle school to high school. Mobile students can change schools in between school years, such as during the summer, or during the school year. But no matter when it occurs, student mobility not only can harm the students who change schools, it can also harm the classrooms and schools they attend.

The Extent of Student Mobility

Student mobility is widespread in the United States. According to the 1998 National Assessment of Educational Progress (NEAP), one-third of fourth graders, 19 percent of eighth graders, and 10 percent of twelfth graders changed schools at least once in the previous two years. Student mobility was even more widespread among poor and minority students. The incidence of student mobility is also higher when viewed over a student's entire elementary and secondary career. Based on data from a national longitudinal study of a cohort of eighth graders in the United States, more students made non-promotional school changes during their elementary and secondary school careers than remained in a stable pattern of attending a single elementary, middle, and high school. School changes were more common during elementary school than during secondary school. In fact, mobility is the norm during elementary school, while it is the exception during high school.

Student mobility not only varies widely among students, but also among schools. It is especially high within large, predominantly minority, urban school districts. In the Chicago public schools, for example, an average of 80 percent of students in the district remained in the same school from September 1993 to September 1994 and only 47 percent remained in the same school over a four-year period. Fifteen percent of the schools lost at least 30 percent of their students in only one year.

The Impact of Mobility on Students

Existing research finds that students can suffer psychologically, socially, and academically from mobility. Mobile students face the psychological challenge of coping with a new school environment. Mobile students also face the social adjustment to new peers and social expectations. Research has demonstrated that mobility is related to misbehavior and youth violence—it is easier to commit crimes against strangers. Studies have also found that mobile high school students are less likely to participate in extracurricular activities.

Mobility can hurt students academically. Several studies have examined the impact of mobility at the elementary level. Studies that do not control for the background characteristics of students consistently find that mobile students have lower achievement than non-mobile or stable students. Yet studies that do account for background differences find that mobility may be more of a symptom than a cause of poor school performance. In other words, mobile students came from poorer families and had lower academic performance before they were mobile, a finding supported by other studies.

At the secondary level, several additional studies have examined the impact of mobility on two indicators of student performance—test scores and high school graduation. The impact of mobility of secondary test scores appears to be mixed. Two studies of middle school students, one by Carolyn Hofstetter and the other by Valerie Lee and Julia Smith, found that mobile students had significantly lower test scores after controlling for other student and classroom characteristics. Several studies, based on the same national longitudinal survey of eighth graders who were tracked for six years, found that the impact of mobility was sometimes negative and sometimes positive. These studies suggest that the timing of mobility matters during high school, which is supported by a California study of mobility in which some students made "strategic" school moves to improve their educational prospects, while other students made "reactive" school moves to get out of poor or dangerous situations.

The strongest impact of mobility is on high school graduation. There is overwhelming evidence that mobility during high school diminishes the prospects for graduation. Yet one study found that early school changes as well as changing residences between grades eight and ten and between grades ten and twelve increased the odds of dropping out at twelfth grade, but that early school changes decreased the odds of dropping out at twelfth grade among tenth graders who had not already left school. This suggests that mobility has a negative impact on some students, but may have a positive impact on others.

Although a substantial body of research shows that students can suffer psychologically, socially, and academically from changing schools, the impact of mobility depends on such factors as the number of school changes, when they occur, the reason for the changes, and the student's personal and family situation. Some mobility can actually be beneficial if the reason and timing represent a "strategic" move to a better educational placement. Yet most mobility is not beneficial. What accounts for the generally negative impact of mobility on achievement and why, in some cases, does mobility not impact achievement or even improve it? The answer depends, in part, on the reasons students change schools.

Causes of Mobility

The leading cause of student mobility is residential mobility. A national study by Russell Rumberger and Katherine Larson found that 70 percent of all school changes between grades eight and twelve were accompanied by a change of residences. But there are many reasons students change schools. In one study parents of twelfth grade students who changed schools over the previous four years reported three types of reasons for changing schools. The most frequent reason was the family moving (58%). But almost half of the reasons were because students asked to change schools, often to take advantage of a specific educational program, or asked to be transferred to a public, private, or magnet school. The least frequent reason was because the school asked the adolescent to transfer either because of disciplinary or academic problems.

Research has identified some specific factors that predict student mobility. Interestingly, mobility does not seem to be strongly related to family income and socioeconomic status, but it does appear to be related to family structure: families without both biological parents have higher incidence of residential moves and higher rates of school moves. Several student-related factors have also been identified. Low school performance (grade point average), behavior problems, absenteeism, and low educational expectations all predicted school changes during high school after controlling for family factors. School-related factors also predict student mobility: Schools with high concentrations of at-risk and minority students have lower mobility rates even after controlling for differences in student factors, while schools with higher teacher salaries and better teachers have lower mobility than other schools.

Current literature suggests two ways that schools affect student mobility (as well as school dropout rates). One way is indirectly, through general policies and practices that are designed to promote the overall effectiveness of the school. These policies and practices, along with other characteristics of the school (student composition, size, etc.), may contribute to voluntary student turnover by affecting conditions that keep students engaged in school. This perspective is consistent with several existing theories of school dropout and departure that view student engagement as the precursor to withdrawal. The other way is directly, through explicit policies and conscious decisions that cause students to *involuntarily* withdraw from school. These rules may concern low grades, poor attendance, misbehavior, or being overage and can lead to suspensions, expulsions, or forced transfers. This form of withdrawal is school-initiated and contrasts with the student-initiated form mentioned above. This perspective considers a school's own agency, rather than just that of the student, in producing dropouts and transfers. One metaphor that has been used to characterize this process is discharge: "students *drop out* of school, schools *discharge* students (Riehl, 1999, p. 231). Finally, additional conditions found in large, urban and high minority schools that could contribute to student turnover include open enrollments and overcrowding. Open enrollment allows students to readily change schools if they can find one with sufficient space, while overcrowding prompts schools to transfer students even if they wanted to enroll them.

There are several reasons why mobility may negatively impact student achievement. Mobile students must adjust to new academic standards and expected classroom behaviors. Mobile students sometimes get placed in classes that do not contribute to high school completion or they get placed in classes where the curriculum differs from their previous school—a condition referred to as "curricular incoherence."

But why do some students seem to be adversely affected by changing schools and others do not? The answer may depend, in part, on the reasons students change schools. In one study, students who made "strategic" school changes to seek a better educational placement, in general, reported positive academic impacts, while students who made "reactive"

school changes due to intolerable social or academic situations were more likely to report negative academic impacts from changing schools. The idea of strategic school changes is consistent with the finding that changes early in a student's high school career may not be harmful or can even be beneficial, while changes late in a student's high school career are generally harmful. On the other hand, mobility due to misbehavior or involuntary transfers are more likely to harmful, especially if the change of schools fails to address the underlying problem that lead to the transfer in the first place.

The Impact of Mobility on Schools

Mobility not only impacts students who change schools, it impacts classrooms and schools who must deal with mobile students. It can also adversely impact non-mobile students. In one Rumberger study of mobility in California (1999), school personnel characterized the overall affects of student mobility at the school level as a "chaos" factor that affects classroom learning activities, teacher morale, and administrative burdens—all of which can influence the learning and achievement of all students in the school. Teachers were very adamant about how disruptive and difficult it is to teach in classrooms with constant student turnover. Similarly, a Chicago study by Julia Smith, BetsAnn Smith, and Anthony Byrk found that the pace of instruction was slower in schools with high rates of student mobility. School administrators reported how time-consuming it is to simply process students when they enter and exit a school. Beyond the administrative costs, school personnel also identified other impacts, such as the fiscal impacts that result from mobile students failing to turn in textbooks, and impacts on school climate.

Conclusions

Student mobility is a common feature of American schooling. Although mobility is largely initiated by students and parents due to changing residences, some mobility results from the policies and actions of schools and districts—such as open enrollment, overcrowded schools, and zero-tolerance policies—that can lead to voluntary or involuntary school transfers. Consequently, schools and districts can help reduce the incidence of "needless" mobility and help to mitigate its potentially damaging effects. School reform efforts can help reduce mobility by making schools more attractive to students and parents. Schools can also initiate a number of strategies to help transfer students adjust to their new school setting and to quickly provide the educational and support services that transfer students may require.

With increasing pressure on schools to adopt reforms and raise test scores, addressing the issue of mobility may not seem a high priority for schools. But failing to do so could easily undermine those efforts as well as hurt the students and families the schools are charged to serve.

See also: SCHOOL DROPOUTS.

BIBLIOGRAPHY

ALEXANDER, KARL L.; ENTWISLE, DORIS R.; and DAUBER, SUSAN L. 1996. "Children in Motion: School Transfers and Elementary School Performance." *The Journal of Educational Research* 90:3–12.

AUDETTE, ROBERT; ALGOZZINE, ROBERT; and WARDEN, MICHELLE. 1993. "Mobility and School Achievement." *Psychological Reports* 72:701–702.

BECK, LYNN G.; KRATZER, CINDY C.; and ISKEN, JO ANN. 1997. "Caring for Transient Students in One Urban Elementary School." *Journal for a Just and Caring Education* 3:343–369.

BOWDITCH, CHRISTINE. 1993. "Getting Rid of Troublemakers: High School Disciplinary Procedures and the Production of Dropouts." *Social Problems* 40:493–509.

BRYK, ANTHONY S., et al. 1998. *Academic Productivity of Chicago Public Elementary Schools.* Chicago: Consortium on Chicago School Reform.

CHICAGO PANEL ON SCHOOL POLICY. 2000. *Staying Put: A Mobility Awareness Action Plan.* Chicago: Chicago Panel on School Policy.

ELLICKSON, PHYLLIS L., and McGUIGAN, KIMBERLY A. 2000. "Early Predictors of Adolescent Violence." *American Journal of Public Health* 90:566–572.

FINE, MICHELLE. 1991. *Framing Dropouts: Notes on the Politics of an Urban Public High School.* Albany: State University of New York Press.

FINN, JEREMY D. 1989. "Withdrawing from School." *Review of Educational Research* 59:117–142.

HAVEMAN, ROBERT, and WOLFE, BARBARA. 1994. *Succeeding Generations: On the Effects of Investments in Children.* New York: Russell Sage Foundation.

HEINLEIN, LISA M., and SHINN, MARYBETH. 2000. "School Mobility and Student Achievement in an Urban Setting." *Psychology in the Schools* 37:349–357.

HESS, ALFRED G., JR., et al. 1986. *Where's Room 185? How Schools Can Reduce Their Dropout Problem.* Chicago: Chicago Panel on Public School Policy and Finance.

HOFSTETTER, CAROLYN H. 1999. "Toward an Equitable NAEP for English Language Learners: What Contextual Factors Affect Math Performance." Paper presented at the annual meeting of the American Educational Research Association, Montreal, April 19–23.

HOLLAND, J. V.; KAPLAN, D. M.; and DAVIS, S. D. 1974. "Interschool Transfers: A Mental Health Challenge." *Journal of School Health* 44:74–79.

INGERSOLL, GARY M.; SCAMMAN, JAMES P.; and ECKERLING, WAYNE D. 1989. "Geographic Mobility and Student Achievement in an Urban Setting." *Educational Evaluation and Policy Analysis* 11:143–149.

JASON, LEONARD A., et al. 1992. *Helping Transfer Students: Strategies for Educational and Social Readjustment.* San Francisco: Jossey-Bass.

KERBOW, DAVID. 1995. *Pervasive Student Mobility: A Moving Target for School Reform.* Chicago: Chicago Panel on School Policy.

KERBOW, DAVID. 1996. "Patterns of Urban Student Mobility and Local School Reform." *Journal of Education of Students Placed at Risk* 1:147–169.

LEE, VALERIE E., and BURKAM, DAVID T. 1992. "Transferring High Schools: An Alternative to Dropping Out?" *American Journal of Education* 100: 420–453.

LEE, VALERIE E., and SMITH, JULIA B. 1999. "Social Support and Achievement for Young Adolescents in Chicago: The Role of School Academic Press." *American Educational Research Journal* 36:907–945.

NELSON, P. S.; SIMONI, J. M.; and ADELMAN, HOWARD S. 1996. "Mobility and School Functioning in the Early Grades." *Journal of Educational Research* 89:365–369.

PRIBESH, SHANA, and DOWNEY, DOUGLAS B. 1999. "Why Are Residential and School Moves Associated with Poor School Performance?" *Demography* 36:521–534.

RIEHL, CAROLYN. 1999. "Labeling and Letting Go: An Organizational Analysis of How High School

Students Are Discharged as Dropouts." In *Research in Sociology of Education and Socialization,* ed. Aaron M. Pallas. New York: JAI Press.

RUMBERGER, RUSSELL W., et al. 1999. *The Educational Consequences of Mobility for California Students and Schools.* Berkeley, CA: Policy Analysis for California Education.

RUMBERGER, RUSSELL W., and LARSON, KATHERINE A. 1998. "Student Mobility and the Increased Risk of High School Drop Out." *American Journal of Education* 107:1–35.

RUMBERGER, RUSSELL W., and THOMAS, SCOTT L. 2000. "The Distribution of Dropout and Turnover Rates among Urban and Suburban High Schools." *Sociology of Education* 73:39–67.

SCHALLER, J. 1975. "The Relation between Geographic Mobility and School Behavior." *Man-Environment Systems* 5:185–187.

SIMPSON, GLORIA A., and FOWLER, MARY GLENN. 1994. "Geographic Mobility and Children's Emotional/Behavioral Adjustment and School Functioning." *Pediatrics* 93:303–309.

SMITH, JULIA B.; SMITH, BETSANN; and BRYK, ANTHONY S. 1998. *Setting the Pace: Opportunities to Learn in Chicago's Elementary Schools.* Chicago: Consortium on Chicago School Research.

SWANSON, CHRISTOPHER B., and SCHNEIDER, BARBARA. 1999. "Students on the Move: Residential and Educational Mobility in America's Schools." *Sociology of Education* 72:54–67.

TEACHMAN, JAY D.; PAASCH, KATHLEEN; and CARVER, KAREN. 1996. "School Capital and Dropping Out of School Early." *Journal of Marriage and the Family* 58:773–783.

TUCKER, C. JACK; MARX, JONATHAN; and LONG, LARRY. 1998. "Moving On: Residential Mobility and Children's School Lives." *Sociology of Education* 71:111–129.

U.S. GENERAL ACCOUNTING OFFICE. 1994. *Elementary School Children: Many Change Schools Frequently, Harming Their Education.* Washington, DC: General Accounting Office.

WEHLAGE, GARY G., et al. 1989. *Reducing the Risk: Schools as Communities of Support.* New York: Falmer Press.

WOOD, DAVID, et al. 1993. "Impact of Family Relocation on Children's Growth, Development, School Function, and Behavior." *Journal of the American Medical Association* 270:1334–1338.

RUSSELL W. RUMBERGER

STUDENT ORIENTATION PROGRAMS

Starting college can cause much anxiety in the heart of a new college student because of all the unknowns—"What should my major be? Will I make any friends? How will I find all of my classes? Whom do I ask if I have a question?" New student orientation programs are designed to guide students in answering all of these questions. Prior to the beginning of classes, students are given an overview of the complete realm of university life, from academics to social activities, through a period of days referred to as orientation. Typically, a staff member or team coordinates the orientation programs within the university and provides the leadership to bring the entire university together. Depending on the size and mission of the institution, the format of orientation will vary from a one-day program to a week-long event. However, regardless of the nature of the program, three objectives should be present in all orientation programs: 1) introducing students to college life; 2) acclimating students to their new surroundings; and 3) providing an opportunity for the university to meet the newest members of the community. It is the duty of the coordinator of orientation to design a program that will bring these three goals together.

Introduction to College Life

Introducing students to college life requires presenting as full a view as possible of all the university has to offer. Therefore, academics as well as extracurricular activities should be presented. During orientation, students should be made aware of opportunities to be socially integrated into the college culture. If students do not become socially integrated within the first few weeks of their arrival, they are less likely to stay at that institution. Social activities can include parties, games, concerts, icebreakers, and "hang-out" time. Students also can learn about the various student organizations in which they can be involved. However, orientation programs should not be purely fun and games, for college is more than just fun and games. While the social aspect does play a significant role in one's collegiate experience, the importance of academics should not be overlooked. While a student may focus on one more than the other, both work together in forming the college experience.

Orientation programs begin before classes start; therefore students usually will need to register for classes during orientation. Because new students need some direction and guidance in enrolling for classes, faculty members should have an opportunity to provide academic advising at orientation. An academic component to orientation will give the new students the advantage they will need in making the transition from high school to college. By giving a strong overview of academic expectations, students will be better prepared to meet the challenges of collegiate academics. Therefore, in order to give the most accurate view of an institution, there must be both an academic and social component to the orientation program.

Becoming Familiar with the New Environment

The second aspect of the role of orientation is acclimating students to their new environment. After moving into a new neighborhood, one would ideally like a few days to learn one's way around the new neighborhood. Likewise, orientation should allow students to get their bearings in their new home. For some students, going to college is their first time away from home, so orientation should give them time to become familiar with their new surroundings. New students should meet their roommates and find their classrooms. Through guided tours, campus maps, or even time to just wander, orientation provides a safe avenue for new students to find their way around campus. By moving on campus before classes starts, the new students are able to learn the ropes and not seem so green by the time the academic year begins. Students should become familiar with both physical locations and the workings of the environment during orientation.

Welcome to the Community!

The university community should not only be involved in the preparation and implementation of orientation programs but also have an opportunity to meet the new students. Unlike some of the other programs within campus life, orientation requires the cooperation and the resources of the entire campus community including faculty, dining services, housing, facilities management, and student activities groups. Depending on the size of the institution,

the level of community involvement may vary. The administration of a small, liberal arts college may have more opportunities to meet and greet students than that of a large, public school. Whether through receptions, meetings, and even help on move-in day, the university community should be involved in welcoming the new students. For example, faculty may meet new students prior to the beginning of classes. By making a connection, this interaction with the community may in turn even strengthen the student's persistence in college.

Students, as well as faculty and staff, have an important role in orientation. Selecting a specific number of current students to be orientation leaders allows the new students to meet upperclassmen. The orientation leaders can give the new students the inside scoop on college life since they too have been in the new students' shoes. Many institutions use orientation leaders to lead the new students through a series of workshops, campus tours, and social activities. New students may be more open to receive information from the orientation leaders than from a lecturer in a main auditorium. Orientation leaders can also explain some of the details of university life that some administrators would never think of telling them. For instance, orientation leaders can share things such as where to hang out between classes, where to find the best food in town, how to use the laundry room, and how to get involved in campus activities. Often new students have the most contact during orientation with the orientation leaders, so it is imperative that these leaders be properly trained. Therefore, planning orientation leader training should be just as important as planning the actual program. Leaders need to understand the vision of orientation so that it becomes their own and they can communicate that to the new trainees. When selecting orientation leaders, one should look for a good representation of the student body as well as for those who are willing to go the extra mile in helping new students. The readiness of the orientation leaders is the key to the implementation of a successful orientation program.

Conclusion

When designing an orientation program, one must first understand the culture of the institution and the students. A good program for one university may not be conducive to the size or mission of another. In addition, some programs may work better than others depending on the type of student who attends the institution. Even though most orientation programs are designed with the eighteen-year-old, first-time college student in mind, some institutions may have more transfer students or even nontraditional (older) students. Therefore, programs should be implemented to orient them into the academic community as well. Another factor to consider is the orientation of parents. Because parents can aid in the student's transition into college life, the university needs to inform parents as well as students about the structure of the university and where to find additional information.

Orientation programs serve as a foundation for college success. In many instances, orientation programs create a lasting impression for new students and their families. While it is not possible to tell new students everything they will need to know for their entire collegiate experience, orientation programs should create a framework in which students will know where to go, whether it be the tutoring center or health services, if they have additional questions. Orientation is the designated time for the entire university to say, "We welcome you, and we are glad that you are here!" Likewise, orientation is a time to show the new students why they made a good decision in their college choice.

Orientation is a much-needed program that when planned correctly can aid all participants—new students, parents, faculty, staff, administration, and current students. Orientation is designed to answer questions before they are asked and to provide solutions before problems occur. By planning appropriately and using all campus resources, orientation should relieve anxieties and prepare the new students for success.

See also: ACADEMIC ADVISING IN HIGHER EDUCATION; ADJUSTMENT TO COLLEGE; COLLEGE STUDENT RETENTION.

BIBLIOGRAPHY

ASTIN, ALEXANDER W. 1993. *What Matters in College? Four Critical Years Revisited.* San Francisco: Jossey-Bass.

MULLENDORE, RICHARD H., and BILLER, GARY M. 1994. "Orientation Standards, Evaluation, and Assessment." In *Designing Successful Transitions: A Guide for Orienting Students to College,* ed. Lee M. Upcraft. Columbia: National Resource Center for the Freshmen Year Experience, University of South Carolina.

ROBINSON, DEBRA A.; BURNS, CARL F.; and GAW, KEVIN F. 1996. "Orientation Programs: The Foundation for Student Learning and Success." *New Directions for Student Services* 75:55–68.

SMITH, BECKY F., and BRACKIN, RICHARD. 1994. "Components of a Comprehensive Orientation Program." In *Designing Successful Transitions: A Guide for Orienting Students to College,* ed. Lee M. Upcraft. Columbia: National Resource Center for the Freshmen Year Experience, University of South Carolina.

TINTO, VINCENT. 1993. *Leaving College: Rethinking the Causes and Cures of Student Attrition.* Chicago: University of Chicago Press.

STEPHANIE D. LEE

STUDENT SERVICES

COLLEGES AND UNIVERSITIES
Maureen E. Wilson
COMMUNITY COLLEGES
U. Monique Robinson-Wright
Sonya G. Smith

COLLEGES AND UNIVERSITIES

Student affairs professionals have always been concerned with the development of the "whole student" or a student's intellectual capacity and achievement, emotional make-up, physical condition, social relationships, vocational aptitudes and skills, moral and religious values, economic resources, and aesthetic appreciations. Although the activities of student affairs have changed over time, the basic tenets of helping students reach their full potential and attending to them as a human beings—not simply those in need of intellectual training—has remained constant.

History

Several developments in higher education gave rise to student affairs. In colonial colleges, faculty were responsible for enforcing regulations on students. Colleges acted *in loco parentis* or in place of parents. By the mid-nineteenth century, extracurricular activities such as literary clubs, athletic teams, and eating clubs were founded by students in response to the classical course of study. The rise of research universities and the subsequent changes in the roles of college presidents and faculty, and the increase in women's colleges and coeducation, led to the first appointments of student personnel workers—deans of men and deans of women—who among other duties, relieved college presidents of their role as disciplinarian and resolved student problems. The first dean, LeBaron Briggs, was appointed at Harvard University in 1891, and his duties also included personal counseling of students.

The *Student Personnel Point of View*, a report issued by the American Council on Education in 1937 and revised in 1949, serves as a foundation document for student affairs. It was developed on a philosophy stressing the importance of educating the whole student. It describes a number of services that are adapted according the specific mission, aims, objectives, and student demographics of individual campuses. Also emphasized is the need to coordinate student personnel functions with other programs and services on campus.

In 1914 Columbia University's Teachers College awarded the first master's degree for "Adviser of Women." Esther Lloyd-Jones earned the first doctorate in the field in 1929 and men were admitted for the first time in 1932. As of 2002, eighty-four institutions are listed in the Directory of Graduate Preparation Programs and there are additional ones as well. Entry-level professional positions in student affairs typically require a master's degree in college student personnel or a related field, and advancement to senior management positions often requires a doctorate.

Professional organizations reflect the development of professional positions in student affairs. The National Association of Deans of Women began in 1916; became the National Association of Women Deans, Administrators, and Counselors in 1972; changed its name to the National Association for Women in Education in 1991; and folded in 2000. Founded in 1919, the National Association of Deans and Advisers of Men became the National Association of Student Personnel Administrators in 1951. The American College Personnel Association began in 1924 as the National Association of Appointment Secretaries, assisting in job placement for teachers and other college graduates. Other specialized organizations serve various functional areas (e.g., Association of College Unions International, Association of College and University Housing Officers—International, and National Orientation Directions

Association) and state and regional organizations serve members as well.

Functions

On college and university campuses, the division of student affairs provides services to students and supports the educational mission of the institution. These services may include academic support services, academic advising, admissions, alcohol and drug education programs, career services, campus ministries, community service and service learning, counseling, financial aid, food services, fraternities and sororities, health centers, housing and residence life, multicultural programs, orientation, recreational sports, student activities, student discipline, and wellness programs.

All these programs and services have had to adapt to increasingly diverse student bodies. In the colonial era, higher education was for white males from well-to-do families. The establishment of women's colleges and historically black institutions in the late nineteenth century broadened the scope of higher education. Legislation including the Morrill Land Grant Act of 1862 and Servicemen's Readjustment Act of 1944 (G.I. Bill) allowed new populations access to higher education. Student affairs programs and services expanded accordingly.

At the beginning of the twenty-first century, the majority of undergraduates are more than twenty-one years old. More than 40 percent are enrolled part-time. Nearly 27 percent are people of color. About 65 percent of high school graduates attend college, although far fewer graduate. Furthermore, many students lack adequate preparation for college-level courses. Effective student affairs organizations are able to deliver programs and services to serve diverse populations and assist in the recruitment and retention of students.

Trends

Like all departments on campus, student affairs has had to make critical decisions in the face of rising costs and reduced budgets. Fee-for-service arrangements can mitigate some expenses. Hence, students may have to pay for counseling, health, and other services sometimes covered in student activity fees. Privatization is another issue facing campuses. In an effort to control costs in the face of dwindling budgets, administrators are outsourcing various functions including health services, dining services, maintenance, housekeeping, and bookstores. Although many question the move and raise concerns about job security, quality control, and incompatible operating philosophies, financial considerations are often compelling. Furthermore, private companies have increased competition with campus departments. For instance, off-campus apartment complexes attract students out of campus residence halls and into facilities that are often located close to campus. They may provide shuttle services, swimming pools, workout rooms, cable television, Internet access, laundry machines, and other attractive amenities at very competitive rates. Finally, to remain competitive and meet student demand, many campuses have increased board plan options for students and changed dining facilities and programs. Food courts (often offering popular fast-food chains), a la carte dining options, and expanded service hours now supplement traditional, all-you-can eat dining commons.

Contemporary efforts in student affairs have attempted to refocus student affairs on creating intentionally the conditions that enhance student learning and development, encouraging student commitment to educationally purposeful activities in and out of the classroom, and assessing those initiatives. Increasing the quality of student–faculty interactions and linking in-class and extracurricular activities through living-learning centers in residence halls are two strategies to promote student success. To be involved in the central missions of college and universities, student affairs must affirm its commitment to student learning and development.

See also: ADJUSTMENT TO COLLEGE; COLLEGE STUDENT RETENTION; COLLEGE STUDENTS WITH DISABILITIES, *subentry on* ACCOMMODATING; PERSONAL AND PSYCHOLOGICAL PROBLEMS OF COLLEGE STUDENTS; STUDENT SERVICES, *subentry on* COMMUNITY COLLEGES.

BIBLIOGRAPHY

AMERICAN COLLEGE PERSONNEL ASSOCIATION. 1994. *The Student Learning Imperative: Implications for Student Affairs.* Washington, DC: American College Personnel Association.

AMERICAN COLLEGE PERSONNEL ASSOCIATION AND NATIONAL ASSOCIATION OF STUDENT PERSONNEL ADMINISTRATORS. 1997. *Principles of Good Practice in Student Affairs.* Washington, DC: American College Personnel Association and National Association of Student Personnel Administrators.

AMERICAN COUNCIL ON EDUCATION. 1937/1949. *The Student Personnel Point of View.* Washington, DC: American Council on Education.

COOMES, MICHAEL, and TALBOT, DONNA, eds. 1999. *Directory of Graduate Preparation Programs in Student Affairs.* Washington, DC: American College Personnel Association.

NATIONAL ASSOCIATION OF STUDENT PERSONNEL ADMINISTRATORS. 1987. *A Perspective on Student Affairs.* Washington, DC: National Association of Student Personnel Administrators.

NUSS, ELIZABETH M. 1996. "The Development of Student Affairs." In *Student Services: A Handbook for the Profession.,* ed. Susan R. Komives et al. San Francisco: Jossey-Bass.

THELIN, JOHN R. 1996. "Historical Overview of American Higher Education." In *Student Services: A Handbook for the Profession.,* ed. Susan R. Komives et al. San Francisco: Jossey-Bass.

MAUREEN E. WILSON

COMMUNITY COLLEGES

Institutions of higher education vary in composition and structure, as do the characteristics of the students they serve. Community colleges are but one type of institution that educates and trains students, though they constitute a diverse group of institutions, ranging from comprehensive two-year colleges to technical colleges. These types of colleges offer students certificates, associate of applied science, associate of science, and associate of arts degrees. In contrast, four-year institutions also provide training and education, but usually offer baccalaureate, graduate, and professional degrees.

The demographics of higher education institutions, both community colleges and universities, shifted during the last decade of the twentieth century. In particular, increasing numbers of minorities, different ethnic groups, a larger female population, older adult students, international students, and students of varying academic abilities began to make up a major percentage of postsecondary students.

Overview of Student Service Organizational Structure

According to Robert Fenske (1989), the organizational foundations of student services can be found in a desire to foster the intellectual, social, moral, and spiritual development of students. Based on the community college or university mission, the functions included in the area of student services may vary. Divisions within student services may be linked to the philosophy of the higher education institution, with some institutions stressing a more student-centered approach and others, particularly universities, focusing more on research. Smaller liberal arts colleges, which are also four-year institutions, may emphasis teaching the humanities and maintaining a small student population with a greater student-centered focus. However, it is unnecessary to compromise the needs of student services or a student-centered climate due to institutional missions.

The functions typically associated with student services, at both two-year and four-year institutions, include admissions and recruitment, retention, international student services, counseling, testing, orientation, career services, student activities, disability services, financial aid, and athletics. The most common administrative philosophy is to enhance and support students' experiences, from initial enrollment through graduation. Additionally, four-year institutions usually focus on student programming, such as speakers, symposia, and other student activities, to complement the learning experiences in the classroom.

Whether at a two-year institution or a university, there are several administrative offices that may or may not be a part of the division of student services, depending on the campus organizational structure. Campus security is one such office, and on some campuses security personnel are actually certified campus police, especially if the campus is an urban environment. The offices of admissions, recruitment, and retention also may report to either the student services department or the academic affairs department.

Athletics, though typically within the realm of student services, is a distinct entity—depending on institutional type, National Collegiate Athletic Association (NCAA) designation, and conference. Community colleges generally have fewer athletic programs and the emphasis is less competitive compared to Division I universities. The athletic recruiting process at two-year colleges is also less competitive—athletes may often walk on to a team. Additionally, because athletics at four-year institutions (particularly football and basketball) generate large revenues and the recruitment of top athletic talent is fierce, university athletics may be within the general university administration, or the athletic director may report directly to the president of the university. It should be noted that revenue usually generated from athletics at four-year colleges and universities is much more significant than at community colleges. Additionally, civil rights laws such as Title IX have had a direct impact on both community college and university athletics by requiring equality in men's and women's sports and equity in payment of coaches and athletic facilities and equipment.

Common to two and four-year colleges and universities is the office of career services. Although this office may report to the academic affairs department, it facilitates students' movement into the workforce, and at most institutions it is still considered a student affairs function. Both community colleges and four-year institutions typically invite employers to interview students on campus. While four-year schools may hold career or employment fairs for teachers, engineers, or graduate programs such as nursing and law, the community colleges may put more emphasis on workforce retraining.

Judicial services can usually be found at both two- and four-year campus. These services deal with disciplinary issues and misconduct, which are generally governed by a student handbook outlining rules and regulations and an honor code that covers plagiarism, cheating, or other academic misconduct. Additionally, four-year institutions have an office of fraternity and sorority affairs, which primarily deals with Greek organizations. This is less common at two-year institutions, but some community colleges do have sororities and fraternities. Although these groups are a common source of bonding and service on both types of campuses, incidents of hazing, alcohol abuse, and Greek on-campus housing often present dilemmas that must be carefully monitored.

Recruitment, Retention, and Counseling Services

Recruitment for community colleges is often different than that for four-year colleges and universities. "Because the community colleges try to serve as many members of the community as feasible, they have frequently engaged in extensive recruitment activities" (Cohen and Brawer, p. 193). Community colleges employ recruitment strategies such as partnering with surrounding community colleges to offer classes to high school seniors. Other strategies include working with local businesses, state government, and the local chamber of commerce to develop specialized courses or training programs to meet the needs of industry, businesses, and the state's economy.

The recruitment and admissions function at four-year institutions usually involves admissions counselors working with area high schools and community agencies to recruit students. Additionally, many universities have a national draw, and there are national recruitment forums in urban areas and high schools in which representatives from four-year institutions nationwide assemble to meet and speak with prospective students and their parents.

Prospective four-year students must take the SAT or ACT Assessment, complete an application, write a personal statement, and submit a high school transcript and letters of recommendation. The ACT or SAT may be waived for nontraditional older students who have been in the workforce for a significant amount of time, but they may be required to take a basic standardized test administered by the university to assess their level of academic functioning in basic areas such as English, mathematics, writing, and reading.

In terms of the admissions process, graduate and professional programs at universities are usually even more competitive and also require standardized testing, and medical and law schools may require interviews. Similar recruitment tools may be used, such as online applications, recruitment forums, visiting local colleges, and use of alumni.

Retention is often difficult for two-year colleges compared to other institutional types. The diversification of the student population and commuter campuses both create obstacles to retention. Thus, students often spend less time together and with faculty at two-year colleges than students at four-year schools do. With changing demographics, retention can be difficult due to adults with children and child-care issues and four-year institutions reducing remedial and development programs. Additionally, although some two-year schools have on-campus housing and residential living, some students find it difficult to feel a sense of community. Typically, commuter students often work and have less time for student activities, which often increases a feeling of community and belonging on campus. In four-year schools with residence halls and students who often have more time for student organization, stu-

dents are usually easier to retain. Nevertheless, adjusting to college life, whether at a four-year or two-year institution, can be difficult. Unlike high school, there is usually much less oversight of absenteeism, and large students bodies make it difficult to assess changes in student behavior that may need intervention.

This does not mean that colleges and universities do not realize that adult students are undergoing many psychological and development changes as they enter college. On the contrary, campus counseling services are an integral part of student affairs. "The contention has been that community college students need help in moving into the college and out again into careers and/or transferring to other colleges, and that individualized instruction through counseling and other nonclassroom-based activities is essential" (Cohen and Brawer, p. 194). Since two-year college students possess varying academic abilities, the goal is to help students assess their abilities and limitations, and "community college counselors try to help students clarify their goals and values" (Cohen and Brawer, p. 195). Though four-year colleges and universities campus counseling services provide similar services, they tend to deal more with student socialization issues and, to a lesser degree, academic issues.

New student orientation is a major tool used to introduce students to campus life and to aid in their adjustment at both and two- and four-year institutions. "In determining appropriate formats for these introductory sessions, staff members consider their college's mission statements, campus culture, and student population to tailor an appropriate orientation program for their newest students" (Cohen and Brawer, p. 199). Each college and university designs orientation to suit the populations they serve. This may mean several orientation sessions offered at a variety of times, and use of formats such as video or the Internet. Orientation is closely connected to retention and, as such, is carefully executed to ensure student satisfaction and academic persistence. Encouraging students to participate in orientation, however, can be problematic.

Disability Services

All higher education institutions are required to provide reasonable accommodations for students with qualified disabilities under the Americans with Disabilities Act (ADA) and Section 504 of the Rehabilitation Act of 1973. An office of disability services works with students with disabilities, faculty, and campus officials who may need accommodations. Students are often required to provide medical documentation certifying their disability. They also have the option of voluntarily disclosing to the disability office whether or not they qualify for disability services. In order to receive accommodations and to develop an accommodation plan to meet an individual students needs, however, documentation must be provided.

Students may qualify as students with disabilities due to learning disabilities or visual, hearing, or mobility impairments. These students may need note-takers, special equipment, translators, extended test time, computer-aided testing, and other accommodations to allow them to compete equally in the classroom and to participate equally in other campus activities.

Financial Aid

All students who wish to apply for financial aid must complete the Free Application for Federal Student Aid (FAFSA), which can be completed online or via direct mail. Male students ages eighteen to twenty-five must also register for the Selective Service in order to qualify for any form of federal aid. Each institution may also have its own financial aid forms that must be completed. There are usually priority deadlines for financial aid eligibility.

It should be noted that the ability to pay ever-increasing tuition and fees makes financial aid vitally important to today's college students. Thus, to some, community colleges are the school of choice because of their affordability.

Students who meet certain economic qualifications may qualify for either federal or state grants to assist with college tuition at both two- and four-year colleges. These grants usually do not have to be paid back as long as a student is enrolled for the full academic term or semester. There are few federal and state grants to assist graduate and professional students at the university level.

Many students need to apply for student loans. Stafford Loans are the most common source of education loan funds loans available. Direct Stafford Loans are available through the William D. Ford Federal Direct Loan Program, and FFEL Stafford Loans are available through the Federal Family Education Loan (FFEL) Program. The major differences between the two are the source of the loan funds,

some aspects of the application process, and the available repayment plans. Under the Direct Loan Program, the student receives the loan directly from the U.S. government, while through the FFEL Program, the funds come from a bank, credit union, or other participating lender.

Perkins Loans may also assist students, but are limited in funds. A Federal Perkins Loan is a low-interest loan for an undergraduate or graduate student with exceptional financial need. The student's institution is the lender, and the loan is made with government funds plus a share contributed by the school. The student must repay a Perkins Loan to his or her educational institution.

Parents of undergraduate students may qualify for specific federal loan programs also, but they may be required to pay the interest immediately upon borrowing. Students should be aware that borrowing for their educational needs is very serious, and it is advisable only to borrow what is needed to fund one's education. Usually, there is a six-month grace period after graduation before repayment begins, but if a student withdraws before completing a degree, repayment may be required immediately. Students should be aware that there are often private loan vendors for both undergraduate and graduate programs. Additionally, student default increased somewhat in the closing years of the twentieth century, prompting credit checks to be used by some loan agencies. Following graduation, students may consider consolidating student loans to reduce payments.

Both two- and four-year students should seek out campus-based aid, such as college work-study, institutional loans, and need-based and merit-based scholarships. Scholarships may also be available for underrepresented groups in certain fields. Additionally, in order to remain eligible for any form of financial aid, students must remain in good academic standing.

Residential Life

As previously stated, most two-year schools are basically commuter schools, though some have residential halls. Most four-year colleges and universities have some type of housing, including specialty housing such as faculty-in-residence, fraternity and sorority housing, and off-campus housing. Many residence halls provide food services and technology such as computer labs. Residential life, or special event, programs organized by student and professional campus housing staff are designed to facilitate the growth of students in all aspects of their social development.

Student Organizations and Activities

Community colleges and four-year colleges and universities offer a bevy of student organizations. Both two- and four-year colleges have organizations that are centered around a student's academic, religious, social, or political interests, including volunteer, community service, and cultural organizations. Student government associations, social-activity coordinating bodies, and campus publications are just a few examples. Typically, fraternities and sororities are relegated to four-year colleges and universities. Funding for student organizations usually comes from student fees, and at both public and private institutions student-fee usage has been an issue. Questions regarding the use of these student fees to fund certain politically affiliated or religious organizations—or other controversial groups—have become a source of sometimes heated debate.

The Evolving Concept of Student Services Personnel

Over the years, student services have evolved at both community colleges and four-year higher education institutions. The concept of student services, or student affairs, as simply keeping watch over student behavior or nurturing parents has given way to the concept of an institutional life that is supportive of the growth of the "whole" student.

The *whole student* concept involves the development of a living and learning environment in which student services personnel work with faculty, administrators, students, staff, employers, and the community to integrate academic and student activities outside the classroom in order to prepare students to live in a complex world. Student events, activities, organizations, and departments under the umbrella of *student services* are designed to not only complement the learning environment, but also to allow students to develop intellectually, spiritually, physically, emotionally, and vocationally—and in their capacity to serve as leaders and bring about change.

Future Trends in Student Services

With the increase in technological advances and distance education, student services at both the community college level and at four-year institutions must be able to adapt quickly to change. Online programs, video courses, weekend courses, executive weekend programs, and off-site programs have a significant impact on the way student services are provided. Both community colleges and universities are beginning to rely more on websites, e-mail, chatrooms, and online applications to attract and communicate with students in the technological age. Additionally, a student's ability to apply and monitor application decisions directly online and through Internet portals, which allow prospective students to converse in "real time" with admissions professionals, will greatly impact student services and students' expectations.

In addition, a diverse student body requires student services personnel to be equipped with new skills, including second-language proficiency and sensitivity to disabled, culturally different, and gay and lesbian students. Also, an increase in nontraditional adult students necessitates new approaches to student services, including services at alternative times to meet the needs of part-time and working adults.

Finally, shrinking resources, particularly in light of modern technology, will cause student services personnel to have to justify their place in higher education. Demands for fiscal accountability may one day requires colleges and universities to discuss the elimination of certain student services.

See also: ADJUSTMENT TO COLLEGE; COLLEGE FINANCIAL AID; COLLEGE STUDENT RETENTION; COLLEGE STUDENTS WITH DISABILITIES, *subentry on* ACCOMMODATING; COMMUNITY COLLEGES; PERSONAL AND PSYCHOLOGICAL PROBLEMS OF COLLEGE STUDENTS; STUDENT SERVICES, *subentry on* COLLEGES AND UNIVERSITIES.

BIBLIOGRAPHY

ADELMAN, CLIFFORD. 1994. "The Way We Are: The Community College as American Thermometer." In *Community Colleges*, ed. James L. Ratcliff. Needham Heights, MA: Simon and Schuster.

COHEN, ARTHUR M., and BRAWER, FLORENCE B. 1996. *The American Community College.* San Francisco: Jossey-Bass.

FENSKE, ROBERT H. 1989. "The Historical Foundation of Student Services." In *Student Services: A Handbook for the Profession,* ed. Ursula Delworth, Gary R. Hanson, and Associates. San Francisco: Jossey-Bass.

GELLMAN-DANLEY, BARBARA, and TEAGUE, ROBERT G. 1998. "Navigating the Organizational Maze: Reengineering to Advance the Technology Agenda." In *Integrating Technology on Campus: Human Sensibilities and Technical Possibilities,* ed. Kamala Anandam. San Francisco: Jossey-Bass.

GRACIE, LARRY W. 1998. "Measurable Outcomes of Workforce Development and the Economic Impact of Attending a North Carolina Community College." In *Determining the Economic Benefits of Attending Community College,* ed. Jorge R. Sanchez and Frankie Santos Laanan. San Francisco: Jossey-Bass.

RICHARDSON, RICHARD C., JR. 1994. "Responding to Student Diversity: A Community College Perspective." In *Community Colleges,* ed. James L. Ratcliff. Needham Heights, MA: Simon and Schuster.

SANCHEZ, JORGE R. and LAANAN, FRANKIE SANTOS. 1998. "Economic Benefits of a Community College Education: Issues of Accountability and Performance Measures." In *Determining the Economic Benefits of Attending Community College,* ed. Jorge R. Sanchez and Frankie Santos Laanan. San Francisco: Jossey-Bass.

TWOMBLY, SUSAN B. 1994. "What We Know About Women in Community Colleges." In *Community Colleges,* ed. James L. Ratcliff. Needham Heights, MA: Simon and Schuster.

U. MONIQUE ROBINSON-WRIGHT
SONYA G. SMITH

STUDENT TEACHING

See: EARLY CHILDHOOD EDUCATION, *subentry on* PREPARATION OF TEACHERS; ELEMENTARY EDUCATION, *subentry on* PREPARATION OF TEACHERS; TEACHER EDUCATION; TEACHING, *subentry on* LEARNING TO TEACH.

STUDY ABROAD

Until the 1970s, study abroad programs for American college students mostly followed the general education/liberal arts model that was pioneered in the 1920s by the University of Delaware, and later by Smith College. More recently, significant shifts in international involvements, in U.S. higher education, and in the characteristics and interests of college students have greatly altered the aims, programs, and clienteles of study abroad. The model of sending students (mainly female) to western Europe, typically for an academic year and primarily for foreign language and culture learning, has largely been abandoned.

The multipolarity of the world today, by expanding the demand for cross-culturally competent professionals in an increasingly globalized economy, is influencing the new shapes and goals of study abroad. Learning a foreign language has eroded as an aim of study abroad as the United States has become more than 30 percent Hispanic, and as English has become the new *lingua franca* of the world. Moreover, a study abroad experience is no longer seen as mainly for private college students, but as an essential foundation for international careers—and most careers now are international in their contexts, content, or dimensions.

Study Abroad Programs Today

Probably the main characteristic of the study abroad programs of U.S. colleges and universities is their diversity. There is no typical program. Students in an increasingly wide array of majors seek to study abroad and to pursue coursework while abroad that counts toward their major, whether business, sociology, environmental engineering, or nursing. Small wonder that the foci of study abroad programs are correspondingly diverse.

Driving this diversity, as well as contributing to it, are two additional and interrelated factors. First, the concern of students to enhance their professional qualifications for their future careers leads them to prefer short-term programs (a few weeks or a summer) over longer ones, such as an academic semester or year. Job concerns also make internships and work placements abroad attractive to American students, and programs with a thematic, rather than general education, emphasis, are preferred.

The second factor affecting diversity is the growing appreciation of the importance of cross-cultural skills (though not foreign language competence) in both the domestic and international arenas on the part of employers, students, and faculty. U.S. businesses operating across borders increasingly recognize the need for staff who can communicate, even if only in English, with people from other cultures and countries. Study abroad programs designed to enhance cross-cultural skills bring new goals and strategies to the experience. More programs are located in countries and regions other than the traditional western European ones; and more include experiential learning, immersion in the host culture, and community service as important vehicles for cross-cultural learning. These programs also tend to give more encouragement to independent study and to interdisciplinary and multidisciplinary studies than do the more traditional programs.

As already emphasized, there is no typical program of study among the study abroad programs of U.S. colleges and universities. This should be viewed as a plus rather than an inadequacy, reflecting as it does an important flexibility and pragmatism on the part of U.S. institutions. American universities have become more "user-friendly" to academic programs abroad taught in English, partly because the language has become a dominant factor in the globalization of the economy worldwide. In addition, countries seeking to attract more foreign students want to design programs geared to their needs and interests—whether it be English as a second language (ESL), shortened MBA programs, or post-degree job counseling and opportunities. The combination of more and more academic work offered in English, and the move worldwide towards an academic credit and transfer system comparable to the Educational Credit Transfer System (ECTS) of the European Community (EC) has attracted more U.S. study abroad students to nontraditional destinations.

Paralleling the widening of study abroad destinations has been a shortening of the time spent abroad: the percentage of students studying abroad for more than a semester dropped from 18 percent in 1985 to 10 percent in 1995. Whereas it is widely agreed that longer is better, the conflicting truism that something is better than nothing increasingly prevails. It is ironic that the shorter period that U.S. students spend studying abroad reflects a greater student and faculty appreciation of its importance as part of a quality undergraduate education. For students who must forgo part-time work to afford college or whose family situations or degree requirements (such as engineering majors) preclude more than a short time abroad, the increase in one- to

four-week study or intern options abroad provides an opportunity for foreign study that would not otherwise exist. A significant trend in U.S. study abroad is that more and more colleges and universities integrate the academic work students do abroad into their degree programs. This is fundamental to increasing participation and affirming the academic contribution of study abroad.

Some U.S. institutions are developing creative ways to enable students to have an international experience despite existing deterrents. Some universities offer study abroad opportunities in the sciences to second semester sophomores who cannot leave campus their junior year. A few institutions offer online coursework from the home campus to students studying abroad who require specific courses not available in their study abroad program. Another strategy, exemplified in a course (Cultural Codes in Communication) taught at the University of Massachusetts at Amherst involves the professor and a professor colleague at a university in Finland showing the same film clips on Finland and the U.S. to their respective students. This program does not involve study abroad in the sense of the geographic move, but does involve direct contact with people in another country, focusing on cultural differences and stimulating international learning. The vastly different reactions of the Finnish and American students illustrates how the culture of each nation shapes how they look at the clips. The lively Internet communication that ensues between the Finnish and U.S. students is an integral part of the cross-cultural learning experience.

While the study abroad programs of U.S. colleges and universities share many features, they do tend to be of two markedly different types. One wants its students to be as integrated as possible into a cooperating or "partner" institution abroad, and, with appropriate pre-departure preparation, to mostly fend for themselves. In this type of program, students pay little or no more than for the same period at their home institution. The second type of program tends to provide special academic advising for the U.S. students, extra excursions for them, supplementary assistance with their housing, and day-to-day mentoring on top of what is offered by the host institution abroad. The first program type is quite similar to the EC's Socrates/Erasmus student exchange program in the goals of student integration into their host institutions abroad, little extra cost, and little special assistance by the sending institutions. The second program type aims to respond to the concerns of the kinds of students—and their parents and home institutions—that enroll in them. To a large extent, private college students, their parents, and their sponsors tend to look for special assistance, going well beyond what local university students may receive.

Study Abroad Curricula, Living Arrangements, and Locations

U.S. study abroad programs are increasingly diverse in their curricula, living arrangements, and locations. More and more programs offer a so-called full curricula that includes many of the traditional academic disciplines. Those that focus on language, culture, and social science subjects tend to be in foreign language countries, especially those of the less commonly taught languages in East Asia, North Africa, the Middle East, and eastern Europe. Living arrangements vary from residence halls, home stay, and apartments to such accommodation as the students arrange for themselves. Since 1990 U.S. students have more and more sought to make their own housing arrangements, usually helped by local staff.

The greatest diversification has been in study abroad program locations. Although the largest portion are still in western Europe, few countries are overlooked or left out, other than those with severe unrest or other conditions that may threaten students' safety. Shifts in international politics and economic conditions may significantly affect program locations. Thus, post-normalization China, post–Velvet Revolution Czechoslovakia, and post–cold war Africa have become more attractive U.S. study abroad destinations.

Future Developments

At the beginning of the twenty-first century, there were developments underway internationally, especially in western Europe, that were likely to affect the priorities in curricula and country sites of U.S. study abroad programs. In the Bologna Declaration of June 1999, twenty-nine European countries pledged to reform the structures of their higher education system to include a common framework for degrees and a convergence of their systems, possibly with degrees similar to the U.S. system. These reforms should facilitate increased mobility and cooperation, not only among European higher education institutions, but also with institutions in the United States and other regions worldwide. Just as globalization

has created an increasingly borderless world, so this growing interchange can increase commonalties among higher education systems.

See also: ACADEMIC MAJOR, THE; CURRICULUM, HIGHER EDUCATION, *subentry on* NATIONAL REPORTS ON THE UNDERGRADUATE CURRICULUM; INTERNATIONAL STUDENTS.

BIBLIOGRAPHY

BURN, BARBARA B., ed. 1991. *Integrating Study Abroad into the Undergraduate Liberal Arts Curriculum: Eight Institutional Case Studies.* Westport, CT: Greenwood Press.

BURN, BARBARA B.; CERYCH, LADISLAV; and SMITH, ALAN, eds. 1990. *Study Abroad Programmes.* London: Jessica Kingsley Publishers.

DAVIS, TODD, ed. 2000. *Open Doors 1998–1999: Report on International Educational Exchange.* New York: Institute of International Education.

HOFFA, WILLIAM, and PEARSON, JOHN. 1998. *NAFSA's guide to Education Abroad for Advisors and Administrators.* Washington, DC: NAFSA Publications.

MARCUM, JOHN A., and ROCHNIK, DAVID. 2001. "What Direction for Study Abroad? Two Views." *Chronicle Review* XLVII (36):7–10.

SCHNEIDER, ANN IMLAH, and BURN, BARBARA B. 2000. *Federal Funding for International Studies: Does it Help? Does it Matter?* Amherst, MA: University of Massachusetts International Programs Office.

SCOTT, PETER. 1998. *The Globalization of Higher Education.* Buckingham, Eng.: Open University Press.

BARBARA B. BURN

SUB-SAHARAN AFRICA

Sub-Saharan Africa, referred to as "Africa" in this article, comprises the forty-two countries on the African continent south of the Sahara and the six island nations close to it. Africa's rich cultural and ethnic traditions reflect different heritages in all countries—an early Christian heritage in the Nile Basin, a strong Islamic influence in the north, and Christian influences dating from colonialism in many central and southern African countries.

Geographically and economically, Africa is diverse and fragmented. In 1999 the region's population was about 640 million. Six countries had fewer than 1 million people. Nigeria had 124 million people and Ethiopia 64 million. Within the continent, communications and travel are difficult. Gross national product (GNP) per capita averaged $500 in 1999, ranging from less than $200 in the Burundi, Ethiopia, Malawi, Niger, and Sierra Leone to more than $3,200 in Botswana, Gabon, Mauritius, and South Africa. On the whole, the region's GNP growth and human development indicators lag behind those of other regions.

Poverty is pervasive across the region. More than 290 million people live on less than $1 per day. With the region's rapidly growing population, 5 percent annual growth is needed to keep the number of poor from increasing. According to the World Bank, halving the incidence of poverty by 2015 would require annual per capita gross domestic product (GDP) growth rates of at least 7 percent. Unsustainable external indebtedness has diverted scarce resources away from priority social needs. Waste in the public sector and weak governance structures continue to act as major constraints to development in many countries.

Overview

Education systems in the region reflect differences in geography, cultural heritage, colonial history, and economic development progress. The impact of French, English, and other countries' colonial policies toward education has had a lasting impact on the objectives, structure, management, and financing of education systems in the region. When African countries gained independence from colonial rule around 1960, the region lagged far behind other regions on nearly every education indicator. Dramatic progress—with large national variations—occurred in the 1960s and 1970s. Primary enrollments jumped from 11 million in 1960 to almost 53 million in 1980. Growth at the secondary and tertiary levels was even more dramatic, with secondary enrollments increasing by fifteen times and tertiary enrollments by twenty times.

The economic crisis of the 1980s severely affected education in Africa. Declining public resources and private economic hardship resulted in an erosion of quality and primary level participation rates. As of the early twenty-first century, these setbacks have not yet been reversed. At every level, education

facilities are too few, while those that exist are often in poor repair and inadequately equipped. Teachers are often underpaid and underqualified and rarely receive the support and supervision they need to do an effective job. The number of hours spent in the classroom by most African students is far lower than the international standard. Instructional materials are often in desperately short supply. Not surprisingly, learning achievement is almost always far below the instructional objectives specified in the curricula. While country experiences vary a great deal, the reality for too many Africans is one of education systems characterized by low quality and limited access.

Africa has the lowest enrollment rate at every level and is the only region where the number of out-of-school children continues to rise. The average African adult has fewer than three years of schooling, lower than the attainment level for any other region. Almost one in three males and one in two females is illiterate. Gender inequalities persist at all levels of schooling. Female enrollments are about 80 percent of male enrollments at the primary and secondary levels and less than 55 percent at the tertiary level.

As disturbing as the low levels of literacy and education attainment is the marked decline in the capacity of many African countries to generate knowledge as a resource for tertiary level instruction and for research and technology development. A 1992 study estimated that Africa had only 20,000 scientists and engineers, or 0.36 percent of the world's total. In 1996 Senegal had only 3 researchers engaged in research and development per million people, Burkina Faso had only 16 and Uganda had 20, compared with 149 in India and 350 in China. Few African researchers are integrated in the worldwide scientific knowledge networks. A continuing brain drain exacerbates these problems. Reasons vary from country to country but usually relate to a lack of employment opportunities in the modern sector, limited research budgets in universities, the lack of freedom of speech, and the fear of political repression in countries with authoritarian regimes. An estimated 30,000 Africans holding doctoral degrees live outside the continent, and 130,000 Africans study in tertiary institutions outside Africa.

Social and economic progress in Africa will depend to a large extent on the scope and effectiveness of investments in education. If living standards are to be raised, sustained efforts will be needed to narrow the gaps in educational attainment and scientific knowledge between Africa and other regions and to bridge the digital divide. Decades of research and experience in Africa and elsewhere have shown the pivotal role of a well-educated population in initiating, sustaining, and accelerating social development and economic competitiveness. Numerous studies show that education, particularly primary education, has a significant positive impact on economic growth, earnings, and productivity.

But clearly, primary education cannot expand and African economies cannot grow without an education system that trains a large number of students beyond the basic cycle, including graduate students at universities. To be sustainable, educational development must be balanced. It must ensure that systems produce students at different levels with qualifications that respond to the demand of the labor market, providing a continuous supply of skilled workers, technicians, professionals, managers, and leaders.

Yet, lasting education development will take place only when the extensive armed conflicts come to an end and the HIV/AIDS pandemic stalls. Restoring peace and stability in the region is an urgent priority. At least one in five Africans lives in a country severely disrupted by war. Between 1990 and 1994 more than 1 million people died because of conflict. And in 2000, approximately 13.7 million people in Africa were refugees or internally displaced. Few opportunities for schooling exist in the African conflict zones.

Africa has been the region hardest hit by the HIV/AIDS pandemic, accounting for 23 million of the 33 million people affected worldwide. By killing people in their most productive years, the pandemic is destroying the social and economic fabric of the worst affected countries and reversing hard-won human development gains. Replacing education sector staff lost to AIDS-related illnesses while national resources are being diverted from education to the health sector and providing an education to children affected by AIDS are urgent ongoing challenges.

Stalled Progress in Primary Education

Primary enrollment growth slowed in the 1980s. The gross enrollment rate (total number of children enrolled as a proportion of the number of children of the relevant age group) fell from 80 percent in 1980 to 75 percent in 1990, largely as a result of declining male participation rates, and by 1997 had recovered

to only 77 percent. Yet other coverage indicators showed considerable improvement (see Table 1). Net enrollment rates (number of children of the relevant age group enrolled as a proportion of the number of children of relevant age) increased from 54 percent in 1990 to 60 percent in 1998; apparent intake rates (total number of children admitted in grade 1 as a proportion of the total number of children of the school entry age) from 70 percent to 81 percent; and net intake rates (number of children of entry age admitted in grade 1 as a proportion of the total number of children of the school entry age) from 33 percent to 43 percent. Although not available for all countries, these data suggest that more school-age children are in school, the decline in boys' participation has reversed, and more children are enrolling in first grade. But many children still enroll late (only two-thirds of the new entrants in 1998 were the official age for school enrollment), the gap in girls' initial enrollment rate has increased, and more than 40 percent of school-age children are not in school.

Country experiences vary a great deal, however. Botswana, Cape Verde, Mauritius, Namibia, the Seychelles, Swaziland, and Zimbabwe sustained education progress. Uganda and Mauritania implemented policies that resulted in a sudden increase in primary enrollments and then began struggling to deal with the consequent challenges. Burkina Faso, Guinea, Mozambique, and Senegal opted for a gradual approach. Most other countries are formulating comprehensive long-term strategies for educational development, including universal primary education.

Nevertheless, access to primary education remains problematic. Of the forty-four countries with data for 1996, only ten (Botswana, Cape Verde, Congo, Malawi, Mauritius, Namibia, South Africa, Swaziland, Togo, and Zimbabwe) had a primary gross enrollment rate of 100 percent. Seven (Burkina Faso, Burundi, Ethiopia, Liberia, Mali, Niger, and Somalia) had a primary gross enrollment rate below 50 percent. And between 1985 and 1997 the primary gross enrollment rate actually declined in seventeen countries—Angola, Burundi, Cameroon, Central African Republic, Comoros, Côte d'Ivoire, the Democratic Republic of Congo, Kenya, Lesotho, Liberia, Madagascar, Mozambique, Nigeria, Sierra Leone, Somalia, Tanzania, and Zambia. Together, these seventeen countries include more than half of Africa's school-age population.

TABLE 1

Primary school enrollment and intake rates, 1990, 1995, and 1998						
	1990		**1995**		**1998**	
	Boys	Girls	Boys	Girls	Boys	Girls
Gross enrollment rate	81.9	67.6	83.8	69.4	84.1[b]	69.4[b]
Net enrollment rate	59.8	49.9	64.2	52.9	67.6	54.2
Apparent intake rate	75.7	65.3	83.4	70.0	88.3	73.5
Net intake rate[a]	34.7	31.9	41.4	40.6	44.5	41.6

[a] 1994 [b] 1997.

SOURCE: Based on United Nations Educational, Scientific and Cultural Organization. 2000. *Education for All (2000): Report from the Sub-Saharan Africa Zone, Assessment of Basic Education in SSA*. Harare, Zimbabwe: United Nations Educational, Scientific and Cultural Organization.

The challenge is clear. In almost all countries, access has expanded far too slowly to achieve international education targets for gender equity and universal primary education. About 12 percent of the world's children aged six to eleven live in Africa, yet the region accounts for more than one third of the world's out-of-school children. Unless these trends reverse, Africa will account for three-quarters of out-of-school children by 2015.

Participation problems are exacerbated by the absence of an environment for effective learning. Children are taught in overcrowded classrooms by underqualified and frequently unmotivated teachers who are often poorly and irregularly paid and receive little managerial support. Teacher absenteeism is widespread, disrupting learning and eroding public confidence in the value of public education. Shortages of learning materials further constrain learning. In ten of eleven countries surveyed by UNESCO (1998b), more than one-third of the students had no chalkboards in their classrooms. In eight countries, more than half of the students in the highest grade had no math books. Most African children spend roughly half the time in the classroom that children in other countries do.

Poverty-related deprivation further contributes to low educational attainment in Africa. Poor children spend more time than other children contributing to household work. As a result they are less likely to spend out-of-school hours on schoolwork, more likely to be absent from school during periods of peak labor demand, and more likely to be tired and ill-prepared for learning when they are in the classroom. More than 40 percent of children in Afri-

ca are stunted, while almost one-third are underweight. Primary school-age children are especially susceptible to illnesses that affect poor people, in particular gastrointestinal and respiratory problems. Malnourished and sick children are less likely than healthy children to learn in school and are more likely to be absent from lessons. And if private costs for education are substantial, parents in poor households are more likely to withdraw their children from school early in the school cycle. All these effects are exacerbated by the rapid spread of HIV/AIDS, which affects the attendance of teachers and students and strains household resources.

Unsurprisingly, students who complete primary school often have an unacceptably low level of learning. In 1990–1991 Botswana, Nigeria, and Zimbabwe participated in a thirty-one-country survey of ninth grade reading skills (described by Warwick B. Elley in 1992). Students in these three countries registered the lowest scores, performing considerably worse than students in the other four developing countries participating in the survey (the Philippines, Thailand, Trinidad and Tobago, and Venezuela). More recently, the Southern Africa Consortium for Monitoring Educational Quality assessed the reading skills of sixth grade students in Mauritius, Namibia, Zambia, and Zanzibar. The average percentage of correct answers ranged from 38 percent to 58 percent.

Poor learning often results in high repetition rates and low completion rates. In fifteen countries more than 20 percent of students are repeaters—in Côte d'Ivoire more than half of all primary students are repeating a grade at any time. More than one-third of school entrants fail to reach the final grade. In the Central African Republic, Chad, Congo, Madagascar, and Mozambique, fewer than half the children who enroll in primary school complete five years. Many of the students drop out early in the primary cycle, before they acquire even rudimentary literacy and numeracy skills. In Chad, Ethiopia, and Madagascar more than one-third of the children who enter school never complete second grade.

Increased learning and participation will require a combination of policies, including:

- Increased funding for primary education

- Increased resource availability at the school level

- Allocation of resources to inputs that directly enhance learning

- Meaningful community participation in school development and management

- Increased responsibility of local education authorities for resource allocation, professional support, and personnel management decisions

- Explicit national responsibility for setting standards, monitoring of performance, and mobilizing adequate resources for the system

Beyond Primary Education

Few African countries provide adequate opportunities for education and training needed by twelve- to seventeen-year-olds or for adults. The gross secondary enrollment rate in 1997 was 26 percent for Africa, compared with 52 percent for all developing countries. Many Africans are looking for opportunities to either continue formal schooling or acquire skills that will equip them to enter the world of work.

Education and training for youths is not only an economic imperative. In many countries young people's dissatisfaction and disillusionment with their prospects for education and work threaten social cohesion and stability. Reaching this age group through formal and nonformal education is also vital to the success of targeted interventions in such areas as HIV/AIDS and reproductive health education and of programs to raise awareness of civic rights and responsibilities. Yet only one-fourth of youths in this age group have access to secondary education, and only 6 percent are reached by vocational and nonformal education programs. Access to new communication, information, and computer technology is limited in secondary and public-sector training institutions in Africa. The lack of instruc-

tional equipment and materials further inhibits learning. Many publicly funded skills development programs—especially those teaching vocational subjects in secondary schools—are of poor quality, depend heavily on external financing, and carry high costs per student. Such programs often are also poorly attuned to labor market demand and fail to lead to income-earning opportunities. Skills-training programs typically are geared to formal sector employment at a time when the formal sector in most African countries absorbs only a small minority of labor market recruits. The balance of the evidence suggest that strategies need to:

- Ensure good quality primary and secondary programs as a basis for further education and skill development

- Ensure that investment in skill development programs is firmly grounded in economic and labor market analysis

- Encourage private-sector delivery by creating a favorable policy environment, strengthening employer training, and reducing regulation

- Improve publicly provided training by strengthening linkages with enterprises, improving responsiveness to market forces, increasing efficiency of resource utilization, and diversifying sources of funding beyond government subsidies

Education opportunities for adults remain equally limited. The mass literacy campaigns of the 1970s fell far short of their objectives. Only a few countries—Uganda and Ghana are examples—continue to support large-scale literacy programs. But in the late 1990s countries such as Senegal began to experiment with small-scale highly targeted programs, often implemented with the support of nongovernmental organizations. Skill development programs are delivered for the most part by private-sector institutions and sponsored by employers.

Unprecedented Expansion of Tertiary Education

In 1960 Africa (excluding South Africa) had six universities with fewer than 30,000 students. In 1995 the region supported nearly 120 universities enrolling almost 2 million. Yet, tertiary enrollment, which reached 3.9 percent for Africa in 1997, is still far below the 10 percent average for all developing countries. In many African countries universities are the only national institutions with the skills, equipment, and mandate to generate new knowledge through research and to adapt global knowledge to solve local problems. A few have long traditions and were world-class institutions through the 1970s. Yet many others are weak. Early curriculum links to religious studies and civil-service needs have often promoted the humanities and social sciences at the expense of the natural sciences, applied technology, business-related skills, and research capabilities. Inappropriate governing structures, misguided national policies, weak managerial capacity, political interference, and campus instability have further hampered effectiveness. The experience with subregional academic cooperation has been disappointing, although many institutions are too small and recruit from too small a national pool of talent to develop a high-level teaching and research capacity across a wide range of academic subjects.

Dwindling resources during a period of growing enrollments have caused a severe decline in the quality of education in many institutions. Among countries for which data are available for the years 1990 and 1996, expenditures per pupil at the tertiary level as a percentage of GNP per capita decreased in fifteen countries and increased in seven. Yet African higher education remains expensive by international standards. In 1992 public education spending per pupil as a percentage of per capita GNP was 15.1 percent at the preprimary and primary levels, 53.7 percent at the secondary level, and 507 percent at the tertiary level. This disparity makes the strategic management of higher-education resources a central concern of any educational development policy. Some universities are charging increased tuition and fees. Others have started income-generating activities. As an alternative to the traditional higher-education model of full-time study on residential campuses, several provide instruction through distance education programs and extended educational services—the University of South Africa, which enrolled 130,000 students in the mid-1990s, is actually the largest institution of this kind in the world. A number of universities are beginning to use Internet-based technologies. A consensus on reform strategies appears to be emerging, although in practice implementation has been slow and politically controversial. Key elements are:

- Encouraging differentiation of institutions and delivery modes, including the development of open and distance education universities, private institutions, and nonuniversity tertiary institutions

- Providing incentives for public institutions to diversify sources of funding, including cost sharing with students

- Targeting of social expenditures on the most needy students

- Improving the efficiency of resource utilization, with an increased share allocated to teaching and research

- Access to new technologies needed to connect universities to international scientific networks

- Increased institutional autonomy and strategic planning

- Introducing policies explicitly designed to give priority to quality and equity objectives

Private Education

The private sector is an increasingly important provider of education in Africa. Most registered private schools in Africa are nonprofit community and religious schools. Several countries are also increasing the role of private providers in delivering support services such as textbook publishing, classroom construction, and university catering. The private sector plays a small—although an increasingly important—role at the primary level, but its share in meeting secondary, vocational, and tertiary education needs has increased significantly since the mid-1980s. In Côte d'Ivoire 36 percent of general secondary students and 65 percent of technical students are enrolled in private schools. In Zambia almost 90 percent of the students taking technical and vocational examinations were trained outside public institutions.

At the tertiary level the number of private institutions has increased rapidly. In the 1990s private institutions were established in countries such as Kenya, Mozambique, Senegal, Sudan, Uganda, and Zimbabwe. In South Africa alone there are probably more that 500 private tertiary institutions.

These institutions reduce the financial burden on governments, give parents more choice and control, and improve accountability. They help to meet some of the excess demand for education, provide special programs that the government is unable or unwilling to provide and reduce geographical imbalances in provision. Nevertheless, while many private training institutions have been successful, many others are of poor quality raising important issues of accreditation or other means of quality control.

Registration requirements usually call for the provision of basic infrastructure and staff. Kenya has established a Commission for Higher Education for the accreditation of tertiary institutions. In most other countries the ministry of education typically has this responsibility.

Efficiency

The efficiency of resource use varies considerably within and between countries. In some countries, especially in the Sahel (the southern fringe of the Sahara), high teacher salaries make it difficult to mobilize the resources required to reach universal primary education in the foreseeable future. In other countries teacher salaries are so low that teachers are forced to take additional jobs. Teacher deployment often creates further inefficiencies when teachers are not deployed according to rational criteria such as the number of students. For example, in Niger the teacher-student ratio in primary schools of 200 students ranges from 1:100 to 1:20.

In 1999 Keith Lewin and Francoise Caillods argued that developing countries with low secondary enrollments, including most African countries, cannot finance substantially higher participation rates from domestic public resources with current cost structures. Secondary schooling is the most expensive level relative to GNP per capita in countries with the lowest enrollment rates. In Africa secondary schools use resources such as teachers and buildings much less efficiently than primary schools. One reason may be that in the poorest countries, secondary schools are still organized along traditional lines to educate a small elite.

Limited public resources and competing public spending priorities have prevented many governments from addressing the challenges of education development. Since the mid-1980s the share of GDP spent on education has decreased in eleven and increased in twelve African countries for which data are available. Perhaps more significant, this share is still less than 3 percent in ten countries for which data is available for 1996 or after. At a given level of education spending as a share of GDP, participation and attainment levels in Africa compare unfavorably with those in other low-income countries (see Table 2). Inefficient and inequitable use of scarce resources in a context of high population growth and demand for general public financing of education by politically powerful pressure groups adds to the fiscal challenge. Thus countries must set priorities for public spending and identify possible efficiency gains from and opportunities for mobilizing additional public and private resources.

Prospects

The imperative of accelerated education development in Africa is clear. Africa will not be able to sustain rapid growth without investing in the education of its people. Many lack the education to contribute to—and benefit from—high economic growth. Meeting this challenge will require a major effort by Africans and their development partners during a long period—a decade or more in many cases. Many governments will need to implement changes in the way education is financed and managed—changes that are often politically controversial. Partnership of governments, civil society, and external funding agencies will need to be established or reconfigured to ensure national ownership and sustainability of programs of reform and innovation.

Yet, at the start of the twenty-first century the opportunity to effectively address the often intractable problems of education was perhaps better than at any time in the 1980s and 1990s. The economic performance improved markedly beginning in 1995, with consecutive years of per capita growth in many countries for the first time since the 1970s. In several countries additional resources have or will become available through debt relief provided under the Highly Indebted Poor Countries (HIPC) initiative, the coordinated effort of the industrialized countries to bring down debtor developing countries' debt to sustainable levels. Information and communications technology offers new opportunities to overcome constraints of distance and time. Political commitment to education development is strong almost everywhere. At the World Education Forum in Dakar, Senegal, in April 2000, the 185 participating countries adopted a Framework for Action toward the 2015 goal of Education for All, which gives special attention to the needs of Sub-Saharan Africa. Promising reforms and innovations have been implemented. Many funding agencies are committed to increasing their support for education in Africa. New aid relationships are being piloted in the context of sectorwide development programs replacing the increasingly ineffective individual project approach.

But progress will be achieved and sustained only where efforts are underpinned by genuine commitment to a clear set of guiding principles. First, with-

TABLE 2

Comparative indicators of education spending efficiency, 1993

Country	Education spending/GDP (percent)	Primary education spending/ GDP (percent)	Gross enrollment ratio (percent)	Years of schooling per 1 percent of GDP	Primary teacher salary/GDP per capita
French-speaking Sub-Saharan African countries	3.48	1.45	63	1.42	6.3
English-speaking Sub-Saharan African countries	3.70	1.70	81	1.95	3.2
Non-African (GNP less than $2,000 per capita)	3.50	1.70	94	2.47	2.7

SOURCE: Based on Mingat, Alain, and Suchet, Bruno. 1998. *Une analyse économique comparative des systèmes éducatifs Africains.* Dijon, France: Université de Bourgogne, Institut de Recherche sur l' Economie de l'Education.

out a relentless pursuit of quality, expanded education opportunities are unlikely to achieve their purpose—that is, the acquisition of useful knowledge, reasoning abilities, skills, and values. Second, an unwavering commitment to equity is vital to ensuring that disadvantaged groups—rural residents, the poor, and females—have equal access to learning opportunities at all levels. This will require explicitly targeted strategies for hard-to-reach groups and better analysis of the mechanisms by which people are excluded from education. Third, African countries will need to ensure education development strategies are financially sustainable. Setting spending priorities, spending the resources that have been allocated effectively, diversifying funding sources, and in many cases mobilizing additional funding from sources outside the public sector—especially for postprimary education beyond the basic level—are areas where tough decisions need to be made and then adhered to. Finally, an up-front emphasis on capacity building of institutions and of individuals is needed for accelerated education development to happen. Effective planning, implementation, and evaluation of reforms depend upon effective incentives, reasonable rules, efficient organizational structures, and competent staff. Without these, no strategy for education development can succeed.

See also: INTERNATIONAL EDUCATION; MIDDLE EAST AND NORTH AFRICA; POVERTY AND EDUCATION.

BIBLIOGRAPHY

ASSOCIATION FOR THE DEVELOPMENT OF EDUCATION IN AFRICA. 1999. *Newsletter* 11(1). Paris: Association for the Development of Education in Africa.

ASSOCIATION FOR THE DEVELOPMENT OF EDUCATION IN AFRICA. 2001. *What Works and What's New in Education: Africa Speaks! Report from a Prospective, Stocktaking Review of Education in Africa.* Paris: Association for the Development of Education in Africa.

BARRO, ROBERT J. 1991. "Economic Growth in a Cross-Section of Countries." *Quarterly Journal of Economics* 106:407–444.

ELLEY, WARWICK B. 1992. *How in the World Do Students Read?"* Hamburg, Germany: International Education Association.

INSTITUT NATIONAL D'ETUDE ET D'ACTION POUR LE DEVELOPPEMENT DE L'EDUCATION. 1997. *Projet SNERS: L'évaluation du rendement pédagogique du français écrit dans l'enseignement primaire: Les résultats au CM2 et sciences CM2.* Dakar, Senegal: Institut National d'Etude et d'Action pour le Developpement de l'Education.

INTERNATIONAL INSTITUTE FOR EDUCATION PLANNING. 1999. *Private Education in Sub-Saharan Africa: A Re-examination of Theories and Concepts Related to Its Development and Finance.* Paris: International Institute for Education Planning/United Nations Educational, Scientific and Cultural Organization.

LAU, LAWRENCE J.; JAMISON, DEAN T.; and LOUAT, FREDERIC F. 1991. *Education and Productivity in Development Countries: An Aggregate Production Function Approach.* Policy Research Working Paper 612. Washington, DC: World Bank, Development Economics and Population and Human Resources Department.

LEWIN, KEITH M., and CAILLODS, FRANCOISE. 1999. *Financing Education in Developing Countries.*

Paris: International Institute of Educational Planning, Strategies for Sustainable Secondary Schooling.

LOCKHEED, MARLAINE E.; JAMISON, DEAN T.; and LAU, LAWRENCE. 1980. "Farmer Education and Farm Efficiency: A Survey." *Economic Development and Cultural Change* 29(1):37–76.

LOCKHEED, MARLAINE E., and VERSPOOR, ADRIAAN. 1991. *Improving Primary Education in Developing Countries.* New York: Oxford University Press for the World Bank.

MIDDLETON, JOHN; VAN ADAMS, ARVIL; and ZIDERMAN, ADRIAN. 1993. *Skill for Productivity: Vocational Education and Training in Developing Countries.* New York: Oxford University Press for World Bank.

MINGAT, ALAIN. 1998. *Assessing Priorities for Education Policy in the Sahel from a Comparative Perspective.* Dijon, France: Université de Bourgogne, Institut de Recherche sur l'Economie de l'Education.

MINGAT, ALAIN, and SUCHET, BRUNO. 1998. *Une analyse économique comparative des systèmes éducatifs Africains.* Dijon, France: Université de Bourgogne, Institut de Recherche sur l'Economie de l'Education.

NEHRU, VIKRAM, and DHARESHWAR, ASHOK M. 1994. *New Estimates of Total Factor Productivity Growth for Developing and Industrial Countries.* Policy Research Working Paper 1313. Washington, DC: World Bank, International Economics Department.

ORGANISATION FOR ECONOMIC CO-OPERATION AND DEVELOPMENT, DEVELOPMENT ASSISTANCE COMMITTEE. 1996. *Shaping the Twenty-First Century: The Contribution of Development Cooperation.* Washington, DC: Organisation for Economic Co-operation and Development, Development Assistance Committee.

OXFAM. 1999. *Education Now: Break the Cycle of Poverty.* Oxford: Oxfam.

PSACHAROPOULOS, GEORGE. 1985. "Returns to Education: A Further International Update and Implications." *Journal of Human Resources* (U.S.) 20:583–604.

SAINT, WILLIAM. 1992. *Universities in Africa: Strategies for Stabilization and Revitalization.* World Bank Technical Paper, 0253-7494, no. 194. Washington, DC: World Bank.

UNITED NATIONS EDUCATIONAL, SCIENTIFIC AND CULTURAL ORGANIZATION. 1998a. *Development of Education in Africa: A Statistical Review.* Seventh Conference of Ministers of Education of African Member States of UNESCO. (MINEDAF VII). Paris: United Nations Educational, Scientific and Cultural Organization.

UNITED NATIONS EDUCATIONAL, SCIENTIFIC AND CULTURAL ORGANIZATION. 1998b. *UNESCO Yearbook, 1998.* Paris: United Nations Educational, Scientific and Cultural Organization.

UNITED NATIONS EDUCATIONAL, SCIENTIFIC AND CULTURAL ORGANIZATION. 1998c. *World Education Report, 1998.* Paris: United Nations Educational, Scientific and Cultural Organization.

UNITED NATIONS EDUCATIONAL, SCIENTIFIC AND CULTURAL ORGANIZATION. 1999a. *Science and Technology in Africa: A Commitment for the Twenty-First Century.* Paris: United Nations Educational, Scientific and Cultural Organization, Office of Public Information.

UNITED NATIONS EDUCATIONAL, SCIENTIFIC AND CULTURAL ORGANIZATION. 1999b. *UNESCO Yearbook, 1999.* Paris: United Nations Educational, Scientific and Cultural Organization.

UNITED NATIONS EDUCATIONAL, SCIENTIFIC AND CULTURAL ORGANIZATION. 2000. *Education for All (2000): Report from the Sub-Saharan Africa Zone, Assessment of Basic Education in SSA.* Harare, Zimbabwe: United Nations Educational, Scientific and Cultural Organization.

UNITED NATIONS CHILDREN'S FUND. 1999. *The State of the World's Children, 1999: Education.* New York: Oxford University Press.

VAWDA, AYESHA, and PATRINOS, HARRY ANTHONY. 1999. "Private Education in West Africa: The Technological Imperative." Paper presented at the Fifth Oxford International Conference on Education and Development, Oxford University.

WORLD BANK. 1991. *Vocational and Technical Education and Training: A World Bank Policy Paper.* Washington, DC: World Bank.

WORLD BANK. 2000. *Can Africa Claim the Twenty-First Century?* Washington, DC: World Bank.

WORLD BANK. 2001a. *A Chance to Learn: Knowledge and Finance for Education in Sub-Saharan Africa.* Africa Region Hunan Development Series. Washington, DC: World Bank.

WORLD BANK. 2001b. *Can Africa Reach the International Targets for Human Development? An Assessment of Progress towards the 1998 Second Tokyo International Conference on African Development (TICAD II).* Africa Region Human Development Series. Washington, DC: World Bank.

WORLD EDUCATION FORUM. 2000. *Sub-Saharan Africa Regional Framework for Action.* Dakar, Senegal: World Education Forum.

ADRIAAN M. VERSPOOR

SUCCESS FOR ALL PROGRAMS

Almost all children, regardless of their home backgrounds, enter school bright, confident, hopeful, and highly motivated, certain that they will succeed in school. However, within just a few years, many of these children will be on a path toward failure. In particular, many students will be reading far below grade level. Research shows that disadvantaged third graders who have failed a grade or are reading well below grade level are extremely unlikely to ultimately graduate from high school. Both research and common sense dictate that prevention and early intervention make more sense than remediation and special education for these children. However, it is not enough to convince school staffs that it is important to ensure that all children start off with success; schools need proven, replicable models highly that are likely to work with at-risk children.

The Success for All Program

The search for such methods led a group at Johns Hopkins University to develop a program called Success for All. Success for All began in the Baltimore City Public Schools in 1987 and (as of school year 2001–2002) exists in more than 1,800 schools in forty-eight states (Maine and New Hampshire are the exceptions). Adaptations of the program are currently in use in Britain, Canada, Mexico, Australia, and Israel. Most Success for All schools are in high-poverty urban and rural districts, but many less-impoverished schools also use the program. The idea behind Success for All is simple: focus resources, attention, and the best instructional methods known on the early grades to make certain that no child ever falls behind, especially in reading.

Students in Success for All schools start at the age of four or five with programs designed to build language, self-esteem, and pre-reading skills. In first grade they start a structured reading program that emphasizes systematic phonics in the context of meaningful, enjoyable stories. Students work in cooperation with each other on reading and writing activities. By the end of first grade almost all students are well on the way to successful reading, and they then move on to work with novels, short stories, and expository content in small groups, with programs emphasizing cooperative learning, through the sixth grade. Programs in math, science, and social studies are also used by many Success for All schools in grades K–6. Extensive professional development, follow-up, and coaching enable teachers to use the programs effectively.

Tutoring

Quality early childhood programs and reading and writing instruction prevent most reading problems from arising, but not all. The next level of intervention is tutoring. Tutors are certified teachers or paraprofessionals who work one-on-one primarily with first graders who are having difficulties learning to read. The tutors work in close collaboration with classroom teachers—if a child is struggling with Lesson 37, the tutor works on that lesson so that the child will be ready for Lesson 38. The tutors teach a reading class during a common reading period, both to reduce class size and to make sure that tutors are thoroughly familiar with the reading program.

Family support is also a key element of Success for All. A family support team in each school works to involve parents in the education of their own children in a variety of ways and also deals with such issues as attendance, behavior problems, health problems, and connections with social agencies. A curriculum for solving social problems, Getting Along Together, is used in all schools.

One of the most important individuals in a Success for All school is the facilitator, a teacher who usually works full time to help other teachers implement the program. The facilitator visits classes to give feedback and support, organizes an eight-week assessment program to monitor the progress of every child, and makes sure that teachers, tutors, and family support staff are all communicating. There are several days of formal training and follow-up for teachers each year, but the facilitator sees to it that professional development occurs every day.

FIGURE 1

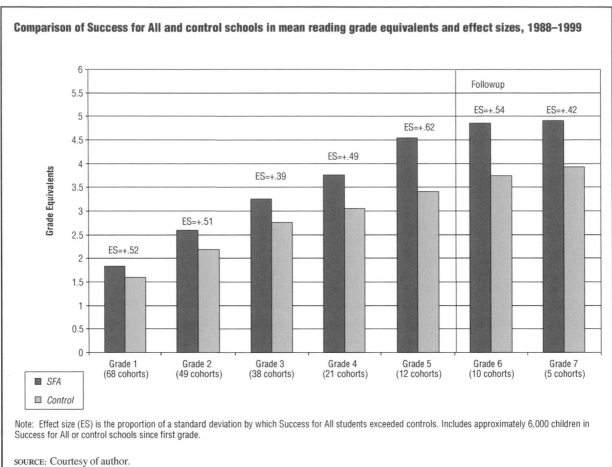

Comparison of Success for All and control schools in mean reading grade equivalents and effect sizes, 1988–1999

Note: Effect size (ES) is the proportion of a standard deviation by which Success for All students exceeded controls. Includes approximately 6,000 children in Success for All or control schools since first grade.

SOURCE: Courtesy of author.

Outcomes

Success for All has been evaluated over time in high-poverty Title I schools throughout the United States. In most evaluations, Success for All schools were compared to matched control schools on individually administered tests of reading. The results have been remarkable in their consistency, breadth, and power. In every district, students in Success for All schools have been found to be reading better than students in control schools. Figure 1 summarizes the average differences between Success for All and control students in reading performance across many studies. The "ES" at the top of each pair of bars refers to *effect size,* the proportion of a standard deviation separating experimental and control schools. The consistent effect size of more than a half standard deviation is considered very large in educational research.

In addition to consistent effects for English-speaking children, strong positive effects have been found for a Spanish version of the program used in bilingual classes and for speakers of many languages learning English as a second language. Effects are especially strong for students who scored in the lowest 25 percent on pretests. Further, assignments to special education for learning disabilities have been cut in half, and retentions have been virtually eliminated.

In addition to the many studies involving individually administered reading measures, many evaluations have found that students in Success for All schools gain significantly more than other students on assessments used in state accountability programs. Based on these findings, an independent review by Rebecca Herman found Success for All to be one of only two comprehensive reform models to meet the highest standards of evaluation rigor, replication, and effectiveness.

See also: ELEMENTARY EDUCATION, *subentry on* CURRENT TRENDS; LANGUAGE ARTS, TEACHING OF; POVERTY AND EDUCATION; SCHOOL REFORM TUTORING, *subentry on* SCHOOL; URBAN EDUCATION.

BIBLIOGRAPHY

HERMAN, REBECCA. 1999. *An Educator's Guide to Schoolwide Reform.* Arlington, VA: Educational Research Service.

HURLEY, ERIC, et al. 2001. "Effects of Success for All on TAAS Reading: A Texas Statewide Evaluation." *Phi Delta Kappan* 82:750–756.

LLOYD, DEE N. 1978. "Prediction of School Failure from Third-Grade Data." *Educational and Psychological Measurement* 38:1193–1200.

SANDERS, WILLIAM L.; WRIGHT, S. PAUL; and ROSS, STEVEN M. 2000. *Four-Year Results for Roots and Wings Schools in Memphis.* Memphis, TN: University of Memphis, Center for Research in Educational Policy.

SLAVIN, ROBERT E., and MADDEN, NANCY A. 1999. "Effects of Bilingual and English As a Second Language Adaptations of Success for All on the Reading Achievement of Students Acquiring English." *Journal of Education for Students Placed at Risk* 4(4):393–416.

SLAVIN, ROBERT E., and MADDEN, NANCY A., eds. 2001. *One Million Children: Success for All.* Thousand Oaks, CA: Corwin.

TRAUB, JAMES. 1999. *Better By Design? A Consumer's Guide to Schoolwide Reform.* Washington, DC: Thomas Fordham Foundation.

INTERNET RESOURCE

SUCCESS FOR ALL FOUNDATION. JOHNS HOPKINS UNIVERSITY. 2002. <www.successforall.net>.

ROBERT E. SLAVIN

SUICIDE

See: RISK BEHAVIORS, *subentry on* SUICIDE.

SUMMER ENRICHMENT PROGRAMS

American society operates on an underlying faith that everyone is "free to perform at the level of his or her ability, motivation, and qualities of character and be rewarded accordingly" (Gardner, p. 22). In other words, individuals should have the opportunity to go where their talents take them. At the same time, Americans hold dear the belief that all people should have an equal opportunity to succeed. Therefore, various education programs (e.g., through Head Start, Title 1), have been established to foster equality, regardless of socioeconomic background. To develop excellence, educational opportunities are provided that are enriching and accelerating so that talented individuals are matched with an environment that draws out their potential. While some truly believe that talented students will make it on their own, research has shown that what is taught, and how it is taught, is important for all students, even the most gifted. High expectations, continuous challenges, and learning something new each day are important for academic success.

Most states and many school districts have developed specialized summer programs that bring together academically talented students and offer an educational experience geared to their high abilities. Such specialized summer enrichment programs have proliferated across the country because research has demonstrated that high-ability students develop higher expectations, feel better about themselves, and engage in higher-level processing or discourse when working with other students of similar abilities. Moreover, summer programs foster independence and good work habits in an intellectually challenging environment that also develops critical thinking skills and creativity.

Types of Programs

Summer programs designed to meet the needs of these high-ability learners include governors' schools, various options developed by local school districts as part of their gifted and talented programming, and precollegiate programs sponsored by colleges and universities on their campuses or at satellite sites. In the past, when funding was available, the National Science Foundation also sponsored such programs through grants to various institutions. Programs can be residential or distanced in nature, and they span the arts, humanities, and sciences. While most are offered in a course format, several programs are devoted to providing research experiences or specialized internships. Most of the residential programs, however, are limited to the secondary grades.

These programs are intended to provide enrichment (and acceleration in some cases) and build motivation in students who are not fully served or are underrepresented by conventional programs. Admission to most summer enrichment programs is highly competitive and selective. While a variety of criteria are often utilized in selecting students (e.g., grades, recommendations, nominations), high demonstrated ability as measured by achievement or aptitude tests is a critical component of any selection system.

Summer Programs: An Example

One of the first summer programs for secondary students was started in 1972 by the Study of Mathematically Precocious Youth (SMPY) at Johns Hopkins University. It became the model for many university-based programs. The Center for Talented Youth (CTY) at Johns Hopkins and other universities across the country (e.g., Duke, Iowa, Iowa State, Northwestern, Vanderbilt) continue this work, adopting and adapting this model for their settings. In such programs, seventh-grade students who have taken the SAT or ACT and whose scores exceed the mean of college-bound seniors are invited to enroll. They are often called Talent Search programs because most students are identified through a talent search. In these summer programs, students can assimilate a full high school course (e.g., chemistry, Latin, math) within three weeks or take a similarly fast-paced course on a topic not offered by their local school. The program's instruction is aimed at the very characteristics that make students so gifted: their ability to make connections among seemingly disparate ideas, to assimilate new information rapidly, and to be challenged by the subject matter. Thus, rather than feeling rushed, these students thrive in such learning environments, which are deeply enriching, and they tend to crave more. Many (as many as 40% in some cases) return the following year for additional learning opportunities developmentally tailored to their level and rate of growth.

Program Success: Some Evaluative Data

While both gifted boys and girls evaluate these programs positively (even twenty years later), a reliable gender difference is characteristically found. Girls tend to report more positive effects. It appears that peer pressure on gifted girls in most schools is harsher than that for gifted boys. When talented girls are placed in an environment without any pressure not to achieve, they not only enjoy the learning experience more fully, but they are especially relieved by the absence of negative peer pressure. Indeed, they often report finally being able to "be themselves." Of course, boys report the same phenomena. It is not known whether participants are more deeply affected academically or socially by these programs. Many highly gifted students feel alienated in a traditional classroom, but not at these programs, where they feel they finally find individuals who understand them.

The identification of intellectually able students and the long-term impact of various educational options upon their development are being studied by SMPY, which is a fifty-year longitudinal study that began in 1971 at Johns Hopkins and in the early twenty-first century is run by the Peabody College of Education and Human Development at Vanderbilt University. This work involves studying, throughout their lives, more than 5,000 mathematically and verbally precocious students. This longitudinal study provides data to not only evaluate but also to refine programs. It also provides information about the development, needs, and characteristics of precocious youth.

The data collected during SMPY's first three decades has shown that, while most SMPY students do achieve their potential for high academic success in high school, college, and even graduate school, intellectually talented students will not necessarily achieve to their full potential unless provided with appropriate educational opportunities, and some of the most satisfying experiences are the summer enrichment programs.

But what does it mean to say that these individuals are doing well, especially if the educational system has intervened in their lives? In the most able cohort of SMPY's longitudinal study, which included individuals who were in the top 1 in 10,000 in ability and who experienced an intensive intervention, individuals have earned doctorates at 50 times the base rate and at twice the rate of individuals in the top 1 percent in ability who received less intervention. One of these individuals became a full professor at a major research university before age twenty-five.

Conclusion

Summer enrichment programs have focused on providing developmentally appropriate learning experiences for talented students, identifying those students who have such needs, which often go undetected, and then providing supplemental educational opportunities that ensure that such students are challenged and that their passions and love for learning are kept alive, rather than extinguished by curricula that are too slow paced and not at the right level. While doing so, they provide an appropriate social experience that is often experienced as healing. It could be said that summer enrichment programs for gifted and talented students are about developing rare human capital.

See also: GIFTED AND TALENTED EDUCATION.

BIBLIOGRAPHY

GARDNER, JOHN WILLIAM. 1961. *Excellence: Can We Be Equal and Excellent Too?* New York: Harper.

CAMILLA BENBOW

SUMMER JOBS

See: EMPLOYMENT, *subentry on* SUMMER.

SUMMER SCHOOL

Summer school programs, also known as extended-year programs, are designed to provide educational opportunities to students during the summer months when schools traditionally observe summer break or summer vacation. Summer school programs generally fit into one of three categories: (1) remediation, (2) enrichment, or (3) extended-year for students with special needs.

Remediation

Remediation summer school programs serve students who have difficulty mastering required core content and skills. Often these students lack the required prerequisites and/or skills needed to graduate from one level to the next, or they lack the required credits to graduate from high school. They may also have failed one or more minimum competency skill examinations required by a local school district or the state.

Remediation programs are designed to deliver a specific curriculum in a condensed period of time, emphasizing the mastery of the student's individual deficiency. These summer school classes are generally longer in length (two to three hours per day) and meet for a shorter duration of time (four to six weeks) than traditional classes, which often meet for forty-five to ninety minutes per day for eighteen weeks. Frequently, students concentrate on one or two areas of study during a typical summer school session.

Enrichment

Summer school enrichment classes are offered in a variety of designs. Some programs follow the same format as remedial programs, only they are designed to assist a student in accelerating their learning during the condensed period of time. Other programs emphasize a particular curricular area, such as science, a second language, or a particular performing or visual art form. These programs are often offered in a camp-type format, and in many cases they are located at an actual camp.

Other enrichment programs are developed in cooperation between a local school system and a college or university. These programs are usually offered on the college or university campus and emphasize an area of strength for the individual student. In a large number of cases, the college or university curriculum is taught.

Private enterprises deliver other forms of summer enrichment programs. These programs generally provide students with accelerated or enriched opportunities to explore a variety of curricular areas. The programs emphasize learning as an enjoyable activity and provide each student with an experience that is designed to create a desire to learn for the sake of learning.

Extended-Year for Students with Special Needs

Under the federal Individuals with Disabilities Education Act (IDEA), each student with special needs must have an Individualized Education Program (IEP). A team consisting of parents, school personnel, support personnel, and, usually, the student develops this plan. IEPs frequently call for an extended-year program to be implemented during the summer months. Because each IEP addresses individual goals for a particular student, each program is intended to be designed to meet the unique needs of that student.

Extended-year programs for students with special needs may take a variety of forms. The program may emphasize the continuation of the overall specific goals established for the student; it may emphasize one or more areas where special attention is needed to meet a particular goal; it may serve as a transition from one setting to another; or it may serve a student who needs the continuity of a structured program to avoid the loss of skills and knowledge due to a prolonged break in attendance. An extended-year program may duplicate the design described earlier for students who need remediation in a particular area of study. In all cases, the program is designed to meet the individual needs of the student.

The History of Summer School

The traditional school calendar in the United States was heavily influenced by the needs of an agrarian society. Since the late spring, summer, and early fall were critical for farming families, school was not in session during these months. As a result, the school calendar traditionally ran from late fall through early spring, when there was less work to do on the farms. This pattern set the groundwork for the development of summer school.

As the nation transformed from an agrarian society to an industrialized society, education changed in many ways, but the traditional nine- to ten-month calendar remained intact. There have been many attempts to alter the traditional agrarian-based calendar, most notably by the advocates of year-round education (YRE), but none have caused widespread national change. As a result, summer has remained a time for vacation, relaxation, and an occasional summer school session.

Sputnik **and the civil rights movement.** The role of summer school in American education is a history of changing expectations. As society has changed, so has the role of summer school. On October 4, 1957, the launch of *Sputnik I* by the Soviet Union changed the world, and American education, forever. A national panic ensued as the country came to grips with its first defeat in the great space race of the 1950s and 1960s. Mathematics and science education became a priority of policymakers and educators. Summer school began to have an increased role in this movement. Students were encouraged to strengthen their mathematics and science skills through increased study. Federal funding became available to create accelerated mathematics and science programs, many of which were delivered in summer school sessions.

As the country became fully involved in the space race, the civil rights movement of the 1960s had an increased impact on education. Schools were seen more and more as institutions to enact social change, and summer schools were expanded to meet this need.

The 1983 publication of *A Nation at Risk: The Imperative for Educational Reform* by the National Commission on Excellence in Education had a profound impact on education. This report contended that the American educational system was inadequate and needed repair. It called for a movement it labeled the *new basics,* meaning a return to traditional academic standards. As schools began to restructure in the wake of this report, more and more summer school programs were implemented to meet the new demand for a return to traditional learning.

During the 1990s there was an increased demand for school accountability. Student test scores were frequently used as the measure of the effectiveness of individual schools and school districts. Students who had substandard test scores were often encouraged, if not required, to attend summer school to make up their deficiencies.

Funding

There are two basic methods of funding summer school. One is through public funding. Schools receive funds from a variety of other governmental taxation sources, such as property taxes, sales taxes, and state run lotteries. Summer school programs are provided funding through these revenues, either on a per-pupil basis or through a lump sum allocation. In either case, funding is usually supplemental and separate from the regular funding dollars. These programs, run by public schools, are a part of the free public education system.

In many other summer school programs the participants pay a fee to cover the costs of the program. These programs are generally operated by private enterprises; however, there are cases where public institutions assess a fee for a summer program that is considered supplemental.

Trends, Issues, and Controversies

As stated earlier, the role of summer school has had a changing mission, depending on the current trends in society at any given time. Summer school has come to be seen as an excellent tool to deliver added emphasis to popular movements. The 1950s and the 1980s saw summer school as an answer to low academic achievement; the 1960s saw summer school as an opportunity to solidify social change; and the 1990s saw summer school as a tool to implement accountability in students and schools.

Advocates of extended-year calendars and year-round education argue that the school calendar, based on the needs of an agrarian society, has outlived its usefulness. They advocate the elimination of the summer vacation, thus ending the need for summer school.

Other researchers have shown that students evidence a profound loss of retention over the summer months, especially those students who come from disadvantaged backgrounds. There is a school of thought, moreover, that questions the value of summer school programs and cites a lack of research showing positive student achievement as a result of participation in a summer school program.

Throughout the history of summer school there have been advocates for requiring low-achieving students to attend summer school. The controversy surrounding this issue runs deep and points to a deeper philosophical argument regarding the overall purpose of American schooling. As long as there is disagreement on this purpose, there will be disagreement on the purpose and role of summer school.

Summer school is as much an American institution as is American education itself. Its development has mirrored the development of an educational system that has struggled to keep pace with the changing demands of a changing society. Summer school has met a variety of needs and will continue to change with our changing society.

See also: ELEMENTARY EDUCATION, *subentries on* CURRENT TRENDS, HISTORY OF; SECONDARY EDUCATION, *subentries on* CURRENT TRENDS, HISTORY OF; YEAR-ROUND EDUCATION.

BIBLIOGRAPHY

BORMAN, GEOFFREY. 2001. "Summers Are for Learning." *Principal* 80(3):26–29.

CAMMAROTA, GLORIA; STOOPS, JOHN A.; and JOHNSON, FRANK R. 1961. *Extending the School Year.* Washington, DC: Association For Supervision and Curriculum Development.

CHMELYNSKI, CAROL. 1998. "Summer School for Meeting Higher Standards." *The Education Digest* 63(9):47–50.

CREMIN, LAWRENCE A. 1970. *American Education: The Colonial Experience 1607–1783.* New York: Harper and Row.

CREMIN, LAWRENCE A. 1980. *American Education: The National Experience 1783–1876.* New York: Harper and Row.

CREMIN, LAWRENCE A. 1988. *American Education: The Metropolitan Experience 1876–1980.* New York: Harper and Row.

DOUGHERTY, JOHN W. 1981. *Summer School: A New Look,* Vol. 158. Bloomington, IN: Phi Delta Kappa.

KULCSAR, MICHAEL. 1999. "Should Students Pay For Summer School?" *American Teacher* 83(8):4.

PIPHO, CHRIS. 1999. "Summer School: Rx for Low Performance?" *Phi Delta Kappan* 81(1):7–8.

U.S. DEPARTMENT OF EDUCATION. 1993. *Summer Challenge: Model Summer Programs for Disadvantaged Students.* Washington, DC: U.S. Department of Education.

DOUGLAS M. DEWITT

SUPERINTENDENT OF LARGE-CITY SCHOOL SYSTEMS

The twenty-first century finds one-third of America's public school children attending one of ten large urban (large-city) school districts. By 2020 approximately one-half of public school enrollment will be clustered in twenty districts. The educational stewardship of a majority of the nations youth rests uncomfortably on the shoulders of a very few large-city school superintendents. Their success and the success of their districts may very well determine the future of American democracy.

Urban districts are typically considered to be those located in the inner core of metropolitan areas having enrollments of more than 25,000 students. The research and literature about large-city school districts portray conditions of poverty, chronic academic underachievement, dropouts, crime, unstable school boards, reform policy churn, and high superintendent turnover.

The typical tenure of a superintendent in the largest large-city districts is two to three years. This brief tenure makes it unlikely a superintendent can develop and implement reform programs that can result in higher academic achievement—let alone rebuild crumbling schools buildings, secure private sector assistance, and build a working relationship with the city's political structure.

The large-city superintendency is a position defined by high expectations, intense stress, inadequate resources, and often a highly unstable politicized board of education.

History of the Urban Superintendent

The first large-city superintendency was established in 1837 in Buffalo, New York. The number of appointed superintendencies grew in parallel with the growth of American cities. These early large-city superintendents were hired to relieve boards of education of managerial tasks and business affairs. The first superintendents generally acted as coordinators ensuring similar practices among schools for purchasing materials, insuring building maintenance, and keeping districts' financial records.

As city school systems grew many quickly became "lighthouse" districts featuring innovative high-quality education programs and services. These district provided a uniform curriculum based upon standards and an extensive array of elective courses taught by specially trained teachers. This was generally an era of social, economic, and political reform and birthplace of the modern large-city superintendency.

The large-city superintendents who shouldered responsibility for educational programs quickly became the most visible and respected educators in the country. Nearly all were men, Protestants, and former schoolmasters of country schools. With assistance from industrial leaders they built the large urban school bureaucracies still in place in the early twenty-first century. An important component of these school bureaucracies was and still is the industrial management practice called *scientific management,* which emphasizes time management, employee specialization, and a top-down type of organization structure. The goal of scientific management was efficiency—a desirable objective for large city superintendents besieged by rapid enrollment growth, construction of new schools, and the management of public tax dollars.

A strong driving force for early large-city superintendents was the Americanization of large numbers of immigrants. This was achieved through a uniform curriculum, compulsory attendance, teacher certification, testing, vocational education, and citizenship. These were the keystones to a "common" education for all children. Many large-city superintendents perceived themselves to be reformers as well as builders of the American dream. Their reforms were built upon practicality and meeting the educational needs of society and the workplace. The vision of schooling held by most of the superintendents was rooted in their experiences of growing up in rural and small-town America.

Despite the stress and strain of leading huge school organizations, the large-city superintendents generally enjoyed lengthy tenure. Their appointments were made by boards of education, themselves appointed by mayors and city councils. Board members were generally prominent doctors, lawyers, and businessmen. Only after the World War II did most large-city districts switch to elected boards.

The pyramid-shaped urban district structure provided the large-city superintendents with an immense amount of personal control. Through hard work they were generally successful in standardizing curriculum and testing procedures that were necessary to select and prepare students for the workforce, high school, and college.

The large-city superintendents not only pioneered the current public school program and organization, but also laid the foundation for a profession. Many superintendents were imposing personalities, adroit politicians, community development activists, and shrewd business executives.

The Profession

Large-city superintendents after World War I were instrumental in creating training programs to identify and prepare their successors. The first of these higher education academic programs was at Teachers College (Columbia University) in New York. Many of the early professors of educational administration were former large-city superintendents.

Elwood Cubberly of Stanford University can perhaps be called the "dean" of the educational administration professorship. Perhaps his most important contribution was conducting large-city studies where he and colleagues studied in detail every operating aspect of a selected large-city school district. Out of these studies came compendiums of best practices on how to build and administer quality school districts. Importantly, Cubberly based his list of best practices and necessary personal attributes on the work of large-city superintendents.

These lists of skills, content knowledge, practices, and leadership traits developed by former large-city superintendents in professorial roles continue to be utilized in the early twenty-first century. Certification standards in many states still reflect the content of the large-city studies. Textbooks about the superintendency were nearly all written by former city superintendents. The establishment of the American Association of School Administrators in 1937 was also due to the efforts of the large-city superintendents.

School Boards

Nearly all large-city superintendents are appointed by elected boards of education. A typical contract length for a large-city superintendent is three or four years. About half of superintendents in the largest twenty-five districts are able complete a four-year contract. Boards of Education in large-city districts usually are comprised of more than nine members elected for four years. The same is true for a growing number of appointed boards found in cities such as Chicago, Cleveland, and Boston.

Large-city district-elected board positions are often contentious, with candidates spending substantial amounts to be elected to a virtually unpaid office. In some districts a modest stipend is paid to board members. Many large-city boards are very politicized, "churning over" both board members and superintendents on a regular basis. Continuity in leadership is a serious problem for many districts.

Most authorities cite the most important decision a board makes to be the selection of a superintendent. In the case of large-city districts it is often very difficult for a majority of board members to agree upon an appointment. Difficulty in choosing a superintendent is usually a harbinger of future intraboard conflict, indecision, and instability. An example is the Kansas City, Missouri, district, which hired nineteen superintendents in a thirty-year period.

Large-city board members often run on single-issue platforms: a typical example, to fire bad teachers and administrators whose incompetence is the reason for low test scores. Also, some board members feel a strong need to report to constituents about the progress they are making in "fixing" the district. These types of attitudes and actions often lead to superintendent and board conflict. Valuable energy and time of boards and superintendents is often spent in endless arguments, intrigue, and political posturing for the media.

In large-city districts superintendent-board conflict seems inevitable due to political interests, attempts by boards to micromanage, and pressures by groups such as unions to pressure board members to discipline superintendents and administrators who do not make decisions to the special interest group's liking.

Characteristics of the Large-City Superintendent

The media often portray the large-city superintendency as an impossible job. At the very least, it is a job of great pain and modest financial gain. The applicant pool for large-city superintendencies has always been reported to be meager in high-quality candidates. Most large-city superintendencies are filled by candidates who reflect the ethnicity of students and community. Racial preferences have kept applicant pools thin because of lack of substantial numbers of qualified African Americans and Hispanics. Women are often found in the position of large-city superintendent.

When a large-city superintendent conflicts with a board the media often takes advantage of the situation. The well-publicized firings of large-city superintendents after tumultuous conflict with boards do not serve as a positive advertisement for large-city superintendencies.

Usually search firms are retained by large-city boards to find a group of qualified candidates. Often a majority of the qualified candidates found by search firms are superintendents in other urban districts. This scenario results in one large-city district making an offer to another districts' superintendent. This creates a public image of the large-city superintendency being recycled.

Another source of large-city superintendents is the inside central office administrator. In large districts there are large number of deputy and assistant superintendents qualified to step up to the higher position. Board members sometimes shy away from inside candidates when those candidates wish to see reform initiatives implemented in the district. However, many of these inside candidates have a vast knowledge of the district, its history, problems, and resources. From experience they know how to get things done within the system. For board members, hiring an inside candidate removes the possibility of possible incompatibility with the new superintendent.

The nontraditional (noneducator) applicant coming from a military or private sector background is infrequently hired by large-city boards permitted to do by state statute. Some large-city boards have hired noneducators to be chief executive officers who in turn hire an educator to lead the educational program. In appearances employing a chief executive officer implies a movement of district management to a corporate model.

A major problem facing the large-city superintendency is attracting a well-qualified applicant pool comprised of women and minorities. Unfortunately, many large-city superintendents are not as well qualified as potential applicants sitting on the sidelines. Many successful superintendents in smaller districts do not wish to take on the "impossibility" of the large-city superintendency.

The Impossibility and Implausibility of the Position

The operational responsibilities of large-city superintendents can be extraordinary. Billion-dollar budgets, a half-million students and 50,000 employees require a chief executive officer capable a leading a large management team. The position is unique in that it also requires the chief executive to be the district's leading educator possessing expert knowledge about teaching, curriculum, testing, special education, and school reform. In addition, due the nature of education financing, the superintendent must be a shrewd politician ensuring that the district receives its share of the public tax dollar.

The superintendent must also be a master communicator working with a political board, forming working relationships with public and private groups, and especially serving as the connecting link between community. In a nutshell this describes the near impossible and implausible role of the large-city superintendent.

The multiple responsibilities and expectations leave large-city superintendents with little choice than to choose a "key set of challenges" to focus their attention upon. The federal government's 1983 report, *A Nation at Risk: The Imperative for Educational Reform*, sparked a national school reform movement and, in reaction, large-city superintendents began to shift from being expert managers to instructional reformers.

Superintendents, especially, in the large urban districts, are pressured for academic accountability. Many at the urging of boards yearly mount multiple reform initiatives promising better test scores. Boards often view reform initiatives as a public demonstration the district is responding to chronic underachievement by poor and minority children.

In response to national school reform efforts, large-city boards search for superintendents who espouse the belief that all children are capable of learning state-imposed standards and that test scores can be raised through improved instructional models. The public persona of many large-city superintendents has been more of a instructional leader rather than chief executive officer. Unfortunately, districtwide success stories of large-city superintendents leading their districts to substantive and lasting reform have been few.

There have been and are successful large-city superintendents. Some of these individuals have failed in one district and succeeded in another possessing more favorable conditions. The deciding factor between success and failure seems to be in mayoral support and board stability. Cities with records of some reform success are those where the mayor perceives the health of the school district to be integral to the city. In several cities, mayoral involvement in school reform has reached the point of mayor's taking control the school board and district.

Perhaps the greatest failing of large-city superintendents is their inability to be political leaders. Large-city schools many times consume more than half of the tax dollars in the city, are a major employer, and provide a critical public service. Competitors for the public tax dollars, such as the city council and agencies, have elected officials with political constituencies with forceful lobbies. School districts boards are comprised of volunteer elected officials without a political power base. Infrequently, a large-city district can mount a strong political offensive that wrests away fiscal resources competitor groups.

The large-city superintendent has to be a keen political observer and be able to form alliances, and work quietly and effectively with the city political power structure. An examination of past and present successful large-city superintendents proves this to be the case. Behind-the-scenes political maneuvering can be more beneficial in obtaining badly needed resources than being a high-profile school reformer making frequent appearances at meetings, conferences and media events.

See also: EDUCATIONAL ACCOUNTABILITY; SCHOOL BOARD RELATIONS, *subentry on* RELATION OF SCHOOL BOARD TO SUPERINTENDENT; SUPERINTENDENT OF SCHOOLS; URBAN EDUCATION.

BIBLIOGRAPHY

CALLAHAN, ROBERT E. 1962. *Education and the Cult of Efficiency.* Chicago: University of Chicago Press.

CARTER, DAVID S.; GLASS, THOMAS E.; and HORD, SHIRLEY M. 1993. *Selecting Preparing and Developing the School District Superintendent.* New York: Falmer.

CARTER, GENE R., and CUNNINGHAM, WILLIAM G. 1997. *The American School Superintendent: Leading in an Age of Pressure.* San Francisco: Jossey-Bass.

CHAPMAN, CAROLYN H., ed. 1997. *Becoming a Superintendent: Challenges of School District Leadership.* New York: Prentice-Hall.

CUBBERLY, ELWOOD C. 1922. *Public School Administration.* New York: Houghton-Mifflin.

GLASS, THOMAS E.; LARS, BJORK; and CRUNNER, CRYSS. 2000. *The Study of the American School Superintendency 2000: A Look at the Superintendent in the New Millennium.* Arlington, VA: American Association of School Administrators.

HESS, FREDERICK M. 1999. *Spinning Wheels: The Politics of Urban School Reform.* Washington, DC: Brookings Institution Press.

HILL, PAUL T., and CELIO, MARY BETH. 1998. *Fixing Urban Schools.* Washington, DC: Brookings Institution Press.

KOWALSKI, THEODORE J. 1995. *Keepers of the Flame: Contemporary Urban Superintendents.* Thousand Oaks, CA: Corwin Press.

MIREL, JEFFREY. 1993. *The Rise and Fall of an Urban System: Detroit: 1907–1981.* Ann Arbor: University of Michigan Press.

TALLERICO, MARILYN. 2000. *Accessing the Superintendency: The Unwritten Rules.* Thousand Oaks, CA: Corwin Press.

TYACK, DAVID, and HANSOT, ELISABETH. 1982. *Managers of Virtue: Public School Leadership in America, 1820 to 1980.* New York: Basic Books.

THOMAS E. GLASS

SUPERINTENDENT OF SCHOOLS

The superintendent of schools is a position of wide influence but one that is narrowly understood. This, in part, stems from its history. Rarely has a position of such centrality grown in such a tangled way. Consequently, there has not been much written or studied about the superintendency, and to this day, not much is known about how it functions and why some people do it well and others do not. Further, because of the tremendous pressure on public education in the twenty-first century, the superintendent's role is changing and moving toward an uncertain future.

The superintendency can be divided into three periods of history. The early period began shortly after the genesis of public education during the 1800s and extends to the early part of the twentieth century. The professional superintendent period covered the first half of the twentieth century and began to end in the 1960s. The modern superintendency is still in transition.

History

The position of superintendent emerged a decade or so after the creation of public schools. Initially there were no superintendents of schools. First, state boards ran schools, and then local lay boards, both without the benefit of professional help.

Public education is the responsibility of the state. The Tenth Amendment to the United States Constitution states that "the powers not delegated to the United States by the Constitution, nor prohibited by it to the states, are reserved to the states respectively, or to the people." Education was not mentioned in the Constitution, and when interest grew in providing education, the states assumed that accountability.

The state legislatures passed laws for public education and allocated small amounts of money to help local communities with their education needs. At the beginning of the nineteenth century, the lawmakers saw the need to have an accounting system for these funds and appointed volunteer committees to oversee the use of state funds. These committees eventually led to the formulation of state and local boards of education to carry out this function. In fact, Massachusetts, which is considered the home of public education because of the work of the educator Horace Mann, still calls its school boards "school committees."

As the number of communities that received funds increased, the time required of the local committees became burdensome. A paid state officer was designated to handle the accounting activities of state education funds as well as an increasing number of other responsibilities. This led to a full-time job and New York is credited with appointing the first state superintendent in 1812. Other states soon planned for similar positions.

With few exceptions, the state superintendents were positions of data collecting and distribution of state funds and had little influence on educational issues. State departments of education evolved with similar functions—establishing and enforcing minimum standards and equalizing educational opportunities through the distribution of state funds.

Many small local school systems formed as the population grew and communities expanded to the west. The state officer was not able to visit, inspect, and oversee all the activities of the new schools, and these responsibilities were gradually delegated to local communities, again usually through county volunteer committees.

History repeated itself: the task of overseeing the daily operations became burdensome and led to the creation of paid county positions to conduct this work. Prior to the Civil War, more than a dozen states adopted the county form of educational supervision and had created county superintendents.

The actual creation of local boards of education dates back to Thomas Jefferson, who in 1779 introduced a proposal in the Virginia Assembly that the citizens of each county would elect three aldermen who would have general charge of the schools. The aldermen were to create an overseer for every ten school districts in the county. The duties included appointing and supervising teachers and examining pupils.

The local superintendency developed simultaneously with the state and county superintendencies. It was established by local initiative, not by constitution or statute, as state and county superintendents were. Some local superintendents supervised a single school district and others oversaw multiple schools.

Buffalo, New York, and Louisville, Kentucky, are credited with establishing in 1837 the first local superintendents. While the idea did not spread quickly, by 1870 there were more than thirty large cities with a superintendent. Until the 1870s local boards without legal authority to do so hired the superintendents. It was felt that local boards had the authority to operate schools and by implication they had authority to hire an individual to administer them.

In 1865 the National Education Association created a Superintendent's Division to serve this growing profession. This later became the American Association of School Administrators, which serves superintendents in the twenty-first century.

Importance in Education

The superintendency—a position that was created by local boards without statutory authority or support—emerged in the twentieth century as a central and powerful position in education. As the number of local districts grew and as the complexity increased, more districts hired superintendents. The high water mark came in the 1960s when there were more than 35,000 superintendents nationally.

Their power also increased and peaked at about the same time. During the first half of the century the superintendent became the most powerful individual in the school district and one of the most visible members of the local community. They were considered civic leaders who held their positions for many years and who wielded enormous authority over the daily life of the school system.

Lay boards were content to turn over the reins of power to these professional educators. The superintendent had little external interference in conducting the work of the school district and boards became secondary in the operations of the school districts. The role of the board of education was, in large part, to support and approve the work of the superintendent.

School districts became big businesses within their local communities, hiring hundreds and in the case of urban districts, thousands of employees and spending millions of tax dollars. Superintendents made most of the major decisions affecting the districts, and were normally supported by the local lay boards who saw their role as supporting this work. Acrimony and disagreements were rare.

By the 1960s the world started to change. The teacher associations, which previously had been considered professional organizations, became more militant and drifted towards the union movement. The advent of the civil rights movement spilled over into the schools with accompanying pressure for local districts to reflect a more "grass roots" quality;

the white-collar board members were replaced by more activist parents and community members. The courts and the federal government became more involved. The passage of the Elementary and Secondary Education Act (ESEA) in 1965 marked a much greater interest on the part of the federal government in education and a series of court cases curtailed the schools' role *in loco parentis* (in place of the parent), authority that had previously been the standard. The civil rights movement and the antiwar movement generated greater student militancy, and schools were faced with dealing with expanded student rights and campus disruptions. This situation led to a dispersal of authority that had once been held by the superintendent, and much greater involvement and scrutiny by the public became the norm. School leaders were no longer trusted to conduct the affairs of the schools without significant external observation and criticism.

New Expectations

During the last quarter of the twentieth century, the country began to change its expectations for what the schools should deliver. For generations, the schools acted as a "sorting device" for society. The segmented society and economy demanded workers and managers, and schools divided their populations into the two groups. As the economy shifted from an industrial system to a more informational/high technology system, it required workers with higher skill sets. This challenge was compounded by federal legislation that placed the education of students with disabilities into the mainstream of schools. It was further exacerbated by the increased immigration of students from all over the world—many arrived without knowledge of English and, in many cases, without the benefit of formal education in their home country.

In 1983 the *Nation at Risk* report was issued by Secretary of Education Terrell Bell and released by President Reagan. The report indicated that the schools of America were caught in a "rising tide of mediocrity" and that serious reform was needed. Although the rising tide was really one of expectations that outstripped the schools' ability to deliver past their traditional role, the pressure on schools and subsequently school leaders became severe. This report was followed by a spate of others and by tremendous media attention that was given to the so-called crisis in schools.

This led to renewed political interest in schools. During the 1980s and 1990s states reasserted their role in education by setting state standards and assessment systems. Even the federal government, despite its lack of constitutional authority, became more aggressive to the point that candidates for president of the United States laid claim to the title "Education President."

This situation further undermined the authority of the superintendency, without alleviating the expectations for greater accountability from the role. At the beginning of the twenty-first century, the role was no longer seen as prestigious or one where power existed, leading to a shortage in the profession.

An Evolving Role

Although it is not clear what the role will become in the future, it seems certain that uncertainty will be the hallmark of the job. That will require a different set of expectations for those entering the profession. The new imperative that "all children be taught" will call for greater educational leadership from the superintendent. Further, the uncertain political climate that now surrounds schools will require the superintendent to be proficient in politics and the art of persuasion. Much of the work will revolve around the ability to create and maintain relationships. The modern superintendent will not be a superintendent of schools whose job is to oversee and manage—he or she will be a superintendent of learning who will have to navigate an uncertain terrain with skill and finesse.

See also: EDUCATIONAL ACCOUNTABILITY; SCHOOL BOARD RELATIONS, *subentry on* RELATION OF SCHOOL BOARD TO SUPERINTENDENT; SUPERINTENDENT OF LARGE-CITY SCHOOL SYSTEMS.

BIBLIOGRAPHY

AUGENSTEIN, JOHN J., and KONNERT, M. WILLIAM. 1990. *The Superintendency in the Nineties: What Superintendents and Board Members Need to Know.* Lancaster, PA: Technomic.

CARTER, GENE R., and CUNNINGHAM, WILLIAM G. 1997. *The American School Superintendent: Leading in an Age of Pressure.* San Francisco: Jossey-Bass.

HOUSTON, PAUL D. 2001. "Superintendents for the Twenty-First Century: It's Not Just a Job, It's a Calling." *Phi Delta Kappan* 82(6):428–433.

PAUL D. HOUSTON

SUPERVISION OF INSTRUCTION

Supervision, as a field of educational practice with clearly delineated roles and responsibilities, did not fall from the sky fully formed. Rather, supervision emerged slowly as a distinct practice, always in relation to the institutional, academic, cultural, and professional dynamics that have historically generated the complex agenda of schooling.

The History of Supervision

In colonial New England, supervision of instruction began as a process of external inspection: one or more local citizens were appointed to inspect both what the teachers were teaching and what the students were learning. The inspection theme was to remain firmly embedded in the practice of supervision.

The history of supervision as a formal activity exercised by educational administrators within a system of schools did not begin until the formation of the common school in the late 1830s. During the first half of the nineteenth century, population growth in the major cities of the United States necessitated the formation of city school systems. While superintendents initially inspected schools to see that teachers were following the prescribed curriculum and that students were able to recite their lessons, the multiplication of schools soon made this an impossible task for superintendents and the job was delegated to the school principal. In the early decades of the twentieth century, the movement toward scientific management in both industrial and public administration had an influence on schools. At much the same time, child-centered and experienced-based curriculum theories of European educators such as Friedrich Froebel, Johann Pestalozzi, and Johann Herbart, as well as the prominent American philosopher John Dewey, were also affecting the schools. Thus, school supervisors often found themselves caught between the demand to evaluate teachers scientifically and the simultaneous need to transform teaching from a mechanistic repetition of teaching protocols to a diverse repertory of instruc-

tional responses to students' natural curiosity and diverse levels of readiness. This tension between supervision as a uniform, scientific approach to teaching and supervision as a flexible, dialogic process between teacher and supervisor involving the shared, professional discretion of both was to continue throughout the century.

In the second half of the century the field of supervision became closely identified with various forms of clinical supervision. Initially developed by Harvard professors Morris Cogan and Robert Anderson and their graduate students, many of whom subsequently became professors of supervision in other universities, clinical supervision blended elements of "objective" and "scientific" classroom observation with aspects of collegial coaching, rational planning, and a flexible, inquiry-based concern with student learning. In 1969 Robert Goldhammer proposed the following five-stage process in clinical supervision: (1) a pre-observation conference between supervisor and teacher concerning elements of the lesson to be observed; (2) classroom observation; (3) a supervisor's analysis of notes from the observation, and planning for the post-observation conference; (4) a post-observation conference between supervisor and teacher; and (5) a supervisor's analysis of the post-observation conference. For many practitioners, these stages were reduced to three: the pre-observation conference, the observation, and the post-observation conference. Cogan insisted on a collegial relationship focused on the teacher's interest in improving student learning, and on a nonjudgmental observation and inquiry process.

The initial practice of clinical supervision, however, soon had to accommodate perspectives coming out of the post-*Sputnik* curriculum reforms of the 1960s that focused on the structures of the academic disciplines. Shortly thereafter, perspectives generated by research on *effective schools* and *effective classrooms* that purported to have discovered the basic steps to effective teaching colonized the clinical supervision process. It was during this period that noted educator Madeline Hunter adapted research findings from the psychology of learning and introduced what was also to become a very popular, quasi-scientific approach to effective teaching in the 1970s and 1980s. These various understandings of curriculum and teaching were frequently superimposed on the three- to five-stage process of clinical supervision and became normative for supervisors' work with teachers. Nevertheless, in many academic circles the original dialogic and reflective process of Cogan and Goldhammer continued as the preferred process of supervision. This original process of supervision has been subsequently embraced by advocates of peer supervision and collegial-teacher leadership through action research in classrooms. Despite the obvious appeal of clinical supervision in its various forms, it is time-consuming and labor-intensive, rendering it impossible to use on any regular basis given the large number of teachers that supervisors are expected to supervise (in addition to their other administrative responsibilities).

Recognizing the time restraints of practicing supervisors, and wanting to honor the need to promote the growth of teachers, Thomas Sergiovanni and Robert Starratt suggested, in 1998, the creation of a supervisory system with multiple processes of supervision, including summative evaluation. Such a system would not require the direct involvement of a formal supervisor for every teacher every year. The supervisory system might cycle teachers with professional status through a three- to five-year period, during which they would receive a formal evaluation once and a variety of other evaluative processes during the other years (e.g., self-evaluation, peer supervision, curriculum development, action research on new teaching strategies, involvement in a school renewal project). The once-a-cycle formal evaluation would require evidence of professional growth. Sergiovanni and Starratt also attempted to open the work of supervision to intentional involvement with the schoolwide renewal agenda, thus placing all stimuli toward professional growth—including the supervisory system—within that larger context.

Roles and Responsibilities of Supervisors

Since supervision is an activity that is part of so many different roles, a few distinctions are in order. First, there are university-based supervisors of undergraduate students in teacher education programs who supervise the activities of novice teachers. Next, a principal or assistant principal may be said to conduct general supervision—as distinct from the more specific, subject-matter supervision conducted by a high school department chair. Other professional personnel involved in supervisory roles include cluster coordinators, lead teachers, mentors, peer coaches and peer supervisors, curriculum specialists, project directors, trainers, program evaluators, and district office administrators. Unfortunately, these professionals, more often than not, carry on their supervisory work without having any professional preparation for it, finding by trial and error what seems to work for them.

Principals not only supervise teachers, but also monitor the work of counselors, librarians, health personnel, secretaries, custodians, bus drivers, and other staff who work in or around the school. This work requires as much diplomacy, sensitivity, and humanity as the supervision of teachers, although it tends to be neglected entirely in the literature. In their everyday contact with students, all of these support personnel may teach multiple, important lessons about the integrity of various kinds of work, about civility and etiquette, and about basic social behavior.

Principals and assistant principals also supervise the work and the behavior of students in the school. As the relationships between students become more governed by legal restrictions—including definitions of racial, ethnic, and sexual harassment, of due process, of privacy and free speech rights—and as the incidents of physical violence, bullying, carrying of weapons to school, and the extreme cases of students killing other students increase, this aspect of supervision becomes increasingly complex. Many system and local school administrators have developed a comprehensive system of low visibility, and restrained, security-oriented supervision that anticipates various responses to inappropriate behavior. Unfortunately, many have not attended to the corresponding need to build a nurturing system of pastoral supervision that sets guidelines for the adults in the school in order for them to build sensitive relationships of trust, care, support, and compassion with the students. This more pastoral approach to student supervision will lessen, though not eliminate, the need for other security-conscious types of supervision.

Supervisors usually wear two or three other hats, but their specific responsibilities tend to include some or all of the following arranged in ascending order of scope or reach:

1. Mentoring or providing for mentoring of beginning teachers to facilitate a supportive induction into the profession.

2. Bringing individual teachers up to minimum standards of effective teaching (quality assurance and maintenance functions of supervision).

3. Improving individual teachers' competencies,

no matter how proficient they are deemed to be.

4. Working with groups of teachers in a collaborative effort to improve student learning.

5. Working with groups of teachers to adapt the local curriculum to the needs and abilities of diverse groups of students, while at the same time bringing the local curriculum in line with state and national standards.

6. Relating teachers' efforts to improve their teaching to the larger goals of schoolwide improvement in the service of quality learning for all children.

With the involvement of state departments of education in monitoring school improvement efforts, supervisory responsibilities have increasingly encompassed the tasks at the higher end of this list. In turn, these responsibilities involve supervisors in much more complex, collaborative, and developmental efforts with teachers, rather than with the more strictly inspectorial responsibilities of an earlier time.

Trends, Issues, and Controversies

A variety of trends can be seen in the field of supervision, all of which mutually influence one another (both positively and negatively) in a dynamic school environment. One trend indicates that teachers will be "supervised" by test results. With teachers being held accountable for increasing their students' scores, the results of these tests are being scrutinized by district and in-house administrators and judgments being made about the competency of individual teachers—and, in the case of consistently low-performing schools, about all the teachers in the school. In some districts, these judgments have led to serious efforts at professional development. Unfortunately, in many districts test results have led to an almost vitriolic public blaming of teachers.

Another trend has been toward a significant involvement of teachers in peer supervision and program development. In the literature, these developments are often included in the larger theme of teacher leadership. Along with this trend comes an increasing differentiation in the available options by which teacher supervision may be conducted, thus leaving the more formal assessment for experienced teachers to once every four or five years. Whatever form supervision takes, it has been sub-

stantially influenced by the focus on student learning (and on the test performances that demonstrate this learning), and by the need to make sure that attention is given to the learning of all students. Thus, the supervisory episode tends to focus more on an analysis of teaching activity only in relation to, rather than independent of, evidence of student learning.

This focus on student learning in supervision is further influenced by the trend to highlight the learning of previously underserved students, namely those with special needs and consistently low-performing students. Supervisors and teachers are expected to take responsibility for high quality learning for all students, a responsibility that necessarily changes how they approach their work together. Finally, all of these trends are combined in the large trend of focusing on schoolwide renewal. This means attending not only to instructional and curriculum issues, but also to structural and cultural issues that impede student learning.

There are a variety of issues in the field of supervision that need resolution—or at least significant attention. To confront the large agenda of school renewal (in which schools are required to respond to state-imposed curriculum standards or guidelines), systems of supervision at the state level, the district level, and the school level need to coordinate goals and priorities. The politics of school renewal tend to lend a punitive, judgmental edge to supervision at the state level, and to some degree at the district level, and that impression poisons supervision at the school level. Test-driven accountability policies, and the one-dimensional rhetoric with which they are expressed, need to take into account the extraordinarily complex realities of classrooms and neighborhood communities, as well as the traditionally underresourced support systems that are needed to develop the in-school capacity to carry out the renewal agenda. If state and district policies call for quality learning for all students, then schools have to provide adequate opportunities for all students to learn the curriculum on which they will be tested. Supervisors are caught in a crossfire. On the one hand, parents and teachers complain that a variety of enriched learning opportunities for children who have not had an opportunity to learn the curriculum are not available; on the other, district and state administrators complain about poor achievement scores on high-stakes tests, while ignoring the resources needed to bring the schools into compliance with reform policies.

Another issue needing attention is the divide between those supervisors who accept a functionalist, decontextualized, and oversimplified realist view of knowledge as something to be delivered, and those who approach knowledge as something to be actively constructed and performed by learners in realistic contexts—and as something whose integrity implies a moral as well as a cognitive appropriation. Assumptions about the nature of knowledge and its appropriation, often unspoken, substantially affect how supervisors and teachers approach student learning and teaching protocols. This is an issue about which all players in the drama of schooling will only gradually reach some kind of consensus. A related issue concerns the degree to which schools and classrooms will accommodate cultural, class, gender, racial, and intellectual diversity. Supervisors cannot ignore the implications of these necessary accommodations for the work of teaching and curriculum development.

Perhaps the biggest controversy in the field is whether supervision as a field of professional and academic inquiry and of relatively unified normative principles will continue to exist as a discernable field. More than a few scholars and practitioners have suggested that supervisory roles and responsibilities should be subsumed under various other administrative and professional roles. For example, principals, acting as "instructional leaders," could simply include a concern for quality learning and teaching under the rubric of instructional leadership and eliminate the use of the word *supervision* from their vocabulary. Similarly, teacher leaders could engage in collegial inquiry or action research focused on improving student learning and teaching strategies, and similarly eliminate the use of the word *supervision* from their vocabulary—terms like *mentoring, coaching, professional development,* and *curriculum development* could instead be used.

Many professors whose academic specialization has been devoted to research and publication in the field of supervision oppose this relinquishing of the concept of supervision, not only because of the vitality of its history, but also because of the fact that the legal and bureaucratic requirements for supervision will surely remain in place. Having a discernible, professional field of supervision, they contend, will prevent the bureaucratic and legal practice of supervision from becoming a formalistic, evaluative ritual. Keeping the professional growth and development aspect of supervision in dynamic tension with the evaluative side of supervision can best be served, they maintain, by retaining a discernible and robust field of scholarship that attends to this balance.

These trends, issues, and controversies will likely keep the field of supervision in a state of dynamic development. However, a lack of attention to the implications of these issues will most certainly cause the field to atrophy and drift to the irrelevant fringes of the schooling enterprise.

See also: MENTORING; PRINCIPAL, SCHOOL; SCHOOL REFORM; TEACHER EVALUATION, *subentries on* METHODS, OVERVIEW.

BIBLIOGRAPHY

ALPHONSO, ROBERT J. 1997. "Should Supervision Be Abolished? No." In *Educational Supervision: Perspectives, Issues, and Controversies,* ed. Jeffrey Glanz and Robert F. Neville. Norwood, MA: Christopher Gordon Publishers.

ANDERSON, ROBERT H. and SNYDER, KAROLYN J. 1993. *Clinical Supervision: Coaching for Enhanced Performance.* Lancaster, PA: Technomic Publications.

BLUMBURG, ARTHUR. 1980. *Supervisors and Teachers: A Private Cold War,* 2nd edition. Berkeley: McCutcheon.

COGAN, MORRIS L. 1973. *Clinical Supervision.* Boston: Houghton-Mifflin.

FIRTH, GERALD R., and PAJAK, EDWARD F., eds. 1998. *Handbook of Research on School Supervision.* New York: Macmillan.

GARMAN, NOREEN. 1986. "Reflection, the Heart of Clinical Supervision: A Modern Rational for Practice." *Journal of Curriculum and Supervision* 2(1):1–24.

GARMAN, NOREEN; GLICKMAN, CARL; HUNTER, MADELINE; and HAGGERSON, NELSON. 1987. "Conflicting Conceptions of Clinical Supervision and the Enhancement of Professional Growth and Renewal: Point and Counterpoint." *Journal of Curriculum and Supervision* 2(2):152–177.

GLANZ, JEFFREY, and NEVILLE, RICHARD F., eds. 1997. *Educational Supervision: Perspectives, Issues, and Controversies.* Norwood, MA: Christopher Gordon Publishers.

GLICKMAN, CARL D. 1985. *Supervision of Instruction: A Developmental Perspective.* Boston: Allyn and Bacon.

GOLDHAMMER, ROBERT. 1969. *Clinical Supervision.* New York: Holt, Rinehart and Winston.

HARRIS, BEN M. 1986. *Developmental Teacher Evaluation.* Boston: Allyn and Bacon.

PAJAK, EDWARD F. 1993. *Approaches to Clinical Supervision.* Norwood, MA: Christopher Gordon Publishers.

SERGIOVANNI, THOMAS J. 1982. "Toward a Theory of Supervisory Practice: Integrating the Scientific, Clinical, and Artistic Views." In *Supervision of Teaching,* ed. Thomas J. Sergiovanni. Alexandria, VA: Association of Supervision and Curriculum Development.

SERGIOVANNI, THOMAS, J. and STARRATT, ROBERT J. 1998. *Supervision: A Redefinition,* 6th edition. New York: McGraw-Hill.

SMYTHE, JOHN. 1988. "A Critical Perspective for Clinical Supervision." *Journal of Curriculum and Supervision* 3(2):136–156.

STARRATT, ROBERT J. 1997. "Should Supervision Be Abolished? Yes." J. In *Educational Supervision: Perspectives, Issues, and Controversies,* ed. Jeffrey Glanz and Richard F. Neville. Norwood, MA: Christopher Gordon Publishers.

TRACY, SANDRA J. 1993. "Restructuring Instructional Supervision." *Contemporary Education* 64:128–131.

WAITE, DUNCAN. 1995. *Rethinking Instructional Supervision: Notes on Its Language and Culture.* London: Falmer Press.

ROBERT J. STARRATT

SUPREME COURT OF THE UNITED STATES AND EDUCATION, THE

Prior to the twentieth century, the United States Supreme Court issued few important decisions concerning education, and virtually none dealing with schooling at the elementary and secondary levels. Schooling has always been considered primarily a state and local government function in America, and it was not until well into the twentieth century that the Court seriously imposed on the states provisions of the U.S. Constitution that have turned out to be importantly relevant to education.

By contrast, in the second half of the twentieth century, the Court became a major force in shaping American education, interacting with most of the key educational policy issues confronting society during that era. Many of these issues have been extraordinarily controversial, both as education questions and as legal questions.

Especially from the mid-1950s through the mid-1970s, the Court largely allied itself with the views of "liberals" and thwarted state and local educational policies that were seen to run counter to "liberal" values. Starting in the late 1970s and continuing into the early twenty-first century, however, the Court has become more cautious about imposing Constitutional restraints on the educational process. The decisive, if changing, role of the Court in American education is illustrated by decisions in three major areas: religion, race, and the individual rights of students.

Religion

Following World War I, nativist movements around the nation prompted some state legislatures to try to restrict, or even close, private schools. But in a series of decisions in the 1920s—most importantly *Meyer v. Nebraska* and *Pierce v. Society of Sisters*—the Court declared that parents have a federal Constitutional right to educate their children in private schools, subject to reasonable regulation of those schools by the state. This legal principle, based in the due process clause of the Fourteenth Amendment to the U.S. Constitution, has helped preserve the Catholic school system that grew up in the nineteenth century in response to Protestant domination of public schools and the insistence at the time on Protestant-based prayer and Bible reading in public schools. In 1972, in an even greater deference to religiously based parental claims, the Court decided in *Wisconsin v. Yoder* that Amish parents, given their long history of responsible other-worldliness, had a due process right to withhold their children from school once they reach age sixteen.

Starting in the 1960s, however, the Court's attention turned to cleansing the public schools of religion. For example, in *Engel v. Vitale* and *School District v. Schempp,* it prohibited government-sponsored school prayer and Bible reading, and in *Epperson v. Arkansas* it voided a ban on the teaching of evolution in public schools as violations of the First Amendment's prohibition against the "establishment" of religion.

At the same time the Court was insisting that the public schools must be secular, it also became leery of direct public financial assistance of private elementary and secondary schools, which were, in the 1960s and 1970s, overwhelmingly Catholic. To be sure, in three earlier cases the Court upheld the public provision of bus rides in *Everson v. Board of Education* and regular textbooks in *Board of Education v. Allen* to children attending nonpublic schools and the exemption of religious schools from the property tax in *Walz v. Tax Commission.* Nevertheless, in the early 1970s the Court announced a series of decisions—most importantly *Lemon v. Kurtzman* and *Committee for Public Education v. Nyquist*—that invalidated financial aid to nonpublic schools and their users. These decisions were based primarily on the theory that the "primary effect" of this funding was the support of religion. Overall, then, by the mid-1970s the Court seemed committed to an interpretation of the First Amendment's "establishment" clause that called for a "high wall of separation" between church and state.

In the last quarter of the twentieth century, the Court held fast to its opposition to prayer in the public schools. In *Wallace v. Jaffree* it extended the ban in 1985 to cover a religiously motivated, required "moment of silence," with the *Lee v. Weisman* decision in 1992 to include invocations and benedictions at public school graduation ceremonies, and in 2000 to student-led prayers at high school football games in the *Santa Fe Independent School District v. Doe* decision. In the same vein, in *Edwards v. Aguillard* in 1987 it struck down as violating the "establishment clause" a law seeking to pair the teaching of evolution with creation science, and in 1994 it invalidated a public school district specially constructed for a group of Hasidic Jews in *Board of Education of Kiryas Joel v. Grumet.*

Yet the Court has also become much more deferential to policies designed to accommodate religious freedom inside schools. Concern for the rights of students to their First Amendment guaranteed "free exercise" of religion has led to the development of "equal access" policies: some adopted by educational institutions; others enacted by legislatures. The Court has upheld these arrangements, allowing student religious groups to use school facilities once that privilege has been accorded to other student groups, in 1981 in *Widmar v. Vincent* at the university level and in *Board of Education of Westside Community Schools v. Mergens* in 1990 at the secondary-school level. Moreover, in 1995, on "free speech" grounds, the Court held in *Rosen-*

berger v. University of Virginia that when college student fees were used to fund various student newspapers, religious student groups had to be included as beneficiaries.

Moreover, on the issue of the aid to private schools, starting in the 1980s the Court began to permit many more types of financial assistance. These have ranged from tax deductions for financial contributions made to private schools in *Mueller v. Allen*; to the provision of a sign language interpreter for a deaf student in a private school in *Zobrest v. Catalina Foothills School District*; reading specialists and similar assistance for low-income private school pupils in *Agostini v. Felton*; and computers and other educational materials to private schools in *Mitchell v. Helms.* At the level of higher education, the Court even upheld a program under which a state would pay for a student's education to become a clergyman in *Witters v. Washington Department of Services for the Blind.*

In sum, the Court has clearly backed away from a rigid adherence to the "high wall of separation" vision of the First Amendment. Yet, the legal doctrine in this area has become so convoluted that in 2001 legal scholars were quite uncertain about whether it is constitutional for states and school districts to adopt, as three had, school choice plans that permit families to pay for tuition at private schools (including religious schools) with publicly funded vouchers.

Race

Starting in 1954 the Court centrally immersed itself in issues of race and American education by taking the lead in dismantling the system of official and intentional segregation that marked American public schools not only in the South, but also in many school districts throughout the nation. Before its famous 1954 decision in *Brown v. Board of Education,* the Court tolerated a scheme of "separate but equal" as in *Plessy v. Ferguson* (1896). During the twenty years leading up to *Brown,* the Court issued several decisions—*Missouri ex rel Gaines v. Canada* and *Sweat v. Painter*—invalidating evasive schemes that pretended to treat whites and blacks equally, but clearly did not. But in *Brown I,* the Court relied upon the "equal protection" clause of the Fourteenth Amendment to declare "separate" inherently "unequal" and a year later, in *Brown II,* it ordered public school desegregation "with all deliberate speed."

Although the Court then became embroiled in "massive resistance" strategies throughout much of the South, it held its ground. For example, in 1964 the *Griffin v. County School Board* decision prevented districts from closing their schools to avoid desegregation. In 1968 it rejected in *Green v. County School Board* purported "choice" plans that left schools identifiably black and white. In 1971 the *Swann v. Charlotte-Mecklenburg Board of Education* decision refused to approve a neighborhood school assignment policy that maintained the prior system of black and white schools. *Norwood v. Harrison* blocked in 1973 desegregation-evading schemes that sought to fund an alternative system of private "white academies," and the *Runyon v. McCrary* decision in 1976 precluded private schools from excluding applicants because they were black.

In 1973 in *Keyes v. School District No. 1,* the Court also extended the reach of *Brown* to northern and western school districts when it could be shown that officials had deliberately drawn school lines, erected new schools, and made other decisions on the basis of race. And with the help of Congressional enactment of the 1964 Civil Rights Act, the intervention of federal government officials from the executive branch, and the tireless work of many federal district judges often working in a hostile local environment, what has became known as formal "de jure" school segregation was rooted out.

Yet over time it became clear that continued racial isolation in public schools and the accompanying continued lower academic achievement of non-white pupils is not so easily blamed on the official racism of identified state and local school officials. The combination of (1) individual residential decisions by white (and non-white) families; (2) the suburbanization of America and the traditional existence outside of the South of many small school districts surrounding the large central city district; (3) national and local housing policies; (4) persistent differences in family poverty between whites and non-whites; and other factors demonstrate that de facto school segregation, especially in urban cities, is not primarily caused by, and can not easily be eliminated by, the deliberate actions of local public school officials.

Although some legal and policy scholars and political leaders called for the end of racial isolation whatever its cause, others began to challenge the fairness, desirability, or feasibility of doing so. By 1974 a closely divided Supreme Court gave an early signal that it was going to start withdrawing the judiciary from this battle. It refused to bring the Detroit suburbs into a proposed metropolitan remedy of a school segregation case in which the federal district judge was presented with a Detroit public school district that had already become overwhelmingly populated by black children in *Milliken v. Bradley*. Starting in the 1990s, it has been telling lower federal courts to relinquish their supervision of school districts, thereby freeing local officials from the affirmative obligation to keep their schools from becoming racially identifiable, for instance *Board of Education of Oklahoma City Public Schools v. Dowell* and *Freeman v. Pitts*. And it voided a remedy adopted by a federal district judge in a Kansas City case that had imposed substantial obligations upon the state and was seen impermissibly to involve the surrounding suburbs in *Missouri v. Jenkins*.

Nonetheless, something of a political turnaround took place in many venues across the nation. Concluding that merely ending obvious official discrimination against minorities was insufficient, many public and private entities (prodded by federal agencies) began to engage in affirmative action. Some saw this as a way to remedy institutional or invisible racism that continued; others viewed it as desirable social policy even in a setting that was no longer officially hostile to racial minorities. Selective colleges and universities began to give preferences to non-white applicants; some employers, including school district employers, did the same; some school districts that had previously fought tenaciously for segregation turned completely about and were now committed to racially balanced schools.

But this practice has generated its own backlash, into which the Court has been drawn. Although a badly divided Court declared in 1978 that race was one of the many factors that colleges could legally employ in order to decide who to admit as students in *Regents of the University of California v. Bakke*, by the mid-1990s the Court had became much more hostile to affirmative action efforts outside of education. If the official action was not racially neutral and was not part of a remedy designed to undo past specific acts of illegal segregation, then the Court decided, in *Adarand Constructors, Inc. v. Pena*, that deliberate race-based actions said to benefit minorities were just as illegal as those adopted to harm them.

As a result, legal scholars in 2001 were uncertain whether affirmative action engaged in by selective high schools and selective colleges was still permissible. Indeed, it was unclear whether racially prompted school busing and other school assignment decisions at the elementary and secondary school levels could be kept in place once a formerly discriminating school district had been declared "unitary" by having eliminated the past vestiges of official segregation.

Individual Rights of Students

The Court's dealing with free speech and other constitutional rights of individual public school children has undergone something of a zig-zag as well. During World War II, the Court relied upon the First Amendment's "free speech" clause to uphold the refusal of religiously motivated Jehovah's Witnesses to participate in the flag salute at school in *West Virginia Board of Education v. Barnette.* Student free speech rights were much further strengthened during the Vietnam War, when the Court protected affirmative student rights of expression at school in the form of non-disruptive wearing of antiwar arm bands in *Tinker v. Des Moines School District.* In that same period, the Court extended to students the right to a hearing before serious disciplinary penalties are imposed on them, thereby bringing the Fourteenth Amendment's "procedural due process" clause into the schoolhouse in *Goss v. Lopez.* Later, in *Board of Education Island Trees Union Free School District No. 26 v. Pico,* the Court, on free speech grounds, thwarted religiously inspired efforts to rid school libraries of books that offended some parent groups.

But in subsequent cases, starting in the late 1970s, the Court has drawn back from this pro-student rights' agenda. It allowed public officials to discipline a student who gave a "lewd" speech at an assembly in *Bethel School District No. 403 v. Frazer;* to delete pages from a high school student newspaper in *Hazelwood School District v. Kuhlmeier;* to impose corporal punishment on public school children in *Ingraham v. Wright;* and to search student posses-

sions (e.g., purses) under circumstances that would be illegal if done to adults in normal circumstances in *New Jersey v. T.L.O.* The Court also declined to get involved with academic dismissals at the college level in its decision *Board of Curators of the University of Missouri v. Horowitz.*

Hence, while it remains true that students do not "shed their constitutional rights to freedom of speech or expression at the schoolhouse gate," it is also now quite clear that school children have many fewer rights than adults have.

Although the Court has involved itself in many additional important issues as well (e.g., teachers' rights, gender discrimination, bilingual education, and the rights of disabled children), the three areas discussed illustrate not only the Court's great importance to American education, but also the Court's own shifting view of its role.

See also: AFFIRMATIVE ACTION COMPLIANCE IN HIGHER EDUCATION; SEGREGATION, LEGAL ASPECTS.

BIBLIOGRAPHY

ALEXANDER, KERN, and ALEXANDER, DAVID. 2000. *American Public School Law,* 5th edition. Belmont, CA: West/Thomson Learning.

GOLDSTEIN, STEPHEN R.; DANIEL, PHILIP T.; and GEE, E. GORDON. 1995. *Law and Public Education: Cases and Materials,* 3rd edition. Charlottesville, VA: Michie.

MCCARTHY, MARTHA M.; CAMBRON-MCCABE, NELDA H.; and THOMAS, STEPHEN B. 1997. *Public School Law: Teachers' and Students' Rights,* 4th edition. Boston: Allyn and Bacon.

REUTTER, E. EDMUND. 1998. *The Law of Public Education,* 4th edition. Westbury, NY: Foundation.

YUDORF, MARK G.; KIRP, DAVID L.; LEVIN, BETSY; and MORAN, RACHEL F. 2001. *Educational Policy and the Law.* Belmont, CA: West/Thomson Learning.

STEPHEN D. SUGARMAN

T

TABA, HILDA (1902–1967)

Curriculum theorist, curriculum reformer, and teacher educator, Hilda Taba contributed to the theoretical and pedagogical foundations of concept development and critical thinking in social studies curriculum and helped to lay the foundations of education for diverse student populations.

Taba was born in a small village in southeastern Estonia at a time when the country was in transition politically. Taba was introduced to Progressive education ideas at Tartu University by her philosophy professor in the period following the Russian Revolution, when John Dewey's ideas about democracy and education were celebrated in Russia and eastern Europe. She pursued her interests in Progressive education and the relationship between democracy and curricula at Bryn Mawr College (M.A. 1927) and Teachers College, Columbia University (Ph.D. 1932), where she studied the work of Progressive education pioneers William Kilpatrick, John Dewey, and Boyd H. Bode, to whom she dedicated her dissertation, *The Dynamics of Education*.

Taba's dissertation established a foundation for much of her subsequent work. Three key ideas in the work are particularly important for curriculum history in the twentieth century. First, she argued that learning and the study of learning should be modeled after dynamic models derived from contemporary physics. Rather than relying on observation, prediction, and measurement of static phenomena, educators should see learning as a dynamic interactive phenomena that is informed by the developing field of cognitive psychology. Thus she established a paradigm that was appreciably different from a simple transmission model of education and evaluation.

Second, she argued that education for democracy was a critical component of contemporary schooling and curricula, and that it needed to be experiential, where children learn to solve problems and resolve conflicts together. Her thinking in democratic education foreshadowed constructivist curricula. Third, she argued that educators had to provide conceptually sound curriculum that was organized and taught effectively, and that student understanding had to be evaluated using appropriate tools and processes. This last goal led to her groundbreaking work in evaluating social attitudes in Progressive education curricula.

Over the next four decades, Taba's work as a curriculum theorist developed. The combination of her considerable intellect, her appreciation for democracy, which grew as intellectual freedom in Estonia diminished in the middle years of the twentieth century, her belief in the power of individuals and groups in educational contexts to realize significant social goals, and her expressed commitment to demonstrate empirically the effects of social education established her leadership in curriculum generally and in three major twentieth century projects specifically.

Evaluation

The Eight-Year Study, also known as the Commission on the Relation of School and College, was an ambitious research project that was to evaluate how students from Progressive secondary schools would fare in colleges. Ralph Tyler was responsible for overall evaluation in the Eight-Year Study and he invited Hilda Taba to join him following a meeting at the Dalton School in New York. The significance of the study was that it included curriculum goals that were important to Progressive educators but were not easily measured on standardized tests, such as social responsibility and cooperative behavior.

Taba's contribution to the study was evaluation of social sensitivity, which was related to the general goal of preparing students for effective democratic participation. Using multiple means of evaluation that included group activities, informal conversations, anecdotal records, reading records, and book reviews, Taba delved under the surfaces of social phenomena to identify the attitudes and problems in students' social life that would contribute to a particular phenomena. She tackled a challenging area of social studies curriculum, the measurement of attitudes about race, class, and ethnicity and at the same time provided authentic alternatives to paper and pencil assessment.

Taba's work on evaluation, conducted at the Ohio State University, led to a productive collaboration with Ralph Tyler and the design of a general framework and theoretical rationale for developing curriculum. It also led to a position as director of the Curriculum Laboratory at the University of Chicago in 1938 and her subsequent leadership in intergroup education in the 1940s.

Intergroup Education

In response to racism, anti-Semitism, and perceived threats to national unity, a collaboration was created in 1934 between the National Conference of Christians and Jews and the American Council on Education. This collaboration, focused on the reduction of prejudice and conflict through education, was known as the Intergroup Education in Cooperating Schools Project. Taba developed an association with the project in 1944 when she headed a summer work shop at Harvard that resulted in a yearbook for the National Council for Social Studies titled *Democratic Human Relations*. She assumed the directorship of the project beginning in 1945, and then served as director of the Center for Intergroup Education at the University of Chicago until 1951.

Taba brought a staff of eight educators together, who fanned out across eighteen sites and seventy-two schools over a period of two years to work with local site faculty on issues of prejudice and discrimination. The Intergroup education project tackled the issues of newcomers, economic instability, housing patterns, and community relations, using typically Taba-type interactive curriculum and processes such

as literature groups, conflict resolution, and role playing. The project constitutes a landmark in social education and foreshadowed multicultural education projects of the 1970s and 1980s.

The Taba Curriculum Framework

In 1951 Taba left the Intergroup Education Center to take a position at San Francisco State College, where her third curriculum reform project developed. Working collaboratively with teachers and administrators in Contra Costa County, California, a San Francisco Bay area community, Taba formulated, researched, and wrote about the foundations of curriculum development. Taba and her colleagues from the college and the county schools explicated and documented the complex processes associated with concept formation by children using social studies curriculum. She and her staff organized and implemented staff development for teachers, and documented the processes for research purposes.

Taba's close associate, Mary Durkin, a teacher and curriculum specialist from the Contra Costa County schools, anchored the critical bridge between Taba's theoretical work and her practice of teaching classroom teachers about concept attainment and writing curriculum.

The Taba Spiral of Curriculum Development is a graphic organizer, which was designed to illustrate concept development in elementary social studies curriculum that was used by teachers in Taba workshops in the 1960s. That graphic tool has sustained its utility and is found in curriculum texts in the early twenty-first century. Taba's theorizing and curriculum development processes provided a blueprint for curriculum development in the twentieth century. She comprehended and articulated the complex connections between culture, politics, and social change; cognition and learning; and experience and evaluation in curriculum development—and the significance of all three for teacher preparation and civic education. Her in-service work with teachers in the San Francisco Bay area and in communities around the United States and in Europe left a permanent imprint on curriculum development discourse.

See also: Eight-Year Study; Multicultural Education; Progressive Education; Social Studies Education, *subentries on* Overview, Preparation of Teachers; Tyler, Ralph.

BIBLIOGRAPHY

BERNARD-POWERS, JANE. 1999. "Composing Her Life: Hilda Taba and Social Studies History." In *"Bending the Future to Their Will": Civic Women, Social Education and Democracy,* ed. Margaret Smith Crocco and Orzo Luki Davis Jr. Boulder, CO: Rowman and Littlefield.

TABA, HILDA. 1932. *The Dynamics of Education.* New York: Harcourt, Brace.

TABA, HILDA. 1936. "Social Sensitivity." In *Evaluation in the Eight Year Study.* Columbus, OH: Progressive Education Association.

TABA, HILDA. 1962. *Curriculum: Theory and Practice.* New York: Harcourt, Brace.

TABA, HILDA; DURKIN, MARY; FRAENKEL, JACK; and MCNAUGHTON, ANTHONY A. 1971. *Teachers' Handbook to Elementary Social Studies: An Inductive Approach,* 2nd edition. Reading, MA: Addison-Wesley.

TABA, HILDA, and VAN TEL, WILLIAM, eds. 1945. *Democratic Human Relations: Promising Practices in Intergroup and Intercultural Education in the Social Studies.* Sixteenth Yearbook of the National Council of Social Studies. Washington, DC: National Council of Social Studies.

JANE BERNARD-POWERS

TAXONOMIES OF EDUCATIONAL OBJECTIVES

Educational objectives describe the goals toward which the education process is directed—the learning that is to result from instruction. When drawn up by an education authority or professional organization, objectives are usually called *standards.* Taxonomies are classification systems based on an organizational scheme. In this instance, a set of carefully defined terms, organized from simple to complex and from concrete to abstract, provide a framework of categories into which one may classify educational goals. Such schemes can:

- Provide a common language about educational goals that can bridge subject matter and grade levels

- Serve as a touchstone for specifying the meaning of broad educational goals for the classroom

- Help to determine the congruence of goals, classroom activities and assessments

- Provide a panorama of the range of possible educational goals against which the limited breadth and depth of any particular educational curriculum may be contrasted

The First Taxonomy of Educational Objectives: Cognitive Domain

The idea of creating a taxonomy of educational objectives was conceived by Benjamin Bloom in the 1950s, the assistant director of the University of Chicago's Board of Examinations. Bloom sought to reduce the extensive labor of test development by exchanging test items among universities. He believed this could be facilitated by developing a carefully defined framework into which items measuring the same objective could be classified. Examiners and testing specialists from across the country were assembled into a working group that met periodically over a number of years. The result was a framework with six major categories and many subcategories for the most common objectives of classroom instruction—those dealing with the cognitive domain. To facilitate test development, the framework provided extensive examples of test items (largely multiple choice) for each major category. Here is an overview of the categories that make up the framework:

1.0. **Knowledge**

  1.1. Knowledge of specifics

    1.1.1. Knowledge of terminology

    1.1.2. Knowledge of specific facts

  1.2. Knowledge of ways and means of dealing with specifics

    1.2.1. Knowledge of conventions

    1.2.2. Knowledge of trends and sequences

    1.2.3. Knowledge of classifications and categories

    1.2.4. Knowledge of criteria

    1.2.5. Knowledge of methodology

  1.3. Knowledge of universals and abstractions in a field

    1.3.1. Knowledge of principles and generalizations

    1.3.2. Knowledge of theories and structures

2.0. **Comprehension**

  2.1. Translation

  2.2. Interpretation

  2.3. Extrapolation

3.0. **Application**

4.0. **Analysis**

   4.1. Analysis of elements

   4.2. Analysis of relationships

   4.3. Analysis of organizational principles

5.0. **Synthesis**

   5.1. Production of a unique communication

   5.2. Production of a plan, or proposed set of operations

   5.3. Derivation of a set of abstract relations

6.0. **Evaluation**

   6.1. Evaluation in terms of internal evidence

   6.2. Judgments in terms of external criteria

The categories were designed to range from simple to complex and from concrete to abstract. Further, it was assumed that the taxonomy represented a cumulative hierarchy, so that mastery of each simpler category was prerequisite to mastery of the next, more complex one. A meta-analysis of the scanty empirical evidence available, which is described in the Lorin Anderson and David Krathwohl taxonomy revision noted below, supports this assumption for Comprehension through Analysis. The data were ambiguous, however, with respect to the location of Knowledge in the hierarchy and for the order of Evaluation and Synthesis.

The taxonomy has been used for the analysis of a course's objectives, an entire curriculum, or a test in order to determine the relative emphasis on each major category. The unceasing growth of knowledge exerts constant pressure on educators to pack more and more into each course. Thus, these analyses repeatedly show a marked overemphasis on Knowledge objectives. Because memory for most knowledge is short, in contrast to learning in the other categories, such findings raise important questions about learning priorities.

Along these same lines is the taxonomy's use to assure that objectives, instructional activities, and assessment are congruent (aligned) with one another. Even when instruction emphasizes objectives in the more complex categories, the difficulty of constructing test items to measure such achievement often results in tests that emphasize knowledge measurement instead. Alignment analyses highlight this inconsistency.

The taxonomy has also commonly been used in developing a test's blueprint, providing the detail for guiding item development to assure adequate, and appropriate curriculum coverage. Some standardized tests show how their test items are distributed across taxonomy categories.

The Affective Domain

In addition to devising the cognitive taxonomy, the Bloom group later grappled with a taxonomy of the affective domain—objectives concerned with interests, attitudes, adjustment, appreciation, and values. This taxonomy consisted of five categories arranged in order of increased internalization. Like the cognitive taxonomy, it assumed that learning at the lower category was prerequisite to the attainment of the next higher one. Here is an overview of the categories:

1.0. **Receiving** (Attending)

   1.1. Awareness

   1.2. Willingness to receive

   1.3. Controlled or selected attention

2.0. **Responding**

   2.1. Acquiescence in responding

   2.2. Willingness to respond

   2.3. Satisfaction in response

3.0. **Valuing**

   3.1. Acceptance of a value

   3.2. Preference for a value

   3.3. Commitment

4.0. **Organization**

   4.1. Conceptualization of a value

   4.2. Organization of a value system

5.0. **Characterization by a value or value complex**

   5.1. Generalized set

   5.2. Characterization

In addition, Elizabeth Simpson, Ravindrakumar Dave, and Anita Harrow developed taxonomies of the psychomotor domain.

Revision of the Taxonomy

A forty-year retrospective of the impact of the Cognitive Taxonomy by Lorin Anderson and Lauren Sosniak in 1994 (dating back to its preliminary edition in 1954) resulted in renewed consideration of a revision, prior efforts having failed to come to fruition. In 1995, Anderson and Krathwohl co-chaired a group to explore this possibility, and the group agreed on guidelines for attempting a revision. Like the original group, they met twice yearly, and in 2001 they produced *A Taxonomy for Learning, Teaching and Assessing: A Revision of Bloom's Taxonomy of Educational Objectives*, hereinafter referred to as the *revision*. Whereas the original was unidimensional, the revision had two dimensions, based on the two parts of objectives: (1) nouns describing the content (knowledge) to be learned, and (2) verbs describing what students will learn to do with that content; that is, the processes they use in producing or working with knowledge.

The Knowledge dimension. The Knowledge category of the original cognitive taxonomy included both a content aspect and the action aspect of remembering. These were separated in the revision, so that the content aspect (the nouns) became its own dimension with four categories:

A. **Factual Knowledge** (the basic elements students must know to be acquainted with a discipline or solve problems in it)
   a. Knowledge of terminology
   b. Knowledge of specific details and elements

B. **Conceptual Knowledge** (the interrelationships among the basic elements within a larger structure that enable them to function together)
   a. Knowledge of classifications and categories
   b. Knowledge of principles and generalizations
   c. Knowledge of theories, models, and structures

C. **Procedural Knowledge** (how to do something, including methods of inquiry and criteria for using skills, algorithms, techniques, and methods)
   a. Knowledge of subject-specific skills and algorithms
   b. Knowledge of subject-specific techniques and methods
   c. Knowledge of criteria for determining when to use appropriate procedures

D. **Metacognitive Knowledge** (knowledge of cognition in general, as well as awareness and knowledge of one's own cognition)
   a. Strategic knowledge
   b. Knowledge about cognitive tasks, including appropriate contextual and conditional knowledge

   c. Self-knowledge

The Process dimension. In the revision, the concepts of the six original categories were retained but changed to verbs for the second (process) dimension. The action aspect of Knowledge was retitled as *Remember*. Comprehension became *Understand*. Synthesis, replaced by *Create*, became the top category. Subcategories, all new, consisted of verbs in gerund form. In overview, the dimension's categories are:

1.0. **Remember** (retrieving relevant knowledge from long-term memory)
   1.1. Recognizing
   1.2. Recalling

2.0. **Understand** (determining the meaning of instructional messages, including oral, written, and graphic communication
   2.1. Interpreting
   2.2. Exemplifying
   2.3. Classifying
   2.4. Summarizing
   2.5. Inferring
   2.6. Comparing
   2.7. Explaining

3.0. **Apply** (carrying out or using a procedure in a given situation)
   3.1. Executing
   3.2. Implementing

4.0. **Analyze** (breaking material into its constituent parts and detecting how the parts relate to one another and to an overall structure or purpose)
   4.1. Differentiating
   4.2. Organizing
   4.3. Attributing

5.0. **Evaluate** (making judgments based on criteria and standards
   5.1. Checking
   5.2. Critiquing

6.0. **Create** (putting elements together to form a novel, coherent whole or make an original product)
   6.1. Generating
   6.2. Planning
   6.3. Producing

FIGURE 1

A taxonomy table with "X's" showing the classification of the objective: "The student should be able to recognize which facts or assumptions are essential to an argument."

The Knowledge Dimension	The Cognitive Process Dimension					
	1. Remember	2. Understand	3. Apply	4. Analyze	5. Evaluate	6. Create
A. Factual Knowledge				X		
B. Conceptual Knowledge				X		
C. Procedural Knowledge						
D. Metacognitive Knowledge						

SOURCE: Courtesy of author.

The Taxonomy Table

With these two dimensions one can construct a taxonomy table in which one can locate the junction of the classifications of an objective's verb and noun. Consider the objective: "The student should be able to recognize the facts and/or assumptions that are essential to an argument." The opening phrase, "The student should be able to," is common to objectives—it is the unique part of the objective that we classify. The verb is "recognize" and the noun is really a noun clause: "the facts and assumptions that are essential to an argument."

First, it is determined what is meant by "recognize." Initially, the term appears to belong to the category Remember because *recognizing* is Remember's first subcategory. But *recognizing*, the subcategory, refers to something learned before, which is not its meaning here. Here, it means that, on analyzing the logic of the argument, the student teases out the facts and assumptions on which the argument depends. The correct classification is Analyze.

The noun clause, "the facts or assumptions that are essential to an argument," appears to include two kinds of knowledge. "The facts" is clearly Factual Knowledge, and "the assumptions"—as in assuming an argument's facts are true—may also be Factual Knowledge. But assuming a principle or concept as part of an argument (e.g. evolution) would be classified as Conceptual Knowledge. So this objective would fall into two cells of the taxonomy table—the junction of Analyze with Factual Knowledge and with Conceptual Knowledge, as shown by the X's in Figure 1.

Just as objectives can be classified in a table, so can classroom activities used to attain them. Likewise, one can construct a table for assessment tasks and test items. If goals, activities, and assessments are aligned, the X's should fall in identical cells in all three tables. To the extent that they do not, the goals may be only partially attained and/or measured, and steps can be taken to restore alignment.

Comments inserted into classroom vignettes in the revision explain the classification of objectives, activities, and assessments as they lead to three completed taxonomy tables. The three tables are then compared to show the alignment, or lack of it, in each vignette. The six vignettes include different subject matters in elementary and secondary education.

Alternative Classification Frameworks

Since the publication of the original framework, numerous alternatives have appeared—intended to supplement, improve upon, or replace it. Chapter 15 of the revision analyzes nineteen such frameworks in relation to the original and revised Taxonomies. Eleven are unidimensional, while eight include two or more dimensions. Some use entirely new terms, and a few include the affective domain.

For example, in 1981 Robert Stahl and Gary Murphy provided these new headings: Preparation, Observation, Reception, Transformation, Information Acquisition, Retention, Transfersion, Incorporation, Organization, and Generation. The Organization heading bridges to the affective domain. David Merrill, in 1994, devised a framework similar to the revised taxonomy, using two dimensions, each with four categories, to form a Performance-Content matrix with a student performance dimension (Remember-Instance, Remember-

Generality, Use, and Find) and a subject matter dimension (Fact, Concept, Procedure, and Principle). The 1977 framework of Larry Hannah and John Michaelis is even more similar. Alfred DeBlock (1972) and others have developed frameworks with more than two dimensions, while Dean Hauenstein's 1998 framework provided taxonomies for all three domains. Marzano's taxonomy (2001) proposes a combination of three kinds of knowledge—Information (often called declarative knowledge), Mental Procedures (procedural knowledge), and Psychomotor Procedures. Marzano also develops a processing model of actions that successively flow through three hierarchically related systems of thinking: first the Self System, then the Metacognitive system, and finally the Cognitive system (which includes Retrieval, Comprehension, Analysis, and Knowledge Utilization).

See also: CURRICULUM, *subentry on* SCHOOL.

BIBLIOGRAPHY

ANDERSON, LORIN W., and KRATHWOHL, DAVID R., eds. 2001. *A Taxonomy for Learning, Teaching, and Assessing: A Revision of Bloom's Taxonomy of Educational Objectives.* New York: Longman.

ANDERSON, LORIN W., and SOSNIAK, LAUREN A., eds. 1994. *Bloom's Taxonomy: A Forty-Year Retrospective.* Ninety-third Yearbook of the National Society for the Study of Education. Chicago: University of Chicago Press.

BLOOM, BENJAMIN. S., ed. 1956. *Taxonomy of Educational Objectives: The Classification of Educational Goals; Handbook I, Cognitive Domain.* New York: David McKay.

DAVE, RAVINDRAKUMAR H. 1970. "Psychomotor Levels." In *Developing and Writing Behavioral Objectives,* ed. Robert J. Armstrong. Tucson AZ: Educational Innovators Press.

DEBLOCK, ALFRED, et al. 1972. "La Taxonomie des Objectifs pour la Discipline du Latin." *Didactica Classica Gandensia* 17:12–13, 119–131.

FLEISHMAN, EDWIN A., and QUAINTANCE, MARILYN K. 1984. *Taxonomies of Human Performance: The Description of Human Tasks.* Orlando, FL: Academic Press.

HANNAH, LARRY S., and MICHAELIS, JOHN U. 1977. *A Comprehensive Framework for Instructional Objectives: A Guide to Systematic Planning and Evaluation.* Reading, MA: Addison-Wesley.

HARROW, ANITA J. 1972. *A Taxonomy of the Psychomotor Domain: A Guide for Developing Behavioral Objectives.* New York: David McKay.

HAUENSTEIN, A. DEAN. 1998. *A Conceptual Framework for Educational Objectives: A Holistic Approach to Traditional Taxonomies.* Lanham, MD: University Press of America.

KRATHWOHL, DAVID R.; BLOOM, BENJAMIN S.; and MASIA, BERTRAM B. 1964. *Taxonomy of Educational Objectives: The Classification of Educational Goals; Handbook II: The Affective Domain.* New York: David McKay.

MARZANO, ROBERT J. 2001. *Designing a New Taxonomy of Educational Objectives.* Thousand Oaks, CA: Corwin Press.

MERRILL, M. DAVID. 1994. *Instructional Design Theory.* Englewood Cliffs, NJ: Educational Technology Publications.

SIMPSON, BETTY J. 1966. "The Classification of Educational Objectives: Psychomotor Domain." *Illinois Journal of Home Economics* 10(4):110–144.

STAHL, ROBERT J., and MURPHY, GARY T. 1981. *The Domain of Cognition: An Alternative to Bloom's Cognitive Domain within the Framework of an Information-Processing Model.* ERIC Document Reproduction Service No. ED 208511.

DAVID R. KRATHWOHL
LORIN W. ANDERSON

TAYLOR, HAROLD (1914–1993)

Philosopher of education, college president, and social activist, Harold Taylor was a recognized spokesperson for Progressive education at the postsecondary level. Taylor was born in Toronto and, upon completion of the B.A. and M.A. degrees at the University of Toronto, received a fellowship to study philosophy at Cambridge University. Shortly after his arrival he questioned the social significance of analytical philosophy and, ultimately, transferred to a doctoral program at University of London. Upon completion of the Ph.D. in philosophy in 1938, Taylor accepted a faculty position at the University of Wisconsin, where he served for six years. In 1945, at age thirty, Taylor assumed the presidency of Sarah Lawrence College, a highly progressive, experimental school outside of New York City. Taylor held this position for fourteen years, during which time he became a national leader for Progressive education, the liberal arts curriculum, international education, and the arts in the United States. While at Sarah Lawrence he worked closely with Eleanor Roosevelt and Adlai Stevenson as a consultant on human rights. Taylor left the presidency of Sarah Lawrence in 1959 and proceeded to establish a career as public intellectual, independent writer and lecturer, and adjunct faculty at the New School for Social Research and the City University of New York. In addition, he served as president of the Agnes de Mille Dance Theatre, vice-chair of the Martha Graham School of Contemporary Dance, and president of the American Ballet Theatre. Taylor also maintained a lifelong friendship with Duke Ellington and was instrumental in arranging for the preservation of the John Dewey professional papers.

By assuming the presidency of Sarah Lawrence College at the young age of thirty, Taylor was immediately thrown into a national spotlight and compared to Robert M. Hutchins of the University of Chicago, another former "boy president." During Taylor's years at Sarah Lawrence College, one of the first Progressive, experimental colleges in the United States, he fostered a setting where there were no formal departments or academic ranks. Everyone on the faculty was considered a teacher and a member of a community of equals, each of whom was responsible for assisting students in creating their own course of study. No examinations or grades were given; students learned to judge the quality of their own work with the help of their teachers and fellow students. Since there were no required courses, the curriculum was built by a series of conscious choices made by the student. Theater, dance, music, painting, sculpture, design, and graphics were central to the overall-all curriculum and integrated with the humanities and sciences course of study. Within the context of this "open curriculum" Taylor sought opportunities to bring to the Sarah Lawrence campus cultural figures with provocative ideological, social activist, liberal, and radical views. This led anticommunist Senator Joseph McCarthy to identify Sarah Lawrence College as a target for attack during the hearings of the House Committee on Un-American Activities.

While Taylor became a leading spokesperson for peace education, academic freedom, and world education, a main theme throughout his academic career was the crucial role of students as active learners where they would be involved in making college policy and in running their own lives. In *Students without Teachers* (1969), considered by many as a blueprint for radical change, Taylor condemned colleges and universities for being out of touch with their students and with the surrounding intellectual community. He objected to the trend of colleges turning from dynamic cultural centers devoted to intellectual freedom and democracy to large bureaucracies that trained students and were managed by "corporate faculty." In essence, Taylor foresaw the impending "moral collapse" of the university (as noted in the 1990s) and sought to encourage student and university political activism at the national level. Taylor's call for postsecondary reform reoriented the learning–teaching system so that students collaborated with professors in the instruction of courses and were actively involved with the selection and organization of the curriculum. Running throughout this point of view was a strong Progressive education ideology, guided by the writings of John Dewey, as Taylor emphasized the importance of democracy and experience. Taylor questioned the traditional liberal arts curriculum with its concentration upon knowledge independent of the student's experience, and he argued for a curriculum embodying personal development, social and cultural activism (social agency), and the unity of intellect and emotions in the educational process. Taylor's position adopted a more tangible form in *How to Change Colleges: Notes on Radical Reform* (1971) which, in essence, constituted a manifesto-manual for postsecondary reform. Taylor advocated reconstructing the college departmental system as learning centers, abolishing the lecture system, required courses, and tests. Implicit within these and other recommendations was Taylor's belief in the importance of bringing the arts into the mainstream of American education and students' life.

While Taylor addressed many administrative and instructional issues at the postsecondary level, he was also active in the area of teacher education. *The World as Teacher* (1969) represents a three-year study of teacher education and combined Taylor's interests in the development in the early 1960s of the World College program and the International Baccalaureate. Taylor charged that teachers must understand the world, and their education must not be composed of mere courses in foreign cultures. Instead, he recommended ways for teachers to participate in international service learning projects and other educational experiences that would initiate broader, cultural perspectives. As the universities transformed in the 1950s and 1960s into corporate, multiversity conglomerates, Harold Taylor was one of the few university spokespeople who maintained a Progressive education perspective for postsecondary school reform and who championed the university as the most appropriate venue for discussion and debate of pressing societal and cultural problems.

See also: HIGHER EDUCATION IN THE UNITED STATES, *subentry on* HISTORICAL DEVELOPMENT; PROGRESSIVE EDUCATION.

BIBLIOGRAPHY

TAYLOR, HAROLD. 1969. *Students without Teachers: The Crisis in the University.* New York: McGraw-Hill.

TAYLOR, HAROLD. 1969. *The World as Teacher.* New York: Doubleday.

TAYLOR, HAROLD. 1971. *How to Change Colleges: Notes on Radical Reform.* New York: Holt, Rinehart, and Winston.

TAYLOR, HAROLD. 1988. "Meiklejohn and Dewey in the 1950s." *Teaching Education* 2(1):20–29.

CRAIG KRIDEL

TEACHER

The role and responsibilities of elementary and secondary school teachers have undergone a significant evolution since the publication of the first edition of the *Encyclopedia of Education.* Historically, teachers have been viewed as purveyors of content knowledge and academic skills, but teachers in the early twenty-first century have also become ambassadors to multicultural communities and promulgators of democracy. As expectations for teacher performance have increased, so too has the status of teaching—the term *teaching profession* has become commonplace.

Conventionally viewed as dispensers of knowledge, teachers are increasingly perceived as facilitators or managers of knowledge. They are often thought to be colearners with their students. Few modern teachers would try to claim intellectual hegemony in the classroom; such a claim would not stand the challenge of increasingly sophisticated students. There is too much to know and too many sources of knowledge outside the classroom that can easily be brought to bear within school walls by students themselves. Teachers teach, of course, but they do not simply dispense information to their students. Teachers are also intellectual leaders who create opportunities for students to demonstrate what they know and what they know how to do.

Responsibilities of Elementary and Secondary School Teachers

Public school teachers spend an average of 49.3 hours per week meeting their responsibilities, including 11.2 hours per week on noncompensated duties. Customary responsibilities for teachers include planning and executing instructional lessons, assessing students based on specific objectives derived from a set curricula, and communicating with parents.

This list of seemingly simple tasks belies the complexity of the job. It was once the norm for teachers to address the needs of large groups of students via standard lesson plans and stock practice. This is no longer the case. Teachers of the early twenty-first century must create and modify lessons, fitting them to the diverse instructional needs and abilities of their students. The Individuals with Disabilities Education Act ensures that any student with an identified disability receive a written Individualized Education Program stating the modifications that must be implemented by any teacher working with that particular child. Students' needs run the gamut from learning disabilities to giftedness—a broad range that compels teachers to behave in certain ways.

Unlike their predecessors, twenty-first-century teachers expect to deal with the dictates of standardized testing and curricula to match. Signed in 2002 by President George W. Bush, the No Child Left Behind Act is simply one very visible indication of the emphasis on local accountability for student performance. The bill requires that all schools display proof of meeting a minimal set of academic standards, as defined by each state. States must begin implementing annual high-stakes testing—testing upon which important decisions such as passing and failing depend. These tests will concentrate, at least initially, on reading and mathematics in grades three through eight.

As always, teachers are responsible for classroom management and discipline. This aspect of a teacher's job shows no signs of growing easier—quite the contrary. According to the U.S. Department of Education, during the period from 1992 to 1996, 1,581,000 teachers were victims of nonfatal crimes that occurred while at school. Recognizing the challenge of student discipline, the No Child Left Behind Act includes steps for providing a safer work environment for teachers as well as students. Opportunities for professional development and training in positive methods of discipline abound.

Teachers are expected to use computer-based technology with increasing frequency and proficiency. The technology boom of the 1990s was accompanied by many efforts to help teachers integrate technology into their teaching and into students' learning. Although there is legitimate concern about the ultimate value of the use of technology in schools, there is little doubt that considerable resources have been expended to advance the digital revolution. The E-rate, for example—a federal program that provides targeted discounts to schools and libraries with the goal of increasing access to the Internet and other telecommunications services—funneled $3.65 billion into schools from 1997 to 2002. The federal government spent another $275 million from 1999 to 2002 to train teachers to use technology via the PT3 program.

Changing societal demographics have forced changes in the practice of teaching. There are, for instance, more than ninety languages spoken in Fairfax County Public Schools in Virginia. Teachers all over the nation work with students and parents from many different cultures. Teachers themselves are students of culture. They create classroom environments to celebrate various ethnic and religious traditions. They are expected to treat children and their families sensitively so as to avoid the proliferation of stereotypical images of races, cultures, or religions.

Teachers continue to exhibit a rich history of participation in educational and political groups, committees, and events. In 1996, 42 percent of public school teachers participated in committees dealing with local curriculum. On the national level, teachers are members of unions that include the American Federation of Teachers (AFT) and the National Education Association (NEA), as well as their local affiliates.

Qualifications of Elementary and Secondary Teachers

State governments determine their own requirements for a teaching license. In addition to a college degree with course work in appropriate areas, more than thirty states require a national teacher examination, such as the Praxis Series. Developed by the Educational Testing Service, the Praxis Series is designed to assess a teacher's knowledge of basic subject matter including reading, writing, and mathematics. Praxis also evaluates a prospective teacher in two other areas: general knowledge of the field of education and knowledge within the teacher's specialty content area.

Many states recognize licenses earned in other states, thus a license earned in one state may be used to work in another state. This process is referred to as "reciprocity" of licensing. Teachers who are interested in pursuing additional endorsements—that is, approvals to teach other specialties—do so most often by taking additional college course work. They can also attempt to acquire national certification through the National Board for Professional Teaching Standards, but they may still have to gain a state license in order to teach in a public school. In 2001 the NEA estimated that there would be 100,000 National Board Certified teachers by 2005.

Teachers also join professional honorary societies. For example, teachers may be invited to become a member of Kappa Delta Pi, an international honor society in education that seeks to inspire high teaching standards. Kappa Delta Pi and other education honorary societies recognize the actions of individual teachers and through membership distinguish them as exceptional educators.

There were approximately 2.78 million public school teachers working in K–12 education during the 1998–1999 academic year. It was estimated that by 2008 the number of teachers needed to meet the demands of a growing student population would be 3.46 million. To address an increasing teacher shortage, the No Child Left Behind Act suggests that state governments and school districts use alternative means of licensing and endorsing teachers, including fast-track teacher education programs for professionals outside education. The act also supports various incentives to keep teachers on the job, including merit pay for practicing educators and performance-based bonuses.

Research on Elementary and Secondary Teachers
Teacher quality has been said to be the number one school-related influence on student achievement. Although research on what constitutes a quality teacher is often the subject of debate, there are some findings on teacher quality that are rarely contested. These suggest that it is what teachers do in classrooms that matters. Research has shown that teachers can improve student achievement when they communicate high expectations, avoid criticism, reward truly praiseworthy behavior, and provide abundant opportunities for success (academic learning time) on material over which students are tested.

Demographics

According to the first edition of the *Encyclopedia of Education,* the average salary in 1969 for a public school teacher was $8,320 at the elementary level and $8,840 at the secondary level. The average salary for a male secondary public school teacher was $9,160, and the average for a female public school secondary teacher was $8,670. While the average salaries have increased, the differences in salaries between elementary and secondary teachers as well as the disparity in salary between male and female educators have diminished. These changes in salaries reflect changes in attitudes about equal pay for equal work and the increasing responsibilities of female educators. The current public school teacher workforce is approximately 74 percent female.

A survey performed in 1995–1996 by the NEA found elementary and secondary public school teachers with a mean salary of $35,549. The range of salaries, however, is quite remarkable. Connecticut consistently ranks number one; in 1999–2000 its average teacher salary was $52,401. South Dakota falls on the opposite end of the spectrum, with an average salary that year of $29,072.

With approximately 90 percent of public school teachers classified as white in 2001, the racial demographics of teachers have not changed as noticeably as the student populations they serve. What has changed significantly is the number of advanced degrees obtained by teachers. In 1970, 25 percent of public school teachers received an advanced degree. The NEA reported in 1997 that this number had more than doubled to 56 percent—54 percent with master's degrees and 2 percent with doctoral degrees.

See also: AMERICAN FEDERATION OF TEACHERS; INTERNATIONAL TEACHERS ASSOCIATIONS; NATIONAL EDUCATION ASSOCIATION; NO CHILD LEFT BEHIND ACT, 2001; TEACHER EDUCATION; TEACHER EMPLOYMENT; TEACHER EVALUATION; TEACHER LEARNING COMMUNITIES; TEACHER UNIONS.

BIBLIOGRAPHY

BROPHY, JERE E., and GOOD, THOMAS L. 1986. "Teacher Behavior and Student Achievement." In *Handbook of Research on Teaching,* 3rd edition, ed. Merlin C. Wittrock. New York: Macmillan.

Individuals with Disabilities Education Act of 1997. U.S. Public Law 105-17. *U.S. Code.* Vol. 20, secs. 1400 et seq.

NATIONAL CENTER FOR EDUCATION STATISTICS. 1998. *Indicators of School Crime and Safety: 2001.* Washington, DC: National Center for Education Statistics.

NATIONAL EDUCATION ASSOCIATION. 1997. *Status of the American Public School Teacher, 1995–96: Highlights.* Washington, DC: National Education Association.

NATIONAL EDUCATION ASSOCIATION. RESEARCH DIVISION. 1970. *NEA Research Bulletin.* Washington, DC: National Education Association.

SOLMON, LEWIS C., and FIRETAG, KIMBERLY. 2002. "The Road to Teacher Quality." *Education Week* 21(27):48.

INTERNET RESOURCES

AMERICAN FEDERATION OF TEACHERS. 2000. "Teacher Salaries Fail to Keep Up with Inflation: AFT Releases Annual State-by-State Teacher Salary Survey." <www.aft.org/research/salary/home.htm>.

CUBAN, LARRY. 1998. "Cuban Speech." *Tapped In.* <www.tappedin.org/info/teachers/debate2.html>.

NATIONAL EDUCATION ASSOCIATION. 2001. "Teachers and Students Excelling Together: Ensuring the Quality Teachers America Needs." <www.nea.org/lac/bluebook/execsum.html>.

KIMBERLY B. WAID
ROBERT F. MCNERGNEY

TEACHER EDUCATION

HISTORICAL OVERVIEW
Edward R. Ducharme
Mary K. Ducharme
INTERNATIONAL PERSPECTIVE
Michael J. Dunkin

HISTORICAL OVERVIEW

Can teaching be taught? Do individuals learn to teach or are they endowed with an innate gift for pedagogy? Are certain individuals born teachers? Do individuals learn about teaching from copying others, from listening to lectures, from reading about it? Are some ways of preparing teachers better than others? These and related questions about teaching and teacher education persist.

Didactic and Evocative Teaching

Joseph Axelrod describes two types of teaching as "the *didactic* modes, employed by teacher-craftsmen, and the *evocative* modes, employed by teacher-artists" (p. 5). Didactic teaching implies passing on traditional knowledge or lore, or teaching how to do something. Teachers use lecture to inculcate knowledge or demonstration to model actions, after which students demonstrate they have learned what was taught either by reciting or writing the material or by repeating the demonstration, as in a science class experiment. Much state and national testing relies on rote recall of material. In this context, learning means being able to reproduce what has been taught or demonstrated. For example, students should recall key facts of American history such as the order of the American presidents. Emphases are often on learning facts and conditions, not on understanding complexity and drawing conclusions.

Early in human history, most teaching was didactic. Poets recited ancient myths and stories and a few listeners learned them by rote. Individuals acquired skills by observing their elders who were fishers, artisans, lawyers, or anything else, and emulating what they saw. Seeing teaching as a process of passing on knowledge has persisted. Paul Woodring argues that "The oldest form of teacher education is the observation and emulation of a master. Plato learned to teach by sitting at the feet of Socrates. Aristotle, in turn, learned from Plato" (p. 1).

Much observation and emulation still go on. In *The Teacher Educator's Handbook,* Sharon Feiman-Nemser and Janine Remillard note that "Like much of our society, prospective teachers believe that teaching is a process of passing knowledge from teacher to student and that learning involves absorbing or memorizing information and practicing skills. Students wait like empty vessels to be filled and teachers do the filling" (p. 70).

Most teaching in early America was highly didactic. Teachers taught both the processes of learning to read and the morals attendant to a proper life through moralistic texts. Children learning their letters in the early nineteenth century read in the *New England Primer* under the letter A, "In Adam's fall, we sinned all"; under the letter F, "The idle fool Is wipt at school"; and under the letter J, "Job feels the rod Yet blesses God" (pp. 12–13). Students thus simultaneously learned their letters, religious lessons, and injunctions about behavior.

Not all teaching in the past was didactic; not all learning was rote. Socrates relied on the relationship between himself and his students to arrive at truths of human existence; he was, in Axelrod's sense, an evocative teacher. Socrates corrected occasionally and enjoined his students, but rarely taught didactically. The Socratic, or evocative, method places responsibility for knowledge growth on the students.

Using the evocative method, social studies teachers might teach geographical lessons from which they expect students to describe how communities develop relative to the natural world surrounding them. Teachers might present students with a computer program describing an environment near a river, with large forests, good soil, and a moderate climate. Students would then describe how they believe a community might evolve, given these circumstances. The teacher's role is to elicit conclusions, probabilities, and hypotheses from the students and have them assiduously pursue the most likely correct answers. Learning means being able to gather and assimilate data and evidence and draw conclusions based on sound thinking.

Neither didactic nor evocative teaching alone will suffice because learners vary widely in how they learn. Some individuals learn material effectively when teachers present it sequentially or chronologically; others may learn better when teachers present material thematically. Some learners have an affinity for concreteness while others prefer abstraction. Teachers require tolerance and understanding for these and other differences in learners. Although some learners may master a variety of ways of learning, teachers more often than not appeal to what they discern to be the learner's most comfortable way of learning. Ideally, teachers attach neither special praise nor stigma to different ways of learning. They recognize not all individuals learn in similar ways. However, in many classrooms, teachers fail to teach a variety of ways of learning. This can frustrate many learners.

Didactic teaching and evocative teaching are merely two modes of instruction among other related ways teachers teach and learners learn. Little exists to suggest one mode is superior to all others. Nearly all teachers use a variety of modes of instruction as they go about their daily teaching tasks. Teacher education must provide opportunities for prospective and practicing teachers to master a range of teaching modes.

Teaching and Teacher Education in Early America

In his biography of John Adams, David McCullough points out that in colonial America, teaching was something men did if they did not have anything better to do. He notes that in 1755 John Adams, not having the money for the fee to apprentice to a lawyer, although "untried and untrained as a teacher, immediately assumed his new role in a one-room schoolhouse at the center of town" (p. 37). It is interesting that McCullough uses the phrase "untried and untrained." The fact is there was no training for teachers in 1755. The first formal teacher preparation began in the 1820s with the establishment of "normal schools" in Vermont and Massachusetts.

The establishment of normal schools became a movement later in the nineteenth century; almost every state had at least one of them. The normal schools' purpose was perfectly straightforward: the preparation of teachers. Cities were desperate for teachers. By the early 1900s, nearly every city with a population of more than 300,000 had a normal school, often tied in with the high schools. Normal schools were technically oriented toward the practice of teaching. Modeled on earlier established European institutions for teacher training, these schools provided very specific training.

In *The Salterton Trilogy* (1986), Robertson Davies provides a fictional but accurate picture of what transpired in many normal school classrooms. "They [normal school teachers] taught how to teach;

they taught when to open the windows in a classroom and when to close them; . . . they taught ways of teaching children with no talent for drawing how to draw; they taught how a school choir could be formed and trained where there was no instrument but a pitchpipe . . . they taught how to make hangings, somewhat resembling batik, by drawing in wax crayon on unbleached cotton, and pressing it with a hot iron" (p. 79). These examples illustrate the didactic mode of teacher education in which prospective teachers learn how to *do* things, not how to *think about* the whys and wherefores of doing things. Didactic teacher education treats teaching as craft. It suggests that individuals can acquire the essential skills to impart knowledge, facts, and even abilities through lecture and demonstration. By contrast, the evocative mode, as applied to the education of teachers, suggests that teaching is an emergent art in which teachers evoke from students what they already know and lead them to the acquisition of new knowledge and skills.

By the 1940s, most normal schools had expanded, first into four-year state teachers colleges or liberal arts colleges emphasizing teacher education, and then, during the higher education expansion in the 1960s and 1970s, into state universities. For example, by the 1960s, the three former normal schools in Vermont had become four-year liberal arts colleges with new campuses and diminished teacher education programs.

Into the Twenty-First Century

As the normal schools morphed into four-year colleges and eventually state universities, established state universities that did not already have them began to develop teacher preparation programs. University and college teacher education programs grew rapidly as states developed specific licensure requirements often based on college level coursework. As accreditation of secondary schools grew, the need for teachers with college degrees also grew. The norm became a combination of a degree with a major in an academic subject and completion of required education courses. Scholars argue that universities were anything but altruistic in their development of teacher preparation programs. Reasons included a desire to show some public service commitment, a need to increase revenues from enrollment of teacher education students, and the development of graduate programs in educational administration.

In 2002, most universities had firmly entrenched teacher preparation programs on their campuses. Campus programs remain the major place of preparation for teachers. State universities continue to be major sources of beginning teachers. Institutions such as Utah's Brigham Young University, South Florida University, Indiana University, and Wayne State University, in Detroit, Michigan, annually graduate hundreds of licensed teachers. In addition, liberal arts colleges with small teacher preparation programs consistently graduate licensed teachers. More than 1,200 institutions continue to provide teacher preparation programs.

During the last decades of the twentieth century a variety of nontraditional centers of activity evolved. The combination of the need for teachers in critically short areas such as mathematics and science and the public criticism of campus-based teacher education produced situations in which individuals and groups developed alternative routes for teacher preparation. Periodic shortages in teachers, particularly in urban and rural settings, led to a variety of ways of circumventing licensure regulations and university requirements. Teacher education was occurring through a variety of vehicles, including colleges and universities, public schools, state departments of education, special projects such as Teach for America, and district and university affiliated programs such as a New York City project for recruiting non-traditional candidates.

Intellectual Caliber and Content of Teacher Education

College and university-based teacher education is often the target of many critics contending that students in teacher education programs are academically weaker than students in other programs, that preparation programs are vacuous, and that the faculty are second-rate. Despite reliable studies responding to these criticisms and demonstrating some of the criticism as ill founded, the attacks continue. The alleged low quality of teacher education students has led to a lack of acceptance by higher education faculty of teacher education on the campus.

Burton Clark and Harry Judge have noted a certain university reluctance to *own* teacher education despite its major presence on campuses. Clark shows how faculty at state universities that had been normal schools or state teachers colleges resent the influence of "education people"; Judge believes that such institutions, their faculties, and their adminis-

trations have little respect for teacher preparation. He contends that the further away from direct involvement in teacher preparation the education faculty are, the better they feel about themselves. Thus, although teacher education has a long history on campuses, the relationship between it and the broader campus remains strained.

Chester Finn, a vitriolic critic of teacher education, argues that colleges of education "are the most-despised institutions in the education universe" (p. 223). Even among the friends of teacher education, criticism is severe. In his 1990 book, *Teachers for Our Nation's Schools,* John Goodlad notes, "Teachers and teacher educators don't know enough about how to teach, and they don't know enough about how to understand and influence the conditions around them" (p. 108).

J. Palmer describes the tenuous nature of teacher education: "Training programs that were established tended to disappear after a few years. Then, as now, public universities were not certain how to deal with teacher education or if they wanted it. The low status of teacher education in state universities was established early, and it has persisted" (p. 52). A reason for the low status of teacher education faculty may be that they prepare people who work with the young in schools: preschool staffs, day care center employees, elementary and secondary school teachers—all groups that are held in low esteem by various segments of society.

Programs to prepare teachers remain remarkably consistent. They generally consist of a general arts and sciences component, advanced study in a discipline, a teacher preparation component, and field experiences. In *The Teacher Educator's Handbook* (1996), Barbara Senkowski Stengal and Alan Tom note that "Traditional teacher education programs are typically marked by three components: foundations of schooling and learning, teaching methodology, and practice teaching" (p. 593). Foundations of schooling and learning include the vital areas of psychology, philosophy, and learning principles, a pattern first established in the normal schools.

Teacher Education and Field Experiences

Teacher education has always provided opportunities for prospective teachers to practice teaching in school settings while still in their preparation programs. For decades, these experiences occurred during the last year of the preparation program and lasted approximately six to eight weeks. In many programs, this was the only experience that prospective teachers had in a school or with students. The typical experience included assigning the student to an experienced teacher in the school who would provide guidance and supervision. A teacher education faculty member would provide a minimum of three visits to observe the prospective teacher teach.

In the 1960s, programs began requiring early experiences in the schools for undergraduate students, often during their freshman year and continuing throughout the four years, culminating in a full semester of student teaching or internship. Preparation programs began placing clusters of four or five students in the same school so as to provide a collective experience rather than a private ordeal for future teachers.

Changes in the requirements of preparation programs regarding field experiences coincided with changes in what teacher education faculty were required to do and expectations of what schools should do. In 1986 and 1990 the Holmes Group argued for professional development schools (PDSs). In a PDS, a teacher preparation program or institution would commit to providing a school population with a cadre of prospective teachers, several higher education faculty, and curriculum assistance over a period of several years. The goals of a PDS are to provide better field experiences for the teacher education students, increased faculty cooperation with the schools, and sustained curricular improvement in schools and in teacher education programs.

Many variations have occurred and will continue to occur in the field experiences of prospective teachers. The reactions of student teachers to their experiences will likely continue to be consistent. Study after study reveals that the student teaching experience is rated most important of all their preparation programs. And why not? It is the one time that they have sustained interaction with the young people that they have professed a desire to spend their working lives with.

Teacher Education Faculty

Who teaches the teachers? Who is a teacher educator? The broadest conception of who is a teacher educator includes everyone who teaches prospective and practicing teachers, from their freshman English professors and those who teach special methods courses to those who supervise student teaching. Teacher educators may be defined specifically as "those who hold tenure-line positions in teacher preparation in higher education institutions, teach beginning and advanced students in teacher education, and conduct research or engage in scholarly studies germane to teacher education" (Ducharme, p. 6).

Research on teacher educators began in the 1980s as Heather Carter, Edward Ducharme and Russell Agne, Judith Lanier and Judith Little, and others began publishing research studies of teacher education faculty. In *The Handbook of Research on Teacher Education,* published in 1996, Nancy Zimpher and Julie Sherrill describe the teacher education professoriate as majority male and more than 90 percent Anglo. Summarizing several studies, they note that males dominate in the higher ranks, publish more than females, and work less in schools. Ducharme offers the observation that "there is a contradiction between a commitment to prepare a professional cadre of students, a majority of whom are female, to become powerful teachers and effective advocates for youth in which the female faculty are in roles and positions implying an inequity between the genders" (p. 120).

The ethnic makeup of the teacher education professoriate is heavily skewed toward white males. The Anglo population of the professoriate is between 91 and 93 percent. Candidates for teaching remain heavily white. With the exception of faculty in the historically black colleges, there are few black or other minority professors in teacher education. As the schools become more and more multicultural, those who teach teachers remain majority white and male; those who teach children in elementary schools remain mostly female and white; those who teach adolescents remain majority female and mostly white.

Teacher Education Themes

Many teacher education programs have defining characteristics. Programs generally lean toward one of several thematic patterns: behaviorist or competency-based, humanistic, and developmental. The 1960s and 1970s were the heydays of the competency-based teacher education (CBTE) and performance-based teacher education (PBTE) programs. In CBTE, researchers attempted to isolate what they perceived as the discrete tasks of teaching, develop protocols for training teachers to master the tasks, and produce tests to assess whether or not the teachers could perform the tasks. The CBTE movement soon degenerated into lists of hundreds of competencies as proponents attempted to outdo one another through elaborate lists. Instead of a system designed to help manage teacher education, it became an unmanageable process.

In *Teacher Education* (1975), N. L. Gage and Philip Winne defined PBTE as "teacher training in which the prospective or inservice teacher acquires, to a prespecified degree, performance tendencies and capabilities that promote student achievement of educational objectives" (p. 146). Both CBTE and PBTE derived from beliefs in relationships between teaching practices and student learning. Intensely behaviorist, both CBTE and PBTE grew in part from a desire for accountability in education, a concern that has persisted into the twenty-first century. Although the nomenclature of CBTE and PBTE has largely vanished from higher education teacher education syllabi, the concerns for accountability and the premises underlying the movements persist.

Other programs emphasize a more developmental approach, typically focusing on field experiences integrated with coursework, analyses of classrooms, journal writing, and reflective practice. The 1980s and 1990s saw emphasis on reflective practice as a program keynote in many institutions.

Accreditation

Teacher education, like other fields in higher education that prepare professionals, has used accreditation as a means of quality control. In 1948 the newly formed American Association of Colleges for Teacher Education (AACTE) began accrediting institutions that prepared teachers. By 1950 AACTE had issued the first of several versions of *Revised Standards and Policies for Accrediting Colleges for Teacher Education.* In 1954, perhaps recognizing the possible conflicts inherent in being the organization of those institutions preparing teachers and also being responsible for managing the accrediting process, AACTE gave up responsibility for accreditation. The National Council for the Accreditation of Teacher Education (NCATE) was created and has dominated the accrediting process at the national level since. Over the years, several versions of its standards, policies, and practices have emerged. Most states have processes for accrediting teacher preparation programs and many work collaboratively with NCATE.

Almost six hundred institutions are NCATE accredited.

The accreditation movement has not been without controversy, controversy that combined with concerns for quality produced a series of revisions of standards and practices over the years. Major controversies include the voluntary nature of NCATE accreditation; the standards used; and the complexity, costs, and time required to complete the process. Perhaps as a result of controversy over these and other issues, an alternative accrediting body, the Teacher Education Accreditation Council, began in the 1990s and by 2002 had more than sixty member institutions.

Thus institutions had two agencies from which to seek professional accreditation. However, the combination of NCATE's longevity and the number of states working together on accreditation suggest that NCATE will continue to be the major accrediting body.

Summary

Paul Woodring, quoting the seventeenth-century writer Comenius, notes that the main object of teacher education is "to find a method of instruction by which teachers may teach less but learners may learn more" (Woodring, p. 1). This brief article suggests the difficulties inherent in finding flawless ways of teaching and of preparing teachers. Despite many research studies purporting to show that one way of doing things is superior to others, finding a way to prepare teachers so that students will learn more remains problematic. Yet if the past is prologue to the present, teacher educators in the many preparation environments that exist and that will evolve will continue to seek better ways so that all may learn.

See also: TEACHER EVALUATION, *subentries on* METHODS, OVERVIEW; TEACHING, *subentry on* LEARNING TO TEACH.

BIBLIOGRAPHY

AMERICAN ASSOCIATION OF COLLEGES FOR TEACHER EDUCATION. 1987–1994. *RATE Studies in Teacher Education.* Washington, DC: American Association of Colleges for Teacher Education.

AXELROD, JOSEPH. 1973. *The University Teacher as Artist.* San Francisco: Jossey-Bass.

BORROWMAN, MERLE. 1965. *Teacher Education in America: A Documentary Study.* New York: Teachers College Press.

CARTER, HEATHER. 1981. *Teacher Educators: A Descriptive Study.* University of Texas, Research and Development Center for Teacher Education. ED 255 354.

CARTER, HEATHER. 1984. "Teachers of Teachers." In *Advances in Education,* Vol. 1, ed. Lillian Katz and James Raths. Norwood, NJ: Ablex Publishing.

CLARK, BURTON R. 1987. *The Academic Life: Small Worlds. Different World.* Princeton, NJ: The Carnegie Foundation for the Advancement of Teaching.

CLIFFORD, GERALDINE J., and GUTHRIE, JAMES W. 1988. *Ed School.* Chicago: University of Chicago Press.

DAVIES, ROBERTSON. 1986. *The Salterton Trilogy.* New York: Viking Penguin.

DUCHARME, EDWARD R. 1993. *The Lives of Teacher Educators.* New York: Teachers College Press.

DUCHARME, EDWARD R., and AGNE, RUSSELL. 1982. "The Education Professoriate: A Research-Based Perspective." *Journal of Teacher Education* 33(6):30–36.

FEIMAN-NEMSER, SHARON, and REMILLARD, JANINE. 1996. "Perspectives on Learning to Teach." In *The Teacher Educator's Handbook,* ed. Frank B. Murray. San Francisco: Jossey-Bass.

FINN, CHESTER. 1991. *We Must Take Charge: Our Schools and Our Future.* New York: Free Press.

GAGE, N. L., and WINNE, PHILLIP. 1975. "Performance-Based Teacher Education." In *Teacher Education,* Seventy-fourth Yearbook of the National Society for the Study of Education, ed. Kevin Ryan. Chicago: University of Chicago Press.

GOODLAD, JOHN. 1990. *Teachers for Our Nation's Schools.* San Francisco: Jossey-Bass.

HOLMES GROUP. 1986. *Tomorrow's Teachers: A Report of the Holmes Group.* East Lansing, MI: Holmes Group.

HOLMES GROUP. 1990. *Tomorrow's Schools: A Report of the Holmes Group.* East Lansing, MI: Holmes Group.

HOWEY, KENNETH, and ZIMPHER, NANCY. 1989. *Profiles of Preservice Teacher Education.* Albany: State University of New York Press.

HOWEY, KENNETH, and ZIMPHER, NANCY. 1996. "Patterns in Prospective Teachers: Guides for Designing Preservice Programs." In *The Teacher Educator's Handbook,* ed. Frank B. Murray. San Francisco: Jossey-Bass.

JUDGE, HARRY. 1982. *American Graduate Schools of Education: A View from Abroad.* New York: The Ford Foundation.

LANIER, JUDITH, and LITTLE, JUDITH. 1986. "Research in Teacher Education." In *Handbook of Research on Teaching,* 3rd edition, ed. Merlin C. Wittrock. New York: Macmillan.

McCULLOUGH, DAVID. 2001. *John Adams.* New York: Simon and Schuster.

MURRAY, FRANK B., ed. 1996. *The Teacher Educator's Handbook.* San Francisco: Jossey-Bass.

PALMER, J. 1985. "Teacher Education: A Perspective from a Major Public University." In *Colleges of Education: Perspectives on their Future,* ed. Charles C. Case and William A. Matthes. Berkeley, CA: McCutchan Publishing Company.

SIKULA, JOHN, ed. 1996. *Handbook of Research on Teacher Education.* New York: Simon and Schuster.

STENGAL, BARBARA SENKOWSKI, and ALAN, TOM. 1996. "Changes and Choices in Teaching Methods." In *The Teacher Educator's Handbook,* ed. Frank B. Murray. San Francisco: Jossey-Bass.

WARREN, DON, ed. 1989. *American Teachers: Histories of a Profession at Work.* New York: Macmillan.

WOODRING, PAUL. 1962. "The Need for a Unifying Theory of Teacher Education: A Reappraisal." In *Teacher Education: A Reappraisal,* ed. Elmer R. Smith. New York: Harper and Row.

WOODRING, PAUL. 1975. "The Development of Teacher Education." In *Teacher Education,* Seventy-fourth Yearbook of the National Society for the Study of Education, ed. Kevin Ryan. Chicago: University of Chicago Press.

ZIMPHER, NANCY, and SHERRILL, JULIE. 1996. "Professors, Teachers, and Leaders in SCDES." In *Handbook of Research on Teacher Education,* ed. John Sikula. New York: Simon and Schuster.

INTERNET RESOURCE

GETTYSBURG COLLEGE SPECIAL COLLECTIONS. 2002. *The New England Primer* (1805). <www.

gettysburg.edu/~tshannon/his341/colonial
amer.htm>.

EDWARD R. DUCHARME
MARY K. DUCHARME

INTERNATIONAL PERSPECTIVE

In 1995 there were approximately 46 million primary and secondary school teachers in the world's formal education systems. A little more than 3 million
of them were in the United States and Canada.

Initial teacher education throughout the world
has five main features, all representing decisions regarding key issues. These are: recruitment, curriculum, structure, governance, and accreditation and
standards. This article focuses on the first three issues.

Recruitment

Among the most important features of teacher education are the criteria and procedures by which candidates are selected or recruited for entry to
programs and institutions. Unlike some other professions, teaching often suffers from a shortage of
qualified candidates for admission. Therefore, teaching often does not enjoy the privilege of being able
to select the best qualified from among a large pool
of applicants. The problem for a system is, first, ensuring that there is a large enough pool of qualified
graduates to meet the needs of the professions and,
second, attracting enough qualified applicants to
enter teaching in competition with the other professions.

How much schooling should a candidate for admission to teacher education have? How valuable are
experiences outside school for prospective teachers?
If the demand for fully qualified applicants for admission to teacher education programs is greater
than the supply, are there alternative qualifications
that might satisfy the demand? These are some of the
issues confronted in attempts made to recruit candidates for entry to teaching. Factors influencing recruitment include the status of the teaching
profession; the supply of, and demand for, teachers;
and the economic resources of the system.

An example of the status of the profession affecting recruitment can be seen in Thailand. In 1996
it was reported that the low status of the teaching
profession in Thailand was discouraging competent
people from entering teaching and that some en-

trants were not seriously committed to becoming
teachers. For Thailand, therefore, the need to improve the status of teaching and to provide other incentives for joining the profession was important.

Raymond Bolam pointed out that the career
structure of the profession is also influential, contrasting the situation in the United Kingdom, where
a head teacher might earn four times as much as a
beginning teacher, with the situation in Spain, where
head teachers received only a small increase in salary
above that of their colleagues. Presumably, in Spain,
candidates motivated by prospects of economic advancement are less likely to enter teaching than they
are in the United Kingdom, other things being equal.

Another important aspect of recruitment concerns the number of years of schooling candidates
have completed before entry to training institutions.
While in most developed countries completion of a
full eleven or twelve years of schooling is a normal
requirement, that is an unrealistic expectation in a
country that is unable to produce a sufficient number of such graduates to meet its needs for teachers.
Toward the end of the twentieth century, in the central and south Asian countries of Afghanistan, Pakistan, India, Sri Lanka, Bangladesh, and Nepal, the
mean number of years of schooling required before
entry to teacher training was 10.7 years. In the
southeast Asian countries of Thailand, Malaysia,
Singapore, Indonesia, and the Philippines, it was
10.5 years, while in the Latin American countries of
Brazil, Chile, Cuba, Peru, Venezuela, and Colombia,
it was 9.3 years. In the African countries of Algeria,
Ghana, Nigeria, Ivory Coast, Morocco, and Kenya,
the mean was 9.6 years.

This is not to say that the only qualifications accepted for entry to teacher education are the number
of years of schooling or level of academic achievement. In some countries, candidates are recruited
without completing the full secondary education
available because of their valuable experience in
other types of activities beyond formal schooling,
such as employment and community development
work, and their strong motivation to become teachers. In Australia, for example, universities like the
University of Sydney offer such candidates programs
specially designed to take advantage of their
strengths.

Structure

Most systems provide teacher education in face-to-
face situations to students attending institutions of

higher education. However, many teachers around the world receive substantial components of their training through distance education. Beginning near the end of the 1950s, this approach involved the use of postal services for the delivery of learning materials to students remote from an institution, and the sending back of completed assignments by the students. The correspondence elements of this model were supplemented with tutorials conducted at centers located within reach of enough students to form a group. On a number of occasions tutors would meet with the groups to render the process in more motivating social contexts and to deal with students at a more personal level. Sometimes students traveled to the campuses for residential schools. Telephone hook-ups were also arranged by land line or even satellite. Two Australian universities, the University of New England and the University of Queensland, pioneered this approach to distance teacher education. As technical electronic advances occurred with the introduction of personal computers and electronic mail the process became much faster and more efficient. Distance education is a relatively inexpensive approach that is especially useful in locations where populations are sparse and distances are great.

The duration of teacher education programs varies across systems from a year or less to four or even five years. That range exists in quite a variety of countries and seems not always to depend on the economic development level of the countries concerned. Among the African developing countries of Algeria, Ghana, Nigeria, Ivory Coast, Morocco, and Kenya, the range in 1990 was from one to five years. In Australia, recruits who have completed three- or four-year university bachelor's degrees can complete a professional teaching qualification in one year, while most choose to enter teaching immediately after completing secondary schooling and then take up to four years to complete a bachelor of education degree.

The crucial factor is the foundation on which the professional training is based. Sometimes systems try to compensate for lack of a full secondary education in its recruits by adding time to the training program in which to supply missing knowledge and skills. However, this can increase the costs of teacher education to prohibitive levels.

One of the chief controversies in initial teacher education in more developed countries in the second half of the twentieth century was whether pro-

fessional components of programs should be offered concurrently with academic components or consecutively. It became commonly accepted that concurrent programs were preferable. However, fluctuations in teacher supply and demand, and the demands of other programs in universities often resulted in decisions being adopted on the basis of practicalities rather than ideals, so that consecutive programs began to take precedence. Continuous, or concurrent, programs tend to introduce professional components early and in close association with general education and specialist academic studies. Consecutive programs, sometimes called "end-on" programs, delay the introduction of professional components until general and specialist studies have been completed.

Especially controversial during the 1970s, 1980s, and 1990s were the relationships between the university or college offering the programs and the schools for which the student teachers were being prepared. Traditionally, schools provided professional experiences during the *practicum* component of the program, perhaps for up to three periods of three or four weeks a year. However, the role of the schools in initial teacher education generally became greater during those decades. In some cases, the school became the locus of the program, with student teachers being based in schools rather than in universities or colleges. Crucial to this controversy was the role of experienced teachers employed in the schools. Whereas it had been more usual for them to act as advisers and supervisors of initial school experience, they now sometimes undertook much more onerous responsibilities, such as designing and coordinating the whole program, with universities providing a supporting role and awarding the final qualification.

The types of institutions offering initial teacher education programs also vary from system to system. In some places, teacher education, especially at the elementary level, is offered in single purpose, state-run or private colleges known often as teachers colleges or colleges of education. In other countries, teacher education is offered by multipurpose institutions, sometimes called polytechnics, which are tertiary education institutions emphasizing training for a variety of occupations, for example paramedical services, occupational therapy, and journalism. During the 1990s both England and Australia restructured their higher education systems so that all such institutions became new universities or additional components of existing universities.

All of these institutions work in conjunction with early childhood, elementary, and secondary schools, which provide practice teaching experiences for teacher education students.

Curriculum

What do student teachers need to learn in order to become effective teachers in the contexts in which they will be employed? That is the most fundamental of all the questions that can be asked about teacher education. Initial teacher education programs usually have five strands: general education, specialist subjects, education foundation studies, professional studies, and the practicum, including practice teaching.

General education programs attempt to ensure that intending teachers have a sound grounding in the predominant knowledge, attitudes, and values of the cultures in which they are preparing to teach. General studies in history, the arts, science, mathematics, philosophy, ethics, government, psychology, and sociology are common components of this strand.

Specialist subjects involve studies in depth, which qualify students to teach specific areas of knowledge. Literature and literacy, languages, history, geography, mathematics, science, computing, domestic science, physical education, and industrial arts are examples. Student teachers preparing to teach in elementary schools are usually expected to teach a broader range of content, whereas postelementary teachers are usually more specialized.

Education foundation studies include studies of the history of educational thought, principles of learning and teaching, human growth and development, comparative education, and sociology of education. Curriculum and instruction subjects provide units on principles and practice of planning, delivering and assessing learning experiences for students and include such matters as programming, classroom management skills, test construction, individualizing instruction, small group teaching methods, laboratory instruction, and cooperative learning techniques.

In some systems, the distinction between these theoretical and applied learnings is eschewed on the grounds that theoretical studies have little relevance to newcomers unless they are seen to arise from practice, and attempts are made to integrate the two. This was well exemplified in England in 1992, when, partly on the grounds that the content of teacher education was too theoretical, Kenneth Clarke, then the Secretary of State for Education, announced that 80 percent of programs in secondary teacher education should be "school-based." In North America, Bruce Joyce and Beverly Showers, among others, called for a more central role of the school in teacher education. A somewhat similar complaint about the excess of theory in the curriculum of teacher education programs was reported in 1991 by Andrea B. Rugh and colleagues with reference to Pakistan, and in 1986 by Linda A. Dove regarding Papua New Guinea.

In some parts of the world, the role of the teacher is wider than in others and the curriculum of teacher education is adjusted accordingly. In 1991 Beatrice Avalos described situations in Tanzania and Papua New Guinea that are useful examples of the risks encountered in such widening of the curriculum. In Tanzania, adherence was given to the belief that education should produce citizens who were self-reliant, especially as most children would not receive more than a basic education. Schools were to be community schools that inculcated "socialist" work habits; were self-supporting financially; emphasized knowledge and skills useful to the village or rural community; and encouraged the participation of the community in school activities. Pursuit of these goals necessitated a broadening of the teacher education curriculum at the same time as the length of the program was shortened in order to produce graduates more quickly. In consequence of these changes, the curriculum became overcrowded and content-centered with little time for practical components. Avalos claimed that the teachers did not even achieve sufficient competence to teach basic literacy and numeracy, and concluded that great caution needs to be exerted in training teachers for more than one purpose.

Providing actual teaching experience in real school situations (the practicum) is one of the most challenging tasks for planners of teacher education. Traditionally, in the elementary school context, the student teacher was placed with a volunteer school teacher and would be assigned lessons to design, prepare, and present under that teacher's guidance. Usually these lessons would number about three per day, after an initial period of orientation and observation, for about three weeks each year of the program. The teacher would provide feedback on a selection of those lessons but, in order to develop confidence and independence, would not be present for all of the lessons, especially toward the end of the period of practice teaching. The college or university in which the student teacher was enrolled would usually appoint one of its own faculty to supervise this process and that person would visit and observe the student teacher on several occasions and would have the responsibility of reporting on progress and awarding a grade, after discussing the experience with both the student and the cooperating teacher. Student teachers would often have other assignments to complete as well as those involving face-to-face teaching. For example, they might be required to establish a file on school organization and curriculum resources in the school. In the context of the secondary school, in which the student teacher might be obtaining experience in a number of specialist subject areas involving more than one school department, a corresponding number of cooperating teachers and college or university supervisors might be appointed.

This traditional approach to the practicum has been criticized on the grounds that it militates against bridging the gap between theory and practice, when the two might be learned more effectively if integrated. In some cases the problem was approached by trying to make the university or college the site of more practically orientated school experiences. Thus, such innovations as laboratory schools were established at the university. Over the last three decades of the twentieth century, the bridge was sought in the form of simulations, such as microteaching. Microteaching usually occurred on the campus of the college or university. It consisted of scaled-down teaching situations in which shorter than normal lessons would be taught to smaller groups of students with limited numbers of teaching skills to be practiced in pursuit of a small number of learning objectives. Usually, teaching spaces were developed and built specifically for the environment of microteaching. The lessons would be videotaped, so that the student teacher could view the lesson, often in consultation with peers and a supervisor or mentor, and obtain feedback which could be used in replanning the lessons.

While the controlled context in which microteaching occurs has facilitated much research on its effectiveness, there has been concern about the extent to which skills developed under microteaching conditions are transferred to normal classroom situations. It has been argued that there is no adequate substitute for real experience in normal classrooms and seldom, if ever, was reliance placed on microteaching as a complete substitute for actual classroom experience. Indeed, some systems have sought to make school experience the central component of teacher education in what has become known as "school-based teacher education" or, at least, by providing much more enduring periods of school experience at some stage of the teacher education program. A medical model has sometimes been applied, with student teachers approaching the end of their programs becoming "interns" attached to schools for a semester, or even a year.

Critics often claimed that professional experiences gained through such innovations as microteaching and such models as "performance-based" or "competency-based" teacher education gave too much emphasis to the "performance" or "behavioral" aspects of teaching at the expense of insight and reflection. Accordingly, calls for more reflective approaches were made and were accepted. The concept of reflective teacher education generated much literature in the 1980s and 1990s. In 1998, Marvin Wideen and colleagues, after an extensive review of research on the effectiveness of innovations in teacher education, including reflective practice, found little encouragement for their adoption, and concluded that such innovations have little ability to affect beginning teachers within teacher education structures common at the end of the twentieth century.

Challenges

Major challenges for initial teacher education in the twenty-first century include:

1. The raising of the status of the teaching profession to a level at which it attracts the best qualified applicants.

2. Harnessing rapidly developing technology to provide maximum learning opportunities for student teachers, especially those in remote areas and those in developing countries, where conventional resources such as libraries are impossible to resource adequately.

3. Discovering the optimum balance between theory and practice in the curriculum of teacher education in the many and varying contexts in which it is provided.

4. Developing teacher education structures and

curricula that provide optimal balances among the academic, humanitarian, aesthetic, and moral domains of human experience.

5. Designing research that takes account of the many complex factors that impinge upon the process of teacher education, so that a greater understanding may be gained of the ways in which students learn to teach in the myriad of contexts in which they live.

See also: ELEMENTARY EDUCATION, *subentry on* PREPARATION OF TEACHERS; TEACHER PREPARATION, INTERNATIONAL PERSPECTIVE.

BIBLIOGRAPHY

AVALOS, BEATRICE. 1991. *Approaches to Teacher Education: Initial Teacher Training.* London: Commonwealth Secretariat.

BEN-PERETZ, MIRIAM. 1995. "Curriculum of Teacher Education Programs." In *International Encyclopedia of Teaching and Teacher Education,* 2nd edition, ed. Lorin W. Anderson. Oxford: Pergamon.

BOLAM, RAYMOND. 1995. "Teacher Recruitment and Induction." In *The International Encyclopedia of Teaching and Teacher Education,* 2nd edition, ed. Lorin W. Anderson. Oxford: Pergamon.

E. ANNE WILLIAMS. 1995. "An English Perspective on Change in Initial Teacher Education." *Asia Pacific Journal of Teacher Education* 23:5–16.

DOVE, LINDA A. 1986. *Teachers and Teacher Education in Developing Countries.* London: Croom Helm.

GHANI, ZULKIPLE ABD. 1990. "Pre-service Teacher Education in Developing Countries." In *Teachers and Teaching in the Developing World,* ed. Val D. Rust and Per Dalin. New York: Garland.

JOYCE, BRUCE, and SHOWERS, BEVERLY. 1995. *Student Achievement through Staff Development: Fundamentals of School Renewal,* 2nd edition. New York: Longman.

JUDGE, HARRY, et al., ed. 1994. *Oxford Studies in Comparative Education,* Vol. 4: *The University and the Teachers: France, the United States, England.* Wallingford, Eng.: Triangle Books.

RUGH, ANDREA B.; MALIK, AHMED M.; and FAROOQ, R. A. 1991. *Bridges Report Series, No. 8: Teaching Practices to Increase Student Achievement: Evidence from Pakistan.* Cambridge, MA: Harvard University.

UNITED NATIONS EDUCATIONAL, SCIENTIFIC AND CULTURAL ORGANIZATION (UNESCO). 1998. *World Education Report: Teachers and Teaching in a Changing World.* Paris: UNESCO Publishing.

WIDEEN, MARVIN; MAYER-SMITH, JOLIE; and MOON, BARBARA. 1998. "A Critical Analysis of the Research on Learning to Teach: Making the Case for an Ecological Perspective on Inquiry." *Review of Educational Research* 68:130–178.

MICHAEL J. DUNKIN

TEACHER EMPLOYMENT

By 2005 America's schools will be serving more children (54 million) than ever before, and the total number of teachers will have grown to more than 3.5 million (up from 2.5 million in 1980). Because of rising student enrollments, growing numbers of teacher retirements, the reduction of class sizes, new curriculum requirements, and high rates of attrition among beginning teachers, the United States will need to hire 2 million new teachers by 2010.

Despite reports of shortages in some areas, the United States annually produces many more new teachers than its schools hire. Nevertheless, only about 60 percent of newly prepared teachers nationwide actually teach after they graduate.

Still, there is a stark maldistribution of qualified teachers. Many schools are hiring increasing numbers of teachers from nontraditional routes into teaching, many of which offer very little preparation or mentoring support. Furthermore, teachers report that they cannot find jobs because they are not trained to teach in subjects and/or in geographic areas where vacancies exist or they are not willing to work for the salaries offered or where poor working conditions are present.

To be sure, noncompetitive salaries and inadequate incentives contribute to the nation's teacher recruitment problems. The average teacher salary was $40,574 in 1999. When accounting for inflation, however, the 1999 average salary gave teachers only a $135 raise from the average earned in 1972.

Improving salaries is critical but not sufficient to address teacher supply, demand, and quality issues. Most districts and states lack a coherent teaching policy framework that can link the ways teachers are recruited, prepared, inducted, evaluated, paid, developed, and retained. This entry outlines the latest trends in teacher supply and demand, licensure, and other employment policies that bear on these matters.

Inequities in Who Is Taught by Whom

In some communities, especially in high-poverty urban and rural locations, schools report increasing difficulties in recruiting qualified teachers in critical subject areas such as physical science, mathematics, bilingual education, and special education. As a result, schools often assign teachers outside of the field in which they have prepared. For example, in 1994, 28 percent of mathematics teachers and 55 percent of physical science teachers did not have the equivalent of a college minor in the subjects they were teaching.

Across the nation there is a need for more teachers of color to meet schools' desires for a teaching force that reflects growing student diversity. The teaching profession continues to be about three-fourths female and white. While only 13 percent of teachers are minorities, nearly one-third of the students are minorities. About 15 percent of students in teacher preparation are individuals of color—but, if past trends hold true, only two thirds of these will find their way into teaching.

In 1996 William Sanders and June Rivers found that African-American students are nearly twice as likely to be assigned to the most ineffective teachers and about half as likely to be assigned to the most effective teachers; poor children and those of color are more likely to be assigned out-of-field, lesser prepared, and nonlicensed teachers than their counterparts. Schools serving larger numbers of low-income students offer teachers fewer salary schedules and poorer teaching conditions (e.g., class sizes, availability of supplies and materials) than those who serve more affluent schools. Ronald Ferguson found in 1991 that academically able teachers were less likely to teach in lower socioeconomic schools unless salaries were raised. Beginning salaries can make a difference in terms of the numbers and quality of teachers recruited and in commitment to teaching.

Recruiting High-Quality Teachers

Newly licensed teachers have been found to be more academically qualified than those who enter without preparation. A 2001 review of teacher certification studies has shown that teachers who entered without preparation had lower scores on teacher tests. These numbers and findings stand in stark contrast to reports that surfaced in the 1980s, indicating that prospective teachers were disproportionately drawn from the bottom quartile of college students.

Yesterday's standards of teacher quality may not be tomorrow's standards. Growing evidence suggests that effective teachers must possess content-specific pedagogical knowledge—that is, they must have knowledge not only of the subjects they are assigned to teach but also of how to teach their content in different ways that make sense to increasingly diverse students. Given growing student diversity, teachers of all grades and subjects need to know how to teach literacy skills and respond to the needs of second-language learners or students with learning disabilities.

Preparing and Supporting Teachers

The extent to which teachers are well-prepared and the degree to which newly hired teachers are supported and assessed in their initial years of teaching can determine whether they remain in teaching and are effective over time. While as many as 30 percent of new teachers leave within five years, high-quality preparation combined with induction programs lowers attrition and enhances effectiveness. New teachers who have had student teaching are twice as likely to stay in teaching for more than five years. Graduates of five-year preparation programs are more self-assured and highly rated and have lower attrition rates than those from four-year programs in the same institutions. Teachers who have left the profession point not only to poor salaries but also to poor working conditions as having the most detrimental impact on their decision to leave teaching. They cite problems with administrative support and leadership, student behavior, school atmosphere, and a lack of autonomy.

Hiring and Selecting Teachers

School districts do not always hire the most qualified and highly ranked teachers in their applicant pools because of inadequate management information systems and hiring procedures that discourage good applicants for several reasons: the large numbers of steps in the application process, demeaning treatment, and lack of timely action. Some prospective teachers report that they decided not to enter teaching after having their files lost, experiencing interviews in which their qualifications were barely reviewed, failing to receive responses to repeated requests for information, and receiving late notification of job availability. These problems have been particularly acute in large urban districts. Other problematic practices that hinder the hiring of the best candidates include: (1) salary caps on experienced candidates, (2) cumbersome interstate licensure reciprocity, (3) limited ability to transfer pension benefits for mobile teachers, and (4) placement of beginning teachers in the most difficult assignments. While some school districts have eliminated these problems by professionalizing teaching and investing more in teachers, these lessons have not translated easily to other school districts.

Teacher Licensure and Certification

In the 1990s twenty-five states created new standards for teacher licensure. By the early twenty-first century, forty-three states were testing teachers, using almost 600 different tests. In 2001 the National Academy of Sciences found that even the relatively well-developed tests do not provide adequate information for distinguishing moderately from highly qualified teachers. Current teacher tests are designed to assess limited competencies, and states use a variety of unclear methods to set passing scores.

Several states are working to create three-tiered licensure systems based upon more rigorous standards. By 2002 only Connecticut had fully implemented such a system, and did so in combination with substantial salary increases. Indiana was in the process of mirroring the Connecticut system. Ohio and Georgia are using a standardized classroom observation system as part of its process, while North Carolina is devising its own portfolio system to assess new teachers. Most states still use simple paper and pencil tests.

In addition, more than 115 alternative certification programs are operating in forty states. While some of these programs expect teachers to meet the same standards as those in traditional certification programs, many do not. For example, in Texas, where about 17 percent of new hires come from alternative routes, there are no SAT score minimums, no requirements to have a content major in the field the teacher will be teaching, and virtually no mentoring guidelines. Studies show that alternative programs have added minorities and men to the teaching ranks in urban areas. A 1997 analysis by Jianping Shen, however, revealed that those who entered teaching through short-term alternate routes had lower academic qualifications, were less likely to stay in teaching, and were more likely to be teaching in inner-city schools that serve more economically disadvantaged students.

Regular certification standards vary widely across the states as well. Some states, such as Connecticut, require a master's degree in addition to a strong subject matter degree, substantial education course work, and a lengthy internship, for a full standard certification. Meanwhile, other states, such as Louisiana, do not require a minor in the field to be taught and specify few education course-work hours or clinical training demands.

States that hold high teaching standards, however, do not necessarily enforce them. For example, 67 percent of all mathematics teachers nationwide in 1994 had a major in mathematics and held full state certification; more than 80 percent met this standard in Minnesota and Wisconsin, while only 39 percent did in Alaska.

Teacher Evaluation and Compensation

States often do not have a standard teacher evaluation process. Principals often have little training in evaluation and find it difficult to balance evaluation with other responsibilities. Inadequate teacher evaluations contribute to difficulty in dismissing ineffective teachers. In the early twenty-first century, more states are passing legislation to create new standards-based evaluation systems, some with measures of student improvement. Value-added student assessments are being considered for teacher evaluation and pay systems, although a number of technical issues need to be resolved.

New salary plans are beginning to emerge. In early 2000 the Cincinnati school district and teacher unions crafted a plan for overhauling teachers' career paths, using standards established by the National Board for Professional Teaching Standards (NBPTS). The process includes administrators and peer review, along with detailed portfolios focused on student and teacher learning. Teachers can advance on a career ladder and earn an additional $9,000. In 2000 Iowa passed a $40 million package that frames new teaching standards, reinvents the evaluation system, and creates a bonus plan for teachers. Teachers will be able earn substantially more, but many issues are yet to be resolved, including how principals, many of whom supervise at least forty teachers each, will have time to conduct valid evaluations.

Supported by new research linking NBPTS certification to improved student learning, forty-four states established policies to encourage teachers to receive NBPTS certification. In about half of the states and about eighty-five districts, teachers receive salary supplements for completion. Some states are offering up to $7,500 annual bonuses to those who have earned certification, and in California, National Board Certified Teachers can earn an additional $20,000 (over four years) by teaching in low-performing schools. These policies are quite new and represent groundbreaking developments in dismantling the traditional lockstep teacher salary schedule.

Proactive and coherent teacher development policies help ensure an adequate supply of well-qualified teachers. At the state level, Connecticut took significant strides to recruit and retain qualified teachers in 1986. By raising and equalizing beginning salaries, while simultaneously raising standards for teacher education and licensing and introducing a well-managed teacher induction program, the state eliminated shortages and created a surplus of teachers by 1990. The state has few unqualified teachers teaching in its public schools and posted some of the highest student achievement gains on the National Assessment of Educational Progress.

The overall problem is not a shortage of people willing to consider teaching but an array of labor, market, and occupational factors. Wealthy districts that pay high salaries and offer good working conditions rarely experience shortages. Districts that have more difficulty recruiting and retaining teachers tend to serve low-income students, pay teachers less, offer larger class sizes and pupil loads, provide fewer materials, and present less desirable working conditions, including less professional autonomy. Thus, teacher supply should not be evaluated in terms of gross numbers of teachers needed in relation to gross demand, but in terms of specific qualifications and characteristics of the teaching force and in terms of the demands of schooling all of the nation's students well.

See also: TEACHER EDUCATION; TEACHER EVALUATION.

BIBLIOGRAPHY

AMERICAN FEDERATION OF TEACHERS. 2000. *Survey and Analysis of Teacher Salary Trends, 2000.* Washington, DC: American Federation of Teachers.

ANDREW, MICHAEL, and SCHWAB, RICHARD L. 1995. "Has Reform in Teacher Education Influenced Teacher Performance? An Outcome Assessment of Graduates of Eleven Teacher Education Programs." *Action in Teacher Education* 17:43–53.

BAINES, LAWRENCE; MCDOWELL, JACKIE; and FOULK, DAVID. 2001. "One Step Forward, Three Steps Backward: Alternative Certification Programs in Texas, Georgia, and Florida." *Educational Horizons* (fall):32–37.

BERLINER, DAVID C. 1986. "In Pursuit of the Expert Pedagogue." *Educational Researcher* 15(7):5–13.

BOLAM, RAY. 1995. "Teacher Recruitment and Induction." In *The International Encyclopedia of Teaching and Teacher Education,* ed. Lorin W. Anderson. Oxford: Elsevier Science.

BOLICH, ANJANETTE M. 2001. *Reduce Your Losses: Help New Teachers Become Veteran Teachers.* Atlanta, GA: Southern Regional Education Board.

BOND, LLOYD.; SMITH, TRACY W.; BAKER, WANDA K.; and HATTIE, JOHN A. 2000. *The Certification System of the National Board for Professional Teaching Standards: A Construct and Consequential Validity Study.* Greensboro: University of North Carolina, Center for Educational Research and Evaluation.

DARLING-HAMMOND, LINDA. 1997. *Doing What Matters Most: Investing in Quality Teaching.* New York: National Commission on Teaching and America's Future.

DARLING-HAMMOND, LINDA. 2000. *Solving the Dilemmas of Teacher Supply and Quality: Policies to Ensure a Caring and Competent Teacher for Every Child.* New York: National Commission on Teaching and America's Future.

DARLING-HAMMOND, LINDA. 2001. *The Research and Rhetoric on Teacher Certification: A Response to "Teacher Certification Reconsidered."* New York: National Commission on Teaching and America's Future.

DARLING-HAMMOND, LINDA, and BERRY, BARNETT. 1999. *Teacher Supply and Demand.* Washington, DC: American Council of Education.

DARLING-HAMMOND, LINDA; WISE, ARTHUR E.; and KLEIN, STEVE P. 1995. *A License to Teach: Building a Profession for Twenty-First Century Schools.* Boulder, CO: Westview Press.

DENTON, JON J., and PETERS, WILLIAM H. 1988. *Program Assessment Report: Curriculum Evaluation of a Non-traditional Program for Certifying Teachers.* College Station: Texas A&M University.

FEISTRITZER, EMILY. 2000. *Alternative Teacher Certification: A State-by-State Analysis.* Washington, DC: National Center for Education Information.

FERGUSON, RONALD. 1991. "Paying for Public Education: New Evidence on How and Why Money Matters." *Harvard Journal on Legislation* 28:465–498.

GRAY, LUCINDA; CAHALAN, MARGARET; HEIN, S.; LITMAN, C.; SEVERYNSE, J.; WARREN, S.; WISAN, G.; and STOWE, PETER. 1993. *New Teachers in the Job Market: 1991 Update.* Washington, DC: U.S. Department of Education, Office of Educational Research and Improvement.

GREENWALD, RONALD; HEDGES, LARRY V.; and LAINE, RICHARD D. 1996. "The Effect of School Resources on Student Achievement." *Review of Educational Research* 66:361–396.

HANUSHEK, ERIC A. 1989. "The Impact of Differential Expenditures on Student Performance." *Educational Researcher* 18(4):45–52.

HANUSHEK, ERIC A.; KAIN, JOHN; and RIFKIN, STEVEN G. 2002. *Why Public Schools Lose Teachers.* Washington, DC: National Bureau of Economic Research.

HENKE, ROBIN R.; CHEN, XIANGLEI; GEIS, SONYA; and KNEPPER, PAULA. 2000. *Progress through the Teacher Pipeline: 1992–93 College Graduates and Elementary/Secondary School Teaching as of 1997.* Washington, DC: U.S. Department of Education, National Center for Education Statistics.

HIRSCH, ERIC. 2001. *Teacher Recruitment: Staffing Classrooms with Quality Teachers. A Report of the SHEEO Project Enhancing the Teaching Profession: The Importance of Mobility to Recruitment and Retention.* Denver, CO: National Conference of State Legislatures.

INGERSOLL, RICHARD. 1998. "The Problem of Out-of-Field Teaching." *Phi Delta Kappan* 79:773–776.

INGERSOLL, RICHARD. 2001. *A Different Approach to Solving the Teacher Shortage Problem.* Seattle: University of Washington, Center for the Study of Teaching and Policy.

JACOBSON, STEVEN. 1988. "The Effects of Pay Incentives on Teacher Absenteeism." *Journal of Human Resources* 24:280–286.

NATIONAL ACADEMY OF SCIENCES. 2001. *Testing Teacher Candidates: The Role of Licensure Tests in Improving Teacher Quality.* Washington, DC: National Academy of Sciences.

NATIONAL COMMISSION ON TEACHING AND AMERICA'S FUTURE. 1996. *What Matters Most: Teaching for America's Future.* New York: Columbia University, Teachers College.

NATIONAL EDUCATION ASSOCIATION. 1992. *Status of the American Public School Teacher, 1990–91.* Washington, DC: National Education Association.

RICHARDS, CRAIG. 1988. "State Regulation of Entry Level Teacher Salaries: Policy Issues and Options." *Educational Policy* 2:307–322.

SANDERS, WILLIAM, and RIVERS, JUNE C. 1996. *Cumulative and Residual Effects of Teachers on Future Student Academic Achievement.* Knoxville: University of Tennessee, Value-Added Research and Assessment Center.

SCHLECTY, PHIL, and VANCE, VICTOR. 1983. "Recruitment, Selection, and Retention: The Shape of the Teaching Force." *Elementary School Journal* 83:469–487.

SHEN, JIANPING. 1997. "Has the Alternative Certification Policy Materialized Its Promise? A Comparison of Traditionally and Alternatively Certified Teachers in Public Schools." *Educational Evaluation and Policy Analyses* 19:276–283.

SNYDER, JON. 1999. *New Haven Unified School District: A Teaching Quality System for Excellence and Equity.* New York: National Commission on Teaching and America's Future.

STANFORD RESEARCH INTERNATIONAL. 2001. *The Status of the Teaching Profession, 2000: An Update to the Teaching and California's Future Task Force.* Santa Cruz, CA: Center for the Future of Teaching and Learning.

U.S. BUREAU OF THE CENSUS. 1998. *Current Population Survey.* Washington, DC: U.S. Bureau of the Census.

U.S. DEPARTMENT OF EDUCATION, NATIONAL CENTER FOR EDUCATION STATISTICS. 1999. *Digest of Education Statistics.* Washington, DC: U.S. Department of Education, National Center for Education Statistics.

WILSON, SUZANNE; DARLING-HAMMOND, LINDA; and BERRY, BARNETT. 2001. *A Case of Successful Teaching Policy: Connecticut's Long Term Efforts to Improve Teaching and Learning.* Seattle: University of Washington, Center for the Study of Teaching and Policy.

WISE, ARTHUR E.; DARLING-HAMMOND, LINDA; and BERRY, BARNETT. 1987. *Effective Teacher Selection: From Recruitment to Retention.* Santa Monica, CA: RAND.

BARNETT BERRY

TEACHER EVALUATION

OVERVIEW
  Robert F. McNergney
  Scott R. Imig
METHODS
  Mari A. Pearlman

OVERVIEW

Baseball is known as the national pastime of the United States, but teacher evaluation beats it hands down. Everybody does it—some with a vengeance, others with the casual disregard that physical and emotional distance afford. Most enthusiasts grow up with the game, playing a sandlot version as they go through school. Indeed, familiarity with the job of teaching and the widespread practice of judging teachers has shaped the history of teacher evaluation.

History of Teacher Evaluation

Donald Medley, Homer Coker, and Robert Soar (1984) describe succinctly the modern history of formal teacher evaluation—that period from the turn of the twentieth century to about 1980. This history might be divided into three overlapping periods: (1) The Search for Great Teachers; (2) Inferring Teacher Quality from Student Learning; and (3) Examining Teaching Performance. At the beginning of the twenty-first century, teacher evaluation appears to be entering a new phase of disequilibrium; that is, a transition to a period of Evaluating Teaching as Professional Behavior.

The *Search for Great Teachers* began in earnest in 1896 with the report of a study conducted by H. E. Kratz. Kratz asked 2,411 students from the second through the eighth grades in Sioux City, Iowa, to describe the characteristics of their best teachers. Kratz thought that by making desirable characteristics explicit he could establish a benchmark against which all teachers might be judged. Some 87 percent of those young Iowans mentioned "helpfulness" as the most important teacher characteristic. But a stunning 58 percent mentioned "personal appearance" as the next most influential factor.

Arvil Barr's 1948 compendium of research on teaching competence noted that supervisors' ratings of teachers were the metric of choice. A few researchers, however, examined average gains in student achievement for the purpose of *Inferring Teacher Quality from Student Learning.* They assumed, for good reason, that supervisors' opinions of teachers revealed little or nothing about student learning. Indeed, according to Medley and his colleagues, these early findings were "most discouraging." The average correlation between teacher characteristics and student learning, as measured most often by achievement tests, was zero. Some characteristics related positively to student achievement gains in one study and negatively in another study. Most showed no relation at all. Simeon J. Domas and David Tiedeman (1950) reviewed more than 1,000 studies of teacher characteristics, defined in nearly every way imaginable, and found no clear direction for evaluators. Jacob Getzels and Philip Jackson (1963) called once and for all for an end to research and evaluation aimed at linking teacher characteristics to student learning, arguing it was an idea without merit.

Medley and his colleagues note several reasons for the failure of early efforts to judge teachers by student outcomes. First, student achievement varied, and relying on average measures of achievement masked differences. Second, researchers failed to control for the regression effect in student achievement—extreme high and low scores automatically regress toward the mean in second administrations of tests. Third, achievement tests were, for a variety of reasons, poor measures of student success. Perhaps most important, as the researchers who ushered in the period of *Examining Teaching Performance* were to suggest, these early approaches were conceptually inadequate, and even misleading. Student learning as measured by standardized achievement tests simply did not depend on a teacher's education, intelligence, gender, age, personality, attitudes, or any other personal attribute. What mattered was how teachers behaved when they were in classrooms.

The period of *Examining Teaching Performance* abandoned efforts to identify desirable teacher characteristics and concentrated instead on identifying effective teaching behaviors; that is, those behaviors that were linked to student learning. The tack was to describe clearly and precisely teaching behaviors and relate them to student learning—as measured most often by standardized achievement test scores. In rare instances, researchers conducted experiments for the purpose of arguing that certain teaching behaviors actually caused student learning. Like Kratz a century earlier, these investigators assumed that "principles of effective teaching" would serve as new and improved benchmarks for guiding both the evaluation and education of teachers. Jere Brophy and Thomas Good produced the most conceptually elaborate and useful description of this work in 1986, while Marjorie Powell and Joseph Beard's 1984 extensive bibliography of research done from 1965 to 1980 is a useful reference.

Goals of Teacher Evaluation

Although there are multiple goals of teacher evaluation, they are perhaps most often described as either *formative* or *summative* in nature. Formative evaluation consists of evaluation practices meant to shape, form, or improve teachers' performances. Clinical supervisors observe teachers, collect data on teaching behavior, organize these data, and share the results in conferences with the teachers observed. The supervisors' intent is to help teachers improve their practice. In contrast, summative evaluation, as the term implies, has as its aim the development and use of data to inform summary judgments of teachers. A principal observes teachers in action, works with them on committees, examines their students' work, talks with parents, and the like. These actions, aimed at least in part at obtaining evaluative information about teachers' work, inform the principal's decision to recommend teachers either for continuing a teacher's contract or for termination of employment. Decisions about initial licensure, hiring, promoting, rewarding, and terminating are examples of the class of summative evaluation decisions.

The goals of summative and formative evaluation may not be so different as they appear at first glance. If an evaluator is examining teachers collectively in a school system, some summary judgments of individuals might be considered formative in

terms of improving the teaching staff as a whole. For instance, the summative decision to add a single strong teacher to a group of other strong teachers results in improving the capacity and value of the whole staff.

In a slightly different way, individual performance and group performance affect discussions of merit and worth. *Merit* deals with the notion of how a single teacher measures up on some scale of desirable characteristics. Does the person exhibit motivating behavior in the classroom? Does she take advantage of opportunities to continue professional development? Do her students do well on standardized achievement tests? If the answers to these types of questions are "yes," then the teacher might be said to be "meritorious." Assume for a moment that the same teacher is one of six members of a high school social studies team in a rural school district. Assume also that one of the two physics teachers just quit, the special education population is growing rapidly, and the state education department recently replaced one social science requirement for graduation with a computer science requirement. Given these circumstances, the meritorious teacher might not add much value to the school system; that is, other teachers, even less meritorious ones, might be worth more to the system.

The example of the meritorious teacher suggests yet another important distinction in processes of evaluating teachers: the difference between *domain-referenced* and *norm-referenced* teacher evaluation. When individual teachers are compared to a set of externally derived, publicly expressed standards, as in the case of merit decisions, the process is one of domain-referenced evaluation. What counts is how the teacher compares to the benchmarks of success identified in a particular domain of professional behavior. In contrast, norm-referenced teacher evaluation consists of grouping teachers' scores on a given set of measures and describing these scores in relation to one another. What is the mean score of the group? What is the range or standard deviation of the scores? What is shape of the distribution of the scores? These questions emanate from a norm-referenced perspective—one often adopted in initial certification or licensure decisions.

The work of John Meyer and Brian Rowan (1977) suggests that there are yet other goals driving the structure and function of teacher evaluation systems. If school leaders intend to maintain public confidence and support, they must behave in ways that assure their constituents and the public at large that they are legitimate. Schools must innovate to be healthy organizations, but if school leaders get too far ahead of the pack—look too different, behave too radically—they do so at their own peril. When they incorporate acceptable ideas, schools protect themselves. The idea that teachers must be held accountable, or in some way evaluated, is an easy one to sell to the public, and thus one that enhances a leader's or system's legitimacy.

Trends, Issues, and Controversies

With the standards movement of the late 1990s came increased expectations for student performance and renewed concerns about teacher practice. Driven by politicians, parents, and, notably, teacher unions, school districts began an analysis of teacher evaluation goals and procedures. The traditional model of teacher evaluation, based on scheduled observations of a handful of direct instruction lessons, came under fire. "Seventy years of empirical research on teacher evaluation shows that current practices do not improve teachers or accurately tell what happens in classrooms" (Peterson, p. 14). Not surprisingly, in this climate, numerous alternative evaluative practices have been developed or reborn.

In the early twenty-first century, the first line of teacher evaluation consists of state and national tests created as barriers for entry to the profession. Some forty states use basic skills and subject matter assessments provided by the Praxis Series examinations for this purpose. Creators of the examinations assume teachers should be masters of grammar, mathematics, and the content they intend to teach. Though many states use the same basic skills tests, each sets its own passing score. The movement to identify and hire quality teachers based on test scores has resulted in some notable legal cases. Teachers who graduate from approved teacher education programs yet fail to pass licensure tests have challenged the validity of such tests, as well as the assignment of culpability. If a person pays for teacher education and is awarded a degree, who is to blame when that person fails a licensure examination? This is not an insignificant concern. In 1998, for example, the state of Massachusetts implemented a new test that resulted in a 59 percent failure rate for prospective teachers. Once a teacher has assumed a job, however, that teacher is rarely, if ever, tested again. In-service teachers typically succeed at resisting pressure to submit to periodic examinations because of the power of their numbers and their political organization.

Despite the well-known difficulties of measuring links between teaching and learning, the practice of judging teachers by the performance of their students is enjoying a resurgence of interest. Polls indicate that a majority of the American public favors this idea. School leaders routinely praise or chastise schools, and by implication teachers, for students' test results. Despite researchers' inabilities to examine the complexity of life in schools and in classrooms, studies of relationships between teaching and learning often become political springboards for policy formulation. For example, William Sanders (1996) suggests that teacher effectiveness is the single greatest factor affecting academic growth. His work has been seized upon by accountability proponents to argue that teachers must be held accountable for students' low test scores.

Although there may be much to be gained from focusing educators on common themes of accountability through the use of standards and accompanying tests, there may be much to lose as well. The upside can be measured over time in greater collective attention to common concerns. The downside results when people assume teachers can influence factors outside their control—factors that affect students' test scores, such as students' experiences, socioeconomic status, and parental involvement. A focus on scores as the sole, or even primary, indicator of accountability also creates the possibility for academic misconduct, such as ignoring important but untested material, teaching to the test, or cheating.

As researchers have demonstrated, those schools that need the most help are often least likely to get it. Daniel L. Duke, Pamela Tucker, and Walter Heinecke (2000) studied sixteen high schools involved in initial efforts to meet the challenges of new accountability standards that emphasize student test scores. These schools represented various combinations of need and ability. The researchers found that the schools with high need and low ability (those with poor test scores and low levels of financial resources) reported the highest concerns about staffing, morale, instruction, and students. Thus, the schools that needed the most help, the ones that were the primary targets of new accountability efforts, appeared in this study to be put at greater risk by the accountability movement.

Teachers' jobs involve far more than raising test scores. An evaluation strategy borrowed from institutions of higher education and business, sometimes referred to as *360-degree feedback,* acknowledges the necessity of considering the bigger picture. The intent of this holistic approach is to gather information from everyone with knowledge of a teacher's performance to create a complete representation of a teacher's practice and to identify areas for improvement. Multiple data sources, including questionnaires and surveys, student achievement, observation notes, teacher-developed curricula and tests, parent reports, teacher participation on committees, and the like, assure a rich store of information on which to base evaluation decisions. Current models tend to place the responsibility with administrators to interpret and respond to the data. To be sure, there are risks involved. The strategy asks children to evaluate their teachers, and it gathers feedback from individuals who possess only a secondary knowledge of a teacher's practices, namely parents and fellow teachers. Nonetheless, different kinds of information collected from different vantage points encourage full and fair representation of teachers' professional lives.

Toward Evaluating Teaching as Professional Behavior

At the turn of the twenty-first century, people continue to debate whether teaching is a true profession. Questions persist about educators' lack of self-regulation, the nebulously defined knowledge base upon which teaching rests, the lack of rigid entrance requirements to teacher education programs (witness alternative licensure routes), the level of teachers' salaries, and the locus of control in matters of evaluation. Yet school districts, state governments, the federal government, and national professional and lay organizations appear intent as never before on building and strengthening teaching as a profession.

One simple example of a changing attitude toward teaching as a profession is that of the use of peer evaluation. Two decades ago, in Toledo, Ohio, educators advanced processes of peer review as a method of evaluation. At its most basic level, peer review consists of an accomplished teacher observing and assessing the pedagogy of a novice or struggling veteran teacher. School districts that use peer review, however, often link the practice with teacher intervention, mentoring programs, and, in some instances, hiring and firing decisions. Columbus, Ohio's Peer Assistance and Review Program, seemingly representative of many review systems, releases expert teachers from classroom responsibilities to act as teaching consultants. Driven by the National Education Association's 1997 decision to reverse its opposition to peer review, the idea has enjoyed a resurgence of popularity in recent years.

Founded in 1987, the National Board for Professional Teaching Standards (NBPTS) is yet another example of people from different constituencies working together to advance the concept of teaching as a profession. The NBPTS attempts to identify and reward the highest caliber teachers, those who represent the top end of the quality distribution. Based on the medical profession's concept of board-certified physicians, the NBPTS bestows certification only on those teachers who meet what board representatives perceive to be the highest performance standards. By the end of the year 2000, nearly 10,000 teachers had received board certification—though this amounts to a tiny fraction of the nation's 2.6 million teachers. Widespread political and financial support, from both political conservatives and liberals, suggests this idea may have staying power.

Teacher evaluation will grow and develop as the concept of teaching as a profession evolves. Computer technology is only beginning to suggest how new methods of formative and summative evaluation can alter the landscape. Perhaps most important is that as reformers confront the realities of life in schools, public knowledge of what it means to be a teacher increases. More people in more walks of life are recognizing how complex and demanding teaching can be, and how important teachers are to society as a whole. Teacher evaluators of the future will demonstrate much higher levels of knowledge and skill than their predecessors, leaving the teaching profession better than they found it.

See also: SUPERVISION OF INSTRUCTION.

BIBLIOGRAPHY

BARR, ARVIL. 1948. "The Measurement and Prediction of Teaching Efficiency: A Summary of Investigations." *Journal of Experimental Education* 16(4):203–283.

BROPHY, JERE, and GOOD, THOMAS. 1986. "Teacher Behavior and Student Achievement." In *Handbook of Research on Teaching,* ed. Merlin C. Wittrock. New York: Macmillan.

GAGE, NATHANIEL L., and NEEDELS, MARGARET C. 1989. "Process-Product Research on Teaching: A Review of Criticisms." *The Elementary School Journal* 89(3):253–300.

GETZELS, JACOB. W., and JACKSON, PHILIP W. 1963. "The Teacher's Personality and Characteristics." In *Handbook of Research on Teaching: A Project of the American Educational Research Association.* ed. Nathaniel L. Gage. New York: Macmillan.

DOMAS, SIMEON J., and TIEDEMAN, DAVID V. 1950. "Teacher Competence: An Annotated Bibliography." *Journal of Experimental Education* 19:99–210.

DUKE, DANIEL L.; TUCKER, PAMELA; and HEINECKE, WALTER. 2000. *Initial Responses of Virginia High Schools to the Accountability Initiative.* Charlottesville, VA: Thomas Jefferson Center for Educational Design, University of Virginia.

HERBERT, JOANNE M. 1999. "An Online Learning Community: Technology Brings Teachers Together for Professional Development." *American School Board Journal* March:39–40.

MCNERGNEY, ROBERT F.; HERBERT, JOANNE M.; and FORD, R. E. 1993. "Anatomy of a Team Case Competition." Paper presented at the Annual Meeting of the American Educational Research Association, Atlanta, Georgia.

MEDLEY, DONALD M. 1979. "The Effectiveness of Teachers." In *Research on Teaching: Concepts, Findings, and Implications,* ed. Penelope L. Peterson and Herbert J. Walberg. Berkeley, CA: McCutchan.

MEDLEY, DONALD M.; COKER, HOMER; and SOAR, ROBERT S. 1984. *Measurement-Based Evaluation of Teacher Performance: An Empirical Approach.* New York: Longman.

MEYER, JOHN W., and ROWAN, BRIAN. 1977. "Institutionalized Organizations: Formal Structure as Myth and Ceremony." *American Journal of Sociology* 83(2):340–363.

PETERSON, KENNETH D. 2000. *Teacher Evaluation: A Comprehensive Guide to New Directions and New Practices,* 2nd edition. Thousand Oaks, CA: Corwin Press.

POWELL, MARJORIE, and BEARD, JOSEPH W. 1984. *Teacher Effectiveness: An Annotated Bibliography and Guide to Research.* New York: Garland.

SANDERS, WILLIAM L. and RIVERS, JUNE C. 1996. *Cumulative and Residual Effects of Teachers on Future Student Academic Achievement.* Knoxville: University of Tennessee Value-Added Research and Assessment Center.

SCRIVEN, MICHAEL. 1967. "The Methodology of Evaluation." In *Perspectives of Curriculum Evaluation,* ed. Ralph W. Tyler, Robert M. Gagné, and Michael Scriven. Chicago: Rand McNally.

ROBERT F. MCNERGNEY
SCOTT R. IMIG

METHODS

In the decade from 1991 to 2001, a number of developments in public policy and assessment practices significantly altered the landscape for teacher evaluation practices. The single most important shift in the public policy arena has been the emergence of a tidal wave of support for what is loosely called "teacher accountability." What this seems to mean in effect is a growing insistence on measurement of teacher quality and teacher performance in terms of student achievement, which is often poorly defined, crudely measured, and unconnected to what educators regard as significant learning.

Because there is still little consensus about acceptable ways to meet the very substantial challenges posed by links between measures of student achievement and consequent conclusions about teacher effectiveness, the fact that this issue dominates current discourse about teacher evaluation is very significant, and somewhat alarming. This is not a new effort or a new issue, but the heated insistence on its power as the single most important criterion for establishing a teacher's effectiveness is new. Simply put, most efforts to connect student achievement to individual teacher performance have foundered in the past on the following weaknesses:

- The measurement does not take into account teaching context as a performance variable.

- The measurement is unreliable, in part because it does not include time as a variable—both the teacher's time with a cohort of students; and some model or models of sufficient time to see learning effects in students.

- The measures used to reflect student achievement are not congruent with best practice and philosophy of instruction in modern education.

The link between teacher performance and student achievement is both so intuitively compelling as a major part of a teacher's performance evaluation and so very difficult to implement that it has never really been systematically achieved in the United States. The pressure to forge such links is immense in the early twenty-first century, and it is critical to the health and vitality of the education workforce that the link be credible and valid. A foundational validity issue is, of course, the quality and integrity of the methods states and districts have developed or adopted to measure student achievement. The teaching workforce has long disdained standardized national tests, the most commonly used assessments in school districts across the United States to represent student achievement, arguing persuasively that actual local and state curricula—and thus instruction—are not adequately aligned (or aligned at all) with the content of these tests. Furthermore, education reformers have almost universally excoriated these tests for two decades as reductive and not representative of the skills and abilities students really need to develop for the new millennium.

An evaluative commentary on the use of student tests for the purpose of high stakes accountability decisions was given by incoming American Educational Research Association President Robert Linn (2002), who evaluated fifty years of student testing in the U.S. education system, and the effects of that testing:

> I am led to conclude that in most cases the instruments and technology have not been up to the demands that have been placed on them by high-stakes accountability. Assessment systems that are useful monitors lose much of their dependability and credibility for that purpose when high stakes are attached to them. The unintended negative effects of the high-stakes accountability uses often outweigh the intended positive effects. (p. 14)

Given the policy climate in the early twenty-first century, this is a sobering and cautionary conclusion, coming as it does from such a major figure in the measurement community, and one known for his even-handed and judicious treatment of measurement issues. It is clear that the most widely used current measures of student achievement, primarily standardized norm-referenced multiple-choice tests developed and sold off-the-shelf by commercial test publishers, are useful for many educational purposes, but not valid for school accountability. Indeed, they may be positively misleading at the school

level, and certainly a distortion of teaching effectiveness at the individual teacher level. Concerns about the increased dependence on high-stakes testing has prompted a number of carefully worded technical cautions from important policy bodies as well. Although it is possible to imagine a program of student testing that aligns the assessments used to the standards for learning and to the curriculum actually taught, and that employs multiple methods and occasions to evaluate student learning, the investment such a program would demand would increase the cost of student assessment significantly. Furthermore, involving teachers in the conceptual development and interpretation of assessment measures that would be instructionally useful (particularly when those measures may have a direct effect on the teachers' performance evaluation and livelihood) is no closer to the realities of assessment practice than it has ever been —it is, in general, simply not part of the practice of school districts in the United States.

The emphasis on teacher quality has gained considerable momentum from the body of empirical evidence substantiating the linkage between teacher competence and student achievement. The "value-added" research, typified by the work of William Sanders and colleagues (1996; 1997; 1998) reinforces the assumption that the teacher is the most significant factor that affects student achievement. Sanders's work in this area is the best known and, increasingly, most influential among policymakers. In the measurement community, however, independent analyses of Sanders's data and methods have just begun. There appear to be controversial issues associated with both the statistical model Sanders uses and replicability of his findings.

Teacher Evaluation

At the beginning of the twenty-first century there is more teacher testing for various purposes than ever before. Some of this testing serves traditional purposes; for example, for admission into programs of professional preparation in colleges and universities or for licensure. For the first time in the United States there is a high-stakes assessment for purposes of certification, the National Board for Professional Teaching Standards (NBPTS) certification assessments, which are modeled on medical specialty board certification. Finally, there is a growing use of performance assessments of actual teaching for both formative purposes—during a teacher's initial years of practice, or the induction period—and for summative purposes, to grant an initial or more advanced teaching license. Performance-assessment-based licensure has been implemented in Connecticut since 2000 and is being implemented in 2002 in Ohio and in 2003 in Arkansas. In addition, California plans to implement a teaching performance assessment for all beginning teachers in California beginning in 2004.

Both the policy climate and the standards movement have had profound effects on teacher testing. States set passing standards on licensing tests, often rigorous, for demonstrations of sufficient skill and knowledge to be licensed. For example, as of the year 2000, thirty-nine states require all licensed teachers to pass a basic skills test (reading, mathematics, and writing), twenty-nine require secondary teachers to pass subject-specific tests in their prospective teaching fields, and thirty-nine require prospective secondary teachers to have a major, minor, or equivalent course credits for a subject-specific license. This means that a number of states require all three hurdles to be cleared before granting a license. In addition, most states require that the teacher's preparation institution recommend the candidate for the license. In every state but New Jersey, however, the state has the power to waive all of these requirements "either by granting licenses to individuals who have not met them or by permitting districts to hire such people" (Edwards, p. 8). And, perhaps most discouraging, only about twenty-five of the fifty states even have accessible records of "the numbers and percentages of teachers who hold various waivers" (Jerald and Boser, p. 44). Thus, reliance on rigorous state testing and preparation requirements to assure the quality of the education workforce is likely to lead to disappointment.

In 2000, thirty-six of the thirty-nine states that require teachers to pass a basic skills test waived that requirement and permitted a teacher to enter a classroom as teacher of record without passing the test. In sixteen states, this waiver can be renewed indefinitely, so long as the hiring school district asserts its inability to find a qualified applicant. Of the twenty-nine states that require secondary teachers to pass subject matter exams—most often only multiple-choice tests, even though more sophisticated tests are available—only New Jersey denies a license and therefore a job to candidates who have not passed the tests. Eleven of these twenty-nine states allow such candidates to remain in the job indefinitely, and all twenty-nine but New Jersey waive the course

work completion requirement for secondary teachers if the hiring district claims that it cannot find a more qualified applicant for the position.

Thus, while initial licensing tests have become increasingly sophisticated—they are based on K–12 student and disciplinary standards and offer both multiple-choice and constructed response formats—the requirements for their use are not only widely variable, but also not rigorously enforced.

As of 2001 the NBPTS certification assessments represent the first-ever, widely accepted national recognition of excellence in the teaching profession. The program has grown exponentially since 1994 when eighty-six teachers, the first National Board Certified Teachers, were announced. In 2001 approximately 14,000 candidates in nineteen different fields were assessed; the NBPTS expects that the number of National Board Certified Teachers nationwide will rise from 9,534 (2000) to approximately 15,000. The certification assessment consists of a classroom-based portfolio, including videotapes and student work samples with detailed analytical commentaries by the teacher-candidates, and a computer-delivered written assessment focused primarily on content and pedagogical-content knowledge. The NBPTS assessments have established a number of new benchmarks for teacher evaluation. The assessments themselves are both elaborate and very rigorous; it takes approximately nine months for a teacher to complete the assessment process. Almost universally regarded by candidates as the single most profound learning and professional development experience they have ever had, the assessment process is being widely used as a model for teacher professional development. The scoring process, which requires extensive training of peer teachers, is itself a substantial professional development opportunity.

In addition, the actual technical quality of the scoring has contradicted long-held opinions that complex human judgments sacrifice reliability or consistency for validity, or credibility. The NBPTS scoring reliability is extremely high. The expense of the assessment—$2,300 per candidate in 2002—has been borne largely by states and local governments as part of their support for teacher quality initiatives. That level of public support for a high-stakes, voluntary assessment is unprecedented in education in the United States. In 2001, the NBPTS published the first in a series of validity studies that showed substantive differences between National Board Certified Teachers and non-certified teachers in terms of what actually goes on in the classrooms and in student learning.

The third area of change and innovation in teacher evaluation has taken place in states' provision for mentoring and formative assessment in the initial period of a beginning teacher's career, a period commonly called the induction period. States vary in the nature of the support they provide, with twenty-eight states requiring or providing funds for beginning-teacher induction programs, but only ten states doing both. The most sophisticated induction programs exist in Connecticut (the Connecticut BEST program), California (the CFASST program), and Ohio (the Ohio FIRST program). Each of these programs uses structured portfolio-based learning experiences to guide a new teacher and a mentor through a collaborative first year of practice.

Few states assess the actual teaching performance of new teachers. Twenty-seven states require that the school principal evaluate each new teacher. As of 2000, only four states (Kentucky, Louisiana, Oklahoma, and South Carolina) go beyond this requirement and require that the principal and a team of other educators from outside the school, trained to a common set of criteria, participate in the new teacher's evaluation. As of 2001 Connecticut, New York, and Ohio will all have performance-based licensure tests for beginning teachers at the end of the first or second year of teaching. Connecticut requires a subject-specific teaching portfolio; New York requires a videotape of teaching; Ohio will use an observation-based licensing assessment developed by Educational Testing Service called Praxis III. In 2002 Arkansas will begin using Praxis III as well; by 2004 California will make its work-sample-based Teaching Performance Assessment operational for initial licensure of all California teachers.

See also: TEACHER EDUCATION; TEACHER EMPLOYMENT; TEACHER UNIONS, *subentry on* INFLUENCE ON INSTRUCTION AND OTHER EDUCATIONAL PRACTICES.

BIBLIOGRAPHY

BOND, LLOYD; SMITH, TRACY; BAKER, WANDA K.; and HATTIE, JOHN A. 2000. *The Certification System of the National Board for Professional Teaching Standards: A Construct and Consequential Validity Study.* Washington, DC: National Board for Professional Teaching Standards.

EDWARDS, VIRGINIA B. 2000. "Quality Counts 2000." *Education Week* 19(18)[entire issue].

EDWARDS, VIRGINIA B., ed. 2000. "Who Should Teach? The States Decide." *Education Week* 19(18):8–9.

ELMORE, RICHARD F., and ROTHMAN, ROBERT, eds. 1999. *Testing, Teaching, and Learning: A Guide for States and School Districts.* Washington, DC: National Academy Press.

FEUER, MICHAEL J., et al., eds. 1999. *Uncommon Measures: Equivalence and Linkage Among Educational Tests.* Washington, DC: National Academy Press.

HEUBERT, JAY P., and HAUSER, ROBERT M., eds. 1999. *High Stakes: Testing for Tracking, Promotion, and Graduation.* Washington, DC: National Academy Press.

JERALD, CRAIG D., and BOSER, ULRICH. 2000. "Setting Policies for New Teachers." *Education Week* 19(18):44–47.

KORETZ, DANIEL, et al. 2001. *New Work on the Evaluation of High-Stakes Testing Programs.* Symposium conducted at the National Council on Measurement in Education's Annual Meeting, Seattle, WA.

LINN, ROBERT L. 2000. "Assessments and Accountability." *Educational Researcher* 29:4–16.

MADAUS, GEORGE E., and O'DWYER, LAURA M. 1999. "A Short History of Performance Assessment: Lessons Learned." *Phi Delta Kappan* 80:688–695.

MILLMAN, JASON, ed. 1997. *Grading Teachers, Grading Schools. Is Student Achievement a Valid Evaluation Measure?* Thousand Oaks, CA: Corwin.

SANDERS, WILLIAM L., and HORN, SANDRA P. 1998. "Research Findings from the Tennessee Value-Added Assessment System (TVASS) Database: Implications for Educational Evaluation and Research." *Journal of Personnel Evaluation in Education* 12:247–256.

SANDERS, WILLIAM L., and RIVERS, JUNE C. 1996. *Cumulative and Residual Effects of Teachers on Future Student Academic Achievement.* Knoxville, TN: University of Tennessee Value-Added Research and Assessment Center.

WRIGHT, S. PAUL; HORN, SANDRA P.; and SANDERS, WILLIAM L. 1997. "Teacher and Classroom Context Effects on Student Achievement: Implications for Teacher Evaluation." *Journal of Personnel Evaluation in Education* 11:57–67.

INTERNET RESOURCES

AMERICAN EDUCATIONAL RESEARCH ASSOCIATION. 2000. "AERA Position Statement Concerning High-Stakes Testing in PreK–12 Education." <www.aera.net/about/policy/stakes.htm>.

BARTON, PAUL. 1999. "Too Much Testing of the Wrong Kind: Too Little of the Right Kind in K–12 Education." <www.ets.org/research/pic>.

MARI A. PEARLMAN

TEACHER LEARNING COMMUNITIES

Although they are seldom mentioned in the educational literature or in professional educators' organizations before the early 1980s, it has become commonplace to refer to certain projects, programs, networks, and collaboratives of prospective or experienced teachers as *teacher learning communities*. The term combines two basic concepts—*teacher learning* and *community*—that are part of the discourse in teacher education, professional development, school reform, and educational policy in the early twenty-first century.

Teacher Learning and the New Professional Development

It has become understood that teachers are linchpins in educational reforms of all kinds. In fact, Michael Fullan, a well-known contemporary writer on educational change, suggests that "teachers' capacities to deal with change, learn from it, and help students learn from it will be critical for the future development of societies" (p. ix). This means that teacher learning—how, what, and under what conditions teachers learn to respond to the needs of a changing society—is among the most important issues in educational policy and practice. A strong emphasis on teacher learning is part of what has been referred to as a new paradigm of professional development or a new model of teacher education. The new professional development is conceptualized as continuous teacher learning over time. Early research about how teachers think about their work prompted a shift in emphasis away from what teachers do and toward what they know, what their sources of knowledge are, how those sources influence their work in classrooms, and how they make decisions and construct curriculum within conditions that are ultimately uncertain and changing.

With its focus on teachers as "knowers" and thinkers (not just do-ers), the concept of teacher learning is more constructivist than transmission-oriented. The concept carries with it the idea that both prospective and experienced teachers (like all learners) bring prior knowledge and experience to all new learning situations, which are social and specific, and that active learning requires opportunities to link previous knowledge with new understandings. This means that teachers are acknowledged as not just receivers of information or implementers of teaching methods and curriculum, but also translators and interpreters of subject matter, inventors of teaching strategies, and generators of knowledge, curriculum and instruction.

For prospective teachers, the concept of teacher learning replaces earlier notions of "teacher training," a one-time process prior to the beginning of the teaching career wherein undergraduates were equipped with content, methods in the subject area, and information about educational foundations and then sent out to "practice" teaching. Similarly, for experienced teachers, the notion of teacher learning replaces the concept of periodic "in-service staff development" wherein experienced teachers were congregated to receive the latest information about effective teaching processes and techniques from various educational experts. Rather, it is generally understood that teacher learning takes place over time rather than in isolated moments in time and that teacher learning occurs over the entire professional life span (i.e., prior to and during formal preparation and initial teaching but also during the induction period and the early and later career years) rather than beginning during the formal preparation period and ending once a teacher has achieved a particular professional benchmark (e.g., tenure in a school system, permanent state licensure, national board certification) or position (e.g., mentor teacher, teacher leader, teacher on special assignment). It has also been widely acknowledged that teacher learning projects are most effective when linked to students' learning and curricular reform that is embedded in the daily life of schools and when focused on what Ann Lieberman and Lynn Miller call "culture-building," not skills training.

The concept of teacher learning is part of a new perspective on teacher education and professional development. It is used to emphasize that across the career lifespan, the professional education of teachers is a process of learning to adapt and invent strategies, manage competing agendas, interpret and construct subject-specific and interdisciplinary curriculum, and build classroom and school cultures within conditions that are ultimately uncertain.

Community

Although long used in other fields, the term *community* is relatively new in the mainstream literature about teacher education, professional development, and educational change. In literary theory, "interpretive community" has been used by Stanley Fish and other theorists to refer to a network of people with similar meaning perspectives. In sociolinguistics, "speech community" has been used by Dell Hymes, John Gumperz, and other linguistic anthropologists to refer to a group of people who engage in face-to-face interaction within a specific context. Jay Lemke defines community as "systems of doing, of social and cultural activities or practices, rather than as systems of doers, of human individuals per se" (p. 93). In the field of composition, Joseph Harris has suggested that the term "discourse community" draws on the everyday meaning of community as a group with common goals and interests as well as the literary concept of interpretive community and the sociolinguistic notion of speech community. In this sense discourse communities are real groupings of readers and writers who share a kind of larger mission, but they also become networks of "citations and allusions" that refer to texts both within the speech community and outside of it.

According to social theorists such as Joel Westheimer, the central features of community include "interaction and participation, interdependence, shared interests and beliefs, concern for individual and minority views, and meaningful relationships" (p. 12). Along different lines, John McKnight suggests that community is the primary location for the development of relationships and commitments among citizens. In teacher education and professional development, the terms *inquiry communities* and *teacher research groups* have been used for some time to describe groups of education practitioners who meet together to inquire systematically about aspects of their own work in schools and classrooms.

Communities of practice is a term that has become prominent in the literature on learning. Drawing on the social psychology of learning, particularly on research about situated cognition and activity theory, the notion of communities of practice is developed in the work of Jean Lave and Etienne Wenger. Lave and Wenger suggest that "learning, thinking, and knowing are relations among people engaged in activity *in, with, and arising from the socially and culturally structured world*" (p. 67, emphasis in original). This means that learning is a process that occurs when more and less experienced people work together within communities of practice, which are "the social configurations in which our enterprises are defined as worth pursuing and our participation is recognizable as competence" (Wenger, p. 5). Communities of practice organized around a common goal are the site for participants' learning new roles that are connected to new knowledge and skills. From this perspective, it is not simply learning that takes place within communities of practice, but—since knowing and being are intimately connected to one another—it is also identity formation itself. The idea of professional communities has also been used to understand variations in teachers' interpretations of their opportunities and challenges within the social and organizational structures of schools.

Conceptually, *community* has been used in a number of different ways in education theory and research and in the social sciences to denote groups of people engaged in particular kinds of work or other activity and linked by a common purpose. Community members typically exchange meaning perspectives and ideas about what it means to be actively engaged in a particular activity or enterprise.

Teacher Learning Communities

"Teacher learning communities" (TLCs) is a term that combines many of the meanings of the two concepts above to refer to projects, programs, cooperatives, and collaboratives of prospective or experienced teachers—often in partnership with university-based educators—that support the ongoing education of participants. TLCs are social groupings of new and experienced educators who come together over time for the purpose of gaining new information, reconsidering previous knowledge and beliefs, and building on their own and others' ideas and experiences in order to work on a specific agenda intended to improve practice and enhance students' learning in K–12 schools and other educational settings. Conceptually, *teacher learning community* refers to an intellectual space as much as it designates a particular group of people and, sometimes, a physical location. In this sense, communities are the intellectual, social, and organizational configurations that support teachers' ongoing professional growth by providing opportunities for teachers to think, talk, read, and write about their daily work, including its larger social, cultural, and political contexts in planned and intentional ways.

Key Characteristics. Although TLCs vary considerably (as discussed below), they have several key characteristics: ways of spending and organizing time, planned and intentional patterns of structuring talk and written texts in their work together, and a shared purpose or understanding about the central tasks of teaching.

Organizing time. TLCs need sufficient chunks of time in which to work and sufficient longevity as a group over time. Generally, TLCs function over relatively long periods—at least an academic year—and often on an ongoing basis wherein group membership is basically stable although membership changes from time to time. In TLCs that include both experienced and prospective teachers, as is the case in some projects that combine pre-service teacher education with ongoing professional development, the experienced educators may be members of the community over time, while the prospective teachers may change with every program cycle or cohort. When members of a community make a commitment to work over time, there is the potential for ideas to develop, trust to build in the group, and participants to feel comfortable raising sensitive issues. Over time, many communities that support teacher learning develop their own histories and, in a certain sense, their own culture—a common discourse, shared experiences that function as touchstones, and a set of procedures that provide structure and form for continued experience.

Structuring talk and texts. Second, TLCs have particular ways of using language in their work together—both oral conversations and written texts. In communities that support teacher learning, groups develop ways of describing, discussing, debating, reflecting on, writing about, and reading about teaching, learning, and schooling. In some TLCs, groups engage in joint construction of knowledge through conversation by making their tacit knowledge more visible, questioning assumptions about common practice, and examining together school and classroom data and artifacts that make possible the generation and consideration of alternative explanations and analyses. Some TLCs use very

structured formats for oral inquiries into teaching, such as reflections on practice or descriptive reviews of students described by Patricia Carini of the Prospect School. Other communities do not use formal conversation formats, but they do talk in distinctive ways about teaching and learning. In communities that support teacher learning, all talk does not contribute directly to the joint construction of knowledge about teaching and schooling. Rather, teachers also swap classroom stories, share specific ideas, seek one another's advice, and trade opinions about issues and problems in their schools and larger educational arenas. In TLCs, this "small talk" has an important function—it helps to create and sustain the interpersonal relationships necessary for the larger project or purpose of the community.

In addition, many TLCs use a wide range of texts in their work together, not all of which are published or widely disseminated. These texts often include books and journal articles from the extensive theoretical and research literature in fields related to teaching and learning as well as subject matter literature, including history, fiction, drama, and scientific accounts. Some communities focus on teacher research, action research, and other forms of practitioner inquiry as the primary vehicle for teacher learning. In these TLCs, then, the texts also include teacher research and action research reports in the form of journals, essays, and studies as well as teachers' written records and accounts, transcriptions of classroom interactions, students' writing and other work, school forms and documents, demographic data, and curriculum guidelines and materials. Teacher learning in communities is a fundamentally social and constructive activity that depends on the collective and cumulative power of the community to disseminate ideas, stimulate discussion, and widen the oral and written discourse about schools and schooling.

Shared purpose. Finally, although the specific purposes of various TLCs can be quite different from one another, most TLCs are organized around a common purpose or goal. Almost always, a fundamental goal of TLCs is some kind of improvement or change in professional practice, school culture, community partnerships, or school routines and procedures, in order—ultimately—to enhance students' learning opportunities and increase their life chances. How this task is understood, however—that is, what it means to enhance students' learning and what it takes to increase life chances—varies enormously. Some TLCs focus on the improvement of curriculum and teaching in a particular subject matter or disciplinary area, such as writing, mathematics, or science. Others focus on a broad-based educational agenda such as restructuring or reinventing urban schools, or incorporating the ideals of progressive education across curriculum, assessment, and teaching. Some TLCs are more specifically focused, such as those intended to improve the conditions and outcomes of teaching and learning in particular local schools with a population that has been traditionally under-served by the mainstream educational system.

TLCs in particular school districts may be organized to improve teachers' work in a general area, such as supporting the language growth and development of English language learners or improving early reading instruction in the primary grades. TLCs are sometimes focused on a particular curriculum package, such as "Success for All" or "Reading Recovery," or a particular school district goal, such as improving students' scores on state-wide standardized high stakes tests. Some communities aim to help teachers learn about a particular approach to subject matter teaching, such as cognitively guided instruction in mathematics, process writing, or problem-based approaches to science teaching and learning. Generally speaking, TLCs are most effective and long-lived when teachers choose to participate and when they play a significant role in constructing the issues that are important. This includes participation and choice in community governance and structures—planning, timing, topics, strategies, speakers, evaluation procedures, dissemination activities, and so on. However, in some cases, teachers choose to take on and eventually come to "own" an already-established agenda or purpose and agree to work collaboratively toward a goal set by a school or school district.

Knowing More, Teaching Better: Differences among TLCs

The surface characteristics of many TLCs are similar, and in a general sense, all TLCs are aimed at teachers knowing more and teaching better. However, different TLCs are initiated and motivated by quite different ideas about what it means to "know more" and "teach better." A useful way to sort out some of the differences among TLCs, then, is in terms of their underlying assumptions about teaching knowledge and professional practice and about how these are related in teachers' work. Although competing, three major ideas about the relationships of knowledge and practice co-exist in the world of educational policy, research, and practice and are invoked by differently positioned people in order to justify quite different approaches to improving teaching and learning through TLCs.

The first approach is "knowledge-for-practice," where it is assumed that knowing more (e.g., more subject matter, more educational theory, more pedagogy, more instructional strategies) leads more or less directly to more effective practice. Here, knowledge for teaching consists primarily of what is commonly called formal knowledge, or the general theories and research-based findings on a wide range of foundational and applied topics that together constitute the basic domains of knowledge about teaching, widely referred to by educators as the knowledge base. The idea here is that competent practice reflects the state of the art —that is, that highly skilled teachers have deep knowledge of their content areas and of the most effective teaching strategies for creating learning opportunities for students. From this perspective, the purpose of TLCs is to provide access to the knowledge base and help teachers implement, translate, or otherwise put into practice the knowledge they acquire from experts outside the classroom. TLCs that operate according to these assumptions often include school district groups working with coaches or content area experts to implement a new curriculum, institute strategies intended to raise test scores, or make instruction consistent with state or national curriculum standards.

The second approach is "knowledge-in-practice," wherein it is assumed that some of the most essential knowledge for teaching is what many people call practical knowledge, or, what very competent teachers know as it is expressed or embedded in the artistry of practice, in teachers' reflections on practice, in teachers' practical inquiries, or in teachers' narrative accounts of practice. A basic assumption here is that the knowledge teachers need to teach well is acquired through experience and through considered and deliberative reflection about or inquiry into experience. To improve teaching, then, teachers need opportunities to work in communities to enhance, make explicit, and articulate the tacit knowledge embedded in experience and in the wise action of very competent professionals. Teacher learning communities with these underlying assumptions often include facilitated teacher groups, dyads composed of more and less experienced teachers, and other kinds of collaborative arrangements that support teachers' working together to reflect in and on practice. TLCs that operate according to these assumptions often include pre-service contexts where prospective teachers learn how experienced teachers plan and reflect on their work, induction programs wherein novice teachers work with experts, and school-based groups where teachers share stories and experiences.

The third approach is "knowledge-*of*-practice," wherein it is assumed that the knowledge teachers need to teach well is generated when teachers treat their own classrooms and schools as sites for intentional investigation at the same time that they treat the knowledge produced by others as generative material for interrogation and interpretation. In this sense, teachers learn when they generate local knowledge of practice by working within the contexts of inquiry communities to theorize and construct their work and to connect it to larger social, cultural, and political issues. Here basic questions about what it means to generate knowledge, who generates it, what counts as knowledge and to whom, and how knowledge is used and evaluated in particular contexts are always open to question. From this perspective, new information is not necessarily expected to be used or applied to an immediate situation but may also shape the interpretive frameworks teachers develop to make judgments, theorize practice, and connect their efforts to larger efforts. Teacher research groups, action research groups, inquiry communities, and other school or cross-school collectives in which teachers and others conjoin their efforts to construct knowledge are the major kinds of TLCs that work from this set of assumptions.

Finally, it is important to point out that although TLCs share the goal of enhancing students' learning and improving the quality of schooling, all communities do not share the same ideas about the ultimate purposes of teachers' work and educational change. Some TLCs are overtly committed to working for social change and social justice by altering the fundamental arrangements of schooling and society. Others are more in keeping with the basic goals of the current educational system. Some TLCs fit comfortably with a university's or a school district's stated commitment to teacher leadership, site-based management, or curricular revision. At other times,

members of TLCs challenge fundamental school practices such as tracking, promotion and retention policies, testing and assessment practices, and school-community-family relationships, as well as what counts as teaching and learning in classrooms. To the extent that TLCs fit comfortably with a university or school district's institutional agenda for reflective practice, increased professionalism, and teacher accountability, they can be regarded as compatible with ongoing efforts toward teacher education and professional development. But sometimes TLCs critique and seek to alter cultures of collegiality; ways that school or program structures promote or undermine collaboration; ratios of teacher autonomy to teacher responsibility; norms of teacher evaluation; relationships among student teachers, teachers, and their university colleagues; and the ways power is exercised in teacher-to-teacher, mentor-to-teacher, and school-university partnerships. What this suggests is that there is a whole range of TLCs —some that are more readily integrated into the existing social and institutional arrangements of schools, school systems, and universities than others.

Examples of Teacher Learning Communities

There are scores of TLCs in the United States and in many other countries worldwide. Many are school-based and/or develop from a local or regional teachers' network or from a particular need, e.g., preparing for National Board Certification. A relatively small number of school-based professional communities have been treated in the literature. Many TLCs are subject-centered and offer teachers opportunities to learn from their own experiences as learners. In the area of literacy, teacher inquiry communities have been sponsored by a range of social and organizational structures, including the federal government, national professional organizations, national networks, foundations and centers, and university centers and university-generated networks. With a few notable exceptions, those connected to universities are most likely to disseminate their work through presentations and publication. A few of these are described here to provide a sense of the range and variation across communities.

Many TLCs have been formed with participants in the National Writing Project, perhaps the most prominent subject-centered teacher professional network nationally. The Multicultural Collaborative for Literacy and Secondary Schools (M-CLASS) teacher research network, based at the University of

California Berkeley, began in 1990 as a collaborative of twenty-four teacher researchers from four U.S. cities and has grown to include seventy-five additional teachers who are teacher-credential candidates or part of a university-teacher-research collaborative or members of school-change teams. All M-CLASS teacher researchers seek to improve literacy learning in their urban multicultural classrooms and to communicate the results of their research to other professionals. The Philadelphia Writing Project (PhilWP) is an urban teacher collaborative network of more than 500 Philadelphia K–12 teachers and educators at the University of Pennsylvania. A site of the National Writing Project since 1986, the community utilizes a wide variety of oral and written inquiry formats to support its many projects, all of which are designed to improve the teaching/learning of writing and literacy by strengthening the critical linkages among language, access to literacy, social justice and educational change. Since its inception in 1986, PhilWP has organized and received funding from various foundations and other sources for more than fifteen teacher inquiry communities, lasting from two to six years each and many linked with other TLCs nationally. The National Writing Project sponsors the Teacher Inquiry Communities Network, a consortium of groups formed by NWPs around the country.

Other TLCs exemplify local collaborations between school districts and area universities. The Madison Metropolitan School District Classroom Action Research Professional Development program has been in existence since 1990. More than 500 teachers and administrators have participated in this program within small groups facilitated by teachers or staff development staff. The research studies, which are published by the school district each year, employ an action research model and use a variety of mostly qualitative research methods. Collaborations have existed since 1990 between this program and teacher education programs at the University of Wisconsin–Madison. In another example of university–school collaboration, school- and university-based teachers in the Athens, Georgia, area have formed fluid, evolving study groups such as LEADS (Literacy Educators for a Democratic Society) and PhOLKS (Photographs of Local Knowledge Sources), and collaborative action research teams (e.g., the Kings Bridge Road Research Team, and the eight-year collaboration of Shockley, Michelove, and Allen [1995] who wrote the "engaging children/

families/teachers" series). Using mediating dialogue and action research, they inquire into issues of culturally engaged teaching, educational equity, and social justice.

Often TLCs evolve and take different shapes over time as membership changes and groups develop new purposes and interests. Led by Susan Florio-Ruane and Taffy Raphael, the Teachers Learning Collaborative Network, for example, brought together a diverse group of teachers who lived and taught in school districts across southeast Michigan. The Network comprised three study groups, all focused on improving their understandings and teaching practices in literacy and diversity. Activities included reading and writing autobiography and autobiographical fiction, developing curriculum to support struggling readers, and engaging in school reform of literacy instruction and assessment practices. Another example of teachers working with a university-based faculty member is Kathryn Au's work with the Ka Lama Teacher Education Initiative, established in 1996. This is an effort to create a community of teachers committed to working on the Leeward Coast, a rural area in which the majority of residents are Native Hawaiian. The initiative emphasizes the themes of literacy, multicultural education, and Hawaiian studies, and teachers engage in a variety of inquiry activities, including creating literacy portfolios, writing family educational histories, and developing Hawaiian studies units with challenging academic content.

Some TLCs connected to universities reflect the priorities of academic research centers or departments. For example, The Action Research Group (ARG), an affiliated program of Community Psychology's "Partners for Progress" at the University of Illinois, Urbana, is one part of a long-term commitment by staff from a university and public school to work together to develop awareness and sustain initiatives that will make connections between communities in order to enhance student achievement in a predominantly low-income, African American area. In addition to dialogue about work in classrooms, the "Partners" group has worked on a school-based course in "Race and Teaching," a community garden on the school site, and a community arts project. It is currently involved in efforts to develop more project-based learning through regular planning meetings of grade-level teams, to create an evaluation of students' learning that goes beyond standardized test scores, and to develop a practice-based course in "Teaching for Social Justice." Since the early 1990s Sarah Michaels and the Hiatt Center for Urban Education at Clark University have worked closely with a number of Worcester Public School teachers in a variety of teacher research activities. These include university and school-based seminars, informal teacher research groups that meet after school over a period of years, and a number of Spencer Foundation supported efforts from their Practitioner Research, Mentoring, and Communication grant program. This work has resulted in the publication of books, videos, articles, and presentations at national conferences. A common thread in this work is the focus on talk and the importance of the teacher's role as orchestrator of rigorous, coherent, and equitable classroom conversations.

Quite a number of TLCs function outside any school or university context. Among the most prominent and widely published is the Brookline Teacher Researcher Seminar founded in 1989 as a collaborative of seven teacher researchers whose members have adapted the research tools of sociolinguistics and ethnography to the classroom in order to explore their own questions, dilemmas, and concerns for equity through the study of "talk" or classroom discourse. The weekly meeting serves as a central part of the methodology where teachers assist one another as each member, through collaborative exploration of an individual's data, begins to uncover new understandings of children's meanings and to cast away habitual ways of seeing and thinking. Also widely known is the Philadelphia Teachers' Learning Cooperative, which is closely related to Patricia Carini's work at the Prospect School in Vermont, founded in 1965. Using the documentary processes developed at Prospect, the Philadelphia TLC has been meeting weekly for more than twenty years. Beginning, new, and experienced teachers use structured oral inquiry processes to examine children's work and classroom/school life. Members of this group and others connected with Prospect consult with other TLCs—locally and nationally—to acquaint others with ways to use these processes in different contexts and for various purposes. The work of Prospect and the Philadelphia TLC is disseminated through summer institutes and a growing number of publications.

Electronic Teacher Learning Communities

Many TLCs—particularly those that involve local, regional, or national teacher networks—have developed online technologies integral to their collaborative work. One of the oldest and best known, The Bread Loaf Teacher Network, creates online communities of teachers who have attended one of the campuses of Middlebury College designed to bring together rural and urban teachers for intensive graduate work related to teaching writing, theater, literature, and multicultural studies. For more than ten years, Bread Loaf has been giving teachers financial assistance for ongoing research and has used major grant support to make it possible for rural and more recently urban teachers to participate in summer graduate work designed to foster learning communities supported by technology. Linked across sites by an electronic network called Breadnet, many Bread Loaf teachers focus on teacher and student generated collaborative and community-based projects that combine action research, service, and advocacy. Increasingly, teacher learning communities are using electronic media to disseminate their work for other audiences.

The examples above represent a small number of the teacher learning communities that have burgeoned over the last several decades. In contrast to training programs for teachers or transmission-oriented, in-service staff development programs, this growth is not yet well-documented. Teacher learning communities represent a major cultural shift with considerable potential for promoting lifespan learning in the teaching profession and altering the cultures of teaching and teachers' work. Realizing this potential clearly depends upon the willingness of teachers to engage with each other in a joint search for meaning in the work of teaching and schooling. But it also depends upon support at all levels of the educational system to reconceptualize teaching as learning and teacher education and professional development as continuous work in learning communities. The rapid growth of learning communities signals that practicing teachers can effectively self-organize for intellectual work, collaborate with consultants and university partners, generate new knowledge about daily practice that is of value beyond their local community, and contribute meaningfully to the transformation of schools and districts.

See also: COOPERATIVE AND COLLABORATIVE LEARNING; INSTRUCTIONAL STRATEGIES; TEACHER; TEACHER EDUCATION; TEACHING, *subentry on* LEARNING TO TEACH.

BIBLIOGRAPHY

Au, Kathryn Hu-Pei. 2002. "Communities of Practice: Engagement, Imagination, and Alignment in Research on Teacher Education." *Journal of Teacher Education* 53(3).

Ballenger, Cynthia. 1998. *Teaching Other People's Children: Literacy and Learning in a Bilingual Classroom.* New York: Teachers College Press.

Barnes, Henrietta. 1989. "Structuring Knowledge for Beginning Teaching." In *Knowledge Base for the Beginning Teacher,* ed. Maynard C. Reynolds. New York: Pergamon Press.

Bransford, John D.; Brown, Ann L.; and Cocking, Rodney R., eds. 2000. *How People Learn: Brain, Mind, Experience, and School.* Washington, DC: National Academy Press.

Brown, Ann L., and Campione, Joseph. 1994. "Guided Discovery in a Community of Learners." In *Classroom Lessons: Integrating Cognitive Theory and Classroom Practice,* ed. Kate McGilly. Cambridge, MA: MIT Press.

Carini, Patricia F. 2001. *Starting Strong: A Different Look at Children, Schools, and Standards.* New York: Teachers College Press.

Cochran-Smith, Marilyn. 1991. "Reinventing Student Teaching." *Journal of Teacher Education* 42(2):104–118.

Cochran-Smith, Marilyn, and Lytle, Susan S. 1993. *Inside/Outside: Teacher Research and Knowledge.* New York: Teachers College Press.

Cochran-Smith, Marilyn, and Lytle, Susan S. 1999. "Relationship of Knowledge and Practice: Teacher Learning in Communities." In *Review of Research in Education,* Vol. 24, ed. Ali Iran-Nejad and P. David Pearson. Washington, DC: American Educational Research Association.

Darling-Hammond, Linda. 1994. *Professional Development Schools: Schools for a Developing Profession.* New York: Teachers College Press.

Edgar, Christopher, and Wood, Susan Nelson. 1996. *The Nearness of You: Students and Teachers Writing Online.* New York: Teachers and Writers Collaborative.

Feiman-Nemser, Sharon. 1990. "Teacher Preparation: Structural and Conceptual Alternatives." In *Handbook of Research on Teacher Education,* ed. W. Robert Houston. New York: Macmillan.

Fish, Stanley. 1980. *Is There a Text in This Class: The Authority of Interpretive Communities.* Cambridge, MA: Harvard University Press.

Florio-Ruane, Susan. 2001. *Teacher Education and The Cultural Imagination: Autobiography, Conversation, and Narrative.* Mahwah, NJ: Erlbaum.

Florio-Ruane, Susan, and Raphael, Taffy E. 2001. "Reading Lives: Learning about Culture and Literacy in Teacher Study Groups." In *Talking Shop: Authentic Conversation and Teacher Learning,* ed. Christopher M. Clark. New York: Teachers College Press.

Freedman, Sarah Warshauer; Simon, Elizabeth Radin; Calin, Julie Shalhope; Casareno, Alex; and M-CLASS of Teacher Researchers. 1999. *Literacy and Learning: Teacher Research in the Multicultural Classroom.* New York: Teachers College Press.

Fullan, Michael G. 1993. *Change Forces: Probing the Depths of Educational Reform.* London: Falmer Press.

Gallas, Karen. 1994. *The Language of Learning: How Children Talk, Write, Dance, Draw, and Sing Their Understanding of the World.* New York: Teachers College Press.

Gallas, Karen. 1995. *Talking Their Way into Science.* New York: Teachers College Press.

Gallas, Karen. 1998. *Sometimes I Can Be Anything.* New York: Teachers College Press.

Goswami, Dixie, and Stillman, Peter. 1987. *Reclaiming the Classroom: Teacher Research as an Agency for Change.* Upper Montclair, NJ: Boynton/Cook.

Grimmett, Peter, and Neufeld, Jon. 1994. *Teacher Development and the Struggle for Authenticity: Professional Growth and Restructuring in the Context of Change.* New York: Teachers College Press.

Grossman, Pam, ed. 1990. *The Making of a Teacher: Teacher Knowledge and Teacher Education.* New York: Teachers College Press.

Gumperz, John. 1982. *Discourse Strategies.* Cambridge, Eng.: Cambridge University Press.

Hargreaves, Andy. 1994. *Changing Teachers, Changing Times: Teachers' Work and Culture in the Postmodern Age.* New York: Teachers College Press.

Hargreaves, Andy, and Fullan, Michael G. 1992. *Teacher Development and Educational Change.* Philadelphia: Falmer Press.

Harris, Joseph. 1989. "The Idea of Community in the Study of Writing." *College Composition and Communication* 40:11–22.

HAWLEY, WILLIS D., and VALLI, LINDA. 1999. "The Essentials of Effective Professional Development: A New Consensus." In *Teaching as the Learning Profession: Handbook of Policy and Practice,* ed. Linda Darling-Hammond and Gary Sykes. San Francisco: Jossey-Bass.

HIMLEY, MARGARET, and CARINI, PATRICIA F. 2000. *From Another Angle: Children's Strengths and School Standards.* New York: Teachers College Press.

HOLLINGSWORTH, SANDRA. 1994. *Teacher Research in Urban Literacy Education: Lessons, Conversations in a Feminist Key.* New York: Oxford Press.

HYMES, DELL. 1974. *Foundations in Sociolinguistics.* Philadelphia: University of Pennsylvania Press.

LAMPERT, MAGDALENE. 1985. "How Do Teachers Manage to Teach? Perspectives in Practice." *Harvard Educational Review* 55(2):178–194.

LAVE, JEAN, and WENGER, ETIENNE. 1991. *Situated Learning: Legitimate Peripheral Participation.* Cambridge, MA: Cambridge University Press.

LEMKE, JAY L. 1995. *Textual Politics: Discourse and Social Dynamics.* Philadelphia: Taylor and Francis.

LIEBERMAN, ANN, and MILLER, LYNNE. 1991. *Staff Development for Education in the '90s.* New York: Teachers College Press.

LIEBERMAN, ANN, and MILLER, LYNNE. 1994. "Problems and Possibilities of Institutionalizing Teacher Research." In *Teacher Research and Educational Reform,* ed. Sandra Hollingsworth and Hugh Sockett. Chicago: University of Chicago Press.

LITTLE, JUDITH WARREN. 1993. "Teachers' Professional Development in a Climate of Educational Reform." *Educational Evaluation and Policy Analysis* 15(2):129–151.

LYTLE, SUSAN L. 2000. "Teacher Inquiry in the Contact Zone." In *Handbook of Reading Research Vol. III,* ed. Michael L. Kamil, Peter Mosenthal, David Pearson, and Rebecca Barr. Mahwah, NJ: Erlbaum.

MCLAUGHLIN, MILBREY WALLIN. 1993. "What Matters Most in Teachers' Workplace Context?" In *Teachers' Work,* ed. Judith Warren Little and Milbrey Wallin McLaughlin. New York: Teachers College Press.

MCLAUGHLIN, MILBREY WALLIN, and TALBERT, JOAN E. 2001. *Professional Communities and the Work of High School Teaching.* Chicago: University of Chicago Press.

PHILADELPHIA TEACHERS LEARNING COOPERATIVE. 1984. "On Becoming Teacher Experts: Buying Time." *Language Arts* 6:731–735.

SHOCKLEY, BETTY; MICHELOVE, BARBARA; and ALLEN, JOBETH. 1995. *Engaging Families: Connecting Home and School Literacy Communities.* Portsmouth, NH: Heinemann.

SHULMAN, LEE S. 1987. "Knowledge and Teaching: Foundations of the New Reform." *Harvard Educational Review* 51:1–22.

STEIN, MARY KAY; SMITH, MARGARET SCHWAN; and SILVER, EDWARD A. 1999. "The Development of Professional Developers: Learning to Assist Teachers in New Settings in New Ways." *Harvard Educational Review* 69(3):237–269.

WELLS, GORDON. 1994. "Text, Talk, and Inquiry: Schooling as Semiotic Apprenticeship." In *Language and Learning,* ed. Norman Bird. Hong Kong: Institute of Language in Education and the University of Hong Kong, Department of Curriculum Studies.

WENGER, ETIENNE. 1998. *Communities of Practice: Learning, Meaning, and Identity.* Cambridge, MA: Cambridge University Press.

WESTHEIMER, JOEL. 1998. *Among School Teachers: Community, Autonomy, and Ideology in Teachers' Work.* New York: Teachers College Press.

INTERNET RESOURCE

CARNEGIE ACADEMY FOR THE SCHOLARSHIP OF TEACHING AND LEARNING. 2002. <www.carnegiefoundation.org>.

MARILYN COCHRAN-SMITH
SUSAN L. LYTLE

TEACHER PREPARATION

TEACHER PREPARATION, INTERNATIONAL PERSPECTIVE

All nations have established specialized institutions and particular processes by which prospective teachers are educated; however these institutions and processes vary in their structure, goals, and organization around the world. The variation is not only due to expected differences across countries and cultures, but also to a major transition that the field of teacher education has been undergoing in developed countries since the late 1980s. At the beginning of the twenty-first century this transition has also begun to affect several developing nations. For years, the preparation of teachers was described as teacher *training;* this label reflected the actual process of giving prospective teachers or noncertified in-service teachers some subject matter knowledge and some pedagogical tools so that they could transfer information to their students. That is still the case in a majority of developing countries, particularly in Africa, Asia, and Latin America where the shortage of certified teachers still is found to be a major factor in the kind of teacher education offered.

However, the trend is to use *teacher training* only to refer to specific short-term training that teachers may receive, mostly on the job, to learn a particular skill (for example, a training session or unit on the use of computers) and to refer to the preparation of teachers as *professional development,* as it reflects more effectively the fact that teachers are professionals, their job is a complex process of helping students learn, and thus their preparation is not a one-shot training, but rather a lifelong process of learning and development. Professional development includes formal experiences (such as completing a program of initial teacher preparation, and also attending workshops, institutes, and professional meetings, mentoring, completing research, etc.) and informal experiences (such as reading professional publications, viewing television specials related to an academic discipline, joining study groups with other teachers, etc.).

New Paradigm in Teacher Education

This perspective of teacher education as a long-term process that includes regular opportunities and experiences planned systematically to promote growth and development in the profession has been welcomed by educators everywhere. This shift has been so dramatic that many have referred to it as a new image of teacher learning, a new model of teacher education, a revolution in education, and even a new paradigm of professional development.

This new paradigm of teacher education has several characteristics. First of all, it is based on constructivism rather than on a transmission-oriented model. As a consequence, teachers are treated as active learners who are engaged in the concrete tasks of teaching, assessment, observation, and reflection. Several research studies have shown that when the constructivist method is used in the preparation of teachers, the results are quite positive: teachers who are engaged, reflective, thoughtful, and effective. A few new studies, however, have been critical of this method, as it appears to be most effective only with middle-class learners, or only when used in very specific contexts and under certain conditions, something that could potentially limit the effectiveness of its use in teacher education.

It is also conceived of as a long-term process, as it acknowledges that teachers learn over time. As a result, connected experiences (rather than one-shot presentations) are thought of as most effective as they allow teachers to relate prior knowledge with new experiences. Regular follow-up support is perceived as an "indispensable catalyst of the change process" (Schifter, Russell, and Bastable, p. 30).

This approach to teacher education is conceived as a process that takes place in a particular context. Contrary to the traditional staff development opportunities that did not connect the "training" with the actual experiences in the classroom, the most effective professional development is based in schools, connected to the daily activities of teachers and learners. Schools are transformed into communities of learners, communities of inquiry, professional communities, and caring communities because teachers are engaged in professional development activities. The most successful teacher development opportunities are "on the job learning" activities such as study groups, action research, and portfolios.

Many identify this process as one that is intimately linked to school reform since professional development is a process of culture building, and not just skill-training, that is affected by the coherence of the school program. In this case, teachers are empowered as professionals; they should be treated in the same ways as society expects them to treat students. Teachers' professional development that is not supported by school and curriculum reform is not effective.

With this approach to teacher education and professional development, a teacher is considered a reflective practitioner, someone who comes into the profession with a certain knowledge base and who will build new knowledge and experiences based on that prior knowledge. For this reason, the role of professional development is to facilitate teachers' building new pedagogical theory and practice and help teachers improve their expertise in the field.

Professional development is regarded as a collaborative process. Even though there may be some opportunities for isolated work and reflection, most effective professional development happens when there are meaningful interactions, not only among teachers, but also with administrators, parents, and other community members.

Professional development may look and be very different in diverse settings, and even within one setting there may be a variety of dimensions. There is not "one best" form or model of professional development that can be implemented anywhere. Schools and educators must evaluate their needs and cultural beliefs and practices to decide which professional development model may be most successful in that particular context. It is clear in the literature that workplace factors (one significant variable of "the context") such as school structure and school culture can influence teachers' sense of efficacy and professional motivation. Apparent contradictory results reported in the literature (such as the fact that some studies conclude that the best professional development is that designed and implemented at a smaller scale, while others say that it is better at a larger, system-approach scale) may be explained not by deciding that one study is more accurate than an-

other, but by examining the contexts in which the different studies were completed. In his 1995 article, "Results-Oriented Professional Development: In Search of an Optimal Mix of Effective Practices," Thomas Guskey argues strongly about the importance of paying attention to context so that the "optimal mix" of professional development processes can be identified and planned. In other words, professional development has to be considered within a framework of social, economic, and political trends and events. In another 1995 article, "Professional Development in Education," Guskey writes: "The uniqueness of the individual setting will always be a critical factor in education. What works in one situation may not work in another . . . . Because of the enormous variability in educational contexts, there will never be 'one right answer.' Instead, there will be a collection of answers, each specific to a context. Our search must focus, therefore, on finding the *optimal mix*—that assortment of professional development processes and technologies that work best in a particular setting" (p. 117).

This new form of teacher education has had a significant positive impact on teachers' beliefs and practices, students' learning, and on the implementation of education reforms. In fact, Linda Darling-Hammond noted in a 1999 article in the *Journal of Staff Development* that "investments in teachers' knowledge and skills net greater increases in students' achievement [in the United States] than other uses of an education dollar" (p. 32).

What Do Teachers Need to Know?

For years, educators and other related professionals have argued whether teacher preparation should emphasize content knowledge or pedagogical knowledge. Under this new model of teacher professional development, there is a recognition that the work of teachers is complex and thus needs a broad and inclusive perspective. Authors including Anne Grosso de Leon, Anne Reynolds, Robert Glaser, Hilda Borko and Ralph Putnam, and Olugbemiro Jegede, Margaret Taplin, and Sing-Lai Chan have offered lists of types of knowledge, skills, dispositions, and values that effective teachers must have a mastery of. They include:

- General pedagogical knowledge. This includes knowledge of learning environments and instructional strategies; classroom management; and knowledge of learners and learning.

- Subject-matter knowledge. This includes knowledge of content and substantive structures and syntactic structures (equivalent to knowledge about a discipline).

- Pedagogical content knowledge. A conceptual map of how to teach a subject; knowledge of instructional strategies and representations; knowledge of students' understanding and potential misunderstandings; and knowledge of curriculum and curricular materials.

- Knowledge of student context and a disposition to find out more about students, their families, and their schools. Knowledge and disposition to involved families in the day-to-day work of the schools.

- A repertoire of metaphors in order to be able to bridge theory and practice.

- External evaluation of learning.

- Clinical training.

- Knowledge of strategies, techniques, and tools to create and sustain a learning environment or community, and the ability to employ them.

- Knowledge, skills, and dispositions to work with children of diverse cultural, social, and linguistic backgrounds. A multicultural perspective in teacher preparation is crucial for an effective program of teacher education and professional development.

- Knowledge and attitudes that support political and social justice as social realities make teachers very important agents of social change. In some extreme situations (such as that of South Africa after the apartheid regime and Namibia after gaining independence), this aspect of the professional work of a teacher is more emphasized and thus institutions of teacher preparation have adopted this as a requirement of their programs. Michael Samuel, Katarina Norberg, and others argue that the development of this critical consciousness should be part of teacher preparation, not only in extreme cases, but also in all countries and contexts.

- Knowledge and skills on how to use technology in the curriculum. In a 2001 article in *Language Arts,* Evangeline Pianfetti lists a number of "virtual opportunities for professional development," and also a number of Internet sites with information about grant providers that support professional development efforts to educate teachers about new technologies in the classroom.

Twenty-First Century Trends in Teacher Education and Professional Development

Most countries acknowledge that initial or pre-service teacher education is just the first step in a longer process of professional development, and not the only preparation teachers will receive. A majority of countries are beginning to require the same level of preparation for all teachers, regardless of the level they will teach, and the worldwide trend is toward requiring a minimum of a bachelor's degree to enter programs that prepare teachers.

In terms of the content of teacher preparation programs, different countries vary in their emphasis on particular components of the curriculum or the time devoted to each one. But in general, most include courses and experiences that address subject matter, foundation of education courses, professional studies (such as pedagogy and methods courses), and child development, and a practicum, or student teaching. The tendency in a majority of countries is to emphasize the teaching of content in the initial preparation and to emphasize the pedagogy in the practicum and programs of induction for new teachers as well as other professional development opportunities.

There are trends to increase the length of teacher preparation programs and to increase the amount of time pre-service teachers spend in practicum sites. Pre-service programs that provide opportunities for supervised practice teaching throughout the duration of the course are the most effective. There is a wide variation of length for this practical experience of student teachers in the world. In some countries where the practicum is short, teachers are required to have extensive in-service opportunity to practice under serious supervision.

In a number of developed and developing countries, the need for more teachers and the lack of candidates entering the profession have been fertile ground for the creation of a number of alternative teacher certification programs. These programs usually include a heavy component of in-service training and usually begin with a "crash course" on pedagogical knowledge that is completed in a very short amount of time. The creation and proliferation of such programs has generated great controversy in most countries where they exist.

Among more recent developments is a tendency to offer new teachers some support in the form of "induction programs." Induction programs are planned and systematic programs of sustained assistance to beginning teachers. Finally, the trend in "in-service education" is to offer a variety of opportunities for professional development that go beyond the "one-shot" short course or workshop traditionally offered to experienced teachers.

See also: ELEMENTARY EDUCATION, *subentry on* PREPARATION OF TEACHERS; INTERNATIONAL TEACHERS ASSOCIATION; TEACHER EDUCATION, *subentry on* INTERNATIONAL PERSPECTIVE; TEACHING AND LEARNING.

BIBLIOGRAPHY

ABDAL-HAQQ, ISMAT. 1996. *Making Time for Teacher Professional Development.* ERIC Digest. Washington, DC: ERIC Clearinghouse on Teaching and Teacher Education.

ALIDOU, HASSANA. 2000. "Preparing Teachers for The Education of New Immigrant Students from Africa." *Action in Teacher Education* 22(2):A.

ANGESS, JACQUELINE. 2001. "Teacher Learning at the Intersection of School Learning and Student Outcomes." In *Teachers Caught in the Action: Professional Development That Matters,* ed. Ann Lieberman and Lynne Miller. New York: Teachers College Press.

BAKER, SCOTT, and SMITH, SYLVIA. 1999. "Starting Off on the Right Foot: The Influence of Four Principles of Professional Development in Improving Literacy Instruction in Two Kindergarten Programs." *Learning Disabilities Research and Practice* 14(4):239–253.

BEN-PERETZ, MYRIAM. 1995. "Curriculum of Teacher Education Programs." In *International Encyclopedia of Teaching and Teacher Education,* 2nd edition, ed. Lorin W. Anderson. London: Pergamon Press.

BERRY, BARNETT. 2001. "No Shortcuts to Preparing Good Teachers." *Educational Leadership* 58(8):32–36.

BORKO, HILDA, and PUTNAM, RALPH T. 1995. "Expanding a Teacher's Knowledge Base: A Cognitive Psychological Perspective on Professional Development." In *Professional Development in Education: New Paradigms and Practices,* ed. Thomas R. Guskey and Michael Huberman. New York: Teachers College Press.

CLEMENT, MIEKE, and VANDENBERGHE, ROLAND. 2000. "Teachers' Professional Development: A Solitary or Collegial (Ad)Venture?" *Teaching and Teacher Education* 16:81–101.

COBB, VELMA. 1999. *An International Comparison of Teacher Education.* ERIC Digest. Washington, DC: ERIC Clearinghouse on Teaching and Teacher Education.

COCHRAN-SMITH, MARILYN, and LYTLE, SUSAN L. 2001. "Beyond Certainty: Taking an Inquiry Stance on Practice." In *Teachers Caught in the Action: Professional Development That Matters,* ed. Ann Lieberman and Lynne Miller. New York: Teachers College Press.

COHEN, DAVID K. 1990. "A Revolution in One Classroom: The Case of Mrs. Oublier." *Educational Evaluation and Policy Analysis* 12(3):311–329.

DADDS, MARION. 2001. "Continuing Professional Development: Nurturing the Expert Within." In *Teacher Development: Exploring Our Own Practice,* ed. Janet Soler, Anna Craft, and Hilary Burgess. London: Paul Chapman Publishing and The Open University.

DARLING-HAMMOND, LINDA. 1998. "Policy and Change: Getting Beyond Bureaucracy." In *International Handbook of Educational Change,* ed. Andy Hargreaves et al. Great Britain: Kluwer Academic Press.

DARLING-HAMMOND, LINDA. 1999. "Target Time Toward Teachers." *Journal of Staff Development* 20(2):31–36.

DARLING-HAMMOND, LINDA, and McLAUGHLIN, MILBREY W. 1995. "Policies That Support Professional Development in an Era of Reform." *Phi Delta Kappan* 76(8):597–604.

DHARMADASA, INDRANIE. 2000. *Pre-service Teachers' Perspectives on Constructivist Teaching and Learning.* Paper presented at the Annual Meeting of the Mid-South Educational Research Association. Bowling Green, Kentucky, November 15–17, 2000.

DUDZINSKI, MARYANNE; ROSZMANN-MILLICAN, MICHELE; and SHANK, KATHLENE. 2000. "Continuing Professional Development for Special Educators: Reforms and Implications for University Programs." *Teacher Education and Special Education* 23(2):109–124.

EDUCATIONAL TESTING SERVICE. 1998. *Professional Development: A Link to Better Learning.* New Jersey: Educational Testing Service.

FALK, BEVERLY. 2001. "Professional Learning Through Assessment." In *Teachers Caught in the Action: Professional Development That Matters,* ed. Ann Lieberman and Lynne Miller. New York: Teachers College Press.

GANSER, TOM. 2000. "An Ambitious Vision of Professional Development For Teachers." *National Association of Secondary School Principals Bulletin* 84(618):6–12.

GAY, GENEVA, and HOWARD, TYRONE C. 2000. "Multicultural Teacher Education for the 21st Century." *The Teacher Educator* 36(1):1–16.

GLASER, ROBERT. 1987. "Thoughts on Expertise." In *Cognitive Functioning and Social Structure Over The Life Course,* ed. Carmi Schooler and K. Warner Schaie. Norwood, NJ: Ablex.

GORSKI, PAUL; SHIN, GENE-TEY; and GREEN, MARTHA, eds. 2000. *Professional Development Guide for Educators.* (The Multicultural Resource Series, Volume 1). Washington, DC: National Education Association of the United States.

GRACE, DONALD. 1999. "Paradigm Lost (and Regained)."*Independent School* 59(1):54–57.

GROSSO DE LEON, ANNE. 2001. *Higher Education's Challenge: New Teacher Education Models for a New Century.* New York: Carnegie Corporation of New York.

GUSKEY, THOMAS R. 1995. "Professional Development in Education: In Search of the Optimal Mix." In *Professional Development in Education: New Paradigms and Practices,* ed. Thomas R. Guskey and Michael Huberman. New York: Teachers College Press.

GUZMAN, JOSE LUIS. 1995. *Formando Los Maestros y Maestras de Educacion Basica del Siglo XXI.* San Salvador, El Salvador: Universidad Centroamericana Jose Simeon Canas.

JACKSON, ROBERT K., and LEROY, CAROL A. 1998. "Eminent Teachers' Views on Teacher Education and Development." *Action in Teacher Education* 20(3):15–29.

JARVINEN, ANNIKKI, and KOHONEN, VILJO. 1995. "Promoting Professional Development in

Higher Education Through Portfolio Assessment." *Assessment and Evaluation in Higher Education* 20(1):25–36.

JEGEDE, OLUGBEMIR; TAPLIN, MARGARET; and CHAN, SING-LAI. 2000. "Trainee Teachers' Perception of Their Knowledge About Expert Teaching." *Educational Research* 42(3):287–308.

JENLINK, PATRICK M., and KINNUCAN-WELSCH, KATHRYN. 1999. "Learning Ways of Caring, Learning Ways of Knowing Through Communities of Professional Development." *Journal for a Just and Caring Education* 5(4):367–385.

KING, M. BRUCE, and NEWMANN, FRED M. 2000, April. "Will Teacher Learning Advance School Goals?" *Phi Delta Kappan* 576–580.

LIEBERMAN, ANN. 1994. "Teacher Development: Commitment and Challenge." In *Teacher Development and the Struggle for Authenticity: Professional Growth and Restructuring in the Context of Change,* ed. Peter P. Grimmett and Jonathan Neufeld. New York: Teachers College Press.

LOUCKS-HORSLEY, SUSAN, and MATSUMOTO, CAROLEE. 1999. "Research on Professional Development for Teachers of Mathematics and Science: The State of the Scene." *School Science and Mathematics* 99(5):258–271.

MCGINN, NOEL, and BORDEN, ALLISON. 1995. *Framing Questions, Constructing Answers: Linking Research with Education Policy for Developing Countries.* Cambridge, MA: Harvard University Press.

MCLAUGHLIN, MILBREY W., and ZARROW, JOEL. 2001. "Teachers Engaged in Evidence-Based Reform: Trajectories of Teachers' Inquiry, Analysis, and Action." In *Teachers Caught in the Action: Professional Development That Matters,* ed. Ann Lieberman and Lynne Miller. New York: Teachers College Press.

MINTROP, HEINRICH. 2001. "Educating Students to Teach in a Constructivist Way—Can It All Be Done?" *Teachers College Record* 103(2):207–233.

MORALES, FRANCISCO. 1998. *Participacion de Padres en la Escuela: Component para la Formacion de Profesores.* Santiago, Chile: Centro de Investigación y Desarrollo de la Educación.

NATIONAL COMMISSION ON TEACHING AND AMERICA'S FUTURE. 1996. *What Matters Most: Teaching for America's Future.* New York: National Commission on Teaching and America's Future.

NATIONAL COMMISSION ON TEACHING AND AMERICA'S FUTURE. 1997. *Doing What Matters Most: Investing in Quality Teaching.* New York: National Commission on Teaching and America's Future.

NORBERG, KATARINA. 2000. "Intercultural Education and Teacher Education in Sweden." *Teaching and Teacher Education* 16:511–519.

PIANFETTI, EVANGELINE S. 2001. "Teachers and Technology: Digital Literacy Through Professional Development." *Language Arts* 78(3):255–262.

REYNOLDS, ANNE. 1992. "What Is Competent Beginning Teaching? A Review of the Literature." *Review of Educational Research* 62(1):1–35.

RICHARDSON, VIRGINIA, ed. 1997. *Constructivist Teacher Education: Building New Understandings.* Washington, DC: Falmer Press.

RICHARDSON, VIRGINIA, ed. 2001. *Handbook of Research on Teaching.* Washington, DC: American Educational Research Association.

SAMUEL, MICHAEL. 1998. "Changing Lives in Changing Times: Pre-service Teacher Education in Post-Apartheid South Africa." *Tesol Quarterly* 32(3):576–585.

SCHIFTER, DEBORAH; RUSSELL, SUSAN JO; and BASTABLE, VIRGINIA. 1999. "Teaching to the Big Ideas." In *The Diagnostic Teacher: Constructing New Approaches to Professional Development,* ed. Mildred Z. Solomon. New York: Teachers College Press.

SCRIBNER, JAY PAREDES. 1999. "Professional Development: Untangling the Influence of Work Context on Teacher Learning." *Educational Administration Quarterly* 35(2):238–266.

TATTO, MARIA TERESA. 1999. *Conceptualizing and Studying Teacher Education Across World Regions: An Overview.* Paper prepared for the Conference on Teachers in Latin America: New Perspectives on their Development and Performance. San Juan, Costa Rica.

VAN STRAT, GEORGENA, and GIBSON, HELEN. 2001. *A Longitudinal Study of the Impact of Constructivist Instructional Methods on the Attitudes Toward Teaching and Learning Mathematics and Science.* Paper presented at the Annual Meeting of the National Association for Research in Science Teaching, St Louis, MO, March 26–29, 2001.

VILLEGAS-REIMERS, ELEONORA, and REIMERS, FERNANDO. 1996. "Where Are 60 Million Teachers? The Missing Voice in Educational Reforms Around the World." *Prospects* 26(3): 469–492.

WALLING, BRENDA, and LEWIS, MARK. 2000. "Development of Professional Identity Among Professional Development School Pre-Service Teachers: Longitudinal and Comparative Analysis." *Action in Teacher Education* 22: 2A.

WEISMAN, EVELYN M. 2001. "Bicultural Identity and Language Attitudes: Perspectives of Four Latina Teachers." *Urban Education* 36(2):203–225.

WOOD, FRED, and McQUARRIE, FRANK. 1999. "On-The-Job Learning." *Journal of Staff Development* 20(3):10–13.

WOODS, P. 1994. "The Conditions for Teacher Development." In *Teacher Development and the Struggle for Authenticity: Professional Growth and Restructuring in the Context of Change,* ed. Peter P. Grimmett and Jonathan Neufeld. New York: Teachers College Press.

YOUNG, PETER. 2001. "District and State Policy Influences on Professional Development and School Capacity." *Educational Policy* 15(2):278–301.

INTERNET RESOURCE

GUSKEY, THOMAS. 1995. "Results-Oriented Professional Development: In Search of an Optimal Mix of Effective Practices." North Central Region Educational Laboratory (NCREL). <www.ncrel.org/sdrs/areas/rpl_esys/pdlitrev.html#4>.

ELEONORA VILLEGAS-REIMERS

TEACHER UNIONS

OVERVIEW
David W. Kirkpatrick
INFLUENCE ON INSTRUCTION AND OTHER
EDUCATIONAL PRACTICES
Willis D. Hawley
Donna Redmond Jones

OVERVIEW

The best-known teacher unions in the United States are the National Education Association (NEA) and the American Federation of Teachers (AFT). However, not all public school teachers are their members, nor are all of their members public school teachers. Membership also includes support staff in the public schools, such as secretaries, bus drivers, and cafeteria workers, and some outside the schools, such as hospital nurses.

Other teacher groups include Independent Education Associations (IEAs) at the local, state, and national levels, which remain largely unknown, and Local Only Teacher Unions (LOTUs) which are almost totally unknown. There are also public school teachers who are not members of any organizations, plus private school teachers, few of whom are organized except for the National Association of Catholic Teachers. This organization, headquartered in Philadelphia, represents some, but not all, of the teachers in Catholic schools.

The National Education Association

The National Education Association was founded in 1857 in Philadelphia as the National Teachers' Association. For the first century it grew slowly, with fewer than 2,400 members in 1900 and 330,000 as late as 1964, the point at which its most rapid growth was getting underway. By 2001 NEA membership exceeded 2.3 million in more than 13,000 local affiliate organizations.

A handful of key events led to the evolution of the NEA to its characteristics at the beginning of the twenty-first century. The first was external, in the form of the victory in New York City at the beginning of the 1960s of the American Federation of Teachers local affiliate, the United Federation of Teachers, which emerged as the dominant union from what had been more than 100 groups. Subsequent AFT victories in other urban areas, plus Wisconsin's 1962 passage of the first collective bargaining law for educators, forced the NEA to begin a transformation that initially faced both internal and external problems.

In 1960 the NEA assembly had rejected a resolution endorsing representative negotiations. Although this position was reversed the next year, for much of the 1960s the NEA stressed that it was an association and referred to *professional negotiations,* rather than *collective bargaining,* because of the resistance of many of its own members to identification as a union.

The early 1970s saw a number of major internal changes. Until then the NEA permitted members to join any combination of the local, state, and national units, although some local and state affiliates had different rules. A 1975 provision added to the NEA Constitution established a unified membership, whereby those who did join would have to do so at all three levels. Until then the NEA included departments with specific professional interests, such as administrators, math or science, and curriculum or instruction, in both basic and higher education. With the introduction of unified dues many local affiliated organizations dropped out. These included not only the professional interest groups but even the Missouri state association, which had been one of the NEA's charter members in 1857. These losses were more than compensated by the addition of huge numbers of individual members at the state and national level, most of whom, as they had always done, joined the local association at the urging of their colleagues, whether or not they had any understanding of, commitment to, or even interest in, the state and national organizations.

This membership growth was both accompanied and accelerated by the NEA's establishment of its Uniserv program, which led to the creation of hundreds of offices across the nation in cooperation with its state and local affiliates. The state affiliates employ the Uniserv staff but, with financial and coordinating support from the NEA, these staff function as quasi-NEA employees. Within less than thirty years there were 1,800 of these staff members.

In 1972 the NEA also became the first national education organization with a political action committee, one that remains among the nation's largest and most influential. By the 1990s the NEA came to have one of the largest delegations to the quadrennial Democratic National Convention and a smaller delegation at the Republican National Convention. One example of its influence was the establishment of the U.S. Department of Education by Congress in 1979, with the support of President Jimmy Carter, whom the NEA had endorsed in 1976, despite the opposition of the AFT. Teacher unions also benefit from advantages that Congress has granted unions in general, such as exemption from laws prohibiting conspiracies in restraint of trade.

Ironically, at the peak of their power and influence, the NEA and AFT face more pressures and opposition than ever before. Internal problems for the NEA include the tendency of newer teachers to show less interest in joining. A 1997 membership survey commissioned by the NEA warned that it faced "organizational death." While that is probably overly pessimistic, the NEA recognizes there are difficulties even beyond what might be expected in an influential organization with a budget of nearly $250 million, a national staff of nearly six hundred and, with its affiliates, an additional staff of thousands.

One source of tension is that nearly all of NEA's political endorsements go to Democrats, although its Democratic members, while they comprise a larger political block than either Republicans or Independents, still make up less than 50 percent of its membership. Reportedly 40 percent of NEA members regularly vote contrary to the organization's recommendations and sometimes more than half do so, as in President Ronald Reagan's 1980 and 1984 campaigns. There is also unhappiness with the NEA's adoption of positions on social issues such as abortion and gun control, which many members feel detracts from the attention that should be paid to educational issues.

Externally, both unions face challenges not only from the private school sector but from such growing trends in education as home schooling, tuition vouchers, and charter schools, all of which weaken teachers' perceived need for a union. Unions face a dilemma in dealing with these issues. If they oppose vouchers, charter schools, and private schools, it becomes extremely difficult for them to appeal to teachers in such schools once they are established. As a result, very few charter schools or private schools are unionized. While it is unlikely that the NEA will disappear, some of its leadership advocates a "new unionism," and its future depends upon how it deals with these challenges.

The American Federation of Teachers

Four local teacher unions met in Chicago in April 1916. After charters were granted to other local organizations, an application to the American Federation of Labor for affiliation was granted to the four local unions the next month and the American Federation of Teachers was established. Shortly after World War I, its membership briefly exceeded that of the older but still small NEA.

In 1952 teacher Al Shanker joined the New York Teachers Guild, which had been founded in 1917 with American educator and philosopher John Dewey as a charter member. Shanker edited the Guild's newspaper and began organizing individual schools with colleagues such as David Selden; both

men subsequently became presidents of the national AFT. It was the Guild that triumphed in the 1961 election resulting in the United Federation of Teachers (UFT) local in New York City. Much of the subsequent history of the AFT is the history of Al Shanker. Shanker served first as UFT President, and then from 1974, when he succeeded Selden, until his death in 1997, as president of the AFT. For part of that time he was president of both the UFT and AFT, a result of AFT rules that permit holding multiple offices and an unrestricted number of terms.

This continuity of officers, and its representation of teachers in key urban areas, especially in such media centers as Washington, D.C., and New York City, has enabled the AFT and its presidents to develop greater visibility than the NEA and its leaders, thus partially offsetting the advantages the NEA enjoys because it represents far more people and resources and has a virtually universal distribution of its membership throughout society. The AFT embraced collective bargaining earlier and more enthusiastically than the NEA, but changing circumstances and the competition between the two organizations resulted in victories and growth for both, including legislative and political victories that saw collective bargaining laws adopted in more than half of the states by the early 1970s.

During the tumult of the 1960s AFT membership increased five-fold, from 60,000 in 1961 to 300,000 in 1970 and to 820,000 in 1993, by which time, except for Nevada, the AFT had affiliates in every state plus the District of Columbia, in U.S. territories such as Guam and Puerto Rico, and in ten other nations. But these members represent fewer than 2,300 local organizations, far less than the NEA's more than 13,000. Additionally, nearly half of the locals were in New York state.

Union Influence

The AFT's 900,000 members at the start of the twenty-first century, coupled with the NEA's 2.3 million, give the two unions representation of about three-quarters of all public school teachers; 40 percent of all unionized public employees; a total income at the local, state, and national levels of nearly $1.5 billion; 6,000 employees, more than both major political parties combined; and a distribution of membership and power from rural areas to urban centers such as New York City. On average, there are nearly 7,000 teachers in each congressional district, over 5,000 of whom are organized. As in most unions, NEA and

AFT leaders tend to rise from the ranks but, unlike in most other unions, the leaders who emerge from the ranks are college graduates. These conditions explain the influence the two unions have, and not just on education.

Despite individual strengths, emerging challenges have led to strong efforts by both organizations to merge. The AFT was prepared to accept a merger in 1998 but, at its annual convention that year, the NEA's delegates defeated a proposal by nearly a three to two margin. While there are still efforts to bring about a merger, in the interim, the two groups are seeking to cooperate more, compete less, and maximize their effectiveness against what they perceive as common enemies and obstacles.

Another effort at cooperation developed in the late 1990s when a number of locals of both unions met to establish the Teacher Union Reform Network (TURN) to forward their own reform agenda to counter those coming from other sources. Within a few years twenty-three local organizations had joined, mostly from major urban areas including New York City, Los Angeles, Denver, Seattle, and San Francisco. Their ability to meet contemporary challenges remains to be seen.

Other Teacher Groups

While they do not yet comprise a national force, there are now dozens of local and state teacher groups and one emerging national group—these groups are often referred to as Independent Education Associations (IEAs). The IEA associations in Georgia, Missouri, and Texas are larger than either the NEA or AFT affiliates in those states; the one in Texas has more than 100,000 members. Most reject the union title and oppose strikes or the agency shop model, whereby nonmembers are required to pay a fee to the bargaining representative. Many are in non-union, or right-to-work states, and strongly advocate remaining that way. The national group, known as the American Association of Educators (AAE), was founded in 1994. By 2002 it had 33,000 members and a dozen state affiliates.

There are also an undetermined number of Local Only Teacher Unions (LOTUs), with at least ten in Indiana and others in Ohio. The largest, the Akron Education Association, does proclaim itself to be a union, utilizes the agency shop provision for nonmembers, and has conducted a strike.

There are an estimated 300,000 unorganized public school teachers and as many or more who be-

long to the IEAs and LOTUs. These 600,000 individuals could have a national influence on education but they lack the cohesiveness, organizational structure, or visibility to do so. The AAE may prove to be the group that can counteract the national dominance of the NEA and the AFT. It planned to move from its original base in California to the Washington, D.C. area in 2002. Such a move should provide it the opportunity to become better known to the national media and to other teachers, thus making it more significant in education affairs.

See also: AMERICAN FEDERATION OF TEACHERS; INTERNATIONAL TEACHERS ASSOCIATION; NATIONAL EDUCATION ASSOCIATION; TEACHER UNIONS, *subentry on* INFLUENCE ON INSTRUCTION AND OTHER EDUCATIONAL PRACTICES.

BIBLIOGRAPHY

BRAUN, ROBERT J. 1972. *Teachers and Power, The Story of the American Federation of Teachers.* New York: Simon and Schuster.

CHAPMAN, MICHAEL. 1999. "The NEA's Political Lesson Plan." *Investor's Business Daily* January 5, p. A1.

CHASE, BOB. 1998. *America's Children, America's Promise.* Washington, DC: Proceedings of the 1997 National Education Association Representative Assembly.

FREEDMAN, SAMUEL G. 1990. *Small Victories.* New York: Harper and Row.

GRANT, WILLIAM R. 1975. "School Desegregation and Teacher Bargaining: Forces for Change in American Schools." In *The Politics of Education: Challenges to State Board Leadership,* ed. Stuart Sandow and Wesley Apker. Bloomington, IN: Phi Delta Kappa.

HAAR, CHARLENE; LIEBERMAN, MYRON; and TROY, LEO. 1994. *The NEA and AFT, Teacher Unions in Power and Politics.* Rockport, MA: Pro Active Publications.

HILL, DAVID. 1996. "The Education of Al Shanker." *Teacher Magazine* (February):22–29.

KIRKPATRICK, DAVID W. 1993. "Teacher Unions and Collective Bargaining in Retrospect." *Government Union Review* Fall Issue. Vienna, VA: Public Service Research Foundation.

KIRKPATRICK, DAVID W. 1996. "Teacher Unions and Education Reform." Unpublished monograph prepared for the Education Policy Institute, Washington, DC.

KIRKPATRICK, DAVID W. 1997. *Alternative Teacher Organizations: Policy Study 231.* Los Angeles: Reason Public Policy Institute.

LAMBERT, SAM. 1970. "Report of the Executive Secretary." *Addresses and Proceedings of the 108th Annual Meeting.* Washington, DC: National Education Association.

LARSON, REED. 1999. *Stranglehold: How Union Bosses Have Hijacked Our Government.* Ottawa, IL: Jameson Books.

LIEBERMAN, MYRON. 1996. *Local Only Teacher Unions (LOTUs).* Washington, DC: Education Policy Institute.

LIEBERMAN, MYRON. 1997. *The Teacher Unions.* New York: The Free Press.

NATIONAL EDUCATION ASSOCIATION. 1990. *Charter, Bylaws and Constitution.* Published for NEA Representative Assembly, Kansas City, July 1990. Washington, DC: National Education Association.

O'NEILL, JOHN. 1970. "The Rise and Fall of the AFT." In *Schools Against Children,* ed. Annette T. Rubenstein. New York: Monthly Review Press.

SANDOW, STUART, and APKER, WESLEY, eds. 1975. *The Politics of Education: Challenges to State Board Leadership.* Bloomington, IN: Phi Delta Kappa.

WASSERMAN, MIRIAM. 1970. *The School Fix, NYC, USA.* New York: Outerbridge and Diestenfrey.

WOOSTER, MARTIN MORSE. 1994. *Angry Classrooms.* San Francisco: Pacific Research Institute for Public Policy.

DAVID W. KIRKPATRICK

INFLUENCE ON INSTRUCTION AND OTHER EDUCATIONAL PRACTICES

Schools cannot be significantly improved without improving the quality of teaching. Teacher unions significantly influence how teachers view their work. Not all teachers belong to teacher unions, but more than 90 percent of the 2.6 million public school teachers belong to either the American Federation of Teachers (AFT) or the larger National Education Association (NEA). While teachers do not blindly fol-

low union leaders, it seems unlikely that substantial school improvement can occur without the support and resources of teacher unions.

Overview

Historically, many educational policymakers and researchers have viewed efforts of teacher unions as antithetical to school reform. Most teacher union activity has involved aggressive efforts to raise teacher salaries, improve teachers' working conditions, and protect teachers' rights, even if this entailed protests that limited or suspended teachers' work with students. Although school improvement has been on the agenda of the AFT and the NEA for decades, most observers, and union leaders themselves, have recognized that there has been a tension between fighting for rights that are most beneficial to its members and pressing for reform that is most beneficial for students.

In the 1990s both national unions substantially increased their engagement in direct efforts to increase student achievement by improving instructional strategies and school conditions that support good teaching and student learning. These initiatives—which have been dubbed the "new unionism"—have been motivated by demands of newer members, by the recognition that effective teaching requires new structures and relationships in schools, and by perceived needs to build public and political support for the unions. In spite of national resolutions and new alliances that promote union leadership in reform, some informed observers, such as Gregory Moo and Myron Lieberman, have expressed doubts about the viability of new unionism. Moreover, as federated organizations, both the NEA and AFT propose national stances that are loosely coupled with the practices of state and local affiliates that believe in the unions' more traditional mission of advocating teachers' rights and benefits.

Teacher unions influence instruction and other educational practices of interest to those who define themselves as school reformers in four general ways: (1) electoral politics and lobbying, (2) collective bargaining, (3) reform initiatives focused on their members, and (4) dissemination of information about best practice.

Electoral Politics and Lobbying

Teacher unions engage in direct political action at national, state, and local levels to secure the election of candidates who support their priorities and to promote or oppose the adoption of ballot issues—such as support for increases in education funding and opposition to school vouchers. Likewise, teacher unions seek to influence legislative initiatives and executive actions through the provision of information, promises of electoral support or opposition, and efforts to shape public opinion. As is the case for most political interest groups, teacher unions may be more effective in opposing policies than in getting policies adopted that they favor.

Collective Bargaining

Since the 1960s a hallmark of the traditionally adversarial relationships between union and school district leaders has been their engagement in industrial-style collective bargaining often characterized by divergent labor-management interests, standardized work rules, and equal treatment of teachers who have varying degrees of skill and marketability. Studies, such as Joe A. Stone's 2000 research, have generally found few connections between collective bargaining and improved student achievement. The "new unionism," however, calls for "interest-based bargaining" in which labor and management enter into discussions about what they see as important in efforts to find solutions to problems instead of focusing on prerogatives and issues of control. According to Charles Kerchner, unions can work to enhance teaching quality by promoting teacher leadership and collaboration in initiatives such as peer review, teacher induction, professional development, and performance rewards.

Peer Review

Peer Assistance and Review (PAR) is a union-initiated teacher evaluation system in which veteran teachers jointly selected by union and district representatives are released from their classroom duties to assist beginning teachers or improve the competence of poorly performing, tenured teachers. At the end of the year, the veteran teachers recommend renewal or nonrenewal of the beginning and tenured teachers' contracts. Union support of an evaluation system that could lead to the termination of tenured teachers who are not responsive to remediation attempts is a dramatic departure from a stance that has typically privileged the protection of teachers' jobs. The American Federation of Teachers and National Education Association both favor PAR and argue that it places teachers in charge of setting and enforcing the standards of the profession.

Induction

Although some union locals have not amassed enough support or funding for Peer Assistance and Review programs, a number have established peer assistance programs to provide mentoring to new or veteran teachers expressing a need for help. At the national level, unions provide grants to locals that form partnerships with their districts and local universities to provide intensive training and support for new teachers. On the other hand, contract provisions that give experienced teachers options to move to schools with vacant positions often result in new teachers being assigned to schools with underperforming students, and this contributes to teacher turnover and to low student achievement.

Professional Development

Beyond using the contract to provide time or compensation for teachers engaging in professional development, a growing number of local unions are using contracts to define characteristics of effective professional development, insisting that their districts provide teachers with "ongoing" opportunities for "job-embedded" professional development connected to school and district student achievement objectives. Union contracts can also have negative effects on professional development by reducing flexibility in the how time is used and how teachers are rewarded for their participation in learning new knowledge and skills.

Performance-Based Pay

Although most union-district contracts provide for salary increases to teachers that are based on their years of service or attainment of graduate credits, a number of union affiliates are pushing for pay-for-performance compensation structures that would provide higher compensation to teachers who are exemplary practitioners and who choose to engage in leadership and professional development. Some affiliates also propose to cut the pay of teachers failing to meet high standards. Whether or not student achievement as measured by standardized tests should be a part of the criteria used to determine teacher pay is controversial.

Programmatic Reform Initiatives

In the early twenty-first century, both national unions are engaged in numerous programs that seek to respond to member interests in school improvement and to influence both public policy and public opinion by demonstrating their commitment to student learning. The demand that these activities place on union resources has increased dramatically. In 2001, thousands of schools were involved in a broad array of NEA-supported programs dealing with a broad range of concerns that include changing school conditions that support effective teaching and organizational efficiency and accountability, jumpstarting reform in low-performing schools, teacher education, and the implementation of charter schools. The AFT has placed organizational priority on toughening curriculum standards and preschool education. Both national organizations have programmatic initiatives aimed at improving the teaching of reading and promoting school safety and both are actively involved in promoting teacher involvement in certification by the National Board for Professional Teaching Standards.

Dissemination of Information about Best Practice

Both national unions have made efforts to make useful information about educational practice available to their members. Both publish professional journals and specialized newsletters focused on particular segments of their membership as well as books and reports on dozens of topics. The AFT supports the Educational Research and Dissemination program that helps teachers apply research findings to their classroom practice. These efforts to influence their members' actions have grown substantially and have become more prescriptive in the sense that explicit endorsement of particular strategies is now common. Both organizations, at the national level and in many states and districts, have elaborate websites that both provide information and allow members to engage in professional discussions. During elections and with respect to specific policies under consideration, teacher unions have sought to influence public opinion through press releases, media events, and political advertising. The effort to shape popular thinking about best practice transcends these overtly political actions. Teacher unions buy space in leading newspapers, support cable and public television programming that draws attention to the importance of good teaching, and form partnerships with other educational organizations to disseminate and advocate for research-based practices.

Effect on Educational Reform

There is little research that systematically examines the effects of union actions on improving instruc-

tion and on school reform more generally. It is clear however, that certain policies frequently advocated by would-be reformers would not be as far along as they are now without teacher union cooperation and leadership. These steps include peer review of teacher competence, more robust induction programs, job-embedded professional development, and performance-based pay. It is also clear that the greater emphasis on school improvement and student achievement that has characterized teacher union priorities in the late twentieth century is unlikely to be reversed. This redirection is being institutionalized in organizational structures and new staff positions in state and national units, in organizational initiatives such as the Teacher Union Reform Network, and in relationships at all levels with other professional educators, from principals and superintendents in local schools and districts to national partnerships, such as the Learning First Alliance.

See also: AMERICAN FEDERATION OF TEACHERS; NATIONAL EDUCATION ASSOCIATION; TEACHER EMPLOYMENT; TEACHER EVALUATION; TEACHER LEARNING COMMUNITIES; TEACHER UNIONS.

BIBLIOGRAPHY

AMERICAN FEDERATION OF TEACHERS AND THE NATIONAL EDUCATION ASSOCIATION. 1998. *Peer Assistance and Peer Review: An AFT/NEA Handbook.* Washington, DC: American Federation of Teachers and the National Education Association.

JOHNSON, SUSAN MOORE, and KARDOS, SUSAN M. 2000. "Reform Bargaining and Its Promise for School Improvement." In *Conflicting Missions? Teachers Unions and Educational Reform,* ed. Thomas Loveless. Washington, DC: Brookings Institute.

KERCHNER, CHARLES. 2001. "Deindustrialization." *Education Next* (fall):46–50.

KERCHNER, CHARLES; KOPPICH, JULIA; and WEERES, JOSEPH G. 1997. *United Mind Workers.* San Francisco: Jossey-Bass.

LIEBERMAN, MYRON. 1998. *Teachers Evaluating Teachers: Peer Review and the New Unionism.* New Brunswick, NJ: Transaction.

McDONNELL, LORRAINE. 1992. "Unions." In *Encyclopedia of Educational Research,* 6th edition, ed. Marvin C. Aiken. New York: Macmillan.

McDONNELL, LORRAINE, and PASCAL, ANTHONY. 1988. *Teacher Unions and Educational Reform.*

Santa Monica, CA: Rand Corporation and the Center for Policy Research in Education.

MOO, GREGORY. 1999. *Power Grab.* Washington, DC: Regency.

STONE, JOE A. 2000. "Collective Bargaining and Public Schools." In *Conflicting Missions? Teachers Unions and Educational Reform,* ed. Thomas Loveless. Washington, DC: Brookings Institute.

URBANSKI, ADAM, and JANEY, C. 2001. "A Better Bargain." *Education Week* 20(37):53.

WILLIS D. HAWLEY
DONNA REDMOND JONES

TEACHING

KNOWLEDGE BASES OF
Ralph T. Putnam
LEARNING TO TEACH
Sharon Feiman-Nemser
METHODS FOR STUDYING
James Calderhead

KNOWLEDGE BASES OF

Researchers and other scholars seeking to understand and define the knowledge and thinking underlying teaching have focused on numerous issues and bring multiple perspectives to bear on this complex domain. Much of this work has addressed some combination of three sets of interrelated questions:

1. What do (or should) teachers know? What domains or categories of knowledge are important for teaching?

2. How do teachers know? What is the nature or form of various kinds of knowledge needed for teaching?

3. How do teachers think? What thought processes underlie teaching?

Efforts to address these questions are motivated, in part, by the connection between how teachers teach and what teachers think, know, and believe.

Historical Overview

During the first half of the twentieth century the substance and nature of teachers' knowledge was relatively unproblematic. Judging from various assessments for teacher certification of the period, teachers needed to know the content that they would teach students and have some knowledge of pedagogical practice. As systematic programs of research on teaching began to emerge in the 1960s, attention shifted to various teacher characteristics and behaviors associated with increased student achievement. Although this research did not directly examine the knowledge or thinking of teachers, it was grounded in an assumption that knowledge of relationships established through systematic research could provide a "scientific basis for the art of teaching," as the title of the 1978 book by Nathaniel L. Gage suggested.

As psychology shifted from behavioral to cognitive perspectives, scholars of teaching followed suit and began to focus on the mental life of teachers. By the 1980s, cognitive psychologists had established that the accumulation of rich bodies of knowledge is critical to expert performance in various domains, ranging from chess playing to medical diagnosis. Scholars of teaching began trying to characterize the expert knowledge that is needed for good teaching. In 1986 Lee S. Shulman catalyzed interest in the systematic study of the knowledge underlying teaching, arguing especially for the importance of understanding the role of teachers' knowledge of the content they teach.

Domains of Knowledge for Teaching

Teaching is a complex act, requiring many kinds of knowledge. Some of this knowledge is general and fairly enduring—such as knowledge of subject matter content or of general pedagogical principles; some is more specific and transient—such as knowledge of the particular students being taught and what has taken place in a particular class. Various systems for describing the knowledge needed for teaching have been developed with varying emphases and purposes. With any set of categories or domains of knowledge, it is important to keep in mind that these systems are used to bring conceptual order to knowledge that is in reality complex and interrelated. The various categories of knowledge are not discrete entities, and the boundaries between domains are fuzzy at best. With these caveats in mind, the following set of categories of teacher knowledge is loosely based on a 1987 article by Shulman:

- Knowledge of subject matter content
- Knowledge of general pedagogical principles and strategies
- Knowledge of learners, their characteristics, and how they learn
- Knowledge of educational contexts

• Knowledge of educational goals, purposes, and values

Because they are central to the daily work of teachers, general pedagogical knowledge, knowledge about learners, and knowledge of subject matter have been the focus of considerable research and scholarly discourse.

General pedagogical knowledge/knowledge about learners. These closely related categories of teacher knowledge include knowledge about teaching, learning, and learners that is not specific to the teaching of particular subject matter content. One large component of this domain is knowledge of classroom management—knowledge of how to keep groups of students engaged with various classroom tasks. Teachers must have repertoires of routines and strategies for establishing classroom procedures, organizing classroom events, keeping activities on track, and reacting to student misbehavior. Teachers also draw upon knowledge of instructional strategies for arranging classroom environments and conducting lessons to promote student learning. Experienced teachers have repertoires of strategies and routines for conducting lessons, keeping them running smoothly, and promoting student engagement.

Teachers' knowledge about managing classrooms and conducting lessons is intertwined with knowledge and beliefs about learners, learning, and teaching. Theories about how students learn guide teachers' instructional decisions and interactions with students, often in an implicit way. For example, a teacher who conceives of the learner's role as a passive recipient of knowledge teaches differently than one who conceives of the learner's role as an active participant in the learning process. The former typically presents information that students are expected to attend to, followed by rehearsal and practice of the presented information. The latter is apt to present problem-solving situations designed to stimulate students' thinking and knowledge-building.

Content knowledge. Obviously, teachers must know something about the content they teach. In drawing attention to the need for more attention to the role of content knowledge in teaching, Shulman in 1986 distinguished three kinds of content knowledge: subject matter content knowledge, pedagogical content knowledge, and curricular knowledge. Subject matter content knowledge is what a content specialist knows, for example what a mathematician knows about mathematics. Pedagogical content knowledge is specialized knowledge needed for teaching the subject, such as understanding how key ideas in mathematics are likely to be misunderstood by learners, and multiple ways of representing important ideas in the domain. Curricular knowledge is knowledge of materials and resources for teaching particular content, including how subject matter content is structured and sequenced in different materials.

Early research sought but failed to establish a clear relationship between teachers' subject-matter knowledge—as measured by the amount of coursework, grades, and tests—and teaching effectiveness; taking more university mathematics courses did not necessarily make one a better teacher of mathematics. Nevertheless, when researchers examined what was learned and hence known by teachers, they were able to establish a connection between the degree of disciplinary knowledge and teaching effectiveness. In general, teachers with rich subject matter knowledge tend to emphasize conceptual, problem solving, and inquiry aspects of their subjects; less knowledgeable teachers tend to emphasize facts, rules, and procedures. Less knowledgeable teachers may stick closely to detailed plans or the textbook, sometimes missing opportunities to focus on important ideas and connections to other ideas. When the goal is fostering student understanding and meaningful learning, as promoted by many U.S. educational reform efforts of the 1980s and 1990s, the demands on a teacher's content knowledge intensify. Helping students understand important ideas in a discipline and how these ideas can be use in varied contexts requires that a teacher know more than the facts, concepts, and procedures they are teaching. They must also know how these ideas connect with one another and to other domains.

Often, when one thinks of understanding a discipline—such as mathematics, biology, or history—one means knowing important concepts and principles in the field, how they are related to one another, and how they connect to ideas in other domains. Additionally, to be truly knowledgeable, or "literate," in a particular field involves knowing how experts in that field think. Knowing science, for example, entails knowing something about rules for evidence and how scientific knowledge is established. Knowing literature involves knowing what makes a good critique or argument about a literary point. To teach particular disciplines well, a teacher must be aware of these aspects of disciplinary knowledge and be able to make them explicit in ways that are accessible to learners.

Nature and Form of Teacher Knowledge

A potential danger in describing various categories of knowledge for teaching is coming to think of teachers' knowledge itself as organized into abstract, discrete categories. In fact, what teachers know is complexly intertwined with other knowledge and beliefs and with the specific contexts in which teachers work. Numerous scholars have posed constructs to try to capture the complex contextualized nature of teachers' knowledge. Some researchers have argued that teachers' personalities and life experiences play a major role in shaping the kind of knowledge they develop about teaching, calling this knowledge "personal practical knowledge." In 1987 Kathy Carter and Walter Doyle argued that much of what experienced teachers know is "event-structured knowledge"—knowledge organized around the activities and events they have experienced in classrooms. Others have argued for the importance of articulating the "craft knowledge" of teaching—the implicit theories, skills, and ways of perceiving that teachers develop through their work.

In the late twentieth and early twenty-first centuries, such efforts to understand knowledge for teaching have intersected and been informed by a more general movement in psychology and education to view knowledge and cognition as *situated*. Situative theorists posit that how and where a person learns a particular set of knowledge and skills become a fundamental part of what is learned. An individual's knowledge is intertwined with the physical and social contexts in which it was acquired. All of these efforts to characterize the ways in which knowledge for teaching is intertwined with contexts, other people, and personal histories help one appreciate the rich and complex nature of what teachers need to know. A number of important implications arise from this work.

What teachers know and how they know it are tied to particular contexts. Developing expertise in teaching entails working and learning in the contexts of teaching. Much of what teachers know is connected to particular tools—such as textbooks and instructional materials. Much of what teachers know is routinized and automatic. Just as a person driving a car with a manual transmission is not conscious of the coordination of movements of feet and hands as they drive—unless a problem arises—much of how

teachers interact with students is similarly guided by routine. It is having much of what they know embedded in these routines that enables teachers and students to manage in a highly complex social environment. A downside of much of teachers' knowledge being routinized and automatic is that it can be difficult to examine and change when desired.

Teacher Thinking

As psychological perspectives shifted from behavioral to cognitive in the 1970s, a number of researchers began to focus on the thinking processes entailed in teaching. Much of this research focused on teachers' planning and decision-making. Research on planning suggests that it occurs at different levels (e.g., across a year, across a unit, across a day), that it is mostly informal (i.e., formal written plans play less of a role than does informal thinking about what to do), and that planning requires a broad knowledge base (i.e., of the various categories discussed above). Research that focused on the decisions made during interactive teaching itself found that teachers made few decisions as they taught and that those decisions dealt primarily with keeping planned activities on track. Other research suggests, however, that the well-established routines that teachers and students have developed do much to determine the nature of instruction and minimize conscious on-the-spot decision-making.

See also: ENGLISH EDUCATION; HISTORY, TEACHING OF; LANGUAGE ARTS, TEACHING OF; MATHEMATICS EDUCATION; READING; SCIENCE EDUCATION; SOCIAL STUDIES EDUCATION; TEACHER EDUCATION; TEACHER EVALUATION; TEACHING, *subentry on* LEARNING TO TEACH; WRITING, TEACHING OF.

BIBLIOGRAPHY

ANDERSON, LINDA M. 1989. "Learners and Learning." In *Knowledge Base for the Beginning Teacher,* ed. Maynard Clinton Reynolds. Oxford: Pergamon.

BORKO, HILDA, and PUTNAM, RALPH T. 1996. "Learning to Teach." In *Handbook of Educational Psychology,* ed. David C. Berliner and Robert C. Calfee. New York: Macmillan.

BROPHY, JERE, ed. 1991. *Advances in Research on Teaching,* Vol. 2: *Teachers' Subject Matter Knowledge.* Greenwich, CT: JAI Press.

CALDERHEAD, JAMES. 1986. "Teachers: Beliefs and Knowledge." In *Handbook of Educational Psy-*

chology, ed. David C. Berliner and Robert C. Calfee. New York: Macmillan.

CARTER, KATHY. 1990. "Teachers' Knowledge and Learning to Teach." In *Handbook of Research on Teacher Education,* ed. W. Robert Houston, Martin Haberman, and John P. Silkula. New York: Macmillan.

CARTER, KATHY, and DOYLE, WALTER. 1987. "Teachers' Knowledge Structures and Comprehension Processes." In *Exploring Teachers' Thinking,* ed. James Calderhead. London: Cassell.

CLARK, CHRISTOPHER M., and PETERSON, PENELOPE L. 1986. "Teachers' Thought Processes." In *Handbook of Research on Teaching,* ed. Merlin C. Wittrock. New York: Macmillan.

CONNELLY, F. MICHAEL, and CLANDININ, D. JEAN. 1985. "Personal Practical Knowledge and the Modes of Knowing." *Review of Research in Education* 16:3–56.

DOYLE, WALTER. 1986. "Classroom Organization and Management." In *Handbook of Research on Teaching,* ed. Merlin C. Wittrock. New York: Macmillan.

GAGE, NATHANIEL L. 1978. *The Scientific Basis of the Art of Teaching.* New York: Teachers College Press.

LEINHARDT, GAEA. 1990. "Capturing Craft Knowledge in Teaching." *Educational Researcher* 19(2):18–25.

LEINHARDT, GAEA, and GREENO, JAMES G. 1986. "The Cognitive Skill of Teaching." *Journal of Educational Psychology* 78:75–95.

PUTNAM, RALPH T., and BORKO, HILDA. 2000. "What Do New Views of Knowledge and Thinking Have to Say about Research on Teacher Learning?" *Educational Researcher* 29(1):4–15.

SHULMAN, LEE S. 1986. "Those Who Understand: Knowledge Growth in Teaching." *Educational Researcher* 15(2):4–14.

SHULMAN, LEE S. 1987. "Knowledge and Teaching: Foundations of the New Reform." *Harvard Educational Review* 57(1):1–22.

RALPH T. PUTNAM

LEARNING TO TEACH

The meaning of the phrase *learning to teach* seems clear and straightforward, but in fact, its definition raises a host of empirical, conceptual, and normative questions. What do teachers need to know, care about, and be able to do in order to teach effectively in different contexts? How do teachers build a strong teaching practice and develop a professional identity over time? What role should teacher education play in learning to teach? How do the conditions of teaching shape the content of teacher learning? How do views of teaching shape theories of learning to teach?

Learning to teach is an emerging priority for policymakers and educational reformers. For example, the report of the National Commission on Teaching and America's Future, issued in 1996, placed teacher learning at the heart of its comprehensive blueprint for reform. The report asserts that what students learn is directly related to what teachers teach, and what teachers teach depends on the knowledge, skills, and commitments they bring to their teaching.

Myths About Learning to Teach

Conventional wisdom about learning to teach is rooted in social attitudes toward teaching and the experience of being a student. Some of these ideas contain half truths; some have influenced educational policy.

Teachers are born, not made. Some people believe that the ability to teach is a natural endowment like being musical. Some teachers seem to be "naturals" and some theorists posit an innate tendency in human beings to explain things. Even the founders of the common school believed that teaching was "women's true profession" because it tapped their instinct for nurturing the young. Still, the belief that teachers are born, not made rests on a narrow view of the intellectual and personal requirements of teaching. It ignores the growing understanding of teaching as a complex, uncertain practice, and minimizes the role of professional education on the grounds that the practice of teaching cannot be taught.

If you know your subject, you can teach it. Whatever else teachers need to know, they need to know their subjects. There are teachers whose abundant knowledge and love of their subject make them extremely effective even though they have had no special preparation for teaching. Other teachers who possess extensive subject matter knowledge are unable to present this knowledge clearly or help others learn it. Research is beginning to clarify what it means to "know" one's subject for purposes of teaching it, and why conventional measures of subject matter knowledge are problematic.

Historically, a liberal arts education was considered sufficient preparation for teaching secondary school. Policies that require academic majors for both elementary and secondary teaching candidates represent a contemporary variation on this theme. There is mounting evidence of teachers with a major in their subject not being able to explain fundamental concepts in that subject; this situation raises questions about such policies.

Scholars have identified three dimensions of subject matter knowledge for teaching: knowledge of central facts, concepts, theories and procedures; knowledge of explanatory frameworks that organize and connect ideas within a given field; and knowledge of the rules of evidence and proof in a given field. How is a proof in mathematics different from a historic explanation or a literary interpretation? In addition, teachers must be able to look at their subjects through the eyes of students, anticipating what students might find difficult or confusing, framing compelling purposes for studying particular content, and understanding how ideas connect across fields and relate to everyday life. Future teachers are unlikely to acquire this kind of knowledge in academic courses.

Teacher education prepares people to teach. Whereas the previous myths reflect considerable skepticism about teacher education, this myth reflects confidence that pre-service programs prepare people to teach. The typical program consists of a two-year sequence of education courses and field experiences. Common components include educational psychology, general and subject specific methods, and student teaching. What these components consist of varies across institutions.

Some studies show that teacher education is a weak intervention compared with the socializing effects of teachers' own elementary and secondary schooling, and the influence of on-the-job experience. Other studies suggest that intense, coherent teacher education programs do make a difference. Even the best program, however, cannot prepare someone to teach in a particular setting. Some of the most important things teachers need to know are local and can only be learned in context. Pre-service preparation can lay a foundation for this complex,

situation-specific work, but the early years of teaching are an intense and formative phase in practice of learning to teach.

Phases in Learning to Teach

It is hard to say when learning to teach begins. From an early age, people are surrounded by teaching on the part of parents and teachers, and these early experiences with authority figures unconsciously shape teachers' pedagogical tendencies. The experience of elementary and secondary schooling has a particularly strong impact. From thousands of hours of teacher watching, prospective teachers form images of teaching, learning, and subject matter that influence their future practice unless professional education intervenes.

Liberal studies affect the way teachers think about knowledge and approach the teaching of academic content, although not always in educative directions. At their best, education courses and field experiences cultivate a professional understanding of and orientation toward teaching. Learning to teach begins in earnest when novices step into their own classroom and take up the responsibilities of full-time teaching.

Efforts to describe the stages teachers go through in learning to teach generally posit an initial stage of survival and discovery, a second stage of experimentation and consolidation, and a third stage of mastery and stabilization. These stages are loosely tied to years of experience, with stabilization occurring around the fifth year of teaching. Self-knowledge is a major outcome of early teaching. Novices craft a professional identity through their struggles with and explorations of students and subject matter. Over time, teachers develop instructional routines and classroom procedures and learn what to expect from their students. Experience generally yields greater self-confidence, flexibility, and a sense of professional autonomy. After five to seven years most teachers feel they know how to teach. Whether we call these teachers "masters" or "experts" depends on what kind of teaching is valued and how mastery and expertise are defined.

Models of teacher development serve as a reminder that the process of learning to teach extends over a number of years; however, the current structure of professional education and the conditions of beginning teaching do not reflect this. Continuity of learning opportunities between pre-service preparation and new teacher induction is rare. The assignment of beginning teachers does not reflect their status as learners. Most beginning teachers have the same responsibilities as their more experienced colleagues, and often get the most difficult classes because they lack seniority.

The rise of formal induction programs signals a recognition on the part of some educators and policymakers that learning to teach occurs during the early years of teaching. About thirty states have support systems for beginning teachers and most urban districts offer some induction support, usually in the form of mentor teachers. Still, few programs rest on a robust understanding of teacher learning or help novices learn the kind of ambitious teaching advocated by reformers. Many programs treat induction as short-term support designed to ease the novice into full-time teaching.

What might a developmental curriculum for learning to teach entail? Which tasks belong to initial preparation and which to the induction phase? Despite gaps in knowledge and a lack of consensus about the best ways to prepare teachers and support their learning over time, it is possible to conceptualize a continuum of learning opportunities for teachers.

Teacher Preparation and Learning to Teach

If teachers are to learn a version of teaching that they have not experienced as pupils, they need to develop new frames of reference for interpreting what goes on in classrooms and making decisions about what and how to teach. Positioned between teachers' past experience as students and their future experience as teachers, university-based teacher education is well situated to encourage this shift in thinking. Unless pre-service teachers reconstruct their early beliefs about teaching, learning, students, and subject matter, continuing experience will solidify these beliefs, making them even less susceptible to change.

A second task of teacher preparation particularly suited to university-based study is helping future teachers develop conceptual and pedagogical knowledge of their teaching subjects. Current educational reforms have prompted renewed interest in teachers' subject matter knowledge because they call for a kind of teaching that engages students not only in acquiring knowledge, but also in building and communicating about knowledge. This task depends on contributions from arts and sciences, and education.

To build bridges between subject matter and students, teachers must understand what children are like at different ages, how they make sense of their world, how their ways of thinking and acting are shaped by their language and culture, how they gain knowledge and skills, and develop confidence as learners. This background knowledge becomes increasingly critical as teachers work with children whose racial, cultural, and socioeconomic backgrounds differ from their own.

In order to learn from teaching, teacher candidates must develop the necessary tools and dispositions. This includes skills of observation, interpretation and analysis, the habit of supporting claims about student learning with evidence, the willingness to consider alternative explanations. If teacher candidates work on these skills with others, they may begin to see colleagues as resources in learning to teach.

Although teachers need to know many things, effective teaching depends on the ability to use knowledge appropriately in particular situations. Pre-service teachers can begin developing a repertoire of approaches to curriculum, instruction, and assessment during pre-service preparation. Learning to adapt and use this knowledge in practice is an appropriate task for teacher induction.

Teacher Induction and Learning to Teach

Induction happens with or without a formal program; however, the presence of a strong program can minimize the survival mentality that grips so many beginning teachers and orient their learning in productive directions. Beginning teachers need to learn the goals and standards for students at their grade level, and how these expectations fit into a larger framework of curriculum and assessment. They must get to know their students and community, and figure out how to use this knowledge in developing a responsive curriculum.

If teacher preparation has been successful, beginning teachers will have a vision of good teaching and a beginning repertoire consistent with that vision. A major task for beginning teachers is acquiring the local understandings and developing the flexibility of response to enact this repertoire. The challenges of teaching alone for the first time can discourage new teachers from trying ambitious pedagogies. Induction support can keep them from abandoning such approaches in favor of what they perceive as safer, less complex activities. It can also help novices focus on the purposes and not just the management of learning activities and their meaning for students.

To teach in ways that respond to students and move learning forward, teachers must be able to elicit and interpret students' ideas and generate appropriate teaching moves as the lesson unfolds. Listening to what students say and constructing responses on a moment-to-moment basis; and attending to the needs of the group while attending to individuals requires considerable skill and practice: It represents a demanding learning task for beginning teachers. Beginning teachers must create and maintain a classroom learning community that is safe, respectful, and productive of student learning. Issues of power and control lie at the heart of this task that is tied up with novices' evolving professional identity. Often beginning teachers struggle to reconcile competing images of their role as they evolve a coherent professional stance.

If teachers are asked how they learned to teach, they will say they learned to teach by teaching. Although experience plays an important role in learning to teach, there is a big difference between "having" experience and learning desirable lessons from that experience. To learn from the experience of teaching, teachers must be able to use their practice as a site for inquiry. This means turning confusions into questions, experimenting with new approaches and studying the effects, and framing new questions to extend their understanding.

The ongoing study and improvement of teaching is difficult to accomplish alone. Teachers need opportunities to talk with others about teaching, to analyze samples of student work, to compare curricular materials, to discuss problems and consider different explanations and actions. Many reformers believe that this kind of intellectual work can best be accomplished by groups of teachers working together over time.

See also: LANGUAGE ARTS, TEACHING OF; MATHEMATICS EDUCATION, *subentry on* PREPARATION OF TEACHERS; MOTIVATION, *subentry on* INSTRUCTION; READING, *subentry on* TEACHING OF; SCIENCE EDUCATION, *subentry on* PREPARATION OF TEACHERS; SOCIAL STUDIES EDUCATION, *subentry on* PREPARATION OF TEACHERS; TEACHER EDUCATION; TEACHER LEARNING COMMUNITIES; WRITING, TEACHING OF.

BIBLIOGRAPHY

BALL, DEBORAH, and COHEN, DAVID. 1999. "Developing Practice, Developing Practitioners: Toward a Practice-Based Theory of Professional Education." In *Teaching as the Learning Profession: Handbook of Policy and Practice,* ed. Linda Darling-Hammond and G. Sykes. San Francisco: Jossey-Bass.

BALL, DEBORAH, and MCDIARMID, WILLIAM. 1990. "The Subject Matter Preparation of Teachers. In *Handbook of Research on Teacher Education,* ed. W. Robert Houston. New York: Macmillan.

BORKO, HILDA, and PUTNAM, RALPH. 1996. "Learning to Teach." In *Handbook of Educational Psychology,* ed. David C. Berliner and Robert C. Calfee. New York: Simon and Schuster.

FEIMAN-NEMSER, SHARON, and REMILLARD, JANINE. 1996. "Perspectives on Learning to Teach." In *The Teacher Educator's Handbook: Building a Knowledge Base for the Preparation of Teachers,* ed. Frank B. Murray. San Francisco: Jossey-Bass.

FIDELER, ELIZABETH, and HASELKORN, DAVID. 1999. *Learning the Ropes: Urban Teacher Induction Practices in the United States.* Belmont, MA: Recruiting New Teachers.

GROSSMAN, PAMELA. 1990. *The Making of a Teacher.* New York: Teachers College Press.

LORTIE, DAN. 1975. *Schoolteacher: A Sociological Study.* Chicago: University of Chicago Press.

NATIONAL COMMISSION ON TEACHING AND AMERICA'S FUTURE. 1996. *What Matters Most: Teaching for America's Future.* New York: National Commission on Teaching and America's Future.

REYNOLDS, MAYNARD, ed. 1989. *Knowledge Base for the Beginning Teacher.* Oxford: Pergamon Press.

RYAN, KEVIN. 1970. *Don't Smile until Christmas.* Chicago: University of Chicago Press.

SCHON, DONALD. 1987. *Educating the Reflective Practitioner.* San Francisco: Jossey-Bass.

SHULMAN, LEE. 1986. "Those Who Understand: Knowledge Growth in Teaching." *Educational Researcher* 15(2):4–14.

SHARON FEIMAN-NEMSER

METHODS FOR STUDYING

Teaching has been the subject of systematic inquiry for several decades. The first American Educational

Research Association *Handbook of Research on Teaching,* edited by Nathaniel L. Gage, appeared in 1963 and later editions have appeared at approximately ten-year intervals. Since the 1960s there have also been a number of significant reviews of this research, such as Arnold Morrison and Donald McIntyre's 1969 and 1973 editions of *Teachers and Teaching* and Penelope L. Peterson and Herbert J. Walberg's *Research on Teaching* (1979). Such reviews have highlighted both the complexity of teaching and the fact that it is amenable to study from a number of perspectives, using a variety of methods.

Inquiry into teaching has been pursued for essentially three different purposes. First, researchers and practitioners aim to understand better the processes involved, to develop the knowledge base of teaching, and to contribute to theoretical frameworks, which help to conceptualize teaching. Second, inquiry into teaching has also been pursued for the purposes of improving practice. This is particularly the case, for instance, in action research studies that generally follow a cycle, beginning with the identification of a practical problem or area of concern, followed by the gathering of evidence using various research methods, decisions about how to change practice, and then the gathering of further evidence to monitor the effects of the change. Such cycles are frequently repeated and provide a means of constantly monitoring and improving practice as well as developing an enhanced self-critical awareness. Third, inquiry is intrinsic to professional preparation, and research methods may be employed by student teachers, for example, in helping to make sense of their observations of teaching and in developing their own practice. Classroom interaction schedules, for example, have frequently been used to help student teachers to structure their observations and to note the ways in which teachers ask questions, or move from one task to another within the classroom, or deal with student behavior problems. Any one research project, however, may be being pursued for any or all of these purposes and could draw upon a variety of different research methods in order to achieve its aims.

Research Methods

Various methods have been used to gather information about teaching. The most common fall into the following categories: systematic observation, case study and ethnography, survey techniques, simulations, commentaries, concept mapping, and narra-

tives. Each yields its own distinctive type of data about teaching, and may be more or less appropriate for different purposes as discussed below.

Systematic observation. Ned Flanders in 1970 was the first to popularize the use of observation schedules in the study of teaching. His Flanders Interaction Analysis Categories (FIAC) identified ten categories of behavior that characterised teacher-student interaction within the classroom. Observers, once trained in identifying and categorizing these behaviors, could then code their observations, which would later be studied for interaction patterns. Flanders's work has since been elaborated with numerous schedules designed for specific purposes. Observation schedules essentially provide a checklist of behaviors that the researcher is interested in, and enable a sample of teachers' interactions to be described in quantitative terms. Sometimes the schedule is more oriented towards studying a sequence of teaching behavior rather than the quantity of different types of behavior and may be used to identify the ways in which behaviors change over time or as a result of an experimental intervention.

The major advantage of systematic observation is that it provides a relatively objective account of classroom behavior. For instance it might describe the proportion of questions that a teacher asks that are open-ended, or the proportion of teacher commands that have a disciplinary focus, or the relative number of times that teachers or students initiate interaction. The method, however, is rarely able to offer much information about the context of particular interactions, and is unable to illuminate the interpretations that teachers and students place upon their own and others' behavior. A question directed toward a student, for instance, may be a matter of simple recall for one, an intellectually challenging task for another, a largely social exchange in one context or an implied reprimand in a different context, and the observer may be unable to distinguish sufficient cues to appreciate fully its significance. Systematic observation may be useful, therefore, in considering the general impact of new curriculum materials on instructional behavior, for example, but may have limited value on its own in identifying the full complexities of teachers' work, why teachers behave as they do, and the reasoning that guides their actions.

Case study and ethnography. Some have argued that case study and ethnography refer more to approaches to research than methods in themselves.

Frequently they draw upon interviews and semi-structured observations, though occasionally on other evidence as well, in order to come to an understanding of a particular teacher's practice. One of their distinguishing features is that they involve in-depth study. Over a lengthy period of time, the researcher is able to appreciate the context in which a teacher works, and through interaction with the teacher about their practice is able to develop insights into how they view their work. These insights can then be tested against future observations or other data. Gaea Leinhardt (1988), for example, observed several mathematics lessons taught by one teacher and interviewed her at length both about her teaching and about her past experiences of mathematics. As a result, she was able to piece together an understanding of the ways in which the teacher's own learning of mathematics as a student and her experiences of professional training had come to influence her approach to teaching the subject. Case studies have frequently highlighted the ways in which teachers cope with the complex competing demands that they face in their work or the ways in which beginning teachers encounter and overcome the initial difficulties of learning to teach.

Case studies and ethnographies frequently involve the analysis of very large amounts of qualitative data, and some writers have drawn attention to the possibility that researchers can extract from these their own particular interpretations. The potential of ethnographic research to yield generalizations about teaching has also been debated, with some researchers arguing that the merit of the approach lies in the insights about particular aspects of teaching that such studies can provide.

Survey techniques. Surveys on teachers and teaching have relied on the use of questionnaires, structured interviews, checklists, tests, or attitude scales. Surveys have been used to describe the characteristics of teachers as a professional group, such as their attitudes towards children, their opinions about a particular innovation, or their own aspirations and feelings of job satisfaction. They have also been used to collect teachers' own descriptions of their practices or the professional concerns they have at different stages of their careers.

Surveys allow data to be collected about large numbers of teachers, and if appropriate sampling techniques are used and a sufficiently high return rate is obtained, it is possible to make generalizations about teachers as a whole or about particular groups of teachers, such as elementary school teachers, or teachers in a particular subject area or geographical region. Surveys, however, can only collect information that teachers can easily report, and other methods are required if the researcher wishes to penetrate more deeply into the complex interactions of teachers' thinking and behavior and the contexts in which they work.

Simulations. A variety of simulation techniques have been developed that involve presenting teachers with a task or situation similar to one that would be encountered in their normal work and observing how systematic variations in the nature of different tasks or situations affects the ways teachers aim to deal with them. Such techniques have been used to investigate how teachers plan lessons, how they are influenced in their decision-making by external constraints, or how they are influenced in their interactions with students by different student attributes. Mary M. Rohrkemper and Jere E. Brophy (1983), for example, provided teachers with descriptions or vignettes of children in a variety of classroom situations, each presenting a particular challenge to the teacher. By examining the relationship between the teachers' judgements or decisions and the factors varying within the vignettes, it was possible to identify those features of children that are influential in teachers' thinking about problem situations. Simulations can be used to elicit the knowledge that teachers have and use in their everyday practice and that might be difficult to access through other methods.

Commentaries. Understanding the processes of teaching involves understanding the meaning teachers attribute to their actions and the rationales they have for behaving as they do. Attempts to access the ongoing thinking and decision-making of teachers have necessitated the use of methods particularly geared toward eliciting teachers' knowledge and thought processes. This has included think-aloud protocols where teachers, while engaged in a planning or assessment task, for example, have attempted to verbalize their thoughts at the same time. The thinking and decision-making of teachers during active teaching have been elicited using stimulated recall techniques in which a lesson is videotaped and later played back to the teachers who attempt to recall their thinking at the time. Some researchers have also used the notes taken from observation of lessons to structure interviews with teachers afterwards in order to construct a commentary on what the teacher was doing and the reasons for their actions.

Research in this area has raised several issues about the status of teachers' verbal reports on their practice: Do they genuinely reflect teachers' real thinking at the time, or are they after-the-event justifications? And can the thought that accompanies practical action be adequately represented in terms of words alone, or is "real" thought as much tied up with images, metaphors, and feelings? There are several conceptual issues concerning this type of research method, and clearly care must be taken to consider potential sources of distortion in self-report data. Nevertheless, steps can be taken to minimize such influences, and these methods have been used effectively to explore some of the cognitive aspects of teachers' work.

Concept mapping. Several techniques, loosely labelled as concept mapping, have been used to represent teachers' understanding of various aspects of their work. They generally follow a three-stage process, beginning with brainstorming on a particular topic to identify concepts, followed by a process of indicating how these concepts are interrelated, and finally naming the relationships between the concepts. The end product is a visual representation of teachers' understanding as it relates to a particular topic. Greta Morine-Dershimer (1991), for example, used the technique to identify the ways in which different student teachers think about classroom management: some student teachers, for example, would link classroom management to concepts of personal relationships, classroom climate, and an ethos of mutual respect, whereas others would link it to concepts of rules, sanctions, rewards, and praise. Such techniques can help to illuminate the different understandings that student teachers hold of key concepts or may be used to identify the changes that occur in teachers' understandings over time or as a result of inservice training or curriculum development.

Narratives. Narrative studies aim to provide an account of teaching in teachers' own words. They support an experiential approach to describing teachers' work, taking particular note of the teachers' "voice" and placing teachers' experience within the context of other life events. Narrative researchers have frequently argued against more mechanistic approaches to describing teaching and have argued for a storytelling approach in which the researcher acts as a facilitator helping teachers to recount their experience with due recognition of the personal and contextual factors within which it is framed. D. Jean

Clandinin (1986), for example, develops narrative accounts of three primary teachers. Each narrative highlights a key image or guiding metaphor that is influential in shaping how the teacher thinks about teaching and learning. One teacher, for instance, held an image of "language as the key" and language was perceived as the basis of all classroom activity. Another held the image of "classroom as home" and this image manifested itself in her relationships with children and in her organization of the classroom. In 1994 J. Gary Knowles, Ardra L. Cole, and Colleen S. Presswood charted the difficulties of student teachers on field experience through the construction of narratives, drawing largely on the students' own autobiographies, diaries, and discussions. This approach to research has grown rapidly in recent years and has stimulated several debates about the status and veracity of narratives.

Conclusion

Research on teaching has involved a wide range of different methods. Each has its own advantages as well as its drawbacks. Each has the potential to illuminate particular aspects of the teaching process. Different methods are appropriate for different questions. Moreover, certain orientations towards research—such as cognitive or experiential—predispose researchers to certain types of inquiry and therefore particular methods. Teaching, however, is a complex process and the rich and diverse modes of inquiry currently available enable researchers to pursue those complexities and to contribute to their understanding more fully.

See also: RESEARCH METHODS; TEACHER EDUCATION; TEACHER EVALUATION.

BIBLIOGRAPHY

ATKINSON, PAUL, et al. 2001. *Handbook of Ethnography.* London: Paul Chapman.

BEYERBACK, BARBARA A. 1988. "Developing a Technical Vocabulary on Teacher Planning: Preservice Teachers' Concept Maps." *Teaching and Teacher Education* 4(4):339–374.

BIDDLE, BRUCE J., and ANDERSON, DONALD S. 1986. "Theory, Methods, Knowledge and Research on Teaching." In *Handbook of Research on Teaching,* 3rd edition, ed. Merlin C. Wittrock. New York: Macmillan.

BORKO, HILDA, and CADWELL, JOEL. 1982. "Individual Differences in Teachers' Decision Strategies:

An Investigation of Classroom Organization and Management Decisions." *Journal of Educational Psychology* 74(4):598–610.

BROWN, SALLY, and MCINTYRE, DONALD. 1993. *Making Sense of Teaching.* Buckingham, Eng.: Open University Press.

CALDERHEAD, JAMES, and SHORROCK, SUSAN B. 1997. *Understanding Teacher Education: Case Studies in the Professional Development of Beginning Teachers.* London: Falmer.

CARTER, KATHY. 1993. "The Place of Story in the Study of Teaching and Teacher Education." *Educational Researcher* 22(1):5–12, 18.

CLANDININ, D. JEAN. 1986. *Classroom Practice: Teacher Images in Action.* London: Falmer.

CLARK, CHRISTOPHER M., and YINGER, ROBERT J. 1987. "Teacher Planning." In *Exploring Teachers' Thinking,* ed. James Calderhead. London: Cassell.

CROLL, PAUL. 1998. *Systematic Classroom Observation,* 2nd edition. London: Taylor and Francis.

EVERTSON, CAROLYN M., and GREEN, JUDITH L. 1986. "Observation as Inquiry and Method." In *Handbook of Research on Teaching,* 3rd edition, ed. Merlin C. Wittrock. New York: Macmillan.

FLANDERS, NED. 1970. *Analyzing Teaching Behavior.* Reading, MA: Addison-Wesley.

FLODEN, ROBERT E., et al. 1981. "Responses to Curriculum Pressures: A Policy Capturing Study of Teacher Decisions about Context." *Journal of Educational Psychology* 73:129–141.

FULLER, FRANCES F., and BOWN, OLIVER H. 1975. "Becoming a Teacher." In *Teacher Education: Seventy-Fourth Yearbook of the National Society for the Study of Education,* ed. Kevin Ryan. Chicago: University of Chicago Press.

GAGE, NATHANIEL L., ed. 1963. *Handbook of Research on Teaching.* Chicago: Rand McNally.

HARGREAVES, DAVID H.; HESTER, STEPHEN K.; and MELLOR, FRANK J. 1975. *Deviance in Classrooms.* London: Routledge and Kegan Paul.

HUBERMAN, MICHAEL. 1993. *The Lives of Teachers.* New York: Teachers College Press.

KNOWLES, J. GARY; COLE, ARDRA L.; and PRESSWOOD, COLLEEN S. 1994. *Through Preservice Teachers' Eyes; Exploring Field Experiences Through Narrative and Inquiry.* New York: Merrill.

LEINHARDT, GAEA. 1988. "Situated Knowledge and Expertise in Teaching." In *Teachers' Professional Learning,* ed. James Calderhead. London: Falmer.

MILES, MATTHEW B., and HUBERMAN, A. MICHAEL. 1984. *Qualitative Data Analysis.* Newbury Park, CA: Sage.

MORINE-DERSHIMER, GRETA. 1991. "Learning to Think Like a Teacher." *Teaching and Teacher Education* 7(2):159–168.

MORINE-DERSHIMER, GRETA, et al. 1992. "Choosing Among Alternatives for Tracing Conceptual Change." *Teaching and Teacher Education* 8(5/6):471–484.

MORRISON, ARNOLD, and MCINTYRE, DONALD. 1969. *Teachers and Teaching.* Harmondsworth, Eng.: Penguin.

MORRISON, ARNOLD, and MCINTYRE, DONALD. 1973. *Teachers and Teaching,* 2nd edition. Harmondsworth, Eng.: Penguin.

MORTIMORE, PETER, et al. 1988. *School Matters: The Junior Years.* Wells, Eng.: Open Books.

PETERSON, PENELOPE L., and CLARK, CHRISTOPHER M. 1978. "Teachers' Reports of Their Cognitive Processes During Teaching." *American Educational Research Journal* 15(4):555–565.

PETERSON, PENELOPE L., and WALBERG, HERBERT J., eds. 1979. *Research on Teaching: Concepts, Findings and Implications.* Berkeley, CA: McCutchan.

ROHRKEMPER, MARY M., and BROPHY, JERE E. 1983. "Teachers' Thinking about Problem Students." In *Teacher and Student Perceptions: Implications for Learning,* ed. John M. Levine and Margaret C. Wang. Hillsdale, NJ: Erlbaum.

STENHOUSE, LAWRENCE. 1980. "The Study of Samples and the Study of Cases." *British Educational Research Journal* 6(1):1–6.

WOODS, PETER. 1979. *The Divided School.* London: Routledge and Kegan Paul.

YINGER, ROBERT J. 1980. "A Study of Teacher Planning." *Elementary School Journal* 80:107–127.

ZUBER-SKERRITT, ORTRUN, ed. 1996. *New Directions in Action Research.* London: Falmer.

JAMES CALDERHEAD

TEACHING AND LEARNING

HIGHER EDUCATION
Michael Theall

INTERNATIONAL PERSPECTIVE
Joseph P. Farrell

HIGHER EDUCATION

Student learning in higher education is a function of both formal and informal experiences. Formal learning takes place as a result of a classroom or related activity structured by a teacher and/or others for the purpose of helping students to achieve specified cognitive, or other, objectives. Informal learning encompasses all the other outcomes of students' participation in a higher education experience. In both cases, the more extended or comprehensive the experience, the greater the potential effect. In a comprehensive 1991 review, Ernest Pascarella and Patrick Terenzini described the ways in which college affects students with respect to many kinds of learning. While they found that formal learning related to academic and cognitive skills, and to subject-matter competence, informal learning was shown to impact on many other areas.

Complications arise, however, because of the number and variety of variables affecting college learning. For example, while the differences between being a residential student and a commuter student do not seem to greatly affect cognitive or subject-matter learning, they are relatively influential with respect to psychosocial change, intellectual and cultural values, independence, and similar factors. Is this purely an on-campus versus off-campus difference? Age may be an intervening variable in such cases, because one would expect older, working adults (a constantly growing student population in all of higher education) to represent a substantial percentage of students living off-campus. Given that less psychosocial change might be expected with such learners—because their attitudes and values are already well established—the observed differences between on- and off-campus learning could be a function of student demographic differences such as age, as well as the environment itself. For example, while the influence of college on the intellectual and cultural values of resident students is significant, this effect derives much of its impact from immersion in the college environment and the maturation of younger learners who may not have had a broad range of experience. Adult, non-resident learners may have more firmly-held beliefs and a broader range of experience and by simple maturation, may already have developed more refined sets of values. Thus it is not simply location that makes the difference, but the combination of location and characteristics of the learners.

The Theory behind the Practice

When the first edition of this encyclopedia was published in 1971, the prevailing approach to teaching and learning was the *behaviorist model*. Developed by B. F. Skinner and others in the 1950s, this model considered stimuli such as instructional events or activities, the responses of learners to these stimuli, and contingencies or consequences based on those responses. The basic proposition was that learning occurred when the desired responses were elicited by the stimuli. Robert Mager's work with *instructional objectives* (precise statements of intended behaviors along with measurement criteria) and Benjamin Bloom and colleague's 1956 *taxonomies* (classification schemes) of objectives were also major influences on the ways in which instruction was designed and delivered. The taxonomic levels are knowledge, comprehension, application, analysis, synthesis, and evaluation. A practical problem for teachers is that there can be objectives for literally every instructional activity and every kind of behavior—from acquiring basic knowledge to classroom attentiveness and the development of value systems. While behaviorism has been largely replaced as an instructional theory, the underlying value of clear objectives, appropriate measurement criteria, and the specification of various types of desired learning have remained as important basics for designing effective instruction.

Cognitive theory, essentially the position that learning involves the learner's associations of new stimuli with existing concepts and categorization schemes, regained some support in the 1970s and has continued to develop in its applications since that time. Marilla Svinicki (1999) outlined five general strategies for teaching that derive from the early theory: (1) directing students' attention through verbal or visual cues; (2) emphasizing how material is organized, again with various cues; (3) making information more meaningful by providing associations with other material or applications; (4) encouraging active checking of understanding through questioning and feedback; and (5) compensating for limits of information processing and memory systems with smaller amounts of information, review, breaks, and focusing attention.

Metacognition, or thinking about thinking, went beyond simple associations and brought learners more into the process of actively manipulating new information and incorporating it into both their own conceptual schemes and those of the subject involved. Svinicki suggests that instructors should model and describe their own thinking as they work through problems, stress problem solving and other activities that provide opportunities for practicing thought processes, and even teach specific strategies when necessary. The teacher, as the expert in a specific field, becomes a cognitive mentor and uses such techniques to help students move from positions as novices in the discipline to more seasoned practitioners. Teachers thus provide students with tools for understanding and dealing with future, more complex material. Since efficient problem-solving strategies enhance performance, the additional benefit is motivational: it increases students' expectations for successful completion of the work and strengthens their beliefs about their ability to do the work.

Learner-centered instruction is a term that refers to attending to a learner's individual needs, differences, and abilities, as well as to sharing responsibility for learning. Research by Paul Pintrich (1995) has established that students who are able to control their own behavior, motivation, and cognition are generally successful in college. Such students self-regulate their learning in three ways. First, they exercise active control by monitoring what they do, why they do it, and what happens—and then making adjustments. Second, they have goals that mark desired performance levels and they use these when deciding what adjustments to make. Third, they accept that the control must be theirs rather than someone else's. These procedures revolve around the important underlying concept that learners can exercise control and influence educational outcomes, and that doing so has many benefits.

Collaborative learning is the practice of actively engaging learners in joint discovery, analysis, and use of information. It has its roots in the power of peer and other groups to influence the development of understandings, values, and beliefs. From a pragmatic perspective, collaborative learning is also a more representative model of contemporary practice in the working world. In an interesting irony, however, students who have been generally successful in teacher-centered models tend, at first, to reject collaborative learning as an abdication of the teacher's responsibility, assuming that the job of delivering content has been transferred to other students. This is a misinterpretation of the purpose of collaboration, and it poses an additional problem for teachers: planning and structuring collaborative work so that learners' roles and responsibilities are clear, and also making it apparent that the teacher is serving different, but equally important roles as a resource, a guide, a mentor, an assessor, and any of several other roles. Students are not expected to teach each other, they are expected to work together to reach appropriate goals. The value of self-regulated learning is apparent in this context. Well-constructed collaborative work identifies learner responsibilities, sets goals, provides learners with opportunities to consider the goals and to structure their own efforts accordingly, and supports cooperative effort. Svinicki proposes the following methods for promoting learner-centered instruction: (1) encourage self-regulation; (2) use collaborative methods; (3) employ problem-solving activities that connect content to real-world situations; and (4) provide models of the processes, strategies, and habits of thought of the discipline being taught.

Teaching and Its Outcomes

There is not sufficient space here to provide details of all the relationships between various kinds of learning and teaching techniques. More complete descriptions are available in Kenneth Feldman and Michael Paulsen's 1998 discussion of college teaching and learning and in *How College Affects Students* (1991) by Pascarella and Terenzini. Some basic findings from that work are extracted and outlined below, and the organization of the following paragraphs follows that of the chapters in Pascarella and Terenzini's text.

For verbal, quantitative, and subject-matter learning, lecturing appears to be a valuable method, particularly in learning material at the knowledge and comprehension levels of the Bloom et al. taxonomy. Individualized instruction in various forms seems reasonably effective in teaching similar content. More sophisticated cognitive objectives and affective objectives appear better learned when opportunities for interaction occur, as in smaller classes and those that use discussion and active learning methods. Collaborative learning also provides learners with numerous alternative explanations that must be reconciled, and efforts in this direction support achievement of both complex cognitive and affective objectives for learning content material.

When general cognitive skills and intellectual growth are desired, a process involving exploration of information, developing explanations, and reaching generalizations is useful. Like the *experiential model* of David Kolb (1984), this process is reiterative, and its strength is in the need for learners to go beyond memorization of facts and into solving problems through locating relevant information, testing possible theories, and arriving at conclusions. The cognitive practice involved in such activities provides useful training that can be transferred. Additionally, the need to discuss and debate the merits of conflicting arguments provides opportunities to develop written and spoken communication skills. Similar methods support intellectual growth, critical thinking, and the ability to deal with conceptually complex issues. However, a single course experience may not produce large effects; more time and exposure are generally necessary.

The psychosocial changes described by Pascarella and Terenzini include internal matters such as identity and self-esteem, as well as external factors such as relationships with people and constructs in the outside world. In the internal psychosocial realm, there do not seem to be many effects that can be directly attributed to college teaching and learning, or even to the overall college environment. One reason offered by Pascarella and Terenzini for the lack of significant or important findings is the difficulty in measuring such changes. Research lacks a generally accepted set of theories to guide the work, and measurement itself is imprecise. They also note the variety of college environments and the difficulty in generalizing from data gathered across these environments. Another reason may be that attending college does not guarantee a progressively positive set of experiences. Academic difficulties can have large negative effects on self-esteem, and research suggests that many students leave college because of a sense of isolation and loneliness. Such negative outcomes can counterbalance the positive effects of college, thus diminishing the overall strength of the findings.

There are things that can be done to avoid such problems. Arthur Chickering and Zelda Gamson (1987) developed a list of "Seven Principles for Good Practice in Undergraduate Education." They suggest that instruction that encourages social and academic interaction, cooperative efforts, active learning, regular feedback, high expectations about both student effort and outcomes, and the creation of respect and trust among individuals and groups are all critical to success.

In terms of changes with respect to external factors, Pascarella and Terenzini report general student gains in independence, nonauthoritarian thinking, tolerance, intellectual orientation, maturity, personal adjustment skills, and personal development. They note that "the largest freshman-senior changes appear to be away from authoritarian, dogmatic, and ethnocentric thinking and behavior" (p. 257).

Teachers can do much to support the kinds of growth that have been found in the external psychosocial area. The use of cooperative and collaborative methods of teaching and learning supports the development of social skills and team membership skills, and also exposes students to a variety of opinions and ideas. Teachers can present diverse points of view and engage students in exploration, analysis, and synthesis of these views. Indeed, most instruction that addresses the upper levels of the Bloom taxonomy (i.e., analysis, synthesis, and evaluation) requires students to weigh the merits of alternative ideas and approaches, and to make evidence-based judgments. As students move from entry-level courses through graduation and into graduate education, there is an increasingly heavy stress on independent learning and the development of the ability to carry out one's own analyses and arrive at one's own conclusions. It is not surprising then, that one of the best-documented effects of college is an increase in the *internality* of students' locus of control. Locus is one aspect of *attribution theory,* and it refers to the student's perception of the extent to which she or he has the power to influence outcomes. Those students whose locus is more internal (those who are generally successful) feel capable of exercising some control and they take action to do so, while students who exhibit external tendencies are generally less successful and have few feelings of power or the ability to affect outcomes. They are often more passive and attribute their failures (and sometimes, even their successes) to external factors such the skill of the teacher, their classmates, course difficulty or simplicity, and even, to luck.

As with external psychosocial factors, a number of attitudes and values seem to change in college, and there seems a reasonable relationship between these kinds of changes in terms of their nature as well as in the kinds of instruction that can promote growth. Attitudinal changes occur in cultural, aesthetic, and intellectual areas and are marked by greater sophistication and interest in broader ranges of music, literature, philosophy, creative activities, history, and the humanities. Other changes are found in educational and occupational values, including such things as interest in a liberal education and the desire for a fulfilling career. More change seems to occur in the early years of college than does in the latter years. Programs and institutions that support (particularly) younger learners from the outset—and that combine sound instructional methods, the development of a sense of engagement in an intellectual community, and readily available support services—create many opportunities for success.

Insofar as moral development is concerned, attending college appears to consistently promote growth in the direction of principled moral reasoning. This growth takes place primarily in the early years of college and it is reflected in both in-college and postgraduation behavior. Pascarella and Terenzini report this change as one of the most prominent, but they also note that evidence of change does not tell how or why such change takes place. There are some logical connections to teaching strategies in this area, and they are similar to those noted above. For example, use of the discussion method, collaborative learning, peer review, and other techniques that require students to consider alternative points of view and to reconcile differences among these alternatives, can lead to more openness to new ideas, more cultural sensitivity, and more awareness of social/ethical issues. Such techniques can be used in many disciplines and are not limited to particular courses dealing with moral reasoning, ethics, and related subjects. In these or other courses, exposing students to real-world ethical issues and requiring them to propose alternative solutions to problems using the perspectives of the various stakeholders is one way to demonstrate the complexities of making such decisions. Such an approach can also help expand the students' range of understanding of differing points of view.

One of the advantages of higher education's emphasis on diversity and multicultural issues is that the range of experiences and opinions available for discussion is considerably broadened. This advantage relates to research findings that moral reasoning does not develop as much, or as consistently, in contexts where there is a high degree of similarity among students. Homogeneity tends to reduce the conflicting opinions that are the basis for discussion and synthesis.

The Importance of Individual Differences and Motivation

Despite a great deal of discussion and the development of a large number of schema and indicators of individual difference, some caution is necessary when considering their effects. Individual differences—such as general intelligence, affinity for certain subjects, level of knowledge, prior training, personal experience, and cultural and related differences—can be identified reasonably well and taken into account. Other variables, however, are less understood and more difficult to reconcile when instruction is designed. One area of debate is over that group of differences known as teaching and learning *styles*.

While it is generally agreed that each person may have some unique combinations of characteristics, and that certain of these characteristics can be identified and categorized, it is dangerous to make simplistic assumptions about style. Indeed, there are so many different classifications of style and individual difference, that it is all too easy to assume unilateral reliance on any one, or to attempt to include too many. Research suggests that since most learners have a repertoire of styles, simply using a variety of instructional methods will provide the majority with sufficient opportunities to learn. While students may use some approaches more frequently than others, they can adapt to new situations by using whatever alternative approaches seem most suitable at the moment. It is those few learners who have limited repertoires who have the greatest difficulty and for whom the greatest accommodations are necessary. Useful interventions for these learners include individual assistance, making instruction more concrete and relevant through relating content to real-world situations or to their own experiences, explaining processes for organizing content information, teaching general study skills as well as specific problem-solving strategies, using frequent assessment techniques, and providing regular feedback.

Motivation is a well-researched area, and though there are several descriptions of the elements of motivation, these elements are quite similar. Michael Theall's 1998 distillation of thirteen motivational approaches resulted in a six-item conceptualization that applies to higher education students and faculty. The elements were: inclusion, attitude, meaning, competence, leadership, and satisfaction. Of the models reviewed, one that can be directly connected to college teaching is that of John Keller (1983). Keller proposed a model for the *motivational design of instruction.* The model outlines a cycle of inputs, events, and consequences that could result in positive or negative outcomes. Students and teachers enter into a teaching-learning situation with sets of values and expectations that affect the extent and nature of the effort they expend. Positive attitudes (e.g., the student is interested in the subject; the teacher has done research on the topic) and expectations (e.g., the students believe themselves to be able in the content area; the teacher expects the course to be well received) lead to greater effort, and effort directly affects performance. Strong performance leads to both satisfaction (via the consequences of good grades, the sense of a "job well done" and the recognition of effective learning) and heightened value and expectations for the future (which further motivate effort). However, in the negative direction, certain attitudes (e.g., the students do not want to take the class; the teacher is tired of teaching the material) and expectations (e.g., a student's subject anxiety; the teacher's concerns about the course) can diminish effort and lead to reduced performance and disappointment, thus reinforcing negative attitudes and expectations.

Raymond Wlodkowski (1998) stresses that *intrinsic motivation* is more powerful that *extrinsic motivation.* In other words, the older view of motivation as something that is done to someone is less relevant than the understanding that success involves promoting or creating sets of conditions under which the individual is the one who actually provides the motivation. A typical case in college learning would be a teacher's creation of sets of experiences that arouse the students' interest and allow engagement in activities that both promote growth and provide opportunities for success. In this scenario, satisfaction comes internally from accomplishment, while grades are only a documentation of the learning and satisfaction, rather than after-the-fact rewards that drive performance.

Determining Outcomes

The growth of both evaluation and assessment has been exponential, and with this growth have come expectations that teachers and institutions will be able to document their performance, and that of their students, in meaningful ways. Classroom tests are no longer sufficient as evidence. Certification and licensure are important in certain professional fields, but many disciplines do not require such standardized demonstrations of learning, and many have questioned even these more carefully constructed measures in terms of their ability to truly describe learning.

Moreover, the interest of accrediting bodies is not only in what kinds of data are collected in what ways, but also in what actions have been taken as a result of assessments. In other words, assessment has become a process for continuous revision and improvement. Assessment is concerned with the results of teaching and the educational experience, and of determining as precisely as possible what was learned. This role differs from that of evaluation, which is more a process to determine merit or worth. Evaluation is a more global, formal, quantitative, and occasional process, while assessment is often more narrow, informal, qualitative, and ongoing. This is because assessment's objectives are often at the level of the individual learner and less amenable to social science research methods that depend on samples of adequate size to allow statistical inference. Interestingly, both evaluation and assessment use the terms *formative,* meaning a process for exploration, revision, and improvement; and *summative,* meaning a process for determining merit and making administrative decisions about people or programs.

The most widely circulated and complete source of assessment information is *Classroom Assessment Techniques* (1993) by Thomas Angelo and K. Patricia Cross. This book contains numerous techniques for assessing learning in the immediate context of the classroom, as well as in the broader context of the full course, the college semester, and beyond. In the 1990s, this work and the concurrent interest in Ernest Boyer's conception of the *scholarship of teaching* led to the development of methods for classroom research that are, according to Cross and Mimi Steadman (1996), learner-centered, teacher-directed, collaborative, context-specific, scholarly, practical/relevant, and continual. Very much like assessment in its emphasis on learning, classroom research provided a bridge that connected investigation of classroom learning with the more formal research that had previously held exclusive rights to the term *scholarship.* In effect, evaluation and assessment methods were blended to provide a vehicle for the teacher-scholar to carry out the scholarship of teaching.

Adult Learning and the Growth of Technology

A new and unique set of circumstances arose during the 1990s due to the increase in the number of adult learners and programs accessible at a distance. Not only was this population of students very different from traditional, residential students, but the contexts of teaching and learning were also markedly different. Stephen Brookfield (1991) suggests six principles for effectively working with adult learners: (1) voluntary participation and engagement by learners; (2) respect among participants and acknowledgement of learners' experiences and knowledge; (3) collaborative rather than directive facilitation of learners' experiences; (4) praxis and constant integration of activities into a unified whole; (5) critical reflection; and (6) promoting self-directed efforts and a sense of empowerment. But since the majority of adult learners are commuters or students taking courses away from the traditional campus setting, the benefits of the traditional communities of the college campus are not readily available to this population, and opportunities for informal dialogue, for developing social relationships, and for spending concentrated time on course requirements are limited.

At the same time that these issues about new student populations were being discussed, the rapid growth of distance education programs, especially courses and curricula delivered entirely, or almost entirely, via the Internet, was raising questions about how instruction could be delivered in a disembodied form. Rena Palloff and Keith Pratt (2001) suggest that the following lessons have been learned so far: (1) course development needs to focus on interactivity, not content, because even if course content is known and established, there remains the need to deliver it in ways that facilitate learning; (2) faculty and student roles need to change, with less emphasis on one-sided delivery and more on active and interactive modes; (3) faculty and student training on the use of the technology, as well as the new modes of instruction, is critical to success; (4) faculty and students need to have substantial support networks throughout the course experience; (5) institutions must develop strategic plans that go well beyond technological requirements and deal with everything from pedagogical support to intellectual property rights; (6) institutions must have tested and reliable infrastructure in place, and the systems used should be accessible and usable; (7) technologies should be chosen by teams of users, and choices should be based in instructional as well as technical parameters.

Summary

Since 1970 there have been many changes in higher education—changes that center on different student populations, different methods of delivering instruction, and different conceptions of what a college education is and how it should be pursued. This change process will continue, but despite dire predictions that technology will replace the need for college campuses, it is likely that the residential experience of undergraduate education and the intensive nature of graduate training will continue to require opportunities for interaction and apprenticeship that can only be provided on traditional campuses.

See also: COLLEGE TEACHING; COOPERATIVE AND COLLABORATIVE LEARNING; INDIVIDUAL DIFFERENCES; LEARNING THEORY; LEARNING TO LEARN AND METACOGNITION; MORAL DEVELOPMENT; MOTIVATION.

BIBLIOGRAPHY

ANGELO, THOMAS A., and CROSS, K. PATRICIA. 1993. *Classroom Assessment Techniques: A Handbook for College Teachers,* 2nd edition. San Francisco: Jossey-Bass.

BLOOM, BENJAMIN S.; ENGLEHART, MAX D.; FURST, EDWARD J.; HILL, WALTER H.; and KRATHWOHL, DAVID R. 1956. *Taxonomy of Education Objectives.* New York: David McKay.

BOYER, ERNEST L. 1990. *Scholarship Reconsidered: The Priorities of the Professoriate.* San Francisco: Jossey-Bass.

BROOKFIELD, STEPHEN. 1991. *Understanding and Facilitating Adult Learning.* San Francisco: Jossey-Bass.

CHICKERING, ARTHUR, and GAMSON, ZELDA. 1987. "Seven Principles of Good Practice in Undergraduate Education." *The Wingspread Journal* 9(2):1–11.

CROSS, K. PATRICIA, and STEADMAN, MIMI H. 1996. *Classroom Research: Implementing the Scholarship of Teaching.* San Francisco: Jossey-Bass.

FELDMAN, KENNETH A. and PAULSEN, MICHAEL B. 1998. *Teaching and Learning in the College Class-*

room, 2nd edition. Needham Heights, MA: Simon and Schuster.

JOHNSON, DAVID; JOHNSON, ROGER T.; and HOLUBEC, ERNEST. 1989. *Cooperation in the Classroom.* Edina, MN: Interaction.

KELLER, JOHN M. 1983. "Motivational Design of Instruction." In *Instructional Design Theories and Models: An Overview of Their Current Status.* ed. Charles M. Riegeluth. Hillsdale, NJ: Erlbaum.

KOLB, DAVID. 1984. *Experiential Learning: Experience as the Source of Learning and Development.* Englewood Cliffs, NJ: Prentice-Hall.

MAGER, ROBERT, F. 1962. *Preparing Instructional Objectives.* Palo Alto, CA: Fearon.

PALLOFF, RENA M., and PRATT, KEITH. 2001. *Lessons from the Cyberspace Classroom: The Realities of Online Teaching.* San Francisco: Jossey-Bass.

PASCARELLA, ERNEST, and TERENZINI, PATRICK. 1991. *How College Affects Students.* San Francisco: Jossey-Bass.

PINTRICH, PAUL R., ed. 1995. *Understanding Self-Regulated Learning.* San Francisco: Jossey-Bass.

SCRIVEN, MICHAEL. 1967. "The Methodology of Evaluation." In *Perspectives of Curriculum Evaluation,* ed. Ralph Tyler, Robert Gagne, and Michael Scriven. Chicago: Rand McNally.

SKINNER, B. F. 1953. *Science and Human Behavior.* New York: Free Press.

SVINICKI, MARILLA. 1999. "New Directions in Learning and Motivation." In *Teaching and Learning on the Edge of the Millenium: Building on What We Have Learned,* ed. Marilla Svinicki. San Francisco: Jossey-Bass.

THEALL, MICHAEL. 1998. "What Have We Learned: A Synthesis and Some Guidelines." In *Motivation from Within: Approaches for Encouraging Faculty and Students to Excel,* ed. Michael Theall. San Francisco: Jossey-Bass.

WEINER, BERNARD. 1986. *An Attributional Theory of Motivation.* New York: Springer-Verlag.

WLODKOWSKI, RAYMOND. 1998. *Enhancing Adult Motivation to Learn.* San Francisco: Jossey-Bass.

MICHAEL THEALL

INTERNATIONAL PERSPECTIVE

A curious paradox can be seen as one considers schooling and teaching across the many cultures of the world. On the one hand there is enormous variation among cultures—and within most cultures—in the ways in which people learn. At the same time there is a remarkable similarity across nations in the ways in which opportunities to learn are provided through formal schools and school systems.

Anthropologists, and educators who have taught in a variety of cultural settings, have long noted differences in the ways that children born into different cultural settings *learn to learn.* While there are variations within any cultural group—sometimes across a narrow range of difference, and sometimes across a wide range (such differences are frequently referred to as *individual learning styles*)—clearly observable modal differences among cultural groups have been well documented. Such differences are analyzed in the literature of European settler states, such as the United States, Canada, Australia, and New Zealand, which contain references to differences in approaches to, and understanding of, learning between the European settler/colonizer groups and the original aboriginal inhabitants, and between settlers and more recently arrived immigrant groups from areas of the world other than Europe. These differences have also figured prominently in analyses of education in other colonial and postcolonial (or neocolonial) states around the world. Yet, with an increasing awareness of these considerable variations in learning, there has simultaneously spread throughout the world a standard model of schooling, which often does not take these differences into account, and thus often does considerable damage to the learning potential of children.

It is frequently forgotten that *schooling,* as it has come to be known, is only one of a vast array of social institutions that humans have invented to provide opportunities for young people to learn. It is, in fact, a human invention of relatively recent origin, at least on a mass scale. The broad-scale provision of education as an instrument of statecraft and state development was effectively "invented" in Prussia after, and as a result of, the Napoleonic invasion of that nation. It spread quickly throughout Europe and other relatively wealthy nations of the time, and more gradually across the world through colonial imposition and, in some cases, through cultural borrowing. But in the broad sweep of history it is a quite new social institution. In its fundamental forms (hence the term *formal education*) it was set by the experience, attitudes, and understanding of the mid- to late-nineteenth century elites in the then newly industrialized nations. As those basic forms have spread around the world they have hardly changed, even in the wealthiest nations, for well over a century. That standard model generally comprises, around the world, the following basic elements.

- One hundred to several hundred children/youth assembled (often compulsorily for a period of years) in a building called a school, from approximately the age of six or seven up to somewhere between age eleven and sixteen.

- Instruction lasts for three to six hours per day, five or six days per week.

- Students are divided into groups of twenty to sixty individuals.

- Students work with a single adult (a "certified" teacher) in a single room for (especially in the upper grades) discrete periods of forty to sixty minutes, each devoted to a separate subject.

- Subjects are studied and learned in a group of young people of roughly the same age, with supporting learning materials, such as books, chalkboards, notebooks, workbooks and worksheets, and, increasingly, computers (and in technical areas such things as laboratories, workbenches, and practice sites).

- There is a standard curriculum, set by an authority level much above the individual school (normally a central or provincial/state government), and which all students are expected to cover in an age-graded fashion.

- Adults, assumed to be more knowledgeable, teach, and students receive instruction from them.

- If they are to go any higher in the schooling system, students are expected and required to repeat back to the adults what they have been taught.

- Teachers and/or a central examination system evaluate students' ability to repeat back to them what the students have been taught, and also provide formal recognized credentials for passing particular grades or levels.

- Most or all of the financial support comes from national or regional governments, or other kinds of authority centers (e.g. church-related schools) well above the local community level.

There are a variety of explanations or theories regarding how and why this particular pattern of organizing and providing teaching for young people has become almost universally overlaid upon the wide diversity of ways in which young people learn to learn. Within this cross-national paradox, there is irony. While it has been clearly demonstrated that this standard model of teaching and schooling has frequently proven very dysfunctional for learning among children from cultural groups different from its place of origin, the accumulated literature from cognitive and learning psychology, anthropology, and comparative education has increasingly demonstrated that it is also inherently dysfunctional for children (and adults for that matter) from those very cultures of origin.

The system, in short, is inherently inefficient and ineffective. People of every age and culture simply do not learn well under these arrangements. These traditional, but now nearly universal, patterns of teaching and schooling are an artifact of the misconceptions of a different time and, for much of the world, a different place. But now that patterns are in place, it seems nearly impossible to get rid of them, and even the richest nations are able to alter them only slightly at great effort and cost, and usually only over very long periods of time.

In the closing decades of the twentieth century, however, a new pattern began to appear in developing nations where the European system has proven to be so often dysfunctional for learning. School systems have begun to appear that are breaking the forms of formal schooling in quite fundamental ways, and that are producing remarkable learning gains among extremely poor and marginalized children. As of 2002 more than 100 of these teaching/school programs have been documented, some involving tens or hundreds of schools, others tens of thousands of schools. Some common features of these alternative forms of schooling are these:

- Child-centered rather than teacher-driven pedagogy
- Active rather than passive learning
- Multigraded classrooms with continuous progress learning
- Peer-tutoring—older and/or faster learning children assist and "teach" younger and/or slower learning children
- Carefully developed self-guided learning materials, which children, alone or in small groups, can work through themselves, at their own pace, with help from other students and teachers as

necessary—the children are responsible for their own learning

- Combinations of fully trained teachers, partially trained teachers, and community resource people—parents and other community members are heavily involved in the learning of the children, and in the management of the school
- Active student involvement in the governance and management of the school
- Free flows of children and adults between the school and the community
- Community involvement includes attention to the nutrition and health needs of young children long before they reach school age
- Locally adapted changes in the cycle of the school day or the school year
- Ongoing monitoring/evaluation/feedback systems allowing the "system" to learn from its own experience, with constant modification of/experimentation with the methodology
- Ongoing and very frequent in-service teacher development programs, with heavy use of peer mentoring

Early indications suggest that they are far more flexible and successful in adapting their teaching/schooling approaches to the variations among cultures in how people learn to learn. But little serious research has been done to try to understand how and why these new programs seem to work so well in promoting learning among very diverse groups. That is a challenge for the twenty-first century.

See also: INDIVIDUAL DIFFERENCES; LEARNING TO LEARN AND METACOGNITION.

BIBLIOGRAPHY

CASE, ROBBIE. 1985. *Intellectual Development: Birth to Adulthood.* Orlando, FL: Academic Press.

FARRELL, JOSEPH P. 1997. "A Retrospective on Educational Planning in Comparative Education." *Comparative Education Review* 41(3):277–313.

FARRELL, JOSEPH P., and MFUM-MENSAH, O. 2002. "A Preliminary Analytical Framework for Comparative Analysis of Alternative Primary Education Programs in Developing Nations" Paper presented at the annual meeting of the Comparative and International Educational Society, Orlando, Florida.

FULLER, BRUCE. 1991. *Growing Up Modern: The Western State Builds Third World Schools.* New York: Routledge.

HALL, EDWARD T. 1986. "Unstated Features of the Cultural Context of Learning." In *Learning and Development: A Global Perspective,* ed. A. Thomas and E. Ploman. Toronto: Ontario Institute for Studies in Education Press.

KNOWLES, MALCOMB. 1984. *The Adult Learner: A Neglected Species.* Houston: Gulf Publishing.

KOCHAN, ANNA. 2001. *Community Educational Projects Database: An International List of Community Education Programs,* Toronto: Ontario Institute for Studies in Education/University of Toronto Comparative International and Development Education Centre.

SCHIEFELBEIN, ERNESTO. 1991. *In Search of the School of the 21st Century: Is Colombia's Escuela Nueva the Right Pathfinder?* Paris: United Nations Educational, Scientific and Cultural Organization.

TYACK, DAVID, and CUBAN, LAWRENCE. 1995. *Tinkering Toward Utopia: A Century of Public School Reform.* Cambridge, MA: Harvard University Press.

ZAALOUK, MALAK. 1995. *The Children of the Nile: The Community Schools Project in Upper Egypt.* Paris: United Nations International Children's Emergency Fund.

JOSEPH P. FARRELL

TEACHING AND RESEARCH, THE RELATIONSHIP BETWEEN

Faculty members' work accomplishes the core teaching, research, and service goals of colleges and universities. Teaching enhances the development of students, research advances the development of new knowledge, and service contributes to the growth of nonacademic, professional, or college and university communities. Observers have debated since the late 1800s whether faculty work roles enhance each other or conflict. The debate focuses in particular on teaching and research, and concerns the best way to organize individual faculty work, departments, institutions, and the entire loosely coupled United States higher education system for maximum research productivity and teaching effectiveness.

Alternative Perspectives

Analysts who perceive that teaching and research enhance each other argue that active researchers are informed and engaging teachers and that teaching stimulates faculty creativity and enthusiasm for research. Economic theory suggests that teaching and research are complementary. Because they use many of the same resources, facilities, and personnel, producing teaching and research together is more efficient than producing each separately. Similarly, individual faculty may improve their efficiency and productivity if they sometimes engage in activities that accomplish both teaching and research goals at the same time. Arguments for integrating teaching and research are consistent with a view that colleges and universities should respond to increasing environmental and technical complexity by considering faculty as professionals—highly qualified, flexible, and complex workers who are able to relate associated tasks in creative ways and to handle unpredictable problems independently.

Analysts, such as Ronald Barnett, who perceive that teaching and research are separate and incompatible argue that faculty members' preoccupation with research interferes with teaching, or that teaching limits precious time available for research. System and organization level arguments suggest that different people in different locations should conduct teaching and research. To some extent, such organizational fragmentation already exists in the United States. For example, most faculty at community colleges focus exclusively on teaching, while many faculty at four-year institutions engage in some combination of teaching and research. Similarly, some university faculty working within institutes or centers focus primarily on research, while many tenure-track faculty in departments engage in both teaching and research. Some analysts suggest that even in institutions that produce both teaching and research, responsibilities for the two roles should be assigned to different faculty according to their varying interests and strengths. Many departments already partially subdivide labor in this way. Adjunct or part-time faculty focus primarily on either teaching or research, while tenure-track faculty are usually expected to do both. At the individual level, teaching and research may be separated by time. In the short-term, some faculty teach during the academic year and save summers for doing research. In the long-term, some faculty may be more effective if they focus primarily on research at one stage in their careers and on teaching at another career stage. Arguments for formalizing de facto fragmentation of faculty work roles are consistent with a view that colleges and universities should respond to increasing environmental and technical complexity by subdividing work, thereby increasing organizational complexity and administrative control.

Perceptions of a positive or negative relationship between teaching and research depend on how observers define the content of the two roles. Teaching is often defined as activities involved in delivering formal classroom instruction to registered students. Some analysts, however, suggest that teaching also includes advising, informal instruction, and training students to conduct research. Similarly, research is often defined as publications. In 1990, however, Ernest Boyer of the Carnegie Foundation asserted that research should be more broadly defined as the scholarships of discovery, integration, application, and teaching. Those who define teaching and research in terms of classroom instruction and publications are less likely to perceive a positive relationship between the two faculty roles than those who define the roles more broadly.

Research Findings

Studies that investigate the relationship between teaching and research also vary in the ways they define the nature of the two roles. One line of inquiry defines teaching and research in terms of measurable outputs. Other lines of inquiry define teaching and research as activities that use time.

Measurable outputs. Many investigators have attempted to determine whether there is some measurable correlation between teaching and research quality. They typically measure teaching effectiveness by student ratings of formal classroom instruction and research productivity by numbers of publications. Most of these studies were conducted at one or only a few institutions and included relatively small (less than 300) samples of faculty. To attain more comprehensive results applicable to more faculty, two meta-analytic studies synthesized the results of multiple studies. In 1987, Kenneth Feldman analyzed the combined results of twenty-nine studies of the relationship between teaching effectiveness and research productivity, and found a very small (0.12) positive correlation. A meta-analysis conducted by John Hattie and Herbert W. March in 1996 analyzed the combined results of fifty-eight studies, and found an even smaller (.06) positive correlation between teaching effectiveness and research productivity. There are several possible reasons for their findings of a relationship so close to zero that it may be considered a null relationship.

A null relationship suggests that teaching and research outputs are completely independent, neither enhancing nor detracting from each other. The substantive reasons frequently given for no relationship discuss inputs and processes for producing effective teaching or large numbers of publications rather than outputs themselves. For example, the organizational resources, production processes, and faculty abilities and personality traits needed for teaching and research may be different while not competing with each other. A methodological reason for finding a statistically null relationship may be that mediating factors that contribute to a negative relationship between research and teaching are effectively canceled out by other mediating factors that contribute to a positive relationship.

There are both individual and organizational explanations for a possible partially negative teaching-research relationship. Some personality characteristics and abilities needed to teach effectively and produce many publications may compete with each other. Students may see extroverts as better teachers, for example, while introverts may be well suited to writing alone about ideas and abstractions. Organizational context may contribute to competition between teaching and research when evaluation and reward policies systematically fragment the two roles. According to James Fairweather, "faculty rewards emphasize the discreteness, not the mutuality, of teaching and research" (p. 110), and faculty are rewarded more for research productivity than for effective teaching. Therefore, faculty may neglect teaching to attain rewards for research.

A partially positive relationship between teaching and research may also be explained by individual and organizational reasons. Individual characteristics that may contribute to success in both teaching and research include general ability, organization, and intellectual curiosity. Organizational evaluation of faculty work as an integrated whole might increase evaluators' and faculty members' own perceptions of a positive association between teaching and research.

Variations in discipline and type of institution may also affect whether the relationship between teaching and research outputs is null, negative, or positive. Although scholars have described comprehensive models that could account for relative impact of many organizational and individual factors on the relationship, no such model has yet been tested.

Time on tasks. Studies that analyze the time faculty take to engage in tasks that meet institutional teaching and research goals define the content of the two roles more broadly than studies that analyze measurable outputs. Time on teaching involves preparing and delivering classroom instruction, grading students' work, meeting students in office hours, advising, and training students to conduct research. Time on research includes reading foundational literature, gathering and analyzing data, supervising assistants, securing funding, writing reports, and presenting findings.

Findings of either a negative or a positive relationship between teaching and research time are primarily a consequence of research methods used. Most workload surveys that ask faculty to estimate the time they devote to their primary work roles define teaching, research, and service as mutually exclusive. A negative relationship between teaching and research emerges by design, because time spent teaching is inevitably not time engaged in research. These studies have been conducted with department, institution, state, and representative national faculty samples.

In contrast, a few workload surveys asked faculty to cross reference time on tasks with institutional teaching, research, and service goals. One such workload survey conducted at the University of Arizona in 1998 found, on average, that faculty engaged in tasks that met all three goals, and teaching and research goals 14 and 18 percent of their time, respectively. A 1998 study by Carol L. Colbeck that observed English and physics faculty on the job found they engaged in integrated teaching and research activities nearly 19 percent of the time. In both studies, the degree of positive relationship—the amount of time spent in activities that accomplished both teaching and research goals—varied by discipline. Studies that account for time spent meeting both teaching and research goals have been conducted at either a single or a few universities and with very small faculty samples.

Conclusion

Evidence indicates that the outputs from teaching and research neither enhance nor interfere with each other, and that faculty engage in activities that meet both teaching and research goals some of the time. Perhaps because of the limitations of small sample size and simple models, however, faculty, administrators, and policy analysts still debate whether the relationship is positive or negative. Evidence that may resolve the debate will require research designs and methods that consider teaching and research both as uses of time and as outputs, take into account mediating factors, and include large samples of faculty across many disciplines and types of institutions.

See also: COLLEGE TEACHING; FACULTY PERFORMANCE OF RESEARCH AND SCHOLARSHIP; FACULTY ROLES AND RESPONSIBILITIES.

BIBLIOGRAPHY

BARNETT, RONALD. 1992. "Linking Teaching and Research: A Critical Inquiry." *Journal of Higher Education* 63:619–636.

BECKER, WILLIAM E., JR. 1975. "The University Professor as a Utility Maximizer and a Producer of Learning, Research, and Income." *Journal of Human Resources* 10:107–115.

BOYER, ERNEST L. 1990. *Scholarship Reconsidered: Priorities of the Professoriate.* Princeton, NJ: The Carnegie Foundation for the Advancement of Teaching.

BRAXTON, JOHN M., ed. 1996. *Faculty Teaching and Research: Is There a Conflict?* San Francisco: Jossey-Bass.

CLARK, BURTON R. 1997. "The Modern Integration of Research Activities with Teaching and Learning." *Journal of Higher Education* 68:241–255.

COLBECK, CAROL L. 1998. "Merging in a Seamless Blend: How Faculty Integrate Teaching and Research." *Journal of Higher Education* 69:647–671.

FAIRWEATHER, JAMES S. 1996. *Faculty Work and Public Trust: Restoring the Value of Teaching and Public Service in American Academic Life.* Boston: Allyn and Bacon.

FELDMAN, KENNETH A. 1987. "Research Productivity and Scholarly Accomplishment of College Teachings as Related to their Instructional Effectiveness: A Review and Exploration." *Research in Higher Education* 26:227–298.

HATTIE, JOHN, and MARSH, HERBERT W. 1996. "The Relationship Between Research and Teaching: A Meta-Analysis." *Review of Educational Research* 66:507–542.

HOPKINS, DAVID S. P. 1990. "The Higher Education Production Function: Theoretical Foundations and Empirical Findings." In *The Economics of American Universities,* ed. Stephen A. Hoenack, and Eileen L. Collins. Albany: State University of New York Press.

KRAHENBUHL, GARY S. 1998. "Faculty Work: Integrating Responsibilities and Institutional Needs." *Change* 30(6):18–25.

CAROL L. COLBECK

TEACHING, COLLEGE

See: COLLEGE TEACHING.

TEAM TEACHING

Team teaching involves a group of instructors working purposefully, regularly, and cooperatively to help a group of students of any age learn. Teachers together set goals for a course, design a syllabus, prepare individual lesson plans, teach students, and evaluate the results. They share insights, argue with one another, and perhaps even challenge students to decide which approach is better.

Teams can be single-discipline, interdisciplinary, or school-within-a-school teams that meet with a common set of students over an extended period of time. New teachers may be paired with veteran teachers. Innovations are encouraged, and modifications in class size, location, and time are permitted. Different personalities, voices, values, and approaches spark interest, keep attention, and prevent boredom.

The team-teaching approach allows for more interaction between teachers and students. Faculty evaluate students on their achievement of the learning goals; students evaluate faculty members on their teaching proficiency. Emphasis is on student and faculty growth, balancing initiative and shared responsibility, specialization and broadening horizons, the clear and interesting presentation of content and student development, democratic participation and common expectations, and cognitive, affective, and behavioral outcomes. This combination of analysis, synthesis, critical thinking, and practical applications can be done on all levels of education, from kindergarten through graduate school.

Working as a team, teachers model respect for differences, interdependence, and conflict-resolution skills. Team members together set the course goals and content, select common materials such as texts and films, and develop tests and final examinations for all students. They set the sequence of topics and supplemental materials. They also give their own interpretations of the materials and use their own teaching styles. The greater the agreement on common objectives and interests, the more likely that teaching will be interdependent and coordinated.

Teaching periods can be scheduled side by side or consecutively. For example, teachers of two similar classes may team up during the same or adjacent periods so that each teacher may focus on that phase of the course that he or she can best handle. Students can sometimes meet all together, sometimes in small groups supervised by individual teachers or teaching assistants, or they can work singly or together on projects in the library, laboratory, or fieldwork. Teachers can be at different sites, linked by video-conferencing, satellites, or the Internet.

Breaking out of the taken-for-granted single-subject, single-course, single-teacher pattern encourages other innovations and experiments. For example, students can be split along or across lines of sex, age, culture, or other interests, then recombined to stimulate reflection. Remedial programs and honors sections provide other attractive opportunities to make available appropriate and effective curricula for students with special needs or interests. They can address different study skills and learning techniques. Team teaching can also offset the danger of imposing ideas, values, and mindsets on minorities or less powerful ethnic groups. Teachers of different backgrounds can culturally enrich one another and students.

Advantages

Students do not all learn at the same rate. Periods of equal length are not appropriate for all learning situations. Educators are no longer dealing primarily with top-down transmission of the tried and true by the mature and experienced teacher to the young, immature, and inexperienced pupil in the single-subject classroom. Schools are moving toward the inclusion of another whole dimension of learning: the lateral transmission to every sentient member of society of what has just been discovered, invented, created, manufactured, or marketed. For this, team members with different areas of expertise are invaluable.

Of course, team teaching is not the only answer to all problems plaguing teachers, students, and administrators. It requires planning, skilled management, willingness to risk change and even failure, humility, open-mindedness, imagination, and creativity. But the results are worth it.

Teamwork improves the quality of teaching as various experts approach the same topic from different angles: theory and practice, past and present, different genders or ethnic backgrounds. Teacher strengths are combined and weaknesses are remedied. Poor teachers can be observed, critiqued, and improved by the other team members in a nonthreatening, supportive context. The evaluation done by a team of teachers will be more insightful and balanced than the introspection and self-evaluation of an individual teacher.

Working in teams spreads responsibility, encourages creativity, deepens friendships, and builds community among teachers. Teachers complement one another. They share insights, propose new approaches, and challenge assumptions. They learn new perspectives and insights, techniques and values from watching one another. Students enter into conversations between them as they debate, disagree with premises or conclusions, raise new questions, and point out consequences. Contrasting viewpoints encourage more active class participation and independent thinking from students, especially if there is team balance for gender, race, culture, and age. Team teaching is particularly effective with older and underprepared students when it moves beyond communicating facts to tap into their life experience.

The team cuts teaching burdens and boosts morale. The presence of another teacher reduces student-teacher personality problems. In an emergency one team member can attend to the problem while the class goes on. Sharing in decision-making bolsters self-confidence. As teachers see the quality of teaching and learning improve, their self-esteem and happiness grow. This aids in recruiting and keeping faculty.

Disadvantages

Team teaching is not always successful. Some teachers are rigid personality types or may be wedded to a single method. Some simply dislike the other teachers on the team. Some do not want to risk humiliation and discouragement at possible failures. Some fear they will be expected to do more work for the same salary. Others are unwilling to share the spotlight or their pet ideas or to lose total control.

Team teaching makes more demands on time and energy. Members must arrange mutually agreeable times for planning and evaluation. Discussions can be draining and group decisions take longer. Rethinking the courses to accommodate the team-teaching method is often inconvenient.

Opposition may also come from students, parents, and administrators who may resist change of any sort. Some students flourish in a highly structured environment that favors repetition. Some are confused by conflicting opinions. Too much variety may hinder habit formation.

Salaries may have to reflect the additional responsibilities undertaken by team members. Team leaders may need some form of bonus. Such costs could be met by enlarging some class sizes. Nonprofessional staff members could take over some responsibilities.

All things being considered, team teaching so enhances the quality of learning that it is sure to spread widely in the future.

See also: ELEMENTARY EDUCATION, *subentries on* CURRENT TRENDS, HISTORY OF; INSTRUCTIONAL STRATEGIES; SECONDARY EDUCATION, *subentries on* CURRENT TRENDS, HISTORY OF.

BIBLIOGRAPHY

BEGGS, DAVID W., III. 1964. *Team Teaching: Bold New Venture.* Bloomington: Indiana University Press.

BUCKLEY, FRANCIS J. 1998. *Team Teaching: What, Why, and How?* Thousand Oaks, CA: Sage.

DAVIS, HAROLD S. 1967. *Team Teaching Bibliography.* Cleveland, OH: The Educational Research Council of America.

MAEROFF, GENE I. 1993. *Team Building for School Change.* New York: Teachers College Press.

McKEACHIE, WILBERT JAMES. 1994. *Teaching Tips: Strategies, Research, and Theory for College and University Teachers.* Lexington, MA: D.C. Heath.

MORSINK, CATHERINE V.; THOMAS, CAROL C.; and CORREA, VIVIAN. 1991. *Interactive Teaming.* New York: Prentice Hall.

PARKER, GLENN M. 1990. *Team Players and Teamwork.* San Francisco: Jossey-Bass.

WEIMER, MARYELLEN. 1993. *Improving Your Classroom Teaching.* Thousand Oaks, CA: Sage.

FRANCIS J. BUCKLEY

TECHNOLOGY EDUCATION

Technology education (TE) in the United States is a field of elementary and secondary education that until the 1980s was commonly referred to as *industrial arts.* Its focus is on promoting technological knowledge and skills.

The notion of teaching children about contemporary technology and industry has been a recurring international theme throughout the history of education. Modern American technology education took form in the first quarter of the twentieth century, mainly in the Northeast. In 1923 Frederick Bonser and Lois Coffey Mossman laid out the view of industrial arts as a general school subject for boys and girls in pre-secondary education. As a subject, industrial arts was a branch of the social studies, with content focused primarily on food, clothing, and shelter. As a method of teaching, it provided a constructional basis for curricular integration. Thus Bonser and Mossman, in the larger context of the Activity and Progressive-education movements of the time, attempted to subsume traditional home economics and manual training topics into a participatory curriculum that went beyond tool manipulation to include larger social issues.

Ostensibly, the Bonser and Mossman conception of industrial arts guided most American industrial arts teacher preparation, as well as the philosophy of the predominant professional organization, the American Industrial Arts Association (AIAA), from the late 1930s until the 1980s, when the AIAA changed its name to the International Technology Education Association (ITEA). But most leaders and practitioners did not observe the progressive ideals of Bonser and Mossman and instead focused mainly on educating high school boys in traditional manual-training subjects such as woodworking, metalworking, and drawing. As recently as the late 1990s, these three subjects were still the most popular technology education courses in the United States. Thus in describing TE one must differentiate between theory and practice.

Philosophies

While the purpose of technology education is often encapsulated as "learning by doing," the relative importance of knowledge and activity is a subject of debate. Specifically, most technology teacher educators and theoreticians regard the primary purpose of technology education either as content, method, or process.

The content philosophy views technology education as an academic discipline with a well-defined taxonomy of knowledge related to industries and technologies such as manufacturing, construction, communication, and transportation. That technology is an important subject of study for children at all grade levels is the essential precept of "Standards for Technology Education: Content for the Study of Technology" (2000), a multimillion dollar ITEA project funded by the National Science Foundation and NASA.

Proponents of the method philosophy see technology education primarily as a means of teaching the subjects of the K–12 curriculum. In this view, technology education takes the form of constructional activities in which children manipulate tools and materials to create products and, in so doing, learn about social studies, science, and other subjects. Advocates of the method philosophy put secondary focus on technological content, emphasizing that any content may be taught via technology education. This conception is most common in the elementary grades.

In the process philosophy, teaching technology education is tantamount to fostering competence in problem solving and solution design. The content of technology education in the process view is any and all knowledge needed to design solutions to problems, and technology activities constitute a context for the entire K–12 curriculum. This philosophy has re-emerged in U.S. technology education literature and teacher education due to its popularity abroad, especially in Anglophone Europe and Australia.

Because it is espoused by the major U.S. technology teachers' organizations and enjoys the financial support of well-known U.S. government agencies, the view of technology education as a con-

tent area dominates teacher education, textbooks, curriculum, funded projects, and doctoral research. Scholarly discourse also favors this view, but to a smaller extent. *The Standards for Technology Education* represents an attempt by the field to position itself as an academic subject by emulating the efforts of educators in the mathematics, science, language arts, social studies, and fine arts fields in the standards movement of the 1980s and 1990s. It is also the most comprehensive effort in the field's history to arrive at consensus as to the nature of American technology education.

Approaches to Curriculum

It is clear that in classroom practice, the most common approaches to technology education do not correspond neatly to these three philosophies. Surveys revealing that high school technology course offerings closely resemble those from the early twentieth century have been a source of consternation to leaders in the field since the 1960s, yet schools and teachers in the United States have been very slow to shift curricula from traditional industrial courses, such as woodworking and drafting, to technological studies like manufacturing or communications. The most prominent leaders in the field have advocated this change in focus since the late 1940s. Their primary success has been in the nearly nationwide name change from *industrial arts* to *technology education*, accomplished in the 1980s and 1990s.

A 1999 survey found that the four most frequently taught middle and high school technology courses had not changed since 1963: general technology education, drafting, woodworking, and metalworking. Other popular courses include automotives, architectural drafting, communications, electricity/electronics, and manufacturing.

In American elementary schools, technology education is rare. Where it is included in the curriculum, it is usually the responsibility of the classroom teacher rather than of a technology specialist. In other nations, however, elementary-school technology education has been a growing area since the 1970s.

In the 1980s and 1990s professorial exchange programs, international tours, and an notable increase in foreign authors publishing in American journals led to a growing interest in overseas curricula, especially process-oriented technology education from the United Kingdom, where *design and technology* is compulsory at the primary level. The first American critiques of late-twentieth-century British design and technology deemed it intriguing but inferior in content depth and tool and machine instruction. But when it became clear that the primarily pre-secondary British model was being compared to traditional high school courses in the United States, design and technology began to be presented as a supplement to, and in some cases a replacement for, the prevailing American curriculum.

Trends and Prospects

As suggested by the titles of the most frequent technology-education offerings in American high schools, the field has always been associated with vocationalism. The connection is downplayed or rejected in many teacher-education curricula, but in practice, educators both within and without the field often see technology education as a branch of vocational education. In fact, the Association for Career and Technical Education (ACTE), by far the largest association for vocational educators in the United States, has maintained a Technology Education (or Industrial Arts) Division since the 1940s. Especially in the western United States, practitioners make very little distinction between career-oriented technology education, supported by the ACTE, and the view of technology education as a general subject matter, advocated by the ITEA. As the career and technical education field continues to style itself as appropriate for all students, the distinction may disappear for all but the most doctrinaire technology educators.

Another challenge which may prove central to the field's future is its failure to identify unique ways in which technology education contributes to K–12 education. Much of its nonvocational content would appear to the lay person to overlap significantly with social studies and science education, as technological content is already included in each of these fields' standards documents. Neither is technology education the sole provider of problem-solving and design skills, two of its most frequently cited benefits to children. Further, research has not demonstrated that technology education practice is efficient as a method of teaching other school subjects.

In addition to these identity concerns, the field has two significant demographic obstacles to its continued growth. First, most states in the United States are experiencing severe shortages of technology

teachers, and both the number of institutions preparing technology teachers and the number of pre-service technology teachers graduated each year have been declining since the 1970s. The second problem is more systemic and has existed as long as technology education has: the field's inability to shed its image as an antiquated program intended primarily for boys. Research has confirmed that technology teachers are primarily conservative and overwhelmingly male Caucasians, and that boys elect technology classes much more frequently than girls do. There is also concern that technology education offerings are being reduced or eliminated in urban areas much more often than in suburban areas. Thus technology education does not always seem to be "for all Americans" (Scott, p.195).

But the ideals of technology education are more democratic than those of any field with its level of implementation in American schools. Its potential as a means of achieving curricular integration, student-centered learning, and the authentic assessment of critical thinking is considerable, and technology teacher education and curriculum are designed to deliver these very goals.

See also: CURRICULUM, SCHOOL; ELEMENTARY EDUCATION, *subentries on* CURRENT TRENDS, HISTORY OF; MEDIA AND LEARNING; SECONDARY EDUCATION, *subentries on* CURRENT TRENDS, HISTORY OF; TECHNOLOGY IN EDUCATION, *subentry on* SCHOOL; VOCATIONAL AND TECHNICAL EDUCATION.

BIBLIOGRAPHY

BONSER, FREDERICK GORDON, and MOSSMAN, LOIS COFFEY. 1923. *Industrial Arts for Elementary Schools.* New York: Macmillan.

LEWIS, THEODORE. 1998. *Toward the 21st Century: Retrospect, Prospect for American Vocationalism.* Columbus, OH: ERIC Clearinghouse on Adult, Career, and Vocational Education.

MALEY, DONALD. 1973. *The Maryland Plan.* New York: Bruce.

MOSSMAN, LOIS COFFEY. 1929. *Principles of Teaching and Learning in the Elementary School.* Boston: Houghton Mifflin.

PETRINA, STEPHEN. 2000. "The Politics of Technological Literacy." *International Journal of Design and Technology Education* 10(2):181–206.

SCOTT, MICHAEL L. 2000. "Technology for Some Americans?" In *Technology Education for the*

Twenty-First Century: Forty-Ninth Yearbook of the Council on Technology Teacher Education, ed. G. Eugene Martin. New York: Glencoe/McGraw-Hill.

TECHNOLOGY FOR ALL AMERICANS. 2000. *Standards for Technology Education: Content for the Study of Technology.* Reston, VA: International Technology Education Association.

ZUGA, KAREN F. 1994. *Implementing Technology Education : A Review and Synthesis of the Research Literature.* Columbus, OH: ERIC Clearinghouse on Adult, Career, and Vocational Education.

PATRICK N. FOSTER

TECHNOLOGY IN EDUCATION

CURRENT TRENDS
Susan M. Williams
SCHOOL
Howard D. Mehlinger
Susan M. Powers
HIGHER EDUCATION
Roger G. Baldwin

CURRENT TRENDS

Computers and Internet connections are becoming widely available in schools and classrooms. In 1999, 99 percent of teachers in the United States had access to a computer in their schools, and 84 percent had one or more computers in their classrooms. At the same time, Internet connections were also widespread, with 95 percent of schools and 63 percent of classrooms having access. Worldwide, many countries are making the creation and diffusion of information and communications technology (ICT) an important priority. Even in developing countries, usage is increasing dramatically. As ICT becomes more widely available, teachers and policymakers are turning their attention to the difficult task of understanding how best to integrate this technology into learning environments.

ICT can be used in many different ways, and how it is integrated into educational settings depends largely on teachers' instructional goals and strategies. Changes in the goals of education during the latter part of the twentieth century, coupled with increases in the amount and type of available technology, has created changes in teachers' use of technology. In the 1970s and early 1980s the primary goal of instruction was to have students memorize important information and procedures. Instruction was teacher-led and dominated by lectures, followed by practice using worksheets and short-answer tests. Students worked alone to complete assignments, and when help was needed they consulted parents, teachers, or textbooks for assistance. If computers were available in classrooms during this time period, their use mirrored this dominant mode of instruction; that is, they were primarily used to present passages of text and test students' comprehension and memory for information contained in the passages.

Research on learning has demonstrated the shortcomings of this type of instruction. Students often forget memorized information, or they fail to apply it in situations where it would be useful. They need help in connecting new information to what they already know and in extending and applying their knowledge to new problems. Researchers in the early twenty-first century believe that students learn best when they work to combine their own past experience with new information in order to solve problems that are personally meaningful to them.

In addition to changes in the understanding of how students learn, there have been substantial changes in what educators and policymakers believe students should know how to do. The exponential growth in information since 1950 has shifted the purpose of education. Information has become abundant and easily accessible. Rather than reading the unified perspective typically presented by a textbook, students have access to many different points of view. Instead of memorizing, students now need assistance in learning how to find and select relevant information for problems they need to solve. They need to learn how to collaborate with others as they solve these problems and communicate their solutions to their teachers and to the world beyond their classroom.

Along with changes in what students should know and an increased understanding of how they learn, new approaches to instruction are being advocated. Instead of listening to lectures and memorizing facts and procedures, educational reforms suggest that students learn best in the context of solving complex, realistic problems. Traditional computer-assisted instruction (CAI) and many integrated learning systems (ILSs) deliver precisely this form of instruction in a range of subject-matter areas. Typically computers dedicated to ILSs are clustered in computer laboratory settings, rather than being located in individual teacher's classrooms. Students who acquire new information as they solve problems are able to understand its usefulness, remember it, and use it to solve problems in the future. Solving interesting problems is more likely to stimulate a student's interest than memorizing isolated facts, and this interest has been shown to positively affect learning. Students solving real problems view their efforts as real work and have a sense of purpose and value.

Organizing instruction around problem solving makes new demands on teachers, including locating meaningful problems and projects and providing students with the resources and guidance for solving them. Teachers are finding that ICT can help them meet these demands, and they are integrating it into their instruction in many new and exciting ways.

Technology and New Forms of Instruction

Using technology to find and represent educational problems. One major challenge for teachers interested in problem-based learning is locating problems that are appropriate for their students and for the topics that they need to learn. Problems must be complex enough to support sustained exploration and encourage collaboration, and they should have multiple interrelated parts to develop students' ability to break problems down and organize their solutions. Representing and communicating such complex problem situations is an important function of technology. Unlike problems that occur in the real world, technology can incorporate graphics, video, animation, and other tools to create problems that can be explored repeatedly. Multimedia representations are easier to understand than problems presented as text. One example of using technology to present problems is the mathematical problem-solving series, *The Adventures of Jasper Woodbury.* Each problem in the *Jasper* series is presented as a video story that ends when the main character experiences a problem that can be solved using math. Using technology that can be easily searched and paused for inspection, students search the video looking for clues to help them understand and solve the problem. In one episode, students explore a variety of transportation methods and routes to rescue a wounded bald eagle. They compare their solution plans and develop ways to determine which plan is best.

Microworlds are another type of technology used to present problems. One example is *Thinkertools,* a computer-based learning environment that simulates aspects of Newtonian physics. Using the *Thinkertools* microworld, students can manipulate various aspects of the environment, observe the results, and attempt to discover the rules that govern this simulation.

Internet and videoconferencing technology allow students to participate in projects sponsored by researchers around the world. In the *Jason Project,* satellite and Internet technology bring classroom students into direct real-time contact with leading scientists, conducting scientific research expeditions around the globe. Each year the project explores a different location in order to help students understand the earth's biological and geological development. Some of the past expeditions have studied deep-sea archaeology, compared shallow and deep ocean habitats, studied plate tectonics and volcanoes, and compared conditions experienced in space and under the oceans. In addition to observing research activities, students are able to ask questions and get immediate answers from the scientists.

Whatever type of technology is used, an important goal is to create problem representations that are interactive and under the learner's control. The student creates a plan for investigating the problem, and the technology creates an environment that makes flexible exploration possible.

Using technology to find educational resources. A second function of technology in problem-based learning environments is locating information needed to solve problems or do other kinds of research. In the past, teachers attempting a problem-based curriculum felt the need to limit problems to those for which they had expertise or the local library had resources. Now the World Wide Web brings a seemingly endless amount of information on almost any subject, and it is possible for students to choose topics based on personal interest rather than availability of resources.

Internet research projects are gaining rapidly in popularity. In the spring of 1998, 30 percent of teachers surveyed (and 70% of those with high-speed Internet connections) reported they had assigned Internet research tasks for their students during the school year. Use of the Internet to gather information for solving problems sometimes resembles a modern version of library research, in which students gather and synthesize information from published reports. Despite the fact that the task seems traditional, the characteristics of this new medium require special skills for students. The sheer volume of information allows students to study almost any topic, but also makes it more difficult to locate precisely the right information from among the thousands, or even millions, of sites that might be located. In addition, the ease of publishing and accessing materials on the Internet increases the likelihood that students will encounter inaccurate or biased information. As a result, students must learn new strategies for conducting searches and evaluating the information that they retrieve.

In addition to its function as a source of information, the Internet's capability for communication and interaction provides many innovative educational opportunities. Many times students are unable to find or understand the available resources. In such cases, teachers are also turning to ICT to link their students with mentors and subject-matter experts. In one such project, fourth- and fifth-grade students in McAllen, Texas, compared the experiences of their families on the Texas *La Frontera* to colonial life in the original thirteen U.S. colonies, with the help of the director of a historic preservation center and museum in Fredericksburg, Virginia.

Students carrying out scientific investigations can use the Internet to make observations and collect data. For example, fourth and fifth graders in California collected insects and sent them to San Diego State University. Using two-way audio and video connecting the school and the university, scientists guided the students in using an electron microscope to examine their specimens. Technology has made it possible to collect data from places students could never visit. In recent projects, high school students explored the floor of the Monterey bay by studying video from remotely operated robots, and middle school students were given time to use the Hubble telescope.

Students also use technology to collect data in their schools and communities. For example, using handheld computers outfitted with various types of probes, students can monitor the water quality at various locations in nearby streams or lakes. By transmitting their individual readings to a laptop computer in a field laboratory they can quickly graph their data and visually compare readings.

Using technology to summarize and present findings. In the past, students memorized and used formulas and models created by others to solve problems. Students often used these formulas, especially in the early stages of learning, with little understanding. In the early twenty-first century computer tools provide the opportunity for students to construct and test their own models using tools such as spreadsheets or concept maps. This type of instruction deepens students' understanding of abstract concepts and allows these concepts to be taught at an earlier age.

Once students have summarized their data and other information, they typically communicate their findings to others. In the past, this meant writing a report to be read by the teacher. Writing reports is still the most widespread use of ICT, with 61 percent of U.S. teachers assigning students word processing tasks. In addition to text, students also use computer-created graphics, video, and animations to communicate their ideas.

The teacher is not the only audience for students' presentations. Students are frequently expected to present their work and receive feedback from their peers and the world outside their classroom. Whether they are using presentation software to accompany a face-to-face presentation or developing materials to put on the Web, the trend is for students to be able to communicate and defend their work to a broad audience. This increases students' perception that problem-based learning is real work for real audiences.

Using technology for collaboration and distance education. There are many opportunities for individual students to use technology to enhance their learning. These include online courses that provide students in remote locations with opportunities for customized curriculum and advanced placement courses. These courses are conducted entirely online and offer asynchronous interaction among faculty and students. Because they allow students to participate anytime and from anywhere, online courses are becoming increasingly popular among postsecondary students whose job and personal commitments do not allow them to meet a regular class schedule.

Opportunities for interaction with peers from other countries can also contribute to knowledge and understanding of other cultures. ICT makes this type of communication possible for anyone with Internet access. For example, the KIDLINK project encourages students up to age fifteen to use the Internet to build a global network of friends.

KIDLINK participants discuss issues ranging from how to make and keep friends to war and peace.

Teachers' Integration of Technology in Instruction

Although ICT is creating opportunities for fundamental changes in the way teachers teach and the way students learn, a recent survey indicated that only one-third of teachers feel prepared to use it effectively. This includes being able to use word processing, spreadsheet, presentation, and Internet-browsing software. Such tools help teachers increase their productivity by preparing reports or lesson plans, taking notes, and communicating with colleagues and parents. These basic skills are necessary, but not sufficient, for creating changes in instruction. Changes require that teachers are familiar with ICT tools and materials in the subjects they teach. They must also be able to incorporate these resources into classroom activities that accomplish important learning goals.

Research has shown that learning to incorporate technology into instruction occurs over time and follows a pattern. Initially, teachers incorporate new technologies into the things that they traditionally do. Then, after observing changes in their students—including improvements in behavior, absenteeism, collaboration, and independent learning—teachers gradually begin to experiment and use technology to teach in new ways. It often takes four years or more from initial attempts until changes in student learning can be observed.

Research indicates that change at all levels will be necessary to bring about widespread and effective use of technology. Successful programs must devote a substantial portion of their budget to extensive professional development and technical support; they must encourage a culture of collaboration in which teachers work together to explore more effective uses of technology; and they must modify their assessment systems to measure changes, such as deeper understanding and improved problem solving, that result from effective technology use.

Future Trends

Advances in hardware and software have the potential to bring about fundamental changes in how technology is integrated and even in education itself. Computers formerly tethered to desktops by cables are being rapidly replaced by wireless laptop and palmtop models that free students to move about the school; collect, share, and graph data on field trips; and communicate their whereabouts and progress to teachers and parents.

Monitoring students' independent learning in these flexible environments will be supported by sophisticated new assessment technologies that will help teachers collect and analyze student data and make instructional decisions. These tools will continually assess students' work and provide feedback to them and their teachers. Such assessment has the potential to make time-consuming standardized testing unnecessary and to personalize the curriculum for every student. Ubiquitous, well-integrated technology tools will bring educators closer to redefining the educational enterprise and providing customized, just-in-time solutions for the learning needs of adults and children.

See also: ASSESSMENT TOOLS, *subentry on* TECHNOLOGY BASED; INTERNATIONAL ASSESSMENTS, *subentry on* IEA STUDY OF TECHNOLOGY IN THE CLASSROOM; INTERNATIONAL GAP IN TECHNOLOGY, THE; MATHEMATICS LEARNING, *subentry on* LEARNING TOOLS; SCIENCE LEARNING, *subentry on* TOOLS; TECHNOLOGY EDUCATION.

BIBLIOGRAPHY

BECKER, HENRY JAY. 1999. *Internet Use by Teachers: Conditions of Professional Use and Teacher-Directed Use.* Teaching, Learning and Computing: 1998 National Survey of Schools and Teachers, Report 1. Irvine: Center for Research on Information Technology and Organizations, University of California, Irvine.

BIRCHARD, KAREN. 2001. "Distance Education: European Commission Adopts $13.3-Billion Plan That Is Expected to Promote Online Education." *Chronicle of Higher Education* April 16.

BRANSFORD, JOHN D.; BROWN, ANN L.; and COCKING, RODNEY R. 1999. *How People Learn: Brain, Mind, Experience, and School.* Washington, DC: National Academy Press.

COGNITION AND TECHNOLOGY GROUP AT VANDERBILT. 1997. *The Jasper Project: Lessons in Curriculum, Instruction, Assessment, and Professional Development.* Mahwah, NJ: Erlbaum.

DWYER, DAVID. 1994. "Apple Classrooms of Tomorrow: What We've Learned." *Educational Leadership* 51(7):4–10.

MEANS, BARBARA. 2000. *Accountability in Preparing Teachers to Use Technology.* Paper prepared for the Educational Technology Leadership Conference, Washington, DC, January 13-14.

PELLEGRINO, JAMES W.; CHUDOWSKY, NAOMI; and GLASER, ROBERT, eds. 2001. *Knowing What Students Know: The Science and Design of Educational Assessment.* Washington, DC: National Academy Press.

REIL, MARGARET. 2000. *New Designs for Connected Teaching and Learning.* White paper commissioned for The Secretary's Conference on Educational Technology Evaluating the Effectiveness of Technology, Washington, DC, September 11–12.

REIL, MARGARET., and BECKER, HENRY JAY. 2000. *The Beliefs, Practices, and Computer Use of Teacher Leaders.* Paper presented at the annual meeting of the American Educational Research Association. New Orleans, LA, April.

SHEINGOLD, KAREN, and HADLEY, MARTHA. 1990. *Accomplished Teachers: Integrating Computers into Classroom Practice.* New York: Center for Technology in Education, Bank Street College.

TINKER, ROBERT. 2000. *Ice Machines, Steamboats, and Education: Structural Change and Educational Technologies.* White paper commissioned for The Secretary's Conference on Educational Technology Evaluating the Effectiveness of Technology, Washington, DC.

THORNBURG, DAVID D. 1999. *Technology in K–12 Education: Envisioning a New Future.* White paper commissioned for the Forum on Technology in Education: Envisioning the Future, Washington, DC.

WHITE, BARBARA Y., and FREDERIKSEN, JOHN R. 2000. "Metacognitive Facilitation: An Approach to Making Scientific Inquiry Accessible to All." In *Teaching in the Inquiry-Based Science Classroom,* ed. Jim Minstrell and Emily H. van Zee. Washington, DC: American Association for the Advancement of Science.

INTERNET RESOURCES

CHEN, MILTON. 2002. "Bugscope: Magnifying the Connection Between Students, Science, and Scientists." <http://glef.org/bugscope.html>.

ELECTRONIC EMISSARY PROJECT. 2001. <http://emissary.ots.utexas.edu/emissary/>.

KIDLINK. 2002. <www.kidlink.org>.

NATIONAL CENTER FOR EDUCATION STATISTICS. 2000. "Internet Access in U.S. Public Elementary and Secondary Schools." <http://nces.ed.gov/pubsearch/pubsinfo.asp?pubid=2000102>.

PASSPORT TO KNOWLEDGE. 2001. <http://passporttoknowledge.com/hst/>.

UNITED NATIONS DEVELOPMENT PROGRAM. 2001. "Human Development Report 2001: Making New Technologies Work for Human Development." <www.undp.org/hdr2001/>.

UNIVERSITY OF WASHINGTON, TACOMA 2001. "Conductivity and Temperature Study." <www.Tacoma.Washington.edu/education/intel/Projects/Morrison_photo.htm>.

SUSAN M. WILLIAMS

SCHOOL

The term *educational technology* refers to the use of technology in educational settings, whether it be elementary and secondary schools, colleges and universities, corporate training sites, or independent study at home. This discussion, however, will focus on educational technology in grades K–12.

Educational technology has both general and specialized meanings. To the lay public and to a majority of educators, the term refers to the instructional use of computers, television, and other kinds of electronic hardware and software. Specialists in educational technology, in particular college and university faculty who conduct research and teach courses on educational technology, prefer the term *instructional technology* because it draws attention to the instructional use of educational technology. This term represents both a process and the particular devices that teachers employ in their classrooms. According to the Association for Educational Communications and Technology, one of the principal professional associations representing educational technologists, "Instructional Technology is a complex, integrated process involving people, procedures, ideas, devices, and organization for analyzing problems, and devising, implementing evaluating, and managing solutions to these problems, in situations in which learning is purposive and controlled." (p. 4). Educational technologists often employ the term *instructional media* to represent all of the devices that teachers and learners use to support learning. However, for many educators the terms *educational technology, instructional media,* and *instructional technology* are used interchangeably, and they are used so here. In addition, the principal focus will be upon the most modern computational and communication devices used in schools today.

History of Educational Technology

The history of educational technology is marked by the increasing complexity and sophistication of devices, exaggerated claims of effectiveness by technology advocates, sporadic implementation by classroom teachers, and little evidence that the technology employed has made a difference in student learning. Although technology proponents have from time to time claimed that technology will replace teachers, this has not occurred. The typical view among educators is that technology can be used effectively to supplement instruction by providing instructional variety, by helping to make abstract concepts concrete, and by stimulating interest among students.

The terms *visual education* and *visual instruction* were used originally because many of the media available to teachers, such as three-dimensional objects, photographs, and silent films, depended upon sight. Later, when sound was added to film and audio recordings became popular, the terms *audiovisual education, audiovisual instruction,* and *audiovisual devices* were used to represent the variety of media employed to supplement instruction. These were the principal terms used to describe educational technology until about 1970.

The first administrative organizations in schools to manage instructional media were school museums. The first school museum was established in St. Louis, Missouri, in 1905. Its purpose was to collect and loan portable museum exhibits, films, photographs, charts, stereographic slides, and other materials to teachers for use in their classrooms. District-wide media centers, common in school systems today, are descendants of school museums.

By the first decade of the twentieth century, silent films were being produced for instructional use. In 1910 George Kleine published the *Catalogue of Educational Motion Pictures,* which listed more than 1,000 titles of films that could be rented by schools. In 1913 Thomas A. Edison asserted, "Books will soon be obsolete in schools . . . . Our school system will be completely changed in the next ten years" (Saettler 1968, p. 98). In 1917 the Chicago public schools established a visual education department to take responsibility for the ordering and management

of films, and by 1931, thirty-one state departments of education had created administrative units to take charge of films and related media. Despite these efforts, films never reached the level of influence in schools that Edison had predicted. From evidence of film use, it appears that teachers used films only sparingly. Some of the reasons cited for infrequent use were teachers' lack of skill in using equipment and film; the cost of films, equipment, and upkeep; inaccessibility of equipment when it was needed; and the time involved in finding the right film for each class.

Radio was the next technology to gain attention. Benjamin Darrow, founder and first director of the Ohio School of the Air, imagined that radio would provide "schools of the air" (Saettler 1990, p. 199). In 1920 the Radio Division of the U.S. Department of Commerce began to license commercial and educational stations. Soon schools, colleges, departments of education, and commercial stations were providing radio programming to schools. Haaren High School in New York City is credited with being the first to teach classes by radio, broadcasting accounting classes in 1923. Peak activity for radio use occurred during the decade between 1925 and 1935, although some radio instruction continued through the 1940s. Nevertheless, radio did not have the impact on schools its advocates had hoped. In the beginning, poor audio reception and the cost of equipment were cited as obstacles to use. When these problems were overcome in later years, the lack of fit between the broadcasts and teachers' instructional agendas became more important factors. Ultimately, efforts to promote radio instruction in schools were abandoned when television became available.

World War II provided a boost for audiovisual education. The federal government and American industry were faced with the challenging task of providing training for large numbers of military recruits and for new industrial workers. Ways had to be found to train people swiftly and effectively. The U.S. government alone purchased 55,000 film projectors and spent $1 billion on training films. In addition to films, the military used overhead projectors to support lectures, slide projectors to support training in ship and aircraft recognition, and audio equipment for teaching foreign languages. Experience gained from the wartime use of these media fueled their subsequent use in schools in the decades to follow.

Instructional television was the focus of attention during the 1950s and the 1960s. This attention was stimulated by two factors. First, the 1952 decision by the Federal Communications Commission (FCC) to set aside 242 television channels for educational purposes led to a rapid development of educational (now called public) television stations. A portion of their mission was to provide instructional programs to school systems in their viewing area. The second factor was the substantial investment by the Ford Foundation. It has been estimated that during the 1950s and the 1960s the Ford Foundation and its related agencies invested more than $170 million in educational television. One of the most innovative efforts at this time was the Midwest Program on Airborne Television Instruction (MPATI) which employed airplanes to transmit televised lessons over a six-state area.

By the 1970s much of the enthusiasm for instructional television had been exhausted. Educational television stations continued to provide some programming, and school systems and state departments of education formed consortia to pool funds to provide for the cost of program development. Congress also provided funds to support instructional television via satellite transmission in an effort to help rural schools, in particular, to obtain courses that might not otherwise be available to their students. However, instructional television appeared to prosper only where there was substantial public, corporate, or commercial support. Schools found it difficult to meet the substantial costs incurred for program development and the purchase and maintenance of equipment. Moreover, despite repeated efforts, it proved nearly impossible to broadcast instruction when individual teachers needed it.

The next technology to capture the interest of educators was the computer. Some of the earliest work on instructional applications of computing took place in the 1950s and the 1960s, but these efforts had little impact on schools. It was not until the 1980s, and the appearance of microcomputers, that many educators and public officials became enthusiastic about computers. By January 1983, computers were being used for instructional purposes in 40 percent of all elementary schools and 75 percent of all secondary schools in the United States. These percentages can be misleading, however. In most cases, students had only limited access to computers, often in a computer laboratory and only for an hour or so a week. In 1995 the Office of Technology Assessment estimated that the optimum ratio of computers to students was five to one, and by the year 2000 the National Center for Educational Statistics reported that there was, in fact, an average of one computer for every five students, with 97 percent of schools having Internet connections.

Technology and Learning

A primary purpose for employing instructional technology in schools is to enhance student learning. Has technology been successful in helping students learn more effectively and efficiently? Much research has been done on this question, but the answer is far from certain. Most research on educational technology has consisted of media comparison studies. After assigning comparable students to control groups or to experimental groups, the researcher presents the experimental group of students with instruction that employs the new media, while the control group experiences the same content without the new media. The researcher then compares the achievement of the two groups.

After reviewing hundreds of such studies, educational technologist Richard Clark concluded that "there are no learning benefits to be gained from employing any specific medium to deliver instruction," and that "media do not influence learning under any conditions," but are "mere vehicles that deliver instruction but do not influence student achievement any more than the truck that delivers our groceries causes changes in our nutrition" (1983, p. 445). According to Clark, any positive results that were gained by experimental groups over the control groups were easily accounted for by differences in instructional strategy.

Clark's findings were controversial and have been disputed by other reputable scholars. Nevertheless, Clark's opinions are useful in clarifying technology's role in instruction. Technology is neutral; there is nothing inherent about the media that assures learning. A poorly designed computer program is unlikely to advance learning and may even hinder it.

This relationship between learning and technology is further complicated by disagreements over what constitutes learning. During the first half of the twentieth century, *transfer-of-learning* theories were popular among classroom teachers. According to these theories, the principal task of the teacher was to transfer the teacher's knowledge and textbook content to the students' minds and, through periodic examinations, determine if the transfer occurred. The task of instructional media was to assist in that transfer process by means of accurate and compelling presentations of content.

During the second half of the century, educators embraced other theories of learning. At least two of these theories have influenced the development of instructional media for schools. One of these theories is *behaviorism;* the other is *constructivism.*

Although the intellectual roots of behaviorism can be traced to the beginning of the twentieth century, behaviorism did not have much impact on education until the 1960s. Drawing upon B. F. Skinner's concepts, educators promoting behaviorism emphasized the importance of providing clear statements of what learners should be able to do following instruction. These educators also sought to break complex units of knowledge and skills into smaller and simpler units, sequencing them in ways that would lead to mastering the more complex skills and content. Frequently, their goal was also to individualize instruction as much as possible. Thus, the focus of instruction shifted from presentation of content knowledge before a group of students to a focus on the behavior of individual learners, an analysis of the steps needed to ensure learning, and the reinforcement of desirable behavior when it occurred.

The interest in behaviorism occurred about the same time that the first computer-assisted programs (CAI) were being developed. It is not surprising that the first CAI programs were essentially computer applications of printed, programmed learning books. Computers appeared to offer a good solution. Students could be assigned to a computer to work at their own pace, and the computer would keep track of students' work and provide a record of each student's progress for the teacher. Such programs evolved into what were later called *individualized learning systems* (ILS). ILS software and hardware were installed in school computer laboratories; they provided *drill and practice* exercises that were judged valuable, especially for students with learning difficulties. The behavioral movement also had an impact on the educational technology profession. The belief that it was possible to design instruction so that all students could learn led to an interest in the design of learning materials and in a systems approach to instruction.

During the last half of the twentieth century, cognitive theories of learning gained ascendancy over behaviorism among psychologists, and some of the views of cognitive psychologists, represented by the term *constructivism,* began to influence education. Constructivists argued that learners must construct their own understanding of whatever is being taught. According to this perspective, the teacher's task is not primarily one of promoting knowledge transfer, nor is it one of ensuring that students perform consistently according to a predetermined description of knowledge and skills. The teacher's role is to create an environment in which students are able to arrive at their own interpretations of knowledge while becoming ever more skillful in directing their own learning.

Many constructivists were initially critical of the use of computers in schools because they equated the use of computers with behaviorist theories of learning. Other constructivists recognized the computer as a potential ally and designed programs that took advantage of constructivist beliefs. The result has been computer-based programs that promote higher-level thinking and encourage collaborative learning.

Current Technologies Used in Schools

Whatever learning theory a teacher may embrace, many technologies exist in schools to enhance instruction and to support student learning. While teachers vary greatly in their use of these technologies, teachers select media they believe will promote their instructional goals. Following are a few examples of computers being used to support four goals: building student capacity for research, making student inquiry more realistic, enabling students to present information in appealing forms, and offering students access to learning resources within and beyond the school.

Student research. Students once relied upon local and school libraries and their printed reference materials to research topics. Now, however, computer technologies provide access to digital versions of these references—and to libraries worldwide. Encyclopedias on CD-ROMs provide information, digital images, video, and audio, and also provide links to websites where students access tools such as live web cameras and global positioning satellites. Dictionaries and thesauruses are built into word processors. Through the Internet students can gain access to a wide variety of primary and secondary sources, including government documents, photographs, and diaries.

Student inquiry. Educational reformers believe education needs to be real and authentic for students. Technology can engage students in real-world activities. In the sciences, electronic probes allow science students to collect precise weather or chemical reaction data and digitally trace trends and answer hypotheses. Graphing calculators, spreadsheets, and graphing software provide mathematics students with the ability to visualize difficult mathematical concepts. In the social sciences, electronic communication tools (e.g. Internet conferencing, e-mail, electronic discussion groups) allow students to communicate with their peers from many parts of the world. In the language arts, students use handheld computers and wireless networks to create joint writing exercises and read electronic books that allow them to explore related topics. Concept-mapping software provides all students with the opportunity to build the framework for a story or report and to map out linkages among complex characters, such as those in a play by Shakespeare. In the arts, students can explore images of original artwork through the Internet; with appropriate software they can create original digital artwork or musical compositions. Physical education students can use electronic probes to learn about the relationship between the impact of physical movement and physiological changes.

Authentic student inquiry extends beyond data collection. It also implies the opportunity for students to investigate questions or issues that concern them. Communications technology allows students to contact experts such as scientists, book authors, and political leaders. Electronic communication tools support interactions and increase the probability of prompt responses. Students who want to learn more about a current event, such as an experiment on an international space station, scientific endeavors in the Antarctic, an international meeting of environmentalists, or a musher during the Iditarod dogsled race in Alaska, can use the Internet to investigate the topic, participate in a virtual field trip to the event, and watch the event as it unfolds through a web camera. In this manner, instructional technology assists students who wish to investigate their own questions and concerns.

Constructing new knowledge. James Pellegrino and Janice Altman (1997) believe the penultimate use of technology occurs when students use technology to move from being knowledge consumers to being knowledge producers. Results of original student inquiry usually take the form of printed reports or oral presentations. With advanced technologies, students can present their original data or newly interpreted data by integrating digital video, audio, and text into word-processed documents, multimedia presentations, videos, or web-based documents. Local, state, national, and international media fairs provide opportunities for students to demonstrate the new knowledge representations that students are capable of creating when given the opportunity. Media fairs showcase photographs, original digital images, overheads, videos, and interactive multimedia projects from students of all ages.

In the past, award-winning projects have included a video created by fourth graders that demonstrates their feelings regarding acceptance, diversity, and compassion; an interactive, multimedia presentation by second graders about the water cycle; and an interactive multimedia project by a high school student depicting the history of war experienced by one family. Each of these projects illustrates student generated knowledge that could have been demonstrated through a traditional paper or research report. However, the instructional technology tools provided students with a way to express their knowledge in a more interesting manner.

Access to learning resources. Some schools lack the resources to provide all of the courses that students may need or want. Advanced placement and foreign language courses can be particularly expensive for a school system to offer when there is not a high level of student demand. A variety of technologies (e.g. interactive television, Internet videoconferencing) provide students the opportunity to participate in a class that is located in a different school, in a different town, and even in a different state or country. Instructional technologies can also serve the instructional needs of students who may be unable to attend classes in the school building. Students who are homebound, home schooled, or who may be forced to drop out of school can take advantage of coursework offered over the Internet. Virtual high schools, online college credit courses, and for-profit companies all make courses available to students through the Internet. Through an online program, students can obtain their high school diplomas or GED without attending a particular school.

Instructional technologies also provide some students important access to traditional classroom instruction. Students who have physical or learning disabilities can use a variety of assistive technologies in order to be an active member of a mainstreamed class. Braille writers and screen readers allow students with sight limitations to use a computer for work and communication. Various switches allow students with limited mobility to use a computer to speak for them and complete assignments. *Switches,* similar to a computer mouse, manipulate the computer through a touch pad, by head or eye movement, or even by breath. Handheld computing devices and specialized software allow students with learning disabilities to function in traditional classrooms by helping them organize thoughts, structure writing, and manage time. Instructional technology is also used to provide alternative forms of assessment for disabled students, including digital portfolios that electronically capture the accomplishments of students who are not able to complete traditional assessments.

Approaches to Computer Use in Schools

The function of computers in schools differs from that of other educational technologies. In the case of films, radio, instructional television, overhead projectors, and other instructional media, educational technology is used to support and enhance the teacher's role as instructor. Teacher support has also been one of the justifications for the introduction of computers in schools, but it has not been the only, nor the most important, justification. Computers are also promoted as an important part of the school curriculum. Learning about computers and acquiring computer skills have been accepted by educators and the lay public as a necessary curricular requirement because they give students tools needed to function effectively in modern American society. The role and function of computers in schools can be classified according to three categories: (1) computer literacy, (2) computers as tools, and (3) computers as a catalyst for school transformation.

Computer literacy. Beginning in the 1980s it was assumed that all children should become computer literate. While the meaning of the term *computer literacy* has changed over time, all children are expected to graduate with knowledge about the role of computers in society and essential skills in their operation. Educators continue to debate what skills are essential and when and how they are best learned, but there is little controversy about whether students should be competent in the use of computers. No such discussion surrounds the school use of film, radio, and instructional television.

Computers as tools. With the continuing increase in computer power and the decline in cost, schools have steadily increased the numbers of computers in schools and their use by students. Rather than place computers in specialized laboratories where students have access to them for only a limited period each week, computers have increasingly been placed in libraries and in classrooms. Beginning in the 1990s the goal became to make computers ubiquitous and to integrate them across the curriculum. Computers had become something more that a curriculum topic; they had become a tool that students needed in order to perform their work. Students were expected to use the Internet to gather information and to use word processing and multimedia software to produce their reports. While other instructional media were seen as tools for teachers, computers are accepted as tools for both teachers and students.

Computers as a catalyst for school reform. Throughout the twentieth century, technology zealots have heralded one technology or another as having the capacity to transform schools, but such transformations have not occurred. Film, radio, television, and other instructional media have enriched the classroom resources available to teachers. However, rather than challenging traditional classroom practices, they were used to maintain traditional practices. The culture of schooling, with teachers in charge of instruction before a class of students, has remained relatively constant. Some proponents believe that computers have the power to transform schools because they empower learners in ways that previous technologies were unable to, because they challenge the authority of teachers to be the sole source of information, and because they encourage an active, rather than a passive, learner. Computers may eventually provide the catalyst that will result in school transformation.

Current Issues Relating to the Use of Educational Technology

The effective use of technology in schools involves more than the purchase of educational technologies and their integration into the curriculum. The existence of technology within a school can create special concerns—particularly regarding legal issues, ethical issues, media literacy, and funding—that must be addressed.

Legal issues. Software piracy (the installation of nonlicensed software) is an important legal concern. When software is purchased, generally the buyer obtains one license, which allows that software to be installed on only one computer. Schools may purchase site licenses that permit the software to be installed on multiple computer stations. While the practice of loading software without licenses onto multiple computers (piracy) may seem benign to school officials, it is a form of theft that results in billions of dollars in lost revenue to vendors, and it can result in fines to school corporations.

Technology also raises important legal issues regarding copyright and privacy. Technology allows for easy duplication of many types of media. With a videocassette recorder, a teacher can record a television program for reuse in the classroom. Artwork, photos, and articles can be scanned and reproduced digitally. The Internet provides easy access to digital images, movies, music, and written works from all over the world; these can be downloaded and used in multiple formats, raising not only questions about copyright, but also plagiarism.

When a student or a teacher uses a piece of media that is not in the public domain (copyright-free), they must be certain that they have not violated the doctrine of *Fair Use.* Fair Use (Section 107 of the 1976 Copyright Act) considers the purpose of the use, the nature of the copyrighted work, the amount used in comparison to the entire piece, and the impact of classroom use on the work's commercial value. Therefore, while showing videotape in a classroom to illustrate a point of history may be permissible, the downloading of images from the Internet into a calendar for the student council to sell is probably not.

The right to privacy and free speech is considered an essential American ideal. However, with computer technologies and the Internet, there is little actual privacy. All electronic communications (e-mail, web forums, etc.) pass through multiple computer sites before arriving at a destination. During that process, information is saved that can be read by anyone who has the knowledge to do so. In order to ensure the safety and security of everyone, students and teachers need to be informed that electronic communications from their school are not private and can be accessed. In 2000 Congress passed the Children's Internet Protection Act (CIPA) and the Neighborhood Children's Internet Protection Act (NCIPA), which require all schools and libraries that receive federal technology funds to have an Internet safety policy to protect children from visual depictions that are obscene, contain child pornography, or are otherwise harmful to children. An adequate technology protection measure can be an Internet block or filtering software that prevents the objectionable material from being displayed. However, blocking software and other practices to eliminate access to websites raises issues relating to rights of free speech guaranteed by the U.S. Constitution. The conflict about free speech, privacy, and the obligation of schools to protect children make this issue quite controversial within some school systems.

Ethical issues. Ethical issues often relate to whether schools are providing students with equal access to technology. Gender-equity issues arise when girls are treated differently than boys in terms of the use of, and encouragement to use, technology. Girls tend to enroll in fewer computer classes, spend fewer hours on the computer either at home or at school, and are less likely to choose majors in computer-related fields than do boys. For example, in 2000 only 15 percent of the students who took the Advanced Placement Computer Science exam were girls. There are a number of factors that contribute to this gender difference, including the limited number of female role models in computer-related fields, adults who especially encourage boys to use the computer and computer games, and software that tends to targets boys' interests more than that of girls.

The *digital divide* is the division that exists between the information rich and the information poor. Advanced technologies, and the Internet in particular, provide easy access to vast amounts of information. Digital inequities can exist along racial, economic, academic achievement (low-achieving versus high-achieving classes), and geographic (rural, urban, and suburban) lines. A student in a rural school that lacks fast Internet connections does not have the same access to information as a student near a major city.

The digital divide also extends beyond the school. More economically advantaged children usually have access to information sources through Internet connections and microcomputers at home. Those who are more disadvantaged must rely upon limited school and public library resources. Minority students may be discouraged from accessing online content because of an absence of exposure to computers in general or because of a lack of racially and ethnically diverse information on the Internet. Finally, computers are often used as a reward for high achieving students, leaving out those students with poorer academic records, while some students are simply not encouraged to use technology to fuel their interest in academics.

Media literacy. Media literacy is the ability to access, evaluate, and produce information. Teachers themselves not only need to be media literate, but they must also ensure that their students are able to access the information they need, are capable of determining the relative merits of the information obtained, and are able to represent the information they have gathered in new ways using the different forms of media available to them (print, video, audio, digital). The concept of media literacy is not unique to computer technology. For decades, child advocates have expressed concern about the impact of movies and television on children and about whether children can distinguish the illusion presented to them from what is real. Media literacy has become an even greater teaching responsibility for educators, as the Internet provides access to vast quantities of information, much of which is inaccurate or represents biased views.

Adequate funding. The Office of Technology Assessment described four barriers to technology integration in instruction: inadequate teacher training, a lack of vision of technology's potential, a lack of time to experiment, and inadequate technical support. Each of these obstacles stems in part from weak or inconsistent financial support for technology. Much of the money used to support technology in schools has been provided through special governmental appropriations or by private funds. Technology funds have rarely become a part of the regular, operating budget of school systems. For technology to achieve its potential, funds are needed to provide adequate training for teachers, to keep equipment repaired and up-to-date, and to provide the time necessary for teachers and administrators to plan ways to use technology effectively. Only then will the schools be able to experience the advantages afforded by technology.

See also: ASSESSMENT TOOLS, *subentry on* TECHNOLOGY BASED; INSTRUCTIONAL DESIGN; MEDIA AND LEARNING; SCHOOL REFORM; TECHNOLOGY EDUCATION.

BIBLIOGRAPHY

ANGLIN, GARY J., ed. 1995. *Instructional Technology: Past, Present, and Future,* 2nd edition. Englewood, CO: Libraries Unlimited.

ASSOCIATION FOR EDUCATIONAL COMMUNICATIONS AND TECHNOLOGY. 1996. "The Definition of Educational Technology: A Summary." In *Classic Writings on Instructional Technology,* ed. Donald P. Ely and Tjeerd Plomp. Englewood, CO: Libraries Unlimited.

CATTAGNI, ANNE, and FARRIS, ELIZABETH. 2001. *Internet Access in U.S. Public Schools and Classrooms: 1994–2000.* Washington, DC: National Center for Educational Statistics.

CLARK, RICHARD E. 1983. "Reconsidering Research on Learning from Media." *Review of Educational Research* 53(4):445–449.

CLARK, RICHARD E. 1994. "Media Will Never Influence Learning." *Educational Technology Research and Development* 42(2):21–29.

COMMISSION ON BEHAVIORAL AND SOCIAL SCIENCES AND EDUCATION, NATIONAL RESEARCH COUNCIL. 2000. *How People Learn: Brain, Mind, Experience, and School.* Washington, DC: National Academy Press.

CUBAN, LARRY. 1986. *Teachers and Machines: The Classroom Use of Technology Since 1920.* New York: Teachers College Press, Columbia University.

EDUCATION WEEK. 2001. "Technology Counts 2001: The New Divides." *Education Week,* special issue 20(35).

INTERNATIONAL SOCIETY FOR TECHNOLOGY IN EDUCATION. 2000. *National Educational Technology Standards for Students: Connecting Curriculum and Technology.* Eugene, OR: International Society for Technology in Education.

JONASSEN, DAVID H., ed. 1996. *Handbook of Research for Educational Communications and Technology.* New York: Macmillan Library Reference USA.

JOSSEY-BASS. 2000. *The Jossey-Bass Reader on Technology and Learning.* San Francisco: Jossey-Bass.

KERR, STEPHEN T., ed. 1996. *Technology and the Future of Schooling.* The Ninety-Fifth Yearbook of the National Society for the Study of Education. Chicago: University of Chicago Press.

LeBARON, JOHN F., and COLLIER, CATHERINE. 2001. *Technology in Its Place: Successful Technology Infusion in Schools.* San Francisco: Jossey-Bass.

LOCKARD, JAMES, and ABRAMS, PETER D. 2001. *Computer for Twenty-First Century Educators,* 5th edition. New York: Longman.

MEANS, BARBARA. 2000. "Technology in America's School: Before and After Y2K." In *Education in a New Era,* ed. Ronald S. Brandt. Alexandria, VA: Association for Supervision and Curriculum Development.

MOURSAND, DAVID, ed. 2001. "Closing the Digital Divide." *Learning and Leading with Technology,* special issue 28(5).

OFFICE OF EDUCATIONAL RESEARCH AND IMPROVEMENT. 1996. *Getting America's Students Ready for the 21st Century.* Washington, DC: U.S. Department of Education, Office of Educational Research and Improvement.

PELLEGRINO, JAMES W., and ALTMAN, JANICE E. 1997. "Information Technology and Teacher Preparation: Some Critical and Illustrative Solutions." *Peabody Journal of Education* 72(1):89–121.

REISER, ROBERT A. 1987. "Instructional Technology: A History." In *Instructional Technology: Foundations,* ed. Robert M. Gagné. Hillsdale, NJ: Erlbaum.

REISER, ROBERT A. 2001. "A History of Instructional Design and Technology. Part I: A History of Instructional Media." *Educational Technology Research and Development* 49(1):53–64.

SAETTLER, PAUL. 1968. *A History of Instructional Technology.* New York: McGraw Hill.

SAETTLER, PAUL. 1990. *The Evolution of American Technology.* Englewood, CO: Libraries Unlimited.

U.S. CONGRESS, OFFICE OF TECHNOLOGY ASSESSMENT. 1995. *Teachers and Technology: Making the Connection.* Report Summary. Washington, DC: U.S. Government Printing Office.

INTERNET RESOURCES

AMERICAN LIBRARY ASSOCIATION. 2000. "Title XVII Children's Internet Protection." <www.ala.org/cipa/law.pdf>.

U.S. DEPARTMENT OF EDUCATION. 2000. "E-Learning: Putting A World-Class Education at the Fingertips of All Children. The National Education Technology Plan." <www.ed.gov/Technology/elearning/index.html>.

HOWARD D. MEHLINGER
SUSAN M. POWERS

HIGHER EDUCATION

Colleges and universities have generally been quick to adopt new technologies, often even before their educational value has been proven. Throughout its history, higher education has experimented with technological advances as diverse as the blackboard and the personal computer. Some technologies have become permanent parts of the higher education enterprise. Others, such as the slide rule and the 16-millimeter movie projector, have been replaced as more sophisticated or more cost-effective technologies have emerged to take their place.

At the dawn of the twenty-first century, new and rapidly improving technologies are in the process of transforming higher education. Each year since 1994, the Campus Computing Survey has shown increased use in college classrooms of technology-dependent resources such as e-mail, the Internet, course web pages, and computer simulations. Technology has the potential to revolutionize the traditional teaching and learning process. It can eliminate the barriers to education imposed by space and time and dramatically expand access to lifelong learning. Students no longer have to meet in the same place at the same time to learn together from an instructor. Fundamentally, modern technologies have the ability to change the conception of a higher education institution. No longer is a higher education institution necessarily a physical place with classrooms and residence halls where students come to pursue an advanced education. Thanks to recent developments in technology, the standard American image of a college or university as a collection of ivy-covered buildings may need to be revised for the first time since the founding of Harvard in 1636.

Computers and telecommunications are the principal technologies reshaping higher education. Due to advances in each of these domains, electronic mail, fax machines, the World Wide Web, CD-ROMs, and commercially developed simulations and courseware are altering the daily operations and expanding the missions of colleges and universities.

Forces Promoting and Inhibiting Technology Use

Powerful forces are promoting higher education's adoption of new technologies. The rapid advance of globalization that is lowering international barriers and transforming the business world is also expanding the potential reach of colleges and universities.

With sophisticated communication technologies, institutions of higher education are no longer limited to student markets or educational resources in their geographic regions. Likewise, the growing need for lifelong learning opportunities to keep pace with social, economic, and technological changes fuels demand for accessible alternatives to traditional real-time, campus-based instruction. In addition, competition among higher education institutions contributes to technology's advance within colleges and universities. Not wishing to be outpaced by competitors, many institutions are active participants in a technology "arms race" that requires the rapid adoption of new technological innovations as soon as they become available. The alternative is to fall behind other schools that are attempting to recruit the same students, faculty, and donors.

In spite of technology's promise, its integration throughout higher education has not been rapid or painless. Many barriers to technology-based innovations exist within colleges and universities. Academic traditions, such as the faculty-centered lecture, make many professors reluctant to adopt alternative instructional strategies using the computer or telecommunication devices. The cost of many technological applications also prohibits their easy adoption at many resource-limited institutions. Before technology became such a central part of institutional operations, many colleges paid for new or improved technologies from funds left over at the end of their annual budget cycle. Now that technology has become an essential and recurring investment, most schools must locate additional funds to meet their increasing needs for technology resources.

Limited support to help faculty and staff members learn how to take full advantage of technology is another factor inhibiting more widespread use of technology in colleges and universities. According to the 2000 Campus Computing Survey, the single most important educational technology challenge facing colleges and universities is helping faculty integrate information technology into their teaching. The second most important challenge is providing adequate user support. According to Kenneth Green, director of the Campus Computing Project, higher education's investment in technology hardware is, by itself, not sufficient to reap the full benefits of new technology advances. Green concludes that "the real [information technology] challenge is people, not products" (p. 1). Technology will nei-

ther reap its full potential nor revolutionize higher education if these barriers to its adoption are not resolved satisfactorily by individual institutions or the educational system as a whole.

Impact on Teaching and Learning

No aspect of higher education remains untouched by the technological developments of the 1980s and 1990s. Academic administration, as well as the instructional process, has been dramatically altered by new technologies. When compared to other college and university operations such as student services, housing, and administration, however, the teaching and learning process probably is being changed most dramatically by technology.

Traditionally, professors have used much of their class time with students to disseminate information through lectures and follow-up discussion. This was especially the case in introductory-level courses, where students lack a foundation in the basic concepts and principles of a field. In an era of advanced technology, this approach to instruction seems archaic and inefficient. Computers, especially web-based resources, can disseminate basic information more efficiently and more cost effectively than human beings can. For example, Gregory Farrington recommends that instructors use the web to do what it can do well. This includes presenting information to students in a variety of formats, twenty-four hours per day. Students can access course material when it is most convenient for them and return to it as often as they need to achieve basic comprehension, competence, or mastery.

This approach to information dissemination can save precious class time "for the intellectual interactions that only humans can provide" (Farrington, p. 87). Following this revised method of facilitating learning, traditional lectures can be replaced or pared down. In their place, classes can be more informal, seminar-like sessions with more free flowing discussion structured by students' interests, questions, and concerns. In other words, appropriate use of technology applications can help instructors to structure more active learning opportunities. Research shows that active engagement in the learning process helps to motivate students and enhance their learning outcomes. New technologies can facilitate active engagement in learning by reducing the amount of class time where students sit passively listening to lectures.

Technology can also help to make education a much more interactive and collaborative process. E-mail, course-based websites, and computer-based chat rooms are some of the technology-enabled resources that facilitate communication and teamwork among students. Research by education scholars has shown that collaborative learning opportunities enhance recall, understanding, and problem solving. Technology can greatly ease the work of collaborative design teams, peer writing groups, and other types of collaborative learning groups, even among students who do not live in the same geographic area and who cannot meet face to face.

While technology helps to promote collaborative learning, it also helps to personalize and individualize education. By reducing the need to deliver vast amounts of information, technology can free an instructor to devote more time to individual students. With more time to interact and get acquainted, professors can adapt their teaching strategies and assignments to bring them more in line with the interests and needs of the students in their classes. Technology's capacity to deliver large quantities of information over networks also expands the potential for tailoring educational programs to the specific needs of each learner. Dewayne Matthews argues that technology-enhanced programs "can be custom-designed around the needs and interests of the recipient instead of around the scheduling and resource needs of the provider" (p. 3). With the help of technology, educational programs—even full degrees—can be structured around flexible course modules that students can combine in a variety of forms to meet their personal and professional objectives. Matthews suggests that technology-mediated education makes traditional academic calendars and rigid curriculum structures obsolete because it can adapt education so well to individual learning interests and needs.

If education's goal is to help the learner reach his or her full potential, why should education be designed for the convenience of the instructor or the educational institution? Essentially, technology is empowering learners to take more control of their education than ever before. The expanded reach that technology affords educational institutions has encouraged many new providers to offer educational services. This increased competition enables consumers to choose the learning opportunities that best meet their needs within the constraints of their life circumstances. As technology transforms the educational marketplace, the balance of power is shifting from the education provider to the education consumer. Education consumers are now freer to pick and choose, from a variety of sources, the learning opportunities that meet their goals. In this fluid educational environment, the old system of accumulating credits from one or two nearby institutions becomes too restrictive for many students who are balancing a variety of personal and professional roles.

There is a related shift underway as technology transforms the teaching and learning process. The traditional higher education measure of educational achievement, the credit hour, is also being questioned. Matthews argues that "learning outcomes, as measured by student competencies [rather than course credits], is the quality measure that makes the most sense to consumers" (p. 4). In the new educational environment defined by technology, innovative institutions such as Western Governors University award degrees by certifying that students have achieved certain required competencies, regardless of where those competencies were acquired. Such a dramatic shift in the way educational achievement is documented would have been unthinkable before the advent of the free market educational system stimulated by the technology advances of the late twentieth century. Measuring competencies rather than credit hours represents another shift in favor of the consumer. As long as a student can document competence in a subject or skill area, it makes no difference where or how the learning occurred.

Technology's potential to lower the cost of education has been one of its principal appeals. The ability of computers and telecommunications to reach large audiences with the same high-quality educational programs has raised hopes for economies of scale never possible in the very labor-intensive traditional forms of instruction. To date, technology's promise to lower instructional costs has not been realized. Developing the infrastructure to support technology-mediated teaching and learning has been a very expensive proposition. The possibility remains, however, that new, advanced technologies may eventually lower the costs of higher education as researchers and educators learn how to blend technology-delivered and traditional instruction in a more cost-effective manner.

Impact on Professors' Roles

Technology has already changed the lives of college professors in significant ways. As the twenty-first century unfolds, professors' roles will most likely evolve further as computers and telecommunications media are more fully integrated into higher education. Professors can now use technology to prepare for classes, conduct research, deliver instruction, and keep in touch with their students and colleagues in far away places. Electronic mail, fax machines, computerized databases and search engines, and high-tech classrooms are some of the technologies that have transformed the work of college professors. Many experts on teaching and learning and instructional technology are suggesting that a fundamental shift in faculty duties is underway as more technology applications are adopted in higher education. Because technology calls into question the professor's role as a knowledge transmitter, educational reformers such as James Duderstadt, former president of the University of Michigan, suggest that professors should become "designers of learning experiences, processes, and environments" (p. 7).

Rather than serving primarily as a subject expert who shares specialized knowledge with students, this new type of professor acts more as a consultant or coach. With the aid of technology, his primary instructional role is to inspire and motivate students, to construct an environment that promotes learning, and ultimately to manage an active learning process. Ideally, in this carefully designed context, students take more responsibility for their learning and construct meaning themselves, rather than passively absorbing information from a professor. According to conventional wisdom in contemporary higher education, the professor has moved from being "a sage on the stage to a guide on the side." This individual knows his subject deeply, but is also skilled at constructing situations conducive to learning. Effective utilization of instructional technology is part of the twenty-first-century professor's redefined duties.

There has been some discussion that technology may eventually make many instructional positions obsolete, the same way it eliminated the need for telephone operators or police to direct traffic at busy intersections. Why employ undistinguished professors to lecture in classes when sophisticated telecommunications technology can bring world-renowned authorities into classrooms via satellite or the World Wide Web to inspire students and share the latest information in their fields? Critics of this proposal counter by arguing that big academic "stars" do not hold office hours, grade papers, construct exams, or counsel troubled students. They believe that professors should not lose their jobs to automation. According to this view, there will always be a need for many of the conventional faculty functions, such as designing learning opportunities, motivating students, and evaluating performance.

The future probably lies somewhere between these two contrasting options. Higher education will undoubtedly supplement its local talent with other human resources that have become easily accessible through technology. Yet it will also continue to employ professional staff members to design curriculum, manage academic programs, and work closely with students.

Technology is loosening professors' control of the curriculum. Faculty and academic administrators once wielded nearly absolute power over the academic programs their institutions offered. However, technology has now made it possible—and commercially viable—for publishers, software companies, and other providers to design and distribute a wide variety of courseware and instructional modules. This alternative to "in-house" production of courses and academic programs is appealing for financial as well as educational reasons. Spreading the development costs of technology-enhanced educational products permits the integration of sophisticated instructional strategies, such as gaming and simulations, into educational programs. On the other hand, moving the design of educational programs further from those who know an institution's students best causes many educators some concern. Technological advances usually lead to trade-offs. In this case, the benefit of being able to integrate high-tech elements into courses is counterbalanced by the reduction in local control of the curriculum.

Rethinking the Concept of College

Since higher education institutions first emerged, they have been physical places where people gather together to learn. Although higher education institutions have grown and become more complex over time, their basic essence has remained constant. Technology now calls into question the very idea of a college or university. Some accredited institutions of higher education, such as Jones International University, now exist entirely in cyberspace with no campus, classrooms, or athletic teams to tie together the academic community. The traditional campus-based institutions that have served the United States so well are being challenged in the early twenty-first century by a host of nontraditional competitors that offer education at a distance. Many of these entrepreneurial institutions are aided by an assortment of technologies, including computers, satellites, and electronic streaming video. Technology has vastly expanded the demand for education over the course of a lifetime. It has also released education from the confines of the conventional classroom. It has even removed the restrictions imposed by the clock by enabling people who have access to Internet technology to convene for the purpose of shared learning.

The multipurpose American university was so successful because it brought together the array of facilities, experts, students, and funding needed to educate the masses and expand the boundaries of knowledge in service to humanity. The university assembled the critical mass of talent and resources necessary to meet the knowledge needs of a dynamic society. Although this formula worked throughout the twentieth century, technology is challenging this comfortable arrangement. It has enabled many other organizations, such as corporate colleges and for-profit firms, to provide educational services such as degree programs, professional certificate programs, and a host of outreach services that were once monopolized by the higher education community.

The result of this "unbundling" of higher education roles remains in doubt. Technology has led to a vast expansion of the postsecondary education market, and it is calling into question conventional views of what a higher education institution is or should be. However, no one knows precisely what a college or university (physical or virtual) will look like once the other side of the technology revolution is reached. In the past, when higher education adopted technological innovations, the educational system became more open, more complex, and more dynamic. If the past history of higher education can serve as a guide to its future, the technologies now working their way into the system will lead to a more diverse and responsive educational enterprise. How that enterprise resembles the system that functioned throughout the 1900s remains to be seen.

Special Challenges of Technology

In spite of its nearly irresistible appeal, technology presents higher education with difficult challenges. Systematic planning of technological enhancements to educational programs is difficult when technology changes so quickly and unpredictably. Academic planners are continually playing catch-up to implement new technology applications that appear more quickly than a careful planning process can anticipate. Similarly, paying for new technologies with exciting educational applications remains troublesome for institutions with more needs than resources. Authors who wrestle with the funding issues raised by technology argue that new budgeting strategies are necessary to keep institutions from lurching from one technology-funding crisis to the next. Institutions must view technology as a routine expense, not an exceptional special expenditure.

Training faculty and staff members to utilize technology effectively remains a challenge that many colleges and universities have not resolved satisfactorily. It seems clear that building a physical technological infrastructure is not enough. It is also necessary to build a human resource infrastructure for technology to fulfill its promise to higher education.

Finally, adequate evaluation of technology's contribution to higher education remains a challenge. For example, in *Teaching with Technology*, Wake Forest University vice president David Brown concludes that "the case for computers [in collegiate education] rests on scant amounts of hard evidence" (p. 5). Much of the immense investment in technology that occurred in the 1980s and 1990s was to a large extent an act of faith. Brown argues that the logic in favor of using technology in higher education is compelling, however. He believes that "more choice leads to more learning" (p. 4), and that technology greatly enhances the "box of tools" a professor can employ to reach diverse students. According to Brown, most of the evidence that supports using computers in education is indirect. In his view, research demonstrates that repetition, dialog (question and answer, point and counterpoint), collaborative learning, and visualization and animation (using pictures to support learning) enhance learning. Because computers and other technologies can support these proven educational strategies, Brown concludes that the weight of logic comes down firmly on the side of technology use in colleges and universities. Although Brown makes a strong case for technology, more empirical evidence is needed to justify higher education's massive investment in computers, high-tech classrooms, distance-learning programs, and other technology-based initiatives.

An Emerging New System

Duderstadt asserts that the United States needs a new educational paradigm in order to deliver educational opportunity to a broader spectrum of humanity. The advanced technologies available at the beginning of the twenty-first century are laying the foundation of a new higher education system, better equipped to meet the needs of a complex and rapidly changing society. The outlines of this system, transformed by technology, have begun to appear. The educational system that George Connick believes will eventually result from the current technology revolution has four defining attributes. First, it is easier to access than the old campus-based system. Second, it is unconstrained by the barriers of time and space because technology can liberate education from the restrictions imposed both by the clock and geography. Third, it is student-centered because technology can increase students' learning options. Fourth, it is cost-effective because technology can reduce the labor-intensive nature of higher education and permit the reorganization necessary to make institutions more responsive and competitive.

No one knows what higher education will look like in 2025 or 2100. It is certain, however, that colleges and universities will be very different places than they were in the year 2000. Many factors will contribute to the changes that will occur as the higher education system moves into the future. There is no doubt that technology will be one of the driving forces contributing to the educational transformation that is already well underway.

See also: DISTANCE LEARNING IN HIGHER EDUCATION; FACULTY ROLES AND RESPONSIBILITIES; MEDIA AND LEARNING.

BIBLIOGRAPHY

BROWN, DAVID G. 2000. "The Jury Is In!" In *Teaching with Technology,* ed. David G. Brown. Bolton, MA: Anker.

CONNICK, GEORGE P. 1997. "Issues and Trends to Take Us into the Twenty-First Century." In *Teaching and Learning at a Distance,* ed. Thomas E. Cyrs. San Francisco: Jossey-Bass.

DUDERSTADT, JAMES J. 1999. "Can Colleges and Universities Survive in the Information Age?" In *Dancing with the Devil,* ed. Richard N. Katz. San Francisco: Jossey-Bass.

FARRINGTON, GREGORY C. 1999. "The New Technologies and the Future of Residential Under-graduate Education." In *Dancing with the Devil* ed. Richard N. Katz. San Francisco: Jossey-Bass.

HANNA, DONALD E. 2000. *Higher Education in an Era of Digital Competition: Choices and Challenges.* Madison, WI: Atwood Publishing.

JOHNSON, DAVID W.; MARUYAMA, GEOFFREY; JOHNSON, ROGER; NELSON, DEBORAH; and SKON, LINDA. 1981. "Effects of Cooperative, Competitive, and Individualistic Goal Structures on Achievement: A Meta-Analysis." *Psychological Bulletin* 89:47–62.

STUDY GROUP ON THE CONDITIONS OF EXCELLENCE IN AMERICAN HIGHER EDUCATION. 1984. *Involvement in Learning: Realizing the Potential of American Higher Education.* Washington, D.C.: National Institute of Education.

INTERNET RESOURCES

CLAREMONT GRADUATE UNIVERSITY. 1996. "Use of Instructional Technology Jumps on College Campuses." <www.ksu.edu/committees/citac/references/claremont.html>.

GREEN, KENNETH C. 1999. "The Real IT Challenge: People, Not Products." *Converge Magazine.* <www.convergemag.com/Publications/CNVGJan00/DigitalTweed/DigitalTweed.shtm>.

GREEN, KENNETH C. 2000. "Campus Computing, 2000: The 2000 National Survey of Information Technology in U.S. Higher Education." <www.campuscomputing.net>.

MATTHEWS, DEWAYNE. 1998. "The Transformation of Higher Education Through Information Technology." <www.educase.edu/nlii/keydocs/finance.html>.

MCCOLLUM, KELLEY. 1999. "Colleges Struggle to Manage Technology's Rising Costs." *Chronicle of Higher Education* <http://chronicle.com/free/v45/i24/24a00101.htm>.

ROGER G. BALDWIN

TECHNOLOGY TRANSFER

Technology is information or knowledge that is put to use in order to accomplish a particular task. *Technology transfer* is the application of information into use.

American research universities have become increasingly involved in various technology-transfer activities by establishing technology/business incubators, technology parks, venture capital funds for start-up companies, university research foundations, and technology licensing offices. This trend toward what Sheila Slaughter and Larry Leslie (1997) call *academic capitalism* is also illustrated by an increase in the number of university-based research centers—and by the tendency for some universities to retain partial ownership in the start-up companies that spin out of university research.

Through this variety of boundary-spanning activities, research universities seek to facilitate the transfer of technological innovations to private companies in order to: (1) create jobs and contribute to local economic development, and (2) earn additional funding for university research. Technology transfer from research universities has been increasingly recognized as an engine for economic growth in the United States. This relatively new role for research universities has been greeted with considerable discussion and debate. One question that has been raised concerns what role American research universities can, and should, play in transferring research results to private companies in the form of licensed technologies.

A *research university* is an institution whose main purposes are to conduct research and to train graduate students in how to conduct research. The first research universities developed in Germany; the University of Göttingen (founded in 1737) and the University of Berlin (established in 1810) were among the earliest examples. The idea of the research university spread to the United States, first to Johns Hopkins University (in 1876) and Clark University (in 1890), and then to Stanford University (1891) and the University of Chicago (1892). In the early twenty-first century, several hundred U.S. universities consider themselves research universities.

While some U.S. research universities established an office of technology licensing as early as 1925 (the University of Wisconsin at Madison), 1935 (Iowa State University), and 1940 (Massachusetts Institute of Technology [MIT]), most research universities did not adopt this idea until after 1970. Wisconsin, and later Stanford, served as the models for many other research universities as they became increasingly involved in technology transfer. The Patent and Trademark Law Amendments Act of 1980, commonly known as the Bayh-Dole Act and amend-

ed by Public Law 98-620 in 1984, facilitated patenting and licensing on a broad scale by research universities. This legislation shifted the responsibility for the transfer of technologies stemming from federally funded research from the federal government to the research universities that conducted the research.

Since the early 1980s the rise of biotechnology research and development and, more generally, of research in the life sciences has also boosted the number of research universities with offices of technology licensing—and increased the incomes earned by these offices. Today, some 70 percent of all technology royalties earned by universities come from the life sciences, with the remainder mainly derived from the physical sciences, including engineering. David Mowery et al. (1999) found that most invention disclosures, patents, and licensing at Columbia University were concentrated in a very small number of departments, including electrical engineering, computer science, and the medical school.

The spread of university offices of technology licensing followed the S-shaped curve that is characteristic of the cumulative rate of adoption of an innovation, with larger, more research-oriented universities tending to adopt first, followed over ensuing years by universities with a smaller amount of external research funding that devote fewer resources to research and development and technology transfer.

Detractors of university patenting and licensing point to such potential problems as conflicts of interest that may be created for faculty members, delays in publication of research results to accommodate patent filing or to benefit university-licensed companies, and the possible shift from basic research to more applied research, which has a higher potential for yielding patents and licenses. However, Mowery et al. found that there has been very little shift to more applied research due to the Bayh-Dole Act at Columbia University, Stanford University, or in the University of California System.

U.S. universities that are relatively more involved in technology transfer (indicated by invention disclosures, patents filed, start-up companies, and licensing royalties) are characterized by: (1) higher average faculty salaries; (2) a larger number of support staff for technology licensing; (3) a higher value of private gifts, grants, and contracts; and (4) larger research and development expenditures from industry and from federal sources.

See also: FACULTY AS ENTREPRENEURS; FACULTY CONSULTING; UNIVERSITY-INDUSTRIAL RESEARCH COLLABORATION.

BIBLIOGRAPHY

DEVOL, ROSS C. 1999. *America's High-Tech Economy: Growth, Development, and Risk for Metropolitan Areas.* Santa Monica, CA: Miliken Institute.

MASSING, DONALD E. 1998. *AUTM Licensing Survey: FY 1997.* Norwalk, CT: Association of University Technology Managers.

MOWERY, DAVID C.; NELSON, RICHARD R.; SAMPAT, BHAVEN N.; and ZIEDONIS, ARVIDS A. 1999. "The Effects of the Bayh-Dole Act on U.S. University Research and Technology Transfer." In *Industrializing Knowledge: University-Industry Linkages in Japan and the United States,* ed. Lewis M. Branscomb, Fumio Kodama, and Richard Florida. Cambridge, MA: MIT Press.

ROGERS, EVERETT M. 1995. *Diffusion of Innovations,* 4th edition. New York: Free Press.

ROGERS, EVERETT M.; HALL, BRAD J.; HASHIMOTO, MICHIO; STEFFENSEN, MORTON; SPEAKMAN, KRISTEN L.; and TIMKO, MOLLY K. 1999. "Technology Transfer from University-Based Research Centers: University of New Mexico Experience." *Journal of Higher Education* 70(6): 687–705.

ROGERS, EVERETT M.; YIN, JING; and HOFFMANN, JOERN. 2000. "Assessing the Effectiveness of Technology Transfer Offices at U.S. Research Universities." *Journal of the Association of University Technology Managers* 12:43–80.

SLAUGHTER, SHEILA, and LESLIE, LARRY L. 1997. *Academic Capitalism: Politics, Policies, and the Entrepreneurial University.* Baltimore: Johns Hopkins University Press.

EVERETT M. ROGERS

TELEVISION

See: MEDIA, INFLUENCE ON CHILDREN.

TERMAN, LEWIS (1877–1956)

Lewis M. Terman was a psychologist who developed some of the earliest and most successful measures of individual differences. He was raised on an Indiana farm and, after an early career as a schoolteacher and high school principal, received his doctorate in psychology from Clark University in 1905. After four years of teaching pedagogy at the Los Angeles State Normal School, he joined the education faculty at Stanford University in 1910. In 1922 he became head of Stanford's Psychology Department, a position he held until his retirement in 1942.

At Stanford, Terman followed up his doctoral research on mental testing by working on a revision of Alfred Binet's 1905 scale of intelligence. Collaborating with graduate students, Terman's revision was published in 1916 as the "Stanford-Binet." An innovative feature of the Stanford-Binet was the inclusion of the "Intelligence Quotient" or IQ, an index that had not been previously used in mental tests. Although there were several competitive versions, Terman's revision of the Binet test utilized the largest standardized sample and, by the 1920s, became the most widely used individually administered intelligence scale.

The success of the Stanford-Binet brought Terman professional acclaim. In 1917 he played a key role in the development of intelligence tests for the army. These group-administered tests were largely based on the Stanford-Binet. Such tests enabled large numbers of individuals to be tested at one time and, after the war, Terman endeavored to utilize this efficient form of test administration in the schools. In collaboration with a committee of psychologists who had worked on the army tests, he developed the "National Intelligence Tests" for grades three to eight, which were ready for use in 1920. Throughout the 1920s he played a leading role in establishing the widespread use of various group intelligence tests in schools so that students could be classified into homogeneous ability groups, in what became termed a *tracking system.* This educational practice became well established in American schools by the 1930s. Terman was also a leader in the development of group achievement tests, which assessed school learning. He collaborated on the construction of the Stanford Achievement Test, the first test battery of its kind.

Terman viewed the widespread adoption of tests in the schools as a reflection of how testing could be of use to American society. It was to be the major means of achieving his vision of a meritocracy; a social order based on ranked levels of native ability. Consistent with the views of other leaders of the

American mental testing movement, Terman believed that mental abilities were primarily a product of heredity. The highest purpose that testing could serve was the identification of intellectually gifted children—the potential leaders of society.

To achieve his goals, Terman launched a longitudinal study of gifted children in 1921, the first longitudinal study in psychology to use a large sample. Canvasing elementary and secondary schools in California, Terman and his research team came up with a sample of close to 1500 children with IQ scores of at least 135. In an attempt to dispel the popular notion that gifted children were underdeveloped in nonintellectual areas, Terman included measures of personality, character, and interests. Compared with a control group of California schoolchildren, Terman reported that gifted children excelled in measures of academic achievement. The profiles of gifted children also revealed that they were emotionally as well as intellectually mature. This sample was followed as the participants moved through adolescence, adulthood, and the retirement years. The study of the gifted over the lifespan demonstrated that they had achieved career success well above the average of college graduates and attained a high degree of personal satisfaction.

As a consequence of his research with the gifted, Terman devoted the latter part of his career to assessing nonintellectual personality traits. This work centered on the measurement of gender identification, which was viewed as a composite of motivational and emotional traits that differentiated the sexes. In 1936, with his research associate Catharine Cox Miles, he produced the first questionnaire measure of masculinity–femininity. The test was standardized on a sample, primarily made up of high school juniors and college sophomores. In essence, the test reflected the gender norms of the 1930s, though Terman was insensitive to the cultural and historical limits of his measure. He chose to emphasize the need to raise and educate girls and boys so that they would conform to the existing gender norms that fostered a clear distinction between the sexes.

He extended his interest in gender differences to the study of marital adjustment. He conducted a large-scale survey of several thousand married and divorced couples. In his study, he stressed that the key to marital happiness was the extent to which each spouse accepted the other's needs and feelings, and did not fight to get their own way. Happily married women were therefore characterized as being cooperative and content with their subordinate status. Terman's conventional views on gender thus carried over from his masculinity–femininity study to his marital research.

Terman's seminal contributions to the development of testing and the study of the intellectually gifted ensure his position as one of the pioneers of American psychology. Like many other psychologists of his time, however, he was insensitive to the cultural bias inherent in psychological testing, and did not anticipate the harmful effects that testing could have on those who were not in the mainstream of American society, especially poor and racial minority children. The changing social context of the 1960s therefore brought about a more critical evaluation of Terman's accomplishments in the testing field.

See also: BINET, ALFRED; EDUCATIONAL PSYCHOLOGY; INDIVIDUAL DIFFERENCES; INTELLIGENCE, *subentry on* MEASUREMENT.

BIBLIOGRAPHY

BORING, EDWIN G. 1959. "Lewis Madison Terman: 1877–1956." *Biographical Memoirs of the National Academy of Sciences* 33:414–440.

CHAPMAN, PAUL DAVIS. 1988. *Schools as Sorters: Lewis M. Terman, Applied Psychology, and the Intelligence Testing Movement, 1890–1930.* New York: New York University Press.

MINTON, HENRY L. 1988. *Lewis M. Terman: Pioneer in Psychological Testing.* New York: New York University Press.

SEAGOE, MAY V. 1975. *Terman and the Gifted.* Los Altos, CA: Kaufmann.

TERMAN, LEWIS M. 1916. *The Measurement of Intelligence.* Boston: Houghton Mifflin.

TERMAN, LEWIS M., et al. 1925. *Genetic Studies of Genius:* Vol. 1, *Mental and Physical Traits of a Thousand Gifted Children.* Stanford, CA: Stanford University Press.

TERMAN, LEWIS M., et al. 1938. *Psychological Factors in Marital Happiness.* New York: McGraw-Hill.

TERMAN, LEWIS M., and MILES, CATHARINE COX. 1936. *Sex and Personality: Studies in Masculinity and Femininity.* New York: McGraw-Hill.

HENRY L. MINTON

TESTING: COLLEGE ADMISSIONS TESTS

See: COLLEGE ADMISSIONS TESTS.

TESTING

STANDARDIZED TESTS AND EDUCATIONAL POLICY

The term *standardized testing* was used to refer to a certain type of multiple-choice or true/false test that could be machine-scored and was therefore thought to be "objective." This type of standardization is no longer considered capable of capturing the full range of skills candidates may possess. In the early twenty-first century it is more useful to speak of *standards-based* or *standards-linked* assessment, which seeks to determine to what extent a candidate meets certain specified expectations or standards. The format of the test or examination is less important than how well it elicits from the candidate the kind of performance that can give us that information.

The use of standardized testing for admission to higher education is increasing, but is by no means universal. In many countries, school-leaving (exit) examinations are nonstandardized affairs conducted by schools, with or without government guidelines, while university entrance exams are set by each university or each university department, often without any attempt at standardization across or within universities. The functions of certification (completion of secondary school) and selection (for higher or further education) are separate and frequently noncomparable across institutions or over time. In most countries, however, a school-leaving certificate is a necessary but not a sufficient condition for university entrance.

Certification

In the United States, states began using high school exit examinations in the late 1970s to ensure that students met minimum state requirements for graduation. In 2001 all states were at some stage of implementing a graduation exam. These are no longer the "minimum competency tests" of the 1970s and 1980s; they are based on curriculum and performance standards developed in all fifty states. All students should be able to demonstrate that they have reached performance standards before they leave secondary school.

Certification examinations based on state standards have long been common in European countries. They may be set centrally by the state and conducted and scored by schools (France); set by the state and conducted and scored by an external or semi-independent agency (the Netherlands, the United Kingdom, Romania, Slovenia); or set, conducted, and scored entirely within the schools themselves (Russian Federation), often in accordance with government guidelines but with no attempt at standardization or comparability. Since the objective is to certify a specified level of learning achieved, these exit examinations are strongly curriculum-based, essentially *criterion-referenced,* and ideally *all* candidates should pass. They are thus typically medium- or low-stakes, and failing students have several opportunities to retake the examination. Sometimes weight is given to a student's in-school performance as well as to exam results—in the Netherlands, for example, the weightings are 50-50, giving students scope to show a range of skills not easily measured by examination.

In practice, however, when constructing criteria for a criterion-referenced test, norm-referencing is unavoidable. Hidden behind each criterion is norm-referenced data: assumptions about how the *average* child in that particular age group *can be expected* to perform. Pure criterion-referenced assessment is rare, and it would be better to think of assessment as being a hybrid of norm- and criterion-referencing. The same is true of setting standards, especially if they have to be reachable by students of varying ability: one has to know something about the *norm* before one can set a meaningful standard.

Selection

By contrast, university entrance examinations aim to select some candidates rather than others and are therefore *norm-referenced:* the objective is not to determine whether all have reached a set standard, but to select "the best." In most cases, higher education expectations are insufficiently linked to K–12 standards.

Entrance exams are typically academic and high-stakes, and opportunities to retake them are limited. Where entrance exams are set by individual university departments rather than by an entire university or group of universities, accountability for selection is limited, and failing students have little or no recourse. University departments are unwilling to relinquish what they see as their autonomy in selecting entrants; moreover, the lack of accountability and the often lucrative system of private tutoring for entrance exams are barriers to a more transparent and equitable process of university selection.

In the United States the noncompulsory SATs administered by the Educational Testing Service (ETS) are most familiar. SAT I consists of quantitative and verbal reasoning tests, and for a number of years ETS insisted that these were curriculum-free and could not be studied for. Indeed they used to be called "Scholastic *Aptitude* Tests," because they were said to measure candidates' aptitude for higher level studies. The emphasis on predictive validity has become less; test formats include a wider range of question types aimed at eliciting more informative student responses; and the link with curriculum and standards is reflected in SAT II, a new subject test in high school subjects, for example English and biology. Fewer U.S. universities and colleges require SAT scores as part of their admission procedure in the early twenty-first century, though many still do.

Certification Combined with Selection

A number of countries (e.g., the United Kingdom, the Netherlands, Slovenia, and Lithuania) combine school-leaving examinations with university entrance examinations. Candidates typically take a national, curriculum-based, high school graduation exam in a range of subjects; the exams are set and marked (scored) by or under the control of a government department or a professional agency external to the schools; and candidates offer their results to universities as the main or sole basis for selection. Students take only one set of examinations, but the question papers and scoring methods are based on known standards and are nationally comparable, so that an "A" gained by a student in one part of the country is comparable to an "A" gained elsewhere.

Universities are still entitled to set their own entrance requirements such as requiring high grades in biology, chemistry, and physics for students who wish to study medicine, or accepting lower grades in less popular disciplines or for admittance to less prestigious institutions.

Trends in Educational Policy: National Standards and Competence

Two main trends are evident worldwide. The first is a move towards examinations linked to explicit national (or state) *standards*, often tacitly aligned with international expectations, such as Organisation for Economic Co-Operation and Development (OECD) indicators or the results of multinational assessments such as the Third Mathematics and Science Study (TIMSS) or similar studies in reading literacy and civics. The second trend is towards a more *competence-based* approach to education in general, and to assessment in particular: less emphasis on what candidates can remember and more on what they understand and can do.

Standards. The term *standards* here refers to official, written guidelines that define what a country or state expects its state school students to know and be able to do as a result of their schooling.

In the United States all fifty states now have student testing programs, although the details vary widely. Few states, however, have testing programs that explicitly measure student achievement against state standards, despite claims that they do. (Some states ask external assessors to evaluate the alignment of tests to standards.) Standards are also used for school and teacher accountability purposes; about half the states rate schools primarily on the basis of student test scores or test score gains over time, and decisions to finance, close, take over, or otherwise overhaul chronically low-performing schools can be linked to student results. Much debate centers on whether tests designed for one purpose (measuring student learning) can fairly be used to judge teachers, schools, or education systems.

The same debate is heard in England and Wales, where student performance on national curriculum "key stage" testing at ages seven, eleven, fourteen, and sixteen has led to the publication of "league tables" listing schools in order of their students' performance. A painstaking attempt to arrive at a workable "value-added" formula that would take account of a number of social and educational variables ended in failure. The concept of "value added" involves linking a baseline assessment to subsequent performance: the term refers to *relative* progress of pupils or how well pupils perform compared to other pupils with similar starting points and background variables. A formula developed to measure these complex relationships was scientifically acceptable but judged too laborious for use by schools. Nevertheless, league tables are popular with parents and the media and remain a feature of standards-based testing in England and Wales.

Most countries in Central and Eastern Europe are likewise engaged in formulating educational standards, but standards still tend to be expressed in terms of content covered and hours on the timetable ("seat time") for each subject rather than student outcomes. When outcomes are mentioned, it is often in unmeasurable terms: "[Candidates] must be familiar with . . . the essence, purpose, and meaning of human life [and] . . . the correlation between truth and error" (State Committee for Higher Education, Russian Federation, p. 35).

Competence. The shift from content and "seat-time" standards to specifying desired student achievement expressed in operational terms ("The student will be able to . . .") is reflected in new types of performance-based assessment where students show a range of skills as well as knowledge. Portfolios or coursework may be assessed as well as written tests. It has been argued that deconstructing achievement into a list of specified behaviors that can be measured misses the point: that learning is a subtle process that escapes formulas people seek to impose on it. Nevertheless, the realization that it is necessary to focus on outcomes (and not only on input and process) of education is an important step forward.

Apart from these conceptual shifts, many countries are also engaged in practical examinations reform. Seven common policy issues are: (1) changing concepts and techniques of testing (e.g., computer-based interactive testing on demand); (2) shift to standards- and competence-based tests; (3) changed test formats and question types (e.g., essays rather than multiple-choice); (4) more inclusive target levels of tests; (5) standardization of tests; (6) independent, external administration of tests; and (7) convergence of high school exit exams and university entrance.

Achieving Policy Goals

In terms of monitoring the achievement of education policy goals, standards-linked diagnostic and formative (national, whole-population, or sample-based) assessments at set points *during* a student's schooling are clearly more useful than scores on high-stakes summative examinations at the end. Trends in annual exam results can still be informative to policy makers, but they come too late for students themselves to improve performance. Thus the key-stage approach used in the United Kingdom provides better data for evidence-based policy making and more helpful information to parents than, for example, the simple numerical scores on SAT tests, which in any case are not systematically fed back to schools or education authorities.

However, the U.K. approach is expensive and labor-intensive. The best compromise might be sample-based periodic national assessments of a small number of key subjects (for policy purposes), plus a summative, curriculum- and standards-linked examination at the end of a major school cycle (for certification and selection).

See also: INTERNATIONAL ASSESSMENTS; STANDARDS FOR STUDENT LEARNING; STANDARDS MOVEMENT IN AMERICAN EDUCATION; TESTING, *subentries on* INTERNATIONAL STANDARDS OF TEST DEVELOPMENT, NATIONAL ACHIEVEMENT TESTS, INTERNATIONAL.

BIBLIOGRAPHY

CRESSWELL, MICHAEL J. 1996. "Defining, Setting and Maintaining Standards in Curriculum-Embedded Examinations: Judgmental and Statistical Approaches." In *Assessment: Problems, Developments and Statistical Issues,* ed. Harvey Goldstein and Toby Lewis. London: Wiley and Sons.

DORE, RONALD P. 1997. *The Diploma Disease: Education, Qualifications and Development.* London: George Allen and Unwin.

ECKSTEIN, MAX A., and NOAH, HAROLD J. eds. 1992. *Examinations: Comparative and International Studies.* Oxford: Pergamon Press.

GREEN, ANDY. 1997. *Education, Globalization and the Nation State.* Basingstoke, Eng.: Macmillan.

HEYNEMAN, STEPHEN P. 1987. "Uses of Examinations in Developing Countries: Selection, Research and Education Sector Management." *International Journal of Education Development* 7(4):251–263.

HEYNEMAN, STEPHEN P., and FAGERLIND, INGEMAR, eds. 1988. *University Examinations and Standardized Testing.* Washington, DC: World Bank.

HEYNEMAN, STEPHEN P., and RANSOM, ANGELA. 1990. "Using Examinations to Improve the Quality of Education." *Educational Policy* 4(3):177–192.

LITTLE, ANGELA, and WOLF, ALISON, eds. 1996. *Assessment in Transition: Learning, Monitoring and Selection in International Perspective.* Tarrytown, NY: Pergamon.

SCHOOL CURRICULUM AND ASSESSMENT AUTHORITY (SCAA). 1997. *The Value Added National Project; Final Report.* London: SCAA Publications.

STATE COMMITTEE FOR HIGHER EDUCATION, RUSSIAN FEDERATION. 1995. *State Educational Standards for Higher Professional Education.* Moscow: Ministry of Education.

TYMMS, PETER. 2000. *Baseline Assessment and Monitoring in Primary Schools: Achievements, Attitudes and Value-added Indicators.* London: David Fulton.

UNIVERSITY OF CAMBRIDGE LOCAL EXAMINATIONS SYNDICATE (UCLES). 1998. *MENO Higher-Level Thinking Skills Test Battery.* Cambridge, Eng.: UCLES Research and Development Division.

WEST, RICHARD, and CRIGHTON, JOHANNA. 1999. "Examination Reform in Central and Eastern Europe: Issues and Trends." *Assessment in Education: Principles, Policy and Practice* 6(2):71–289.

INTERNET RESOURCES

NATIONAL GOVERNORS ASSOCIATION. 2002. "High School Exit Exams: Setting High Expectations." <www.nga.org/center/divisions/1,1188,C_ISSUE_BRIEF%5ED_1478,00.html>.

NATIONAL CENTER FOR PUBLIC POLICY AND HIGHER EDUCATION. 2002. "Measuring Up 2000." <http://measuringup2000.higher education.org/>.

JOHANNA V. CRIGHTON

STANDARDIZED TESTS AND HIGH-STAKES ASSESSMENT

Assessment is the process of collecting data to measure the knowledge or performance of a student or group. Written tests of students' knowledge are a common form of assessment, but data from homework assignments, informal observations of student proficiency, evaluations of projects, oral presentations, or other samples of student work may also be used in assessment. The word *assessment* carries with it the idea of a broader and more comprehensive evaluation of student performance than a single test.

In an age when testing is controversial, *assessment* has become the preferred term because of its connotation of breadth and thoroughness. The National Assessment of Educational Progress (NAEP) is an example of a comprehensive assessment worthy of the name. Also known as the "Nation's Report Card," NAEP administers achievement tests to a representative sample of U.S. students in reading, mathematics, science, writing, U.S. history, civics, geography, and the arts. The achievement measures used by NAEP in each subject area are so broad that each participating student takes only a small portion of the total assessment. Not all assessment programs, however, are of such high quality. Some administer much more narrow and limited tests, but still use the word *assessment* because of its popular appeal.

Standardized tests are tests administered and scored under a consistent set of procedures. Uniform conditions of administration are necessary to make it possible to compare results across individuals or schools. For example, it would be unfair if the performance of students taking a test in February were to be compared to the performance of students tested in May or if one group of students had help from their teacher while another group did not. The most familiar standardized tests of achievement are traditional machine-scorable, multiple-choice tests such as the California Achievement Test (CAT), the Comprehensive Tests of Basic Skills (CTBS), the Iowa Tests of Basic Skills (ITBS), the Metropolitan Achievement Test (MAT), and the Stanford Achievement Test (SAT). Many other assessments, such as open-ended performance assessments, personality and attitude measures, English-language proficiency tests, or Advanced Placement essay tests, may also be standardized so that results can be interpreted on a common scale.

High-stakes testing is a term that was first used in the 1980s to describe testing programs that have serious consequences for students or educators. Tests are high-stakes if their outcomes determine such important things as promotion to the next grade, graduation, merit pay for teachers, or school rankings reported in a newspaper. When test results have serious consequences, the requirements for evidence of test validity are correspondingly higher.

Purposes of Assessment

The intended use of an assessment—its purpose—determines every other aspect of how the assessment is conducted. Purpose determines the content of the assessment (What should be measured?); methods of data collection (Should the procedures be standardized? Should data come from all students or from a sample of students?); technical requirements of the assessment (What level of reliability and validity must be established?); and finally, the stakes or consequences of the assessment, which in turn determine the kinds of safeguards necessary to protect against potential harm from fallible assessment-based decisions.

In educational testing today, it is possible to distinguish at least four different purposes for assessment: (1) classroom assessment used to guide and evaluate learning; (2) selection testing used to identify students for special programs or for college admissions; (3) large-scale assessment used to evaluate programs and monitor trends; and (4) high-stakes assessment of achievement used to hold individual students, teachers, and schools accountable. Assessments designed for one of these purposes may not be appropriate or valid if used for another purpose.

In classrooms, assessment is an integral part of the teaching and learning process. Teachers use both formal and informal assessments to plan and guide instruction. For individual students, assessments help to gauge what things students already know and understand, where misconceptions exist, what skills need more practice in context, and what supports are needed to take the next steps in learning. Teachers also use assessment to evaluate their own teaching practices so as to adjust and modify curricula, instructional activities, or assignments that did not help students grasp key ideas. To serve classroom purposes, assessments must be closely aligned with what children are learning, and the timing of assessments must correspond to the specific days and weeks when children are learning specific concepts. While external accountability tests can help teachers examine their instructional program overall, external, once-per-year tests are ill-suited for diagnosis and targeting of individual student learning needs. The technical requirements for the reliability of classroom assessments are less stringent than for other testing purposes because assessment errors on any given day are readily corrected by additional information gathered on subsequent days.

Selection and placement tests may be used to identify students for gifted and talented programs, to provide services for students with disabilities, or for college admissions. Because selection tests are used to evaluate students with a wide variety of prior experiences, they tend to be more generic than standardized achievement tests so as not to presume exposure to a specific curriculum. Nonetheless, performance on selection measures is strongly influenced by past learning opportunities. Unlike IQ tests of the past, it is no longer assumed that any test can measure innate learning ability. Instead, measures of current learning and reasoning abilities are used as practical predictors of future learning; because all tests have some degree of error associated with them, professional standards require that test scores not be the sole determiner of important decisions. For example, college admissions tests are used in conjunction with high school grades and recommendations. School readiness tests are sometimes used as selection tests to decide whether children five years old should start school, but this is an improper use of the tests. None of the existing school readiness measures has sufficient reliability and validity to support such decisions.

Large-scale assessments, such as the National Assessment of Educational Progress (NAEP) or the Third International Mathematics and Science Survey (TIMSS), serve a monitoring and comparative function. Assessment data are gathered about groups of students in the aggregate and can be used by policymakers to make decisions about educational programs. Because there is not a single national or international curriculum, assessment content must be comprehensive and inclusive of all of the curricular goals of the many participating states or nations. Obviously, no one student could be expected to master all of the content in a test spanning many curricula, but, by design, individual student scores are not reported in this type of assessment. As a result, the total assessment can include a much broader array of tasks and problem types to better represent the content domain, with each student being asked to complete only a small sample of tasks from the total set. Given that important policy decisions may follow from shifts in achievement levels or international comparisons of achievement, large-scale assessments must meet high standards of technical accuracy.

High-stakes assessments of achievement that are used to hold individual students, teachers, and schools accountable are similar to large-scale monitoring assessments, but clearly have very different consequences. In addition, these tests, typically administered by states or school districts, must be much more closely aligned with the content standards and curriculum for which participants are being held accountable. As a practical matter, accountability assessments are often more limited in the variety of formats and tasks included, both because each student must take the same test and because states and districts may lack the resources to develop and score more open-ended performance measures. Regardless of practical constraints, high-stakes tests must meet the most stringent technical standards because of the harm to individuals that would be caused by test inaccuracies.

A Short History of High-Stakes Testing

Accountability testing in the United States started in 1965 as part of the same legislation (Title I of the Elementary and Secondary Education Act [ESEA]) that first allocated federal funds to improve the academic achievement of children from low-income families. Federal dollars came with a mandate that programs be evaluated to show their effectiveness. The early accountability movement did not assume, however, that public schools were bad. In fact, the idea behind ESEA was to extend the benefits of an excellent education to poor and minority children.

The public's generally positive view of America's schools changed with the famous SAT test score decline of the early 1970s. Despite the fact that a blue-ribbon panel commissioned by the College Board in 1977 later found that two-thirds to three-fourths of the score decline was attributable to an increase in the number of poor and minority students gaining access to college and not to a decline in the quality of education, all subsequent accountability efforts were driven by the belief that America's public schools were failing.

The minimum competency testing movement of the 1970s was the first in a series of educational reforms where tests were used not just as measures of the effectiveness of reforms, but also as the primary drivers of reform. Legislators mandated tests of minimum academic skills or survival skills (e.g., bal-ancing a checkbook), intending to "put meaning back into the high school diploma." By 1980, thirty-seven states had taken action to mandate minimum competency standards for grade-to-grade promotion or high school graduation. It was not long, however, before the authors of *A Nation at Risk* (1983) concluded that minimum competency examinations were part of the problem, not part of the solution, because the "'minimum' [required of students] tends to become the 'maximum,' thus lowering educational standards for all" (p. 20).

Following the publication of *A Nation at Risk*, the excellence movement sought to ratchet up expectations by reinstating course-based graduation requirements, extending time in the school day and school year, requiring more homework, and, most importantly, requiring more testing. Despite the rhetoric of rigorous academic curricula, the new tests adopted in the mid-1980s were predominantly multiple-choice, basic-skills tests—a step up from minimum competency tests, but not much of one. By the end of the 1980s, evidence began to accrue showing that impressive score gains on these tests might not be a sign of real learning gains. For example, John Cannell's 1987 study, dubbed the "Lake Wobegon Report," showed that all fifty states claimed their test scores were above the national average.

Standards-based reforms, which began in the 1990s and continued at the start of the twenty-first century, were both a rejection and extension of previous reforms. Rejecting traditional curricula and especially rote activities, the standards movement called for the development of much more challenging curricula, focused on reasoning, conceptual understanding, and the ability to apply one's knowledge. At the same time, the standards movement continued to rely heavily on large-scale accountability assessments to leverage changes in instruction. However, standards-based reformers explicitly called for a radical change in the content and format of assessments to forestall the negative effects of "teaching the test." Various terms, such as *authentic, direct,* and *performance-based,* were used in standards parlance to convey the idea that assessments themselves had to be reformed to more faithfully reflect important learning goals. The idea was that if tests included extended problems and writing tasks, then it would be impossible for scores to go up on such assessments without there being a genuine improvement in learning.

Effects of High-Stakes Testing

By the end of the 1980s, concerns about dramatic increases in the amount of testing and potential negative effects prompted Congress to commission a comprehensive report on educational testing. This report summarized research documenting the ill effects of high-pressure accountability testing, including that high-stakes testing led to *test score inflation,* meaning that test scores went up without a corresponding gain in student learning. Controlled studies showed that test score gains on familiar and taught-to tests could not be verified by independent tests covering the same content. High-stakes testing also led to *curriculum distortion,* which helped to explain how spurious score gains may occur. Interview and survey data showed that many teachers eliminated science and social studies, especially in high-poverty schools, because more time was needed for math and reading. Teaching to the test also involved rote drill in tested subjects, so that students were unable to use their knowledge in any other format.

It should also be noted that established findings from the motivational literature have raised serious questions about test-based incentive systems. Students who are motivated by trying to do well on tests, instead of working to understand and master the material, are consistently disadvantaged in subsequent endeavors. They become less intrinsically motivated, they learn less, and they are less willing to persist with difficult problems.

To what extent do these results, documented in the late 1980s, still hold true for standards-based assessments begun in the 1990s? Recent studies still show the strong influence that high-stakes tests have on what gets taught. To the extent that the content of assessments has improved, there have been corresponding improvements in instruction and curriculum. The most compelling evidence of positive effects is in the area of writing instruction. In extreme cases, writing has been added to the curriculum in classrooms, most often in urban settings, where previously it was entirely absent.

Unfortunately, recent studies on the effects of standards-based reforms also confirm many of the earlier negative effects of high-stakes testing. The trend to eliminate or reduce social studies and science, because state tests focused only on reading, writing, and mathematics, has been so pervasive nationwide that experts speculate it may explain the recent downturn in performance in science on NAEP.

In Texas, Linda McNeil and Angela Valenzuela found that a focus on tested content and test-taking skills was especially pronounced in urban districts.

In contrast with previous analysts who used test-score gains themselves as evidence of effectiveness, it is now widely understood by researchers and policymakers that some independent confirmation is needed to establish the validity of achievement gains. For example, two different studies by researchers at the RAND Corporation used NAEP as an independent measure of achievement gains and documented both real and spurious aspects of test-score gains in Texas. A 2000 study by David Grissmer, Ann Flanagan, Jennifer Kawata, and Stephanie Williamson found that Texas students performed better than expected based on family characteristics and socioeconomic factors. However, a study by Stephen Klein and colleagues found that gains on NAEP were nothing like the dramatic gains reported on Texas's own test, the Texas Assessment of Academic Skills (TAAS). Klein et al. also found that the gap in achievement between majority and minority groups had widened for Texas students on NAEP whereas the gap had appeared to be closing on the TAAS. Both of these studies could be accurate, of course. Texas students could be learning more in recent years, but not as much as claimed by the TAAS. Studies such as these illustrate the importance of conducting research to evaluate the validity and credibility of results from high-stakes testing programs.

Professional Standards for High-Stakes Testing

The *Standards for Educational and Psychological Testing* (1999) is published jointly by the American Educational Research Association, the American Psychological Association, and the National Council on Measurement in Education. The *Standards* establish appropriate procedures for test development, scaling, and scoring, as well as the evidence needed to ensure validity, reliability, and fairness in testing. Drawing from the *Standards,* the American Educational Research Association issued a position statement in 2000 identifying the twelve conditions that must be met to ensure sound implementation of high-stakes educational testing programs.

First, individual students should be protected from tests being used as the sole criterion for critically important decisions. Second, students and teachers should not be sanctioned for failing to meet new standards if sufficient resources and opportunities to learn have not been provided. Third, test validity must be established for each separate intended use, such as student certification or school evaluation. Fourth, the testing program must fully disclose any likely negative side effects of testing. Fifth, the test should be aligned with the curriculum and should not be limited to only the easiest-to-test portion of the curriculum. Sixth, the validity of passing scores and achievement levels should be analyzed, as well as the validity of the test itself. Seventh, students who fail a high-stakes test should be provided with meaningful opportunities for remediation consisting of more than drilling on materials that imitate the test. Eighth, special accommodations should be provided for English language learners so that language does not interfere with assessment of content area knowledge. Ninth, provision should be made for students with disabilities so that they may demonstrate their proficiency on tested content without being impeded by the format of the test. Tenth, explicit rules should be established for excluding English language learners or students with disabilities so that schools, districts, or states cannot improve their scores by excluding some students. Eleventh, test results should be sufficiently reliable for their intended use. Twelfth, an ongoing program of research should be established to evaluate both the intended and unintended consequences of high-stakes testing programs.

Professional standards provide a useful framework for understanding the limitations and potential benefits of sound assessment methodologies. Used appropriately tests can greatly enhance educational decision-making. However, when used in ways that go beyond what tests can validly claim to do, tests could very likely do more harm than good.

See also: ASSESSMENT; INTERNATIONAL ASSESSMENTS; STANDARDS FOR STUDENT LEARNING; STANDARDS MOVEMENT IN AMERICAN EDUCATION.

BIBLIOGRAPHY

AMERICAN EDUCATIONAL RESEARCH ASSOCIATION; AMERICAN PSYCHOLOGICAL ASSOCIATION; and NATIONAL COUNCIL ON MEASUREMENT IN EDUCATION. 1999. *Standards for Educational and Psychological Testing*. Washington, DC: American Educational Research Association.

BEATTY, ALEXANDRA; GREENWOOD, M. R. C.; and LINN, ROBERT L., eds. 1999. *Myths and Trade-offs: The Role of Tests in Undergraduate Admissions*. Washington, DC: National Academy Press.

CANNELL, JOHN J. 1987. *Nationally Normed Elementary Achievement Testing in America's Public Schools: How All 50 States Are Above the National Average*. Daniels, WV: Friends for Education.

CANNELL, JOHN J. 1989. *The Lake Wobegon Report: How Public Educators Cheat on Achievement Tests*. Albuquerque, NM: Friends for Education.

COLLEGE BOARD. 1977. *On Further Examination: Report of the Advisory Panel on the Scholastic Aptitude Test Score Decline*. New York: College Board.

GRISSMER, DAVID; FLANAGAN, ANN; KAWATA, JENNIFER; and WILLIAMSON, STEPHANIE. 2000. *Improving Student Achievement: What State NAEP Test Scores Tell Us*. Santa Monica, CA: RAND.

KLEIN, STEPHEN P., et al. 2000. *What Do Test Scores in Texas Tell Us?* Santa Monica, CA: RAND.

McNEIL, LINDA, and VALENZUELA, ANGELA. 2000. *The Harmful Impact of the TAAS System of Testing in Texas: Beneath the Accountability Rhetoric*. Cambridge, MA: Harvard University Civil Rights Project.

NATIONAL COMMISSION ON EXCELLENCE IN EDUCATION. 1983. *A Nation at Risk: The Imperative of Educational Reform*. Washington, DC: U.S. Department of Education.

STIPEK, DEBORAH. 1998. *Motivation to Learn: From Theory to Practice*, 3rd edition. Boston: Allyn and Bacon.

U.S. CONGRESS, OFFICE OF TECHNOLOGY ASSESSMENT. 1992. *Testing in American Schools: Asking the Right Questions*. Washington, DC: U.S. Government Printing Office.

INTERNET RESOURCES

AMERICAN EDUCATIONAL RESEARCH ASSOCIATION. 2000. "AERA Position Statement Concerning High-Stakes Testing in Pre-K–12 Education." <www.aera.net/about/policy/stakes.htm>.

NATIONAL ASSOCIATION FOR THE EDUCATION OF YOUNG CHILDREN. 1995. "Position Statement on School Readiness." <www.naeyc.org/resources/position_statements/psredy98.htm>.

LORRIE A. SHEPARD

STATEWIDE TESTING PROGRAMS

State testing programs have a long history. New York State administered its first Regents' Examinations as early as 1865. Several other state programs had their beginnings in the 1920s, when new forms of achievement examinations—objective tests—were developed for and introduced in the schools. In 1937 representatives from fifteen state programs and nonprofit testing agencies met, under the leadership of the American Council on Education's Committee on Measurement and Guidance, to discuss common problems. The group continued to meet annually, except during World War II, for decades.

In 1957 President Dwight D. Eisenhower called attention to state testing programs when he indicated the need for nationwide testing of high school students and a system of incentives for qualified students to pursue scientific or professional careers. The subsequent passage of the National Defense Education Act of 1958 (NDEA) not only encouraged but gave financial support to testing, guidance, and scholarship programs.

The growth in number and importance of state testing programs accelerated rapidly in the 1970s and has continued to grow ever since. The growth in the 1970s reflected, at least in part, the enhanced role of states in education policy. In the academic year 1969–1970, the majority—53 percent—of the funding for schools came from local agencies; states contributed 39 percent and the federal government provided 8 percent. A decade later, however, the state share of education funding had increased to 47 percent, and state governments became the dominant source of funding for schools.

With that increased responsibility came demands for some form of accountability for results, and that meant state tests to determine if students were learning. At the same time, there was growing concern among public officials and the public about the quality of schools, fueled in part by the revelation that average scores on the SAT declined between 1963 and 1977. In response to these concerns, and the interest in accountability, a majority of states in the 1970s implemented some form of minimum competency test, which students were required to pass in order to graduate from high school. The number of states conducting such tests rose from a handful in 1975 to thirty-three in 1985.

The wave of state education reforms enacted following the publication in 1983 of *A Nation at Risk,* the report by the National Commission on Excellence in Education, further accelerated the growth in state testing. That report, which warned of a "rising tide of mediocrity" in America's schools, recommended that states adopt achievement tests to measure student performance, and many states responded to the call. By the end of the 1980s, forty-seven states were operating at least one testing program, up from thirty-nine in 1984.

This growth continued throughout the 1990s as well. The dominant role of states in education policy was symbolized near the beginning of that decade, when President George H. W. Bush called the nation's governors to an extraordinary "education summit" in Charlottesville, Virginia. In the wake of that meeting, the President and the governors agreed to a set of national education goals, which included the pledge that all students would be "competent in challenging subject matter" by the year 2000. The goals were enshrined into federal law in 1994; that same year, President Bill Clinton signed the Improving America's Schools Act, which required states to set challenging standards for student performance and implement tests that measure student performance against the standards. In response to the law, nearly all states revamped their existing tests or developed new tests, and as of 2001, all states except Iowa (where local school districts administer tests) had a statewide testing program; by one estimate, the amount spent by states on testing doubled, to $410 million, between 1996 and 2001.

The No Child Left Behind Act, which President George W. Bush signed into law in 2002, requires a significant increase in state testing. Under the law, states must administer annual reading and mathematics tests in grades three through eight, tests in science in at least three grade levels, and tests at the high school level. At the time of enactment, only nine states met the law's requirements for annual tests in reading and mathematics aligned to state standards.

Types of Tests

Although most state tests consist primarily of multiple-choice questions, there is considerable variation among the states. Thirty-four states include some short-answer questions in at least some of their tests, requiring students to write answers rather than select from among answers already provided, and eighteen states include questions requiring extended responses in subjects other than English language arts.

(Nearly all states administer writing tests that ask for extended responses.) Two states, Kentucky and Vermont, assess student performance in writing through the use of portfolios, which collect students' classroom work during the course of a school year. The portfolios are scored by teachers, using common criteria.

The Maryland state test, the Maryland School Performance Assessment Program (MSPAP), is unusual in that it consists exclusively of open-ended questions. Students work in groups for part of the assessment, and many of the questions are interdisciplinary, requiring students to apply knowledge from English language arts, mathematics, science, and social studies. In addition, the test is designed so that individual students take only a third of the complete assessment; as a result, scores are reported for schools, school districts, and the state, but not for individual students.

The MSPAP, like many state tests, was custom-made to match the state's standards. In Maryland's case, the test was developed by state teachers; other states contract with commercial publishers to develop tests to match their standards. Such tests indicate the level of performance students attained, but do not permit comparisons with student performance from other states. The types of reports vary widely. Maryland, for example, specifies three levels of achievement: excellent, indicating outstanding accomplishment; satisfactory, indicating proficiency; and not met, indicating more work is required to attain proficiency. The state's goal is for 70 percent of students to reach the satisfactory level and 25 percent to reach the excellent level.

Other states, meanwhile, use commercially available tests that provide comparative information. The most commonly used tests are the Stanford Achievement Test, 9th Edition (or SAT-9), published by Harcourt Brace Educational Measurement, and the Terra Nova, published by CTB-McGraw-Hill. These tests are administered to representative samples of students, known as a norm group, and provide information on student performance compared with the norm group. For example, results might indicate that a student performed in the sixty-fifth percentile, meaning that the student performed better than sixty-five percent of the norm group. To provide both information on performance against standards and comparative information, some states employ hybrid systems. Maryland, for example, administers a norm-referenced test in grades in which

the MSPAP is not used. Delaware, meanwhile, has embedded an abbreviated version of the SAT-9 within its state test.

Purposes

State tests are used for a variety of purposes. The most common is to provide information to parents and the public about student, school, and school system performance. The expectation is that this information can improve instruction and learning by pointing out areas of weakness that need additional attention.

In addition to providing reports to parents about their children's performance, forty-three states issue "report cards" on schools that indicate school performance; twenty states require that these report cards be sent to parents. The No Child Left Behind Act requires all states to produce school report cards and to disseminate them to parents.

States also place consequences for students on the results of tests. As of 2001 four states (Delaware, Louisiana, New Mexico, and North Carolina) make promotion for at least certain grades contingent on passing state tests, and another four states are planning to do so by 2004. In other states, school districts set policies for grade-to-grade promotion, and many districts use state tests as criteria for determining promotion from grade to grade. A 1997 survey of large school districts, conducted by the American Federation of Teachers, found that nearly 40 percent of the districts surveyed used standardized tests in making promotion decisions at the elementary school level, and 35 percent used tests in making such decisions at the middle school level. Although the survey did not indicate which tests the districts used, the report noted that statewide tests were among them.

More commonly states use tests as criteria for high school graduation. Seventeen states, as of 2001, make graduation from high school contingent on passing state tests, and another seven are expected to do so by 2008. These numbers are similar to those recorded in the early 1980s at the height of the minimum-competency era. Yet the graduation requirements first implemented in the late 1990s are different than those of the earlier period because the tests are different. Unlike the previous generation of tests, which measured basic reading and mathematical competencies, many of the newer tests tend to measure more complex skills along with, in many cases, knowledge and skills in science, social studies, and other subjects.

In most states with graduation test requirements, the tests are administered in the tenth or eleventh grade, and students typically have multiple opportunities to take the tests before graduation. In some states, such as New York, Tennessee, and Virginia, the graduation tests are end-of-course tests, meaning they measure a particular course content (such as algebra or biology) and are administered at the completion of the course.

States also use tests to reward high-performing students. For most of its existence, the New York State Regents' Examination was an optional test; students who took the test and passed earned a special diploma, called a Regents' Diploma. Beginning in 2000, however, the state required all students to take the examinations. Other states, such as Connecticut, continue to use tests to award special diplomas to students who pass them.

Some states, such as Michigan, provide scholarships for students who perform well on state tests. There, the state awards $2,500 scholarships to students attending Michigan colleges and universities who score in the top level of all four high school tests—mathematics, reading, science, and writing (the scholarships are worth $1,000 for students attending out-of-state institutions).

In addition to the consequences for students, states also use statewide tests to determine consequences for schools. As of 2001 thirty states rate schools based on performance, and half of those states use test scores as the sole measure of performance (the others use indicators such as graduation and attendance rates, in addition to test scores). In Texas, for example, the state rates each school and school district in one of four categories, based on test performance: exemplary, recognized, acceptable/academically acceptable, and low-performing/academically unacceptable. To earn a rating of exemplary, at least 90 percent of students—and 90 percent of each group of students (white, African American, Hispanic, and economically disadvantaged)—must pass the state tests in each subject area. Those with at least an 80 percent pass rate, overall and for each group, are rated recognized; those with a 55 percent pass rate are rated acceptable.

In eighteen states high-performing schools can earn rewards. In some cases, such schools earn rec-

ognition from the state. In North Carolina, for example, the twenty-five elementary and middle schools and ten high schools that register the highest level of growth in performance on state tests, along with those in which 90 percent of students perform at or above grade level, receive a banner to hang in the school and an invitation to a state banquet in their honor. Schools and teachers in high-performing or rapidly improving schools also receive cash awards in some states. In California, for example, 1,000 teachers in the schools with the largest gains on state tests receive a cash bonus of $25,000 each. Another 3,750 teachers receive $10,000 each, and another 7,500 receive $5,000 each. Schools that demonstrate large gains receive awards of $150 per pupil.

States also use test results to intervene in low-performing schools. In 2001 twenty-eight states provide assistance to low-performing schools. In most cases, such assistance includes technical assistance in developing improvement plans and financial assistance or priority for state aid. In some cases, such as in North Carolina and Kentucky, the state sends teams of expert educators to work intensively with schools that perform poorly on state tests. These experts help secure additional support and can recommend changes, such as replacing faculty members.

Twenty states also have the authority to levy sanctions on persistently low-performing schools. Such sanctions include withholding funds, allowing students to transfer to other public schools, "reconstitution," which is the replacing of the faculty and administration, and closure. However, despite this authority, few states have actually imposed sanctions. One that did so was Maryland, where in 2000 the state turned over the management of three elementary schools in Baltimore to a private firm.

The No Child Left Behind Act of 2001 contains a number of provisions to strengthen the role of state tests in placing consequences on schools. Under the law, states are required to set a target for proficiency that all students are expected to reach within twelve years, and to set milestones along the way for schools to reach each year. Schools that fail to make adequate progress would be subject to sanctions, such as allowing students to transfer to other public schools, allowing parents to use funds for supplemental tutoring services, or reconstitution.

Effects of Statewide Testing

The rapid growth in the amount and importance of statewide testing since the 1970s has sparked intense scrutiny about the effects of the tests on students and on classroom practices.

Much of the scrutiny has focused on the effects of tests on students from minority groups who tend to do less well on tests than white students. In several cases, advocates for minority students have challenged tests in court, charging that the testing programs were discriminatory. In one well-known case, African-American high school students in Florida in the 1970s challenged that state's high school graduation test—on which the failure rate for African Americans was ten times the rate for white students—on the grounds that the African Americans had attended segregated schools for years and that denying them diplomas for failing a test preserved the effects of segregation. In its ruling, the U.S. Court of Appeals for the Fifth Circuit upheld the use of the test, but said the state could not withhold diplomas from African-American students until students had no longer attended segregated schools (*Debra P. v. Turlington*).

The court also held that students have a property right to a diploma, but that Florida could use a test to award to diplomas provided that students have adequate notice of the graduation requirement (four years, in that case) and that the test represents a fair measure of what is taught. Although the decision applied only to the states in the Fifth Circuit, the standards the court applied have been cited by other courts and other states since then.

In addition to the legal challenges, state tests have also come under scrutiny for their effects on student behavior—specifically, on the likelihood that students at risk of failing will drop out of school. There is some evidence that dropout rates are higher in states with graduation-test requirements. But it is unclear whether the tests caused the students to decide to drop out of school.

Many testing professionals have also expressed concern that the use of tests to make decisions like promotion or graduation may be inappropriate. Because test scores are not precise measures of a student's knowledge and skills, test professionals warn that any important decision about a student should not rest on a single test score; other relevant information about a student's abilities should be taken into account.

There has been a great deal of research on the effects of state tests on instruction. Since a primary purpose of the state tests is to provide information to improve instruction and learning, this research has been closely watched. The studies have generally found that tests exert a strong influence on classroom practice, but that this influence was not always salutary. On the positive side, the studies found that tests, particularly those with consequences attached to the results, focused the attention of students and educators on academic performance and created incentives for students and teachers to raise test scores. In addition, tests also encouraged teachers to focus on aspects of the curriculum that may have been underrepresented. For example, in states like California that introduced writing tests that assessed students' written prose (as opposed to multiple-choice tests that measured writing abilities indirectly), teachers tended to spend more time asking students to write in class and exposing them to a broader range of writing genres.

On the negative side, studies also found that state tests often encouraged teachers to focus on the material on the test at the expense of other content that may be worthwhile. In states that used exclusively multiple-choice basic skills tests, researchers found that many teachers—particularly those who taught disadvantaged students—spent a great deal of class time on drill and practice of low-level skills, as opposed to instruction on more complex abilities that the tests did not assess. At the same time, researchers found that in some cases teachers devoted a greater proportion of time to tested subjects and less to subjects not tested, like history and the arts, and that teachers spent class time on test-preparation strategies rather than instruction in academic content. The heavy influence of tests on instruction has led some commentators to question whether gains in test scores represent genuine improvements in learning or simply "teaching to the test."

See also: STATES AND EDUCATION; TESTING, *subentry on* STANDARDIZED TESTS AND EDUCATIONAL POLICY.

BIBLIOGRAPHY

EDUCATION WEEK. 2002. "Quality Counts 2002: Building Blocks for Success." *Education Week* 21(17):January 10.

ELMORE, RICHARD F., and ROTHMAN, ROBERT, eds. 1999. *Testing, Teaching, and Learning: A Guide for States and School Districts.* Committee on Title I Testing and Assessment, National Research Council. Washington, DC: National Academy Press.

FUHRMAN, SUSAN H., ed. 2001. *From the Capitol to the Classroom: Standards-Based Reform in the States.* National Society for the Study of Education. Chicago: University of Chicago Press.

HEUBERT, JAY P., and HAUSER, ROBERT M., eds. 1999. *High Stakes: Testing for Tracking, Promotion, and Graduation.* National Research Council, Committee on Appropriate Test Use. Washington, DC: National Academy Press.

LINN, ROBERT L., and HERMAN, JOAN L. 1997. *A Policymaker's Guide to Standards-Led Assessment.* Denver, CO: Education Commission of the States.

OFFICE OF TECHNOLOGY ASSESSMENT. 1992. *Testing in America's Schools: Asking the Right Questions.* Washington, DC: U.S. Government Printing Office.

RAVITCH, DIANE. 1995. *National Standards in American Education: A Citizen's Guide.* Washington, DC: Brookings Institution Press.

ROTHMAN, ROBERT. 1995. *Measuring Up: Standards, Assessment, and School Reform.* San Francisco: Jossey-Bass.

ROBERT ROTHMAN

TEST PREPARATION PROGRAMS, IMPACT OF

Test preparation programs share two common features. First, students are prepared to take one specific test and second, the preparation students receive is systematic. Test preparation programs have been found to have differing degrees of the following characteristics:

1. Instruction that develops the skills and abilities that are to be tested.

2. Practice on problems that resemble those on the test.

3. Instruction and practice with test-taking strategies.

Short-term programs that include primarily this third characteristic are often classified as *coaching*.

There are various shades of gray in this definition. First, the difference between short-term and long-term programs is difficult to quantify. Some researchers have used roughly forty to forty-five hours of student contact time as a threshold, but this amount is not set in stone. Second, within those programs classified as short-term or long-term, the intensity of preparation may differ. One might speculate that a program with twenty hours of student contact time spaced over one week is quite different from one with twenty hours spaced over one month. Finally, test preparation programs may include a mix of the three characteristics listed above. It is unclear what proportion of student contact time must be spent on test-taking strategies before a program can be classified as coaching.

There is little research base from which to draw conclusions about the effectiveness of preparatory programs for achievement tests given to students during their primary and secondary education. This may change as these tests are used for increasingly high-stakes purposes, particularly in the United States. There is a much more substantial research base with regard to the effectiveness of test preparation programs on achievement tests taken for the purpose of postsecondary admissions. The remainder of this review will focus on the effectiveness of this class of programs.

The impact of commercial test preparation programs is a very controversial topic. The controversy hinges in large part upon how program impacts are quantified. Students taking commercial programs are usually given some sort of pretest, a period of preparatory training, and then a posttest. The companies supplying these services will typically quantify impact in terms of average score gains for students from pretest to posttest. Conversely, most research on the subject of test preparation will quantify impact as the average gain of students in the program relative to the average gain of a comparable group of students not in the program. Here the impact of a test preparation program is equal to its estimated causal effect. The latter definition of impact is the more valid one when the aim is to evaluate the costs and benefits of a test preparation program. Program benefits should always be expressed relative to the outcome a person could expect had she chosen *not* to participate in the program. This review takes the approach that program impact can only be assessed by estimating program effects.

Program Effects on College Admissions Tests

Research studies on the effects of admissions test preparation programs have been published periodically since the early 1950s. Most of this research has been concerned with the effect of test preparation on the SAT, the most widely taken test for the purpose of college admission in the United States. A far smaller number of studies have considered the preparation effect on the ACT, another test often required for U.S. college admission. On the main issues, there is a strong consensus in the literature:

- Test preparation programs have a statistically significant effect on the changes of SAT and ACT scores for students taking the test at least twice.

- The magnitude of this effect is relatively small.

How small? The SAT consists of two sections, one verbal and one quantitative, each with a score range from 200 to 800 points. While the section averages of all students taking the SAT each year varies slightly, the standard deviation around these averages is pretty consistently about 100 points. The average effect of test preparation programs on the verbal section of the SAT is probably between 5 and 15 points (.05 and .15 of a standard deviation); the average effect on the quantitative section is probably between 15 and 25 points (.15 and .25 of a standard deviation). The largest effects found in a published study of commercial SAT preparation reported estimates of about 30 points per section. Some unpublished studies have found larger effects, but these have involved very small sample sizes or methodologically flawed research designs.

The ACT consists of four sections: science, math, English, and reading. Scores on each section range from 1 to 36 points and test-takers are also given a composite score for all four sections on the same scale. The standard deviation on the test is usually about 5 points. A smaller body of research, most of it unpublished, has found a test preparation effect (expressed as a percentage of the 5 point standard deviation) of .02 on the composite ACT score, an effect of about .04 to .06 on the math section, an effect of about .08 to .12 on the English section, and a negative effect of .12 to .14 on the reading section.

The importance of how test preparation program effects are estimated cannot be overstated. In most studies, researchers are presented with a group of students who participate in a preparatory program in order to improve their scores on a test they have already taken once. Estimating the effect of the program is a question of causal inference: How much does exposure to systematic test preparation cause a student's test score to increase above the amount it would have increased without exposure to the preparation? Estimating this causal effect is quite different from calculating the average score gain of all students exposed to the program. A number of commercial test preparation companies have advertised—even guaranteed—score gains based on the average gains calculated from students previously participating in their program. This confuses gains with effects. To determine if the program itself has a real effect on test scores one must contrast the gains of the treatment group (students who have taken the program) to the gains of a comparable control group (students who have not taken the program). This would be an example of a controlled study and is the principle underlying the estimation of effects for test preparation programs.

One vexing problem is how to interpret the score gains of students participating in preparatory programs in the absence of a control group. Some researchers have attempted to do this by subtracting the average gain of students participating in a program from the expected gain of the full test-taking population over a given time period. This has been criticized primarily on the grounds that the former group is never a randomly drawn sample from the latter. Students participating in test preparation are in fact often systematically different from the full test-taking population along important characteristics that are correlated with test performance—for example, household income, parental education, and student motivation. This is an example of self-selection bias. Due in part to this bias, uncontrolled studies have been found to consistently arrive at estimates for the effect of test preparation programs that are as much as four to five time greater than those found in controlled studies.

Is Test Preparation More Effective under Certain Programs for Certain People?

In a comprehensive review of studies written between 1950 and 1980 that estimate an effect for test preparation, Samuel Messick and Ann Jungeblut (1981) found evidence of a positive relationship between time spent in a program and the estimated effect on SAT scores. But this relationship was not linear; there were diminishing returns to SAT score changes for time spent in a program beyond 45 hours. Messick and Jungeblut concluded that "the student contact time required to achieve average score increases much greater than 20 to 30 points for both the SAT-V and SAT-M rapidly approaches that of full-time schooling" (p. 215). Since the Messick and Jungeblut review, several reviews of test preparation studies have been written by researchers using the statistical technique known as meta-analysis. Use of this technique allows for the synthesis of effect estimates from a wide range of studies conducted at different points in time. The findings from these reviews suggest that there is little systematic relationship between the observable characteristics of test preparation programs and the estimated effect on test scores. In particular, once a study's quality was taken into consideration, there was at best a very weak association between program duration and test score improvement.

There is also mixed evidence as to whether test preparation programs are more effective for particular subgroups of test-takers. Many of the studies that demonstrate interactions between the racial/ethnic and socioeconomic characteristics of test-takers and the effects of test preparation suffer from very small and self-selected samples. Because commercial test preparation programs charge a fee, sometimes a substantial one, most students participating in such programs tend to be socioeconomically advantaged. In one of the few studies with a nationally representative sample of test-takers, test preparation for the SAT was found to be most effective for students coming from high socioeconomic backgrounds. A similar association was not found among students who took a preparatory program for the ACT.

Conclusions

The differential impact of test preparation programs on student subgroups is an area that merits further research. In addition, a theory describing why the pedagogical practices used within commercial test preparatory programs in the twenty-first century would be expected to increase test scores has, with few exceptions, not been adequately explicated or studied in a controlled setting at the item level. In any case, after more than five decades of research on the issue, there is little doubt that commercial preparatory programs, by advertising average score gains without reference to a control group, are misleading prospective test-takers about the benefits of their product. The costs of such programs are high, both in terms of money and in terms of opportunity. For

consumers of test preparation programs, these benefits and costs should be weighed carefully.

See also: COLLEGE ADMISSIONS TESTS.

BIBLIOGRAPHY

BECKER, BETSY JANE. 1990. "Coaching for the Scholastic Aptitude Test: Further Synthesis and Appraisal." *Review of Educational Research* 60(3):373–417.

BOND, LLOYD. 1989. "The Effects of Special Preparation on Measures of Scholastic Ability." In *Educational Measurement,* ed. Robert L. Linn. New York: American Council on Education and Macmillan.

BRIGGS, DEREK C. 2001. "The Effect of Admissions Test Preparation: Evidence from NELS:88." *Chance* 14(1):10–18.

COLE, NANCY. 1982. "The Implications of Coaching for Ability Testing." In *Ability Testing: Uses, Consequences, and Controversies. Part II: Documentation Section,* ed. Alexandra K. Wigdor and Wendell R. Gardner. Washington, DC: National Academy Press.

DERSIMONIAN, ROBERTA, and LAIRD, NANCY M. 1983. "Evaluating the Effect of Coaching on SAT Scores: A Meta-Analysis." *Harvard Educational Review* 53:1–15.

EVANS, FRANKLIN, and PIKE, LEWIS. 1973. "The Effects of Instruction for Three Mathematics Item Formats." *Journal of Educational Measurement* 10(4):257–272.

JACKSON, REX. 1980. "The Scholastic Aptitude Test: A Response to Slack and Porter's 'Critical Appraisal.'" *Harvard Educational Review* 50(3):382–391.

KULIK, JAMES A.; BANGERT-DROWNS, ROBERT L.; and KULIK, CHEN-LIN. 1984. "Effectiveness of Coaching for Aptitude Tests." *Psychological Bulletin* 95:179–188.

MESSICK, SAMUEL, and JUNGEBLUT, ANN. 1981. "Time and Method in Coaching for the SAT." *Psychological Bulletin* 89:191–216.

POWERS, DONALD. 1986. "Relations of Test Item Characteristics to Test Preparation/Test Practice Effects: A Quantitative Summary." *Psychological Bulletin* 100(1):67–77.

POWERS, DONALD. 1993. "Coaching for the SAT: A Summary of the Summaries and an Update."

Educational Measurement: Issues and Practice (summer): 24–39.

POWERS, DONALD, and ROCK, DON. 1999. "Effects of Coaching on SAT I: Reasoning Test Scores." *Journal of Educational Measurement* 36(2):93–118.

SENOWITZ, MICHAEL; BERNHARDT, KENNETH; and KNAIN, D. MATTHEW. 1982. "An Analysis of the Impact of Commercial Test Preparation Courses on SAT Scores." *American Educational Research Journal* 19(3):429–441.

SLACK, WARNER V., and PORTER, DOUGLASS. 1980. "The Scholastic Aptitude Test: A Critical Appraisal." *Harvard Education Review* 50:51–175.

DEREK C. BRIGGS

NATIONAL ACHIEVEMENT TESTS, INTERNATIONAL

National testing of elementary and secondary students exists in most industrialized countries. Each country's national examinations are based on national curricula and content standards. The difference in weight and consequence of the exams varies tremendously from country to country, as does the use of exams at various levels of education. In France, Germany, Great Britain, Italy, and Japan, examinations at the lower secondary or elementary level are required for admission to academic secondary schools. In the United States, there is a more informal system of tracking students into academic, vocational, or general studies within the same secondary school. In Japan and Korea secondary students take nationally administered examinations that determine their postsecondary placement. Top-scoring students attend the most prestigious public universities. In France the baccalaureate examinations are given to students at academic secondary schools (the *lycée*) as exit examinations and also to determine university placement. In Germany a similar distinction is made between academic and vocational secondary school, and passing the *Abitur* (exit examination from *Gymnasium* or academic secondary school) allows students to continue on to university-level coursework. In Great Britain students study for their A-level examinations for university placement. Finally, in Italy students must pass exit examinations at both the lower- and upper-secondary levels. At the secondary level, the *Esami di maturita* impacts university attendance or employment.

In the United States the SAT (once called either the Scholastic Assessment Test or the Scholastic Aptitude Test) and the ACT (the American College Test) are required for entrance into the more prestigious and rigorous colleges and universities. This system closely mirrors that of Japan, Korea, France, and Germany with the exception of the lack of federal governing. However, the SAT and ACT are not meant to monitor student performance over time and are not national tests of student performance, as are the aforementioned tests specific to other countries.

In contrast to the nations described above, the United States has no national system of education and as such no national or federal assessment that has an impact on students at the individual level. The system of public education in the United States is characterized by a high degree of decentralization. The Tenth Amendment to the U.S. Constitution prohibits direct federal government involvement in education; the provision of education is a state-level function. States and local school districts are the entities charged with policy and curriculum decisions. Nonetheless, there has been a trend toward increased measures of national performance for the past three to four decades. Although the United States has no national curriculum, given the truly global nature of society, curricula are converging in similarity within the United States as well as internationally.

Current Trends in Educational Assessment

In 1965 Congress passed the Elementary and Secondary Education Act, which authorized federal support for the education of disadvantaged and handicapped children. The Elementary and Secondary Education Act (ESEA) made clear the federal government's commitment to equal education for all by mandating fairness criteria for disadvantaged and minority students. With ESEA standardized testing became entrenched in American education, as it required regular testing in schools that receive federal funding for disadvantaged students.

A major surge toward education reform can be linked to the 1983 Department of Education sponsored report, *A Nation at Risk*. While the National Assessment of Educational Progress (NAEP) long-term assessment showed gains for every age group between 1971 and 1992, declining SAT scores drew national attention with pronouncements that the education system in the United States was failing its students and society as a whole.

In 1989 President George Bush and the nation's governors established a set of six national education goals to be achieved by all students in the United States by the year 2000. These six goals plus two more were enacted into law as part of President Bill Clinton's Goals 2000: Educate America Act (1994). The goals stated that by the year 2000, all students would come to school ready to learn, high school graduation rates would increase, students would demonstrate competency in challenging subject matter and would be prepared for life-long learning, U.S. students would be first in the world in science and mathematics, American adults would be literate and productive citizens, schools would be drug- and violence-free, teachers would be more prepared, and parental involvement in education would rise. The education goals set forth by President George Bush and furthered in strength and number by President Bill Clinton with the Educate America Act increased the demands on accountability systems in education at both the state and national levels.

The National Assessment of Educational Progress had been monitoring the nation's student achievement for many years. The new reforms and new goals required more of the NAEP than it could provide. In 1994 NAEP responsibilities and breadth were extended with the reauthorization of NAEP through the Improving America's Schools Act of 1994. As the National Research Council states in its 1999 publication *High Stakes: Testing for Tracking, Promotion, and Graduation,* "recent education summits, national and local reform efforts, the inception of state NAEP and the introduction of performance standards have taken NAEP from a simple monitor of student achievement—free from political influence and notice—into the public spotlight" (p. 25). Linking federal funding with the development of performance-based standards and assessments and accountability only enhanced the attention and emphasis place on the NAEP.

In 2001 President George W. Bush proposed tying federal education dollars to specific performance-based initiatives including mandatory participation in annual state NAEP assessments in reading and mathematics and high-stakes accountability at the state level. The emphasis in Bush's reform "blueprint" is on closing the achievement gap for minority and disadvantaged students. To this end, President Bush signed into law Public Law 107-110

(H.R.1), the No Child Left Behind Act of 2001. The Act contains four major provisions for education reform: stronger accountability for results, expanded flexibility and local control, expanded options for parents, and an emphasis on teaching methods that have been proven to work. Direct accountability based on NAEP is not part of the final public law.

As the nation turned toward an increasing reliance on student assessment so too did the states. States began implementing minimum competency examinations in the 1970s. By 1990 more than forty states in the nation required some form of minimum competency examination (MCE) before awarding the high school diploma. For example, Massachusetts tenth graders are required to pass the Massachusetts Comprehensive Assessment System (MCAS) prior to earning a high school diploma. In Kentucky graduating seniors can distinguish themselves by not only fulfilling the requirements for graduation and a high school diploma but by also fulfilling the requirements for the Commonwealth Diploma that include successful completion of advanced placement credits. Students in Texas must pass secondary-level exit examinations before graduating high school. In North Carolina students must pass exit examinations as part of the requirement set for obtaining a high school diploma. The trend favors the implementation of more examinations with consequences for states at the national level, and for students at the state level.

National Examinations in the United States

In the United States, there are two sets of "national" examinations. The first set includes the SAT, the American College Test (ACT), and the Advanced Placement (AP) examinations, which allow high school seniors to earn college credits for advanced level classes. The second set is known as the National Assessment of Educational Progress (NAEP). These tests have come to be known as "The Nation's Report Card." The NAEP is a federally funded system of assessing the standard of education in the nation. It is the only nationally representative test. It is also the only test given that selects a representative sample of U.S. students, testing the same standard of knowledge over time. It provides no measure of individual student, school, or school district performance.

The National Assessment of Educational Progress (NAEP)

The NAEP is a federally funded national examination that regularly tests a national sample of American students. The National Center for Education Statistics (NCES) of the Department of Education has primary responsibility for the NAEP. The Educational Testing Service (ETS) and Westat currently administer the NAEP. Finally, the NAEP is governed by an independent organization, the National Assessment Governing Board (NAGB) charged with setting policies for the NAEP.

The NAEP has three distinct parts: a long-term trend assessment of nine-, thirteen-, and seventeen-year-olds, a main assessment of the nation, and the state trial assessments. The long-term assessment has been administered to nine-, thirteen-, and seventeen-year-old students every four years since 1969. The main assessment and trial state assessments began in 1990, testing fourth, eighth, and twelfth grades in various subjects. NAEP allows trend evaluations as well as comparisons of performance between groups of students.

NAEP long-term assessment. The NAEP long-term assessment is the only test based on a nationally representative sample of students. It is the only test that can be used to track long-term trends in student achievement. The tests have been given to national samples of nine-, thirteen-, and seventeen-year-old students and have maintained a set of questions such that the results in any given year can be compared to any other year. The long-term or trend assessments are designed to track academic performance over time.

The early tests were given in science, mathematics, and reading, and were administered every four years until 1988 and more frequently after 1988. Writing tests that can be compared over years were given in 1984, and geography, history, civics, and the arts have been tested more recently. Until the early 1980s NAEP results were reported by question, indicating the percentage of students answering a particular question correctly over time.

Overall NAEP scores show small to modest gains. From the early 1970s to 1996, gains occurred in math, reading, and science for nine- and thirteen-year-old students, and in math and reading for seventeen-year-old students. The gains in science were small, approximately .10 standard deviations or three percentile points, for all age groups. Math gains for nine- and thirteen-year-old students were larger, between .15 and .30 standard deviations. Evidence suggests that these trends mask differentiated trends by race and/or ethnic groups.

During the same time period (1970–1996), substantial gains occurred for both Hispanic and black students and for lower-scoring students. For instance, black gains between .30 and .80 standard deviations occurred for almost all subjects in all age groups.

NAEP main assessment and trial state assessments. Between 1984 and 1987 the NAEP underwent an "overhaul" in order to accommodate the increasing demands being placed on it. First, the main assessment and state assessments were added to the NAEP. Second, new instruments were designed to measure not only what students know but also what students *should* know. Third, test items in every subject area were based on rigorous, challenging content standards. Fourth, NAEP's independent governing board, the National Assessment Governing Board (NAGB), identified performance standards or achievement levels at advanced, proficient, basic, below basic knowledge levels.

Main NAEP, or the main assessment, is administered to a nationally representative sample of students, testing overall student achievement. Unlike the long term NAEP, main NAEP test items are content-based, reflecting current curriculum and instructional practices. Test items are designed to test student performance in relation to the national education goals and to monitor short-term trends in academic achievement. The main assessment is given in mathematics, reading, writing, and science to fourth, eighth, and twelfth graders at intervals of two years.

The state-level NAEP is administered to representative samples of students within states. The assessment items are the same as those on the main assessment. The trial state assessment and the main assessment are given in mathematics, reading, writing and science at intervals of two years or more beginning in 1990. Between 1990 and 2000 there were seven math tests: an eighth grade assessment in 1990, and fourth and eighth grade exams in 1992, 1996, and 2000. Reading tests have been administered to fourth graders in 1992, 1994, and 1998. In 1998 an eighth grade assessment in reading was administered for the first time.

Significant short-term trends are being made nationally. Statistically significant trends can be seen across the 1990–1992, 1992–1994, and 1992–1996 testing cycles. The largest gains occurred for eighth grade math tests, where composite gains between 1990 and 1996 are about .25 standard deviation, or eight percentile points. Smaller gains of approximately .10 standard deviation or three percentile points occurred in fourth grade math from 1992 to 1996. Reading scores show a decline of approximately .10 standard deviations per year between 1992 and 1994.

The estimated score gains in mathematics indicate a trend of .03 standard deviations or one percentile point per year made between 1990 and 1996 in math across states. About three-quarters of states show consistent, statistically significant annual gains in mathematics between 1990 and 1996. The rate of change varies dramatically across states, from being flat to gains of .06 to .07 standard deviations per year. The sizes of the later gains are remarkable and far above the historical gains of .01 standard deviation per year on the long-term assessment. These results do not change when the fourth and eighth grade 1998 NAEP Reading Assessment and 2000 Mathematics Assessment are added to the sample. (This trend estimates control for student demographics and home environments. A consensus has been reached in the education research community that school systems—here, states—should be judged on score differences and trends beyond the family characteristics that they face.)

International Assessment of Student Performance

International comparisons of student achievement are of growing concern given the trend toward a more global economy. Poor United States performance on international examinations is inextricably linked in the minds of Americans of decreasing economic competitiveness. Part of the debate over voluntary national testing includes the question of linking the NAEP to international tests of achievement as well as to state achievement tests.

Third International Mathematics and Science Study. In 1995 and 1999 the International Association for the Evaluation of Education Assessment (IEA) administered the Third International Mathematics and Science Study (TIMSS) to students in grades 3–4, 7–8 and the last year of secondary schooling. The TIMSS was an ambitious effort. More than forty-one countries and half a million students participated. Cross-country comparisons place the

United States in the bottom of the distribution in student performance on the TIMSS. International assessments galvanize support for educational improvement. However, recent evidence suggests the overall poor performance of the United States hides the above average performance of several states: Connecticut, Maine, Massachusetts, Indiana, Iowa, North Dakota, Michigan, Minnesota, Vermont and Wisconsin, all of which are states with higher than average levels of median family income and parental educational attainment.

Programme for International Student Assessment. In 2000 the Programme for International Student Assessment (PISA) administered examinations of reading, mathematics, and science literacy. Literacy is defined in terms of content knowledge, process ability, and the application of knowledge and skills. Thirty-two countries participated in PISA 2000 with more than 250,000 students representing 17 million students enrolled in secondary education in the participating countries.

The PISA assessments differ from the TIMSS in that

> "the assessment materials in TIMSS were constructed on the basis of an analysis of the intended curriculum in each participating country, so as to cover the core material common to the curriculum in the majority of participating countries. The assessment materials in PISA 2000 covered the range of skills and competencies that were, in the respective assessment domains, considered to be crucial to an individual's capacity to fully participate in, and contribute meaningfully to, a successful modern society." (Organisation for Economic Co-operation and Development, p. 27.)

The latter assessment form reflects the growing trends in curricula that emphasize the same thing: training students for life-long learning.

PISA performance in reading, mathematics and science literacy is measured on a zero to 500 scale with a standard deviation of 100. The United States performed at the OECD mean score in reading, mathematics, and scientific literacy. The performance of the United States was better in reading than mathematics; reading and scientific literacy were not statistically different. The United States was outperformed in each literacy domain by Japan, Korea, the United Kingdom, Finland, and New Zealand.

Conclusions

Although there are no federal-level examinations in the United States and there is a distinction between national testing, national standards, and federal testing and standards, the federal government is able to indirectly influence what is taught is public schools. First, the adoption of national goals for education provides states with a centralized framework for what students should know. Second, the federal government awards money to states to develop curriculum and assessments based on these goals. And third, states that align their curriculum and testing to the NAEP achieve higher overall performance measures on the NAEP. All of these and more make the National Assessment of Educational Progress truly a "national" examination.

See also: ASSESSMENTS, *subentry on* NATIONAL ASSESSMENT OF EDUCATIONAL ACHIEVEMENT; INTERNATIONAL ASSESSMENTS, *subentry on* INTERNATIONAL ASSOCIATION FOR THE EVALUATION OF EDUCATIONAL ACHIEVEMENT.

BIBLIOGRAPHY

ECKSTEIN, MAX A. and NOAH, HAROLD J., eds. 1992. *Examinations: Comparative and International Studies.* New York: Pergamon Press.

GRISSMER, DAVID W., and FLANAGAN, ANN E. 1998. "Exploring Rapid Test Score Gains in Texas and North Carolina." Commissions paper, Washington, DC: National Education Goals Panel.

GRISSMER, DAVID W.; FLANAGAN, ANN E.; and WILLIAMSON, STEPHANIE. 1998. "Why Did Black Test Scores Rise Rapidly in the 1970s and 1980s?" In *The Black-White Test Score Gap,* ed. Christopher Jenks and Meredith Phillips. Washington, DC: Brookings Institution Press.

GRISSMER, DAVID W., et al. 2000. *Improving Student Achievement: What State NAEP Scores Tell Us.* Santa Monica, CA: RAND.

HAUSER, ROBERT M. 1998. "Trends in Black-White Test Score Differentials: Uses and Misuses of NAEP/SAT Data." In *The Rising Curve: Long-Term Changes in IQ and Related Measures,* ed. Ulric Neisser. Washington, DC: American Psychological Association.

HEDGES, LARRY V., and NOWELL, AMY. 1998. "Group Differences in Mental Test Scores: Mean Differences, Variability and Talent." In *The Black-White Test Score Gap,* ed. Christopher Jenks and Meredith Phillips. Washington, DC: Brookings Institution Press.

INTERNATIONAL ASSOCIATION FOR THE EVALUATION OF EDUCATIONAL ACHIEVEMENT, TIMSS INTERNATIONAL STUDY CENTER. 1996. *Mathematics Achievement in the Middle School Years: IEA's Third International Mathematics and Science Study TIMSS.* Chestnut Hill, MA: Boston College.

NATIONAL RESEARCH COUNCIL. 1999. *Evaluation of the Voluntary National Tests, Year: Final Report.* Washington, DC: National Academy Press

NATIONAL RESEARCH COUNCIL. 1999. *Grading the Nation's Report Card: Evaluating NAEP and Transforming the Assessment of Educational Progress.* Washington, DC: National Academy Press.

NATIONAL RESEARCH COUNCIL. 1999. *High Stakes: Testing for Tracking, Promotion, and Graduation.* Washington, DC: National Academy Press.

NATIONAL RESEARCH COUNCIL. 1999. *Uncommon Measures: Equivalence and Linkage Among Educational Tests.* Washington, DC: National Academy Press.

ORGANISATION FOR ECONOMIC CO-OPERATION AND DEVELOPMENT, PROGRAMME FOR INTERNATIONAL STUDENT ASSESSMENT. 2001. *Knowledge and Skills for Life: First Results from PISA 2000.* Paris, France: Organisation for Economic Co-operation and Development.

RAVITCH, DIANE. 1995. *National Standards in American Education: A Citizens Guide.* Washington, DC: Brookings Institution Press.

ROTHSTEIN, RICHARD. 1998. *The Way We Were? The Myths and Realities of American's Student Achievement.* New York: The Century Foundation Press.

U.S. DEPARTMENT OF EDUCATION, OFFICE OF EDUCATIONAL RESEARCH AND IMPROVEMENT, NATIONAL CENTER FOR EDUCATION STATISTICS. 1995. *Progress of Education in the United States of America—1990 through 1994.* Washington, DC: U.S. Department of Education.

U.S. DEPARTMENT OF EDUCATION, OFFICE OF EDUCATIONAL RESEARCH AND IMPROVEMENT, NATIONAL CENTER FOR EDUCATION STATISTICS. 1997. *NAEP 1996 Trends in Academic Progress: Achievement of U.S. Students.* Washington, DC: U.S. Department of Education.

U.S. DEPARTMENT OF EDUCATION, OFFICE OF EDUCATIONAL RESEARCH AND IMPROVEMENT, NATIONAL CENTER FOR EDUCATION STATISTICS. 1998. *Linking the National Assessment of Educational Progress (NAEP) and the Third International Mathematics and Science Study (TIMSS): Eighth-Grade Results.* Washington, DC: U.S. Department of Education.

INTERNET RESOURCES

EXECUTIVE OFFICE OF THE WHITE HOUSE. 1998. "Goals 2000: Reforming Education to Improve Student Achievement." <www.ed.gov/pubs/G2KReforming>.

EXECUTIVE OFFICE OF THE WHITE HOUSE. 2002. "No Child Left Behind Act of 2001." <www.ed.gov/legislation/ESEA02/107-110.pdf>.

ANN E. FLANAGAN

INTERNATIONAL STANDARDS OF TEST DEVELOPMENT

Standardized tests are used in important ways at all levels of education, and such tests can help educators and policymakers make important decisions about students, teachers, programs, and institutions. It is therefore critical that these tests, and the information that they provide, meet the highest professional and technical standards. Fortunately, the experts who set policies for testing programs, who design and develop tests, and who make use of the scores and other reports adhere to a number of rigorous and publicly available standards, three of which merit a brief summary.

Code of Fair Testing Practices in Education

The *Code of Fair Testing Practices in Education* (the *Code*) is one of the most widely distributed and referenced documents in educational testing. It contains standards related to the development, selection, and reporting of results of assessments in education. Written in nontechnical language, it provides test-takers, parents, teachers, and others with clear statements of what they are entitled to receive from those who develop tests, as well as from those who use test scores to help make decisions.

The *Code* has been endorsed by the leading testing organizations in the United States, including the major nonprofit companies (e.g., the College Board, the Educational Testing Service, ACT Inc.) and the large commercial test publishers (e.g., the California Test Bureau, Harcourt Educational Measurement, Riverside Publishing) who account for a large share of all school district and state-level tests. The *Code* has also been endorsed by major professional organizations in the field of education, whose members make extensive use of tests, including the American Counseling Association, the American Educational Research Association, the American Psychological Association, the American Speech-Language-Hearing Association, the National Association of School Psychologists, and the National Association of Test Directors.

As a result of the widespread acceptance of the *Code,* users of standardized educational tests that are developed by major testing companies can be confident that conscientious efforts have been made to produce tests that yield fair and accurate results when used as intended by the test makers.

Standards for Educational and Psychological Testing

The basic reference source for technical standards in educational testing is *Standards for Educational and Psychological Testing* (the *Standards*). Since 1950, this document has been prepared in a series of editions by three organizations, the American Educational Research Association (AERA), the American Psychological Association (APA), and the National Council on Measurement in Education (NCME). It is a resource that is very useful for individuals with training in psychometrics, but is not very readable by those without such specialized training. Any team involved in the development of a testing program needs to include at least one person with the expertise necessary to understand and assure adherence to the *Standards.*

ATP Guidelines for Computer-Based Testing

As useful as the AERA/APA/NCME Standards are as a resource for technical testing standards, they give relatively little attention to one of the most important trends in testing, the growth of computer-based testing. The Association of Test Publishers (ATP) has addressed this "standards vacuum" by creating the *ATP Guidelines for Computer-Based Testing* (the *Guidelines*). The ATP is the industry association for test publishing, with over 100 member companies, an active program of publishing, a highly regarded annual meeting focused on computer-based testing, and a set of productive divisions.

The *Guidelines* address six general areas related to technology-based test delivery systems:

- Planning and Design
- Test Development
- Test Administration
- Scoring and Score Reporting
- Statistical/Psychometric Analyses
- Communications to Test Takers and Others

The intent of the *Guidelines* is to define the "best practices" that are desirable for all testing systems, without reference to the particular hardware or operating system employed for testing. The fast growth of computer-based testing in education will make these *Guidelines* especially valuable to test makers and test users.

See also: INTERNATIONAL ASSESSMENTS.

BIBLIOGRAPHY

AMERICAN EDUCATIONAL RESEARCH ASSOCIATION; AMERICAN PSYCHOLOGICAL ASSOCIATION; and NATIONAL COUNCIL ON MEASUREMENT IN EDUCATION. 1999. *Standards for Educational and Psychological Testing.* Washington, DC: American Educational Research Association.

ASSOCIATION OF TEST PUBLISHERS. 2000. *Guidelines for Computer-Based Testing.* Washington, DC: Association of Test Publishers.

JOINT COMMITTEE ON TESTING PRACTICES. 1988. *Code of Fair Testing Practices in Education.* Washington, DC: Joint Committee on Testing Practices.

JOHN FREMER

TEXTBOOKS

OVERVIEW
  Joseph P. Farrell
SCHOOL TEXTBOOKS IN THE UNITED STATES
  Daniel Tanner

OVERVIEW

Historical records indicate that for as long as systems of writing and formal schools have existed (whether for secular, religious, or other purposes), textbooks, in one form or another, have also existed, whether on clay tablets; scrolls; bound sheets of papyrus, vellum, or parchment; or modern mass-produced books. There are records of textbooks being used in schools in ancient Greece, Rome, China, India, Sumer, Egypt, and elsewhere. Until the invention in the mid-fifteenth century of printing with moveable type, such textbooks were hand-produced, very rare, and available only to a very small, and generally very privileged, minority of people. The ability to mass-produce books led to an ever-increasing demand for, and supply of, formal schooling, which in turn produced an ever-increasing demand for books specially designed for schools. Thus, the mass-produced textbook for mass schooling was first developed in Europe. Following the patterns of European colonization (and in noncolonized areas through cultural and technological borrowing) it spread to much of the rest of the world. As formerly colonized areas achieved independence, they replaced textbooks originating in the colonizing nation with locally created textbooks reflecting their own national beliefs, aspirations, and creations.

Soon after the United States achieved independence, locally written textbooks began to be created to replace those originating in England, including Noah Webster's speller, grammar, and reader—in which he introduced U.S. writings, history, and geography. As Latin American nations achieved independence from Spain and Portugal in the early 1800s, a similar pattern of replacing European textbooks with locally produced versions occurred. When Canada gained independence from the United Kingdom in 1867, a similar challenge to "localize" textbooks was faced and met. During the great wave of decolonization in Africa and Asia during the late 1940s through the 1960s, the then newly independent nations attempted to alter their textbooks to reflect their independent status. Most recently, with the disintegration of the former Soviet Union (and Yugoslavia) and the collapse of its domination of its former satellite states, there has been yet another wave of changing textbooks to reflect new national realities and aspirations.

These historical changes have never been simple and superficial. For example, as the nations of formerly French West Africa decolonized, they not only had to change their texts to reflect local history, but had also to change commonly used primary readers, which began with the sentence: "All of our ancestors were Gauls." Similarly, in the former Eastern European satellite states, not only did such obvious candidates as history, politics, and economics textbooks have to be changed, but stories in primary readers that glorified "kind Uncle Lenin" or "heroic Young Pioneers" also had to be altered, as did word problems in mathematics texts that reflected a reality that had disappeared (e.g., arithmetic problems that referred to collective farmers or workers in state enterprises). When Canada became independent, the country changed its textbooks to reflect the Canadian view that the War of 1812 was won neither by the United Kingdom nor the United States, but by Canada, since that nation had successfully resisted invasion and attempts at annexation by its neighbor to the south.

Two key points emerge from this history: (1) textbooks are as universal as formal mass schooling—where there are schools there are textbooks (except in some nations so poor that they cannot yet afford universal textbook provision); and (2) textbooks are not just pedagogical instruments—they are intensely political documents whose content reflects a given vision of a people, their history and position in the world, and their values and aspirations. Almost everywhere in the world, disputes over textbooks have been common, heated, and very difficult to resolve. While these disputes are formally over curriculum content, since textbooks basically "carry" the curriculum, the arguments tend to focus on the texts themselves. Thus, arguments in North America about how the curriculum should deal with subjects such as the place of women or racial minorities in society or organized labor, end up as arguments about the place and presence of these groups in the pages and pictures of textbooks. Similarly, arguments about the relative presence of creationism versus evolution as core explanations in science in the curriculum end up as arguments about their presence or absence in textbooks, and arguments in Japan about how to treat that nation's role in World War II in the curriculum turn into disputes about how this role should be depicted in the prescribed textbooks.

Policy Issues

There are two basic policy issues regarding textbooks that all nations face: (1) private versus public publishing, and (2) local versus international control and publishing.

Private versus public publishing. In all nations, governments tend to intervene strongly in the textbook development and provision process. Even in the most market-oriented economies, such as the United States and much of Europe, government agencies (whether at the central, state, provincial or local level) attempt to control and regulate textbook content and provision. In other words, in this field there is no such thing, empirically, as a wholly free market. Nations differ in the degree, locus, and mechanisms of state intervention, and in the extent to which the state formally "owns" the various agencies of design, production, and distribution of textbooks. In some nations, such as the United States, private publishers handle all three of these stages almost exclusively. In other cases the state presence at all three stages is overwhelming. It is very common for both private and public sectors to co-exist at one or more of these stages. In a 1989 study of twenty-one developing nations, Joseph Farrell and Stephen Heyneman found ten different patterns or combinations of public and private sector participation across the three stages. Clearly there is no general, or even particularly common, pattern. In most cases pedagogical and economic pragmatism, in relation to particular national histories and circumstances, have been the guide to these choices, rather than an ideological predisposition toward either the public or private sectors.

Local versus international control and publishing. Since all nations insist upon state influence on school curricula, and hence on textbook content, it is often assumed that a logical extension is that textbook design, production, and distribution must all be done locally, whether by private firms or government agencies. However, that connection has never been as tight as sometimes assumed, and it appears to be getting looser. Even in a nation like the United States, which is large and wealthy enough to support a large multi-firm private textbook publishing industry, in the early twenty-first century almost all textbooks are manufactured (printed and bound) off shore, in low-wage developing nations. For subject areas that "travel well" across cultures (e.g. sciences, mathematics, technology), there has always been considerable international trade in textbooks and textbook publishing, especially for postprimary levels of study. In earlier years this reflected patterns of European colonization. More recently it has reflected the fact that, except in such inherently localized subjects as national history and geography, curricula in most nations have become very similar, leading to textbooks that are quite similar except for the language of instruction. This makes it increasingly easy, and pedagogically and economically sensible, to borrow, adapt, and translate textbook sections, or entire books, for different nations.

This international transfer of textbook material is commonly accomplished through various forms of licensing and contractual arrangements among publishers, and increasingly frequently through plagiarism and international copyright violations. Major centers of international textbook publishing and export include not only former colonial powers such as France and the United Kingdom, but developing nations such as India, Colombia, and Mexico. Even in very large and wealthy nations, textbook publishers routinely borrow from, adapt, and translate material from textbooks already published elsewhere. A lesson learned is that good ideas about how best to communicate and enhance the learning of bodies of knowledge and skill can be found almost anywhere in the world.

Many smaller and/or poorer nations, especially those using languages of instruction that are not widely spoken and read, are finding quite inventive ways to combine local curriculum control with various combinations of local and international publishing in order to provide textbooks for their students that are locally relevant, of high quality, and affordable. For example, a group of relatively poor British Commonwealth nations has a contractual relationship with an international publisher that has produced a set of history books that combine common chapters on world and regional history with specific locally designed chapters on each individual nation's history. By combining local knowledge with international technical expertise, they have produced books that are locally relevant, pedagogically and technically well designed, and relatively inexpensive due to the resultant economies of scale in production. The distinction between local and international in terms of curriculum content and technical production is increasingly difficult to draw cleanly, and many nations are learning that one can combine local curricular control with various combinations of local and international publishing.

Defining the Textbook

What exactly is a textbook? In one sense the answer will seem obvious to anyone who has gone to school: it is that printed and bound artifact with which one was provided, or which one had to buy, for each year and course of study. It contained all of the core content and all sorts of exercises and study questions at the end of sections or chapters. However, the textbook is not that simple.

First of all, textbooks are not at all like other kinds of books. Except in some subject areas in secondary school and in many subject areas at the university level, they are not the product of the creativity and imagination of individual authors. Textbooks are commissioned and written by authors or firms who are hired to write to specifications set by whatever authorities develop the standard curriculum for a system of schools. That is, the curriculum is set, then from it a set of specifications for textbooks are developed, and these specifications are then either delivered to a state textbook agency for book development and production or taken up by private sector publishers for textbook development, according to the specifications, in a competitive market. Indeed, it is commonly the case, certainly in North America, that the authors whose names appear on a textbook have had only a marginal input into the entire book development process. Quite often they are names selected by publishers for market appeal. This is a far cry from the days of Noah Webster, whose textbooks essentially set the curriculum for many schools in the new nation. In the early twenty-first century, authors do not set the curriculum—they write to a curriculum set by state educational authorities. This process has tended to produce textbooks that are formulaic and uninteresting.

Secondly, the boundaries between textbooks and other forms of learning materials have become increasingly blurred in recent years. Early in the development of mass formal schooling (and still the case in many poor nations), the textbook was the primary, or the only, carrier of the set curriculum. As wealth and technology have advanced, other learning materials have appeared in classrooms, to the point where it is often difficult to distinguish between the textbook and all the other forms of learning materials. In the early twenty-first century, schools (or school systems) in wealthy nations typically acquire not simply a book or set of books, but a carefully (one hopes) designed set of all sorts of learning materials, including basic texts, teachers' guides, audiovisual material, charts, maps, student exercise and homework sheets, power-point presentations and computer-access resources, and future resources produced by advancing technology. *Learning materials packages* are increasingly replacing the basic textbook.

But at the core there remains that basic book, which has been there in schoolrooms around the world for several millennia, for good or ill. Research in wealthy nations indicates that even with all of the other learning materials now available, the vast majority of teachers continue to rely heavily on the textbook as their core teaching resource. Recent research in developing nations indicates that the single most important investment poor nations can make for improving the learning of their children is increasing textbook availability and quality. Research regarding the contribution to learning of all the new learning materials is much less clear. The value of all the new learning materials, in nations rich or poor, is less well proven. The content of textbooks is frequently controversial, its forms of presentation often subject to much debate, and which groups actually determine its form and content is a subject of much controversy, but even with all that is available to them, teachers and students throughout history have depended upon this seemingly simple learning tool.

See also: CURRICULUM, SCHOOL; MEDIA AND LEARNING; READING, *subentry on* LEARNING FROM TEXT; WEBSTER, NOAH.

BIBLIOGRAPHY

ALTBACH, PHILIP G. 1983. "Key Issues of Textbook Provision in the Third World." *Prospects* 13(3):315–325.

ALTBACH, PHILIP G. and KELLY, GAIL P., eds. 1988. *Textbooks in the Third World: Policy Context and Content.* New York: Garland.

BENEVOT, AARON; CHA, YUN KYUNG; KAMENS, DAVID; MEYER, JOHN; and WONG, SUK-YING. 1991. "Knowledge for the Masses: World Models and National Curricula, 1920–1986." *American Sociological Review* 56:85–100.

ELLIOTT, DAVID L., and WOODWARD, ARTHUR, eds. 1990. *Textbooks and Schooling in the United States* (89th Yearbook of the National Society for the Study of Education). Chicago: National Society for the Study of Education.

FARRELL, JOSEPH P. 2001. *Transforming the Forms of Formal Primary Schooling: The Emergence of a Radically Alternative Model of Schooling.* Paper presented at the annual meeting of the Comparative and International Education Society, Washington, DC.

FARRELL, JOSEPH P., and HEYNEMAN, STEPHEN P. 1989. *Textbooks in the Developing World.* Washington, DC: The World Bank.

WOODWARD, ARTHUR; ELLIOTT, DAVID L.; and NAGEL, KATHLEEN CARTER. 1988. *Textbooks in School and Society: An Annotated Bibliography and Guide to Research.* New York: Garland.

JOSEPH P. FARRELL

SCHOOL TEXTBOOKS IN THE UNITED STATES

The schoolbook can be traced back to the close of the fifteenth century in Europe, but the actual term *textbook* did not come into general use until the latter part of the eighteenth century in England. In the colonial period in the United States, the religiously oriented *New England Primer* (1690) served as the beginning reader for more than a century and a quarter. Most schoolbooks were imported from England, such as the many editions of *A New Guide to the English Tongue* (1740), which included moral stories and religious selections, and the arithmetic text, *Schoolmaster's Assistant* (1743)— both written by Thomas Dilworth, an English schoolmaster. The turning point for the development of distinctive American textbooks was to emerge dramatically during the national period.

Americanization of Schoolbooks

The Revolutionary War cut off the supply of schoolbooks from England during its duration, and although American-born texts began to appear to meet the pent-up demand following the war, most schoolbooks continued to come from England. The epochal transformation was launched by Noah Webster's *American Spelling Book* (1783), a combined speller and reader, and his dictionaries (1806, 1828). It was Noah Webster who recognized the need for a uniform American language to reflect the ideals and realities of the new country, as opposed to the social-class divisions marked by language in England and Europe. The vehicle for this transformation was his American speller, reader, grammar, and dictionaries, which, according to Henry Commager, made Webster "schoolmaster to America" and assured him "a place among the Founding Fathers" (p. 83).

Webster criticized the emphasis given to Latin and Greek, as well as the traditional uses of the Bible as a textbook. In addition to his school textbooks on American language, he authored other school textbooks in a range of subjects, including history, geography, and science. Although Webster's readers were moralistic and patriotic, he believed that whereas the nations of the Old World had inherited a long history of national identity, America had been created, and needed to establish its own authentic identity by means of education and language.

The McGuffey Readers

In 1836 the first two of what was to become a series of six grade readers appeared in Cincinnati. These were the McGuffey readers. Between 1836 and 1870 some 47 million copies of the McGuffey texts were sold. They became the textbooks of the nation, while also contributing to the establishment of the graded school and a more common curriculum. Heavily moralistic and Protestant in religious preachment, the readers were deemed to promote good character. In writing the readers (and the successive editions), the McGuffey brothers (William and Alexander) seemed oblivious to the Progressive pedagogical practices being transformed by the American experience. Nevertheless, the McGuffey readers served to promote a common curriculum that, according to Henry Commager, was a benevolent, not a chauvinistic, expression of nationalism.

Growth and Development of Textbooks

The educational systems in European nations were traditionally under national ministries, resulting in greater standardization and uniformity of curriculum, with the consequence that textbooks were relatively limited in variety. In contrast, the decentralized American system of education, coupled with the early universalization of public elementary and secondary education in the United States, proved to be fertile ground for the proliferation of textbooks, in both variety and quantity.

Early in the twentieth century, Progressive educators were criticizing rote textbook recitation—and promoting the uses of multiple textbooks and resource books. Units of work, or teaching units, were developed at leading Progressive schools, most notably the Lincoln School at Columbia's Teachers College, in an effort to articulate the new curriculum in the face of the traditionally segmented subject curriculum. A sixth-grade unit on architecture, for example, would require the usage of a vast array of books and other resource materials in integrating several previously isolated subjects. The unit of work also typically required students to become engaged in a corresponding variety of projects. Nevertheless, these developments did not curtail the growth and development of textbooks, but instead stimulated the production of supplementary texts and textbooks more realistically attuned to the nature of the learner and the need to connect subject matter to life experience. Since that time, textbooks have typically identified chapter groupings as *units*, although this practice has been more cosmetic than authentic or functional. Yet the better textbooks contained suggested activities, projects, and lines of inquiry beyond the actual textbook content.

Although Progressive education did not lead to the end of the textbook recitation, an early study by William Bagley (1931) found that while "straight" recitation from the single textbook was being used just about as frequently as the socialized recitation, contemporary educational theory was increasingly affecting teaching practices in a fairly profound fashion and moving it away from textbook-linked recitation. More than half a century later, in 1984, John Goodlad reported in his study of schooling that, although textbooks dominated the instruction in the sciences and mathematics, there was a wide range of textbooks and materials in classrooms. However, heavy emphasis was being given to workbooks and worksheets in various subjects, including mathematics, in a mode not always distinguishable from testing.

The early twenty-first century's national movement for standards and external testing has led to efforts to align the curriculum to the standardized tests and for teachers to engage in teaching the test, with the consequence that workbooks, worksheets, and photocopied exercises are increasingly being used. Just as with programmed instruction, the dominant mode of workbook/worksheet teaching and learning is established-convergent. In contrast, good textbooks will suggest activities, projects, and lines of inquiry that are emergent, and even divergent.

Textbook Controversies

Since the advent of computer-assisted instruction (CAI), much has been made of an impending educational revolution whereby print and paper will no longer be the memory of humanity. In a 1967 publication commemorating the centennial year of the U.S. Office of Education, a scenario of the school was envisioned in which, before the year 2000, textbooks and other books, and even teachers, would be replaced by the computer. Subsequent developments in educational technology have been accompanied by extravagant promises that eventually faded away. Considering the economy, convenience, and durability of the textbook, it is likely that new electronic technology will not replace the textbook, but will find a supplementary place in the teaching-learning process.

Since 1990 the pressure on school administrators to bring computers into schools created all too many instances where, in the face of limited facilities, space for library books was reduced to make room for computer stations. Considerable effort has been expended on integrating the computer into the curriculum, but virtually no thought has been given to integrating the curriculum with the computer. The most common uses of the computer in schools has been as an electronic workbook or worksheet.

A review of issues of the American Library Association's *Newsletter on Intellectual Freedom* finds virtually no instances of censorship of computer-based instruction programs, whereas the cases on censorship of school textbooks are legion. The most notorious case of textbook censorship stems back to 1925, when John T. Scopes, a Tennessee high school teacher, was brought to trial for having violated a state statute prohibiting the teaching of evolution—ironically by using a state-approved biology text. The case generated national and worldwide notoriety as the "World's Most Famous Court Trial," with William Jennings Bryan on the side of the state and Clarence Darrow for the defense. Scopes was convicted and fined $100. On appeal, the Tennessee Supreme Court upheld the law, but reversed the lower court's decision on a technicality. The law in question was eventually replaced by a statute prohibiting the use of any textbook presenting evolution without a qualifying statement that evolution is a theory and not a scientific fact—thereby revealing the legislature's ignorance of what a scientific theory is.

The problem of academic freedom in the schools reached such a critical state in the 1930s that the American Historical Society issued a huge volume of more than 850 pages under the title *Are American Teachers Free?* (1936). The book devoted a lengthy article to the problem of textbook censorship. From the 1930s into the early 1940s, the lead-

ing social studies textbook series for junior and senior high schools, written by Harold Rugg, underwent the full assault of the National Association of Manufacturers, the Advertising Federation of America, the Hearst Press, the American Legion, and other ultra-right-wing groups and individuals seeking to portray the Rugg textbooks as subversive of American ideals and institutions. The Rugg textbooks traced the evolution of modern American democracy in the face of pervasive social problems and issues, but super-patriotic groups viewed any study of unsettling ideas and problems in American life as anti-American. By the early 1940s the Rugg textbooks had been completely removed from the schools. A similar fate befell the widely used *Building America* series (1935–1948) of supplementary pictorial social studies texts during the early years of the cold war. The *Building America* series was focused on thematic problems and issues in the building of American democracy.

Nationalizing Influences on the Textbook

In the wake of the cold war and the space race, an unprecedented national effort was financed with federal funds through the National Science Foundation to support curriculum reform projects in the sciences and mathematics so as to meet the "long range crisis in national security" (Bruner, p. 1). From the 1950s into the early 1970s, the overriding goal of this effort was to produce more scientists and mathematicians to meet the Soviet threat. Early on it had been anticipated that the newer instructional media would play a pivotal role in these national projects, but the mainstay turned out to be the textbook.

Controlled, directed, and promoted by university scholar-specialists, the projects embraced a discipline-centered doctrine focused on specialized, puristic, theoretical, and abstract knowledge. University scholars in the social sciences and other fields soon jumped on the discipline-centered bandwagon. With very few exceptions, the project progenitors avoided controlled research, thereby violating a fundamental principle of scientific inquiry. By the late 1960s and into the early 1970s it was becoming increasingly apparent that what had been heralded as the "new math," "new physics," and so on, had failed to deliver what was promised. The number of college majors in the sciences underwent a sharp decline, and noted scientists and mathematicians who had not been involved in the discipline-centered projects began to examine the school textbooks and proceeded to issue devastating reports criticizing the textbooks and other materials for being too abstract and theoretical for children and adolescents. Nobel Laureate Linus Pauling made a blistering attack on the "new chemistry" texts for covering far too much information and advanced theoretical material, making them incomprehensible to the high school student, and recommended that the chemistry textbooks be reduced to half their size.

In effect, had the textbooks been reviewed by a wider range of authorities from the outset, the massive failure of the national discipline-centered curriculum reforms could have been avoided, and appropriate textbooks could have been created. Clearly the lesson was that textbooks should be subjected to the test of face validity by a cosmopolitan jury of authorities in the field, including educators. Totally neglected in the discipline-centered textbooks were the nature and interests of the learner, practical knowledge applications, and connections of the discipline with bordering fields of knowledge. This was also the case for the national discipline-centered projects in the social sciences and language and literature, which, in the pursuit of puristic knowledge, failed to make connections of the subject matter with the wider social life of American democracy. In following their specializations, the scholars deliberately dismissed the democratic sociocivic function of the curriculum as "ideological bias" (Tanner 1971, pp. 200–201).

More Disputations

The latter half of the 1960s witnessed the full social impact of the civil rights movement, protests against the escalating Vietnam War, and outbursts of civil disobedience in major cities—accompanied by student disruptions on college campuses that filtered down into high schools. The demand in colleges and schools was now for curriculum *relevance*. A host of neoromantic best-selling books appeared calling for laissez-faire pedagogy and even for the elimination of textbooks and the preplanned curriculum. Following a brief period of extreme child-centered classrooms and the uses of *au courant* materials in the secondary schools in the name of relevance, a counterreaction of *back to basics* set in, with emphasis being given to statewide minimum-competency testing.

In a postmortem effort examining the fall of the national disciplinary curriculum-reform projects,

the National Institute of Education formed a task force in 1975. In its report the chair of the task force attributed the collapse of the federally supported projects largely to the forces of censorship, capped by a congressional attack on one of the projects in 1975, and although the new biology textbooks had been attacked by antievolutionists, it was clear that most of the projects were not targets of censorship and were already in a state of imminent collapse by the late 1960s.

Unfortunately, teachers, textbook authors, and publishers sometimes engage in self-censorship. For example, as a means of avoiding attacks by creationists, the leading center for curriculum development in life sciences for schools produced modular materials for one of its projects, rather than a textbook, allowing schools and districts the option of avoiding any of the modules that may be contentious—such as the module on evolution. Whatever the marketing benefits may be, such as the claim of "flexibility," the fact remains that such an approach only segments the curriculum and in the case of evolution, keeps students in ignorance of a foundational paradigm of life sciences.

Dumbing-Down of Textbooks

By the mid-1980s it was becoming increasingly clear that the back-to-basic retrenchment and minimum-competency standards had resulted in a renewed proliferation of worksheets, workbooks, and the *dumbing-down* of textbooks. Despite its reckless language in scapegoating the public schools for the decline in U.S. industrial productivity, the 1983 report of the National Commission on Excellence in Education (*A Nation at Risk*) leveled some cogent criticisms at the minimum-competency tests (required in most of the states) for actually lowering educational standards and recommended that textbooks be made more challenging. The report held that textbook expenditures and related instructional materials had declined by 50 percent over the previous seventeen years and recommended that expenditures for textbooks and other curriculum materials should be raised to between 5 and 10 percent of the operating costs of schools—many times the then current level. In 1984 U.S. Secretary of Education Terrel H. Bell accused publishers of "dumbing down" their textbooks, but he failed to acknowledge that the dumbing-down is the inevitable consequence of curriculum fundamentalism, back-to-basics retrenchment, and censorship pressures.

In 1985, upon the recommendation of the California Curriculum Development and Supplemental Materials Commission, the California State Board of Education rejected many of the science textbooks for having failed to address controversial topics adequately, and many mathematics texts for stressing "apparent mastery" of mechanical skills without conceptual understanding and experiential application in problem-solving situations. Within several months, revised textbook editions appeared. One publisher, which had not even listed the topic of evolution in the index of its textbook, produced a revised edition within a year with an entire chapter on evolution. Based on the California experience, it would appear that a knowledgeable curriculum development commission in other states could serve not only as an antidote to censorship, but also as a vehicle for the continual improvement of textbooks and other curriculum materials. Faculty curriculum committees at the local school level could also serve in this capacity.

Change and Challenge

Good textbooks codify and synthesize knowledge in ways appropriate to the cognitive, affective, and social growth of learners. The durability and popularity of the textbook reside in its economy and flexibility. The fact that textbooks have served historically as prime targets for censorship of ideas is testimony that textbooks are powerful media for emergent, and even divergent, learning. The textbook should not be seen as the syllabus or complete course of study, but should be created as a vehicle for opening up avenues for further inquiry and the use of a range of print materials and other media. Whether the school textbook is designed to meet the function of general education, exploratory education, enrichment education, or even specialized education, to be successful it must be generative in ideas, concepts, and skills for meaningful applications in the life and growth of the learner. Such textbooks should relate to and draw from bordering areas of knowledge. But even the best textbooks depend on the teacher for their successful use as a vehicle for emergent learning.

The programmed textbook failed for many of the reasons cited above—for its narrow-minded behavioristic focus on established-convergent learning, its segmental and mechanical format and approach to knowledge, its mechanistic multiple-choice or fill-in-the blank mentality, and its artificiality in failing

to engage the learner's imagination and life experience, to list just a few shortcomings. Unfortunately the workbook and worksheet persist, while the computer has commonly been used in school as an electronic worksheet aligned to external tests. Over the short history of the programmed textbook, censorship was never a problem. As noted by Judith A. Langer and Richard L. Allington in 1992 and by Daniel Tanner in 1999, the established-convergent programming repertoire found no place for provocative ideas.

In the contemporary scene, publishers would do well to cut down on the uses of readability formulas in the construction of textbooks and instead center reading materials on ideas. Even preschoolers can follow a story line, which requires the development of plot, character, sequential events, and relational ideas. Idea-oriented teaching, rather than error-oriented teaching, is required for a generative curriculum.

For more than a century, Progressive educators have deplored the direct textbook recitation method and the use of the textbook as the sole curriculum source for a subject at each grade level. Teachers have been urged to use multiple texts and a rich variety of material resources and activities beyond the texts. Progressive educators promoted and produced textbooks that stimulated students to investigate problems of persistent personal and social significance. In the early twenty-first century, it is not uncommon to find a beginning college textbook in ecology, for example, perfectly suitable for use at both the college and high school levels. The wide range of appeal stems from the appropriateness of the interdisciplinary material to the life of the learner in the wider society.

The design and function of the textbook at virtually any level should be directed at interrelating or correlating the content with bordering areas of knowledge so as to empower the learner in the uses to which knowledge is put. As Margaret McKeown and Isabel Beck noted in 1998, the textbook should be so designed as to reveal turning points, rather than end points, in the development and uses of knowledge.

In a multicultural society there will always be divided and special interests that will seek to impinge on the teacher's right to teach and the student's right to learn. But an enlightened citizenry requires freedom of inquiry. Historically, those who would seek to curtail the free currency of ideas in the teaching-learning process have focused their efforts on print media, especially the school textbook.

See also: CURRICULUM, SCHOOL; ELEMENTARY EDUCATION, *subentries on* CURRENT TRENDS, HISTORY OF; MEDIA AND LEARNING; SECONDARY EDUCATION, *subentries on* CURRENT TRENDS, HISTORY OF; TECHNOLOGY IN EDUCATION; WEBSTER, NOAH.

BIBLIOGRAPHY

ABELSON, PHILIP H. 1967. "Excessive Educational Pressures." *Science* 156:741.

BAGLEY, WILLIAM C. 1931. "The Textbook and Methods of Teaching." In *The Textbook in American Education* (30th Yearbook of the National Society for the Study of Education, Part II), ed. Guy M. Whipple. Bloomington, IL: Public School Publishing.

BARNES, EMILY A. and YOUNG, BESS M. 1932. *Children and Architecture.* New York: J. J. Little.

BEALE, HOWARD K. 1936. *Are Teachers Free?* Report of the Commission on Social Studies Education, Part XII. New York: Charles Scribner's Sons.

BRUNER, JEROME S. 1960. *The Process of Education.* Cambridge, MA: Harvard University Press.

COMMAGER, HENRY S. 1968. *The Commonwealth of Learning.* New York: Harper and Row.

CARRIER, GEORGE F.; COURANT, RICHARD; ROSENBLOOM, PAUL C.; YANG, C. N.; and GREENBERG, H. J. 1962. "Applied Mathematics: What is Needed in Research and Education." *SIAM Review* 4:297–320.

CREMIN, LAWRENCE A. 1970. *American Education: The Colonial Experience 1607–1783.* New York: Harper and Row.

CREMIN, LAWRENCE A. 1980. *American Education: The National Experience, 1783–1876.* New York: Harper and Row.

CUBBERLEY, ELLWOOD P. 1947. *Public Education in the United States.* Boston: Houghton Mifflin.

CURRICULUM DEVELOPMENT AND SUPPLEMENTARY MATERIALS COMMISSION, STATE OF CALIFORNIA. 1986. *Report on Mathematics Instructional Materials.* Sacramento: California Department of Education.

ELLIOTT, DAVID L., and WOODWARD, ARTHUR, eds. 1990. *Textbooks and Schooling in the United States* (89th Yearbook of the National Society for the Study of Education, Part I). Chicago: University of Chicago Press.

FEYNMAN, RICHARD P. 1965. "New Textbooks for the New Mathematics." *Engineering and Science* 28:9–15.

FISKE, EDWARD B. 1984. "Are They 'Dumbing Down' the Textbooks?" *Principal* 64:44.

GOODLAD, JOHN I. 1984. *A Place Called School.* New York: McGraw-Hill.

JACKSON, PHILIP W. and HAROUTUNIAN-GORDON, SOPHIE, eds. 1989. *From Socrates to Software: The Teacher as Text and the Text as Teacher* (88th Yearbook of the National Society for the Study of Education, Part I). Chicago: University of Chicago Press.

KERR, STEPHEN T. 1989. "Pale Screens: Teachers and Electronic Texts." In *From Socrates to Software: The Teacher as Text and the Text as Teacher,* ed. Philip W. Jackson and Sophie Harotounian-Gordon. Chicago: University of Chicago Press.

KILLIAN, JAMES R., JR. 1965. "Preface to the First Edition." In *Physics,* 2nd edition, ed. Physical Sciences Study Committee. Boston: D.C. Heath.

KING, L. CARROLL. 1967. "High Student Failure Rate Serious Problem." *Chemical and Engineering News* 15:44.

KLINE, MORRIS. 1966. "Intellectuals and the Schools: A Case History." *Harvard Educational Review* 36:505–511.

KOHL, HERBERT R. 1969. *The Open Classroom.* New York: Random House.

KUHN, THOMAS S. 1970. *The Structure of Scientific Revolutions,* 2nd edition. Chicago: University of Chicago Press.

LANGER, JUDITH A., and ALLINGTON, RICHARD L. 1992. "Curriculum Research in Writing and Reading." In *Handbook of Research on Curriculum,* ed. Philip W. Jackson. New York: Macmillan.

LINCOLN SCHOOL STAFF. 1927. *Curriculum Making in an Elementary School.* Boston: Ginn.

MAYER, WILLIAM V. 1978. "The BSCS Past." *BSCS Journal* 1:19.

MCKEOWN, MARGARET C., and BECK, ISABEL L. 1998. "Talking to an Author: Readers Taking Charge of the Reading Process." In *The Reading-Writing Connection* (97th Yearbook of the

National Society for the Study of Education, Part II), ed. Nancy Nelson and Robert C. Caffee. Chicago: University of Chicago Press.

NATIONAL COMMISSION ON EXCELLENCE IN EDUCATION. 1983. *A Nation at Risk: The Imperative for Educational Reform.* Washington, D.C.: U.S. Department of Education.

NEWMAN, ROBERT E., JR. 1960. "History of a Civic Education Project Implementing the Social-Problems Technique of Instruction." Ph.D. diss. Stanford University.

PAULING, LINUS. 1983. "Throwing the Book at Elementary Chemistry." *Science Teacher* 50:25–29.

POSTMAN, NEIL, and WEINGARTNER, CHARLES. 1973. *The School Book.* New York: Delacorte.

ROBINSON, DONALD W. 1983. "Patriotism and Economic Control: The Censure of Harold Rugg." Ph.D. diss. Rutgers University.

SCHAFFARZICK, JON. 1979. "Federal Curriculum Reform: A Crucible for Value Conflict." In *Value Conflicts and Curriculum Issues,* ed. Jon Schaffarzick and Gary Sykes. Berkeley, CA: McCutchan.

SOSNIAK, LAUREN. 1992. "Textbooks." In *Encyclopedia of Educational Research,* Vol. 4, ed. Marvin C. Alkin. New York: Macmillan.

TANNER, DANIEL. 1971. *Secondary Curriculum: Theory and Development.* New York: Macmillan.

TANNER, DANIEL. 1999. "The Textbook Controversies." In *Issues in Curriculum* (98th Yearbook of the National Society for the Study of Education, Part II), ed. Margaret J. Early and Kenneth J. Rehage. Chicago: University of Chicago Press.

TANNER, DANIEL. 2002. *Crusade for Democracy: Progressive Education at the Crossroads.* Albany: State University of New York Press.

TANNER, DANIEL, and TANNER, LAUREL. 1987. *Supervision in Education: Problems and Practices.* New York: Macmillan.

TANNER, DANIEL, and TANNER, LAUREL. 1990. *History of the School Curriculum.* New York: Macmillan.

TANNER, DANIEL, and TANNER, LAUREL. 1995. *Curriculum Development: Theory Into Practice.* New York: Macmillan.

U.S. OFFICE OF EDUCATION. 1967. *OE 100: Highlighting the Progress of American Education.* Washington, DC: U.S. Government Printing Office.

VENEZKY, RICHARD L. 1992. "Textbooks in School and Society." In *Handbook of Research on Curriculum,* ed. Philip W. Jackson. New York: Macmillan.

WEINBERG, ALVIN M. 1967. *Reflection on Big Science.* Cambridge, MA: MIT Press.

WHIPPLE, GUY M., ed. 1931. *The Textbook in American Education* (30th Yearbook of the National Society for the Study of Education, Part II). Bloomington, IL: Public School Publishing.

World's Most Famous Court Trial. Complete Stenographic Report. 1925. Cincinnati: National Book.

DANIEL TANNER

THAYER, V. T. (1886–1979)

Teacher and Progressive education administrator, V. T. Thayer was the author of many books on American education. In his outlook and work, Thayer remained an articulate and persuasive advocate of Progressive education, philosophic naturalism, and secular humanism.

V. T. Thayer received his doctorate in philosophy at the University of Wisconsin in 1922. While studying for that degree he was an instructor in the subject (1919–1922) and additionally acquired wide experience as a teacher and superintendent of schools in Wisconsin. From 1924 to 1928 he held the position of professor of education at Ohio State University and was managing editor of the *American Review* (1923–1927).

Although associated primarily with the philosophy of John Dewey, Thayer was receptive to the educational ideas of Felix Adler and the Ethical Culture Society. In 1928 he was invited to become education director of the Ethical Culture Schools, a position he held until 1948. He was also one of the leaders in the society.

Throughout his life Thayer was frequently in demand as a lecturer and taught at many universities, among them Harvard University; Teachers College, Columbia University; Dartmouth College; the University of Hawaii; the University of Virginia; Johns Hopkins University; the University of Maryland; and Fisk University. He was a member of the Progressive Education Association, the National Education Association, the Advisory Council for Academic Freedom Committee of the American Civil Liberties Union, the Public Education Association, and the Institute on the Separation of Church and State. He was named Pioneer Humanist of the Year by the American Humanist Association in 1964. In 1969 he received the Award for Distinguished Service to Education from the John Dewey Society.

In the early 1930s while serving on the Board of Directors of the Progressive Education Association, Thayer was active in two commissions founded by the association. The first was concerned with liberalizing college admissions procedures. By a special arrangement made between some 100 colleges and a select group of secondary schools (known as the "thirty schools") the latter were able to experiment with curricular revisions without jeopardizing the admission of their students to college. The arrangement was the basis of what has been called the Eight-Year Study. The work of this commission soon revealed the need for a fundamental study of the secondary school curriculum. Accordingly the association formed a second commission with Thayer as chairman, titled the Commission on the Secondary School Curriculum. A group of committees was established in which school and college teachers, anthropologists, sociologists, psychologists, psychiatrists, physicians, and social workers participated. The primary purpose was to stimulate research and suggest materials and methods helpful in curricular experimentation on school and college levels, and to develop guidelines for this experimentation relevant to the needs of young people in contemporary society. Thayer reported on this commission in *Reorganizing Secondary Education* (1939). Fieldston was one of the "thirty schools," and Thayer's activity in both of the commissions stimulated wide interest in the Ethical Culture Schools.

During his directorship Thayer was responsible for several major innovations in the administration and curriculum of the Ethical Culture Schools. He had often emphasized the importance of guidance, with a special concern for individual and social aspects of needs and growth, in contrast to traditional views of a curriculum of discipline and fixed standards. With the cooperation of Caroline B. Zachry, Thayer established a Department of Guidance consisting of professionally trained counselors. This recognition of the role of "needs" in the personal and social formation of an adolescent's life and relationships requiring "guidance" was regarded critically by some educators as giving undue attention to the idiosyncrasies of individual students. Thus in his history of the Ethical Society, Howard Radest charges that in emphasizing the importance of individual student needs, Thayer subverted the teachings of Felix Adler, who held that the goal of the school is to serve "the needs of civilization." However, Radest fails to consider what Adler and Thayer really meant by "needs." Furthermore, Thayer's humanistic conception of individual student needs was not advanced to replace Adler's ideals, nor were their views ever entirely antithetical.

Thayer also initiated an extensive reorganization of the administrative structure of the Ethical Culture Schools. Each functional group in each of the several schools—faculty, parents, alumni—would participate in the formulation of policies through representation in an integrated ascending order of committees. Each school had its executive committee, consisting of faculty representatives, principal, and the director. These committees were in turn represented in one administrative council. Students, parents, and faculty were also represented by membership on the board of governors. Thayer called this organizational structure "functional democratic administration." As a model it was a contribution to educational administration.

A further novel addition to the school curriculum was the development of ways by which the school could contribute to the community. Programs of community service were designed to involve each student in the upper high school (junior and senior grades) in some form of community service. A notable extension of this effort was the development of Junior Work Camps, managed primarily by members of the Fieldston staff and administered by a board of directors of which Thayer was the chairperson. The camps included students of other schools as well as those of Fieldston. Their purpose was to provide young persons of high school age with an opportunity to engage in meaningful and constructive work (i.e., participation in the harvesting of fruits and vegetables, which gave valuable help to truck farmers in a period of labor shortage).

Despite formidable problems of stability and direction due to the depression of the 1930s and the outbreak of World War II, the impressive academic record and successful curricular experimentation of the Ethical Culture Schools under Thayer's leadership occasioned national and international recognition.

In the early twenty-first century, however, he is remembered primarily for his professional activities after he left the Ethical Culture Schools and especially for his many writings on problems and issues of American education. Two well-known books deal with the historical background and philosophical influences and formative ideas that have shaped the school in American society. In these and other writings, Thayer engaged in critical analyses of certain well-publicized proposals for reforming education; he also examined such major problems as federal aid, desegregation, and contesting views of church and state in relation to the schools.

See also: EIGHT-YEAR STUDY; PROGRESSIVE EDUCATION; SECONDARY EDUCATION.

BIBLIOGRAPHY

RADEST, HOWARD B. 1969. *Toward Common Ground: The Story of the Ethical Societies in the United States.* New York: Unger.

THAYER, V. T. 1944. *American Education under Fire.* New York: Harper.

THAYER, V. T. 1945. *Religion in Public Education.* New York: Viking.

THAYER, V. T. 1965. *Formative Ideas in American Education: From the Colonial Period to the Present.* New York: Dodd, Mead.

THAYER, V. T.; ZACHRY, CAROLINE; and KOTINSKY, RUTH. 1939. *Reorganizing Secondary Education.* New York: Appleton-Century.

ZEPPER, JOHN T. 1970. "V. T. Thayer: Progressive Educator." *The Educational Forum* May:495–504.

H. S. THAYER

THORNDIKE, EDWARD L. (1874–1949)

Edward L. Thorndike was an American psychologist, educator, lexicographer, and pioneer in educational research. The groundwork for research into learning was provided in 1913–1914 by his three-volume *Educational Psychology,* which set forth precepts based on his experimental and statistical investigations. These precepts—which covered such wide-ranging topics as teaching practices and individual differences between students and such administrative concerns as promotion decisions and grouping according to ability—came to dominate professional thinking.

While such men as John Dewey and Robert M. Hutchins influenced the philosophy of education, Thorndike and those whom he inspired wrote reading and arithmetic books for pupils, school dictionaries and spelling lists, tests, and pedagogical guidebooks and teachers' manuals. Because, however, it is far more difficult to assess influence in the operations of many thousands of American classrooms than to analyze ideas in the words of educational theorists, Thorndike's contributions are taken largely for granted.

The Man and His Career

In its external details, Thorndike's life was uneventful and circumspect; its drama lay in his genius (his IQ was estimated at nearly 200) and in the tumultuous times to which his work bore such marked reference. Born in Williamsburg, Massachusetts, on August 31, 1874, of a family line resident in New England since 1630, Thorndike, like a surprising number of other notables of his day, was reared in a clergyman's household. But in an era when science was challenging religion as a source of truth, when inquiry and universal education threatened dogmatism and sectarian inculcation, and when a career in the church was becoming less attractive than life in the laboratory, Thorndike rejected even his father's liberal brand of Methodism for an agnostic secularism. Yet, in his evangelical regard for science, Thorndike transferred to science a religious-like belief in the possibility of personal and societal salvation. Science was, he said repeatedly, "the only sure foundation for social progress."

Thorndike grew up in a household where excellence was expected, for the children of a minister were to be models for the congregation in all matters. In academic performance the Reverend Thorndike's children complied, all earning excellent grades and winning the scholarships which made college studies possible. In addition, all established academic careers: Ashley as a professor of English, Lynn as a historian, and Mildred as a high school English teacher; eventually all three Thorndike brothers taught at Columbia University. Edward Thorndike's children continued this scholastic brilliance but turned, like father, from literary to scientific and mathematical careers. All four children earned Ph.D.

degrees: Elizabeth Frances in mathematics, Edward Moulton and Alan in physics, and Robert Ladd in psychology. Thus, from his own boyhood, when his parents encouraged early reading and supervised homework, to his own close guidance of his children's schooling, Thorndike brought high degree of personal involvement to his professional study of education.

Because of the church's requirement that a minister be moved regularly, Thorndike grew in eight New England towns before 1891, when he left home to enter Wesleyan University in Middletown, Connecticut. Never feeling at home anywhere in his childhood, when he possessed the power to decide for himself he chose to stay put: he spent forty years at Teachers College, Columbia University, spurning other positions offered, and built a home at Montrose, New York, at age thirty-three. He died there on August 9, 1949, near age 75, leaving his widow, Elizabeth Moulton, whom he married in 1900, and their four grown children.

The early moving about left Thorndike with pronounced shyness and social uneasiness, helping to make the lonely privacy of research a comfortable world. His educational work also displays a certain nonsocial cast. Unlike the psychologies of the Progressive educators with whom he shared many beliefs, Thorndike's educational psychology was not a social one. To him learning was an essentially private, organic undertaking, something that happened under one's skin, in the nervous system; the "connections" of interest to the teacher were properly those between stimulus and response—not the interactions between individual students, which concern those who view a class primarily as a social group.

During Thorndike's youth the United States fully entered the age of industrialization and urbanization. The mill towns of New England were part of the industrial revolution that was attracting hundreds of thousands of immigrants a year to manufacturing jobs and making Boston, Pittsburgh, Chicago, and New York great, if trouble-plagued, cities. Coming to New York City in 1897 to complete his doctoral studies at Columbia University, Thorndike was to remain there for the rest of his life, except for a brief tenure from 1898 to 1899 as a teacher of psychology and pedagogy at the College for Women of Western Reserve University in Cleveland, Ohio.

It was understandable that an urban setting would be attractive to the modern academic man, particularly to the man of science; it was in the cities that industrial wealth built museums, libraries, and laboratories, and it was there that philanthropic foundations had their headquarters. Such foundations as the Carnegie Corporation of New York, the General Education Board, and the Commonwealth Fund established the Institute of Educational Research at Teachers College, to which Thorndike devoted his energies almost exclusively from 1921. It was at this time that the wealth and centrality of New York City were helping to make Columbia a great national university and its Teachers College the most important center for the training of the leaders in public education in the United States. By 1900 all leading American universities were, like Columbia, in urban settings. Moreover, the leadership of public education nationally was passing into the hands of the superintendents of big-city school systems and to their counterparts in the state capitals and in the Federal Bureau of Education.

By the turn of the century, elementary education in the United States was virtually universal; thereafter, the task was to extend secondary schooling to the entire nation. The need for teachers was great. Although the normal schools, frequently rural institutions, continued to train many teachers, departments of education became common within universities after 1900. Thorndike first arrived at Teachers College in 1899, when its status was changing from that of a private normal school to the education department of Columbia University. Because universities were preeminently places of research, their departments for training teachers and school administrators partook of the prevailing atmosphere favoring scholarly and scientific inquiry. In leaving Western Reserve for Teachers College, Thorndike abandoned a traditional training school for a place which he quickly helped make a center for the scientific study of education and for the training of educational researchers. As its dean, James Earl Russell, recalled: "In developing the subject of educational psychology . . . for students in all departments, Professor Thorndike has shaped the character of the College in its youth as no one else has done and as no one will ever again have the opportunity of doing" ("Personal Appreciations" 1926, p. 460).

In addition to urban resources and leadership for research and to the prestige accorded science by the universities, there was another incentive for expanding educational research: the widespread desire in educational circles to have teaching recognized as a profession. Schoolmen were aware of the high total of public spending for education and shared the prevailing faith in schools as critical agencies of character training and national development. Even in an occupation marked by low prestige, minimal preparation, a preponderance of women, high turnover, and legal dependence upon boards of laymen, professional status was regarded as an attractive, realizable goal.

One of the characteristics claimed by an occupational group seeking professional status is its possession of a large and growing body of expert knowledge. The function of research was to replace the folklore of the teaching craft with scientifically verifiable assertions. Thorndike acknowledged after thirty years of work that research had yielded only a few answers to the practical questions raised by school operations. He maintained, however, that a true profession awaited those who patiently researched fundamental educational questions. The principal barrier was not, he believed, the limitations of science, but the traditional conservatism and inertia characteristic of institutionalized education.

A Psychology for Educators

At Teachers College, Thorndike taught psychology to large numbers of teachers and school administrators. In his early courses and in such books as his *Notes on Child Study* (1901a), *Principles of Teaching, Based on Psychology* (1906), and *Education: A First Book* (1912), he tried to inform educators of what was already known of human nature and human variation, of what had been written about behavior and learning by such creative psychological thinkers as Scotland's Alexander Bain and William James at Harvard, under whom Thorndike had once studied. Increasingly, however, he turned away from concentrating his efforts on converting teachers to a scientific attitude and away from deducing educational precepts from existing psychological thought. Instead, he began to construct a new educational psychology—one more in keeping with the experimental quantified directions laid out by the "new psychology" being developed in German and American research centers.

The scientific requirement. As much as he admired the brilliance, humane perceptiveness, and stylistic elegance of William James's *Principles of Psychology*, Thorndike was of that new generation of younger

psychologists who, after 1895, sought to sever psychology's ties with "mental philosophy" by rejecting armchair theorizing, avoiding such philosophical concepts as "soul," and opting for the methods, language, and standards of physics and experimental biology. He was deeply impressed by the painstakingly precise observations of animal behavior by Charles Darwin, by the methodological controls in the memory studies of Hermann Ebbinghaus, and by the statistical inventiveness of Sir Francis Galton and Karl Pearson. Discussions in the summer of 1900 with the famed experimentalist Jacques Loeb at the Marine Biology Laboratory at Woods Hole, Massachusetts, finally convinced Thorndike that his talent lay in "doing science," and that he "ought to be shut up and kept at research work" (Jonçich, p. 265).

Lacking mechanical aptitude, Thorndike never incorporated into his research the elaborate instruments found in Wundt's Leipzig laboratory and among Titchener's students at Cornell, or favored by Charles Judd, another important educational psychologist. Thorndike's approach was basically observational and problematic: place the subject in some problem (test) situation—seeking to escape from a confining place, having to rank his attitudes, choosing the correct response among several alternatives to avoid a mild shock—then observe the behavior aroused and report it in quantitative form. The typical Thorndike experiment was a simple paper-and-pencil investigation, like the first he ever attempted: as a Harvard graduate student he tried to measure children's responsiveness to unconscious cues by giving candy rewards to those correctly guessing the number or object he had in mind.

Lessons from animal studies. Despite his typically simple approach, Thorndike is credited with two research techniques basic to modern psychological studies of animal behavior: the maze and the problem box, both of which were invented for his now-classic study of learning, *Animal Intelligence* (1898). A thoroughgoing Darwinist, Thorndike was convinced that, because of evolutionary continuity, the study of animal behavior is instructive to human psychology. Hence, when he had difficulty in securing human subjects, Thorndike switched easily from children to chickens in his Harvard studies.

A significant portion of *Animal Intelligence* is a critique of the uncontrolled observation and casually acquired anecdotal reportage prevalent in what little comparative psychology existed in the 1890s. The faulty methods, Thorndike declared, contributed

spurious data and led to unwarranted interpretations. The most serious error was attributing to animals a higher order of intelligence than would be
justified by scientific observations of animal behavior. His own painstaking research with cats and
dogs, and later with fish and monkeys, convinced
Thorndike that the process of animal learning rested
not on some form of reasoning and not even on imitation. Learning depends, instead, upon the presence
of some situation or stimulus (S) requiring the animal to make various, more or less random responses
(R); as a result of such trial and error, the correct,
or most adaptive, response is eventually made (for
example, hitting a lever to escape a box or to reach
food). The effect produced by the appropriate response is a sort of reward: it may be escape, food,
sex, or a release of tension (in animals and humans)
or an experienced feeling of success or other learned
rewards (in humans alone). The effect acts physio-
logically, creating or reinforcing a neural connection
between that response and the situation which pro-
voked it; repetition of that or a similar stimulus becomes more readily able to produce the previously
successful response, and inappropriate responses are
forgone. Learning has taken place.

Reward: the key to learning. The basic principle
which Thorndike formulated to account for the S-R
connection is the law of effect; in the language of
such later psychologists as Clark Hull and B. F. Skinner, this is a reinforcement theory of learning.

If, as Thorndike maintained, human behavior
represents primordial attempts to satisfy native and
learned wants, then an effective, positive, and humane pedagogy is one which facilitates the making
of desired and successful responses, forestalls incorrect responses, and is generous with rewards; a poor
teaching method, on the other hand, carelessly permits wrong responses and then must punish them
to prevent their becoming established as bad habits.
Initially Thorndike assumed that reward and punishment were equal opposites, effects evenly capable
of causing learning. Reward is preferable since it is
more efficient to forestall inappropriate responses by
producing and rewarding desired behavior than by
punishing incorrect responses; a positive pedagogy
is preferable to a punitive one. As a result of empirical studies undertaken in the late 1920s and 1930s,
however, Thorndike concluded that he had been
mistaken earlier. Punished responses are not weak-
ened as rewarded connections are strengthened; despite common sense and tradition, punishment may

actually enhance the probability that an undesired
response will be repeated.

Thorndike was virtually the first educator to
give theoretical and empirical attention to effect, although reward and punishment had been given
practical attention by generations of schoolmen.
Still, the pedagogical emphasis at the turn of the century centered on punitive and repressive measures
and on fault-finding. In 1906 Thorndike warned
teachers that the most common violation of human
nature was the failure to reward desired behavior. In
propounding the law of effect, then, Thorndike gave
a psychologist's support to those educational philosophers, like John Dewey, and those founders of Progressive schools, like Marietta Johnson, who wished
to make schools more humane and to have them
better relate educational methods to the nature of
childhood. However, because of his articulation of
another law of learning—the law of exercise—
Thorndike's psychology differed from that Progres-
sivist thinking which emphasized spontaneity and
favored student selection of activities and freedom
from a planned curriculum sequence and from drill.
(The law of exercise states that once a given response
is made to a particular stimulus, each recurrence of
that stimulus tends to recall that response; hence, an
S-R bond is being strengthened. The educational implication of the law promotes drill, or practice, of desired responses and careful teacher attention to
forming appropriate habits.)

Education as Specific Habit Formation

Accepting William James's views, Thorndike wrote:

> Intellect and character are strengthened not
> by any subtle and easy metamorphosis, but
> by the establishment of particular ideas and
> acts under the law of habit . . . . The price
> of a disciplined intellect and will is eternal
> vigilance in the formation of habits . . . .
> Habit rules us but it also never fails us. The
> mind does not give us something for noth-
> ing, but it never cheats. (1906, pp. 247–248)

A radical educational theory stressing freedom,
spontaneity, inner direction, and "unfolding," one
that "stands out of nature's way," was to Thorndike
a "something for nothing" pedagogy. In its place,
Thorndike's psychology required the careful ordering of learning tasks, as in the *Thorndike Arithmetics*
(1917), which he prepared for school use; practice
(exercise, drill) with reward; and measurement of

progress through frequent testing, preferably by standardized tests so that more reliable estimates of learning could be had.

Another "something for nothing" educational theory—this one from the conservative, formalistic right wing of educational opinion—was the belief in mental (formal) discipline: that various mental or perceptual faculties are strengthened by being exercised upon some formal, preferably difficult task; that the study of a rigorously logical subject, like geometry, promotes logical behavior; and that practice in accurate copying transfers to other behavior, making one more accurate generally.

Some skepticism about transfer of training had already developed, on a priori grounds, before Thorndike published the first major empirical challenge to this widely held theory. The proponents of more modern subjects—vocational courses, the modern languages, physical education, even the sciences—had attacked formal discipline and faculty psychology because the defenders of the classical studies had based classical domination of the curriculum primarily on the grounds that these difficult and abstruse subjects, which were unappreciated by pupils, had tremendous transferability value, just as lifting the heaviest weights develops muscle power better than lighter burdens do. Between 1901 and 1924, Thorndike's research supported those educational reformers who believed that a subject or skill should be included in the curriculum because of its intrinsic value, and not because of unproved assertions about transfer power.

Education as a Science

In his *Educational Psychology,* Thorndike wrote: "We conquer the facts of nature when we observe and experiment upon them. When we measure them we have made them our servants" (1903, p. 164). Equally as important as empiricism to Thorndike's psychology was his emphasis on measurement and quantification; poorly prepared by the schools in mathematics and largely self-taught in statistics, Thorndike became the educational world's exponent of the use of science's universal language of description, numbers. His theme was, all that exists, exists in some amount and can be measured. He introduced the first university course in educational measurement in 1902, and two years later he wrote the first handbook for researchers in the use of social statistics, *An Introduction to the Theory of Mental and Social Measurements.*

Educational and intellectual tests. The movement toward testing was the primary outcome of attempts to translate qualitative statements (Mary seems to be having trouble in reading) into quantitative and comparable terms (In grade 5.6, Mary tests at 4.4 in reading comprehension and 4.7 in vocabulary knowledge). Standardized achievement tests in school subjects were built on centuries of use of teacher-made tests. What the twentieth century added was the standardization necessary for reliability and comparison of results from class to class. Professionally written and administered to thousands of pupils, using norms based on nationwide samples of students, achievement tests were created for every level of schooling, from primary through graduate school, including tests for out-of-school adults at various age levels. In 1921 use of these tests was established when 2 million pupils took standardized tests of academic achievement; thereafter, growth in the use and development of tests was virtually taken for granted. Thorndike contributed several works on construction of tests and devised various tests of his own: rating scales for handwriting, drawing, and composition; tests of oral and silent reading skill, geographical knowledge, English usage, spelling, reading and reasoning; and college entrance tests and law-school entrance examinations.

Intelligence and scholastic aptitude tests have a shorter history but have been even more crucial in shaping school practices (like promotion policies, grouping, and grading) and professional and public thinking. Alfred Binet's point scale, developed in France early in the twentieth century, is the landmark contribution. But before such testing could have great educational or social impact, it was necessary to find means of adapting the individually administered, Binet-type artifact tasks to groups using paper and pencil. This did not come about until World War I, when the U.S. Army commissioned psychologists to prepare and administer tests to aid in classifying recruits. Thorndike was a member of the Committee on Classification of Personnel from 1917 to 1919 and supervised work on the Beta form (the form for illiterate recruits); it and the Alpha form (for literates) were administered to 2 million soldiers by 1919, the world's first effort in the mass measurement of intelligence. Within three years, 1 million schoolchildren took similar tests, many of them the National Intelligence Test which a group of former army psychologists, including Thorndike, had developed. He later devised the CAVD (sentence completion, arithmetic, vocabulary, following directions) intelligence examination and a nonlanguage scale (for illiterates).

Aside from the kind of general intelligence measurements which concern educators most, Thorndike was interested in other types of aptitudes, believing that intelligence is not a unitary or general factor but is constituted of millions of discrete stimulus-response bonds; any intelligence test is simply a selective sample-taking of all the possible learned connections that might be present. Thorndike believed that since individuals differ, primarily by heredity, in their relative ability to form connections (that is, to profit from experience, to learn), and since any one individual is unevenly endowed in the ability to form connections of different types, tests of intelligence-in-general may miss certain aptitudes useful for vocational counseling, hiring programs, or selection of employees for special training programs.

In 1914 Thorndike began devising tests for use in locating persons with clerical aptitudes and interests and thereby fathered personnel-selection psychology in business and industry. In 1918 he headed the wartime search for men with aptitude for learning to fly. To try to prophesy flying success was itself a pioneering venture in a day when hardly a flying school existed in the United States and the aircraft industry was yet unborn. Such wartime experience in measuring aptitudes was continued in Thorndike's later research into vocational guidance for schools. He advocated special efforts and new departures in vocational education for those schoolchildren—perhaps as much as a third of the total—who "may learn only discouragement and failure" from much of the existing curriculum (Jonçich, p. 473). The vocational education movement lagged, however, with the decline of public interest in the 1920s and massive unemployment of the 1930s.

Studying human variation. The new instruments for measuring ability and achievement and especially the widespread use of these instruments inspired new knowledge of and intensified concern with individual differences. "It is useless to recount the traits in which men have been found to differ, for there is no trait in which they do not differ," Thorndike wrote in *Individuality* (1911, p. 6). The new educational psychology, he said, must reject classical psychology's assumption of a typical mind from which pattern there were only rare departures; it must study individual minds, be a differential psychology

which describes, explains, and seeks to make predictions about human variation.

Society's commitment to universal schooling must not, Thorndike believed, obscure its responsibility to every individual and its respect of difference. While psychology will, as a science, search for universal laws explaining human behavior, the pedagogical art, Thorndike believed, must recognize that it is individuals who act, who learn or refuse to learn.

> The practical consequence of the fact of individual differences is that every general law of teaching has to be applied with consideration of the particular person [for] the responses of children to any stimulus will not be invariable like the responses of atoms of hydrogen or of filings of iron, but will vary with their individual capacities, interests, and previous experience. (1906, p. 83)

Of these sources of variation, the most important in Thorndike's view was differing capacities—differences caused primarily by genetic inequalities. To the persisting debate about heredity and environment, Thorndike offered comparative studies of twins, siblings, and unrelated individuals, of family histories, and of school eliminations (dropouts). His findings convinced him that heredity is the primary determinant of intellectual difference and, because such other traits as personal morality, civic responsibility, industriousness, and mental health correlate positively with intelligence, that genetic endowment is the critical variable for welfare and social progress. So, in the interest of improving the human gene pool, he espoused eugenics.

In an age when psychoanalysis introduced arresting concepts of the primitive motivations of mankind, when the arts made a virtue of the "natural," when such educational theorists as G. Stanley Hall espoused a naturalism in education which urged teachers to step aside lest they interfere with nature's way, Thorndike offered dissent. Investigations of original nature and its differing expressions in individuals is not an end in itself, he argued. To find that heredity shapes human potential more than does a favorable environment does not end society's responsibility to improve its institutions, any more than the discovery of gravity was an excuse to cease man's efforts to fly. "The art of human life is to change the world for the better," Thorndike wrote in *Education: A First Book* (1912, p. 1). "Only one thing [in man's nature] is unreservedly good, the power to make it better. This power of learning . . . is the essential principle of reason and right in the world," he wrote in *Educational Psychology* (1913–1914, Vol. 1, pp. 281–282).

It is to institutions called schools and universities that modern societies assign most of the formal stimulation of this power of human learning. For his efforts to improve the abilities of educational institutions to capitalize upon learning potential Thorndike received much recognition during his lifetime: the presidencies of and honorary memberships in numerous American and international scientific and educational associations, honorary degrees from many universities, and election to the National Academy of Sciences. A most appropriate award, the Butler Medal in gold, was bestowed upon Thorndike by Columbia University in 1925 "in recognition of his exceptionally significant contributions to the general problem of the measurement of human faculty and to the applications of such measurements to education" (Jonçich, p. 487).

See also: EDUCATIONAL PSYCHOLOGY; INTELLIGENCE, *subentry on* MEASUREMENT; LEARNING THEORY, *subentry on* HISTORICAL OVERVIEW.

BIBLIOGRAPHY

"Annotated Chronological Bibliography, 1898–1925." 1926. *Teachers College Record* 27(6):466–515.

CALLAHAN, RAYMOND. 1962. *Education and the Cult of Efficiency.* Chicago: University of Chicago Press.

CREMIN, LAWRENCE A. 1961. *The Transformation of the School: Progressivism in American Education, 1876–1957.* New York: Knopf.

CURTI, MERLE. 1935. *The Social Ideas of American Educators.* New York: Scribner.

JONÇICH, GERALDINE. 1968. *The Sane Positivist: A Biography of Edward L. Thorndike.* Middletown, CT: Wesleyan University Press.

LORGE, IRVING. 1949. "Thorndike's Publications from 1940 to 1949: A Bibliography." *Teachers College Record* 51(1):42–45.

MURCHISON, CARL, ed. 1936. *A History of Psychology in Autobiography.* Vol. 3. Worcester, MA: Clark University Press.

O'CONNELL, GEOFFREY. 1938. *Naturalism in American Education.* New York: Benzinger Brothers.

"Personal Appreciations." 1926. *Teachers College Record* 27(6):460–465.

"Publications from 1898 to 1940 by E. L. Thorndike." 1940. *Teachers College Record* 41(8):699–725.

THORNDIKE, EDWARD L. 1898. "Animal Intelligence." *The Psychological Review, Monograph Supplements* 2, no. 4.

THORNDIKE, EDWARD L. 1901a. *Notes on Child Study.* New York: Macmillan.

THORNDIKE, EDWARD L. 1901b. "The Influence of Improvement in One Mental Function Upon the Efficiency of Other Functions." 3 parts. With Robert S. Woodworth. *Psychological Review* 8(3):247–261; (4):384–395; (6):556–564.

THORNDIKE, EDWARD L. 1903. *Educational Psychology.* New York: Lemcke and Buechner.

THORNDIKE, EDWARD L. 1906. *Principles of Teaching, Based on Psychology.* New York: A. G. Seiler.

THORNDIKE, EDWARD L. 1911. *Individuality.* Boston: Houghton Mifflin.

THORNDIKE, EDWARD L. 1912. *Education: A First Book.* New York: Macmillan.

THORNDIKE, EDWARD L. 1913a. *An Introduction to the Theory of Mental and Social Measurements* (1904). 2nd edition, revised. New York: Teachers College Press.

THORNDIKE, EDWARD L. 1913b. *Educational Administration: Quantitative Studies.* New York: Macmillan.

THORNDIKE, EDWARD L. 1913–1914. *Educational Psychology.* Vol. 1: *The Original Nature of Man.* Vol. 2: *The Psychology of Learning.* Vol. 3: *Work and Fatigue, Individual Differences and Their Causes.* New York: Teachers College Press.

THORNDIKE, EDWARD L. 1917. *Thorndike Arithmetics.* Books 1, 2, and 3. Chicago: Rand McNally.

THORNDIKE, EDWARD L. 1923. *Psychology of Algebra.* New York: Macmillan.

THORNDIKE, EDWARD L. 1928. "Curriculum Research." *School and Society* 18:569–576.

THORNDIKE, EDWARD L. 1935. *Thorndike-Century Junior Dictionary.* Chicago: Scott Foresman.

THORNDIKE, EDWARD L. 1940. *Human Nature and the Social Order.* New York: Macmillan.

THORNDIKE, EDWARD L. 1962. *Psychology and the Science of Education: Selected Writings of Edward L. Thorndike,* ed. Geraldine Jonçich. New York: Teachers College Press.

THORNDIKE, EDWARD L., and GATES, ARTHUR I. 1929. *Elementary Principles of Education.* New York: Macmillan.

THORNDIKE, EDWARD L., et al. 1928. *Adult Learning.* New York: Macmillan.

GERALDINE JONÇICH CLIFFORD

TITLE IX

SCHOOL SPORTS
Janet M. Holdsworth
INTERCOLLEGIATE ATHLETICS
Janet M. Holdsworth

SCHOOL SPORTS

Participation in interscholastic athletics programs provides students from diverse backgrounds opportunities to cooperate with and compete against their peers through sport. Participation in school sports may lead to the following benefits to students: improved physical health and fitness, higher self-esteem, a stronger sense of community and purpose, consistent time spent with an adult mentor, and increased academic performance in the classroom. Given the possible benefits associated with school sport participation, both boys and girls should have equitable opportunities to participate in and benefit from sports. Historically, boys have participated in interscholastic athletics programs in greater numbers than their female peers; at the turn of the twenty-first century, however, girls are participating in larger numbers than ever before.

In 1971 approximately 300,000 girls (compared to 3.5 million boys) participated in interscholastic sports programs. By 1999, an estimated 2.5 million girls (compared to about 4 million boys) participated in youth and high school sports. And overall, society is more accepting of this increased rate of girls' participation in school-sponsored sports. The increase in female participation in athletics at all levels across the United States is attributed mainly to the passage of Title IX of the Education Amendments of 1972 to the Civil Rights Act of 1964.

Since its passage in 1972, Title IX has been the main catalyst behind secondary school and college athletics programs creating more athletic opportunities for females. Title IX requires institutions receiving federal funding to provide equitable resources and opportunities for women in a nondiscriminatory way. The legislation states that "no person in the United States shall, on the basis of sex, be excluded from participation in, be denied the benefits of, or be subjected to discrimination under any educational program or activity receiving federal financial assistance." The Department of Education's Office for Civil Rights (OCR) has been responsible for the oversight of Title IX since 1980.

OCR created a three-prong test that is used to assess gender equity compliance in school athletic departments. Schools must meet the criteria of at least one prong to be in compliance with Title IX. To satisfy the first prong of the gender equity test, a school must show that the athletic participation rates by gender are within 5 percent of the enrollment rate for that gender. Schools may also be in compliance if they satisfy the second prong—providing evidence that the school has a history and current practice of program expansion for girls. To meet the requirements of the third prong, the school must demonstrate that it offers an athletic opportunity for girls if there is a sufficient interest and ability in a particular sport. Although schools need to meet only one prong of this three-prong test, most interscholastic athletics programs still have not achieved equity in the three major areas of Title IX that pertain to high school sports: athletic financial assistance, accommodation of student interests and abilities, and other program areas.

Schools do not necessarily need to provide equal funding for boys' and girls' sports. School sports programs are in compliance with Title IX if the quality of the girls' program is equal to that of the boys' program. The funding may not be equitable because of large programs (such as football), but if the total funding for overall programs are equal, then the school is more than likely in compliance. Other program areas that must be equitable by gender include: equipment and supplies, scheduling of practices and contests, travel, access to quality coaches with equitable pay, locker rooms and facilities, access to training facilities and medical services, publicity, and sporting opportunities.

Achieving sports equity in secondary schools is a significant factor in increasing opportunities for girls in sports and in helping to change perceptions about athletes based on traditional gender stereotypes. Gender equity in interscholastic sports translates into students having similar opportunities for participation in a variety of sports and seasons regardless of their gender. Equitable opportunities to benefit from participation in interscholastic sports should exist for all students. Although the number of girls participating in school sports has increased since the passage of Title IX, inequities still exist. Schools need to work with their athletics administrators and designated Title IX officers to ensure compliance is achieved.

See also: FEDERAL EDUCATIONAL ACTIVITIES; FINANCIAL SUPPORT OF SCHOOLS; INDIVIDUAL DIFFERENCES, *subentry on* GENDER EQUITY AND SCHOOLING; PHYSICAL EDUCATION; SPORTS, SCHOOL.

BIBLIOGRAPHY

LICHTMAN, BRENDA. 1997. "Playing Fair: What School Leaders Need to Know about Title IX and Gender Discrimination in Athletic Programs." *American School Board Journal* 184:27–30.

PRIEST, LAURIE, and SUMMERFIELD, LIANE M. 1995. "Promoting Gender Equity in Middle Level and Secondary School Sports Programs." *NASSP Bulletin* 79:52–56.

SOMMERFELD, MEG. 1998. "Parity on the Playing Field." *School Administrator* 55:32–36.

WHITE, KERRY A. 1999. "Girls' Sports: 'The Best of Times, the Worst of Times.'" *Education Week* 19(7):16–17.

INTERNET RESOURCE

WOMEN'S SPORTS FOUNDATION. 2002. "Playing Fair: A Guide to Title IX in High School and College Sports." <www.womenssportsfoundation.org/cgi-bin/iowa/issues/geena/action/record.html?record=818>.

JANET M. HOLDSWORTH

INTERCOLLEGIATE ATHLETICS

Ever since 1852, when Harvard defeated Yale in a regatta, intercollegiate athletics have played an increasingly significant role on American college and university campuses and in their communities. The boat race, set in New Hampshire, marked the first intercollegiate athletic event in the United States, and athletics rapidly became an important, and often controversial, part of collegiate life. The surge of enthusiasm around intercollegiate athletics—both on campus and in the surrounding community—mirrored the infectious competitive spirit of the developing American culture and society in the late nineteenth and early twentieth centuries. Since that first intercollegiate athletic event, undergraduate students competing in this unofficial *extra* curriculum have been transformed into the highly trained, specialized student athletes participating in the nationally visible (and televised) athletic events of the twenty-first century.

After 1900, intercollegiate athletic programs grew expansively on campuses across the United States in terms of the quantity and type of sports offered to undergraduate students, the number of male participants, and the size of operating budgets. Athletic competition for female undergraduates saw limited development, however, with the exception of sports-related activities and contests organized by physical educators, such as intramural and related events. Historically, female athletes faced exclusion in sports, as access to scholarships and facilities, and to playing, coaching, and administrative opportunities, were limited.

From the late nineteenth century until the mid-twentieth century, athletic activities offered to female undergraduates (e.g., basketball, field hockey, softball, and tennis) were meant to provide health benefits, not promote competition or any other seemingly negative and unfeminine characteristic in young women. This general protection and attempted preservation of collegiate women's feminine characteristics on campus paralleled the general perception of society at this time in history. The passage of Title IX of the 1972 Education Amendments to the 1964 Civil Rights Act marked the beginning of a shift from this restrictive climate toward an environment of more opportunities for females in athletics and of a growing awareness on campus and in society that female athletes can compete in the athletic arena in ways comparable to their male peers.

Gender Equity Legislation

Since its passage in 1972, Title IX has fueled the growth in college athletic programs and opportunities for female student athletes. Title IX requires institutions receiving federal funding to provide equitable resources and opportunities for women in a nondiscriminatory way. The legislation states that "no person in the United States shall, on the basis of sex, be excluded from participation in, be denied the benefits of, or be subjected to discrimination under any educational program or activity receiving federal financial assistance." After the legislation was passed, colleges and universities were granted until 1978 to make the necessary changes to programs and procedures in order to be in full compliance with the law.

Subsequent legislation passed by Congress has provided further assurance that institutions will be held accountable for complying with Title IX and its principles. For example, the 1987 Civil Rights Restoration Act specifically requires athletic departments to comply with Title IX. Also, the Equity in Athletics Disclosure Act of 1996 mandates the reporting of intercollegiate athletic participation rates and also requires institutions to report on departmental spending on athletic programs, by gender.

The enforcement of Title IX and gender equity in intercollegiate athletics is the responsibility of the federal government. Specifically, it is the responsibility of the Office of Civil Rights (OCR) in the Department of Education to enforce this law. In 1979, the OCR created and released the Intercollegiate Athletics Policy Interpretation, offering regulatory requirements related to Title IX compliance to assist institutions and athletic administrators in achieving gender equity. The OCR's interpretation of the policy broke down the legislation's application into the following three major categories: (1) athletic offerings; (2) athletic scholarships; and (3) other program areas, including (but not limited to) equipment, facility use, coaching, tutoring services, and publicity.

Gender Equity "Test"

The institutional task of complying with Title IX legislation is challenging, given the language of the law and its policy interpretations. As institutional practices were, and continue to be, questioned, the courts became involved in ascertaining whether or not the athletic interests and abilities of females are accommodated effectively. In order to determine whether or not an athletic department is in compliance, the OCR created a three-prong test for Title IX. An institution's athletic department is found in compliance with achieving gender equity if at least one criterion is met.

The first prong in the OCR's gender equity compliance test is whether or not the intercollegiate athletic participation opportunities for male and female undergraduates are offered in numbers substantially proportionate to their enrollment numbers at the institution in question. The second prong includes an assessment of whether or not the institution is able to show a continuing practice of program expansion for members of the historically underrepresented sex, based on student interest and abilities. The third prong consists of whether or not an institution can establish that the needs and interests of the underrepresented group are satisfied and accommodated by the existing athletic program. Typically, the OCR and courts will examine this third criterion only when it is clear that an institution's athletic department meets neither of the first two criteria.

Opportunities, Challenges, and Debates

Title IX created, and continues to create, positive opportunities for females in intercollegiate athletics; however, real challenges sparking debate about gender equity in sports continue to exist. Despite a growth in undergraduate enrollment and participation and opportunities for females in intercollegiate athletics since the enactment of Title IX, data collected and reports released in the late 1990s suggest that inequities still exist across competition levels, with some divisional and sport differences emerging. These athletic-related inequities include fewer participation opportunities, unequal facilities and services, lagging coaches' salaries, and smaller proportions of operating and recruiting budgets.

According to the General Accounting Office's 2001 report, approximately 400,000 student athletes participated in intercollegiate athletics at four-year colleges and universities during the 1998–1999 school year, with approximately 160,000 being female athletes. While this represented a significant increase from the 90,000 female student athletes who participated in 1981–1982, published gender-equity statistics continue to highlight the underrepresentation of female student athletes, specifically in Division I universities (the institutions offering the majority of athletic scholarships), compared to the proportion of females in the undergraduate student population at these institutions. According to the National Collegiate Athletic Association (NCAA), females made up the majority of the total undergraduate enrollment in Division I institutions in 1997–1998, while only 37 percent of the student athletes were female. The majority of female student athletes are situated in the colleges and universities

2572 TITLE IX: INTERCOLLEGIATE ATHLETICS

that are classified as Division II- and Division III-level institutions. By 2000, approximately 41 percent of athletes competing at the Division III level were female, compared to 38 percent and 32 percent at the Division II and Division I levels, respectively. As debates over the significance of the gains made for women's athletic programs continue to occur, the fact remains that female student athletes are underrepresented in all divisions, especially when the substantial proportionality criterion of Title IX is applied.

Additional gains have been made in gender equity since Title IX, including an increase in spending on women's sports programs. In the late 1990s, women's sports programs and budgets grew at a faster rate than men's sports programs and budgets, though data suggest that men's sports receive approximately twice as much money for recruiting, athletic scholarships, and operating expenses in the top collegiate athletic programs. In 1974 approximately fifty female athletes received athletic-related scholarships for their athletic ability, while 50,000 male student athletes were awarded such scholarships. By 1997, approximately 35 percent of all athletic scholarship dollars were awarded to female student athletes.

Although athletic-based scholarships awarded to female student athletes at the Division I level are increasing, many supporters of Title IX argue that the gap between male and female scholarship recipients is closing at an inexcusably slow rate. Even with an increase in the proportion of operating and recruiting budgets earmarked for women's sports programs, women's sports teams continue to receive less overall funding than men's sports teams. Additional data reveal that the Division II and III colleges and universities spend a larger proportion of their athletic funding on women's sports programs than do Division I institutions.

Despite the gains made by females in attaining midlevel athletic administrative positions in colleges and universities since 1972, women remain underrepresented in top-ranking, intercollegiate athletic leadership positions, including director-level administrative positions and top-paying coaching positions. A related and especially interesting phenomenon has occurred since 1972 in terms of the demographics of the head coaches of women's teams. Approximately 90 percent of female athletic teams had female coaches prior to 1972; however, by 1998, females coached only 47 percent of women's

sports teams. A debate continues over this and related issues as to whether or not, with the passage of gender equity legislation and the male-dominated NCAA assuming leadership over the administration of women's athletics in 1983, women's sports have assimilated into the dominant culture of male sports. With this assimilation, some argue, came the loss of the unique characteristics of women's sports, as well as the female voice in governance issues related to intercollegiate athletics.

A major concern for many athletic departments at the beginning of the twenty-first century is how to commit to gender equity while building powerful and competitive programs, managing shrinking athletic department budgets, and avoiding the decision to eliminate men's teams. Debates over how to achieve equity, and at what cost to institutions and other athletic programs, are widespread in postsecondary institutions at all competition levels. Campus administrators employ various strategies to comply with Title IX, such as adding new facilities and purchasing new equipment and uniforms in an attempt to provide equal opportunities and equitable resources for female student athletes. Some colleges and universities have discovered creative ways to add athletic opportunities for female student athletes without eliminating men's athletic teams, which creates a win-win situation, produces a less threatening climate on campus, and placates both athletes and alumni.

According to Title IX, women in postsecondary institutions must be afforded equal opportunity in the classrooms as well as on the playing fields, courts, and tracks. Gender equity in general, and Title IX specifically, are necessary components to achieving equitable opportunities in the postsecondary education experience for all students, no matter their sex. Female student athletes and other individuals and groups, collectively, have made significant accomplishments in the area of gender equity in intercollegiate athletics. Debates surrounding how best to achieve gender equity in intercollegiate athletics, despite Title IX, additional supportive legislation, and court rulings mandating compliance, are likely to continue well into the first half of the twenty-first century.

See also: COLLEGE ATHLETICS; FINANCE, HIGHER EDUCATION; INDIVIDUAL DIFFERENCES, *subentry on* GENDER EQUITY AND SCHOOLING.

BIBLIOGRAPHY

Acosta, R. Vivian, and Carpenter, Linda J. 1985. "Women in Sport." In *Sport and Higher Education,* ed. Donald Chu, Jeffrey O. Segrave, and Beverly J. Becker. Champaign, IL: Human Kinetics.

General Accounting Office. 2001. *Intercollegiate Athletics: Four Year Colleges' Experiences Adding and Discontinuing Teams.* Washington, DC: U. S. General Accounting Office.

Howell, Reet. 1982. *Her Story in Sport: A Historical Anthology of Women in Sports.* West Point, NY: Leisure Press.

Lazerson, Marvin, and Wagener, Ursula. 1996. "Missed Opportunities: Lessons From the Title IX Case at Brown." *Change* 28:46–52.

National Collegiate Athletic Association. Gender Equity Task Force. 1995. *Achieving Gender Equity: A Basic Guide to Title IX for Colleges and Universities.* Overland Park, KS: National Collegiate Athletic Association.

Shulman, James A., and Bowen, William G. 2001. *The Game of Life: College Sports and Educational Values.* Princeton, NJ: Princeton University Press.

Smith, Ronald A. 1988. *Sports and Freedom: The Rise of Big-Time College Athletics.* New York: Oxford University Press.

Toma, J. Douglas, and Cross, Michael E. 2000. "Contesting Values in American Higher Education: The Playing Field of Intercollegiate Athletics." In *Higher Education: Handbook of Theory and Research,* ed. John C. Smart and William G. Tierney. New York: Agathon Press.

U.S. Department of Education. 1997. *Title IX: 25 Years of Progress.* Washington, DC: U.S. Department of Education and Office for Civil Rights.

Janet M. Holdsworth

TRANSPORTATION AND SCHOOL BUSING

Pupil transportation, also known as school busing, has become one of the most important segments of the American educational system. It is subject to the same rules one might find in the classroom, including the dictates of the Americans with Disabilities Act (ADA) of 1990 and a host of laws and rules governing disabled or special needs pupils.

Pupil transportation is big business. The number of school children riding school buses in the United States has risen dramatically, making school busing one of this nation's greatest service industries. American pupil transportation provides an estimated 10 billion rides to and from school annually.

In 1950, 7 million children were transported in 115,000 school buses. Fifty years later, 448,307 school buses transported 22,675,116 children more than 3,788,427,941 miles to and from public schools. Many of these were pupils with special needs. It is not known how many nonpublic school children are transported or how many school buses are used to transport them.

Public school transportation costs approximately $500 per year per pupil. Only Pennsylvania transports all school children at state expense. The fifty states spent $11,746,576,005 for the 1999–2000 school year, which included expenditures for transportation and capital outlay to purchase new or replacement school buses.

According to a national annual survey done through the state directors of pupil transportation of each state, twenty-two children were killed in school bus loading or unloading accidents during the 1999–2000 school year, whereas eighteen were killed in the 1997–1998 school year. The average annual number of pupils killed in school bus–related accidents during the 1990s is 20.4. The highest toll was during the 1993–1994 school year when thirty-two pupils were killed and the lowest was ten in 1997–1998. More than half of the fatal accidents occurred as pupils were exiting the bus in the afternoon, while approximately one-quarter of the accidents took place in the morning as pupils were waiting for the school bus. As one might expect, most of the victims were elementary school children. Only two of the victims were over the age of twelve. Eleven children were struck by their own bus and another eleven were struck by passing vehicles.

The School Bus

The school bus remains the safest form of surface transportation in the United States. It is far safer than the automobile, truck, public bus, or train. School buses are designed and manufactured specifically for the safety and protection of pupil passengers. Manufacturers must conform to a host of federal standards and certify that each school bus meets all federal and state standards.

The school bus is made up of a straight-body truck chassis with a school bus body mounted on two I-beams. Each area of the school bus body is constructed of a skeletal system beneath the finish and trim elements. The framing elements are heavy-gauge steel collision beams covered by heavy-gauge steel plates. Emergency personnel have to be specially trained in extrication due to this skeletal framework and the safety cushion built around the pupils.

Safety features. School buses are constructed using the concept of *compartmentalization,* which provides a passive restraint system in lieu of seat belts. The passengers are seated higher off the ground so that average-sized opposing vehicles are beneath the pupils' feet. The four-inch cushioned seats and seat backs afford the passenger a padded compartment in case of collision. The seats are closer together than in most vehicles to further create a compartmentalized safety zone. The aisles are twelve inches apart. There are no windshields or door close to the riders to offer paths of ejection from the bus. The passenger windows are placed higher than passenger vehicles. Elementary pupils are housed three to a seat while secondary pupils sit two to a seat. This crowding affords an extra measure of safety because the pupils cannot move far from their seat.

In the case of emergency, evacuation may be through the front service door, the rear emergency door, side emergency-operation windows, or roof hatches designed to offer ventilation or fully open as escape routes. In addition, the front windshield may be kicked out to provide another escape route. Escape is also possible through all side windows, which open eleven inches vertically by twenty-two inches in width. Students are trained through school bus evacuation drills to know what to do in case of an emergency. Emergency evacuation drills are held regularly and include what to do after exiting the school bus or in the event of the driver becoming disabled. Emergency evacuation preparation sessions are also conducted with students with disabilities and wheelchair-bound students.

Federal requirements regulate new vehicles that carry eleven or more people that are sold for transporting students to or from school or school-related events. These vehicles are required to meet all federal motor vehicle safety standards (FMVSS) for school buses. They must have stop arms, as regular buses do, along with many other safety features that exceed those of other passenger vehicles.

The success of the pupil transportation program is more dependent on the professional performance by the school bus driver than any other factor in program service. The welfare of every child is directly related to the skills, attitudes, and decisions of the driver.

History of Pupil Transportation

In 1869 the Commonwealth of Massachusetts passed the first legislation in the United States allowing the use of public funds for transporting school children. By 1919, with the passage of legislation in Delaware and Wyoming, forty-eight states had enacted similar laws. The primary reasons that states passed such legislation appear to be state-mandated, compulsory school attendance and the consolidation of public schools.

The standard means of transporting children to and from school in the nineteenth century was the school wagon, a modified farm wagon converted to carry pupils from the rural areas to the consolidated schools. By World War I motorized trucks began to replace the farm wagons and soon wooden bodies replaced the canvas tarpaulins that covered the farm wagons. Steel bodies emerged to replace the wooden bodies in the 1920s, and the basic concept of the modern school bus had begun to take shape.

With the passage of the National Traffic and Motor Safety Act of 1966, the federal government was authorized to issue regulations and standards to improve the safety of all motor vehicles manufactured in the United States. As of 2001, thirty-three Federal Motor Vehicle Safety Standards that apply to school buses had been issued. Additions and changes to these standards in 1977 substantially upgraded the safety characteristics, particularly the crashworthiness, of school buses manufactured after April 1, 1977.

The newer the school bus, the safer it is. The watershed year for school bus safety was 1977, when requirements for most of the important safety features were put into place. Tragically, it took a fatal school bus accident to accomplish a goal of further safety. As a result of a major accident in Carrollton, Kentucky, in 1988, safety features were studied and later added to the FMVS standards. School buses manufactured after 1992 have even more critical safety equipment such as additional emergency exits, better mirrors for the driver to be able to see around the bus, and swing-out stop arms to alert motorists that children are getting on or off the bus.

Issues in Pupil Transportation

Most issues in pupil transportation cannot be resolved without substantial increases in expenditures. Demands from the public for expanded programs, door-to-door services, and requests for increases in salaries for bus drivers greatly impact budgets. The elimination of on-board disciplinary problems and a reduction in the rate of turnover of school bus drivers tend to be the major factors affected by budgets. Spending tax dollars wisely in the area of pupil transportation continues to be one of the greatest concerns of school administrators.

Ridership. More than 5,000 children under the age of nineteen are killed each year as passengers in motor vehicles other than school buses. More than 800 school-aged children are killed yearly in passenger cars or other private vehicles during normal school hours. It is likely that many of these children were on their way to or from school or a school-related activity. By comparison, an average of eleven children die each year while they are school bus passengers.

Education opportunities for children with disabilities have increased over the years. Transporting children with disabilities to receive education has evolved as well. The passage of the Federal Handicapped Act, Public Law 94-142, and Section 504 of the Federal Rehabilitation Act changed the way schools provide education-related transportation for children with disabilities. Specialized technical and safety equipment have improved greatly to provide safe travel to and from school for students with special transportation needs.

Compartmentalization as a safety feature. In today's school buses compartmentalization is used instead of lap belts to provide an extremely high level of crash protection for student passengers, considering all the types of crashes involving school buses. There are no aggregate statistical data to suggest that a safety problem exists in large school buses that the installation of lap belts would solve. In fact, there is growing concern among safety professionals around the world over the use of lap belts as a form of passenger restraint for young or small children. In August 1998 at a public hearing held by the National Transportation Safety Board (NTSB), five international experts in the field of motor vehicle occupant crash protection expressed their concern about the appropriateness of lap belts in providing crash protection to small children. The unanimous opinion was that lap belts were not a good means of providing crash protection to small children because small children's bone structure, particularly in the area of the hips, is still developing.

An October 1998 study by the Association for the Advancement of Automotive Medicine concluded that children restrained in three-point belts exhibit a similar pattern of injury to those in two-point belts; however, three-point belts appear to be effective for the lumbar spine. The report noted that "seat belt syndrome," which is associated with the use of two-point belts, can include bruising of the abdominal wall, fracture of the lumbar spine, and internal abdominal injuries.

At the outset of the twenty-first century, the National Highway Traffic Safety Administration (NHTSA) is conducting an extensive research program to consider alternative methods of potentially improving federal school bus passenger crash protection requirements. The NHTSA maintains the organizations' position that compartmentalization has proven to be an excellent form of school bus passenger crash protection, but believes it is important to develop the necessary data and science to review and evaluate potential improvements in passenger crash protection for the next generation of school buses.

Pupil discipline. Pupil discipline is probably the most serious issue in pupil transportation. If the riders are misbehaving it takes the driver's attention away from the driving responsibilities. The school bus is considered to be an extension of the classroom, as far as rules and regulations are concerned. While teachers normally have twenty-eight to thirty-two pupils in their class, facing them, school bus drivers have up to eighty-one pupils on a school bus, all sitting behind the driver, who has only an interior rear view mirror to monitor the pupils. Only school buses designated for special needs have aides on board to assist the driver in off-loading pupils.

Drivers must receive the most up-to-date training in pupil discipline methodology in order to provide both safe transportation and a safe environment for all riders. This issue requires serious training for both the drivers and the pupil riders, as well as effective policies to deal with problems. Most offenses are referred to the school administration for action. If riders have come to expect that the school administration will not take action in response to infractions, they are more apt to misbehave.

Methods for minimizing on-board discipline problems include adding personnel or technological means for monitoring behavior, maintaining clear guidelines and consequences for inappropriate activity, and upgrading student education concerning bus behavior. Parent support is also important.

School bus monitors offer a means of altering behavior to reduce discipline problems but cost is a major objection. Video cameras can help promote safe bus behavior, but critics are concerned about the potential for invading student privacy. However, there is no such thing as privacy aboard the school bus except for personal belongings. School bus video cameras are not directed at any person or group but record all that goes on in the school bus.

The use of video cameras mounted inside the bus must be authorized by the state or local boards of education. Prior warning to pupils and parents that video cameras are authorized and in use should be made in writing. A video camera policy should be developed and use of the film should be very limited. School transportation administrators should review tapes when there has been a discipline complaint. They should also review tapes from each school bus on a periodic basis to see if there are problems on that school bus which are not being reported.

Because the video camera and its mounting devices are expensive, most school districts will install the mounting boxes on every school bus and provide one video camera for every ten or so buses. The cameras are mounted in a box with a one-way mirror so that the camera can videotape outward but no one can see through the glass window to see if there is a camera on board the school bus that day. When complaints come in about a particular bus or driver, use of the camera can allay concerns or capture the problems on videotape. The videotape also lets the supervisor know what the driver is doing, although normally the driver is not in direct view while seated in the driver's seat.

Student education is needed as well. It has been estimated that enhanced pupil education programs could be conducted at an additional cost of about one dollar per student per year. Much of the present pupil training relates to loading and unloading the school bus, crossing streets safely, and using emergency exits in case of an accident. Additional education and awareness about appropriate bus behavior could help reduce disciplinary problems.

Suspension of bus riding privileges for rule offenders for one to three days is a common punishment that can act as a deterrent. Parents usually must provide transportation during this time period, because pupils are generally not also suspended from school for bus-related disciplinary problems. As in all aspects of a child's education, parent support is vital in promoting appropriate bus riding behavior.

Driver recruitment and retention. The old adage in the school transportation industry goes, "When the economy is bad, we have all of the school bus drivers we need; however, when the economy is good, we cannot get enough drivers." School bus driving is normally a part-time job. Drivers pick the pupils up in the morning and take them to school, then pick them up at school in the afternoon and take them home. In most cases the job takes no more than one to two hours in the morning and one to two hours in the afternoon.

In the past there was a ready reserve of potential drivers among stay-at-home mothers who would take such a job because the hours were short. They would be at work when their children were in or on their way to school, and they would be off work the same days as their children were out of school, including summers. With fewer stay-at-home mothers, the pool of available drivers has been reduced, even during economic downturns.

Transportation officials now have to be creative, offering incentives and more pay, or creating more employment hours. One way to do this is to have the school utilize the hours between morning and afternoon bus trips by employing these drivers as classroom aides, custodians, groundskeepers, and cafeteria workers.

Retaining drivers is another problem. School transportation departments train their drivers to operate a school bus. Drivers obtain commercial drivers licenses with associated endorsements and through on-the-road training they develop experience. Once school bus drivers have this combination of road experience and commercial license endorsements, they are often recruited by the trucking industry, which benefits from having trained and licensed drivers. Commercial transportation jobs offer full-time employment and a higher rate of pay.

To combat this draining of trained drivers, the pupil transportation industry has been lobbying for a *school bus–specific* commercial driver's license. Several states have adopted this measure but the federal government has not yet endorsed the concept.

Driver training and qualification. The screening and training of drivers is another issue for the school transportation industry. The minimum age for school bus drivers in most states is eighteen, although some states set the minimum at nineteen or twenty-one. Driver training ranges from eight hours of classroom time to forty hours in the classroom as a minimum training requirement. There is also on-the-road training and qualification under the tutelage of a driver trainer for an additional eight to twelve hours. Some states require in-service training on a yearly basis. All states check driving history and require annual or semiannual physical examinations. Thirty-nine states require fingerprinting and submission of state and federal criminal history background checks. All states interview prospective drivers in the selection process.

To ensure uniform safety of students in all fifty states, industry watchers believe there should be mandatory minimum training standards and qualifications in the United States plus yearly in-service training. The National Highway Traffic Safety Administration recommends that school bus safety instruction be provided to children, as well, on at least a semiannual basis.

School planning design. Finally, the issue of school grounds design is of concern to school transportation professionals. When school layouts are designed, the school bus is many times a forgotten or add-on issue. The safety of school children is at stake, and school bus drivers and transportation officials have valuable perspectives on how to increase safety in the vicinity of school buses.

When designing schools, care should be taken to design loading and unloading areas on school grounds that safely allow pupils to board or exit the school bus. This area must be free from conflict with other vehicles and non-bus riders. The drivers must have adequate space designed for entering and exiting the school bus area without backing up their vehicles. Separate locations must be provided for parent pick-up zones and other parking facilities. Transportation officials should be included in the site planning of new schools, and they can also offer assistance in upgrading existing sites for increased safety.

See also: SCHOOL FACILITIES.

BIBLIOGRAPHY

ALLEN, KEITH. 1976. *Guidebook for School Transportation Supervisors.* Mt. Pleasant: Central Michigan University/American Automobile Association.

ASSOCIATION OF SCHOOL BUSINESS OFFICIALS. 1987. *Issues in Pupil Transportation.* Reston, VA: Association of School Business Officials.

MILLER, ANTHONY R. 2001. *Pupil Transportation Management,* 2nd edition. Thousand Oaks, CA: Ramsburg and Roth.

NATIONAL ASSOCIATION OF STATE DIRECTORS OF PUPIL TRANSPORTATION SERVICES. 1994. *Emergency and Rescue Procedures: A Guideline Manual for School Bus Involvement.* Dover, DE: National Association of State Directors of Pupil Transportation Services.

NATIONAL ASSOCIATION OF STATE DIRECTORS OF PUPIL TRANSPORTATION SERVICES. 1999. *Position Paper: Passenger Crash Protection in School Buses.* Dover, DE: National Association of State Directors of Pupil Transportation Services.

NATIONAL HIGHWAY TRAFFIC SAFETY ADMINISTRATION. 1997. *School Bus Safety: Safe Passage for America's Children.* Washington, DC: U.S. Government Printing Office.

NATIONAL TRANSPORTATION SAFETY BOARD. 1999. *Highway Special Investigation Report: Bus Crashworthiness Issues.* Washington, DC: National Technical Information Service.

SCHOOL BUS FLEET MAGAZINE. 2001. *School Bus Fleet 2001 Fact Book.* Torrance, CA: Bobit.

THE THIRTEENTH NATIONAL CONFERENCE ON SCHOOL TRANSPORTATION. 2000. *National School Transportation Specifications and Procedures.* Warrensburg, MO: Central Missouri State University Safety Center.

TRANSPORTATION RESEARCH BOARD OF THE NATIONAL RESEARCH COUNCIL. 1989. *Special Report 222: Improving School Bus Safety.* Washington, DC: U.S. Government Printing Office.

HARLAN TULL

TRIBAL COLLEGES AND UNIVERSITIES

Tribal colleges and universities are unique American institutions that offer opportunities for Native Americans to pursue higher education within their own cultural and regional contexts. Generally located on or near Indian reservations, tribal colleges and universities (also referred to as tribally controlled colleges) aim to preserve and communicate traditional native culture, provide higher education and career or technical opportunities to tribal members, enhance economic opportunities within the reservation community, and promote tribal self-determination.

In 1968 Diné, Inc., an organization established by Native American political and education leaders, founded Navajo Community College (later renamed Diné College). This was the first tribal college to be created on an American Indian reservation. Since then the number of tribal colleges has increased steadily in the United States. As of 2001, thirty-two tribal colleges have emerged, created *by* American Indians tribes *for* American Indians. These colleges are located in areas with large concentrations of Native Americans, principally in the upper Midwest, the Pacific Northwest, and the Southwest.

There are seven tribal colleges in Montana, five in North Dakota, four in South Dakota, three in Minnesota, three in New Mexico, two each in Michigan, Nebraska, and Wisconsin, and one each in Arizona, California, Kansas, and Washington. Inclusive of these, two new colleges in Michigan and Minnesota were added in 2001, highlighting the steady growth that tribal colleges continue to experience in their relatively short history. Among these tribal colleges and universities, twenty-four are community colleges and offer the associate's degree and technical and vocational certificates, six offer the bachelor's degree, and two offer the master's degree. In light of the tribes' federal sovereign status, however, tribal colleges and universities receive little or no state funds. Thus, they are primarily dependent on federal assistance for their core operating expenses through oversight by the Bureau of Indian Affairs.

Students and Faculty

The majority of tribal colleges and universities are located on isolated Indian reservations. As a result, most of them have small enrollments, often less than 1,000 students. While smaller classes enable these tribal colleges to offer more individualized instruction, they also struggle with limited resources in part due to their smaller enrollments. As of 1994 tribal colleges served approximately 15,000 full- and part-time students according to the National Center for Education Statistics. The average age of tribal college students has become younger in recent years, from thirty years of age down to twenty-seven, as students are choosing with greater frequency to enroll directly in a tribal college after graduation from high school. The majority of students are more likely to come from families with lower levels of educational attainment and thus be first-generation college students. Many students also receive some form of federal financial aid.

The modal profile of the typical tribal college student, however, is a single mother with young children, living below the poverty level and often dependent on welfare or her extended family for support. This typical student attends part-time, and is academically underprepared for college, thus in need of some remedial courses. Child care and family services are common needs for these students that tribal colleges try to meet on their campuses. Lack of dependable transportation and available telephone services in isolated reservation areas also impact tribal students' ability to attend regularly or to communicate with college officials when problems arise and they cannot attend classes.

To help overcome these economic and educational obstacles, tribal colleges offer their students opportunities for self-determination and academic and career success. This is done through an array of diverse, comprehensive, academic and technical course offerings; a culturally infused curriculum that incorporates native values, beliefs, and customs; and a variety of academic and student support services. Another important characteristic is that at least 30 percent of the faculty are Native American and Alaska Natives as compared to less than one percent of all faculty at all other public postsecondary institutions. Thus, students have native role models and mentors, some of whom are tribal elders, who bring cultural awareness, sensitivity, and specific curricular expertise to the classroom. As native faculty, they also have a greater understanding of students' academic and personal situations.

Tribal colleges seek to prepare their students to succeed both inside and outside the reservation. In placing a significant value on the students' culture and incorporating it into the college experience in a holistic manner, tribal colleges and universities are able to achieve higher retention and graduation rates for Native American students than mainstream institutions can. In 1994 tribal colleges awarded 69 percent of their associate's degrees, 81 percent of the bachelor's degrees, and 67 percent of the master's degrees to Native American students. By comparison, only 0.9 percent of the associate's degrees, 0.5 of the bachelor's degrees, and 0.4 of the master's degrees awarded by all other institutions were earned by Native American students that year.

Institutional Types

Four types of tribal colleges and universities have emerged over the years for Native American students. The dominant type of tribal institution to emerge is that chartered by one or more federally recognized American Indian tribes. These receive funds from the federal government administered through the Bureau of Indian Affairs, a subgroup of the Department of Interior. Additionally, two colleges are tribally controlled vocational technical institutions: Crownpoint Institute of Technology in New Mexico and United Tribes Technical College in North Dakota. These are funded under the Carl D. Perkins Vocational and Applied Technology Act through the Department of Education.

Two other colleges, Haskell Indian Nations University in Kansas and Southwestern Indian Polytechnic Institute in New Mexico, fall into a third type as federally chartered institutions. The Bureau of Indian Affairs operates them and limits enrollment in these colleges solely to American Indians and Alaska Natives. One school, the Institute of American Indian Arts in New Mexico, is of the fourth type. It is chartered by Congress and governed by a board of trustees appointed by the president.

Accreditation and Funding

All tribal colleges either have full accreditation status from national accreditation boards, or are in the process of earning accreditation, which is the case for the newest institutions. Moreover, except for the third type, all other tribal colleges have open door admissions policies and serve non-Native Americans in their communities as well.

Two important organizations underwrite additional support for the tribal colleges. In 1972 the American Indian Higher Education Consortium (AIHEC) was organized by leaders of fledging tribal colleges to unite and promote their institutions. The

AIHEC secured federal funding for tribal colleges by getting Congress to pass the Tribally Controlled Community College Assistance Act in 1978 (now referred to as the Tribally Controlled College or University Assistance Act). This act provides for construction, technical assistance, and endowment building funds. In keeping with the latter provision, the federal government matches every dollar raised by tribes for contribution to their institutional endowment funds. Also, the annual AIHEC meeting brings members together to discuss common issues and highlight examples of member colleges' programs and research by Native American scholars. In addition, the AIHEC publishes *Tribal College,* a quarterly journal. Another important source of financial support is the American Indian College Fund. It was created in 1989 with the active support of Ernest Boyer, president of the Carnegie Foundation, who procured financial contributions from numerous foundations and individual contributors to get it established.

A major funding change for tribal colleges occurred in 1998 with the reauthorization of the Higher Education Act. An amendment to the act recognized tribal colleges and universities as special focus institutions serving a distinct population of students and placed them under Title V alongside historically black colleges and universities. Administered by the Department of Education, Title V enables tribal colleges to receive additional funds allocated by Congress.

Nonetheless, tribal colleges and universities remain seriously underfunded compared to the varied support received by mainstream higher education institutions. This will continue to be the case as these institutions increase in number and compete among themselves for the limited resources available to them. A shortage of funds already has led to inferior facilities due to delayed building maintenance and construction, limited classroom materials and laboratory equipment, few on-campus residence halls for students, and poorly paid administrators, faculty, and staff.

Despite scarcity of funding, tribal colleges and universities remain unique within higher education in several ways. Overall, these institutions remain locally and culturally controlled by their own tribes. Second, almost one-third of the faculty across the spectrum of tribal colleges is Native American. Third, they offer a distinctive curriculum that centers on their own native language and culture, some taught by tribal elders, to ensure that their cultural heritage is passed on to future generations. Fourth, they are responsive to the economic needs of their communities. Lastly, tribal colleges will continue to increase in number across states as more tribes seek self-determination and greater educational and career success for their members.

See also: HIGHER EDUCATION IN THE UNITED STATES, *subentries on* HISTORICAL DEVELOPMENT, SYSTEM; HISPANIC-SERVING COLLEGES AND UNIVERSITIES; HISTORICALLY BLACK COLLEGES AND UNIVERSITIES.

BIBLIOGRAPHY

HARVEY, WILLIAM. 2001. *Minorities in Higher Education 2000–2001: Eighteenth Annual Status Report.* Washington, DC: American Council on Education.

NATIONAL CENTER FOR EDUCATION STATISTICS. 2001. *American Indians and Alaska Natives in Postsecondary Education.* Washington, DC: National Center for Education Statistics.

PAVEL, D. MICHAEL; INGLEBRET, ELLA; and VANDENHENDE, MARK. 1999. "Tribal Colleges." In *Two-Year Colleges for Women and Minorities: Enabling Access to the Baccalaureate,* ed. Barbara Townsend. New York: Falmer.

STEIN, WAYNE. 1998. "Tribally Controlled Colleges." In *American Indians and Alaska Natives in Postsecondary Education,* ed. D. Michael Pavel, Rebecca Rak Skinner, Elizabeth Farris, Margaret Cahalan, John Tippeconnic, and Wayne Stein. Washington, DC: U.S. Department of Education.

YATES, ELEANOR LEE. 2001. "American Heritage." *Community College Week* 13(11):6–9.

INTERNET RESOURCE

AMERICAN INDIAN HIGHER EDUCATION CONSORTIUM. 1999. *Tribal Colleges: An Introduction.* <www.aihec.org/intro.pdf>.

BERTA VIGIL LADEN

TUTORING

SCHOOL
Lee Shumow

HIGHER EDUCATION
Art Farlowe
INTERNATIONAL TRENDS
Mark Bray

SCHOOL

Tutoring typically involves two individuals, a tutor and a tutee. The tutor is more knowledgeable or expert than the tutee and attempts to help the tutee learn, usually in an academic area. Age is not necessarily a factor in the tutoring relationship—the tutor and tutee may be the same age—as long as the tutor has greater knowledge or skill than the tutee. Traditionally, tutoring has involved one-to-one instruction, but some tutoring programs do involve a tutor and two or three tutees.

Scholars have long considered tutoring the most effective form of instruction. Numerous research studies provide evidence on which to base this conclusion. The American public appears to be aware of the value of tutoring. According to a 1998 *Newsweek* survey, 42 percent of Americans strongly believe that children should receive private tutoring outside of school. In addition to providing extra practice, tutoring appears to be successful because the intensive individualized attention allows the tutor to identify the student's level of expertise. When the tutor has a clear idea of the next steps in the learning process, he or she is then able to present tutees with materials at their precise level of understanding. Tutoring also is thought to be effective because of the social support and modeling inherent in the process.

Tutees run the gamut from students performing far below grade level to students vying for Ivy League admissions. A wide range of options exists for students who need or desire tutoring. Those options vary in cost, availability, quality, and effectiveness.

School-Based Tutoring Programs

Tutoring is a component of numerous educational programs designed for the prevention of, or intervention with, students at risk of educational failure. These programs are to be delivered by professional or paraprofessional teachers in schools. Reading has been the focus of many school-based tutoring programs. For example, tutoring by certified teachers with special training is a component of Success for All, a comprehensive program designed by Robert Slavin for at-risk primary-school children. More than one million students have participated in Success for All. Studies have documented the effectiveness of the program, and it has been extended to other academic subjects with the Roots and Wings program. The Success for All program is most effective in schools that fully implement the model, and when it is maintained into, but not beyond, middle school.

Reading Recovery is another popular program—it was used by more than 9,000 schools in the 1995–1996 school year. Reading Recovery identifies first graders performing in the lower 20 percent of their class in reading, and these students receive thirty minutes of individual tutoring each day beyond the time spent in classroom reading instruction until they can read at grade level (on average, this takes three to five months). Tutors are certified teachers who have been specially trained in Reading Recovery methods. Numerous studies document that participants in Reading Recovery read better than control group students. However, some researchers point out that Reading Recovery has not been effective for somewhere between 10 and 30 percent of participating students.

Many school districts use Title I funds to finance Reading Recovery. Initially, teachers must be trained, a cost that varies from five to eight thousand dollars. In subsequent years, the costs involve teacher time for one-to-one instruction. Some schools have scheduled creatively so as to minimize that cost. Cost estimates are site specific, and vary from $2,500 to $10,000 annually per student, which is less than the cost of special education programs.

Reading One-to-One, a tutorial program for students in kindergarten through eighth grade who are struggling in reading, has been implemented in more than 100 schools in the United States and Mexico. The program builds on concepts of Reading Recovery and Success for All, but uses paraprofessionals rather than professionals to deliver forty minutes of individualized reading instruction several times per week. Only one study has been conducted on the effectiveness of Reading One-to-One. That study used few students, but found significant positive reading gains associated with program participation. The program designers state that seventy sessions are needed for students to make significant gains. Program costs have been estimated to be $600 per child per year to cover books, materials, tutor training, and paraprofessional salary.

Volunteer Tutoring Programs

Some tutoring programs depend on adult volunteers. Numerous schools throughout the country utilize parents as volunteer tutors. These parents often listen to children read, or they practice academic skills with students individually or in small groups. The circumstances, time spent, and the tutor preparation, skill, and knowledge vary enormously between programs. There are very few studies on the effectiveness of using volunteer tutors. Barbara Wasik reviewed the literature in 1997 and found only two programs that had used control groups in the evaluation. Those two programs were evaluated positively, but one of the programs no longer operates. A reading specialist supervised both programs, and training was provided to the tutors. The cost of both programs to the school districts entailed the salary of the reading specialist and any materials used during tutoring.

Dropout prevention has been the purpose of a number of other school-based mentoring programs. Mentors are usually volunteers from school staff or the community. There is some evidence that such programs are successful when mentors meet consistently with students and regularly monitor their progress. Social support and modeling appear to be the mechanisms through which those programs help to lower school dropout rates. The cost of those programs involves the time of the program coordinator at the schools.

Two nonprofit educational literacy organizations, Laubach Literacy and Literacy Volunteers of America, support the provision of free tutoring for older youths and adults who need basic literacy instruction. The two programs agreed to merge in 2002. Together, the program professional managers will support approximately 160,000 volunteers in 1,450 local, state, and regional literacy programs. Educational materials are published for tutees and for tutor training. Tutors receive information about approaches that have been found to be effective through experience and empirically tested theory. Laubach Literacy has developed a rigorous accreditation program for literacy tutoring programs.

Private For-Profit Tutoring

Private tutoring paid for by fees is another tutoring arrangement. There have been no comprehensive studies of private tutoring, so little is known about the extent and effects of private tutoring. Parents choose to send their children to professionally trained tutors at private businesses to address concerns about student's educational progress or preparedness for examinations. Local tutoring businesses operate in affluent communities throughout the nation, and private tutors command as much as $125 per hour in affluent urban enclaves.

Several tutoring chains operate throughout the nation. Huntington, a corporation that has been operating since 1977, has centers located throughout the United States. Local offices provide tutoring in different subject areas and in test preparation for preschoolers through adults. Most instruction for children takes place in a ratio of three students to one certified teacher but individual (one-to-one) tutoring also is available. Tuition depends on the geographic location of the facility and ranges from thirty to forty-five dollars per hour for group tutoring and from forty to sixty dollars per hour for individual tutoring.

Sylvan Learning, which has been operating since 1979, has approximately 900 centers located in North America, Hong Kong, and Guam. Sylvan conducts their own testing to pinpoint student needs. Most instruction at Sylvan takes place with three students and one certified teacher. Sylvan tutors use the mastery learning approach, in which students must demonstrate proficiency on each skill or concept before progressing. Most students attend between 50 and 100 hours of instruction, with a recommendation of two to four hours of instruction per week. Sylvan uses an incentive system based on behaviorist principles of positive reinforcement, in which tutees receive rewards for their cooperation and learning. Several large urban school systems have contracted with Sylvan to provide reading instruction at public schools to those children who are struggling the most in reading. Sylvan has also introduced live online tutoring for students in the third through ninth grades. The electronic system entails having a student and tutor interact electronically, following the same principles as the center-based program.

The Kaplan organization began test preparation centers for standardized college entrance examinations. Kaplan has since expanded by forming Score! Educational Centers, which tutor students in basic skills and subject matter. Kumon Math and Reading Centers, which originated in Japan, have more than 1,000 centers throughout the United States. Kumon focuses on timed drills of basic skills.

Peer Tutoring

Peer tutoring often involves students of the same age or grade teaching each other one-to-one or in small groups. A host of research studies provide evidence that peer tutoring is effective for promoting both student achievement and positive attitudes toward both content material and individual differences. Peer tutoring is vastly improved when students are provided with information about how to increase interaction and provide feedback during tutoring. Some evidence suggests that peer tutoring is especially beneficial for children from ethnic backgrounds where cooperation is valued. Peer tutors often cannot help students in sophisticated ways, however. Instead, it seems that peer tutors help classmates succeed by increasing their attention to the learning task and their involvement in practicing.

Cross-age tutoring involves having older students tutor younger students. This method has been used with a variety of both students and subjects. Evidence suggests that cross-age tutoring can provide benefits for both tutors and tutees. Experts agree that providing tutors with guidance in tutoring techniques, content, and social interaction and behavior management skills increases the effectiveness of the programs. Some evidence suggests that primary-grade students can make gains even when tutored by minimally trained adolescents.

Computer Tutoring

Computer-aided instruction (CAI) is a relatively new form of tutoring that has become more popular as computer availability and use has grown. Three types of CAI are available. The first, and most popular, type involves drill and practice. Drill and practice programs present items for the student to answer and feedback about the correctness of the responses. Such programs sometimes provide helpful suggestions or vary the level of item difficulty based on the user's performance. Tutorial programs teach or reteach material geared to the student's proficiency level as measured by a pretest or performance record. These programs provide alternate paths depending on student responses during tutoring. Simulations present students with problems to solve, and students must learn new material, use existing knowledge, and test ideas to solve the problems.

CAI programs vary widely in quality. Most experts agree that many available programs are not high quality. Drill and practice programs have been criticized for providing less practice than old-fashioned methods. This is because the attention-getting features that have been added to many programs distract students from the material they are meant to learn, and actually result in little direct practice time. Tutorial programs are very expensive to develop and require the expertise of gifted programmers, educators, and instructional designers. Simulation programs might require teachers to be very involved in helping the students negotiate the challenging situations presented, thus necessitating that the teacher spend time with individuals or small groups while others wait for help. In 1999 Yukiko Inoue pointed out that evaluations of intelligent tutoring systems had resulted in little valid research on which to draw conclusions about the effectiveness of such programs.

Conclusion

A wide range of tutoring options exists. Tutoring programs are offered in public schools, by private corporations, and by nonprofit corporations. Tutors might be volunteers, professionals, peers, or computers. More studies are needed to draw conclusions about the effectiveness of tutoring offered by private corporations or by computers, but there is considerable evidence that one-to-one instruction by a more skilled or knowledgeable tutor, whether a professional, volunteer, or peer, contributes to the learning and academic development of students.

See also: COMPENSATORY EDUCATION, *subentry on* UNITED STATES; SCHOOL-LINKED SERVICES.

BIBLIOGRAPHY

ADLER, JERRY. 1998. "The Tutor Age." *Newsweek* 131(13):47–50.

FITZGERALD, JILL. 2001. "Can Minimally Trained College Student Volunteers Help Young At-Risk Children Read Better?" *Reading Research Quarterly* 36(1):28–47.

GINSBURG-BLOCK, MARIKA, and FANTUZZO, JOHN. 1997. "Reciprocal Peer Tutoring: An Analysis of 'Teacher' and 'Student' Interactions as Functions of Training and Experience." *School Psychology Quarterly* 12(2):134–149.

INOUE, YUKIKO. 1999. "Evaluating Intelligent Tutoring Systems." ERIC Document Reproduction Service ED 429101.

JUEL, CONNIE. 1996. "What Makes Literacy Tutoring Effective?" *Reading Research Quarterly* 31:268–289.

MARIUS, SIDNEY E., JR. 2000. "Mix and Match: The Effects of Cross-Age Tutoring on Literacy." *Reading Improvement* 37(3):126–130.

MATHES, PATRICIA; TORGESON, JOSEPH; and ALLOR, JILL. 2001. "The Effects of Peer-Assisted Literacy Strategies for First-Grade Readers With and Without Additional Computer-Assisted Instruction in Phonological Awareness." *American Educational Research Journal* 38(2):371–410.

MURRAY, BRIDGET. 1995. "Good Mentoring Keeps At-Risk Youth in School." *APA Monitor.* 26(9):49.

THROPE, LYNNE, and WOOD, KAREN. 2000. "Cross-Age Tutoring for Young Adolescents." *Clearing House* 73(4):239–242.

WASIK, BARBARA. 1997. "Volunteer Tutoring Programs: Do We Know What Works?" *Phi Delta Kappan* 79(4):282–287.

WEILER, JEANNE. 1998. "Success for All: A Summary of Evaluations." *ERIC/CIU Digest* 139. ERIC Document Reproduction Service ED 425250.

INTERNET RESOURCES

EDUCATION COMMISSION OF THE STATES. 2000. "Reading One-to-One." <www.ecs.org/clearinghouse/18/90/1890.htm>.

EDUCATION COMMISSION OF THE STATES. 2000. "Reading Recovery." <www.ecs.org/clearinghouse/18/91/1891.htm>.

HUNTINGTON LEARNING CENTER. 2002. <www.800canlearn.com>.

LAURBACH LITERACY INTERNATIONAL. 2002. <www.laubach.org>.

LITERACY VOLUNTEERS OF AMERICA. 2002. <www.literacyvolunteers.org>.

SYLVAN LEARNING CENTERS. 2002. <http://educate.com>.

LEE SHUMOW

HIGHER EDUCATION

The practice of an institution's providing tutors is not a new: Early higher education in America was based on small lectures given by a professor to a group of students. Most often, the method of instruction consisted of drills by the instructor and recitation by the student. The phenomena of large lecture halls and examinations administered by graduate teaching assistants on computer scantron sheets was still two hundred years away.

By and large, institutions of higher education are not able to replicate the early classroom instruction. American college campuses, however, have instituted various forms of tutoring programs that provide a small group environment and a modified form of lecture and recitation. These programs include tutoring for student athletes and at-risk first-generation college students, and departmental programs for honors students, among others.

Tutors come from a variety of backgrounds and interests. Many are graduate students who work as tutors to offset the cost of graduate education; others are upper-level undergraduate students who excel in a particular subject area, or full-time teachers or employees of the institution. The role of the tutor is to complement, not replace, classroom instruction. A tutor should review classroom notes and assigned readings, and be prepared to discuss the classroom topics with his/her students. It is not the role of the tutor to re-teach the material that was covered in class; instead, the tutor should help to clarify major points or explain difficult concepts.

An effective tutor should be aware of various learning styles and should be able to recognize different methods of relaying information. For example, a student who is a visual learner may have difficulty in a history class where the instructor employs only a lecture-style mode of instruction. The tutor can assist the student in understanding the material by utilizing maps or pictures from the time period that depicts key events. The tutor must be creative in developing different learning strategies, and must not assume that all students process information in the same manner.

The most successful tutors have completed a training program. Although one may know and understand a particular academic subject, that knowledge does not always translate into the skills needed to be a successful tutor. A tutor should be trained in some theories of educational psychology and learning styles, and be cognizant of signs of learning disabilities in students. Tutors should also be well-informed about techniques that can motivate honor students since not all students who seek tutoring are borderline students.

There are several different types of tutoring programs, depending upon the target student population: for example, student-athletes, honors students, and at-risk students. Most National Collegiate Athletic Association (NCAA) member institutions offer some form of tutoring for student-athletes. At many institutions, first-year athletes are required to attend some type of tutoring during their first year of enrollment. The purposes of the tutoring program for student-athletes are varied. Most important: students receive assistance in meeting their academic goals and meet NCAA eligibility requirements. Tutors working with student-athletes shoulder a great deal of responsibility. These students have tremendous demands on their time in addition to the time commitments of completing academic work. In addition, many of these students are first-generation college students—some come to college ill prepared for the challenges of college work. The tutor not only helps to explain and clarify academic work but can often become a mentor, friend, and role model.

Other tutoring programs such as those for honors, first-generation, at-risk students, or specialty programs such as English, mathematics, or foreign-language centers differ in that students are not required to attend these sessions. Institutions offer these services either at no charge or for a reduced fee to students.

One college, the University of South Carolina, met a demand for tutoring by establishing several tutoring centers in its residence halls through the Department of Housing. These Academic Centers for Excellence (ACE) are partnerships between university housing, the math lab, and the writing center on campus. Students can seek out tutors in the lobbies of their residence halls. Graduate students provide on-site support in mathematics and English at the ACE offices.

Tutoring in higher education cannot be narrowly defined as it is interpreted differently by various institutions. Tutoring is an important component in undergraduate education as it provides students with the opportunity to seek help in a one-on-one basis or small group setting. Depending on the institution, this goal can be accomplished in a myriad of models.

See also: ADJUSTMENT TO COLLEGE; COLLEGE ATHLETICS, *subentry on* ACADEMIC SUPPORT SYSTEMS FOR ATHLETES; COLLEGE STUDENT RETENTION;

TEACHING AND LEARNING, *subentry on* HIGHER EDUCATION.

BIBLIOGRAPHY

BROOKS, DANA, and ALTHOUSE, RONALD, eds. 1993. *Racism in College Athletics*. Morgantown, WV: Fitness Information Technology.

BYERS, WALTER. 1995. *Unsportmanslike Conduct: Exploiting College Athletes*. Ann Arbor: University of Michigan Press.

COLLINSON, VIVIENNE. 1996. *Reaching Students*. Thousand Oaks, CA: Corwin.

JEWLER, JEROME, and GARDNER, JOHN. 1993. *Your College Experience*. Belmont, CA: Wadsworth.

MEYER, EMILY, and SMITH, LOUISE Z. 1987. *The Practical Tutor*. New York: Oxford University Press.

WINSTON, ROGER B. JR.; BONNEY, WARREN C.; MILLER, THEODORE K.; and DAGLEY, JOHN C. 1988. *Promoting Student Development Through Intentionally Structured Groups*. San Francisco: Jossey-Bass.

ART FARLOWE

INTERNATIONAL TRENDS

Private tutoring in academic subjects is defined as tutoring provided on a supplementary basis at the end of the school day, at weekends, or during vacations. In some countries, especially in East Asia, out-of-school supplementary tutoring has long been a major and accepted part of social and educational life. Elsewhere, especially in North America and western Europe, such tutoring has been less significant. It seems, however, to be growing worldwide, including in some countries where it was previously nonexistent. Some observers welcome the phenomenon, but others view it with disquiet.

Scale

Countries in which tutoring is a major enterprise include the following.

- **Egypt.** A 1994 survey of 4,729 households found that 64.0 percent of urban primary children and 52.0 percent of rural ones had received supplementary tutoring.
- **India.** A 1997 survey of 7,879 primary school pupils in Delhi found that 39.2 percent received tutoring.
- **Japan.** A 1993 survey found that 23.6 percent of elementary pupils and 59.5 percent of lower secondary pupils attended tutorial schools known as *juku*.
- **Malta.** A 1997–1998 survey of 1,482 pupils in upper primary and lower secondary schools found that 50.5 percent had received private tutoring at some time.
- **Tanzania.** A 1995 survey of 2,286 grade-six pupils found 44.5 percent received tutoring.

The scale of tutoring appears to have increased during the last few decades. In Japan, for example, attendance at elementary-level *juku* is reported to have doubled from 12.0 percent of pupils receiving tutoring in 1976 to 23.6 percent in 1993; in Singapore surveys in 1982 and 1992 suggested that the proportion of primary pupils receiving tutoring had increased from 27.0 to 49.0 percent. During the 1990s the shift toward a market economy in China and Vietnam permitted and encouraged the emergence of supplementary tutoring in settings where previously it did not exist. Eastern Europe has also undergone economic transition. The partial collapse of public education during the period that accompanied that transition has required families to invest in tutoring on a scale not previously evident. Supplementary tutoring has also become more evident in parts of Australia, Canada, and the United States.

Nature

Tutoring may take diverse forms. They include individual tutorials held in the homes of either tutors or tutees, and large cramming institutions that utilize not only lecture theatres but also overflow rooms in which students watch on a screen what is happening in the main room.

Zeng's 1999 study compared patterns in Japan, South Korea, and Taiwan and focused on "cram schools" in which students gain intensive preparation for examinations. He noted that some tutorial schools are old-fashioned but others are ultramodern. In Japan and South Korea, many tutoring companies have multistory buildings and branch campuses. In Taiwan, by contrast, large operators are much less prominent. This may partly reflect government regulations but also reflects broader economic patterns which emphasize small enterprises more than multibranch chains.

Not all tutees, even within particular locations, receive tutoring for the same duration each day or week. One Malaysian study of 4,340 primary and secondary students indicated that 69.5 percent of students who received tutoring did so throughout the year, while the others only received tutoring prior to important examinations. Over half the students received tutoring in only one or two subjects, but nearly 20 percent received tutoring in five or more subjects.

Determinants

Among the determinants of the scale and nature of tutoring, and thus its geographic spread, are cultural, educational, and economic factors. Many Asian cultures, particularly those influenced by Confucian traditions, stress effort as a factor that explains and determines success. In contrast, European and North American cultures are more likely to emphasize ability. Supplementary tutoring is especially widespread in cultures which stress effort.

The nature of education systems is also important. Private tutoring is more evident where success in examinations can easily be promoted by supplementary tutoring; tutoring becomes more necessary in systems that are teacher-centered rather than child-centered, and/or which are intolerant of slow learners.

A further crucial factor concerns economic rewards. If supplementary tutoring helps people to stay in education systems longer, then for those people it may be a very good investment. Further, some societies have particularly wide differentials in living standards between individuals with different amounts of education. Differentials have long been great in such societies as Singapore and Hong Kong, but less marked in the United Kingdom and Australia. This implies that the rewards from extra levels of schooling, and from supplementary tutoring, are greater in these Asian societies than in western Europe or Australasia.

Private tutoring is more common in urban than in rural areas. This may be partly because incomes are commonly higher in cities than in rural areas. Also, cities may be more competitive and students may be able to find tutors more easily in densely populated locations.

Impact on Mainstream Schooling

Supplementary tutoring may affect the dynamics of mainstream classes. For example, where all students receive tutoring, mainstream teachers may have a decreased workload. Where some students receive supplementary tutoring but others do not, mainstream teachers may be confronted by disparities within their classrooms. Some teachers respond to these disparities by assisting the slower learners, but others take the students who receive tutoring as the norm and permit the gaps between students to grow. In the latter case, parents are placed under greater pressure to invest in private tutoring for their children.

When supplementary tutoring helps students to understand and enjoy their mainstream lessons, it may be considered beneficial. Supplementary tutoring can enable remedial teaching to be undertaken according to individual needs and it may help relatively strong students to receive more out of their mainstream classes. However, students may be bored by their classes if they have already covered the content outside school.

The curriculum emphasized by cram schools may be contrasted with that in mainstream schools. Especially in public education systems, schools are expected to develop rounded individuals who have sporting and musical as well as academic interests, and to promote courtesy, civic awareness, and national pride. Mainstream schools may also keep all students of one grade together, in order to reduce labeling of low achievers. Cram schools, by contrast, cut what they perceive to be irrelevant content in order to focus on examinations, and may have much less hesitation about grouping students by ability. Many analysts view this phenomenon negatively, arguing that the tutorial institutes distort the curriculum, which has been designed with care by specialists. However, the phenomenon may also be seen as an expression of public demand, and perhaps even as a check on curriculum developers who might otherwise be too idealistic.

Social Implications

On the positive side, the pressure created by supplementary tutoring may bring out the best in students and maximize their potential. To some extent, the degree of pressure that is considered appropriate is determined by social and cultural norms. East Asian societies influenced by Confucian traditions tend to place great value on discipline and dedication, and to see the pressure applied by supplementary tutoring as generally beneficial. Also, Russell's 1997 study noted that most children in Japan found the Kumon approach to teaching mathematics (involving considerable repetition and gradual increase in difficulty of exercises) an unthreatening experience. Many parents enroll their children in Kumon classes because the children like the activity.

However, many analysts concerned with other contexts consider the negative aspects of tutoring to outweigh the positive ones. One factor concerns social inequalities. Like other forms of private education, supplementary tutoring is more easily available to the rich than to the poor. Research in Mauritius has shown that in primary grade one the proportion of children receiving private tutoring in the highest income group was 7.5 times greater than the proportion of children in the lowest income group.

A further consideration concerns the types of tutoring. Mass tutoring in Japan and Hong Kong may be inexpensive, but it may also be limited in the extent to which it promotes learning. Richer families can more easily afford one-to-one and small-group tutoring tailored to individual needs, while poorer families must tolerate mass-produced tutoring.

Economic Implications

Advocates of human capital theory may consider supplementary tutoring to be highly desirable. The scale of tutoring may be one reason why Hong Kong, Japan, Singapore, South Korea, and Taiwan became prosperous societies during the second half of the twentieth century.

However, an alternative approach is less positive. Critics argue that most tutorial schools are parasitic, that they waste financial and human resources that could be better allocated to other uses, and that in systems which are dominated by traditional examinations, cramming stifles creativity and can damage the bases of economic production.

These views cannot easily be reconciled. They reflect broader debates on the nature and impact of mainstream education that rest as much on ideological principles as on empirical research. The broad literature on the links between education and development contains many ambiguous findings. No clear formulae can link certain types and amounts of education to certain types and amounts of economic development.

Conclusions

Private supplementary tutoring is widespread in some societies, and in others it is growing. Such tutoring has major social and economic implications, and it can have a far-reaching impact on mainstream education systems. Because the nature of supplementary tutoring varies, different policies are needed for different societies. Some planners may prefer to let the market regulate itself, but others may wish to intervene to alleviate what they perceive to be negative dimensions. The growth of private tutoring may be seen in the context of a worldwide shift toward the marketization of education and reduced government control. In many settings, this shift is viewed with ambivalence. Governments may have positive reasons for withdrawing the dominant role that they have played in many countries; but in some societies the rise of private tutoring appears to be a social response to inadequacies in government quantitative and qualitative inputs.

See also: COMPENSATORY EDUCATION, *subentry on* POLICIES AND PROGRAMS IN LATIN AMERICA; EAST ASIA AND THE PACIFIC; PRIVATE SCHOOLING.

BIBLIOGRAPHY

BRAY, MARK. 1999. *The Shadow Education System: Private Tutoring and its Implications for Planners.* Fundamentals of Educational Planning No. 61. Paris: UNESCO International Institute for Educational Planning.

RUSSELL, NANCY UKAI. 1997. *Lessons from Japanese Cram Schools.* In *The Challenge of Eastern Asian Education: Lessons for America,* ed. William K. Cummings and Philip G. Altbach. Albany: State University of New York Press.

STEVENSON, DAVID L., and BAKER, DAVID P. 1992. "Shadow Education and Allocation in Formal Schooling: Transition to University in Japan." *American Journal of Sociology* 97(6):1639–1657.

ZENG, KANGMIN. 1999. *Dragon Gate: Competitive Examinations and their Consequences.* London: Cassell.

MARK BRAY

TYLER, RALPH W. (1902–1994)

Ralph W. Tyler's long and illustrious career in education resulted in major contributions to the policy and practice of American schooling. His influence was especially felt in the field of testing, where he transformed the idea of measurement into a grander concept that he called *evaluation*; in the field of curriculum, where he designed a rationale for curriculum planning that still has vitality today; and in the realm of educational policy, where he advised U.S. presidents, legislators, and various school leaders on new directions and improvements for public schooling.

After starting his career in education as a science teacher in South Dakota, Tyler went to the University of Chicago to pursue a doctorate in educational psychology. His training with Charles Judd and W. W. Charters at Chicago led to a research focus on teaching and testing. Upon graduation in 1927, Tyler took an appointment at the University of North Carolina, where he worked with teachers in the state on improving curricula. In 1929 Tyler followed W. W. Charters to the Ohio State University (OSU). He joined a team of scholars directed by Charters at the university's Bureau of Educational Research, taking the position of director of accomplishment testing in the bureau. He was hired to assist OSU faculty with the task of improving their teaching and increasing student retention at the university. In this capacity, he designed a number of path-breaking service studies. He made a name for himself at OSU by showing the faculty how to generate evidence that spoke to their course objectives. In this context, Tyler first coined the term *evaluation* as it pertained to schooling, describing a testing construct that moved away from pencil and paper memorization examinations and toward an evidence collection process dedicated to overarching teaching and learning objectives. Because of his early insistence on looking at evaluation as a matter of evidence tied to fundamental school purposes, Tyler could very well be considered one of the first proponents of what is now popularly known as *portfolio assessment*.

Contribution to Testing and Curriculum Development

The years Tyler spent at OSU clearly shaped the trajectory of his career in testing and curriculum development. His OSU ties brought him into the company of the Progressive Education Association and its effort to design a project dedicated to the re-examination of course requirements in American high schools. Known as the Eight-Year Study, the project involved thirty secondary schools that agreed to experiment with various alternative curricula approaches. The purpose of the study was to help colleges and high schools better understand the effects of the high school experience on college performance and other post–high school events. Tyler was chosen as the director of evaluation for the study, recommended for the job by Boyd Bode, who witnessed Tyler's work with faculty at OSU. Tyler designed methods of evaluation particular to the experimental variables of the Eight-Year Study. The details of this work are captured in Tyler and Smith's 1942 book on the evaluative component of the Eight-Year Study. The finding of the Eight-Year Study threw into question the tradition of supporting only one set of high school experiences for success in college and opened the door for more alternative thinking about the secondary school curriculum.

For Tyler, the Eight-Year Study not only provided a venue for his creative perspective on evaluation but it also forced him to think about a rationale for the school curriculum. Answering a call from the participating schools in the study for more curriculum assistance, Tyler designed a curriculum planning rationale for the participating schools. After moving to the University of Chicago in 1938 to take the position of chairman in the Department of Education, Tyler continued to cultivate his ideas on the rationale, using it in a syllabus for his course on curriculum and instruction and eventually publishing it in 1949, under the title *Basic Principles of Curriculum and Instruction*. In the rationale, Tyler conceived of school action as moving across a continuum of concerns that speaks to school purposes, the organization of experiences and the evaluation of experiences. His basic questions are now famous:

1. What educational purposes should the school seek to attain?

2. What educational experiences can be provided that are likely to attain these purposes?

3. How can these educational experiences be effectively organized?

4. How can we determine whether these purposes are being attained?

The rationale also highlighted an important set of factors to be weighed against the questions. Tyler believed that the structure of the school curriculum also had to be responsive to three central factors that represent the main elements of an educative experience: (1) the nature of the learner (developmental factors, learner interests and needs, life experiences, etc.); (2) the values and aims of society (democratizing principles, values and attitudes); and (3) knowledge of subject matter (what is believed to be worthy and usable knowledge). In answering the four questions and in designing school experience for children, curriculum developers had to screen their judgments through the three factors.

Tyler's rationale has been criticized for being overtly managerial and linear in its position on the school curriculum. Some critics have characterized it as outdated and atheoretical, suitable only to administrators keen on controlling the school curriculum in ways that are unresponsive to teachers and learners. The most well-known criticism of the rationale makes the argument that the rationale is historically wedded to social efficiency traditions. Tyler offered no substantive response to these criticisms, believing that criticism of his curriculum development work required some discussion of an alternative, which none of the critics provided.

Tyler's reputation as an education expert grew with the publication of *Basic Principles of Curriculum and Instruction*. Because of the value Tyler placed on linking objectives to experience (instruction) and evaluation, he became known as the father of behavioral objectives. This led many to again characterize his work in the tradition of the social efficiency expert aiming to atomize the curriculum with hyperspecific objectives. Tyler, however, claimed no allegiance to such thinking. To him, behavioral objectives had to be formed at a generalizable level, an idea he first learned in graduate school under Charles Judd, whose research focused on the role of generalization in the transfer of learning. And although Tyler understood that schooling was a normative enterprise, he showed great regard for the exercise of local prerogatives in the school and cited a concern for "children who differ from the norm" as an educational problem needing attention.

Advisory Role

Tyler also exercised enormous influence as an educational adviser. Rising to the position of Dean of Social Sciences at the University of Chicago, Tyler assisted Robert Hutchins in restructuring the university's curriculum in the late 1940s and in founding the university's Center for the Study of Democratic Institutions. During this time Tyler also started his career as an education adviser in the White House. In 1952 he offered U.S. President Harry Truman advice on reforming the curriculum

at the service academies. Under Eisenhower, he chaired the President's Conference on Children and Youth. President Lyndon B. Johnson's administration used Tyler to help shape its education bills, most notably the Elementary and Secondary Education Act of 1965, in which he was given the responsibility of writing the section on the development of regional educational research laboratories. In the late 1960s Tyler took on the job of designing the assessment measures for the National Assessment of Education Progress (NAEP), which are federally mandated criterion-reference tests used to gauge national achievement in various disciplines and skill domains.

After leaving the University of Chicago in 1953, Tyler became the first director of the Advanced Center for Behavioral Science at Stanford University, a think tank for social scientists that Tyler founded with private monies. He formally retired in 1967, taking on the position of director emeritus and trustee to the center and itinerant educational consultant.

Given the longevity of his career in education and wide-ranging influence of his work in the policy and practice of public education, especially in the realm of curriculum development and testing, Tyler could very well be seen as among the most influential of figures setting the course for the American public school during the second half of the twentieth century.

See also: ASSESSMENT, *subentry on* PORTFOLIO ASSESSMENT; EIGHT-YEAR STUDY; TESTING, *subentry on* STANDARDIZED TESTS AND EDUCATIONAL POLICY.

BIBLIOGRAPHY

HLEBOWITSH, PETER S. 1992. "Amid Behavioural and Behaviouralistic Objectives: Reappraising Appraisals of the Tyler Rationale." *Journal of Curriculum Studies* 24(6):553–547.

KIESTER, E. 1978. "Ralph Tyler: The Educator's Educator." *Change* 10(2):28–35.

KLIEBARD, HERBERT. 1970. "The Tyler Rationale." *School Review* 78(2):259–272.

PINAR, WILLIAM F. 1978. "Notes on the Curriculum Field." *Educational Researcher* 7(8):5–12.

RIDINGS-NOWAKOWSKI, JERI. 1981. "An Interview with Ralph Tyler." In *Educational Evaluation:*

Classic Works of Ralph Tyler, eds. George F. Madaus and Daniel L. Stufflebeam. Boston: Kluwer.

TANNER, DANIEL, and TANNER, LAURA. 1979. Emancipation from Research: The Reconceptualist Perspective." *Educational Researcher* 8(6):8–12.

TYLER, RALPH W. 1949. *Basic Principles of Curriculum and Instruction.* Chicago: University of Chicago Press.

TYLER, RALPH W. 1966. "The Objectives and Plans for a National Assessment of Educational Progress." *Journal of Educational Measurement* 3(spring):1–4.

TYLER, RALPH W. 1968. *The Challenge of National Assessment.* Columbus, OH: Merrill.

TYLER RALPH W., and SMITH, EUGENE R. 1942. *Appraising and Recording Student Progress,* Vol. 3, *Adventure in American Education.* New York: Harper.

TYLER, RALPH W., et. al. 1932. *Service Studies in Higher Education.* Columbus: Bureau of Educational Research, Ohio State University.

PETER HLEBOWITSH

U

UNITED NATIONS AND INTERNATIONAL AGENCIES

See: INTERNATIONAL DEVELOPMENT AGENCIES, *subentry on* UN AND INTERNATIONAL AGENCIES.

UNIVERSITY COUNCIL FOR EDUCATIONAL ADMINISTRATION

The University Council for Educational Administration (UCEA) is a consortium of sixty-seven universities that offer doctoral programs in educational administration. UCEA's mission is to advance the preparation and practice of educational leaders for the benefit of all children and schools. UCEA fulfills this purpose collaboratively by (1) promoting, sponsoring, and disseminating research on the essential problems of practice; (2) improving the preparation and professional development of school leaders and professors; and (3) influencing policy and practice through establishing and fostering collaborative networks.

UCEA encourages membership among universities willing and able to commit time and resources to research, development, and dissemination activities toward the ends of improving preparatory programs and solving substantial problems in educational administration. All professors at member universities involved in the preparation program are eligible to participate in and contribute to UCEA activities. Approximately 1,000 professors in the sixty-seven member institutions are involved in various aspect of the UCEA program.

Program

UCEA sponsors and conducts activities through interuniversity cooperation designed to advance and disseminate research on the essential problems of practice, to improve the preparation and professional development of school leaders and professors, and to influence policy and practice. Research is fostered through task forces, program centers, and national conferences. The UCEA headquarters has facilitated large-scale research projects, involving faculty from a number of member institutions, as well as smaller research projects involving a few faculty. Research is also facilitated by UCEA program centers.

UCEA program centers conduct their research and development work in target areas of contemporary importance and interest. The UCEA program centers focus on the study of (1) academic leadership, (2) educational finance, (3) field practices in special education administration, (4) leadership and ethics in educational administration, (5) leadership in urban schools, (6) school site leadership, (7) the superintendency, and (8) patterns of professional preparation in administration. Whenever possible, center directors involve faculty from multiple universities, as well as practicing school administrators and state education agency leaders, in their work.

Dissemination of research findings and knowledge developed through UCEA collaborative efforts is accomplished through workshops, UCEA conventions, UCEA center conferences, publications, and the UCEA website. The UCEA annual convention is designed to share current research and program innovations, to stimulate discussion and debate on reform issues, and to advance an agenda of research on the essential problems of practice. The convention also provides opportunities for graduate-student research mentoring and career development.

UCEA task forces provide opportunities for professors interested in particular issues to explore them cooperatively. Such issues have included program content and pedagogy, internships, university–school district links, social justice, program evaluation and improvement, international issues, professional development, and the recruitment and retention of students and faculty from underrepresented groups in educational administration.

New instructional materials developed by professors, teams of professors, and UCEA are disseminated by UCEA to both member and nonmember universities. The most elaborate of these materials is the Information Environment for Educational Leadership Preparation (IESLP), an Internet-based, data-rich, problem-based learning environment. Other instructional materials available through the UCEA include case studies, texts, and simulations. UCEA also sponsors an online peer-reviewed *Journal of Cases in Educational Administration.*

Three other periodicals are sponsored by UCEA. The organization's newsletter, the *UCEA Review,* published three times per year, contains essays, debates, occasional papers, and news on UCEA activities and programs, member institutions, and state and national policy developments. The *Educational Administration Quarterly* provides a forum for scholars to share cutting-edge research and theory. Finally, the *Educational Administration Abstracts* reviews the content of more than 100 journals to select articles relevant to educational administration scholars and practitioners.

The collaborative networks UCEA has developed through its member institutions, program centers, and other educational organizations enable UCEA to influence educational administration at a national level. UCEA is a founding member of the National Policy Board of Educational Administration; has established two national commissions (the National Commission for Excellence in Educational Administration, 1987, and the National Commission for the Advancement of Educational Leadership, 2001); and works closely with organizations such as the National Council of Professors of Educational Administration (NCPEA), the American Association of School Administrators (AASA), and the American Association of Colleges for Teacher Education (AACTE).

Organizational Structure

A nine-member executive committee formulates UCEA policies. Executive committee members are elected by UCEA plenary session representatives. The UCEA Plenum, which is composed of one representative from each of the member institutions, also establishes goals and priorities, reviews and approves policies, and examines and approves the budget. Representatives to the plenary session serve as official liaison among the universities, the board, and the UCEA executive director. The executive director implements the policies of the executive committee, develops initiatives and programs to achieve organizational goals, coordinates activities, and disseminates information resulting from research and developmental projects.

Financial support for the UCEA comes from the annual fees paid by member universities and from contributions made by its host institution and individual universities, foundations, and governmental agencies for specific programs and projects.

History and Development

UCEA was established in 1956 through the support of the AASA, the Kellogg Foundation, and the Cooperative Program in Educational Administration. The central office for UCEA was located at Teachers College, Columbia University, until 1959, with faculty devoting part of their time to developing the council, its membership, its goals, and its bylaws. Since 1959 the central office of the UCEA has been hosted by member universities, including the Ohio State University, Arizona State University, the Pennsylvania State University, and the University of Missouri.

See also: EDUCATIONAL LEADERSHIP; PRINCIPAL, SCHOOL; SUPERINTENDENT OF LARGE-CITY SCHOOL SYSTEMS; SUPERINTENDENT OF SCHOOLS.

INTERNET RESOURCE

UNIVERSITY COUNCIL FOR EDUCATIONAL ADMINISTRATION. 2002. <www.ucea.org>.

MICHELLE D. YOUNG

UNIVERSITY-INDUSTRIAL RESEARCH COLLABORATION

Historically, university researchers have collaborated with industrial scientists on marketable projects.

News coverage at the turn of the twenty-first century might lead one to believe that this is a current phenomenon. However, science historians have traced collaborations between European companies and university researchers back to the 1800s. In the United States, university-industry research relationships began with the industrial revolution.

Traditionally, industry sought partnerships with universities as a means to identify and train future employees. As global economies shifted, companies wanted access to faculty who created the cutting-edge knowledge and technology central to university research. Knowledge creation and technology development require considerable capital investments, historically provided by governments. However, declining federal, state, and local funds, as well as increased competition for monies allocated to human services, has forced university researchers to seek new sponsors. In 2002 industry-sponsored research accounted for 8 percent of total university research dollars. These contributions occur through grants, contracts (such as consulting agreements), and collaborative training programs. The areas most likely to benefit commercially from these relationships are agriculture, biotechnology, chemistry, computer science, engineering, and medicine. Furthermore, about half of the biotechnology firms have collaborative agreements with universities and account for nearly one-fourth of all funding for biotechnology research.

The interdependent research relationships between universities and companies enable both entities to sustain growth in their areas. While companies rely on university researchers for product innovations, faculty gain prestige through increased external research funds. Just as industry needs innovative ideas to ensure profits, researchers need additional research dollars to sustain faculty productivity.

Since the 1970s the United States government has aggressively promoted the alignment of university and industrial researchers through specific funding programs. The National Science Foundation (NSF) sponsors both the Industry-University Cooperative Research Projects Program (I/UCRPP) and The Industry-University Research Centers Program (I/URCP). Both began as pilot programs in 1972 and expanded in 1978. The I/UCRPP is a traditional consulting arrangement, for which the NSF provides the initial two years of fiscal support. The I/UCRC is more closely related to university-industry relation-

ships that currently exist. The NSF outlays substantial initial funding, with the intention that the collaborative industry-university engineering centers will become self-supporting. The research centers consist of an interdisciplinary team of university faculty and business representatives. The government, in alliance with universities and industry, provides one year of planning and five years of decreasing operational funds. Generally, universities contribute through a waiver of overhead support for the centers, and businesses pay membership fees to participate. As of February 2002 there were fifty-six operational centers devoted to materials science, biotechnology and health care, energy, manufacturing, agriculture, electronics, and chemistry.

The National Science Foundation also provides funds for industry-university collaborations in engineering for twenty centers (as of February 2002). These centers are hybrids that combine basic with applied research projects, and they receive NSF support for up to eleven years.

University-industry research collaborations merge basic and applied research. Incremental research and product development often occur in industrial labs. However, industry scientists report that when they are involved in breakthrough discoveries, it is important to maintain close alliances with university researchers so that they can gain a better understanding of the science that underlies the discovery.

Academic-industry research relationships take other forms, as well. For example, some companies will *gift* scientific equipment to university researchers to conduct their studies. Although it is called *gifting,* companies expect that university researchers will somehow repay their generosity by communicating any cutting-edge research results related to the use of the equipment. This gives companies an edge in innovation, as they can capitalize on the research results and create new, potentially profitable, products.

Frequently, university-industry research collaborations take the form of clinical trials for drugs and medical devices. Universities provide the technical expertise, patients, and physical space to conduct clinical trials while companies supply the drugs, equipment (both diagnostic and therapeutic), and money to operate the trials. The section that describes advantages will address how both researchers and companies benefit from this relationship.

2594 UNIVERSITY-INDUSTRIAL RESEARCH COLLABORATION

Advantages of the Collaborative Relationships

There are numerous benefits that derive from university-industry relationships, including benefits to society, universities, and companies.

Social benefits. Society benefits from university-industry research relationships through innovative products and technologies. Industry-sponsored university research is often developed into practical applications that benefit society. These applications include new improved medical devices, techniques, and therapies; efficient energy development; and innovative electronic technologies such as computers and DVD players. Indirectly, university-industry partnerships may spawn new industries that enhance the U.S. competitive advantage globally. Federal, state, and local tax bases expand because of the growth of new industries. These are just a few examples of the social promise of university-industry research relationships.

University benefits. Interactions with industry are clearly thought out with attention paid to the benefits that will accrue to the university. Some universities seek industrial partnerships because of the potential financial rewards of patents and licenses that result from the commercialization of academic research. This provides a means by which universities can decrease the governmental funding gap. Patents generated through industry-sponsored research are sometimes shared between companies and universities. The intent is that the university will use patent revenues to support activities that are not market oriented, such as the teaching mission of institutions.

Additionally, faculty benefit through the access to cutting-edge scientific equipment not always available in university labs. This equipment enables faculty to pursue additional lines of research that, ultimately, contribute to faculty productivity (such as additional external funds as well as increased publications). Both of these elements combine to enhance institutional prestige—an important component used by institutions to attract top students, establish their legitimacy, and acquire available public funds. Universities also enhance opportunities to find future employment for undergraduate and graduate students through university-industry connections.

Company benefits. University-industry collaborations can stimulate companies' internal research and development programs. University researchers help industrial scientists identify current research that

might be useful for the design and development of innovative processes and potential products. This first look at cutting-edge research gives companies a competitive edge because it decreases the time it takes to move a potential product from the laboratory to the market, which strengthens international economic competition.

The association between universities and company sponsors also enhances a company's reputation. Oftentimes, university and industry researchers will coauthor refereed journal articles that describe research results. Joint publications are used as a public relations tool by companies to add to their prestige.

So far, the more abstract benefits companies realize from university-industry relationships have been described. However, the concrete benefits are the ones that drive these collaborations. When a company becomes involved with academic researchers and "buys" access to new ideas, it builds trade secrets that could lead to new, potentially profitable patents. Furthermore, if university researchers develop a patent, the company that sponsored the research often gains the first right of refusal to license the product. Companies thus become industry leaders.

Universities provide inexpensive lab space in which to conduct industrial research. One area where this is critical is in the arena of clinical trials. Medical companies use university partnerships to conduct clinical trials of drugs, devices, and emergent techniques. This is less costly for industry because university hospitals have access to large numbers of patients.

Finally, university-industry research relationships strengthen companies' research and development (R&D). Either through the generation of innovative products developed from current research or through a redirection of industrial development to more profitable lines, R&D is positively affected. University researchers also help industry scientists solve design and technical problems. Often, company employees learn new research techniques with their university partners.

Disadvantages of the Collaborative Relationships

Despite the benefits of university-industry research relationships, a number of disadvantages are also apparent. Many of these reflect significant normative issues related to the academic enterprise. Professor and business and ethics writer Norman Bowie suggests that a university becomes "caught between two of its compelling interests" because of its relationship with corporate sponsors (p. 12). Academic researchers are compelled to approach research without regard for its commercial benefits; to share the results with peers so they can be examined and validated; and to train future researchers for universities and industries. Universities must balance their relationships with industry to reflect traditional academic norms, as well as those of industry.

High-profile agreements and legal disputes have created concerns that university faculty no longer set their own research agendas. Instead, research topics are based on both available funds and university needs. This is especially problematic because faculty need the academic freedom to pursue any line of inquiry, regardless of where it may lead. If either industry or the university sets the research agenda, many important social benefits will become neglected as resources are targeted solely at those activities that increase income.

Ownership issues can arise between universities and companies who establish research relationships, causing universities to develop more formal relationships with corporate sponsors through contracts that clearly stipulate data ownership as well as interest in any products developed from university-industry research. For example, some company contracts stipulate that university researchers cannot share data or research materials with other academic scientists who request them. The company assumes that the research generated by the university researchers contains proprietary information.

These contracts extend to publication. Most university policies allow publication delays for up to six months while researchers and their sponsors develop patent applications. Oftentimes, publication delays arise because companies want to approve a journal article before it is published. This is especially problematic when the research reflects unfavorably on the product, a situation that occurred in a 1997 case concerning synthetic thyroid medication. A university researcher found that a particular medication was ineffective, but the university legal department had signed a contract that enabled the company to block publication of damaging results. Critics believe that this type of arrangement reduces the quality of university researchers and creates potentially harmful situations for patients.

Some university researchers are not allowed to include pertinent methodology details in either published or presented results. A company will argue that the methods used to conduct the research constitute a company trade secret and must be protected. This creates problems for academicians who need to publish to generate additional research dollars.

Corporations are concerned with their market edge, and they may require that university researchers not publish studies from their sponsored research activities. Market success depends partly on the innovation of specific products, as well as the investment in production necessary to make products available to the public. Secrecy is something companies use to protect trade secrets that emerge from corporate-funded projects. This is contrary to the wide-scale dissemination practiced in universities, where faculty, postdoctoral fellows, and graduate students publish results from the studies in which they participate. Commercial enterprises are more competitive than academic interests as a company must find a way to secure its niche with a new product.

The Role of the Collaboration in Biotech Development and Start-Up Industries

The collaboration between industry funding, university researchers, and start-up companies is complex. Most often, individual entrepreneurial faculty use their research to start a private company. Much of the research on these spin-off companies has looked at academic entrepreneurs. The university is a passive player, while the entrepreneur generates external venture capital. University faculty often leave institutions to manage the new company, or faculty may use the company to support their academic research activities. Universities tend to react unfavorably when faculty operate new companies in tandem with their research agendas. There is an assumption that faculty will neglect their core duties to the university and focus on research and other activities that support their commercial enterprise.

Some start-up companies that universities support are those that develop into *incubation centers.* Incubation centers are units that support faculty or students in the development of their research products. For example, incubators established near colleges and universities house start-up companies based on faculty research. This is the more traditional form of a collaborative university-industry relationship that results in start-ups. Currently, the development of start-up companies from university faculty research is housed in various administrative departments of institutions. For example, Massachusetts Institute of Technology (MIT) was involved in forming the American Research and Development Corporation, which has culminated in a venture capital firm.

The Role of the Collaboration in State Economic Development

Universities often use industry-university collaborations to define their role in economic development. Science policy, for example, has become associated with economic development, especially in light of cases like MIT's and Stanford University's relationships with local economic development. Stanford University faculty played a crucial role in the development of Silicon Valley. Both MIT and Stanford faculty have had profound effects on local and regional economies. Science parks, also associated with economic development, reflect strategies to draw industry and government labs to specific locations to stimulate growth. Research Triangle in North Carolina is an example of this type of enterprise.

A justification for the involvement of universities in economic development is that the government will provide large-scale financial support for university research, provided institutions conduct research that supports and sustains state economies. This is not quite accurate, as reduced federal research dollars have made grant-getting more competitive for university researchers. Thus, there is a greater reliance on industry relationships to help fund these growth areas.

State economic development programs encourage high-tech development through university-industry research relationships. However, the ability to identify any specific economic development agendas by universities is difficult. Many view the industrial-university partnerships as direct contributors to local economies. For example, the Michigan legislature funded a biotechnology center operated at Michigan State University. The legislature believed that the research generated at the center would increase jobs and, ultimately, fill the state coffers. The center did contribute to the creation of commercial products from basic research (e.g., the development of drugs). However, because Michigan lacked the manufacturing infrastructure to support wide-scale production of drugs, the state did not realize a direct economic benefit from its investment in the center. Instead, New Jersey, Illinois, and Indiana reaped the benefits from drug production based on Michigan State's research. The state legislature, disappointed with this outcome, decreased center funding. This story illustrates the misconceptions policymakers have about the direct economic benefits derived from the commercialization of academic research.

There is a belief that, because of their ability to increase external research funds and establish relationships with industry, only research universities contribute to state economic development. However, colleges and universities from multiple sectors play roles in state economic development. For example, community colleges contribute through training the workforce. Typically, comprehensive and community colleges often forge collaborations with industry that do not require a substantial investment in research. Instead, universities collaborate with industry to help reform higher education curricula, train employees for companies, assist local economic development offices, and retrain displaced workers. These important relationships between industry and the university are often overlooked when scholarly writers and journalists focus only on research collaborations that generate tangible goods.

Conclusion

University-industry research relationships have existed in multiple forms since the nineteenth century. Current collaborations are complex and often appear threatening to both the academic and industrial enterprises through value and goal conflicts. However, institutions have developed formalized relationships with industry that alleviate some of the tensions that arise from these relationships.

See also: ACADEMIC FREEDOM AND TENURE; FACULTY AS ENTREPRENEURS; FACULTY CONSULTING; INTELLECTUAL PROPERTY RIGHTS; NATIONAL SCIENCE FOUNDATION; TECHNOLOGY TRANSFER.

BIBLIOGRAPHY

ANDERSON, MELISSA S. 2001. "The Complex Relations between the Academy and Industry: Views from the Literature." *Journal of Higher Education* 72(2):226–246.

BOWIE, NORMAN E. 1994. *University-Business Partnerships: An Assessment.* Lanham, MD: Rowman and Littlefield.

ETZKOWITZ, HENRY, and WEBSTER, ANDREW. 1998. "Entrepreneurial Science: The Second Academic Revolution." In *Capitalizing Knowledge: New Intersections of Industry and Academia,* ed. Henry Etzkowitz, Andrew Webster, and Peter Healy. Albany: State University of New York Press.

ETZKOWITZ, HENRY, and WEBSTER, ANDREW. 1998. "Toward A Theoretical Analysis of Academic-Industry Collaboration." In *Capitalizing Knowledge: New Intersections of Industry and Academia* ed. Henry Etzkowitz, Andrew Webster, and Peter Healy. Albany: State University of New York Press.

FAIRWEATHER, JAMES S. 1996. *Faculty Work and Public Trust: Restoring the Value of Teaching and Public Service in American Academic Life.* Boston: Allyn and Bacon.

FRANKLIN, STEPHEN J.; WRIGHT, MICHAEL; and LOCKETT, ANDREW. 2001. "Academic and Surrogate Entrepreneurs in University Spin-Out Companies." *Journal of Technology Transfer* 26:127–141.

HALL, BRONWYN H.; LINK, ALBERT N.; and SCOTT, JOHN T. 2001. "Barriers Inhibiting Industry from Partnering with Universities: Evidence from the Advanced Technology Program." *Journal of Technology Transfer* 26:87–98.

LEE, YONG S. 2000. "The Sustainability of University-Industry Research Collaboration: An Empirical Assessment." *Journal of Technology Transfer* 25:111–133.

LOUIS, KAREN SEASHORE, and ANDERSON, MELISSA S. 1998. "The Changing Context of Science and University-Industry Relations." In *Capitalizing Knowledge: New Intersections of Industry and Academia* ed. Henry Etzkowitz, Andrew Webster, and Peter Healy. Albany: State University of New York Press.

LOUIS, KAREN SEASHORE; JONES, LISA M.; ANDERSON, MELISSA S.; BLUMENTHAL, DAVID; and CAMPBELL, ERIC G. 2001. "Entrepreneurship, Secrecy, and Productivity: A Comparison of Clinical and Non-Clinical Life Sciences Faculty." *Journal of Technology Transfer* 26:233–245.

SCHARTINGER, DORIS; SCHIBANY, ANDREAS; and GASSLER, HELMUT. 2001. "Interactive Relations Between Universities and Firms: Empirical Evidence from Austria." *Journal of Technology Transfer* 26:255–268.

INTERNET RESOURCE

CHO, MILDRED K.; SHOHARA, RYO; and RENNIE, DRUMMOND. 2002. "What Is Driving Policies on Faculty Conflict of Interest? Considerations for Policy Development." Washington, DC: Office of Research Integrity. <http://ori.dhhs.gov/multimedia/acrobat/papers/cho.pdf>.

LISA M. JONES

UNIVERSITY OF CHICAGO

Identified by American industrialist and philanthropist John D. Rockefeller as "the greatest investment I ever made," the University of Chicago, founded in 1891, became a standard-bearer for modern America's universities by being the first to meld the great English and German traditions of higher education by creating an institution focused on teaching and research.

Early Years

In 1891 the American Baptist Education Society united William Raincy Harper, a dynamic leader, with John D. Rockefeller, an equally magnanimous donor. The union produced the University of Chicago, which became America's shining educational city on a hill. Historian Frederick Rudolph asserted that "no episode was more important in shaping the outlook and expectations of American higher education . . . than the founding of the University of Chicago" (p. 349).

President William Rainey Harper, the "young man in a hurry," was a Hebrew scholar lured from Yale in 1888 to create an institution that would combine the best of German and English higher educational traditions. Harper demanded that Chicago support pure research yet still provide quality instruction and moral guidance. He also revolutionized academic practices by dividing the year into quarters, encouraging year-round attendance, and by allowing students to graduate whenever they completed their degree requirements. Furthermore, Harper introduced *majors* and *minors* to the elective system and thereby provided students with both freedom and direction. Lastly, though founded by Baptists, the university was always nondenominational. Also, it welcomed both women and minority students at a time when many campuses did not.

Harper's vision required deep financial pockets and the deepest were found. John D. Rockefeller, though initially committing to a modest gift, eventually donated more than $35 million to the project. Harper used the funds to construct an English-Gothic-style campus with towers, spires, and gargoyles within Chicago's Hyde Park. This land, valued at the time at more than $8 million, was donated by Chicago department store owner Marshall Field. Harper hired 120 faculty members for opening day. Because he wanted only the best researchers and instructors, he used Rockefeller's generosity to raid the faculties of other elite colleges and universities—especially the strapped Clark University.

Early Twentieth Century

The University of Chicago continued to thrive despite the death of its young president in 1906. Its fifth president, Robert Maynard Hutchins, inaugurated in 1929, like Harper before him left a lasting imprint on Chicago and the nation. Hutchins reduced the dominance of applied science and commercial utility in the nation's great universities by shifting Chicago to an emphasis on perennial issues associated with the humanities. Thus began Chicago's Great Books curriculum, which focused on classics in Western civilization. The program was far more than just reading significant books, however. Rather than relying on professorial lectures for understanding, students engaged their instructors in spirited debate over the treatises. This atmosphere of intense intellectual argument became and remains the essence of the University of Chicago ethos. So popular was this approach that the Great Books were published for a wide reading audience, including discussion groups of laymen that popped up around the country in an effort to capture the Chicago spirit of intellectual discourse.

Not only did Hutchins buck the dominant trends in philosophy and instruction, he also challenged higher education's emphasis on intercollegiate football. Hutchins abolished the university's football team in 1939 because he believed students needed to focus on scholarship and Chicago should play football only if it could remain competitive with major athletic programs. This was a momentous decision as the Maroons were a founding member of the Big Ten Conference and once a national powerhouse under the famed coaching of Amos Alonzo Stagg. In fact, Stagg, who had retired from Chicago in 1933, had been the first coach in the nation to be

a tenured professor, and his large athletics' budget was exempted from normal institutional review. Even as late as 1935, Chicago's Jay Berwanger became the first Heisman Trophy winner, but by 1939 Chicago's scoreboard indicated that the glory days had passed, including a 61–0 loss to Harvard. Therefore, despite the legacies, and partly because of them, after much debate the university dropped football.

Future Directions

Varsity football was resurrected at Chicago in 1969. Other traditions have been maintained without interruption. The University of Chicago has remained a bold innovator, demonstrated again in 1978 when Hanna Gray was appointed president—the first woman to serve as president of a major research university. The University of Chicago continues to adjust its curriculum, always with its emphasis on humanistic education. It proudly claims to be the "teacher of teachers," as one in seven of its alumni follows an academic career path. As such, the original vision for the university continues to stand out as a home of critical inquiry and informed discussion within the nation's higher educational landscape.

See also: HIGHER EDUCATION IN THE UNITED STATES, *subentry on* HISTORICAL DEVELOPMENT; HUTCHINS, ROBERT.

BIBLIOGRAPHY

LESTER, ROBIN. 1995. *Stagg's University: The Rise, Decline, and Fall of Big-Time Football at Chicago.* Champaign: University of Illinois Press.

RUDOLPH, FREDERICK. 1962. *The American College and University: A History.* New York: Random House.

SHILS, EDWARD, ed. 1991. *Remembering the University of Chicago: Teachers, Scientists, Scholars.* Chicago: University of Chicago Press.

JASON R. EDWARDS
ERIC MOYEN
JOHN R. THELIN

UNIVERSITY OF VIRGINIA

The University of Virginia, known since its founding in 1819 as "Mr. Jefferson's University," has personified, in past and present, a distinctive approach to public higher education whose integration of academic vision and architectural environment attracts national and international acclaim.

The University of Virginia remains one of Thomas Jefferson's greatest legacies. The former president led a commission that chose the institution's location, devised the architectural plans for the grounds, and crafted the curriculum. The Board of Visitors nominated Jefferson as the university's first rector. His desire to build a strong faculty encouraged hiring distinguished national and international scholars rather than local clergy.

Early Years

Jefferson's "academical village" consisted of eight independent schools and offered a radical departure from the rigid curriculum, strict discipline, and theological dogmatism that characterized many American colleges. Students chose their own classes and earned a degree after meeting a school's requirements. In place of the customary bachelor of arts, Virginia offered a master of arts degree to students completing programs in five of the colleges. To encourage self-government, the university vested power in the rector and in the faculty chair rather than in a president. Governing rowdy students, however, became a problem. Serious student riots occurred throughout the 1830s and climaxed in 1840 when a student shot and killed a professor. In the wake of this unrest the university implemented a student honor code, one of the institution's greatest legacies. Virginia students displayed both "honor and dishonor" in their conduct before the Civil War. The university's regional provincialism also precluded attracting a true "aristocracy of talent," and its relatively high tuition prevented attendance by modest-income students. Its presumption of racial and gender exclusion also prohibited the enrollment of African Americans and women.

The university prospered during the antebellum years, but the Civil War brought great hardship to Charlottesville. Prewar enrollments exceeded 600, while literary societies and student groups flourished. In contrast, attendance during the Civil War averaged sixty-four students. U.S. General George Armstrong Custer spared the campus from destruction in 1865. Unlike many other universities in the South, Virginia rebounded quickly.

Growing enrollments and institutional complexity prompted the board to appoint a president.

After Woodrow Wilson declined the board's invitation, Edwin Anderson Alderman accepted the presidency in 1904. That same year Virginia accepted a membership invitation from the Association of American Universities, making the university the first southern institution to receive such an honor.

The Twentieth Century and Future Directions

Along with changing curricula, Virginia responded selectively to social justice issues. In 1920 the university first admitted women to some graduate and professional departments, although women were not accepted on the same basis as men in Charlottesville until 1970. African Americans first attended Virginia in 1950. When a court order mandated admission, the university complied and avoided much of the strife that engulfed other southern campuses during the civil rights movement. In 1953 it became the first major university in the South to award a doctorate to an African-American student.

After World War II Virginia expanded its programs while distinguishing itself as one of the nation's best universities. Enrollment for the school year beginning in 2001 totaled 18,848 students. In 2001 Virginia achieved the highest graduation and retention rates of any public institution. The library system includes fifteen libraries with more than 4 million holdings. In addition, the Cavaliers compete in National Collegiate Athletic Association (NCAA) division I athletics as a member of the Atlantic Coast Conference (ACC).

A continuing legacy of the university is its architectural design. Original construction of Jefferson's "academical village" provided a symbol of his Enlightenment faith. On October 27, 1895, fire destroyed the Rotunda, the architectural centerpiece that housed the library. The university rebuilt the structure, which underwent renovation during the 1970s. Other institutional reforms during the late twentieth century included curbing the tradition of excessive student drinking. The historic student honor code faced a severe test in 2001 when a computer program detected widespread plagiarism in a physics class.

During the tenure of John T. Casteen III, who became president in 1990, Virginia's capital campaign raised more than $1.4 billion—the largest effort of any state university. The institution used its good fortune to promote sound educational programs. Casteen's remarkably thoughtful presidential addresses acknowledged Virginia's unfortunate heritage of racial inequity in admissions and committed the university to correcting that social injustice.

Virginia offers forty-eight bachelor's degrees and fifty-five doctoral degrees along with other graduate and professional programs. *U.S. News and World Report* ranked Virginia among the top public universities in the nation for 2002. Its schools, including the McIntire School of Commerce, the Darden Graduate School of Business Administration, the Law School, and the Medical Center, have received national academic recognition. Virginia has accepted its role as a leader in higher education to promote sound educational values of which Mr. Jefferson would be proud.

See also: HIGHER EDUCATION IN THE UNITED STATES, *subentry on* HISTORICAL DEVELOPMENT.

BIBLIOGRAPHY

ABERNETHY, THOMAS PERKINS. 1948. *Historical Sketch of the University of Virginia.* Richmond, VA: Dietz Press.

BRUCE, PHILIP ALEXANDER. 1920–1922. *History of the University of Virginia, 1819–1919.* New York: Macmillan.

DABNEY, VIRGINIUS. 1981. *Mr. Jefferson's University: A History.* Charlottesville: University Press of Virginia.

WAGONER, JENNINGS L., JR. 1988. "Honor and Dishonor at Mister Jefferson's University: The Ante-Bellum Years." *History of Education Quarterly* 26:155–175.

WILSON, GUY, and BUTLER, SARA A. 1999. *The Campus Guide: The University of Virginia.* New York: Princeton Architectural Press.

ERIC MOYEN
JASON R. EDWARDS
JOHN R. THELIN

UNIVERSITY PRESSES

Established by universities to promote scholarly communication, university presses publish books and related material in a wide range of academic, creative, and professional subjects. They provide college and university faculty and other serious researchers with outlets for specialized works and make new ideas and perspectives available to a national and global audience. The sales of university press books are typically very modest by the standards of trade publications. Overall, however, the works issued by university presses play a significant part in shaping the agendas of many disciplines, especially in the humanities and social sciences.

Historical Background

The relationship between universities and printing dates back at least to the fifteenth and sixteenth centuries, not long after the emergence of movable type printing. Printing and publishing activities were established at Oxford, and soon thereafter at Cambridge, under the approval and protection of the crown through various royal charters. Centuries later, these enterprises remain a powerful presence in academic publishing.

In the English-speaking colonies of the present United States, some early attempts at connecting the small colleges and printing were also undertaken. Without a compelling need for in-house publishing activities beyond what a print shop could provide, however, university presses, in the modern sense, were slow to develop. It was not until the nineteenth century and the rise of the university movement in American higher education that conditions favoring the creation of university presses emerged in the United States. That era brought an emphasis on original research and new disciplinary specialization. As universities began to replace the older, undergraduate-focused colleges at the center stage of American higher education, demand grew for new ways to disseminate the fruits of research to the growing audience of faculty and graduate students.

Andrew Dickson White introduced the idea at Cornell University in 1869, in conjunction with his plans to train professional journalists. Although the results were only marginally successful and the press was discontinued in the 1880s, it was an important first step. Among those following Cornell's lead was Daniel Coit Gilman, who promoted the establishment of the Publication Agency at the Johns Hopkins University in 1878. Later known as the Johns Hopkins University Press, it is the oldest continuously operating university press in the United States.

American university presses did not immediately achieve the goals that later would be expected of them. Often, the research published was from the faculty of the parent institution, which sometimes limited the ability of the presses to seek out work of a uniformly high caliber. In addition, universities commonly required the publication of doctoral dissertations, and university presses often fulfilled this task, with the authors subsidizing production costs. In these instances again, the presses exercised less critical judgement about what they would publish than in later years.

In the era following World War II, university presses became more prominent and prestigious in the academic world. As American higher education rapidly grew and academic libraries increased acquisitions activities, university presses achieved a greater and more successful position in the academic environment than before the war. Their reputation for quality grew at the same time. University presses blossomed during this period. By the close of the twentieth century, there were more than eighty university presses in the United States.

Types of Material Published

Unlike trade publishing firms, which usually select and develop books for publication based primarily on commercial appeal, university presses have an overarching mission to produce works of scholarly value even though the audience is usually much smaller than that of a trade book. The financial implications for a publishing project are certainly taken into consideration when a university press contemplates publishing a book. However, as not-for-profit entities, university presses have traditionally placed significantly more weight on the scholarly or creative merits of a book, with much less emphasis on potential profitability. By the closing years of the twentieth century, those traditions were challenged, however, as subsidies from the universities to which they are attached often diminished and budget slumps affected academic libraries' acquisition budgets.

A chief function of university presses lies in their role in selecting topics and perspectives to be brought to the attention of the scholarly community. In the humanities and in many of the social sciences, books about specialized topics (often called *monographs*) remain one of the vital mechanisms for the distribution of scholarly knowledge and critical insight. Such titles continue to be a staple of university press publication lists. (This is less true in the natural sciences, where the more typical mode by which new knowledge is disseminated has been through articles in refereed academic journals.) University presses

also have developed strong reputations for publishing in areas such poetry and regional studies.

As universities and academic disciplines became more complex and subject to specialization over the course of the twentieth century, so, too, did publishing programs become increasingly specialized. This specialization was partly due to practical reasons, since it would be difficult for a university press to maintain a high degree of competence across the whole of the academic spectrum. One benefit of specialization is that by focusing on fewer disciplines and subject areas, individual university presses are often able to develop stronger and more national and international reputations. This, in turn, makes it easier to market the books that are published and to attract additional high-quality manuscripts. In any case, the strengths of a university press usually reflect those of the university of which it is a part.

Book Acquisitions Process and Academic Quality

The claim to high quality is closely linked to the process university presses employ in acquiring manuscripts. In this aspect of publishing, the contrast between university presses and commercial publishers is especially sharp. Because the academic value and integrity of works published is a central concern for a university press book, many of these presses have adopted a rigorous, three-part review process to help ensure that the books reaching publication have the characteristics desired.

The process begins with contact between an editor and a prospective author. Sometimes authors send a letter of inquiry—or, more rarely, a completed manuscript—to a publisher, and sometimes the editors themselves seek out possible authors. If the editor accepts a proposed book, the next step is peer review, which is usually not undertaken until the manuscript has been completed. In this phase, the publisher sends the manuscript for independent evaluation by readers who are selected because of their own academic standing and credentials. Typically, the peer review begins with two readers. A third reader may be consulted if one reader approves and the other has reservations about the manuscript.

If the manuscript receives a positive evaluation from two readers, it proceeds to the final step in which it is reviewed by the press's editorial board. This group is a committee of faculty members, largely from the home institution in most cases, with final authority over whether to proceed to publication of the book.

The university press arena is highly decentralized. Though there are many hurdles to publication at any given press, the existence of many university presses means that a manuscript might be rejected at one press yet still find a home with a different publisher that has differing needs and criteria. In addition, there is also a smaller, but important, group of scholarly publishers in the commercial publishing world, some of which have high standing in various academic fields.

University Presses as Gatekeepers

Commentators have noted that university presses serve as "gatekeepers of ideas." Many more books are proposed than are accepted for publication at a university press, and the greater the prestige ranking of a press, the greater the competition to have one's book published with a given press. Decisions about what to publish—and what not to publish—are important in shaping of the academic agendas for many disciplines. For such reasons, the traditional lack of diversity among university press editors has been the cause of some concern.

In addition to the role that university presses play for the scholarly community at large, they also are important to the lives of individual scholars in many disciplines. In fields of the humanities especially, the publication of a book has been an important measure of scholarly achievement. Book publication in such fields, especially by respected university presses, can be extremely important in tenure and promotion decisions and in enhancing a scholar's reputation outside her or his own institution. Beyond simply having a book published, the academic reputation of the book's publisher has a central importance for a scholar, since the prestige of the publisher is often taken as an indication of the quality of the work itself.

Challenges to University Presses

University presses have faced many challenges, a situation that became increasingly acute in the 1980s and 1990s as economic and technological changes accelerated. University presses, as well as the few commercial presses focusing on scholarly works, saw a long period of decline in sales. In part this was due to severe constraints on the budgets of college and university libraries.

Already, some university presses had begun to seek out a broader audience. A prominent example of this impulse was found in Louisiana State University Press's publication of John Kennedy Toole's novel *A Confederacy of Dunces,* which won the Pulitzer Prize for fiction in 1981. When financial circumstances later became more pronounced among university presses, many of them similarly aimed to augment their publication lists with books that could be sold to a wider audience of readers without compromising the scholarly reputation of the presses themselves.

Technological advances, which constitute a major challenge to book publishing more generally, also deeply have affected university presses. The future viability of printed books was widely debated in 1990s, and university presses explored various ways to take advantage of the opportunities presented by new electronic technologies.

Though they have evolved over the years and face many challenges, university presses remain an integral part of the academic world.

See also: FACULTY PERFORMANCE OF RESEARCH AND SCHOLARSHIP; FACULTY RESEARCH AND SCHOLARSHIP, ASSESSMENT OF.

BIBLIOGRAPHY

ALTBACH, PHILIP G., and McVEY, SHEILA, eds. 1976. *Perspectives on Publishing.* Lexington, MA: Lexington Books.

BUDD, JOHN M. 1991. "Academic Libraries and University Presses." *Publishing Research Quarterly* 7(2):27–38.

HAWES, GENE R. 1967. *To Advance Knowledge: A Handbook on American University Press Publishing.* New York: American University Press Services.

HOROWITZ, IRVING LOUIS. 1991. "Toward a History of Social Science Publishing in the United States." *Publishing Research Quarterly* 7(2):59–68.

KERR, CHESTER. 1949. *A Report on American University Presses.* Washington, DC: Association of American University Presses.

McKITTERICK, DAVID. 1992. *A History of Cambridge University Press.* New York: Cambridge University Press.

PARSONS, PAUL. 1988. "University Presses as 'Gatekeepers of Ideas' within Society." Paper presented at the Annual Meeting of the Association for Education in Journalism and Mass Communication, July 2–5. ERIC, ED 298489.

PARSONS, PAUL. 1990. "Specialization by University Presses." *Book Research Quarterly* 6(2):3–16.

POWELL, WALTER W. 1985. *Getting into Print: The Decision-Making Process in Scholarly Publishing.* Chicago: University of Chicago Press.

SISLER, WILLIAM P. 1978. *One Hundred Years of Scholarly Publishing, 1878–1978.* Baltimore: Johns Hopkins University Press.

GORDON B. ARNOLD

UPWARD BOUND

Upward Bound (UB) is a federal educational program designed to prepare high school students from poverty-level homes for entry and success in college. It was begun in the summer of 1965, when the Office of Economic Opportunity (OEO) funded seventeen summer pilot programs on college campuses under the Community Action component of the Economic Opportunity Amendments of 1965. It formed a miniscule part of President Lyndon Johnson's War on Poverty.

The theoretical basis for the program was taken from the work of Richard Cloward and Lloyd Ohlin's opportunity theory, which addressed the problems of juvenile delinquency and gang behavior. Several members of the President's Commission on Juvenile Delinquency in the Justice Department transferred to OEO and adapted Cloward and Ohlin's basic concepts. They designed programs to increase the chances that youth from disadvantaged backgrounds might enter and succeed in higher education as one way to overcome poverty. Experimental precollege programs funded in the early 1960s by foundations provided ready-made structures for what the programs might look like. Upward Bound gained recognition, though it never became as well known as its sister program for preschool youngsters, Head Start, also housed in OEO. It has been restricted in its possible impact because of underfunding, caused at first by the escalating cost of the Vietnam War and then by the inflation that followed. This pattern continued, and in 2001 it was estimated that only between 1 to 7 percent of the eligible students are being served.

The Higher Education Amendments of 1969 transferred UB from OEO to the Office of Education in the Department of Health, Education and Welfare. There it was joined with two other programs designed to work with different populations of low-income youth to increase the likelihood that they would enter and/or succeed in postsecondary education. These formed what began to be called the TRIO Programs.

The current legislative authority for UB is found in the Higher Education Act of 1965, Title IV, Part A, Subpart 2, Section 402C. 20 U.S.C. 107a-13. Program information and requirements, legislative references, and other current information can be accessed at the Department of Education Federal TRIO Program Internet site.

A call for proposals is published every four years in the *Federal Register.* Four- and five-year grants are awarded to institutional applicants based on ranked scores assigned by peer reviewers. In the 1998 competition, 82 percent of the applicants were funded.

Since 1986 the legislation has directed that "prior experience" be considered and points added to the peer review scores of previously funded projects that met certain criteria. TRIO is unique among federal discretionary grant awards for incorporating this element in the competition process, and it helps provide a quasi permanence to previously funded projects.

The Design of a Project

Regulations require that the students selected have a need for academic support and that two-thirds come from low-income families (defined as income less than 150 percent of poverty level) where neither parent has attained a baccalaureate degree. The student is then defined as a "potential first-generation college student." The remaining one-third must meet only one of these criteria. Participants enter during their ninth or tenth grade and are expected to remain through high school graduation. Most UB programs are located on college campuses and consist of a residential six-week intensive summer program with follow-up during the school year. Many projects offer Saturday and weekday after-school sessions designed to improve student performance in the sciences, mathematics, languages, and computer skills. Other services include college visitations, counseling, test preparation, and various cultural enrichment activities. Students usually receive a small stipend for participation. Programs range in size from 50 to 150 students with an average enrollment of seventy.

Over time, the programs have come to be somewhat standardized and, for the most part, less experimental than in the earlier years. The legislation and regulations have evolved to require more uniform program design and increasingly insist on measurable outcomes. Indicators, such as improvement in student grade point averages, standardized test scores, and enrollment in and graduation from four-year institutions of higher education are monitored by annual performance reports in an attempt to determine whether program goals are being achieved.

Current information on UB as well as links to the home pages of several hundred projects can be accessed through links from the Internet site of the Council for Opportunity in Education (COE), a national organization of TRIO professional staff.

Veteran's Upward Bound

In 1972 Congress authorized a Veteran's Upward Bound program (VUB) in response to the large number of military returning from the Vietnam War. Originally envisioned as lasting for only a short period of time, the VUB has continued to work with veterans from other conflicts despite several attempts to eliminate this component of the UB program. Although the goals of the VUB programs are the same as classic programs, that is, to increase postsecondary enrollment, more latitude is permitted in age range and the types of services offered.

Upward Bound Math/Science

In 1990 an initiative was undertaken to address the concern that students from low-income, first-generation, and minority populations were not well represented in the fields of science and mathematics. Upward Bound Math/Science programs (UBMS) were begun, often drawing participants from a regional area extending over several states and hundreds of miles from the host institution. The emphasis was, and continues to be, the preparation of participants for postsecondary study in fields of mathematics and the sciences. Because participants are spread out over such a large geographic area, these programs face a challenge in continuing follow-up services for participants during the academic year, which follows the summer program at the host institution's campus.

Evaluations of the Program

Many studies have been done on the effectiveness of UB. The most comprehensive evaluation was completed in 1979 and concluded that UB does have a positive effect on overall educational attainment and college enrollment but no effect on high school academic preparation or persistence in college. A current longitudinal study was begun in 1992. It is following a treatment and control group from a nationally representative sample of students and is designed to assess the impact of the program on participants over a ten- to twelve-year period. Preliminary findings indicate that specific subgroups of students receive the greatest benefits from the program: those with lower academic expectations and poorer performance on entry—Hispanic students, boys, and students who qualified solely under the low-income criteria.

Greater impact on both high school and college outcomes becomes more evident the longer a student remains in the program. Because nearly two-thirds of the participants withdraw from the program within two years, this finding highlights the need for retention if the intervention is to become most effective. The large majority of students leaving report that they terminate to take a job. In response to this, the authorizing statute now allows summer students to participate in a work-study component, designed to expose participants to careers requiring a postsecondary degree. However, current funding is not sufficient to allow the $900 to be awarded to participants in most projects.

Upward Bound is the most costly of the federal TRIO programs, which as a group rank among the highest expenditures in discretionary federal dollars for education after student financial aid. In 2001–2002 the Department of Education reported there were 772 UB projects, including forty-five VUB, and 123 additional UBMS projects across the United States and its territories. Funding for classic and VUB projects totaled $251,154,772, serving an estimated 56,564 students; an additional $30,874,003 was awarded to the UBMS projects serving 6,093 students. The average yearly cost per participant in regular UB was $4,440 and $5,063 for UBMS.

See also: FEDERAL EDUCATIONAL ACTIVITIES; U.S. DEPARTMENT OF EDUCATION.

BIBLIOGRAPHY

BENDIXEN, SALLY, and WESBY, JOHN. 1990. "A History of the Veterans Upward Bound Program." *NCEOA Journal* Fall:16–19.

GROUTT, JOHN, and HILL, CALVIN. 2001. "Upward Bound: In the Beginning." *Opportunity Outlook* April:23–36.

MCELROY, EDWARD J., and ARMESTO, MARIA. 1998. "TRIO and Upward Bound: History, Programs, and Issues—Past, Present, and Future." *The Journal of Negro Education* 67:373–380.

MORTENSON, THOMAS. 2000. "TRIO Market Penetration." *Postsecondary Education Opportunity* 95:10–16.

MYERS, DAVID, and SCHRIM, ALLEN. 1999. *The Impacts of Upward Bound: Final Report for Phase I of the National Evaluation, Executive Summary.* Washington, DC: Prepared under contract by Mathematica Policy Research for the U.S. Department of Education, Planning and Evaluation Services.

WOLANIN, THOMAS R. 1977. "The History of TRIO: Three Decades of Success and Counting." *NCEOA Journal* April:2–4.

INTERNET RESOURCES

COUNCIL FOR OPPORTUNITY IN EDUCATION. 2002. <www.trioprograms.org>.

FEDERAL TRIO PROGRAMS. 2002. <www.ed.gov/offices/OPE/HEP/trio/upbound.html>.

TRIO NATIONAL CLEARINGHOUSE. 1999. The Impacts of Upward Bound: Final Report for Phase I of the National Evaluation, Executive Summary. <www.trioprograms.org/clearinghouse>.

JOHN W. GROUTT

URBAN EDUCATION

The dictionary definition of *urban* is simply "a term pertaining to a city or town." In everyday parlance the term is used frequently to distinguish something from the terms *rural, small town, suburban, or ex-urban.*

These objective size and density definitions, however, do not convey the range of meanings intended or received when the term is most commonly used. Perceptions of urban areas differ widely. Rooted in the early history of the United States and illustrated in the writings of Alexander Hamilton is a vision of the urban setting as one that fosters free-doms. This perception defines cities as places of refuge and opportunity, a vision widely accepted in many countries. Also rooted in America's history, as illustrated in the writings of Thomas Jefferson, is the opposing perception of urban as dysfunctional and the cause of many societal problems. In American parlance, "God's country" is used to refer to rural areas or nature preserves, not cities.

During the first half of the twentieth century urban areas were viewed by many as economically dynamic, attracting and employing migrant populations from small towns, rural areas, and abroad. During the second half of the twentieth century, however, the term urban became a pejorative code word for the problems caused by the large numbers of poor and minorities who live in cities. Such negative associations with the term urban profoundly affect education and shape the nature of urban schooling.

Students and Structure

Unlike most other countries where education is a federal or national function, schooling in the United States is decentralized. States are the legally responsible entities but local districts are generally perceived as the accountable units of administration. There were approximately 53 million American children entering public and private schools in the fall of the year 2000. Thirty-five percent were members of minority groups. One in five came from an immigrant household. Nearly one-fifth were living in poverty. Eleven states accounted for more than half of the children in poverty: California, Texas, New York, Florida, New Jersey, Pennsylvania, Ohio, Illinois, Michigan, North Carolina, and Georgia. All these students were overseen by more than 15,000 local districts with almost 90,000 schools. The 120 largest school districts, generally defined as the urban ones, served 11 million students, most of whom were of color or in poverty.

Since 1962 the achievement gap between disadvantaged populations and more affluent ones has widened. At one extreme, urban school districts graduate half or fewer of their students. At the other extreme, 11 percent of American students are among the top 10 percent of world achievers. As one researcher remarked, "If you're in the top economic quarter of the population, your children have a 76 percent chance of getting through college and graduating by age 24. . . . If you're in the bottom quarter, however, the figure is 4 percent" (Loeb, pp. 87–

88). According to educational researcher Gerald W. Bracey, white students' standardized test achievement in reading, mathematics, and science ranks second, seventh, and fourth, respectively, when compared with students worldwide. African-American and Hispanic students, however, rank twenty-sixth, twenty-seventh, and twenty-seventh on these basic skills. Such data describe but do not explain the causes of such wide disparities among educational outcomes. The following section describes some of the challenges which, taken together, help to explain the failure of urban school districts. A final section describes many of the characteristics of successful urban schools.

Special Challenges

Highly politicized school boards. Board politics in major urban school districts often impede judicious decision-making. Several practices contribute to the problem. First, in an effort to better represent diverse constituencies, citywide board seats have given way to narrowly drawn district seats. Board members elected from such districts may find it difficult to support policies and budgets aimed at the good of the total district when doing so is viewed negatively by parents, citizens, and educators in their own neighborhood schools. Second, board members often try to micromanage large, complicated school organizations, thereby abrogating the leadership and accountability of their own superintendent. Finally, it is not unusual for narrow majorities on boards to change after a board election and for superintendents to find prior initiatives no longer supported and even have their contracts bought out.

Superintendent turnover. The average years of service for an urban superintendent has been reported differently in various surveys, with some reporting as low as 2.3 years. As a result a new superintendent may function more as a temporary employee of a school board than as the educational leader of the district and the community. Administrators and teachers are reluctant to throw themselves into new initiatives that are not likely to remain in place long enough to show any results. Constituencies, including governments, businesses, church groups, foundations, and universities, with whom the superintendent must interact may take a "wait and see" attitude rather than become active partners in the new superintendent's initiatives.

Principals as managers and leaders. The size and complexity of most urban schools inevitably lead to a focus on the principal as the manager or CEO of a major business enterprise. This emphasis has led to a transformation of the traditional principal role as an instructional leader. Few urban districts dismiss principals because of low student achievement unless the achievement falls low enough for the school to be taken over by the state or district and be reconstituted. In practice the typical urban principal who is transferred or coaxed into retirement is one that has "lost control of the building." The district's stated system of accountability may place student learning as the highest priority; however, the real basis for defining urban principals as "failing" may be not because they have been unable to demonstrate increasing student achievement but because they have been unable to maintain a custodial institution. As researchers Kathy Kimball and Kenneth A. Sirotnik report, the fact that most urban principals spend the preponderance of their time and energy on management issues demonstrates that they fully understand this reality.

Government oversight. Local and state government officials involve themselves more and more in educational policies that impact urban districts. This politicization of education produces an endless stream of regulations and funding mechanisms, which encourage or penalize the efforts of local urban districts. However the treatments frequently counteract one another or have unintended negative consequences.

Central office bureaucracies. In rural, small town, and suburban districts, classroom teachers comprise 80 percent or more of the school district's employees. In the 120 largest urban districts, the number of employees other than teachers is approaching a ratio of almost 2 to 1; that is, for every classroom teacher there are almost two others employed in the district ostensibly to perform services that would help these teachers. The effect of this distortion is frequently a proliferation of procedures, regulations, interruptions, and paperwork that impedes rather than facilitates student learning. Many teachers leaving urban districts cite paperwork and excessive bureaucratic regulation as among the most debilitating conditions they face.

The self-serving nature of the district bureaucracy frequently impedes initiatives, which would decentralize decision-making and transfer power to individual school staffs. Historically centralized systems are reluctant to change. Prodded by parents, community members, and business leaders, urban districts are gradually allowing more decentralized decision-making at the school level. In response to bureaucratic rigidities, choices are proliferating within public systems. Examples include open enrollment plans, magnet and specialty schools, schools-within-schools, alternative schools, and public choice and charter schools. Urban parents also have increased options outside the public systems through private school voucher programs, but these efforts account for less than one percent of enrollment in urban districts.

School staff accountability. As public school options increase so do calls for accountability. The most frequently tried accountability efforts in the twentieth century have been attempts at merit pay for teachers based on student achievement test scores. Private foundations have funded many of these trials and several have been supported initially by local teachers unions. Thus far, however, there have been no successful models for holding either principals or teachers accountable based on achievement scores. In some cases superintendents have clauses in their contracts stating that their tenure or salaries are dependent on improvements in student achievement. In some districts, school principals' annual evaluations and contract extensions have become tied to improving student achievement.

At the start of the twenty-first century, many states have adopted systems for declaring particular schools (or districts) as failing if a given number of the school's students are below a minimum level of achievement. In these cases the state may mandate that a failing school be reconstituted and may grant the local district the authority to re-staff the school with a new principal and teaching staff. The staff of a failing school is typically permitted to transfer to other schools in the district. This means that while an urban school district is being held accountable based on achievement data, the individual staff members are not. Furthermore the concept of accountability is nonexistent for curriculum specialists, hiring officials, or those who appoint principals, psychologists, safety aides, or other school staff.

Teacher shortages. The public clearly understands the importance of well-prepared teachers: 82 percent believe that the "recruitment and retention of better teachers is the most important measure for improving public schools, more effective than investing in computers or smaller class size" (Education Commission of the States, p. 6). In the early twenty-first century there may be as many as one million new teachers hired because of turnover, retirement, and the fact that the typical teaching career has shortened to approximately eleven years. If the school-age population continues to increase, another million teachers may be needed. While all districts face occasional selected shortages of special education teachers, bilingual teachers, and mathematics or science teachers, the major impact of the current and continuing teacher shortage falls on the urban school districts. These are the teaching positions that many traditionally prepared teachers are unwilling to take. This problem is confounded by the fact that many urban districts must lay off teachers to make up for budget deficits in a given year while they are simultaneously recruiting teachers to remedy their chronic shortages.

In the states that prepare a majority of the teachers in traditional university-based programs, more than half of those who graduate and are licensed never take teaching positions. Of those who do enter the classroom, according to a report from the Education Commission of the States, up to one-third have not only left their initial positions but the teaching profession as well by five years after graduation.

The typical teacher education graduate is a 22-year-old white female, who is monolingual and has little work or life experience. She will teach within fifty miles of where she herself attended school. The profile of teachers who succeed and stay in urban school districts differs in important respects. While they are still predominantly women, they are usually over thirty years of age, have attended urban schools themselves, have completed a bachelor's degree in college but not necessarily in education, have worked at other full-time jobs, and are parents themselves. This successful pool also contains a substantially higher number of individuals who are African American, Latino, and male. Typically, the teacher educators who serve as faculty in traditional university-based teacher preparation programs have had little or no teaching experience in urban school districts while those mentoring teachers in alternative licensure programs typically come from long, successful careers as teachers in urban districts.

State licensure laws. While traditional teacher preparation programs seek to attract more young people into the teaching profession, past experience suggests that many of these graduates will not seek employment in large urban school districts where most of the new hires will be needed. To assist in meeting this urban district need, new kinds of recruiting and training programs are being established to attract older, more experienced, and more diverse candidates into the teaching profession. States differ widely in their response to these new programs. On the one hand there are those whose position is that "the key to attracting better teachers is to regulate entry into the classroom ever more tightly" while others argue that "the surest route to quality is to widen the entryway, deregulate the processes, and hold people accountable for their results" (Thomas B. Fordham Foundation, p. 1). Forty-three states have passed alternative licensure laws that permit the hiring of college graduates who were not trained in traditional programs of teacher preparation. But licensure requirements vary greatly across the states and implementation of new approaches is often controversial even though an increasing number of urban districts now develop a pool of teachers using alternative training programs.

Funding for districts and classrooms. Urban school districts often receive substantially less annual financial support per student than they need. The level of funding in urban districts, however, generally exceeds the per pupil expenditures in small towns and rural areas. Many argue, therefore, that there is no total shortage of funds for urban schools, especially when categorical aids and grants are considered. The overall problem of inadequate funding is often exacerbated after the urban school district receives its funds and distributes the monies from the central office levels to the individual schools. Too often, too much money is expended to maintain central office functions, leaving too little to cover the direct costs of instruction and equipment in specific school buildings. In addition, many urban districts are characterized by buildings that are outmoded, even unsafe, creating conditions that make learning problematic. In New York City, for example, more than 150 school buildings are still heated by coal in the early twenty-first century.

"Projectitis." New school board members and superintendents often believe they must set their personal stamps on the district through new initiatives. It is common for urban districts to claim they are aware of and experimenting with the latest curricula in reading, mathematics, or science, for example. In addition, administrators are pressured to try out new programs against drugs, violence, gangs, smoking, sex, etc. This proliferation of programs and projects results in so many new initiatives being tried

simultaneously it is not possible to know which initiative caused what results. Furthermore, not enough time is devoted to any given program to allow it to demonstrate intended results. The problem is compounded by the fact that many of these new initiatives are not systematically or carefully evaluated. Veteran teachers, when confronted with the latest initiative from the school board or administration, often become passive resisters, simply waiting for the next fad to come along while they continue to maintain the status quo. The constant claims of experts, school boards and superintendents that their latest initiative will transform their schools is frequently stonewalled by the very people who must be the heart of the effort for it to succeed.

Narrowing curriculum and lowering expectations. As presented in state and local district philosophy and mission statements, the list of what the American people generally expect from their public schools is impressive. A typical list is likely to include the following goals for students: the acquisition of basic skills, positive self-concept, and humane, democratic values; motivation to be life-long learners and active citizens; success in higher education and in the world of work; effective functioning in a culturally diverse society and a global economy; technological competence; development of individual talents; maintenance of physical and emotional health; appreciation and participation in the arts. In many suburban and small town schools the parents, community members, and professional school educators maintain a broad general vision about the goals that thirteen years of full-time schooling is supposed to accomplish. But in the urban districts serving culturally diverse students in poverty, these broad missions are frequently narrowed down to "getting a job and staying out of jail" (Russell p. 51).

Narrowing down the curriculum is particularly evident among the burgeoning populations of students labeled as special or exceptional. The urban districts have disproportionately large and, some observers claim, wildly accelerating numbers of students labeled with some form of disability. In urban districts the numbers of special students currently range from 6 percent to 20 percent of the student body. This means that exceptional education may account for between 20 percent and 35 percent of a total urban district's budget. In their 1994 book, *The War Against Children*, Peter R. Breggin and Ginger R. Breggin note that well intentioned but sometimes misapplied state and federal initiatives for special education students encourage the labeling of increasing numbers of students as having learning disabilities, cognitive disabilities, or attention deficit hyperactivity disorder.

It is also not uncommon for many urban teachers who do not have in-depth knowledge of child development to perceive undesirable behavior as abnormal rather than as a temporary stage or as student responses to poor teaching. Thus it is common in urban middle schools to find many students doing well academically who have been labeled as having disabilities in primary grades and who will carry these labels throughout the remainder of their school careers. Teacher expectations are likely to be very modest for such children; testing may be waived. Some low-income parents may be enticed to agree to have their children labeled exceptional because of financial grants. Recent efforts at inclusion for exceptional students in regular classrooms are aimed at breaking the cycle of low expectations and isolation. In urban districts, however, inclusion mandates are most frequently followed in the primary grades but seldom at the high school level. The disproportionate number of children of color, particularly males, labeled exceptional further exacerbates this problem.

Achievement and testing. There are four curricula operating in schools. The first is the broadest. It is the written mission of the school district. The second curriculum is what the teachers actually teach. The third operative curriculum is what the students actually learn, which is considerably less than what a district claims or what the teachers teach. The fourth curriculum is what is tested for, and this is the narrowest of the four.

The "tested-for" curriculum frequently supports the narrowing and lowering of expectations. As total school and district programs are evaluated by norm-referenced tests, the accountability of teachers and principals is also narrowed and lowered to the kinds of learning that can be readily tested. Recognition of this problem has led to a new emphasis on standards-led testing or performance assessment that is closely linked to curriculum, in place of the norm-reference testing that compares student's performance to that of others. Done carefully, such assessment measures the performance of successive cohorts of students against an annual rate of improvement (local or state) that is sufficient to achieve whatever curriculum goals have been set. For the most part, aligning the goals, curriculum, instruction, and testing is yet to be accomplished, however.

After decades of ignoring low student scores in urban schools or explaining them away as predictable because of family income, national attention has shifted to the numerous and widespread examples of individual urban schools in which students' scores are being raised and increasing numbers of low income children are reaching grade level achievement. Educators at all levels are being called upon to focus time, thought and resources on the poorest performing schools and the persistent cultural and racial gaps between high and low performing students.

Research on urban school practices. The research literature in teaching, learning, and best practice is robust. A great deal is known about best practices for teachers, how children learn, and what makes specific urban schools successful. The problem is that schools, even failing schools in urban districts that would be expected as being more amenable to change, are resistant institutions shaped by history, culture, and their economic support systems. Simply knowing what works does not guarantee its implementation.

Schools reflect not only general American norms and values but also their local cultures. Since the mid-1980s the plethora of federal and state laws and local administrative mandates is testimony to the fact that education is also a flourishing political activity. It seems clear that schools reflect culture more than research, or even logic and theory. Schools reflect and maintain a multiplicity of social norms contradicted by research-based knowledge regarding best practice. It is ironic that those seeking to transform failed urban school districts are frequently expected to prove beforehand that their advocacies are research-based while those who stonewall change rely on a rationale of laws, funding mechanisms, school organization, and practices that reflect culture and tradition, unsupported by a research knowledge base.

One example lies in what has been described by Martin Haberman (1991) as the pedagogy of poverty. Teaching in many urban schools consists of ritualized teacher acts, which seldom engage students in meaningful learning that is connected to their lives. Such teaching includes giving directions and information; making assignments; monitoring seatwork; testing and grading; settling disputes and punishing noncompliance. While such activities are part of teaching, the research literature is clear that more is needed if schools are to reach diverse groups of students with widely varied backgrounds, interests, and experiences. Allowing these limited teaching practices to become the typical ones in the urban districts serving diverse student populations of low income students not only "dumbs down" the content of the curriculum but also narrows the pedagogy by which it is offered. It is a process in which students are treated in a disrespectful manner—as if they are incapable of appreciating or responding to the genuine teaching of important knowledge.

Taken together, these formidable urban challenges demand the best of educational practices if children are to succeed. While there are no fully successful urban districts, every district has individual schools that *are* effective. Indeed there are examples of outstanding schools in some of the poorest performing urban districts. This anomaly of how individual schools can be successful in the midst of chaos and failure has been sufficiently documented to enable the stating with some certainty the characteristics that account for their effectiveness.

Characteristics of Successful Urban Programs

The correlates of the effective school literature are as follows: a clearly stated mission; a safe climate for learning; high expectations for students, teachers and administrators; high student time on task; administrators who are instructional leaders; frequent monitoring of student progress; and positive home-school relations. These and other necessary conditions are demonstrated in urban schools in the following ways: First, such schools have outstanding principals who serve as leaders rather than building managers. These individuals are instructional leaders with a deep understanding of the teaching and learning process. They also know, appreciate, and respect the cultures of the ethnic and racial groups the school serves.

Second, there is a critical mass of star teachers or teachers on their way to becoming stars. These are individuals who believe that students and their families are the clients. They believe that student effort rather than ability accounts for success in school and their teaching reflects their ability to generate student effort. These teachers not only know the content and methods of teaching, but also have effective relationship skills that connect them with students. The ideology and behaviors of star teachers have been well documented. While there are numerous exceptions, star urban teachers tend to be people who are more mature with more varied life experience than college youth. They are often people of color who have attended urban schools themselves. Many have experienced poverty firsthand. It is also increasingly likely that they did not go through traditional teacher training.

Third, effective urban schools have a vision of the school's mission commonly held by students, the entire staff, parents, caregivers, and the community. There is a unity of purpose that grows out of everyone who is involved with the school believing, sharing, and contributing to this common vision.

Fourth, there is a deep and growing knowledge of how computers and information systems can be used in classrooms and for all school activities. The students and staff are connected to the full resources of the Internet and to the latest instructional programs and not engaged in merely "drill and kill" activities using a computer.

Fifth, parents are involved in integral ways in the life of the school and not merely as homework tutors or disciplinarians. Parents have a strong voice in all aspects of the school's decision-making processes. They are regarded as resources able to inform school policy and curriculum.

Sixth, the curriculum is aligned with achievement tests. There is also a closed loop so that the results of testing inform and guide curriculum revisions as well as what teachers teach everyday. Student evaluation includes more than norm-referenced tests and places great emphasis on the systematic use of students' work samples and work products. While achievement tests are important, the teachers offer a broad curriculum and do not narrow or dumb it down to prepare for the tests. The acquisition of important knowledge for all students, including those with special needs, is maintained as the school priority.

Seventh, the curriculum is sensitive to issues of equity and social justice. What the teachers plan to teach on any given day can be set aside as students and teachers consider issues that arise in the school. "Problems" are not generally seen as intrusions on the curriculum but are dealt with as opportunities to make learning relevant. The students learn that school is not preparation for living later but rather for learning to deal with issues and challenges now.

Eighth, there are frequent celebrations of student achievements. These take the form of student accomplishments in all areas, which then culminate in exhibits, publications, performances, and displays for other students, parents, and the community. The climate and schedule of the building clearly manifest student learning and accomplishment.

Ninth, the faculty and staff are themselves a community of learners. Teachers and administrators design annual educational plans to develop further as people and as professionals. Such plans include team and cooperative activities to help teachers combat isolation. Professional development occurs during the workday as well as during nonschool periods. It provides "opportunities to build meaningful partnerships with parents, businesses, educational and cultural institutions to create exciting new learning experiences" (Renyi, p. 18).

Tenth, the school provides a healthy, safe environment for learning. The staff is expert at de-escalating rather than escalating student behavior problems. There are few suspensions and expulsions. Every effort is made to continue student learning during a suspension period.

Finally, successful urban schools frequently find ways to extend the time children spend with knowledgeable, caring adults through preschool, extended day, weekend, and summer school programs, often working as partners with their communities.

At the beginning of the twenty-first century the greatest challenge to every major urban school system is to create and replicate these effective conditions, which are already practiced in specific school buildings, throughout the district as a whole.

See also: EDUCATIONAL LEADERSHIP; PRINCIPAL, SCHOOL; SUPERINTENDENT OF LARGE-CITY SCHOOL SYSTEMS; URBAN INSTITUTE.

BIBLIOGRAPHY

ARBANAS, DAVID. 2001. "Dropout Rates by States." *Milwaukee Journal Sentinel.* November 11:1.

ASCHER, CAROL, and FLAXMAN, ERWIN. 1985. "Toward Excellence: An Urban Response to the Recommendations of School Reform." *ERIC/CUE Trends and Issues Series* 2:7–14.

BRACEY, GERALD W. 2002. *Put to the Test: An Educator's and Consumer's Guide to Standardized Tests.* Bloomington, IN: Phi Delta Kappan.

BREGGIN, PETER R., and BREGGIN, GINGER R. 1994. *The War Against Children.* New York: St. Martin's Press.

COHEN, MICHAEL. 2001. *Transforming the American High School.* Washington, DC: The Aspen Institute.

COUNCIL OF THE GREAT CITY SCHOOLS. 2000. "Urban School Superintendents: Characteristics, Tenure and Salary. Second Biennial Survey." *Urban Indicator* 52(2):39–51.

CROSBY, EMERAL A. 1999. "Urban Schools: Forced to Fail." *Phi Delta Kappan* 81(4):298.

CUBAN, LARRY. 2001. "How Systemic Reform Harms Urban Schools." *Education Week* May 30:48.

D'AMICO, JOSEPH J., and CORCORAN, THOMAS B. 1985. *The Impact of Tests and Promotion Standards on Urban Schools and Students.* Philadelphia: Research for Better Schools.

EDUCATION COMMISSION OF THE STATES. 1997. *Redesigning the Urban School District.* Denver, CO: Education Commission of the States.

EDUCATION COMMISSION OF THE STATES. 2000. *In Pursuit of Quality Teaching: Five Key Strategies for Policymakers.* Denver, CO: Education Commission of the States.

FEISTRITZER, EMILY. 1993. *Report Card on American Education: A State by State Analysis.* Washington, DC: National Center on Education Information.

HABERMAN, MARTIN. 1991. "The Pedagogy of Poverty Versus Good Teaching." *Phi Delta Kappan* 734:290–294.

HABERMAN, MARTIN. 1995. *Star Teachers of Children in Poverty.* West Lafayette, IN: Kappa Delta Pi.

HABERMAN, MARTIN. 2001. *The Leadership Functions of Star Principals Serving Children in Poverty.* Houston, TX: The Haberman Educational Foundation.

HILL, PAUL. 1999. "Getting It Right the Eighth Time." In *New Directions,* ed. Marci Kanstoroom and Chester E. Finn, Jr. Washington, DC: Thomas B. Fordham Foundation.

HUNT, JR., JAMES B. 1996. *What Matters Most: Teachers for America's Future.* Woodbridge, VA: National Commission on Teaching and America's Future.

HYMAN, IRWIN A., and SNOOK, PAMELA A. 2000. "Dangerous Schools and What You Can Do About Them." *Phi Delta Kappan* 81(7):488–501.

KIMBALL, KATHY, and SIROTNIK, KENNETH A. 2000. "The Urban School Principal: Take This Job and

. . ." *Education and Urban Society* 32(4):535–543.

KNOTT, JACK H., and MILLER, GARY J. 1987. *Reforming Bureaucracy: The Politics of Institutional Choice.* Englewood Cliffs, NJ: Prentice-Hall.

LANGDON, CAROL A., and VESPER, NICK. 2000. "The Sixth Phi Delta Kappan Poll of Teachers' Attitudes Toward the Public Schools." *Phi Delta Kappan* 81(8):607.

LINN, ROBERT L., and HERMAN, JOAN L. 1997. *A Policymaker's Guide to Standards-Led Assessment.* Denver, CO: Education Commission of the States.

LOEB, PAUL R. 1999. *Soul of a Citizen: Living with Conviction in a Cynical Time.* New York: St. Martin's Griffin.

MALONE, DUMAS. 1948. *Jefferson and His Time.* Boston: Little, Brown.

MCCLAFFERTY, KAREN A.; TORRES, CARLOS A.; and MITCHELL, THEODORE R., eds. 2000. *Challenges of Urban Education: Sociological Perspectives for the Next Century.* Albany: State University of New York Press.

MEYER, ADOLPHE E. 1957. *An Educational History of the American People.* New York: McGraw-Hill.

MITCHELL, LOURDES Z. 2000. "A Place Where Every Teacher Teaches and Every Student Learns." *Education and Urban Society* 32(4):506–518.

OLSON, LYNN. 2000. "2000 & Beyond: The Changing Face of American Schools." *Education Week* 20(4):31–41.

ORTIZ, FLORA I. 1991. "Superintendent Leadership in Urban Schools." Paper presented at the Annual Meeting of the American Educational Research Association, Chicago, April 3–7.

REID, KAREN S. 2002. "City Schools Feel the Pain of Fiscal Bites." *Education Week* 21(19):410.

RENYI, JUDITH. 1996. *Teachers Take Charge of Their Learning.* Washington, DC: The National Foundation for the Improvement of Education.

ROSS, RANDY. 1994. *Effective Teacher Development Through Salary Incentives.* Santa Monica, CA: RAND.

RUSSELL, AVERY, ed. 1986. "The Urban School Principal: The Rocky Road to Instructional Leadership." *Carnegie Quarterly* 31(1):49–68.

SCHUG, MARK, and WESTERN, RICHARD D. 1997. *Deregulating Teacher Training in Wisconsin.* Madison: Wisconsin Policy Research Institute.

SCHUTTLOFFEL, MERYLANN J. 2000. "Social Reconstruction of School Failure." *Education Policy Analysis Archives* 8(45):157–171.

SMITH, B. OTHANEL; SILVERMAN, STUART H.; BORG, JEAN M.; and FRY, BETTY V. 1979. *A Briefing for a College of Pedagogy.* Tampa: University of South Florida.

SPRINTHALL, NORMAN A.; RIEMAN, ALAN J.; and TRIES-SPRINTHALL, LOIS. 1996. "Teacher Professional Development." In *Handbook for Research on Teacher Education,* ed. John Sikula. New York: Rand McNally.

TAYLOR, BARBARA O. 2002. "Effective Schools Process: Alive and Well." *Phi Delta Kappan* 83(5):375–378.

THOMAS B. FORDHAM FOUNDATION. 1999. *The Teachers We Need and How to Get More of Them: A Manifesto.* Washington, DC: Thomas B. Fordham Foundation.

TUNEBERG, JEFFREY. 1996. "The State's Role in Implementing Legislative Mandates: The Urban School Superintendent's Perspective." Paper presented at the Annual Meeting of the American Educational Research Association, New York, April 8–12.

VAN DUNK, EMILY. 1999. *Encouraging Best Practices at MPS.* Milwaukee, WI: The Public Policy Forum.

MARTIN HABERMAN

URBAN INSTITUTE

The Urban Institute, founded in 1968, is a private, nonprofit organization dedicated to conducting independent research on a broad range of social and economic issues of particular importance to improving the quality of life in metropolitan centers in the nation and throughout the developing world. Through statistical research, polling, and interviews, the institute seeks to make available pertinent data that will help in the formulation of state and federal policy. Its published reports, offered in print and on the Internet, are made available to interested individuals, organizations, and researchers free of charge, in the interest of expanding public debate.

Program

The Urban Institute carries out its mission of research and education through the activities conducted by its nine research centers, each of which specializes in particular aspects of the urban experience. For instance, the Education Policy Center generates research on all aspects of education reform, particularly as it relates to the needs of urban public school programs. The Health Policy Center has long concerned itself in studying the changing landscape of insurance availability and, especially, the growing numbers of uninsured and underinsured workers. The Labor and Social Policy Center explores trends in employment and unemployment and, since the late 1980s, has taken a special interest in addressing the problem of rising homelessness in the nation's cities. And the Metropolitan Housing and Communities Center has concentrated on research into standards and availability of low- and middle-income urban housing and on the social and economic effects of housing policy at the state and federal level.

In addition to research, the institute actively seeks to disseminate its findings to interested parties, from policymakers at the state and national level to academic researchers and the general public. To accomplish this goal, the institute makes its data available, free of charge, to all interested parties via its website, and its experts regularly present their research results in a variety of formats, from books and journal articles to interviews, radio addresses, and testimony before congressional committees. "First Tuesdays" is a series of seminars on urban-related topics of current interest, hosted at the institute's headquarters in Washington, D.C., on the first Tuesday of each month from October to June. In addition, the institute participates in a nationally syndicated program, *CityScapes,* in partnership with WAMU-FM, a Washington, D.C., radio station.

Membership and Funding

The institute draws its members from the fields of government and community service, academia, journalism, and business. A small group of senior fellows directs institute-sponsored research with the assistance of a research staff of 400. In addition to directing specific projects, senior fellows also conduct independent research, publish in scholarly and mass-market publications, and represent the institute in the media and while testifying before Congress.

Organization and Funding

The Urban Institute is home to nine separate research centers: the Education Policy Center, the Health Policy Center, the Income and Benefits Policy Center, the International Activities Center, the Justice Policy Center, the Labor and Social Policy Center, the Metropolitan Housing and Communities Center, the Nonprofits and Philanthropy Center, and the Population Studies Center. It receives financial support from government agencies, charitable foundations, corporate sponsors, individual donations, and grants from international organizations such as the World Bank.

History

In the mid- to late 1960s the United States was confronted by increasing urban unrest. Then-president Lyndon B. Johnson had initiated an extensive array of social initiatives, termed the "Great Society," in an effort to address many of the problems facing the nation during that era. In 1968 the Urban Institute was created specifically to evaluate the successes and failings of President Johnson's policies, particularly as they affected key urban issues, such as poverty, educational finance, unemployment, housing, transportation, and welfare. Among the first projects undertaken by the institute was a pioneering effort to use computer modeling to track the results achieved by federal social programs and changes in the tax law and to investigate the impact of these policies on a wide variety of U.S. households.

In the 1970s the institute expanded its areas of interest to develop new management techniques, with the goal of aiding federal and state agencies in improving their performance in delivering their program benefits. These early concerns remain central to the institute's mission today, and the research generated by early institute scholars provided the initial data from which the current databases were built.

In the 1980s the institute devoted much of its resources to producing a detailed chronicle of the urban policy initiatives of the Reagan administration. At the same time, however, other research was still carried out, including an in-depth examination of the proliferation of federal and state programs. One result of this latter research was the recognition that many of these programs were redundant and that overlapping authorities, competing bureaucracies, and a host of contradictory eligibility requirements actually inhibited the implementation of many desired initiatives. To address these problems, the institute developed the concept of the *block grant* approach to federal funding, in an effort to provide states with greater flexibility in addressing the particular needs of their communities. In 1987 the institute also released a groundbreaking study of the problem of urban homelessness. In 1988 it took on the problem of uninsurance and underinsurance, bringing to public awareness the fact that this was not just a problem for the unemployed but for working Americans as well.

The 1990s saw a further broadening of the institute's interests, when the International Activities Center was launched. In 1992 the Los Angeles riots once again brought the institute's attention to the core problems facing the nation's cities, including the problems attendant on the rise in legal and illegal immigration, particularly from Latin America. Meanwhile, increased concerns about problems facing the nation's courts led to the creation, in 1994, of the Federal Justice Statistics Resource Center, a database of trends and issues in criminal justice. In 1997 the institute published its "neighborhood indicators," a progress-assessment checklist designed to help state and local municipalities improve their performance in achieving social and economic goals.

In the year 2000 the institute inaugurated a new project, Assessing the New Federalism. This program, inspired by the trend toward "devolution" (the reversion of control over social and economic policy to the states), monitors the progress of local and state initiatives and makes that information available to the wider public.

INTERNET RESOURCE

URBAN INSTITUTE. 2002. <www.urban.org>.

NANCY E. GRATTON

U.S. DEPARTMENT OF EDUCATION

OVERVIEW
    Christopher T. Cross
    M. René Islas
INTERNATIONAL ROLE
    Lenore Yaffee Garcia
    Rafael Michael Nevarez

OVERVIEW

A persistent debate that the United States has struggled with since its early history is the role of the fed-eral government in the education of its citizenry. Much of this debate has played out in battles over the existence of a national government entity focused on education, such as the U.S. Department of Education.

The divisive issue of the federal role in education stems from an ambiguous charge from the nation's founding fathers. On one hand, they generally professed a limited national government organized to secure the national interest, leaving the responsibility of most public operations to state and local government bodies. On the other hand, the founding fathers were very direct in their belief in the unalienable relationship between a well-educated citizenry and a healthy democracy.

For the most part, advocates of a very limited federal government were victorious in maintaining the responsibility of education at the local and state level. The strength behind their argument was that the U.S. Constitution made no mention of a federal role in education. However, opponents cite the constitutional clause that grants the power to provide for the nation's "general welfare" to Congress, as reasoning for a substantial federal role. The result was that for the "first three-quarters of a century of the country's existence, there was no agency in the federal government specifically concerned with education" (National Library of Education website).

History of the Department

In 1867 the U.S. Congress passed legislation to establish the first Department of Education. President Andrew Jackson signed the legislation that created the department, which was to be a non-cabinet-level agency with a mission of improving American education by disseminating sound education information to local- and state-level authorities. Henry Barnard, a dedicated scholar of education reform, became the first commissioner of the Department of Education; he was given a small staff of three and two rooms in Washington, D.C., to run the agency.

Barnard accepted the challenge and believed that American education, especially practitioners at the state and local level, would benefit from having sound information, data, research, and best practices to emulate. Barnard was responsible for collecting a great deal of data about the nation's schools and disseminating it to practitioners. He focused the department on producing scholarly reports and research to provide a context for education. Despite the miniscule staff, resources, and power that the Department of Education carried, Barnard achieved some success in achieving his mission. However, Congressional opposition did not agree that Barnard's academic approach was cost-effective, charging that the department had become a waste of national resources.

As a result, "the annual appropriations act approved by Congress on July 20, 1868 reduced the funding for the education agency and stated that after June 30, 1869, it would lose its independent status and become the Office of Education within the Department of Interior" (National Library of Education website). Soon thereafter, in 1870, the education agency was renamed the Bureau of Education, and Barnard became discouraged about the new direction and resigned.

Barnard's successor, John Eaton, was immediately appointed as commissioner of the Bureau of Education. Eaton continued Barnard's interest in collecting education statistics, publications, and reports, and in disseminating them to local and state education authorities. In fact, Eaton, recognizing the value of the library collection owned by Barnard and housed in the Bureau of Education, decided to purchase the collection for the Bureau of Education's library. Eaton emphasized the importance of the collection of resources by appointing a librarian and pushing to grow the collection despite a lack of funding support by Congress.

Additionally, Eaton maintained the emphasis on collecting statistics. He realized that there was much to be collected, and he continued Barnard's charge, with some success. In an 1875 report, Eaton stated:

> When the work of collecting educational statistics was begun by the Office, it was found that there was no authentic list of the colleges in the United States, or of academies, or normal schools, or schools of science, law, or medicine, or of any other class of education institutions. The lists of nearly all grades of schools are now nearly complete. Information on all other matters relating to educational systems was equally incomplete and difficult to access. (quoted in Grant)

From 1889 to 1906 the Department of Interior's Bureau of Education continued its focus on collecting and diffusing education information and statistics in the United States. William Torrey Harris was the commissioner during this period, and data collection was greatly expanded. It included private elementary and secondary school enrollment, teachers, and graduates; enrollment by subject field in public high schools; public school revenue receipts by source; and income and value of physical plants of institutions of higher education. The bureau continued along the same path of substantial growth under commissioners such as Eaton, Harris, and Elmer Ellsworth Brown (1906–1911) until 1929, when the Bureau of Education once again became the Office of Education. In 1929 Commissioner of Education William John Cooper took over the newly renamed Office of Education, which was still residing in the Department of the Interior. Cooper maintained the focus on collecting materials for the library.

In 1939 the Office of Education underwent yet another reorganization. This time it was not a cosmetic name change but an actual restructuring. The Office of Education was moved out of the Department of Interior and made part of a new agency called the Federal Security Agency (FSA). The office was granted more autonomy under the reorganization under the direction of another ambitious commissioner of education, John Studebaker.

In 1953, early in the Eisenhower administration, the Department of Health, Education, and Welfare (HEW) was established by merging parts of the Federal Security Agency, including the Office of Education, with related functions in other parts of the government. During the 1950s, more funds became available for education due to political and social circumstances. The United States began to take global competitors seriously, and the government was reminded by the Soviet Union's launch of the satellite *Sputnik* that educating the nation's youth was vital to remaining a world power. The National Defense Education Act (NDEA) of 1958, a direct result of the furor surrounding the launching of *Sputnik,* created major federal education programs in mathematics, science, and foreign languages. When President Lyndon Johnson came into office in 1963, he made education a central element of the War on Poverty, which led to the passage of the Higher Education Act (1965) and the landmark Elementary and Secondary Education Act (ESEA, 1965).

The National Education Association (NEA), the national teachers' union, was a major player in American politics at that time, and the organization was rewarded for its political support with the creation of the cabinet-level U.S. Department of Education in 1980. The decision to raise the status of education to a cabinet-level position was one that did not come without controversy and an interesting series of events.

Independence Achieved

The Carter administration proposed the creation of the Department of Education in 1978, despite the active opposition of HEW secretary Joe Califano. While it easily passed the Senate, due to strong advocates such as Abraham Ribicoff (the Democratic senator from Connecticut) and Jacob Javits (a Republican from New York) the bill faced a tough fight in the House of Representatives. Under House rules, the bill was referred to the Government Operations Committee, where a coalition of Republicans led by John Erlenborn (R-Ill.) and Leo Ryan (D-Calif.) kept the bill from being reported out of committee for full House consideration.

At the end of that session of Congress, Representative Ryan led a delegation to Jonestown, Guyana, to investigate reports of a cult leader, Jim Jones, and his influence on young Americans, many from Ryan's district. Following his meetings, Ryan and four others were murdered as he and his delegation returned to their small planes. When the Congress reconvened in January, the Democratic opposition collapsed in the committee and the bill finally passed the House by the very close margin of 210 to 206. President Carter soon thereafter nominated federal judge Shirley Hufstedler from California as the first secretary of the new department. The department formally came into existence on May 4, 1980. In November, Carter was defeated by Ronald Reagan and Hufstedler left office in January. She was replaced by Reagan nominee Terrel Bell.

In the Carter proposal to create the department, it was anticipated that schools operated by the U.S. Department of Defense on and near overseas military bases would be transferred to the new Department of Education. The legislation scheduled the transfer for several years in the future. Prior to that date, Congress intervened and amended the section of the law deleting the provision to transfer Department of Defense schools to the Department of Education. This was a notable action because it reduced the staff size of the agency by nearly half and removed the department from any direct involvement in operating those schools.

Because Reagan had campaigned on a platform that called for dissolving the U.S. Department of Ed-

ucation, Bell operated under severe handicaps: the budget was cut; there was a major consolidation of programs, and a significant downsizing of staff. While Bell was presiding over a department that the White House wanted to dismantle, he took one action that ensured the continued existence of the department. In 1981 he created the National Commission on Excellence in Education, chaired by David Gardner, then president of the University of Utah and later president of the University of California. In 1983 this little-noticed commission issued a report titled *A Nation at Risk*. Using rhetoric in an extraordinarily powerful fashion, this report, which coined the phrase, "a rising tide of mediocrity," captured the attention first of the White House, and then of the nation.

A Nation at Risk led to the publication of a tidal wave of similar reports, a wave that swept ashore in 1989 when the George H. W. Bush administration held the first joint White House/Governors summit since the Great Depression. That summit led to the creation of National Education Goals, a renewed status and respect for the department, and an ambitious agenda that largely reversed the declines of the first Reagan administration. It was at this point that President Bush appointed a former governor, Tennessee's Lamar Alexander, as the first political leader of the department. Alexander followed Lauro Cavazos, who had followed William Bennett upon Bell's departure in 1984.

The political leadership of the agency continued when Bill Clinton defeated George Bush in 1992 and appointed another former southern governor, Richard Riley of South Carolina, to the secretariat. Riley stayed at the department the entire Clinton presidency, thereby establishing himself as the longest-serving education secretary and creating a record achieved in few other agencies. In 2001, President George W. Bush appointed Rod Paige, then the Houston superintendent of schools, as secretary of education, returning the department to leadership from the education field.

The Department Focuses Its Mission

With the creation of the Department of Education, education became a prominent national issue. The department's major functions were to establish policy for administrators and coordinate most federal assistance to education. According to the Department of Education Organization Act (1979), Congress set out to accomplish seven things by creating the department:

1. Strengthen the federal commitment to ensuring access to equal educational opportunity for every individual.

2. Supplement and complement the efforts of states, local school systems (and other instrumentalities of the states), the private sector, public and private educational institutions, public and private nonprofit educational research institutions, community-based organizations, parents, and students to improve the quality of education.

3. Encourage the increased involvement of the public, parents, and students in federal education programs.

4. Promote improvements in the quality and usefulness of education through federally supported research, evaluation, and sharing of information.

5. Improve the coordination of federal education programs.

6. Improve the management and efficiency of federal education activities, especially with respect to process and procedural funds, as well as the reduction of unnecessary and duplicative burdens and constraints, including unnecessary paperwork, on the recipients of federal funds.

7. Increase the accountability of federal education programs to the president, the Congress, and the public.

In developing its own mission, the Department of Education identified its own basic responsibilities:

1. Establish policies relating to financial aid for education, administer distribution for these funds, and monitor their use.

2. Collect data and oversee research on America's schools, and disseminate this information to the public.

3. Identify major issues and problems in education and focus attention on these problems.

4. Enforce federal statues prohibiting discrimination in programs and activities receiving federal funds and ensure equal access to education.

Organizational Structure

The Department of Education is a horizontally and vertically differentiated agency organized into four levels: management and staff, operations, external relations, and program offices. Each level of the department has its own offices and individual mission that contributes to the attainment of its four stated goals.

Management and staff. The secretary of education is responsible for the overall direction, supervision, and coordination of all activities of the department and is the principal adviser to the president on federal policies, programs, and activities related to education in the United States. The deputy secretary serves as the principal policy adviser to the secretary on all major program and management issues, including student financial assistance. The deputy secretary is also responsible for the internal management and daily operations of the department. The under secretary is responsible for oversight of policy development and administration of the Budget Service and the Planning and Evaluation Service.

The Office of the General Counsel is under the supervision of the general counsel, who serves as principal adviser to the secretary on all legal matters affecting departmental programs and activities. The office has three legal practice areas, each of which is headed by a deputy general counsel, and an operation management staff, headed by an executive officer.

The Office of the Inspector General's mission is to promote the efficiency, effectiveness, and integrity of the department's programs and operations; conduct independent and objective audits, investigations, and inspections; and other activities. The Office of Public Affairs develops the department's communications and outreach strategy, coordinates communication with members of the national and local media, directs the department's speechwriting and publications operations, and oversees its in-house television channel and radio news service.

The Executive Management Committee meets each week to discuss and advise the deputy secretary on decisions about the overall management of the agency and the implementation of its initiatives. Its members are all senior offices whose central purpose is management of the agency.

Operations. The Office of Management is the department's administrative component and is dedicated to promoting customer services, expanding staff performance capacity, using strategic approaches to management, and providing a high-quality workplace for the department.

The Office of the Chief Financial Officer is headed by the chief financial officer, whose primary responsibilities involve supervising the activities of major components and serving as the principal adviser to the secretary on all matters related to discretionary grant-making, cooperative agreements, and procurement, as well as financial management, financial control, and accounting. The office's mission is to provide accurate, timely, and useful grant, contract, and financial management information and services to all of the department's stakeholders.

The Office of the Chief Information Officer develops technological strategies and solutions that enable the Department of Education to provide world-class service to schools, students, and their families.

External relations. The mission of the Office of Legislative and Congressional Affairs is to serve as the principal adviser to the secretary on education and other legislative matters before the Congress, and as the department's liaison in responding to the needs of Congress. The Office of Intergovernmental and Interagency Affairs works with government officials at federal, state, and local levels—as well as with educators, business and community leaders, parents and families, and religious leaders—to encourage their support for the improvement of American schools.

Program offices. The Office of Postsecondary Education is responsible for formulating federal postsecondary education policy and administering programs that provide assistance to postsecondary education institutions and to students pursuing programs of postsecondary education.

The Office of Student Financial Assistance Programs is a performance-based organization (PBO) established as part of the Higher Education Amendments of 1998 to modernize the delivery of student financial aid and improve service to millions of students and the postsecondary institutions they attend. In fiscal year 1998, some 8 million students received more than $46 billion in federal financial aid.

The mission of the Office of Elementary and Secondary Education is to promote academic excellence, enhance educational opportunities and equity for all of America's children and families, and to improve the quality of teaching and learning by providing leadership, technical assistance, and financial support. The office is responsible for directing, coor-

dinating, and recommending policy for programs designed to: (1) assist state and local educational agencies to improve the achievement of elementary and secondary school students; (2) help ensure equal access to services leading to such improvement for all children, particularly children who are educationally disadvantaged, Native American, homeless, or children of migrant workers; (3) foster educational improvement at the state and local levels; (4) and provide financial assistance to local educational agencies whose local revenues are affected by federal activities.

The Office of Educational Research and Improvement (OERI) provides national leadership for educational research and statistics. OERI strives to promote excellence and equity in American education by conducting research and demonstration projects funded through grants to help improve education; collecting statistics on the status and progress of schools and education throughout the nation; and distributing information and providing technical assistance to those working to improve education. OERI houses the National Center for Education Statistics, the primary federal entity for collecting and analyzing data that are related to education in the United States and other nations.

The Office of Bilingual Education and Minority Languages Affairs (OBEMLA) provides national leadership in promoting high-quality education for the nation's population of English language learners (ELLs). Traditionally, this population has been known as limited English proficient (LEP) students. OBEMLA's mission is to include various elements of school reform in programs designed to assist the language minority agenda. These include an emphasis on high academic standards, an improvement of school accountability, an emphasis on professional development, the promotion of family literacy, the encouragement of early reading, and the establishment of partnerships between parents and the community. OBEMLA administers grant programs that help every child learn English and content matter at high levels. It also provides leadership ensuring that policy-related decisions focus principally on the best interests of the ELL child; collaborates with other federal, state and local programs to strengthen and coordinate services for ELLs and promote best practices; monitors funded programs; and provides technical assistance to ensure that funded programs focus on outcomes and accountability.

The Office of Vocational and Adult Education has the mission to help all people achieve the knowledge and skills to be lifelong learners, to be successful in their chosen careers, and to be effective citizens. The Office of Special Education and Rehabilitative Services' mission is to provide leadership to achieve full integration and participation in society of people with disabilities by ensuring equal opportunity and access to, and excellence in, education, employment and community living. In implementing this mission, the office supports programs that help educate children and youth with disabilities, provides for the rehabilitation of youth and adults with disabilities, and supports research to improve the lives of individuals with disabilities.

The mission of the Office for Civil Rights is to ensure equal access to education and to promote educational excellence throughout the nation through vigorous enforcement of civil rights laws.

See also: FEDERAL EDUCATIONAL ACTIVITIES, *subentries on* HISTORY, SUMMARY BY AGENCY; FEDERAL INTERAGENCY COMMITTEE ON EDUCATION; U.S. DEPARTMENT OF EDUCATION, *subentry on* INTERNATIONAL ROLE.

BIBLIOGRAPHY

U.S. CONGRESS. 1979. *Department of Education Organization Act Conference Report.* 96th Congress, 1st session, S. Report 96-326.

VINOVSKIS, MARIS A. 1999. *The Road to Charlottesville.* Washington, DC: National Education Goals Panel.

INTERNET RESOURCES

GRANT, W. VANCE. 2001. "Statistics in the U.S. Department of Education: Highlights from the Past 120 Years." <http://nces.ed.gov/publications/majorpub/120yr/porhigh.txt>.

MURPHY, RETHA. 1995. "U.S. Department of Education." <http://mailer.fsu.edu/~kshelfer/busrefpapers/edu.htm>.

NATIONAL ARCHIVES AND RECORDS ADMINISTRATION. "General Records of the Department of Education." <www.nara.gov/guide/rg441.html>.

NATIONAL LIBRARY OF EDUCATION. 2001. "History: National Library of Education." 2001. <www.ed.gov/NLE/histearly.html>.

CHRISTOPHER T. CROSS
M. RENÉ ISLAS

INTERNATIONAL ROLE

Although the primary mission of the U.S. Department of Education is a domestic one, the department also sponsors international programs, cooperates with other nations, and participates in international organizations, studies, and events. This international role has grown over time with the heightened relevance of global developments for U.S. citizens in an increasingly interdependent world, and the growing awareness of the part played by education in fostering economic, social, and personal development, and in sustaining democracy.

Within these contexts, the department facilitates efforts by U.S. educators, students, researchers, and policymakers to forge partnerships with counterparts abroad who have common interests. The department engages in a variety of international activities with three primary objectives: to strengthen U.S. education, to increase U.S. international expertise, and to facilitate the exchange of information and building of knowledge about education worldwide.

The department's international cooperation helps educators and policymakers understand how U.S. educational performance compares with that of other countries. It also provides information on effective educational policies and practices abroad. The department coordinates U.S. participation in both international assessments of student achievement and the development of internationally comparable educational statistics. Other activities focus on analyzing other countries' best practices in areas in which there have been positive results, as well as learning alongside other nations through joint studies and research projects, on topics ranging from mathematics instruction to migrant education, and from early childhood education to rehabilitation services. Educators and policymakers use such information to improve educational practice in the United States. Other programs support U.S. educational institutions' efforts to build strong partnerships with counterpart institutions abroad.

Through its international activities and grant programs, including those authorized by Title VI of the Higher Education Act and the Fulbright-Hays Act of 1961, the department supports efforts to expand the study of the languages and societies of other nations, as well as opportunities for U.S. students and teachers to study and carry out research abroad. Such programs help U.S. citizens develop a broader understanding of, and communicate more effectively with, other nations, and contribute to national security by developing experts on regions of the world that are of strategic importance to the United States. A significant proportion of U.S. students studying abroad receive financial aid from the department.

The department represents the U.S. government in education-related matters at international meetings and conferences, and provides expertise to the U.S. government's foreign affairs and foreign assistance agencies on matters related to education policy and practice. In doing so, it helps to (1) stimulate discussion and research on topics of priority to the United States; (2) increase the participation of U.S. experts in international policy dialogues; (3) build mutual understanding on social issues with other nations; and (4) improve education both at home and abroad. New technologies facilitate these efforts.

Foreign demand for information regarding U.S. education policy and practices results in frequent information exchanges between the department and colleagues in other countries. The department also receives foreign visitors who request to meet with their counterparts to learn about education in the United States. Visitors (more than 1,500 in the year 2000) range from ministers of education and senior policy advisors to school administrators, teachers, members of legislatures, the press, and the private sector. Many others obtain information on U.S. education via the department's web-based resources.

See also: INTERNATIONAL EDUCATION; INTERNATIONAL STUDENTS.

BIBLIOGRAPHY

PETERSON, TERRY; GINSBURG, ALAN; GARCIA, LENORE; and LEMKE, MARIANN. 2000. "Educational Diplomacy: Using the Untapped Opportunities of International Education." *Education Week* November 22, 48.

INTERNET RESOURCES

NAFSA: ASSOCIATION OF INTERNATIONAL EDUCATORS. 2002. <www.nafsa.org>.

OPEN DOORS ON THE WEB. 2001. "Senate Resolution on International Education Policy for the United States." <www.opendoorsweb.org/Lead%20Stories/National_Policy_Resolution.htm>.

LENORE YAFFEE GARCIA
RAFAEL MICHAEL NEVAREZ

U.S. WAR COLLEGES

Career-long education is a cornerstone tradition of the American military. The capstone of the America's professional military education systems is the War College, or, more correctly, the Senior Service Colleges (SSCs). While each of the four primary SSCs reflects its service origins, students attending each are selected from the five military services, from civilian agencies, and from allied nations. The collective mission of the SSCs is to prepare senior leaders for duties of responsibility and to enhance their ability to make sound decisions in command, staff, and managerial positions. Each SSC provides interdisciplinary instruction in national strategy and operational arts, and seeks to instill a commitment to joint service and combined operations. SSCs also serve as centers for research, doctrinal development, and war gaming, focusing on issues of strategy and international relations, national security policy and mobilization, executive management and leadership, and the operational command of joint and multinational forces.

The oldest of these institutions, the Naval War College (NWC), was established at Newport, Rhode Island, in 1884 to provide an advanced course of professional study for naval officers. Commodore Stephen B. Luce served as its first president. Luce viewed the college as "a place of original research on all questions relating to war, and to statesmanship connected to war, or the prevention of war" (Naval War College website). Instructors were recruited from the Navy, other services, and civilian universities, shaping an interdisciplinary faculty that is characteristic of all the SSCs in the early twenty-first century.

The NWC is actually a university, home to five named colleges and numerous departments and specialized programs. Its SSC-level program for senior officers is housed in the College of Naval Warfare.

The College of Naval Command and Staff educates midcareer officers selected from all five armed services and other governmental agencies. The Naval Command College serves senior naval officers from allied nations, while the Naval Staff College provides training for midgrade allied officers. The College of Continuing Education develops and administers a nonresident program equivalent of the College of Naval Command and Staff. Among its many departments is the War Gaming Department. Battle simulations have been part of the Naval War College curriculum since 1887, and they are used today to train leaders at all levels and to evaluate doctrinal concepts and operational techniques.

The Army War College (AWC) was established by Secretary of War Elihu Root in 1903. Root envisioned a learning institution "not to promote war, but to preserve peace" with a mission "to study and confer on the great problems of national defense, of military science, and of responsible command." Housed at Carlisle Barracks, Pennsylvania, the AWC focuses on education, research, and outreach. Three hundred American and allied students attend the resident course each year, while thousands of others participate in specialized programs and research projects. The Department of Distance Learning conducts an SSC-equivalent nonresident course, employing advanced Internet-based learning tools, and extensive professional readings and written reflection. Specialized programs include the Center for Strategic Leadership, Military History Institute, Peacekeeping Institute, and the Strategic Studies Institute.

The Air University (AU), located at Maxwell Air Force Base in Alabama, was established in 1946, and has a broad education scope. Collectively, its five named colleges seek to "educate Air Force people to develop and lead the world's best aerospace force and to inspire commitment to a war-winning profession of arms" (Air University website). The Air War College educates senior officers to lead at the strategic level in the employment of aerospace forces, including joint operations, in support of national security. The AU also includes the Air Command and Staff College, the College of Aerospace Doctrine, the Department of Research and Education (specializing in war gaming), the College of Enlisted Professional Education, and the Community College of the Air Force.

The National Defense University (NDU), headquartered in Washington, D.C., serves the educational needs of uniformed and civilian officials from the Defense and State Departments and other federal agencies by focusing on the resource component of national power. NDU colleges emphasize material acquisition, industrial mobilization, and joint logistics. NDU oversees the educational and research programs of the Industrial College of the Armed Forces, Joint Forces Staff College, Information Resources Management College, the National War College, the Institute for National Strategic Studies, and the Center for Hemispheric Defense Studies.

Collectively, the Senior Service Colleges, and the professional education systems they represent, are a national education asset of great value. Each employs a full range of advanced teaching techniques and information-age technologies, from case-based learning and simulations to distance learning and across-the-curriculum interdisciplinary studies. Graduation from one of these highly selective programs is the professional equivalent of a doctoral degree in other fields.

See also: MILITARY PROFESSIONAL EDUCATION SYSTEM.

BIBLIOGRAPHY

BALL, HARRY P. 1983. *Of Responsible Command. The History of the U.S. Army War College.* Carlisle Barracks, PA: Alumni Association of the U.S. Army War College.

INTERNET RESOURCES

AIR UNIVERSITY. 2002. <www.au.af.mil/au/schools/awc.html>.

ARMY WAR COLLEGE. 2002. <http://carlisle-www.army.mil>.

NATIONAL DEFENSE UNIVERSITY. 2002. <www.ndu.edu>.

NAVAL WAR COLLEGE. 2002. <www.nwc.navy.mil>.

BRUCE T. CAINE

V

VIOLENCE, CHILDREN'S EXPOSURE TO

GENERAL EFFECTS
Anna Marie Medina
Gayla Margolin
Elana B. Gordis

COMMUNITY VIOLENCE
Joy D. Osofsky
Howard J. Osofsky

DOMESTIC VIOLENCE
Debbie Miller

GENERAL EFFECTS

Children's experience with violence has been linked to a variety of negative outcomes, one of particular importance being children's school adaptation and academic success. Since the early 1980s researchers and professionals working with children have become increasingly aware of the extent to which many children experience or observe violence within the confines of their own homes or within their own neighborhoods. Data from 1999 reports by states to the National Child Abuse and Neglect Data Systems indicate that approximately 826,000 children (nearly 12 out of every 1,000 children) were confirmed by child protective services as victims of maltreatment. With respect to exposure to interparental violence, Murray A. Straus estimated, in a report published in 1992, that more than 10 million children in the U.S. witness physical aggression between their parents each year, with prevalence rates throughout childhood being at least triple the rates of exposure within a given year.

Community violence also has an impact on many children. Estimates of community violence ex-

posure are based on data gathered through interview or survey methods, and generally reflect the number of children who were personally victimized as well as those who witness community violence involving their family members, schoolmates, neighbors, and peers as victims. Whereas attempts are made to keep child abuse and interparental aggression private and secret, community violence is discussed widely, often resulting in rapidly spreading ripple effects. Thus, even children who do not directly observe community violence often have knowledge of violent events within their community or hear repeated accounts of a specific incident, and may form their own mental imagery of the violence. Studies suggest that in inner city neighborhoods, almost all children have been exposed to community violence, and at least one-third of pre-teenage and teenage children have been directly victimized. Exposure to violence (i.e. children's experience as either targets or witnesses to violence) affects children's views of the world and themselves, their ideas about the meaning and purpose of life, their expectations for future happiness, and their moral development. Moreover, exposure to violence often interferes with developmental tasks children need to accomplish in order to become competent members of society.

Two key developmental tasks frequently compromised by exposure to violence are children's adaptation to school and academic achievement. Children exposed to either familial or community violence (or both) often demonstrate lower school achievement and poorer adaptation to the academic environment. Exposure to violence affects these developmental tasks both directly and indirectly. Violence exposure can lead to disturbances in cognitive functioning, emotional difficulties such as depression and anxiety, and behavior and peer problems. Before examining how each of these effects can interfere with children's adaptation to school and academic competence, it is important to consider three issues related to children's violence exposure.

First, violence exposure rarely occurs only once or only in one form. That is, most children who are exposed to violence are rarely exposed to only one incident or one type of violence. Researchers have determined that there are high rates of co-occurrence between exposure to community violence and intrafamilial violence, and within the family, high rates of co-occurrence have been detected between interparental violence and parent-to-child violence. Moreover, it also has become clear that these different forms of violence are frequently recurring events.

A second central issue is that violence exposure often goes hand in hand with numerous other adverse life experiences. Children living with violence typically experience other stressors such as poverty, neglect, poor nutrition, overcrowding, substance abuse, lack of adequate medical care, parents' unemployment, and parents' psychopathology. These factors can exacerbate and extend the negative effects of violence exposure in children. For example, children whose parents suffer from psychopathology or struggle with substance abuse problems may not have had the opportunity or guidance to develop pro-social coping skills with which to deal with violence exposure in their community. Although children exposed to violence may have a greater need for nurturance and protection than children without such stressors, they may actually have less access to social support from their caretakers. Therefore, efforts to grasp the effects of violence exposure on children also must evaluate the context in which the child is embedded.

A third issue is that the effects of violence exposure are developmentally contingent. Children face specific challenges at different points in development. Thus, the impact of violence exposure will vary according to the child's developmental level. Children's abilities to appraise and understand violence, to respond to and cope with danger, and to garner environmental resources that offer protection and support change become refined over the course of development. Moreover, theorists assert that as children mature, the skills required to master current life challenges rest on competencies acquired earlier in development. Accordingly, exposure to vi-

olence early rather than later in development may be more detrimental, particularly if the violence exposure compromises the foundations required to develop future competencies. In a related vein, however, if early violence exposure is terminated, the plasticity in children's developmental processes may promote recovery for any lost or delayed functioning. The implications of length and timing of violence exposure are complicated and require future empirical investigation.

The review that follows examines the cognitive, emotional, behavioral and social effects of violence exposure, and highlights the ways in which these effects can disrupt children's adaptation to school and academic competence. Although the effects of violence exposure are presented here as distinct, in reality the cognitive, emotional, behavioral and social effects of violence are interrelated and contribute to one another. For example, if children who are exposed to violence are less flexible and resourceful in their reasoning, these cognitive processes may be associated with problems with peers and school work, which may then lead to depression and anxiety.

Cognitive Effects

Exposure to violence, particularly parent-to-child violence, has been associated with problems in children's cognitive processes and poor academic functioning. Researchers have linked exposure to chronic abuse and violence with lower IQ scores, poorer language skills, decrements in visual-motor integration skills and problems with attention and memory. Cognitive problems associated with exposure to violence and abuse comprise one of the most direct threats to the developmental task of school adaptation and academic achievement. Deficits in attention regulation, language skills, and memory undermine the child's ability to accomplish the central requirements of academic achievement and school adaptation, namely to encode, organize, recall, and express understanding of new information. Accordingly, physically abused school-age children have been found to score lower than non-abused comparison children on tests of verbal ability and comprehension, reading and math skills, and overall achievement on standardized tests. Similarly, children exposed to community violence tend to show lower school achievement.

The cognitive effects of violence exposure affect more than children's academic performance. Children who have difficulty with attention and memory may not be sensitive to important social cues and expectations, and thus find themselves struggling with school rules, peer relationships, and classroom instructions. Thus, the cognitive effects of violence exposure may disrupt children's successful functioning in the school environment in addition to hindering academic competence.

Emotional Effects

Exposure to violence almost always carries emotional consequences for children. Children's exposure to intrafamilial violence has been linked to depression and more negative self-concept. Studies have shown that both witnessing and/or being a victim of community violence may put children at risk for increased anxiety and depressive symptoms. Violence exposure can be interpreted by the child to mean not only that the world is unsafe but also that the child is unworthy of being kept safe. Whether related to violence in the home or in the community, these attitudes can undermine children's school adjustment and academic achievement by contributing to negative self-perceptions and problems with depression and anxiety.

Another emotional consequence for children exposed to violence is posttraumatic stress disorder (PTSD). Researchers have determined that both chronic and acute exposure to violence is linked to heightened levels of PTSD symptoms, including diminished concentration, sleep disturbance, sudden startling, and intrusive thoughts. These symptoms, as well as the symptoms of anxiety and depression, interfere with children's academic achievement by making it more difficult to attend to school lessons, and by lowering the motivation and disrupting the concentration necessary to complete academic tasks. Similarly, children's adaptation to the school environment may be undermined by the emotional consequences of violence exposure. Violence-exposed children have been rated by teachers and parents as less "ready to learn," less competent in school, and more likely to repeat grades.

In addition, children's efforts to manage the emotional consequences of violence exposure may interfere with school adaptation and academic achievement. Research has shown that children use both behavioral distraction and attentional disengagement to cope with uncontrollable stress and reduce anxiety. Children's efforts to cope with the symptoms of depression, anxiety, and PTSD may have a deleterious effect on their social awareness,

social engagement, ability to problem solve, and their attentional resources. Whereas some children will cope with the emotional toll of violence exposure by isolating themselves and withdrawing from the environment, other children will use behavioral distraction to cope with overwhelming negative emotions. Both coping strategies can create problems in the classroom and on the playground.

Behavioral and Social Effects

Childhood exposure to violence is associated with a variety of aggressive and otherwise maladaptive behaviors that can disrupt children's school adaptation and academic competence. Such behavior problems not only interfere with classroom learning, they also hamper children's efforts to make friends, another essential task of childhood and an important dimension of school adaptation. Exposure to intrafamilial violence has been linked with increased aggression, fighting, "meanness," and generally disruptive behavior. Children exposed to intrafamilial violence are reported to have more disciplinary problems at school than their non-exposed peers, and are more likely to be suspended. Likewise, exposure to community violence has been associated with increases in antisocial behavior and aggression, as reported by teachers and parents.

Behavior problems that emerge following exposure to violence can be thought of as stemming from a lack of appropriate role models, difficulties with emotion regulation skills, and aberrant information processing. Children exposed to adult violence, particularly intrafamilial adult violence, may learn from these adults that aggressive behavior is a viable problem-solving option, and that physical aggression in close relationships is normal. Clearly, such lessons could create problems for children on the playground and later in life.

Researchers have observed that exposure to violence is related to difficulties regulating anger, frustration, and other negative feelings, as well as deficits in understanding and experiencing empathy for the feelings of others. These difficulties can lead to significant behavioral and social problems for children. As noted above, one way in which children deal with overwhelming negative feelings is through behavioral distraction. Performance in academic settings will suffer if violence-exposed children attempt to cope with anger towards other children or frustration with academic material by behaving disruptively. Moreover, children with deficits in emotion regulation, empathy, and understanding emotions tend to be rated as less popular and more rejected by their peers.

Another source of behavior and social problems for violence-exposed children involves aberrant processing of social information. Researchers have observed relations between exposure to violence, problems in the way children think about social relationships, and children's social adjustment in the school peer group. Violence-exposed children have been found to be less interpersonally sensitive and attentive to social cues, less competent at social perspective taking, less able to identify others' emotional expressions and to understand complex social roles, and more likely to ascribe hostile intentions to the neutral behavior of others. The suboptimal processing of social information may contribute to the problem behaviors seen in children exposed to violence.

Long-Term Consequences of Violence Exposure

The impact of violence exposure can go beyond the period of exposure and the immediate aftermath, affecting some individuals into adulthood. Although little is known concerning the effects of exposure to community violence, researchers have examined the adult lives of individuals exposed in childhood to intrafamilial aggression. Adults exposed to such violence as children have been found to have completed significantly fewer years of school and reported more episodes of truancy during their time in school compared to non-exposed peers. In addition, and perhaps related to their lack of schooling, adults exposed to intrafamilial violence in childhood also are at greater risk for arrest for a violent crime, and for earlier and more chronic involvement in criminal behavior.

It is important to recognize, however, that the damaging effects of violence exposure are not inevitable. Researchers have identified a host of protective factors that can buffer the detrimental effects of adverse life events, such as violence exposure. Among these factors are the presence of supportive adults in children's lives, scholastic competence, and realistic educational and vocational plans.

Conclusion

The effects of violence exposure, problematic in their own right, also have a detrimental impact on two key developmental challenges, namely, children's school adaptation and academic achievement.

Both the effects of violence exposure and consequent poor mastery of important developmental challenges set violence-exposed children on a trajectory towards maladaptive outcomes. Much remains to be learned about how violence exposure brings about these effects and how the cognitive, emotional, behavioral and social systems of a child are interconnected. It is important for social scientists and professionals working with children to continue to search for ways to reduce violence exposure and to intervene effectively to keep violence-exposed children on a pro-social track.

Although different types of violence exposure can hold unique effects for children, there are common symptom patterns among children exposed to violence. Difficulties with attention and other cognitive processes, troubling emotional aftereffects, and problems with behavioral and social adaptations are frequent outcomes for children exposed to diverse types of violence. Because children's reactions to violence exposure may be present as common emotional or behavioral symptoms, violence exposure may be overlooked as the underlying problem. From treatment and policy perspectives, it is critical that the assessment of children routinely evaluates for both family and community violence.

See also: AFFECT AND EMOTIONAL DEVELOPMENT; AGGRESSIVE BEHAVIOR; ATTENTION; JUVENILE JUSTICE SYSTEM, *subentry on* JUVENILE CRIME AND JUSTICE.

BIBLIOGRAPHY

BOLGER, KERRY E.; PATTERSON, CHARLOTTE J.; and KUPERSMIDT, JANIS B. 1998. "Peer Relationships and Self Esteem Among Children Who Have Been Maltreated." *Child Development* 69:1171–1197.

BUKA, STEPHEN L.; STICHIK, THERESA L.; BIRDTHISTLE, ISOLDE; and EARLS, FELTON J. 2001. "Youth Exposure to Violence: Prevalence, Risks, and Consequences." *American Journal of Orthopsychiatry* 71(3):298–310.

GARBARINO, JAMES; DUBROW, NANCY; KOSTELNY, KATHLEEN; and PARDO, CAROLE. 1992. *Children in Danger.* San Francisco: Jossey-Bass.

GARMEZY, NORMAN, and MASTEN, ANN S. 1994. "Chronic Adversities." In *Child and Adolescent Psychiatry,* ed. Michael Rutter, Lionel Hersov, and Eric Taylor. Oxford: Blackwell.

LYNCH, MICHAEL, and CICCHETTI, DANTE. 1998. "An Ecological-transactional Analysis of Children and Contexts: The Longitudinal Interplay Among Child Maltreatment, Community Violence, and Children's Symptomatology." *Development and Psychopathology* 10(2): 235–257.

MARGOLIN, GAYLA, and GORDIS, ELANA B. 2000. "The Effects of Family and Community Violence on Children." *Annual Review of Psychology* 51:445–479.

OSOFSKY, JOY D.; WEWERS, SARAH; HANN, DELLA M.; and FICK, ANA C. 1993. "Chronic Community Violence: What Is Happening to Our Children?" In *Children and Violence,* ed. David Reiss, John E. Richters, Marian Radke-Yarrow, and David Scharff. New York: Guilford.

PEREZ, CYNTHIA M., and WIDOM, CATHY SPATZ. 1994. "Childhood Victimization and Long-Term Intellectual and Academic Outcomes." *Child Abuse and Neglect* 18:617–633.

SCHWAB-STONE, MARY E.; AYERS, TIM S.; KAPROW, WESLEY; VOYCE, CHARLENE; BARONE, CHARLES; SHRIVER, TIMOTHY; and WEISSBERG, ROGER P. 1995. "No Safe Haven: A Study of Violence Exposure in an Urban Community." *Journal of the American Academy of Child and Adolescent Psychiatry* 34:1343–1352.

SCHWARTZ, DAVID, and PROCTOR, LAURA. 2000. "Community Violence Exposure and Children's Social Adjustment in the School Peer Group: The Mediating Roles of Emotion Regulation and Social Cognition." *Journal of Consulting and Clinical Psychology* 68:670–682.

SHIELDS, ANN, and CICCHETTI, DANTE. 1998. "Reactive Aggression Among Maltreated Children: The Contributions of Attention and Emotion Dysregulation." *Journal of Consulting and Clinical Psychology* 27:381–395.

SROUFE, L. ALAN, and RUTTER, MICHAEL. 1984. "The Domain of Developmental Psychopathology." *Child Development* 55:17–29.

STRAUS, MURRAY A. 1992. "Children as Witnesses to Marital Violence: A Risk Factor of Lifelong Problems Among a Nationally Representative Sample of American Men and Women." In *Children and Violence: Report of the Twenty-Third Ross Roundtable on Critical Approaches to Common Pediatric Problems,* ed. Donald F. Schwarz. Columbus, OH: Ross Lab.

TRICKETT, PENELOPE K., and MCBRIDE-CHANG, CATHERINE. 1995. "The Developmental Impact of Different Forms of Child Abuse and Neglect." *Developmental Review* 15:311–337.

WERNER, EMMY. 1993. "Risk, Resilience, and Recovery: Perspectives from the Kauai Longitudinal Study." *Development and Psychopathology* 5:503–515.

WIDOM, CATHY SPATZ. 1998. "Childhood Victimization: Early Adversity and Subsequent Psychopathology." In *Adversity, Stress, Psychopathology,* ed. Bruce P. Dohrenwend. New York: Oxford University Press.

INTERNET RESOURCE

U.S. DEPARTMENT OF HEALTH AND HUMAN SERVICES. 1999. "Child Maltreatment 1999: Reports from the States to the National Child Abuse and Neglect Data System." <www.acf.dhhs.gov/programs/cb/publications/cm99/index.htm>.

ANNA MARIE MEDINA
GAYLA MARGOLIN
ELANA B. GORDIS

COMMUNITY VIOLENCE

Many children in the United States are exposed to so much violence that the problem has been characterized as a "public health epidemic." Related in part to transient age-related demographic changes (that is, in the percentage of youth who are at highest risk for violence), children's violence exposure has declined slightly since the early 1990s. The homicide rate, however, is still more than double that reported in 1950 according to the National Summary of Injury Mortality Data, with the 1996 rate being 22 per 100,000 for young people fifteen to twenty-four years old. Further, the United States has the highest level of violence exposure of any developed country in the world. Homicide is the third-leading cause of death for children five to fourteen years of age, the second-leading cause of death for those aged fifteen to twenty-four, and has been the leading cause of death for African-American youth from the early 1980s into the early twenty-first century. It is crucial to understand what such levels of exposure may mean for children in the United States.

In addition to community violence exposure, some estimates, such as those reported by Murray

Straus and Richard Gelles in 1990, indicate that between 8.5 and 11.3 women per 100 are abused by husbands or boyfriends in the United States. Dating violence—that is, the perpetration of an act of violence by at least one member of an unmarried couple on the other member (which can include sexual assault, physical violence, or verbal or emotional abuse)—appears to range from 9 to 65 percent depending on whether threats and emotional or verbal aggression are included in the definition.

While exposure to community violence occurs less frequently for children who do not live in lower socioeconomic neighborhoods, children are also often exposed to violence in their homes and in the media. Exposure to media and family violence crosses socioeconomic and cultural boundaries, occurring in all groups in U.S. society. The effects are often less visible in higher socioeconomic groups, but, nonetheless, such violence impacts significantly on children during their development and influences their later relationship experiences.

Levels of Exposure to Community Violence

Community violence exposure, whether it be isolated, frequent, or unfortunately at times almost continuous, includes frequent and continual exposure to random violence and the use of guns, knives, and drugs. In the early twenty-first century it is rare in urban elementary schools not to find children who have been exposed to such negative events. Children who have been interviewed in several different studies lucidly tell their stories of witnessing violence, including shootings and beatings, as if they were ordinary, everyday events.

In Steven Maran and Donald Cohen's survey of sixth, eighth, and tenth graders in New Haven, Connecticut, in 1992, 40 percent reported witnessing at least one violent crime in the previous year. Very few of these inner-city children were able to avoid being exposed to violence, and almost all eighth graders knew someone who had been killed in a violent incident. In a study by Carl C. Bell and Esther J. Jenkins involving 500 children at three elementary schools on the South Side of Chicago in 1993, one in four had witnessed a shooting and one-third had seen a stabbing. In another study by Jenkins and Bell (published in 1997) surveying 200 Chicago high school students in 1993, almost two-thirds had seen a shooting and close to one-half had seen a stabbing. Three in five of those who witnessed a shooting or stabbing indicated that the incident had resulted in

a death. More than one-fourth of these high school students reported that they had themselves been victims of severe violence.

Even very young children are exposed to high levels of violence. Betsy Groves and colleagues' 1993 survey of parents whose children attended a pediatric clinic at a public hospital in Boston in 1993 found that one of every ten children under the age of six had witnessed a shooting or stabbing. In Marva Lewis, Joy Osofsky, and Mary Sue Moore's 1997 study, African-American third- and fifth-grade children living in a high-violence area of New Orleans were asked to draw pictures of "what happens" in their neighborhoods. They drew in graphic detail pictures of shootings, drug deals, stabbings, fighting, and funerals and reported being scared of the violence and of something happening to them. Children living with domestic and community violence commonly draw similar pictures.

In 1993 John E. Richter and Pedro Martinez conducted an extensive interview study on the exposure to violence with 165 mothers of children, ages six to ten, living in a low-income neighborhood in Washington, DC. According to police statistics, this neighborhood was characterized as having a moderate level of violence; there might be an occasional murder or violent incident, but violence was not a regular event. Concurrently, another study by Joy Osofsky and colleagues gathered similar interview data on fifty-three African-American mothers of children, ages nine to twelve, in a low-income neighborhood in New Orleans, Louisiana. According to police statistics, this neighborhood was characterized as having a high level of violence; a murder or more than one violent incident occurred on a regular basis. Some differences in violence exposure were noted, likely due, to a considerable extent, to differences in the levels of violence in the two neighborhoods being sampled. The data from both studies, however, clearly showed that children frequently are victims of and witnesses to significant amounts of violence. Fifty-one percent of the New Orleans fifth graders and 32 percent of the Washington, D.C., children had been victims of violence, ranging from being chased or beaten to having a gun held to their head.

Xiaoming Li and colleagues, in a 1998 study of 349 low-income black urban children (ages nine to fifteen), found that those who witnessed or were victims of violence showed symptoms of posttraumatic stress disorder similar to those of soldiers coming back from war. The symptoms increased according to the number of violent acts the child had witnessed or experienced. In a 1996 report, Hope Hill and colleagues focused on some of the sociopolitical issues related to violence exposure as well as the importance of support for children by the family, teachers, and community in effective prevention and intervention efforts. This work is consistent with the findings of the Violence Intervention Program, which have indicated the importance of a broad base of support for violence prevention. Deborah Gorman-Smith and Patrick Tolan found that exposure to community violence was related to subsequent symptoms of depression and anxiety as well as to aggressive behaviors as reported by the children, their parents, and teachers. In this 1998 study, having a mother present in the home seemed to be a major factor in mitigating the relationship between community violence exposure and subsequent depressive symptoms in the children.

While specific rates of exposure to community violence vary depending on the definition of exposure and the nature of the sample, children of all ages are being exposed to community violence at an alarming rate. As noted, such exposure has been linked to higher rates of post-traumatic stress symptoms, as well as to depressive symptoms, antisocial behavior, and decreased school performance. In a 2000 article, Stacey Overstreet suggested that repeated exposure to community violence may influence children to become numbed, demonstrating uncaring behavior toward others and desensitization to aggression. Such children may themselves show increased aggression, acting out, and subsequent antisocial behavior.

Impact on Children in School

Exposure to violence is not limited to homes and neighborhoods. For many youth, schools, which should be safe havens, are also places where they can be exposed to violence, which can impact on a student's concentration and ability to be successful in school. Exposure to violence and trauma can lead to feelings of helplessness, hopelessness, and vulnerability in children. Some may react with anger and aggression, which can lead to behavior and discipline problems in school. Others may withdraw and become depressed, which while not drawing as much attention can have a great affect on their ability to concentrate, their self-esteem, and, consequently, their performance. Beyond the psychological and behavioral consequences of exposure to violence that may impact on a child in school, children may learn that violence is an acceptable behavior. They learn violence from what they observe and may believe that fighting and violent behavior is all right either in or outside of the classroom. They do not learn to negotiate to solve problems; rather, they may more quickly lose control of their emotions. Children exposed to violence often do not learn to communicate feelings and may be more easily pressured by peers. They may believe that aggressive behaviors lead to attention and respect. Bullying and intimidating behaviors may be another consequence.

The Centers for Disease Control and Prevention in Atlanta, in their 1998 "Surveillance Summaries," reported survey results from a nationally representative sample of students in grades nine through twelve for selected risk behaviors both at school and outside of school. The survey focused on categories, including students who had carried a weapon, had carried a gun, were in a physical fight, were injured in a physical fight, were threatened or injured on school property, were in a physical fight on school property, and had property stolen or deliberately damaged on school property. The study found alarmingly high incidents of these disturbing behaviors in schools throughout the country.

Children suffer with enormous short-term and long-term consequences from such violence exposure. Students living in urban inner-city environments commonly provide vivid descriptions of the violence they see and experience in their environment, sometimes on a daily basis. Susan Chira's 1994 poll of high school students indicated that 30 percent of white students and 70 percent of African-American students knew someone who had been shot within the previous five years; 19 percent of white students and 37 percent of African-American students identified violence as the biggest problem at school; and 5 percent of white students and 27 percent of African-American students reported worrying about shootings at school. A Harris poll of 2,000 teenagers from around the country indicated that one in eight overall, and almost two in five from inner cities, said that they carried a weapon to protect themselves. In addition, one in nine overall, and one in three in high violence areas, said they had stayed away from school for fear of violence. This 1996 poll was carried out before the many school shootings that later occurred. Despite the previously noted data indicating that the overall incidence of violence exposure has been decreasing slightly (although this may be transient), national surveys demonstrate increased concern and fears about violence in school, especially among older children.

The problem of children's exposure to community violence is significant. Without intervention efforts, it may increase with age shifts in coming years. It is clear that major efforts need to be undertaken to decrease violence exposure and to mitigate the effects of this exposure when it occurs.

See also: AGGRESSIVE BEHAVIOR; JUVENILE JUSTICE SYSTEM, *subentry on* JUVENILE CRIME AND JUSTICE; NEIGHBORHOODS; PARENTING, *subentry on* HIGH-RISK NEIGHBORHOODS; URBAN EDUCATION.

BIBLIOGRAPHY

APPELBONE, PAUL. 1996. "Crime Fear Is Seen Forcing Change in Youth Behavior." *New York Times* January 12.

BELL, CARL C., and JENKINS, ESTHER J. 1991. "Traumatic Stress and Children." *Journal of Health Care for the Poor and Underserved* 2:175–185.

BELL, CARL C., and JENKINS, ESTHER J. 1993. "Community Violence and Children on Chicago's Southside." *Psychiatry* 56:46–54.

CENTERS FOR DISEASE CONTROL AND PREVENTION. 1998. "CDC Surveillance Summaries" 47(SS-3).

CENTERS FOR DISEASE CONTROL AND PREVENTION. DIVISION OF VIOLENCE PREVENTION, FAMILY AND INTIMATE VIOLENCE. 1998. *National Center for Injury Control, 1998.* Atlanta, GA: Centers for Disease Control and Prevention, Division of Violence Prevention, Family and Intimate Violence.

CENTERS FOR DISEASE CONTROL AND PREVENTION. NATIONAL CENTER FOR INJURY PREVENTION AND CONTROL. 1996. *National Summary of Injury Mortality Data, 1987–1994.* Atlanta, GA: Centers for Disease Control and Prevention, National Center for Injury Prevention and Control.

CHIRA, SUSAN. 1994. "Teenagers in a Poll Report Worry and Distrust of Adults." *New York Times* July 10.

FINGERHUT, LOIS A.; INGRAM, DEBORAH D.; and FELDMAN, JACOB J. 1992. "Firearm Homicide among Black Teenage Males in Metropolitan Counties." *Journal of the American Medical Association* 267:3054–3058.

FINKELHOR, DAVID, and DZIUBA-LEATHERMAN, JENNIFER. 1994. "Victimization of Children." *American Psychologist* 49:173–183.

FLANNERY, DANIEL, and HUFF, C. RONALD. 1998. *Youth Violence: Prevention, Intervention, and Social Policy.* Washington, DC: American Psychiatric Press.

GORMAN-SMITH, DIANE, and TOLAN, PATRICK. 1998. "The Role of Exposure to Community Violence and Developmental Problems among Inner City Youth." *Development and Psychopathology* 10:99–114.

GROVES, BETSY M., and ZUCKERMAN, BARRY. 1997. "Interventions with Parents and Caregivers of Children Who Are Exposed to Violence." In *Children in a Violent Society,* ed. Joy D. Osofsky. New York: Guilford.

GROVES, BETSY M.; ZUCKERMAN, BARRY; MARANS, STEPHEN; and COHEN, DONALD. 1993. "Silent Victims: Children Who Witness Violence." *Journal of the American Medical Association* 269:262–264.

HILL, HOPE M.; LEVERMORE, MONIQUE; TWAITE, JAMES; and JONES, L. P. 1996. "Exposure to Community Violence and Social Support as Predictors of Anxiety and Social and Emotional Behavior among African-American Children." *Journal of Child and Family Studies* 5:399–414.

HUESSMAN, L. ROWELL, and ERON, LEONARD D., eds. 1986. *Television and the Aggressive Child: A Cross National Comparison.* Hillsdale, NJ: Erlbaum.

JAFFE, PETER; WILSON, SUSAN; and WOLFE, DAVID. 1986. "Promoting Changes in Attitudes and Understanding of Conflict Resolution among Child Victims of Family Violence." *Canadian Journal of Behavior Sciences* 18:356–366.

JENKINS, ESTHER J., and BELL, CARL C. 1997. "Exposure and Response to Community Violence among Children and Adolescents." In *Children in a Violent Society,* ed. Joy D. Osofsky. New York: Guilford.

LEWIS, MARVA.; OSOFSKY, JOY D.; and MOORE, MARY SUE. 1997. "Violent Cities, Violent Streets: Children Draw Their Neighborhoods." In *Children in a Violent Society,* ed. Joy D. Osofsky. New York: Guilford.

LI, XIAOMING; HOWARD, DONNA; STANTON, BONITA; RACHUBA, LAURA; and CROSS, SHELIA. 1998. "Distress Symptoms among Urban African-American Children and Adolescents: A Psychometric Evaluation of the Checklist of Children's Distress Symptoms." *Archives of Pediatrics and Adolescent Medicine* 152:569–577.

MARANS, STEPHEN, and COHEN, DONALD. 1993. "Children and Inner-City Violence: Strategies for Intervention." In *Psychological Effects of War and Violence on Children*, ed. Lewis Leavitt and Nathan Fox. Hillsdale, NJ: Erlbaum.

MORSE, JODIE. 2000. "The Perception Gap: School Violence." *Time* April 24.

MURRAY, JOHN. 1997. "Media Violence and Youth." In *Children in a Violent Society*, ed. Joy D. Osofsky. New York: Guilford.

NATIONAL COMMISSION ON CHILDREN. 1991. *Speaking of Kids*. Washington, DC: National Commission on Children.

OSOFSKY, JOY D., ed. 1997. *Children in a Violent Society*. New York: Guilford.

OSOFSKY, JOY D.; WEWERS, SARAH; HANN, DELLA M.; and FICK, ANN C. 1993. "Chronic Community Violence: What Is Happening to Our Children?" *Psychiatry* 56:36–45.

OVERSTREET, STACEY. 2000. "Exposure to Community Violence: Defining the Problem and Understanding the Consequences." *Journal of Child and Family Studies* 9(1):7–25.

RICHTERS, JOHN E. 1993. "Community Violence and Children's Development: Toward a Research Agenda for the 1990's." *Psychiatry* 56:3–6.

RICHTERS, JOHN E., and MARTINEZ, PEDRO. 1993. "The NIMH Community Violence Project: I. Children as Victims of and Witnesses to Violence." *Psychiatry* 56:7–21.

ROSENBERG, MARK L., and FENLEY, MARY A. 1991. *Violence in America: A Public Health Approach*. New York: Oxford University Press.

ROSENBERG, MARK L.; O'CARROLL, PATRICK W.; and POWELL, KENNETH E. 1992. "Let's Be Clear: Violence Is a Public Health Problem." *Journal of the American Medical Association* 267:3,071–3,072.

SCHWAB-STONE, MARY E.; AYERS, TIM S.; KASPROW, WESLEY; VOYCE, CHARLENE; BARONE, CHARLES; SHRIVER, TIMOTHY; and WEISSBERG,

ROBERT P. 1995. "No Safe Haven: A Study of Violence Exposure in a Urban Community." *Journal of the American Academy of Child and Adolescent Psychiatry* 34:1343–1352.

STRAUS, MURRAY. 1979. "Measuring Intrafamilial Conflict and Violence: The Conflict Tactics Scales." *Journal of Marriage and Family* 41:75–88.

STRAUS, MURRAY, and GELLES, RICHARD. 1990. *Physical Violence in American Families: Risk Factors and Adaptations to Violence in 8,145 Families*. New Brunswick, NJ: Transaction.

U.S. FEDERAL BUREAU OF INVESTIGATION. 1992. *Uniform Crime Statistics Report*. Washington, DC: U.S. Federal Bureau of Investigation.

JOY D. OSOFSKY
HOWARD J. OSOFSKY

DOMESTIC VIOLENCE

Domestic violence is the greatest public health issue confronting women and children in the United States today. Information from the American Medical Association indicates that:

- Battering is the primary cause of injury to women in the United States.
- The average victim of domestic violence will be physically abused three times per year.
- The total annual health care cost of domestic violence is estimated at over $40 million.
- 20 to 45 percent of all injuries seen in emergency rooms are the result of domestic violence.
- Two-thirds of all women who are murdered die as a result of domestic violence.

Domestic violence is defined as a pattern of behavior that may include physical and sexual violence, threats, insults, and economic deprivation aimed at gaining and maintaining power and control over the mind, body, behavior, and lifestyle of a partner. Under this definition, domestic violence is not limited to married couples or even heterogeneous relationships. Domestic violence can and often does occur within families and across generations.

One of the problems that social scientists, researchers, doctors, and advocates have in documenting the numbers of victims of domestic violence is the stigma attached to an act of violence between family members and intimate partners. One's home is considered a place of safety and refuge, so when violence occurs in that sanctuary, the perpetrators and victims are often reluctant and even fearful to report the incident to outside persons or agencies. When the violence is reported, women and children are overwhelmingly reported as the victims.

In the United States, researchers estimate that one in four women will experience domestic violence at some point in their lifetime. Women who seem most vulnerable to domestic violence are ages sixteen to twenty-four. Data from a 1998 study by the National Violence Against Women Survey indicate that 8 million women are physically, sexually, or emotionally abused every year and 1.9 percent of the women in the United States, which represents 1.9 million women, were physically assaulted in the 12 months prior to the survey.

But physical assault is only a small part of the overall cycle that constitutes domestic violence. The cycle frequently begins with forms of emotional abuse including humiliation, name calling, and making the victim feel guilty. The perpetrator may also use economic abuse, such as preventing the victim from getting a job or taking all the money away and controlling every expenditure. The perpetrator may isolate the victim, limiting the victim's contacts with other family members, friends, and social contacts. As the cycle escalates the perpetrator may use threats of violence against the victim or against children in the home or actual violence such as abusing pets, breaking things, and displaying weapons. Eventually the threats will lead to physical violence causing injury and sometimes death. Physical violence includes beatings, rape, and mutilation.

When the violence is over there may be a period of peace in which the perpetrator asks for forgiveness, apologizes, presents gifts, and blames others, including the victim, for causing the violence. Most often the victim will forgive the perpetrator due to emotional and financial dependence. Victims may also, because of past humiliations and intimidations, feel that they share the blame for causing the violence and the cycle will repeat itself. By definition, domestic violence is a pattern of behavior and not a single act of violence. This pattern or cycle repeats itself many times and it is the repetition that classifies the behavior as domestic violence.

Domestic violence cuts across all areas of culture, class, income, education, profession, race, and age. Internationally an estimated 20 to 50 percent of women have experienced physical violence from an intimate partner or family member. But the true magnitude of domestic violence is hard to assess. In some cultures sexual abuse or rape by an intimate partner is not considered a crime and many incidents of domestic violence are ultimately reported as child injury or abuse when a child is intentionally or unintentionally injured during a violent episode. Even when the situation is made known to legal or social service agencies, treatment or prosecution may be difficult because the victim will not press charges or leave the home.

The Effect of Domestic Violence on Children

Police reports indicate that children are present in the home in 40 to 50 percent of cases involving domestic violence calls. Research indicates that between 3.3 and 10 million children are exposed to domestic violence in the United States every year. Children are significantly affected by this exposure to domestic violence in a number of ways. The most common are that they observe violent acts, they incur injury to themselves, and they suffer neglect by their caretakers.

Children who observe domestic violence react in many ways. External behaviors may include aggressive behavior and conduct problems in home and in school, fighting, cursing, and name calling. Internal behaviors that may also occur include anxiety, depression, low self esteem, guilt, crying; decreased intellectual and academic functioning including inability to concentrate; difficulty with school work, school truancy and failure; and developmental delay. Domestic violence can also affect children's social development, causing them to become isolated and withdrawn from friends and family and demonstrate low levels of empathy. Children affected by domestic violence may also exhibit negative physical health, developing somatic symptoms, poor sleeping and eating habits, headaches, stomach aches, and self-destructive behaviors such as suicide attempts and self-mutilation. A 1998 study indicates that between 45 and 70 per cent of children exposed to domestic violence are also victims of physical abuse. Children in homes with domestic violence are at higher risk of sexual abuse than children in nonviolent homes.

At every stage of a child's life the impact of exposure to violence in the home is evident. Infants or very young children are vulnerable to injury when adults handle them roughly in a moment of violence, but children are also subject to injury when flying objects are thrown or smashed or when weapons are used. They also may be ripped from their caretakers' arms or hurt when the person holding them falls or is knocked down. The victim of domestic violence may neglect the child in an attempt to appease the abuser or in fear that the child might be harmed further if concern is shown. Effects of this neglect can be seen in infants or young children through eating or sleeping disturbances (particularly if the abuse routinely occurs during meal times or after the child has gone to sleep), listlessness, developmental delays (due to lack of stimulation), and failure to thrive (due to lack of nurturing). Exposure to violence interferes with children's ability to develop trust in adults charged with their care. These children commonly exhibit excessive irritability, fear of being left alone, regression in toileting and language skills, and other delays in learning.

School-age children between the ages of five and twelve may exhibit more significant behaviors as a result of observing domestic violence. These children may be aggressive toward other children, exhibit low self-esteem, feel insecure, run away, use drugs, or have problems in school. As the child enters the teen years the child may exhibit more of the behaviors associated with the abuser or the victim. The child who identifies with the victim may come to accept violence as part of an intimate relationship. The child who identifies with the perpetrator learns to use violence to control relationships. Teens may also feel compelled to intervene on behalf of the victim and be injured, or be coerced into participating in the violence. Teens commonly experience shame about what is going on in their home and seek to remove themselves from the situation by running away or attempting suicide. When a victim seeks to remove herself and her children from an abusive situation, the children are frequently separated from their communities, friends, and schools. This puts additional stress on the child.

Given the serious consequence of domestic violence on children, some professionals argue that exposure to domestic violence constitutes a form of child maltreatment. But others argue that not all children are affected in the same way and that, in fact, many children learn to cope with the violence. Thus, witnessing abuse should be viewed as a potential risk factor for child maltreatment rather than conclusive evidence.

Response to Domestic Violence and Child Maltreatment

Since the late 1980s, researchers and practitioners have recognized the relationship between domestic violence and child maltreatment, yet little has been done to coordinate the delivery of services to these populations. The typical service delivery model has different points of entry into the system for adult victims and child victims. Frequently cases are heard in different court systems and those seeking help have to repeat their stories numerous times, fill out similar types of forms at each agency, and receive counseling separately from their children. In some systems the victim is required to seek counseling to receive other services, but the abuser is not required to receive any treatment at all.

As communities have focused on making families safer, new strategies have been developed to address domestic violence treatment and prevention. These strategies focus on building collaboration among law enforcement, child welfare, health care, and domestic violence prevention advocates. Cross-training is one of the most commonly implemented strategies to ensure that police officers, child protective services workers, school personnel, and mental health and medical professionals all recognize the signs of domestic violence and child abuse and know where to refer the victim. Co-location of services to facilitate access to safe housing, counseling, financial support, and legal intervention to victims and children is another effective strategy. But there is still much about prevention, identification, reporting, and treatment of domestic violence victims and abusers that is not known.

Laws on Domestic Violence

In 1984 Congress passed the Family Violence Prevention and Services Act, designed to help states in their efforts to increase public awareness about domestic violence. Ten years later the Violence Against Women Act of 1994 (VAWA) was passed. This act includes provisions to increase the number of programs available to victims of domestic violence. In addition, VAWA directly addresses the impact of domestic violence on children through treatment programs for children who are harmed by these acts.

State laws vary in approaches to domestic violence. For example, all states have provisions for restraining orders to keep the abuser away from the victim, but how long the order lasts, who is included in the order, and how specific courts process such requests vary from state to state. More than half of the states have laws that require that domestic violence be considered when a court makes an award of child custody or visitation. And while this is an improvement over the days when domestic issues were considered irrelevant to the welfare of the child, the laws still leave much discretion to the court.

Societal costs of the effects of domestic violence are enormous. Some costs, such as the cost of mental health and medical treatment, loss of work time for victims and abusers, court proceedings, and law enforcement response, can be estimated. But society cannot begin to estimate the worth of a lost childhood, broken homes, death of a parent, and fear caused by domestic violence.

See also: AGGRESSIVE BEHAVIOR; ATTENTION; CHILD ABUSE AND NEGLECT; DROPOUTS, SCHOOL; PARENTING; STRESS AND DEPRESSION.

BIBLIOGRAPHY

FANTUZZO, JOHN W., and MOHR, WANDA K. 1999. "Prevalence and Effect of Child Exposure to Domestic Violence." *The Future of Children: Domestic Violence and Children* 9(3):21–32.

MATTHEWS, MARTHA A. 1999. "The Impact of Federal and State Laws on Children Exposed to Domestic Violence." *The Future of Children: Domestic Violence and Children* 9(3):50–66.

OSOFSKY, JOY D. 1999. "The Impact of Violence on Children." *The Future of Children: Domestic Violence and Children* 9(3):33–49.

TJADEN, PATRICIA, and THOENNES, NANCY. 1998. "Stalking in America: Findings from the National Violence against Women Survey." Research in brief prepared for the National Institute of Justice and Centers for Disease Control and Prevention. Denver, CO: Center for Policy and Research.

UNITED NATION CHILDREN'S FUND. 2000. "Domestic Violence Against Women and Girls." *Innocenti Digest* 6:2–17.

INTERNET RESOURCES

AMERICAN MEDICAL ASSOCIATION COUNCIL ON SCIENTIFIC AFFAIRS. 2001. "AMA Data on Violence Between Intimates." <www.ama-assn.org/ama/pub/article/2036-5298.html>.

FAMILY REFUGE CENTER. 2001. "Domestic Violence and Children: The Effects of Domestic Violence on Children." <www.familyrefugecenter.com/effecton.html>.

NATIONAL CLEARINGHOUSE ON CHILD ABUSE AND NEGLECT INFORMATION. 2001. "In Harm's Way: Domestic Violence and Child Maltreatment." <www.calib.com/nccanch/pubs/otherpubs/harmsway.cfm>.

PEACE AT HOME. 1995. "Domestic Violence: The Facts—A Handbook to STOP Violence." <www.cybergrrl.com/views/dv/book/def.html>.

DEBBIE MILLER

VISUAL IMPAIRMENTS, EDUCATION OF INDIVIDUALS WITH

The term *blindness* brings to mind many images as well as many unfounded beliefs. Although popular opinion suggests otherwise, individuals with blindness do not possess an extra sense allowing them to intuit the visual world. Likewise, people with visual impairments do not exhibit superhuman abilities in touch and hearing. In fact, most people who are blind can actually see—very few people who are blind are completely blind.

An individual who is legally blind has limited visual acuity relative to either distance (visual acuity of 20/200 or less in his or her better eye even with correction), or field (a field of vision so narrow that its widest diameter subtends an angular distance no greater than twenty degrees). Individuals considered to be partially sighted have visual acuity falling between 20/70 and 20/200 in the better eye, even with correction. Educators commonly use a more functional definition of blindness. Educators use the term *blind* to describe students who are so severely impaired that they must learn to read using braille or aural methods. Children who can read print with magnifying devices or large-print books are often referred to as students with low vision. The different definitions are used in reported prevalence rates. Overall, visual impairment in children is estimated at three per 10,000. In the 1998 through 1999 school year, the Office of Special Education Programs reported more than 26,000 students with visual impairments (approximately .04% of all students ages 6–21).

The causes of partial sight include nystagmus (conditions caused by improper muscle functioning), optic atrophy (conditions including glaucoma), cataracts, and other congenital abnormalities. The main causes of blindness are optic atrophy, retinal conditions, and cataracts and other congenital abnormalities. Although the most serious visual impairments are caused by glaucoma, cataracts, and diabetes, retinopathy of prematurity (ROP) is reemerging as a significant cause of blindness. In the 1940s ROP began appearing in premature infants. Excessive concentrations of oxygen administered to prevent brain damage resulted in scar tissue behind the lens of the eye. More than sixty years later, efforts to save the lives of medically fragile infants that use high concentrations of oxygen are also resulting in ROP.

Although blindness is primarily an adult disability, educational services for individuals with visual impairments include not only training centers and sheltered workshops, but also specialized schools, classrooms, and teachers. The first schools for children with blindness opened in the United States in 1832. The Perkins School for the Blind and the New York Institute for the Education of the Blind were modeled after programs in Europe and led by Dr. John Dix Fisher and Samuel Gridley Howe. These schools and others like them developed sheltered workshops designed to give students skills for employment. Many of these workshops in the early twenty-first century operate independently from educational institutions.

The twentieth century heralded many significant milestones in the provision of services for both children and adults with visual impairment. In 1920, the Smith-Fess Act appropriated state and federal funds for the vocational rehabilitation of people with physical handicaps. Later in 1940, the National Federation of the Blind was formed. This federation began advocating for individuals with blindness and continues to prepare and place people with blindness in suitable jobs. Finally, in 1975 the Education for All Handicapped Children Act (Pub. L. 94-142) was passed. This act guaranteed a free and appropriate education for all children regardless of disability.

In the early 1900s most students with blindness were educated in residential schools; at the beginning of the twenty-first century most attend regular classes with periodic support from a teacher for the visually impaired. However, some professionals still advocate for special schools and programs, arguing that students with blindness need specific services and supplies that cannot be offered in regular classrooms.

The use of braille declined dramatically in the last half of the twentieth century. In opposition to this trend, many professionals, along with the National Federation of the Blind, have argued that knowledge of braille is essential for independent living and that too few teachers are proficient in braille. In the 1997 reauthorization of Public Law 94-142, the U.S. Congress mandated braille services for all students with blindness unless all members of the educational team deemed the services unnecessary. Students with visual impairment also require mobility training. Historically, white canes were not available to young children; however, some experts now contend that cane training should begin as soon as the child is walking independently. This training should be a critical component of preschool programming. Guide dogs are generally not recommended for children because of the care they require.

See also: ASSISTIVE TECHNOLOGY; SPECIAL EDUCATION, *subentries on* CURRENT TRENDS, HISTORY OF.

BIBLIOGRAPHY

BEST, ANTHONY B. 1992. *Teaching Children with Visual Impairments.* Philadelphia: Open University Press.

HALLAHAN, DANIEL P., and KAUFFMAN, JAMES M. 2000. *Exceptional Learners: Introduction to Special Education,* 8th edition, Boston: Allyn and Bacon.

VAUGHAN, C. EDWIN, and VAUGHAN, JOAN. 1998. "Blindness in the United States: From Isolation to Full Inclusion." In *Social and Cultural Perspectives on Blindness,* ed. C. Edwin Vaughan. Springfield, IL: Charles C. Thomas.

DEVERY R. MOCK
DANIEL P. HALLAHAN

VOCABULARY DEVELOPMENT

See: LITERACY, *subentry on* VOCABULARY AND VOCABULARY LEARNING.

VOCATIONAL AND TECHNICAL EDUCATION

HISTORY OF

Vocational education in the United States is the product of an extended evolutionary process. Economic, educational, and societal issues have repeatedly exerted influence on the definition of vocational education, as well as on how, when, where, and to whom it will be provided. There are many legal definitions of vocational education (i.e., how vocational education is defined by law). These legal definitions are critical since they specify how, for what purpose, and to what extent federal monies may be spent for vocational education. All too often this legal definition is interpreted by state and local officials as the only definition of vocational education.

For the purpose of this article, vocational education is defined as a practically illustrated and attempted job or career skill instruction. As such, a variety of components fall under the vocational education umbrella: agricultural education, business education, family and consumer sciences, health occupations education, marketing education, technical education, technology education, and trade and industrial education. The vocational curriculum can be identified as a combination of classroom instruction—hands-on laboratory work and on-the-job training—augmented by an active network of student organizations. Vocational preparation must always be viewed against the backdrop of the needs of society and of the individual. While meeting the demands of the economy, the abilities of individuals must be utilized to the fullest. Meeting the internalized job needs of individuals is a crucial objective of vocational education.

Historical Foundations

The first formalized vocational education system in America can be traced to apprenticeship agreements of colonial times. The first education law passed in America, the Old Deluder Satan Act of the Massachusetts Bay Colony, set specific requirements for masters to teach apprentices academic as well as vocational skills. During the colonial period the colonies frequently cared for orphans, poor children, and delinquents by indenturing them to serve apprenticeships. As apprenticeship declined, other institutions developed to care for these youngsters. By the mid-1880s vocational education in the form of industrial education was synonymous with institutional programs for these youth. The children of defeated Native American leaders were sent to the Carlisle Pennsylvania Indian School, and the curriculum was job training.

After the Civil War Samuel Chapman Armstrong, the founder of Hampton Institute and the ideological father of African-American vocational education, tried to address the racial aspects of the social and economic relations between the former slaves and the white South. His vocational education programs emphasized the need for African Americans to be good, subservient laborers. The prominent educator Booker T. Washington, Armstrong's prize student, took the same values and philosophical views as his former mentor. Washington held firmly to his beliefs that vocational education was the ideal route for most African Americans. W. E. B. Du Bois, also an influential African-American educator, strongly objected to Washington's educational program. He accused Washington of teaching lessons of work and money, which potentially encouraged African Americans to forget about the highest aims of life.

The first land-grant college provisions, known as the First Morrill Act, were enacted by the U.S. Congress on July 2, 1862. The statute articulated the appointment of public lands to the states based on their representation in Congress in 1860. The Morrill Act was one of the first congressional actions to benefit from the post–Civil War constitutional amendments. By the late 1860s Morrill Act funds were being distributed to the states, with the intention that they would foster educational opportunity for all students. Following the Civil War, the expansion of the land-grant college system continued, with its implied focus on educational opportunities. However, with the close of the army's occupation to the old South, funds from the Morrill Act began to flow systemically to schools offering only all-white education. Congress attempted by various legislation to force racial equality, including equality of educational opportunity. However, the U.S. Supreme Court initiated a series of interpretations of the post–Civil War constitutional amendments that ultimately defeated these various legislative efforts. Culminating with its 1882 decision finding the first Civil Rights Act unconstitutional, the Supreme Court held that the Fourteenth amendment only protected against direct discriminatory action by a state government. What followed was a period of nearly seventy-five years when only modest gains were made in higher educational opportunity for minorities. Congress did pass a second Morrill Act (1890), which required states with dual systems of education (all-white and nonwhite) to provide land grant institutions for both systems. Basing their jurisdiction on the 1882 Supreme Court decision, Congress acted to curb direct state-sponsored discrimination. Eventually, nineteen higher education institutions for African Americans were organized as land-grant institutions. These institutions were founded to raise the aspirations of a generation of children of former slaves and to ensure that high quality higher education was provided for Americans of all races. While efforts persisted throughout the late nineteenth and early twentieth centuries to reduce the funding to these colleges, the schools continued to function based on land-grant funds.

Early in the twentieth century, vocational education was a prominent topic of discussion among American educators as schools struggled to meet the labor force needs consistent with the shift from an agrarian to an industrial economic base. In his 1907 address to Congress, President Theodore Roosevelt urged major school reform that would provide industrial education in urban centers and agriculture education in rural areas. A powerful alliance supporting federal funding for vocational education was formed in 1910 when the American Federation of Labor (AFL), who had long opposed such programs as discriminatory, lent its approval to the National Association of Manufacturers' (NAM) promotion of trade instruction in schools. Formed in 1895, one of NAM's first projects was to investigate how education might provide a more effective means to help American manufacturers compete in expanding international markets. The AFL joined the vocational reform movement believing its participation would help protect working-class interests by providing them with a voice at the table on education policy development with the emerging industrial economy. The strength of the combined lobby influenced Con-

gress in 1914 to authorize President Woodrow Wilson to appoint a commission to study whether federal aid to vocational education was warranted. Charles Prosser, a student of social efficiency advocate David Snedden, was principal author of the commission's report to Congress. Prosser considered separately administered, and narrowly focused, vocational training as the best available way to help nonacademic students secure employment after completing high school. In its final report to Congress, the commission chaired by Georgia Senator Hoke Smith declared an urgent social and educational need of vocational training in public schools.

Legislative History and Reforms

Federal support for vocational education began with the Smith-Hughes Act of 1917. Two Democratic lawmakers from Georgia, Senator Hoke Smith and Representative Dudley Mays Hughes, were chiefly responsible for this historic bill, which established vocational education, particularly agricultural education, as a federal program. The act reflected the view of reformers who believed that youth should be prepared for entry-level jobs by learning specific occupational skills in separated vocational schools. According to Harvey Kantor and David B. Tyack, this brand of vocationalism had its critics, including the American philosopher and educator John Dewey, who believed that such specific skill training was unnecessarily narrow and undermined democracy. The Smith-Hughes Act, however, firmly supported the notion of a separate vocational education system and supported courses offered by vocational schools. The act called for specific skill training, focused on entry-level skills, and helped establish separate state boards for vocational education. The Smith-Hughes Act and its successors until 1963 were largely designed to expand these separate vocational education programs, in an effort to retain more students in secondary education, and to provide trained workers for a growing number of semiskilled occupations. These acts focused on basic support, providing funds for teachers and teacher training, and encouraging state support for vocational education through extensive funds-matching requirements.

By the 1960s, the vocational education system had been firmly established, and Congress recognized the need for a new focus. As a result, the 1963 Vocational Education Act, while still supporting the separate system approach by funding the construction of area vocational schools, broadened the definition of vocational education to include occupational programs in comprehensive high schools, such as business and commerce. The act also included the improvement of vocational education programs and the provision of programs and services for disadvantaged and disabled students.

Faced with initial evidence that localities were not responding to the new focus on improving programs and serving students with special needs, the 1968 Amendments to the Vocational Education Act backed each goal with specific funding. This change set the stage for what has become the distinguishing feature of all such legislation since 1968—the manner in which it seeks a compromise between the demands for improved vocational program quality and for increased vocational education opportunities for students with special needs.

Separate funds set aside for disabled and disadvantaged students seemed an effective strategy, as it resulted in more funds expended on these groups and in increased enrollments. Since there are few other sources of federal assistance for secondary special needs students (other than students with disabilities), it is not surprising that other special populations were added to federal vocational education legislation over time. In 1974, the needs of limited English proficient (LEP) students were addressed through provisions for bilingual vocational training; funds for Native American students were also added. In 1976 LEP students were made eligible for part of the disadvantaged set-aside, and provisions to eliminate sex bias and sex stereotyping in vocational education were added.

Education reforms focusing on secondary education began in the early 1980s, prompted by concern about the nation's declining competitiveness in the international market, the relatively poor performance of American students on tests of educational achievement (both nationally and internationally), and complaints from the business community about the low level of skills and abilities found in high school graduates entering the workforce. This reform came in two waves. The first wave, sometimes characterized as academic reform, called for increased effort from the current education system: more academic course requirements for high school graduation, more stringent college entrance requirements, longer school days and years, and an emphasis on standards and testing for both students and teachers. The basic message might be paraphrased, "work more, try harder, strive for excellence."

Beginning in the mid-1980s, a second wave of school reform arose, based in part on the belief that the first wave did not go far enough to improve education for all students. The second wave, sometimes referred to as *restructuring,* called for changes in the way schools and the educational process were organized. While restructuring proposals included school choice and site-based management, of particular interest in this report was the emphasis on improving the school-to-work transition for nonbaccalaureate youth by creating closer linkages between vocational and academic education, secondary and postsecondary institutions, and schools and workplaces.

The reform movement, particularly its first phase, received major impetus from the publication in 1983 of the National Commission on Excellence in Education's report *A Nation at Risk.* This influential report observed that the United States was losing ground in international economic competition and attributed the decline in large part to the relatively low standards and poor performance of the American educational system. The report recommended many of the changes subsequently enacted in first-wave reforms: the strengthening of requirements for high school graduation, including the requirement of a core academic curriculum; the development and use of rigorous educational standards; more time in school or the more efficient use of presently available time; and better preparation of teachers.

The response to this report and related education reform initiatives was rapid and widespread. Marion Asche reported in 1991 that between the early and mid-1980s, more than 275 education task forces had been organized in the United States. By the mid-1980s, forty-three states had increased course requirements for high school graduation; seventeen had developed stronger requirements for admission to state colleges and universities; thirty-seven had created statewide student assessment programs; twenty-nine had developed teacher competency tests; and twenty-eight had increased teacher licensure requirements. Between 1984 and 1986 more than 700 state laws affecting some aspect of the teaching profession had been enacted.

The Carl D. Perkins Vocational Education Act of 1984 (Pub. L. 98-524), known as the Perkins Act, continued the affirmation of Congress that effective vocational education programs are essential to the nation's future as a free and democratic society. The act had two interrelated goals, one economic and one social. The economic goal was to improve the skills of the labor force and prepare adults for job opportunities—a long-standing goal traceable to the Smith-Hughes Act. The social goal was to provide equal opportunities for adults in vocational education. In the late summer of 1990, Congress passed the Carl D. Perkins Vocational and Applied Technology Education Act (Pub. L. 101-392, also known as Perkins II), which amended and extended the Carl D. Perkins Vocational Act of 1984.

The School-to-Work Opportunities Act (STWOA) of 1994 (Pub. L. 103-239) was passed to address the national skills shortage by providing a model to create a highly skilled workforce for the nation's economy through partnerships between educators and employers. The STWOA emphasized preparing students with the knowledge, skills, abilities, and information about occupations and the labor market that would help them make the transition from school to postschool employment through school-based and work-based instructional components supported by a connecting activity's component. Key elements of STWOA included (a) collaborative partnerships, (b) integrated curriculum, (c) technological advances, (d) adaptable workers, (e) comprehensive career guidance, (f) work-based learning, and (g) a step-by-step approach.

On October 31, 1998 President Clinton signed the Carl D. Perkins Vocational and Technical Education Act (Pub. L. 105-332). Two major focus areas of this legislation were to increase accountability and provide states with more flexibility to use funds.

Trends and Issues

In the United States of the early twenty-first century, vocational education has entered a new era. There is increasing acknowledgement that the traditional educational focus on college-bound youth needs to change. Greater attention is being focused on work-bound youth, particularly those who will require less than baccalaureate education. There is increasing concern that the United States is not adequately preparing a growing pool of new workers—women, minorities, and immigrants—for productive, successful roles in the workforce. Education is being urged to change the way it is preparing youth and adults to function in a global economy. All of these trends are bringing new importance to vocational education.

A U.S. General Accounting Office study examined strategies used to prepare work-bound youth for employment in the United States and four competitor nations—England, Germany, Japan and Sweden. Among the findings:

1. The four competitor nations expect all students to do well in school, especially in the early years. U.S. schools accept that many will lag behind.

2. The competitor nations have established competency-based national training standards that are used to certify skill competency. U.S. practice is to certify program completion.

3. All four competitor nations invest as heavily in the education and training of work-bound youth as they do for each college-bound youth.

4. To a much greater extent than in the United States, the schools and employment communities in the competitor countries guide students' transition from school to work, helping students learn about job requirements and assisting them in finding employment.

5. Young adults in the four competitor nations have higher literacy rates than the comparable population segment in the United States.

Generally, research has shown that obtaining workers with a good work ethic and appropriate social behavior has been a priority for employers. Employers complain about the attitude and character of workers—particularly about absenteeism, an inability to adapt, a lack of discipline, and negative work behaviors. In response to criticism about the general employability of the workforce, the Secretary's Commission on Achieving Necessary Skills published in 1991 a range of skills that all workforce participants should have. These include the following:

1. Basic Skills
   a. Reading
   b. Writing
   c. Mathematics
   d. Listening
   e. Speaking
2. Thinking Skills
   a. Creative Thinking
   b. Decision Making
   c. Problem Solving
   d. Knowing How to Learn
   e. Reasoning

3. Personal Qualities

a. Responsibility

b. Self-Esteem

c. Sociability

d. Self-Management

e. Integrity/Honesty

If the United States is to remain at the forefront in the high-tech global marketplace, the workforce must posses the requisite technological competencies and academic skills. As technology continues to influence vocational education, new and innovative educational approaches must be established to provide vocational education students with the enhanced skills and knowledge they will need to participate in the international marketplace.

Technology Education

Most people recognize that technology has changed the world, but few people understand the various aspects of technology and how pervasive technology is in U.S. society. Technology is commonly defined as a discipline or body of knowledge and the application of this knowledge combined with resources to produce outcomes in response to human desires and needs. Technology education draws its content from four universal domains: (1) sciences, (2) humanities, (3) technologies, and (4) formal knowledge. The sciences and humanities domains contain all recorded knowledge of the sciences and humanities. The technologies domain likewise contains all recorded knowledge related to the types of technology. The formal knowledge domain consists of language, linguistics, mathematics, and logic.

Technology education programs are available at the elementary, middle/junior high school, and secondary levels. At the elementary school level, the focus is on technological awareness with classroom activities oriented around the development of motor skills and informed attitudes about technology's influence on society. At the middle school level, the focus of technology education programs is on exploring the applications of technology to solve problems and exploring the various technological careers. A wide variety of problem-solving situations are used, giving students opportunities to create and design. Activities are designed to further promote technological awareness and to promote psychomotor development through processes associated with technology. Secondary technology education pro-

grams are designed to give students experience related to scientific principles, engineering concepts, and technological systems.

The New Vocationalism

Vocationalism is defined as the method used by schools, particularly high schools, to organize their curricula so the students may develop skills, both vocational and academic, that will give them the strategic labor market advantages needed to compete for good jobs. Overall enrollment in vocational courses has fallen. However, an incoming current has brought a growing number of participants into new programs and curricula. While traditional vocational offerings have been geared toward immediate entry into specific occupations, new programs and course sequences are intended to prepare students for both colleges and careers, by combining a challenging academic curriculum with development of work-related knowledge skill. The new combination aims to keep students' options open after high school. They can go to a two-year or four-year college and then work, go to work full-time and then back to college, or engage in paid employment and further education simultaneously.

The overall decline in high school vocational enrollment is evident from student transcript data. Between 1982 and 1994 the average number of vocational credits completed by high school graduates declined form 4.7 to 4.0, or from 22 percent to 16 percent of total credits earned in all subjects. The number of students who completed three or more courses in a single vocational program area slipped from 34 percent to 25 percent. Furthermore, students with disabilities, or with low grades, accounted for a growing proportion of vocational course-taking in high schools during this period. Combining a vocational sequence with college-prep academic courses seems to yield positive results. Several studies have found that high school students who combine a substantial academic curriculum with a set of vocational courses do better than students who omit either one of these two components.

The idea of combining vocational and academic coursework is also central to *High Schools That Work,* a network of more of more than 800 schools engaged in raising academic curriculum with modern vocational studies. It is also a key component of the *New American High Schools* identified by the U.S. Department of Education. Many of these schools are trying to raise academic standards and expectations by structuring the curriculum alignment around students' career-related interests. Charles Benson, in a paper delivered in 1992 and published posthumously in 1997, articulated some of the objectives of the new vocationalism: The first is to enable almost all students, not just the minority, to obtain a thorough working knowledge of mathematics, sciences, and languages. That is, the first objective of the new vocationalism is to help many more students obtain a much higher standard of academic proficiency. The second objective is to help many, many more students gain such a level of occupational proficiency that they enter easily and quickly into productive, rewarding, and interesting careers.

What does the integration of academic and vocational curricula entail? Research has shown that schools bring academic and vocational education together in a number of different ways, which comprise eight different models of integration at the secondary level. These models are summarized as follows:

1. More academic content is incorporated in vocational courses.

2. Academic courses are made more vocationally relevant.

3. Academic and vocational teachers cooperate to incorporate academic content into vocational programs.

4. Curricular alignment is accomplished by modifying or coordinating both academic and vocational curricula across courses.

5. Seminar projects are done in lieu of elective courses and require students to complete a project that integrates knowledge and skills learned in both academic and vocational courses.

6. The academy model is a school-within-a-school that aligns courses with each other and to an occupational focus.

7. Vocational high schools and magnet schools align courses with each other and to an occupational focus for all students.

8. Occupational clusters, career paths, and occupational majors feature a coherent sequence of courses and alignment among courses within clusters.

Work-Based Learning

Work experience programs allow students to learn first-hand about the world of work while still in school. These efforts, broadly referred to as work experience programs, include formal work-based training programs outside the school, such as cooperative education, youth apprenticeship, and school-based enterprises. *Co-op education* is run by individual schools as part of their vocational education programs. Students are provided part-time jobs during the school year in their field of vocational specialization. The job placements are arranged by the classroom vocational instructor or by the school's co-op coordinator. A training plan that clearly states what the student is expected to learn and what the employer is expected to provide is developed. Business and marketing education programs are generally the largest sponsors of co-op education.

The concept of *youth apprenticeship* includes preparation for postsecondary education as well as employment. Youth apprenticeship, typically designed for high school students who may go on to postsecondary education, are different from traditional apprenticeships run by unions or trade associations, that usually enroll young adults who have graduated from high school. There is a growing consensus about the principles that should guide any youth apprenticeship and about the basic design elements that differentiate youth apprenticeships from other models linking school and work. These principles include active participation of employers; Integration of work-based and school-based learning; integration of academic and vocational learning; structured linkages between secondary and postsecondary institutions; and award of a broadly recognized certificate of occupational skill.

The third type of work experience program is *school-based enterprises*. In these programs, students produce goods or services for sale or use to other people. Such enterprises include school restaurants, construction projects, child care centers, auto repair shops, hair salons, and retail stores.

These programs differ from co-ops and apprenticeships in that they do not place students with employers. Rather, the goal of school-based enterprises is to allow students to apply their classroom knowledge to running real-world businesses. School-based enterprises are a viable option in communities where there are too few employers to provide sufficient jobs and training opportunities in the private sector.

As the evolution toward higher technology in the work place continues, the focus of federal support for vocational education must be on redoubling efforts to increase linkages between academic and occupational skill development, secondary and postsecondary education, and business and education.

See also: AGRICULTURAL EDUCATION; BUSINESS EDUCATION, *subentry on* SCHOOL; FAMILY AND CONSUMER SCIENCES EDUCATION; TECHNOLOGY EDUCATION; VOCATIONAL SCHOOL FALLACY.

BIBLIOGRAPHY

ASCHE, MARION. 1991. "Educational Reform and Vocational Education: Review with Implications for Research and Development." *The Journal of Vocational Education Research* 16(3):1–34.

BENSON, CHARLES S. 1997. "New Vocationalism in the United States: Potential Problems and Outlook." *Economics of Education Review* 16(3):201–212.

BOESEL, DAVID; RAHN, MIKALA; and DEICH, SHARON. 1994. *Program Improvement: Education Reform.* Vol. 3: *National Assessment of Vocational Education: Final Report to Congress.* Washington DC: Office of Educational Research and Improvement, U.S. Department of Education.

GORDON, HOWARD R. D. 1999. *The History and Growth of Vocational Education in America.* Needham Heights, MA: Allyn and Bacon.

GRAY, KENNETH C., and HERR, EDWIN L. 1998. *Workforce Education: The Basics.* Needham Heights, MA: Allyn and Bacon.

HYSLOP, EMERY J. 2000. "An Assessment of the Historical Arguments in Vocational Education Reform." *Journal of Career and Technical Education* 17(1):23–30.

JOHNSON, KEITH V. 1996. "Some Thoughts on African Americans' Struggle to Participate in Technology Education." *The Journal of Technology Studies* 22(1):49–54.

KANTOR, HARVEY, and TYACK, DAVID B. 1982. *Work, Youth, and Schooling: Historical Perspectives on Vocationalism in American Education.* Stanford, CA: Stanford University Press.

LEVESQUE, KAREN, et al. 2000. *Vocational Education in the United States: Toward the Year 2000.* National Center for Education Statistics Office of Educational Research and Improvement. Washington, DC: U.S. Department of Education.

NATIONAL COMMISSION ON EXCELLENCE IN EDUCATION. 1983. *A Nation at Risk: The Imperative for Education Reform.* Washington, DC: U.S. Government Printing Office.

SECRETARY'S COMMISSION ON ACHIEVING NECESSARY SKILLS. 1991. *What Work Requires of Schools: A SCANS Report for America 2000.* Washington, DC: U.S. Department of Labor.

SCOTT, JOHN L., and SARKEES, MICHELLE. 1996. *Overview of Vocational and Applied Technology Education.* Homewood, IL: American Technical Publishers.

WALTER, RICHARD A. 1993. "Development of Vocational Education." In *Vocational Education in the 1990s II: A Sourcebook for Strategies, Methodology and Materials,* ed. Craig Anderson and Larry C. Rampp. Ann Arbor, MI: Prakken Publications.

WARNAT, WINIFRED I. 1991. "Preparing a Worldclass Workforce." *Vocational Education Journal* 66(5):23–25.

HOWARD R. D. GORDON

CURRENT TRENDS

The trend in contemporary K–12 vocational education is away from the use of the word *vocational* to label these programs. Most states have selected a broader term, although a few use *vocational technical education.* A number of states have followed the lead of the national vocational education organizations and adopted the term *career and technical education.* Others use variations, such as career and technology education and professional-technical education, and several states include the word *workforce* in describing these programs. The changes in terminology reflect a changing economy, in which technical careers have become the mainstay.

When the term *career education* first became popular in the 1970s, it was distinguished from vocational education by its emphasis on general employability and adaptability skills applicable to all occupations, while vocational education was primarily concerned with occupational skill training for specific occupations. That basic definition of career education remains appropriate today.

The purpose of career and technical education is to provide a foundation of skills that enable high school students to be gainfully employed after graduation—either full-time or while continuing their education or training. Nearly two-thirds of all graduates of career and technical programs enter some form of postsecondary program.

Across the United States, career and technical education programs are offered in about 11,000 comprehensive high schools, several hundred vocational-technical high schools, and about 1,400 area vocational-technical centers. Public middle schools typically offer some career and technical education courses, such as family and consumer sciences and technology education. About 9,400 postsecondary institutions offer technical programs, including community colleges, technical institutes, skill centers, and other public and private two- and four-year colleges. In 2001 there were 11 million secondary and postsecondary career and technical education students in the United States, according to the U.S. Office of Educational Research and Improvement.

The subject areas most commonly associated with career and technical education are: business (office administration, entrepreneurship); trade and industrial (e.g., automotive technician, carpenter, computer numerical control technician); health occupations (nursing, dental, and medical technicians); agriculture (food and fiber production, agribusiness); family and consumer sciences (culinary arts, family management and life skills); marketing (merchandising, retail); and technology (computer-based careers).

Career and technical education programs usually are offered as a sequence of courses supplemented by work-based experiences, such as internships or apprenticeships. These work experiences remain a hallmark of career and technical education.

Rethinking the Mission

For the last two decades of the twentieth century, business led the charge for school reform in order to have better prepared students for the workplace. Yet career and technical education programs, which have the mission of readying young people for employment, continue to be pushed aside by courses designed to prepare students for high-stakes academic assessments. All states have testing requirements for high school students in mathematics, science, English language arts, and sometimes social studies. One result of the emphasis on academic testing is a continuing decline in the number of students enrolled in career and technical education.

To reverse declining enrollments, career and technical education faces a twofold challenge: to re-

structure its programs and to rebuild its image. Traditional vocational programs provided students with job-specific skills that many parents viewed as too narrow for their children.

The trend is for career and technical education programs to rethink their mission by asking how they can prepare students with high-level academic skills and the broad-based transferable skills and technical skills required for participation in the "new economy," where adaptability is key. Programs adopt this dual approach in an effort to make career and technical education a realistic option for large numbers of students to achieve academic success, which will translate into employment for them.

These programs teach broad skills that are applicable to many occupations. This preparation for the world of work is anchored in strong academic skills, which students learn how to apply to real-world situations. These academic skills include the competencies needed in the contemporary workplace as well as the knowledge and skills valued by academic education and measured by state examinations.

The reality is that the academic skills needed for the workplace are often more rigorous than the academic skills required for college. The multidisciplinary approach of most work tasks and the amount of technology and information in the workplace contribute to the heightened expectations of all workers, including entry-level.

For career and technical education programs to flourish in the early twentieth century's test-driven school environment, they must: (1) find ways to continue to prepare students with the skills and knowledge needed in the increasingly sophisticated workplace; (2) embed, develop, and reinforce the academic standards/benchmarks that are tested on the state-mandated assessments; and (3) teach the essential skills that all students need for success in life.

Organizing Programs Around Career Clusters

The workplace requires three sets of skills of most workers:

- Strong academics, especially in English language arts, mathematics, and science, as well as computer skills;
- Career specific skills for a chosen career cluster;
- Virtues such as honesty, responsibility, and integrity.

The U.S. Department of Education Office of Vocational and Adult Education has identified sixteen broad career clusters that reflect a new direction for education. The clusters were created to assist educators in preparing students for a changing workplace. The intent is for secondary and postsecondary educators, employers, and industry group representatives to work together to formulate cluster standards. The careers in each cluster range from entry level through professional/technical management in a broad industry field. Each cluster includes both the academic and technical skills and knowledge needed for careers and postsecondary education. These clusters provide a way for schools to organize course offerings so students can learn about the whole cluster of occupations in a career field. It is an excellent tool to assist students in identifying their interests and goals for the future. The sixteen career clusters are:

- Agriculture and Natural Resources
- Architecture and Construction
- Arts, Audiovisual Technology, and Communications
- Business and Administration
- Education and Training
- Finance
- Government and Public Administration
- Health Science
- Hospitality and Tourism
- Human Services
- Information Technology
- Law and Public Safety
- Manufacturing
- Retail/Wholesale Sales and Services
- Scientific Research/Engineering
- Transportation, Distribution, and Logistics

The preparation of students in the career clusters must include (1) academic skills, (2) cluster-specific standards, and (3) broad transferable skills. All of these aspects of the curriculum must be organized in a continuum. As students grow and develop through this continuum, they will prepare themselves for broader and higher-level opportunities.

The Academic Issues

The 1983 publication of a government report, *A Nation at Risk,* sounded an alarm about the competitiveness of U.S. students in comparison to their international counterparts. Education systems responded by raising standards in mathematics, sci-

ence, English language arts, and, in some states, other disciplines such as social studies as well. States have passed legislation and implemented regulations in hopes of solving the problem.

Because the business community was directly involved in the school reform process, business concepts were applied in schools in the 1980s and 1990s. Examples included Total Quality Management, continuous improvement, and the strategic planning techniques used by senior management to change business organizations.

Many schools also spent a great deal of energy creating vision, mission, and goal statements in their quest for higher student achievement. By the early 1990s, however, it was clear that these endeavors and others, such as site-based management, while well intended, had not improved student performance. Too often, the institutional issues took precedence over the needs of the students.

Schools then made a more aggressive effort to focus instruction on raising achievement, in what became referred to as the "standards movement." Again, this concept was taken directly from business, but industry standards for products and services were not easily transferable to the intellectual development of children. Furthermore, the rules of engagement in education are fundamentally different from the rules of engagement in the business sector. In business, everyone is expendable, whereas in education, nearly everyone is protected. Moreover, education is committed to equity as well as excellence.

Although the standards movement was intended to bring focus and direction to the curriculum, it led instead to a proliferation of content to be taught in the curriculum. This can be seen in research by Dr. Robert Marzano and colleagues in *What Americans Believe Students Should Know: A Survey of U.S. Adults* (1999). The authors examined standards across all subjects and grade levels and identified 200 distinct standards with 3,093 related benchmarks. From teachers' estimates of how long it would take to teach each benchmark adequately, the researchers calculated that it would require 15,465 hours to cover all of them. Yet, students have only 9,042 hours of instructional time over the course of their K–12 careers.

The International Center for Leadership in Education conducted a survey in 1999 to identify the skills and knowledge graduates need for success in the world beyond school. The survey, reported in

The Overcrowded Curriculum (1999), asked respondents to identify the top thirty-five standards—in terms of what a high school senior should know and be able to do—from a list of content topics commonly found in states' exit standards. The top-rated skills in mathematics, science, and English language arts bear a striking resemblance to skills typically covered in career and technical education programs. Many of the lowest-rated topics remain a central focus of instruction in these disciplines.

More School Reform

When the standards movement did not translate into graduates with the skills that corporate America deemed necessary, business leaders pressed elected officials to instill more rigor into the system and to prove that students were mastering what was taught. In response, states initiated or upgraded mandatory statewide testing programs to find out what students know.

Although these testing programs have served some useful purposes, they do not measure a broad scope of knowledge. Schools do not have enough time to teach all the standards, benchmarks, performance objectives, goals, and other subcategories of standards, so states cannot test students on all of them.

While raising academic standards was a central concern of K–12 education for two decades, issues raised by business about students' inability to apply their skills and knowledge on the job did not receive widespread attention. Vocational education was the only area uniformly to embrace the necessity for students to learn how to apply their knowledge in the real world.

The New Workplace

At the conclusion of World War II, the adults in the United States, many of whom grew up during the Great Depression, wanted their children to have a better standard of living than they did. They saw higher education as the ticket to that better life. Meanwhile, Europe and Asia focused more on rebuilding their war-torn countries than on education, thus allowing American colleges and universities to have the highest academic standards in the world for the next several decades.

America's reversal of educational prominence happened at the time when technology began to reshape the workplace. By the early 1990s the academic skills needed in the workplace often surpassed the academic skills required for entry into college. Like the United States, other countries experienced the call for school reform, but they did not need to be convinced of the link between education and work. The United States, with a different value system, retreated to the old ways: raise standards and define excellence through testing. But the reality is that the tests do not measure the skills that underpin the workplace, and U.S. graduates continue to be at a disadvantage in the global and domestic marketplaces.

Another significant event that occurred in the late 1980s was the shift from big business to small business. Companies across the America began to downsize. In small companies, broad skills and the ability to handle multiple tasks are of paramount importance. Even entry-level workers are expected to be jacks-of-all-trades.

The contemporary workplace is dynamic and entrepreneurial. Approximately one-third of jobs is in flux every year, meaning that they have just been added or will be eliminated. The job security once enjoyed in big companies is no sure bet anymore. Employees must continuously reinvent themselves by seeking out the additional training and new skills that will keep them marketable. Skills and adaptability have become the new job security.

The new economy requires that employees be able to apply mathematics, science, and technical reading and writings skills in a variety of job tasks. The trend in career and technical education is to teach transferable skills via the various occupational clusters. These clusters are industry-specific enough to enable students to develop employment skills without being so limited as to track students into narrowly defined or dead-end jobs. To accomplish this, the programs provide a strong academic foundation and teach students the processes of applying this knowledge.

The work environment is always in transition, with changing equipment, tasks, and responsibilities. Technology is progressing too rapidly to train students on the latest equipment, so the trend in career and technical education is to focus on teaching the skills, concepts, and systems that underpin technology rather than how to operate a particular piece of technology.

Use Research about Learning

A growing body of education research supports the efficacy of the methodology used in career and technical education programs. Research documents that the capacity to apply knowledge to practical situations is not only an important ability for students to have, but also an effective way to improve their academic performance. Research also shows that students learn more when they are motivated to do so. In career and technical education, motivation stems from the realization that what they are learning has a practical application to the world of work.

Arnold Packer, Chairman of the Secretary's Commission on Achieving Necessary Skills (SCANS) 2000 Center at the Johns Hopkins Institute for Policy Studies, has found that "solving realistic problems motivates students to work on their academics. They have their own answer to the oft-asked question: "Why do I have to learn this?" This blend of academic, career, and computer learning helps them acquire the skills needed for successful careers while they achieve to meet state standards."

The National Research Council has found that when instruction is based on students' interests and aptitudes and is appropriate to their learning styles, students are more motivated to learn. Academic performance generally improves, for example, when students attend magnet schools and theme academies.

The research suggests that the ability to apply knowledge requires experience in using that knowledge in a variety of ways over a period of time, drawing on the same knowledge base. Career and technical education does a good job in this regard. Skill and knowledge are taught and reinforced through hands-on activities and real-world applications.

The National Research Council's comprehensive 1999 report, *How People Learn: Bridging Research and Practice,* shared key findings of the research literature on human learning, curriculum design, and the learning environment. One of those findings concerned metacognition. Metacognition occurs when a learner takes a new piece of information, debates its validity in relation to what else he or she knows about the subject, and then considers how it expands his or her understanding of the topic. Most career and technical education programs employ more metacognition activities than traditional programs, in which many students spend the school day listening to teachers disseminate knowledge. Learning by doing is the standard approach in their courses, as students use skills and knowledge to create products and model solutions to problems.

Research shows that students will try to rise to the level of expectation established for them. For career and technical education, this means having as high expectations for students' academic performance as for their performance of job-related skills.

In the technological, information-based economy, workers must be able to apply high-level, integrated academic skills on the job. As career and technical education programs redesign curriculum to embed academic standards, their students have an advantage over other students because career and technical education students also learn how to apply these skills.

See also: BUSINESS EDUCATION, *subentry on* SCHOOL; SCHOOL REFORM; TECHNOLOGY EDUCATION; VOCATIONAL SCHOOL FALLACY.

BIBLIOGRAPHY

BOTTOMS, GENE; PRESSON, ALICE; and JOHNSON, MARY. 1992. *Making High Schools Work Through Integration of Academic and Vocational Education.* Atlanta, GA: Southern Regional Education Board.

BUTTON, KENNETH; COX, KENNETH; STOUGH, ROGER; and TAYLOR, SAMANTHA. 2001. *The Long Term Educational Needs of a High-Technology Society.* Washington, DC: 21st Century Workforce Commission.

CAMPBELL, KIM. 2001. "It's Technical, Really." *Christian Science Monitor* May 1.

CHEA, TERENCE. 2000. "Panel Urges Bigger Pool for Tech Jobs." *Washington Post* July 14.

COMMITTEE FOR ECONOMIC DEVELOPMENT RESEARCH AND POLICY COMMITTEE. 2000. *Measuring What Matters: Using Assessment and Accountability to Improve Student Learning.* New York: Committee for Economic Development.

DAGGETT, WILLARD R.; KRUSE, BENEDICT; and FIELDS, GARY M. 2001. *Education as a Business Investment.* Rexford, NY: International Center for Leadership in Education.

DAGGETT, WILLARD R., and OTT, TIMOTHY E. 1999. *The Overcrowded Curriculum: Using Data to Determine Essential Skills.* Rexford, NY: International Center for Leadership in Education.

DONOVAN, M. SUZANNE; BRANSFORD, JOHN D.; and PELLEGRINO, JAMES W., eds. 1999. *How People Learn: Bridging Research and Practice.* Washington, DC: National Research Council Committee on Learning Research and Educational Practice.

HULL, DAN. 1995. *Who Are You Calling Stupid?* Waco, TX: Center for Occupational Research and Development, Inc.

JUDY, RICHARD W., and D'AMICO, CAROL. 1997. *Workforce 2020: Work and Workers in the 21st Century.* Indianapolis, IN: Hudson Institute.

MARZANO, ROBERT J.; KENDALL, JOHN S.; and CICCHINELLI, LOUIS F. 1999. *What Americans Believe Students Should Know: A Survey of U.S. Adults.* Aurora, CO: Mid-Continent Regional Educational Laboratory.

NATIONAL COMMISSION ON EXCELLENCE IN EDUCATION. 1983. *A Nation at Risk: The Imperative for Educational Reform.* Washington, DC: U.S. Government Printing Office.

PACKER, ARNOLD. 2000. "How Lessons Can Compute." *The Baltimore Sun* April 27.

RAVITCH, DIANE. 2000. *Left Back: A Century of Failed School Reforms.* New York: Simon and Schuster.

U.S. DEPARTMENT OF LABOR. 1990. *The Secretary's Commission on Achieving Necessary Skills (SCANS).* Washington, DC: U.S. Department of Labor.

U.S. DEPARTMENT OF LABOR. 1999. *Futurework: Trends and Challenges for Work in the 21st Century.* Washington, DC: U.S. Department of Labor.

WILLARD R. DAGGETT

PREPARATION OF TEACHERS

Most state and local education agencies in the United States have changed the name of vocational education to "career and technical" or "career technical" education to reflect a broader mission. The National Association of State Directors of Career Technical Education Consortium indicated that career technical education "is provided in a variety of settings and levels including middle school career exploration, secondary programs, postsecondary certificates and degrees, and customized training for employees in the workplace. Career Technical Education also provides students and adults (1) the technical skills and knowledge necessary to succeed in occupations and careers, (2) the cross-functional or workplace basics necessary for success in any occupation or career (such as problem solving, teamwork and the ability to find and use information) as well as skills for balancing family and work responsibilities, and (3) the context in which traditional academic skills and a variety of more general educational goals can be enhanced" (National Association of State Directors of Career and Technical Education website). The term *career and technical education,* rather than *vocational education,* will be used throughout this article when describing current programs and activities.

History of Pre-Service Teacher Education

In 1914 a congressional Commission on National Aid to Vocational Education was established to study the skilled worker needs and report its findings to Congress. The findings of this commission resulted in the passage of the Smith-Hughes Act in 1917—the first federally enacted legislation to promote vocational education in public high schools in America. This act provided federal funds for vocational education at the secondary level in the areas of agriculture, trades and industry, and home economics.

The Smith-Hughes Act was also the first federal legislation to make funds available to train teachers. Sections 2, 3, and 4 in the Act authorized the use of funds to be paid to states for the purpose of paying the salaries of teachers, supervisors, and directors and in the preparation of teachers, supervisors, and directors. The George-Deen Act (1936) extended the coverage of vocational education to include distributive education. The George-Barden Act Amendments (1956) extended coverage to include practical nursing and the fishery trades. The Vocational Education Act (1963) included business and office education.

Vocational education teacher requirements have often required a number of years of experience in a craft or trade prior to being employed as a teacher. In some occupational areas, some alternative state certification schemes have allowed those without a college degree, but with extensive occupational experience, to teach vocational education courses.

The educational reform movement of the late twentieth century and the beginning of the twenty-first century has had an important impact on career and technical teacher education programs. Educational reform influences in career and technical teacher education programs include increasing technical and academic achievement; increasing assessment and accountability requirements; designing meaningful instructional tasks based on real world problems; using technology; teaching teamwork and collaboration skills; and developing leadership skills.

A career and technical education teacher must also be prepared to relate to an increasingly diverse student clientele in a manner that results in higher levels of academic and technical proficiency. Furthermore, these students need to be able to reason analytically, solve complex problems, and gather and process information and data.

Organization of Career and Technical Teacher Education

Land-grant universities, state colleges and universities, church-related colleges, and private colleges are important sources of career and technical education teachers. The majority of career and technical teacher education programs are housed in departments or colleges of education. However, they are also found in other colleges or subject area departments such as Food, Agricultural, and Environmental Sciences; Business; Engineering; Human Ecology; and Professional Studies.

Career and technical teacher education faculties are charged with teaching both pre-service and in-service educational programs. Increasingly, colleges and universities are relying on adjunct and part-time faculty to teach career and technical teacher education courses. More programs are offering field-based courses in conjunction with public schools and distance education is also being used to deliver instruction.

Students are generally admitted to a career and technical teacher education program after they have earned at least a 2.5 cumulative grade point average. Other criteria for admission include requirements such as general education courses, work experience, letters of reference and successful passing of the Praxis I (academic skills) examination.

Career and technical teacher education programs include courses such as history and philosophy, methods of teaching, program planning, curriculum development, and field-based inquiry/ student teaching. At the end of their pre-service pro-

gram, students often must pass the Praxis II (subject assessments and principles of learning and teaching) test. Beginning teachers are increasingly required to pass the Praxis III (classroom performance assessments) examination by the end of their first year of teaching. The shortage of certified and/or licensed career and technical education teachers has resulted in the hiring of people from business and industry to fill teacher vacancies. Individuals from business and industry often have the technical skills required but lack the pedagogical skills and understanding needed to establish productive teaching and learning environments. People from business and industry entering teaching are often brought in under temporary licensure and required to obtain, within a specified time period, the educational competencies needed to succeed in the classroom. Individuals entering alternative licensure programs often have the option of being a part of field-based or cohort-based courses.

In-Service and Staff Development Programs

Career and technical education teachers are expected to meet their students' needs for career development, technical and academic achievement, and technology skills. Career and technical education students must also demonstrate higher order skills in reasoning, problem solving, and collaborative work. At the same time, teachers are faced with serving a more diverse student clientele. Finally, the rapidly changing workplace and technological revolution require ongoing curriculum revisions.

Career and technical education teachers participate in professional development using a variety of techniques. These include techniques such as formal education courses, interactions with business and industry, workshops, seminars, conferences, literature, and networking with other career and technical education professionals.

Beginning career and technical education teachers, while facing the same expectations and demands required of all teachers, are also faced with the need to refine their pedagogical skills. Most beginning teachers are required to participate in teacher induction programs designed to help them survive their first year of teaching and pass the Praxis III (classroom performance assessment) examination. Often teacher induction programs are offered through cooperative efforts of local school districts, colleges and universities, state departments of education, and professional career and technical education teachers' organizations.

Major Trends and Issues in Teacher Preparation

Career and technical teacher education is affected by a number of trends and issues. Four of these major trends and issues are: approaches to teaching and learning, infrastructure, teacher licensure and standards, and innovative programs.

Approaches to teaching and learning. Behavioral, cognitive, constructivist, and contextual learning environments have all been used in vocational and career and technical education. However, the psychological approaches in career and technical teacher education changed significantly in the last half of the twentieth century.

From about 1920 to 1970, behaviorists such as B. F. Skinner theorized that human behavior was highly shaped by its consequences. Later, cognitive psychologists portrayed learners as being active processors of information and assigned priority to the knowledge and perspective students bring to their learning. Cognitive theorists stressed the role of thinking in the learning process and believed that the teacher was to provide learners with opportunities and incentives to learn. Cognitive development theorists have more recently taken a constructivist view of learning that incorporates learner-centered teaching practices, problem-based learning, contextual teaching and learning experiences, integrated academic and vocational curriculum, and authentic assessments. Career and technical education teachers, in working with their students, have routinely used learner-centered approaches.

Contextual teaching and learning represents yet another approach to teaching and learning used by career and technical education. Contextual teaching and learning encourages students to employ their academic understandings and abilities in a variety of in- and out-of-school contexts by asking them to solve simulated or real-world problems both alone and with others. Career and technical education teachers often use contextual teaching strategies to help students make connections with their roles and responsibilities as family members, citizens, students, and workers.

Infrastructure. High quality career and technical teacher education programs require personnel (e.g., faculty, staff, and students), productivity tools (such as curriculum, technology, professional develop-

ment opportunities, supplies, and telecommunication technology), and physical facilities (buildings, libraries, classrooms, and laboratories). Unfortunately, higher education—for the most part—has failed to invest in career and technical education personnel, productivity tools, and physical facilities to support quality teacher education programs.

Teacher licensure and standards. The licensure of career and technical teachers varies greatly across states, and can be obtained in a number of different ways depending upon the requirements established by each state. Several types of licenses are available, including initial (or probationary), regular (or permanent), emergency, private school, and alternative. Although numerous routes are available to obtaining a teaching license, very little is known about the effects of these licenses on student achievement.

The National Board for Professional Teaching Standards was created to recognize teachers who have been judged by their peers as being accomplished, making sound professional judgments about students' best interests, and acting effectively on those judgments. As of 2001 there were 342 Nationally Board Certified Early Adolescence through Young Adulthood/Career and Technical Education teachers.

Innovative programs. One of the major suggestions emanating from policy studies for improving education has been to ensure that students are achieving at higher levels of academic and technical competency. Career and technical teacher education has a long history of responding to national needs and initiatives. Among the newer developments in career and technical education are career clusters, career pathways, career academies, and exemplary programs and promising practices.

Seventeen broad clusters have been identified that include all entry-level through professional-level occupations. The goal for these career clusters was to create curricular frameworks designed to organize knowledge and skills in a relevant manner that would help prepare students to transition successfully from high school to postsecondary education and employment in a career area, or both. These career clusters include agriculture and natural resources; business and administration; education and training; health science; human services; law and public safety; government and public administration; scientific research/engineering; arts; audio/video technology and communication; architecture and construction; finance; hospitality and tourism; information technology; manufacturing; retail/wholesale sales and service; and transportation, distribution, and logistics.

Career pathways are a series of academic, technological, and occupational courses and other educational experiences with a career focus in which students participate. Through a continuum of career-focused programs, students are provided with multiple pathways to employment and postsecondary education. Career pathways include rigorous academics as well as technical skills, in order for students to be prepared for both postsecondary education and for careers.

Career academies align clusters of courses around specific career areas, with teachers collaborating to develop integrated academic and vocational programs in a personalized learning environment, delivered over a period of years. These academies are designed to increase engagement and academic performance, students' personal and academic development, preparation for college and work, postsecondary attainment, and successful employment. Many large city school districts, such as Philadelphia, are organizing schools around career academies.

Teacher educators also look for examples of high quality career and technical education programs to use as illustrations in preparing prospective teachers. Wesley Budke, Debra Bragg, and others identified exemplary and promising secondary and postsecondary career and technical education programs in 2000 and 2001. The exemplary secondary career and technical education programs included programs in culinary arts and hospitality services, digital design, tech prep electronics technology, welding technology fabrication, computer graphics design, computer network administrator, culinary academy, and early childhood education/careers in education. The exemplary postsecondary career and technical education programs included programs in associate-degree nursing, telecommunications, integrated manufacturing management, and refugee targeted assistance. This effort to identify and disseminate information about exemplary and promising programs is ongoing.

See also: AGRICULTURAL EDUCATION; BUSINESS EDUCATION, *subentries on* PREPARATION OF TEACHERS, SCHOOL; EXPERIENTIAL EDUCATION; TEACHER EDUCATION; TEACHING, *subentry on* KNOWLEDGE BASES OF; TECHNOLOGY EDUCATION.

BIBLIOGRAPHY

BERNS, ROBERT G., and ERIKSON, PATRICIA M. 2001. *Contextual Teaching and Learning: Preparing Students for the New Economy.* Columbus: Ohio State University, the National Dissemination Center for Career and Technical Education.

BROWN, BETTINA L. 1998. *Applying Constructivism in Vocational and Career Education.* Information Series No. 378. Columbus: Ohio State University, Center on Education and Training for Employment.

BRUENING, THOMAS H.; SCANLON, DENNIS C.; HODES, CAROL; DHITAL, PURANDHAR; SHAO, XIAORONG; and LIU, SHIH-TSEN. 2001. *The Status of Career and Technical Education Teacher Preparation Programs.* Minneapolis: University of Minnesota, the National Research Center for Career and Technical Education.

BUDKE, WESLEY, E., and BRAGG, DEBRA D. 2000. *Sharing What Works: Identifying Successful Programs in Secondary and Postsecondary Career and Technical Education.* Information Series No. 376. Columbus: Ohio State University, the National Dissemination Center for Career and Technical Education.

Carl D. Perkins Vocational and Applied Technology Amendments of 1998. U.S. Public Law 1105-332. *U.S. Code.* Vol. 20, sec. 2301 nt.

EDUCATIONAL RESOURCE INFORMATION CENTER (ERIC). 1998. *Contextual Teaching and Learning: Preparing Teachers to Enhance Student Success in and Beyond School.* Columbus, OH: ERIC Clearinghouse on Adult, Career and Vocational Education and ERIC Clearinghouse on Teaching and Teacher Education.

George Barden Act Amendments of 1957. U.S. Public Law 84-911.

George-Deen Vocational Education Act of 1936. U.S. Public Law 74-673. *U.S. Code.* Vol. 20 ch. 541, 49 Stat. 1428 (20 U.S.C. Sec. 1241). *et seq i.*

JOERGER, RICHARD M., and BREMER, CHRISTINE D. 2001. *Teacher Induction Programs: A Strategy for Improving the Professional Experience of Beginning Career and Technical Education Teachers.* Columbus: Ohio State University, the National Dissemination Center for Career and Technical Education.

McCaslin, N. L., and Parks, Darrell. 2002. *Teacher Education in Career and Technical Education: Background and Policy Implications for the New Millennium.* Columbus: Ohio State University, the National Dissemination Center for Career and Technical Education.

Rojewski, Jay W. 2002. *Preparing the Workforce of Tomorrow: A Conceptual Framework for Career and Technical Education.* Columbus: Ohio State University, the National Dissemination Center for Career and Technical Education.

Skinner, B. F. 1953. *Science and Human Behavior,* 2nd edition. Boston: Allyn and Bacon.

Smith Hughes Act of 1917. U.S. Public Law 64-347. (*Vocational Education Act, 1917.*) *U.S. Code.* Vol. 20, sec. 1145, 16–28.

Vocational Education Act of 1963. U.S. Public Law 88-210. *U.S. Code.* Vol. 20, secs. 1241 *et seq.*

Vocational Education Amendments of 1968. U.S. Public Law 90-576. *U.S. Code.* Vol. 20, sec. 6, 11 nt, 158 nt, 240, 241c, 611, 886nt, 119c 2119c-4, 1201, 1221, 1226, 1241–1248 and others; *U.S. Code.* Vol. 42, sec. 2809 nt.

INTERNET RESOURCES

National Association of State Directors of Career and Technical Education. 2002. "Career and Technical Education: An Essential Component of the Total Education System." <www.nasdvtec.org>.

National Board for Professional Teaching Standards. 2002. <www.nbpts.org/about/index.html>.

U.S. Department of Education. 2000. "Career Clusters." <www.ed.gov/offices/OVAE/clusters/index.html>.

N. L. McCaslin
Darrel Parks

INTERNATIONAL CONTEXT

Education and training have often been considered polar extremes, the first being the development of the mind and the latter the mastery of strictly practical endeavors. But the two worlds of practical and conceptual endeavors are less distant than they may seem, and these simplistic views of education and training are misguided.

Indeed, there are definitional problems concerning education and training, leading to misguided policies. There is a need for a clear understanding of the overlaps and contrasts between the two concepts.

There is a long and old controversy in the literature opposing education and training. The Roman rhetorician Quintilian claimed that oratory was more useful than philosophy, thereby stating the superiority of training over education. But for many centuries education was closer to philosophy than to applied endeavors.

Some educators use the word *training* in a derogatory way, as if to suggest that the learning is intellectually shallow or that it goes with attempts to educate the poor. In contrast, some trainers refer to education as vacuous, fuzzy, and rambling learning that is good only for wasting the time of students.

What Vocational Training Offers

Both views, however, are too narrow and misleading. When dealing with less-schooled students, vocational subjects can be used to motivate and to create an environment that is familiar to them. Good training may function as a conduit for the best possible education for students less ready for abstraction. By using practical situations as start and end points, abstract concepts can be introduced and mastered by students who otherwise would be very low achievers in academic schools.

The environment created by good vocational schools can give students a sense of getting closer to a concrete job. This can in turn generate a degree of motivation and sense of self-efficacy that is conducive to the mastery of abstract concepts that would leave students cold and aloof when taught at academic schools that have difficulties in recreating environments that motivate low-achieving students.

Good vocational training makes use of the context of the practical subjects to teach mathematics, writing, reading, and science. Students are asked to read the instructions of what they are doing and write down the procedures they will execute. Concrete workshop situations are conceived, for instance, to have students convert inches to centimeters, Fahrenheit to Celsius, and so on. In other words, proportion is learned as a by-product of solving shop problems. Mathematics is smuggled into the practicalities of shop work. In fact, good training institutions have different versions of mathematics, one for machinists, another for electricians, and so on.

As research in the psychology of learning suggests, the mastery of subjects increases when the contexts in which phenomena are examined are fully familiar to the students. Experiments have shown that a physical principle is better understood when the students are given the broad context in which it applies. For instance, it has been shown that students acquired a better grasp of the concept of density when they were shown a clip from the film *Raiders of the Lost Ark* in which the hero, Indiana Jones, has to replace a golden skull sitting on a platform with his bag filled with rocks, both which weighed the same. Students were asked to estimate the weight of the golden skull by measuring the approximate volume of a human skull and multiplying it by the relative density of gold. What good training does is to present inside the workshop such concrete problems based on concrete needs arising in the practical tasks to be performed.

Nevertheless, what training offers is merely the possibility to tap into this potential. There is nothing automatic about it. Training can fail to use these opportunities. Training that is only training is bad training or merely too shallow to go beyond the transmission of some dexterity. How to put out a fire or how to unclog a pipe are useful pieces of knowledge in their own right and need to be taught. But they are essentially different from longer training programs that contain more conceptual and theoretical structures.

The "basic skills" movement consists of improving the knowledge of the fundamental literacy and numeracy skills of workers who are learning a trade or have already mastered the more practical and manual aspects of their occupations. The essence of the successful strategies, however, is to use the same workplace operations as a scaffold on which to build the conceptual or cognitive skills that are missing. Workers learn how to read by reading the same manual that they need to read to perform their job correctly.

Vocational contents can be an ideal context in which to plant cognitive development of a higher order. Thinking skills and good reading and writing habits can be developed while doing practical tasks that lead to marketable skills.

By the same token, academic education may also resort to practical endeavors in order to carry the more general message. Laboratory classes try to do this, and the *Indiana Jones* example illustrates more deliberate attempts to bring context to learning. Theory, after all, involves the generalization and conceptualization of real-world observations. Formulas written on the blackboard merely display packaged and sanitized versions of the intense intellectual effort that was required to arrive at them. The idea of having students "rediscover" physical principles goes in the same direction.

Developments in Technology and Work Organization

This reasoning implies that the differences between education and training have always been exaggerated and that most reputable training programs are education as much as training. Recent developments in technology and work organization, however, seem to be blurring even further the distinction between education and training. In industrialized countries, a very significant share of manufacturing activities have changed considerably and incorporate new technologies, particularly those based on microprocessors and the variety of automation techniques that result from them. Some successful industrializing countries are definitely moving in the same direction.

New production technologies require more reading, more writing, more applied mathematics, and more science. In the past, these cognitive skills were, at best, a means to master a trade (e.g., one needs to know how to read to take the machinist course because some of the instruction is written in books or handouts). But these cognitive skills are becoming part and parcel of the occupational profile. For example, reading is directly useful for the performance of the core tasks of the occupation. Could it then be said that reading and mathematics are now vocational subjects? For that reason, most training programs could benefit from a little more emphasis on language, mathematics, and science, as occurs in the best courses and apprenticeships. This is increasingly happening in Germany, in the American tech-prep programs, and in the new generation of SENAI courses in Brazil.

While learning an occupation, the trainee may have an ideal opportunity to develop the same general skills that are taught in academic schools, that is, a general education. But this will not happen spontaneously. The integration of theory and practice, of shop activities with general principles of science, can be the result only of deliberate and well-informed efforts. Training programs should not underestimate the potential offered by such integration or the difficulties of achieving it. But there are good examples of these ideas. For instance, the new versions of the traditional Latin American "methodical series," as well as new methods developed in countries such as the United States (tech prep, School to Work) and Germany (key qualifications), have good track records.

In short, vocational subjects can be used to motivate and to create an environment that is familiar to the students. Good training may function as a conduit for the best possible education for students less ready for abstraction. By the same token, academic education may also resort to practical endeavors in order to carry the more general message.

Differences and Similarities between Training and Education

There are conceptual differences between the roles of vocational training and education. Yet, as mentioned, the borderline between training and education is quite blurred. In its purest version, education is knowledge removed from practical applications (e.g., learning astronomy is pure education, except for those who plan to become professional astronomers). At the other extreme, pure training is a version of skill preparation that does not explore the theoretical implications of the tasks being learned (e.g., learning how to use a saw and a jack plane without learning drafting and the requisite mathematics). In most cases, however, the two are combined.

Good training and a good education are equally good—and actually very similar in nature—when they promote the broad conceptual and analytical development of the trainee. By the same token, a good education is often linked to applied endeavors that turn theoretical knowledge into a practical skill. The difference is mostly one of intention. Education uses the practical or occupational content to obtain a deeper mastery of theory, being somewhat unconcerned with the application of the knowledge in the marketplace. Training starts with the clear goal of preparing for an existing occupation, the theory being a necessary component to prepare a better worker for that position.

Yet, despite all the merits of training, it is not a cost-efficient substitute for good schools for all. By contrast, a solid basic education is the best preparation for a wide range of jobs. In addition, a good basic education shortens the length of training required. In other words, the need to develop a good training system does not replace the (perhaps) stronger imperative to develop a good general education system.

Workers with a good mix of practical skills and conceptual understanding of technology can adjust more easily to new and different occupations, grow in their careers, and adjust to technological changes. The real issue is not general versus superspecialized training but the solidity and depth of the basic skills that go together with specialized training.

A first element to understanding the differences and similarities between training and education is to consider that the presence of training contents that may be applicable at the workplace does not vary inversely with the presence of fundamental concepts and abstraction. Both poetry and solid-state physics are rich in abstraction. The first has scarce direct applicability at the workplace. The second has ample utilization. Basket weaving has hardly any abstraction or conceptualization and finds little demand in modern societies. Cutting hair offers little in abstract thinking but there are ample economic applications for this skill.

It is necessary to stress that theory and practice are not the extremes of a single continuum but independent concepts that admit all possible combinations of highs and lows, as exemplified above. Fortunately, to have the high theoretical and conceptual content that educates and sharpens the mind, one does not have to forego learning the practicalities of life and work. Both what is called vocational training and what is called education of all sorts have both the theory and the practice. The main point here is that occupational training that fetches a good market is as good or better than any other environment to educate the mind in the fundamental concepts that are usually found in good education.

Training should not be understood as something poor in theory and conceptualization. It can be rich or poor. Education should not be understood as something helplessly unpractical. In fact, it may be removed from immediate applications or it may be very close to them. There are no good reasons to be concerned with the differences between education and training instead of offering learning opportunities that have both.

Conclusion

Abstract subjects that are removed from the everyday life of students offer a more arid ground for learning. Such subjects as Latin declensions, French irregular verbs, underground geological layers, the successions of kings of France, and the capitals of African states are not topics that fascinate the average student. Hence, they are not the ideal place to graft the broad basic skills that constitute an education for a modern society. Vocational schools can avoid these motivational difficulties by bringing in the world of the factory, with its practicalities and the inherent motivation of learning some skills that have immediate market value. Nevertheless, not everything that happens in the factory is ideal for the process of learning. In particular, the factory routines teach mostly how to deal with repetitive activities. This is a worthy objective of short training courses and for the preparation of workers who lack the prerequisites for further development. This may be justified in many cases, but it is not what is considered the optimal environment for broad learning. But equally important to understand is that many interesting, motivating, or even fascinating practical applications of the concepts and theories taught in academic schools may fail to have immediate demand in the marketplace—even though, indirectly, all good education ends up being valuable in the world of work. Learning statistics by dealing with Formula 1 auto racing data is as good as any other method of motivating students and leading them to complex concepts. However, newspapers rarely include advertisements for jobs involving the analysis of Formula 1 data.

See also: CURRICULUM, INTERNATIONAL; INTERNATIONAL GAP IN TECHNOLOGY, THE; SECONDARY EDUCATION, *subentry on* INTERNATIONAL ISSUES; VOCATIONAL SCHOOL FALLACY.

BIBLIOGRAPHY

CARNEVALE, ANTHONY; GAINER, LEILA; and MELTZER, ANN. 1988. *Workplace Basics: The Skills Employers Want.* Alexandria, VA: American Society for Training and Development.

CASTRO, CLAUDIO DE MOURA. 1988. "The Right Courses for the Wrong Jobs? Or Vice-Versa?" In *Managing Human Development,* ed. Khadifer Haq and Uner Kirdar. Islamabad, Pakistan: North South Round Table.

CASTRO, CLAUDIO DE MOURA, and ANDRADE, A. C. 1990. "Supply and Demand Mismatches in Training: Can Anything Be Done?" *International Labour Review* 129(3).

CASTRO, CLAUDIO DE MOURA; ANDRADE, A. C.; and OLIVEIRA, J. B. A. 1991. "Education for All and the Roles of Training." Paper prepared for the Regional United Nations Educational, Scientific and Cultural Organization Conference on Educational for All, Cairo, Egypt.

COGNITION AND TECHNOLOGY GROUP AT VANDERBILT. 1991. "Anchored Instruction and Its Relationship to Situated Cognition." *Educational Researcher* 19(6):2–10.

ELAN, M. 1989. *A Critical Introduction to the Post-Fordist Debate: Technology, Markets, and Institutions.* Linkoping, Sweden: Linkoping University, Department of Technology and Social Change.

ELIASSON, GUNNAR. 1987. *The Knowledge Base of an Industrial Economy.* Stockholm, Sweden: Almqvist and Wiksell.

INTERAMERICAN DEVELOPMENT BANK. SUSTAINABLE DEVELOPMENT DEPARTMENT. 2000. "Vocational and Technical Training: A Strategy for the IDB." Washington, DC: Interamerican Development Bank, Sustainable Development Department.

RAIZEN, S. 1994. "Learning and Work: The Research Base." In *Vocational Education and Training for Youth: Toward Coherent Policy and Practice,* ed. Laurel McFarland and Margaret Vickers. Paris: Organisation for Economic Co-operation and Development.

U.S. DEPARTMENT OF LABOR. 1990. *The Bottom Line: Basic Skills in the Workplace.* Washington, DC: U.S. Department of Labor.

CLAUDIO DE MOURA CASTRO

VOCATIONAL EDUCATION

See: VOCATIONAL AND TECHNICAL EDUCATION.

VOCATIONAL SCHOOL FALLACY

Few articles in the field of international and comparative education have been as influential in academic circles and among some donor-agency personnel as Philip Foster's "The Vocational School Fallacy in Development Planning" (1965). This article went to the heart of the long-running (and continuing) debate about whether schools and their curricula can influence society through changing student attitudes towards jobs and work—or whether schools and their pupils are themselves much more influenced by the surrounding economy and by the patterns of work and rewards that exist in the surrounding urban and rural areas. During the period immediately following the independence of many African countries, it was commonplace to suggest that schools could deliver all kinds of attitude change (e.g., towards nation building, good citizenship, and rural development). Foster, however, argued that "schools are remarkably clumsy instruments for inducing large-scale changes in underdeveloped areas" (1965a, p. 144). Foster's message came at a time when a whole series of innovations were being introduced to deal with a sudden surge in unemployment in the developing world among those who had finished primary school, as well as the flight of young people from subsistence agriculture in rural areas. The most famous of these schemes was Education for Self-Reliance, developed by Tanzania's first president, Julius Nyerere.

Foster's warning about the limitations of schooling to change society arrived during the 1960s, a decade that saw many new and more instrumental approaches to schooling (from manpower planning to educational planning). These were frequently about engaging the schools in the creation of high-level manpower for the rapidly Africanizing civil service, but they also implied that schools could directly contribute to the modernization of traditional societies.

Foster's critique of these visions for engaging schools in the transformation of their surrounding societies was derived from an in-depth analysis of Ghana and from a detailed knowledge of its educational history prior to independence in 1957, when it was known as the Gold Coast. Foster was able to argue that, for well over a hundred years, Western education had been responsible for a massive amount of social change in this area, but that schools had very seldom functioned in the manner expected by the educators and the policymakers. In the new era of rational education planning and the new discipline of the economics of education (which involved looking at education as human capital and calculat-

ing the costs and benefits of different mixes of education), Foster's research was a vivid testimony to what he called the "unplanned consequences of educational growth" (1965b, p. 303).

At the heart of this debate lay the issue of vocationalism and its relationship to economic growth. Should not schools, the argument went, and especially those in predominantly agricultural societies where the formal sector of the economy could only absorb a very small proportion of the economically active population, keenly prepare young people with a substantial measure of the practical, agricultural, and technical skills needed for the transformation of their societies? Foster's answer was that, in Ghana, missionary societies, colonial governments, and the new independence government had frequently been attracted by the apparent logic of this position, and had sought to use schools in this instrumental way. But the plain truth was that "the educational history of the Gold Coast is strewn with the wreckage of schemes" based on these assumptions (1965a, p. 145).

Foster's explanation for these failures was that pupils are very realistic and are able to work out what is in their best career interests, regardless of the orientations schools seek to provide. In particular, he argued that schools had been very shrewdly used by pupils as a gateway to the modern sector of the economy—and as an escape from poor prospects in many rural areas. The core argument of the vocational school fallacy, according to Foster, is that "the schools themselves can do little about this. So long as parents and students perceive the function of education in this manner, agricultural education and vocational instruction *in the schools* is [sic] not likely to have a determinative influence on the occupational aspirations and destinations of students. Aspirations are determined largely the individual's perception of opportunities within the exchange sector of the economy, destinations by the *actual* structure of opportunities in that sector" (1965a, p. 151).

Impact of the Vocational School Fallacy

It could be argued that the vocational school fallacy is much better known by students and professors of international and comparative education than by policymakers in ministries of education. Policymakers in many countries continue to be attracted by the possibility of using the school system to change young peoples' attitudes towards different kinds of work and employment. With the reduction in the number of good jobs in the formal sector of many African economies, the school system in the early twenty-first century is being asked to reorient young people towards skills for self-employment. Such optimism tends to be uninformed about the complexity of entering dynamic forms of self-employment.

One exception to the suggestion that policymakers have been largely immune to the message of the vocational school fallacy can be found in the policies of the World Bank. There is strong evidence that acceptance of the vocational school fallacy was one reason why the World Bank, in the late 1970s and early 1980s, turned its back on its earlier widespread policy of supporting *vocationalised,* or *diversified,* secondary education.

The question of whether the vocational school fallacy is still relevant has been addressed in a study conducted by Kenneth King and Chris Martin during 1999 and 2000. This study sought to revisit in Ghanaian secondary schools the same questions and debates that Foster explored in post-independence Ghana. The results confirmed many of Foster's findings about the impact of the economy on education, but, intriguingly, they also suggest that there does, in fact, seem to be a substantial school influence on attitudes towards employment and self-employment and that this is connected in some way to the vocational options in school.

See also: SUB-SAHARAN AFRICA; VOCATIONAL AND TECHNICAL EDUCATION, *subentry on* INTERNATIONAL CONTEXT.

BIBLIOGRAPHY

FOSTER, PHILLIP. 1965a. "The Vocational School Fallacy in Development Planning." In *Education and Economic Development,* ed. Arnold A. Anderson and Mary Jean Bowman. Chicago: Aldine.

FOSTER, PHILLIP. 1965b. *Education and Social Change in Ghana.* London: Routledge.

HEYNEMAN, STEPHEN P. 1985. "Diversifying Secondary School Curricula in Developing Countries: An Implementation History and Some Policy Options." *International Journal of Educational Development* 5(4):283–288.

HEYNEMAN, STEPHEN P. 1987. "Curriculum Economics in Secondary Education: An Emerging Crisis in Developing Crisis." *Prospects* 18(1)63–74.

KING, KENNETH, and MARTIN, CHRIS. 2002. "The Vocational School Fallacy Revisited: Education, Aspiration, and Work in Ghana, 1959–2000." *International Journal of Educational Development* 22:5–26.

KENNETH KING

VOLUNTEER WORK

Volunteer work offers an opportunity for individuals and communities to engage in activities that affect the common good of society. For young people, volunteer work provides a way to gain a variety of useful skills, to understand the community in which they live, and to enhance community life. The community, in turn, fosters the development of a citizenry that is involved in creating a better democracy.

There is an increasing emphasis in schools on the development of character in students, through the study of community issues, actions to address these issues, and reflection on the experience. Many schools are moving students from volunteerism to service-learning initiatives within the curriculum so that students at all levels can develop cooperation, empathy, citizenship, and self-esteem. For example, the Kentucky Education Reform Act of 1990 mandates graduation requirements that emphasize application and integration of community-service work and learning.

Elementary and secondary schools have devised a variety of ways to integrate volunteerism into their schools and community. In some cases, students are left to their own motivations to engage in service to the community through acts of volunteerism. These volunteer experiences can take the form of a one-time involvement in a community agency or event, or can result in a sustained relationship over a period of time with a particular service organization in the community.

Many schools have moved from an emphasis on volunteerism to an involvement by students that connect their service with the curriculum. For example, one elementary school focuses on service to the elderly. As part of the history curriculum, a history of the community was produced after students interviewed older citizens and created a collection of their stories. In art classes, the students produced artwork as gifts for senior members of the community. In math, students helped older adults with grocery shopping, and older adults were able to help students with math problems that arose regarding product pricing.

Some schools have made service a requirement for graduation, though there is debate regarding the merits of requiring service of all students. Some believe that schools should encourage service, but not make it a requirement and that required service is a contradiction in terms. Others argue that service is a responsibility, a debt due to society, and that it is every citizen's civic duty to contribute to the community. Volunteer service requirements vary from having students enroll in a service class in addition to spending a certain amount of hours in a service activity, while other schools require only the service commitment.

Another approach to engage students in volunteer activities is for the school and an organization to partner in a common initiative. Community organizations that have an investment in fostering a service ethic among a new generation of citizens should be sought out by schools for a partnership.

Engaging students with underserved populations and diverse populations in a community usually builds bridges that link the students with individuals and initiatives with whom they might otherwise never have the opportunity to develop and nurture relationships of understanding and reciprocity. Experiences of this nature enable students to ascertain community assets and needs and gain perspective on how to cooperatively develop community-building initiatives. It can also help students understand issues of social injustice and move them toward moral deliberation and critical thinking about societal issues.

Another option schools have implemented is in-school service. Many programs look within the school community for service activities. Cross-age tutoring, school improvement projects, and mentoring are examples of beneficial student service activities.

Institutions of higher education look to create an "engaged campus," where boundaries are blurred between campus and community, and between knowledge and practice. A campus that is engaged with the surrounding community is not just located in a community, but is connected in an intimate way to the public purposes and aspirations of community life itself.

Many campuses also distinguish between acts of volunteerism and academic service-learning experiences. Offices of volunteer activities on college campuses work with community partners to enlist students to provide much needed hands-on aid to the community. These experiences are authorized and supported by the institution in order to contribute to an organized, efficient, effective, and sustainable effort with students and the community. Many of the social organizations on college campuses include volunteerism as a part of their mission of service. In addition, many students act out of their own intrinsic motivation and sense of civic responsibility to become active volunteers in their community.

While volunteerism is supported and promoted in the student affairs divisions of colleges and universities, academic service-learning is being strongly integrated into the curricular offerings of institutions of higher education. Service-learning usually has a two-fold goal: (1) meeting community needs and providing meaningful learning experiences for the students; and (2) enlivening the public service mission of the institution while becoming engaged in the life of the local community.

Volunteerism does not necessarily produce the same outcomes as a service-learning component in the curriculum. When service learning is integrated into the curriculum, it is desired that students learn and develop through active participation in thoughtfully organized service in the community, and that this service meets the needs of the community, is coordinated with school and community activities, helps foster civic responsibility, is integrated into the academic curriculum or educational components of community service programs, and provides structured time for students to reflect on the service experience.

Volunteerism and academic service learning are considered important components in the educational process for building a stronger democracy. Emphasis on curricular and extracurricular means of moving students toward civic engagement has become a focal point of teaching and learning in elementary, secondary, and postsecondary educational institutions.

See also: COMMUNITY EDUCATION; EXPERIENTIAL EDUCATION; SERVICE LEARNING.

BIBLIOGRAPHY

Community Service/Service Learning: An Implementor's Guide and Resource Manual. 1996. ERIC Document ED399239.

DUCKENFIELD, MARTY, and WRIGHT JAN, eds. 1995. *Pocket Guide to Service Learning.* Clemson, SC: National Dropout Prevention Center.

FELTMAN, CARL I. 1994. *Service Learning for All Students.* Bloomington, IN: Phi Delta Kappa Educational Foundation.

GUGERTY, CATHERINE R., and SWEZEY, ERIN D. 1996. "Developing Campus-Community Relationships." In *Service Learning in Higher Education: Concepts and Practices,* ed. Barbara Jacoby. San Francisco: Jossey-Bass.

HOLLANDER, ELIZABETH. 1998. "Picturing the Engaged Campus." In *Service Matters,* ed. Michael Rothman. Providence, RI: Campus Compact.

SHARON SHIELDS
BRAD GRAY

VOUCHERS, SCHOOL

See: CONSTITUTIONAL REQUIREMENTS GOVERNING AMERICAN EDUCATION; PRIVATE SCHOOLING.

VYGOTSKY, LEV (1896–1934)

Fifty years after his death, Lev Semyonich Vygotsky attracted the attention of Western psychologists and educators for his theory of cognitive development. In contrast to other cognitive perspectives, Vygotsky accorded a central role to culture and social interaction in the development of complex thinking. In addition, he advocated the study of children's unfolding development of cognitive processes, and pioneered a research method to accomplish this purpose. He also contributed ideas to pedology (child study) and defectology (special education) that anticipated current views.

A humanist and intellectual, Vygotsky graduated in 1913 with a gold medal from the private Jewish gymnasium in his native Russian province. Fluent in French and German, he studied philosophy and literature at Shanyavsky People's University while completing a master's degree in law at Moscow Uni-

versity. Returning home in 1917, he taught at various institutes, and began reading widely in psychology and education.

Vygotsky's invitation to join the Institute of Experimental Psychology in Moscow in 1924, his official entry into psychology, was an accident of history. The disappearance of old professional hierarchies in the reorganization of Soviet society and the directive to redesign psychology consistent with Marxist philosophy created an opportunity for new ideas. Thus, Vygotsky joined a discipline for which he had had no formal training.

After completing his doctoral dissertation, "The Psychology of Art," in 1925, Vygotsky pursued his goals of reconstructing psychology as a unified social science and explaining both the origins and development of human consciousness. His rationale for this major task, discussed in his paper "The Crisis in Psychology," foreshadowed the views of modern postpositivist philosophers of science. Specifically, research lacked a unifying theory, and as a result, had produced conflicting or unrelated findings. Vygotsky sought to remedy this problem.

In his brief ten-year career, interrupted by severe bouts of tuberculosis, Vygotsky's demanding schedule included lecturing throughout the U.S.S.R., organizing research projects, and conducting clinical work. His writing, undertaken late at night and during his hospitalizations, was banned in the U.S.S.R. in 1936 for twenty years for "bourgeois thinking." This charge originated from the fact that Vygotsky had incorporated ideas from European and American anthropologists, linguists, psychologists, and zoologists into his work. In his thinking, Vygotsky applied dialectical synthesis in which a perspective (thesis) is negated by an opposing view (antithesis). Their interaction produces a synthesis in the form of a novel development or idea. Vygotsky reviewed and contrasted ideas from a variety of fields, fusing many of them into a qualitatively new explanation of cognitive development (synthesis).

Misinterpretations of Vygotsky's work have occurred because, until the 1990s, only a few fragmented ideas, taken out of context, had been translated into English. Thus, the long-term impact of his thinking is yet to be determined.

Cultural-Historical Theory

Applying dialectical synthesis, Vygotsky noted the Marxist concept of the influence of tool invention on human mental life (thesis) and the anthropological view of the role of culture in human development (antithesis). His resolution was the designation of cultural signs and symbols as psychological tools, which he defined as instruments of cognitive development (synthesis). Their importance is that early humans created signs (simple psychological tools) and initiated progress toward complex thinking in the species (phylogeny). For the individual in society, the task is to appropriate the symbol systems of one's culture to develop the related forms of reasoning (ontogeny).

In other words, the traditional role of signs and symbols, such as human speech, written language, and algebraic and mathematical symbols, is to serve as carriers of both meaning and sociocultural patterns. Vygotsky, however, emphasized a second essential role, that of assisting individuals to master complex cognitive functions that are not fully developed prior to adolescence. Referred to by Vygotsky as complex or higher cognitive functions, these capabilities are voluntary (self-regulated) attention, categorical perception, conceptual thinking, and logical memory.

Of particular importance is that Vygotsky considered higher cognitive functioning, the cultural development of behavior, and the mastery of one's behavior by internal processes as equivalent. That is, the higher cognitive functions, which require self-mastery, develop through a complex dialectical process from given biological functions. The process requires the child's mastery of the external materials of cultural reasoning, which become internal mechanisms of thinking.

Vygotsky's conceptualization anticipated subsequent discussions of the need to develop self-regulated learners who can direct and manage their own learning and thinking. Unlike these perspectives, which have had limited success in teaching specific self-regulatory strategies for particular situations, Vygotsky identified two general requirements for developing self-directed thinking. First, higher cognitive functions emerge only after students develop conscious awareness and some control of their own thought processes. Second, school instruction should focus on developing these broad capabilities, which, in turn, develops self-regulation.

The lengthy process required to develop self-mastery and the higher cognitive functions is illustrated in Vygotsky's identification of the four stages

of learning to use symbols for thinking. In developing logical memory, for example, symbol use progresses from preintellectual (child cannot master his or her behavior by organizing selected stimuli) to internalization in which individuals construct self-generated symbols as memory aids.

Essential to cognitive development is the social interaction between the learner and a knowledgeable adult. Development of the higher cognitive functions depends on situations in which the adult commands the learner's attention, focuses his or her perception, or guides the learner's conceptual thinking. Formally stated, any higher cognitive function, such as self-regulated attention, categorical perception, or conceptual thinking, was first external in the form of a social relationship between two people. Then, through the learner's activity, it becomes internalized as an intracognitive function.

Vygotsky's emphasis on the dynamics of development is reflected in his critique of psychological research for studying already developed or fossilized behaviors. Instead, research methods should capture the processes of development. Vygotsky's double-stimulation method placed learners in problem-solving situations that were above their natural capacities. Available nearby were aids, such as colored cards or pictures. Vygotsky and his co-workers studied the ways learners of different ages struggled or successfully used these aids, documenting changes in learner activity and accompanying changes in cognitive functioning.

Education and Cognitive Development

Two influential Vygotskian concepts are *the role of inner speech* and *the zone of proximal development*. In contrast to the Swiss psychologist Jean Piaget, Vygotsky maintained that the child's external self-focused speech during activities did not disappear. Instead, through a dialectical transformation, it became inner speech that guided the child's planning and other emerging thought processes.

Vygotsky's view that learning leads development and the immaturity of students' conscious awareness and mastery of their thinking at school age set the stage for the concept referred to as the zone of proximal development (ZPD). Defined as including higher cognitive functions that are about to mature or develop, the ZPD is determined by the cognitive tasks the learner can complete in collaboration with an adult or an advanced peer. Simply stated, the cognitive operations that the student can complete with the assistance of another today, he or she can accomplish alone tomorrow.

Some discussions of classroom practices credit Vygotsky as supporting or advocating peer collaboration in the classroom. However, translations of his writings indicate that he discussed only teacher-student collaboration in the classroom. Higher cognitive functions develop through the teacher's requiring the learner to explain, compare, contrast, and generalize from subject-matter concepts. In this way, students learn to control their attention, to think conceptually, and to develop logical networks of well-developed concepts in long-term memory.

Applying cultural-historical theory to disabilities such as deafness, Vygotsky emphasized that the child's social deprivation is the factor responsible for defective development. For example, he noted that the blindness of a farmer's daughter and that of a duchess are different psychological situations because their social situations differ. To address the difficulties faced by disabled learners, Vygotsky suggested that societies continue developing special psychological tools that can provide the social and cultural interactions essential for cognitive development.

Finally, Vygotsky's intellectual heritage includes his emphasis on child study as the science of child development. Required is the synthesis of knowledge from different disciplines that addresses both the development of novel cognitive functions and the educational needs of children.

See also: DEVELOPMENTAL THEORY, *subentry on* VYGOTSKIAN THEORY; EDUCATIONAL PSYCHOLOGY.

BIBLIOGRAPHY

VALSINER, JEAN. 1988 *Developmental Psychology in the Soviet Union.* Bloomington: Indiana University Press.

VALSINER, JEAN, and VAN DER VEER, RENÉ. 2000. "Vygotsky's World of Concepts." In *The Social Mind: Construction of the Idea,* ed. Jean Valsiner and René Van der Veer, pp. 323–384. New York: Cambridge University Press.

VAN DER VEER, RENÉ, and VALSINER, JEAN. 1991. *Understanding Vygotsky: A Quest for Synthesis.* Cambridge, MA: Blackwell.

VYGOTSKY, LEV S. 1987. "Problems of General Psychology." *The Collected Works of L. S. Vygotsky.* Vol. 1, trans. Norman Minick. New York: Plenum

VYGOTSKY, LEV S. 1997. *The Collected Works of L. S. Vygotsky.* Vol. 4. *The History of the Development of Higher Mental Functions* (1931), trans. Marie J. Hall. New York: Plenum.

VYGOTSKY, LEV S. 1998. *The Collected Works of L. S. Vygotsky.* Vol. 5. *Child Psychology* (1928–1931), trans. Marie J. Hall. New York: Plenum.

MARGARET E. GREDLER

W

WALLER, WILLARD W.
(1899–1945)

Among education scholars the sociologist Willard W. Waller is known for writing the *Sociology of Teaching* (1932), an early classic in the sociology of education and the first extended treatment of schools as organizations in social contexts. He was born in Murphysboro, Illinois, and died in New York City, just days prior to his forty-sixth birthday. After attending public school in Illinois, Waller completed a B.A. at the University of Illinois in 1920 and then taught Latin and French for six years at the Morgan Park Military Academy. He completed an M.A. degree at the University of Chicago in 1925, followed by his Ph.D. at the University of Pennsylvania. His dissertation study of divorce, *The Old Love and the New* (1929), became his first book.

During his relatively short career, Waller explored a broad range of topics, but much of his written work reflected three major interests. He wrote on the family with special attention to courtship and divorce, on education, and on war and the veteran. Those who read Waller's works and accounts of his life often find the man as intriguing as the scholar. Waller's sociological interests reflected his experiences. His interest in the family stemmed from his own divorce and his awareness of the long and sometimes troubled relationship of his parents. His interests in education reflect his being the son of a school superintendent and his years as a high school teacher at Morgan Park Military Academy. His interest in war and the veteran seem connected to his brief service in the navy at the close of World War I and to his having taught at a military academy, where he was addressed as captain, a rank he had in the Illinois National Guard.

Waller pioneered in his ethnographic analysis of schools as miniature societies with problematic relationships to the larger community. Although Waller's work provided rich conceptual resources for scholars in the sociology of education and in educational administration, his influence on subsequent research on schools was limited. He died young, leaving few disciples; what he believed was a realistic portrayal of schools may well have been seen by others as too bleak and harsh; and social science and educational research moved away from the kind of methods Waller employed to more quantitative techniques.

Although Waller's work did not receive the critical attention it deserved at first, since the 1960s scholars have increasingly recognized the significance and staying power of his pioneering analysis of the sociological characteristics of schools. Waller's *The Sociology of Teaching* (1932) remains a key book in the field. Further indicative of his high standing, the award for the outstanding publication in the sociology of education, presented annually by the American Sociological Association's section on that topic, is named after Waller.

Readers of *The Sociology of Teaching* are often troubled by Waller's account of how teaching affects teachers, and by what David Tyack called Waller's "bleak vision" of schools. David Cohen provided an eloquent discussion of these issues and what he viewed as Waller's ambivalence in "hating school but loving education." As it turns out, Waller's bleak vision of schools and his pessimism about the difficulty of changing schools and teachers were prophetic. The sustained school reform movement that began with the 1983 report by the National Commission on Excellence in Education, *Nation at Risk: The Imperative for Educational Reform,* failed to appreciate until the late 1990s one of Waller's key insights: "The reformation of the schools must begin with the teachers, and no program that does not include the personal rehabilitation of teachers can ever overcome the passive resistance of the old order" (1932, p. 458).

In one way or another, in *The Sociology of Teaching* Waller touched on most of the issues that continue to perplex school reformers. For example, how best to reform schools, from within or without, top-down or bottom-up? How can teaching and the teaching profession be improved? What impedes the quality of teaching and learning? What accounts for goal displacement in schools? What balance should be struck in teaching and learning between control and authority, on the one hand, and freedom and spontaneity on the other hand? Likewise, in managing and governing schools, what balance should be made among the competing interests of students, teachers, administrators, parents, and taxpayers? Waller dealt with all of these and more.

Willard Waller understood acutely what few policymakers have grasped about the fundamental nature of schools: They are highly institutionalized "small societies," run by employees with a strong feeling of vulnerability to pressures, both from within and without. Facing restive students and critical parents and taxpayers, teachers and administrators must strive continuously for control over their enterprise. Consequently, Waller believed that schools are typically run on autocratic principles and often develop a garrison mentality. The result, he argued, is that the school is "a despotism in a state of perilous equilibrium" (1932, p. 10). "The school is continually threatened," he said, "because it is autocratic, and it has to be autocratic because it is threatened" (1932, p. 11). These conditions, dividing teachers from both students and the community, have profound consequences for the attitudes and behavior of teachers. Those who fail to reckon with these consequences, he suggested, will fail in efforts to reform schools. Waller's message of the 1930s is relevant even for the more democratically run schools of the twenty-first century.

BIBLIOGRAPHY

BOYD, WILLIAM L. 1989. "School Reform Policy and Politics: Insights from Willard Waller." In *Willard Waller on Education and Schools: A Critical Appraisal,* ed. Donald J. Willower and William L. Boyd. Berkeley, CA: McCutchan.

COHEN, DAVID. 1989. "Willard Waller, on Hating School and Loving Education." In *Willard Waller on Education and Schools: A Critical Appraisal,* ed. Donald J. Willower and William L. Boyd. Berkeley, CA: McCutchan.

GOODE, WILLIAM J.; FURSTENBERG, FRANK F., JR.; and MITCHELL, LARRY R. 1970. *Willard W. Waller on the Family, Education, and War: Selected Writings.* Chicago: University of Chicago Press.

TESTA, RANDY. 1998. "Willard Waller's 'Sociology of Common Sense': A Tribute at Sixty-Six." *Teachers College Record* 99(4):758–778.

TYACK, DAVID. 1989. "Life in the 'Museum of Virtue': The Bleak Vision of Willard Waller." In *Willard Waller on Education and Schools: A Critical Appraisal,* ed. Donald J. Willower and William L. Boyd. Berkeley, CA: McCutchan.

WALLER, WILLARD W. 1932. *The Sociology of Teaching.* New York: Wiley.

WILLOWER, DONALD J., and BOYD, WILLIAM L., eds. 1989. *Willard Waller on Education and Schools: A Critical Appraisal.* Berkeley, CA: McCutchan.

WILLIAM LOWE BOYD

WASHBURNE, CARLETON (1889–1968)

Superintendent of schools in Winnetka, Illinois, from 1919 to 1943, Carleton W. Washburne is most notably connected with the Winnetka Plan which he developed and promoted. Washburne also served as president of the Progressive Education Association (1939–1943) and on the faculty of Brooklyn College (1949–1960).

Early in his career Washburne was a protégé of Frederic Burk, president of the San Francisco State Normal School which, under Burk's leadership, had gained wide recognition as a center of Progressive education before World War I. Burk and his faculty had launched an attack on the traditional pedagogical practice of classroom recitation and the lockstep system of holding all students to the same pace at each grade level. At the San Francisco State laboratory school, self-instruction booklets were developed in various studies to allow students to progress at their own pace under the "individual system." These booklets garnered wide demand nationally despite Burk's policy against promotional marketing. It was a time when the traditional basis or common essentials were being seen by Progressive educators as "tool studies," denoting the basic skills as instrumental for further learning through practical application as opposed to meaningless and mechanical rote learning.

On Burk's recommendation, Washburne was appointed superintendent at Winnetka where he instituted a plan whereby the school day at the elementary level was divided into two parts—at least half being devoted to common essentials and from one-third to one-half to group work or social-creative activities stemming from the social studies, literature, art, music, and dramatics—involving discussion, projects, and reports. Washburne's extensive writings, however, were centered more on the development of objective tests for the common essentials (multiple choice and fill-in items), and self-instruction booklets with self-correction exercises linked to specific objectives. Pupils were to proceed at their own rates until mastery was demonstrated subject-by-subject. Demonstrated mastery in basic subjects did not usually lead to an individual's promotion to the next grade, but allowed additional time for work in weaker areas and enrichment. A pupil failing to achieve mastery in a subject was usually not held back at the time of class promotion to the next grade, but would continue instructional exercises in the next grade until mastery was attained. Washburne held that nonpromotion was wasteful and it was virtually eliminated under the Winnetka system.

Although Washburne's self-paced program was promoted as individualized instruction, the only factor individualized was the rate of correct items completed and time of testing to certify achievement. Other problems with the Winnetka Plan were raised by William H. Kilpatrick and fellow Progressive educators, who questioned the division of the curriculum into two disconnected and unequal parts, and the designation as the common essentials those subjects that most readily conformed to mechanistic self-instruction exercises and objective items. Further, at the time curriculum-making was moving toward correlation and integration of subjects, a trend supported by mounting research that showed not only positive outcomes when various subjects were

articulated, but also when the skill studies were made meaningful through the widest applications in all studies. The Progressive movement in curriculum development had turned to units of work, projects, enrichment and exploratory studies, and, at the middle-school and secondary level, block-time teaching and a correlated core curriculum in place of the separate subjects.

Nevertheless, Washburne had anticipated the rise of programmed instruction, mastery learning, and the increasing use of the multiple-choice test in determining achievement. By his own account Washburne laid claim to the evolution of his self-instruction booklets into "workbooks," which became a perennial pedagogical instrument in the traditional classroom from that day onward. Few Progressive educators would ally themselves with the workbook then or now.

The widespread interest generated by the Winnetka Plan stemmed in no small measure from its being seen as an answer to the incessant and mounting allegations leveled at Progressive education for neglecting the essentials. Under the dual plan, school administrators could lay claim to embracing the new education while simultaneously giving proof that at least half of every school day was being devoted to the essentials. At the same time they would not be encumbered by the onerous process of developing an articulated curriculum and the task of convincing parents and the wider public of the need for departing from the traditional separate subject curriculum.

Overlooked in accounts of Washburne's work was his establishment of nursery schools in the Winnetka schools and his required course for middle school students and junior high students in family living, which involved laboratory work in the nursery schools. He also engaged leading international architects, who worked in full cooperation with teachers, to build a school described in *Architectural Forum* as the prototype of the modern elementary school.

See also: ELEMENTARY EDUCATION, *subentry on* HISTORY OF; PHILOSOPHY OF EDUCATION; PROGRESSIVE EDUCATION.

BIBLIOGRAPHY

KILPATRICK, WILLIAM H. 1925. "An Effort at Appraisal." In *Adapting the Schools to Individual Differences,* ed. Guy Montrose Whipple. Bloomington, IL: Public School Publishing.

TANNER, DANIEL, and TANNER, LAUREL. 1990. *History of the School Curriculum.* New York: Macmillan.

WASHBURNE, CARLTON W. 1925. "Burk's Individual System as Developed at Winnetka." In *Adapting the Schools to Individual Differences,* ed. Guy Montrose Whipple. Bloomington, IL: Public School Publishing.

WASHBURNE, CARLETON W. 1927. "The Philosophy of the Winnetka Curriculum." In *Curriculum-Making: Past and Present,* ed. William Chandler Bagley. Bloomington, IL: Public School Publishing.

WASHBURNE, CARLETON W. 1953. *What Is Progressive Education?* New York: Day.

WASHBURNE, CARLETON W., and MARLAND, SIDNEY P., JR. 1963. *Winnetka: The History and Significance of an Educational Experiment.* Englewood Cliffs, NJ: Prentice-Hall.

DANIEL TANNER

WASHINGTON, BOOKER T. (1856–1915)

Born a slave on a Virginia plantation five years before the Civil War began, Booker T. Washington's professional life as an educator and leader of African-American interests demonstrates how education, race, public policy, and politics intersected in the United States during the late nineteenth century. Washington's career placed him at the center of a debate among African Americans about the proper path to full citizenship and complete participation in American society economically, politically, and socially.

He was also the instrument of elite white industrialists such as George Foster Peabody, William H. Baldwin Jr., and Robert C. Ogden. They shaped the shift in black American educational focus from universal, state-supported public education with its liberal arts component to an industrial education, a move that accommodated their aims for national industrialization and southern white planters' demands for a subservient African-American working class. As a result of his collaboration, Washington became the primary exponent of white philanthropic–industrial efforts to channel African-American and working-class white education to meet the needs of industrial America. The words *Industrial education* and *Washington* became synonymous between his 1895 Atlanta Cotton Exposition Speech and death in 1915. The legacy of Washington's educational philosophy continues to be the source of an early-twenty-first-century debate among African Americans who attempt to reconcile questions of how education must lead the black working class to life as middle-class Americans. This debate also seeks to ensure that the majority of African-American working people obtain access to a better life with mass education as the primary path to modernization and the technology that transforms black political, economic, and social status in the United States.

Early Years

Booker T. Washington was born to a slave mother and "unknown" father near Hales Ford, Virginia, on James Burroughs's plantation in 1856. He survived chattel slavery and the Civil War. He moved with his mother and siblings to West Virginia to join his stepfather, a Union Army veteran. Living under impoverished circumstances, Washington worked in the local salt mines to assist the family. He attended night school initially and eventually obtained permission from his stepfather to go to the day school while he worked from 4 A.M. to 9 A.M. in the mines. Employed as a houseboy by General Lewis Ruffner, he furthered his early education under Mrs. Viola Knapp Ruffner, a former governess and schoolteacher.

The major transformative event, however, in Washington's personal education occurred at Hampton Institute in Hampton, Virginia, under the direction of former Union Army General Samuel Chapman Armstrong, the school's founder. At Hampton, Washington absorbed Armstrong's industrial education philosophy of manual labor, trade training, economic development, self-help, and normal school training. After brief sojourns in black higher education in Washington, D.C., at Howard University and exploration of the ministry, Washington returned to Hampton Institute to teach. Armstrong recommended his protégé, Washington noted, to a "group of white Alabama gentlemen" in Tuskegee, Alabama, who endeavored to open a school similar to the Hampton model (Washington 1965, p. 82). Washington accepted their invitation to lead this normal and industrial institution.

In 1881 Washington began organizing and building Tuskegee Normal and Industrial Institute, literally from the ground up. His leadership of Tuskegee Institute from 1881 to 1915 would elevate him from obscurity to national prominence. He became not only a leader in black education, but also a patron of such industrialists and education philanthropists as Andrew Carnegie; George Foster Peabody; Charles D. McIver, president of the Southern Education Association; and Edgar Gardner Murphy, racial moderate and distinguished southern educator. Washington also advised U.S. presidents William McKinley, Theodore Roosevelt, and William Howard Taft. With these associates and supporters Washington amassed enough political power to become the most powerful southern politician of his era, 1895 to 1915.

The Black Commitment to Free Education

The emancipated slaves, including Washington, looked to education in 1865 to define their newly earned freedom and citizenship. According to education historian James D. Anderson, black people emerging from slavery committed themselves to universal, state-supported public education. It continued a tradition developed in slavery among African Americans that the ability to read and write were important skills within the slave community. Blacks held in high esteem fellow slaves and free blacks who had mastered literacy. Even Washington, a critic of slaves and black working-class behavior and goals, acknowledged that freedom was a "great responsibility" and that slaves realized they had "to think and plan for themselves and their children" including "the question . . . of a school . . . for colored children" (Washington 1965, pp. 27–28, 32). Education meant self-reliance, self-determination, and the right to control the institutions of education for their benefit. According to William Channing, an American Missionary Association teacher from New England, black people sought free public education that included white assistance but not white control—seemingly contradictory concepts. Black people challenged white planter repugnance against state government control of the education of all children, especially slaves. African Americans contested the rationale of a society that used the law to prohibit reading and writing. Black educator and Booker T. Washington's political rival, W. E. B. Du Bois, asserted that free public education for all citizens in the South was "a Negro idea," proposed by enslaved blacks as a condition of freedom.

Washington observed that black slaves and ex-slaves were determined to educate themselves by securing their own teachers and even paying "for school as best they could" (Washington 1965, p. 33). They made this commitment long before white and black northern American Missionary Association teachers came south during the Civil War. These efforts at self-education served as a foundation for universal schooling as slaves and ex-slaves organized and willingly taxed themselves to keep the private schools they founded on their own initiative. At the beginning of Reconstruction, the Freedmen's Bureau took control of some of these schools founded by slaves. In 1866 the Freedmen's Bureau in Louisiana failed to force blacks to retake responsibility for administering education for African Americans. Blacks in Georgia in 1865 created a free system of schools. Sabbath schools were also free and operated in black churches stressing literacy. Black student enrollment increased in Sabbath schools in the 1870s and 1880s, demonstrating the African-American commitment to free education and literacy. The ability to read and write was a key to black freedom. These skills helped African Americans secure jobs and direct their access to upward mobility. Literacy ensured that ex-slaves could defend their economic rights in written contracts as well as acquire land, the main symbol of freedom.

Black people attained universal, state-supported public education through a union of African Americans and radical members of the Republican Party. Conservative Republicans and southern Democrats opposed universal education. Black Republicans at southern constitutional conventions during Reconstruction, between 1865 and 1868, institutionalized free public education based on state-supported taxation. By 1870 the eleven states of the former Confederacy had installed constitutions that established free education as a basic citizenship right.

Emancipated blacks also viewed education as the key to political, economic, and personal independence. They pursued education to learn how to organize themselves and build institutions they controlled. To achieve this they sought training and development of their intellectual and leadership capacities. In this context, Anderson notes, "black leaders and educators adopted the New England classical liberal curriculum" (p. 28). After attaining political power in 1895, Booker T. Washington objected to classical education for the general black population on the grounds that it was "impractical";

however, working-class African Americans in Alabama and across the south insisted that blacks needed classical, common school, normal, and industrial education to ensure the advancement of the race to full citizenship in the United States.

White southern planters and merchants used their control over land, labor, housing, and wages to undermine universal, state-supported public education. This class had opposed state-supported public education for the working classes (white people who were not part of the landed elite) before the Civil War. The planters, Anderson asserts, "did not believe in giving the Negro any education" (p. 22). Any degree of education eroded the planter's ability to exploit black labor "upon which their agrarian order depended" (p. 23). Southern white leaders used labor to prevent black children from attending school after the Civil War. Between 1869 and 1877 the planters and merchants ousted African-American legislators from southern state governments. The planters and merchants, armed with political power that gave them a dominant position in state government, dismantled universal, state-supported public education utilizing state authority, economic intimidation, and violence. By legal means, white opponents of universal education lowered taxation, challenged compulsory attendance laws, and prevented the passage of new laws that could have reinforced free public education. The planters and merchants wanted to restore slavery and their domination of all societal institutions, which were undermined by the Civil War, Reconstruction, northern capital investment in the south, and the centralization of federal power.

No white group challenged white planter-merchant class antipublic education policies between 1865 and 1880. Beginning in the late 1880s, however, white Populists and Progressive-era reformers who followed the Populists questioned the planter-merchant vision of limiting white working-class education. As the nineteenth century drew to a close white people were forced by black agitation to confront their conflicting views of universal, state-supported public education.

Industrial Education

Industrial education introduced northern educators, industrialists, philanthropists, and Booker T. Washington into the debate between African-Americans' universal, state-supported public education and the white planter-merchant class's efforts to reconstruct antebellum slavery. The partnership formed by General Samuel Chapman Armstrong and Washington at Hampton Institute in the 1870s was part of a broader northern industrial-capital campaign to undercut black adaptation of the New England classical curriculum. The Hampton Institute was not envisioned as an industrial education institution. It was a normal school dedicated to training teachers, such as Washington, who would teach black workers and prepare them for their "place" in the South after Reconstruction. The institute was additionally part of a national movement focused on technological, trade, and manual education for the general American population. Although Hampton focused on teacher training, industrial education as it was originally defined did not involve teacher preparation.

There were three primary areas of vocational training that defined industrial education in the latter part of the nineteenth century. One area was collegiate training in applied science and technology to educate engineers, architects, chemists, and other professionals to work in the newly emerging technologically based twentieth-century economy. A second area encompassed trade schools that taught labor supervision and management. The third area supplemented the academic curriculum to modify or transform the behavior of working people from sloth to "habits of industry," thrift, and morality.

General Armstrong's Hampton Institute was founded in 1868. It utilized daily manual labor as the base of its normal school training. Armstrong wrongly assumed that the newly freed black people had to be guided and controlled because they were incapable of "self-direction" due to slavery's destruction of their minds and moral compasses. He hoped Hampton Institute might train black teachers who would impart the lessons of "work habits, practical knowledge, Christian morality, and acceptance of a subservient role" (Anderson, p. 35) in the post-Reconstruction southern household. Washington completed Hampton's curriculum and became the chief disciple of the Hampton model.

The Hampton model of industrial education was intended to "de-politicize" and "defuse" black challenges to white opposition to universal education. Providing, Anderson asserted, "the equivalent . . . of a fair tenth grade" education, the Hampton model preached an education gospel that emphasized that black people be apolitical (p. 35). Armstrong believed that African Americans should not be "allowed to vote," serve as politicians, or participate in public policy decisions because black people were "not capable of self-government" (p. 37). Armstrong based his assertions on the supposition that black people needed "moral development" as the basis for voting intelligently. He rejected the belief embraced by black people that a "literate culture" created a morally responsible voting electorate. Finally, Armstrong believed that African Americans' real role was to serve the planters' and merchants' needs for cheap non-confrontational labor.

Armstrong created the *Southern Workman,* a monthly magazine founded in 1872 to create a "public forum" on black education and to more broadly disseminate his views on the "place" of black people in the New South's social, political, and economic structure. He aligned his vision of black education with the planter and merchant class and northern industrialists. Armstrong was a friend of Robert C. Ogden, who also served as a Hampton Institute trustee. He wrote Ogden that the southern workman needed to be "a power" who would influence northern philanthropists and white southern racial moderates principally opposed, Anderson contended, "to black higher education, equal job opportunities, civil equality, and equal political rights" (pp. 36–37). Together they hoped to be the critical individuals in determining the direction of black education, especially in the south.

Planter-Merchant and Northern Industrialist Agenda

In 1896, a year after Booker T. Washington's infamous "Atlanta Compromise" speech (partly crafted by industrialist William H. Baldwin Jr.) at the Atlanta Cotton States International Exposition, a conference on "the higher education of the colored people" was convened in Saratoga, New York. Du Bois biographer David Levering Lewis characterized the meeting as a "watershed conclave" where national white leaders decided to forsake and cut off their support for "black higher education" in favor of the Hampton model of industrial education. George Foster Peabody, Hampton trustee and a key distributor of funding to black education in the south, attended the meeting, and alumnus Washington spoke favoring practical education superceding liberal arts instruction. Philadelphia's Baptist leader H. L. Wayland was enthused to hear Washington's industrial education vision was being substituted for Atlanta and Fisk Universities' New England classical

education for black people. Wayland also threatened to terminate funding support to these black liberal arts institutions and shift financial aid to the exponents of the Hampton model, Hampton and Tuskegee Institutes. According to David L. Lewis, William Baldwin Jr. and Robert C. Ogden were determined to let nothing impede "the regional reconciliation [of the north and south] and southern modernization that their kind of educational philosophy and capital investment was intended to foster." With Samuel Armstrong's death three years before this conclave, Washington inherited Armstrong's mantle and the people who had supported his mentor. Washington after 1895 was the instrument of the industrialists and planters to restore the Union, modernize the South, and control black mass education.

The late nineteenth century and early twentieth century was defined by a debate between former slaves establishing a vision and the utility of universal, state-supported public education for all U.S. citizens, especially in the South, and the white planters-merchants and northern industrialists coalition to create a cheap labor force. Black people hoped to utilize education as the means to acquire full citizenship and the key to political participation and economic success. The north-south white elite coalition used education to control blacks politically, economically, and socially, while reconciling the sectional divisions of the Civil War. Washington was at the center of this debate. He represented the white elite and some emerging black middle-class members' thoughts on African-American education for the masses. Political reality in the 1890s and afterward caused Washington to publicly accept white violations of the Fourteenth Amendment that included denying black people the right to vote across the south. Privately, Washington paid lawyers to challenge disfranchisement in the American court system, but even the Supreme Court of the United States endorsed preventing black voting as "an appropriate reform" to remove corruption from politics.

Washington's Legacy

In the late twentieth century and early twenty-first century, the debate about Booker T. Washington's educational legacy has been transformed into a contest between "liberal" thinking African Americans and conservative black intellectuals seeking a viable route to economic success in technology-based America. Specifically, Washington has wrongly become the proponent of a classical education that opened black students' minds to a broader world culture that included the exploration of Latin and the classics. Advocates of this position assert that Washington had a plan for black education that could have ensured African American access to economic success and perhaps middle-class status.

A look back to the Booker T. Washington of the past disregards his criticism of "Latin and Greek" for the newly freed ex-slave as making "a very superior human being . . . something bordering almost on the super natural" (Washington 1965, p. 65). Washington suggested in *Up from Slavery* that "the craze for Greek and Latin learning" was wrongly tied by blacks to "a desire to hold [political] office." He did stress that black people should embrace "manual labor" first and then build to the next levels of human achievement over time. He publicly charged that black working people were not ready for all the avenues of freedom. They would have to work toward attaining these privileges over an unspecified amount of time. This was the public rationale of African Americans for forsaking the right to vote in exchange for access to economic success, which would be supervised by white northern and southern capitalists. The white elite, Washington argued publicly, would see to it that black political rights were protected when black people proved their economic importance to white leaders.

For Washington, Samuel Chapman Armstrong was "the perfect man." Washington was "convinced that there is no education which one can get from books and costly apparatus that is equal to that which can be gotten from contact with great men and women. . . . Instead of studying books . . . how I wish that our schools and colleges might learn to study men and things (1965, p. 49). Washington wanted African Americans to have access to America's material wealth. That objective is still the subject of education reform in the twenty-first century.

See also: EDUCATION REFORM; DuBois, W.E.B.; HISTORICALLY BLACK COLLEGES AND UNIVERSITIES; MULTICULTURAL EDUCATION.

BIBLIOGRAPHY

ANDERSON, JAMES D. 1988. *The Education of Blacks in the South, 1860–1935.* Chapel Hill: University of North Carolina Press.

HARLAN, LOUIS H. 1972. *Booker T. Washington: The Making of a Black Leader, 1856–1901.* New York: Oxford University Press.

HARLAN, LOUIS H. 1983. *Booker T. Washington: The Wizard of Tuskegee, 1901–1915.* New York: Oxford University Press.

LEWIS, DAVID LEVERING. 1993. *W. E. B. Du Bois: Biography of a Race, 1868–1919.* New York: Holt.

WASHINGTON, BOOKER T. 1965. *Up from Slavery.* New York: Dell

WASHINGTON, BOOKER T. 1972–1989. *Booker T. Washington Papers,* Vols. 1–14, ed. Louis H. Harlan, et al. Urbana: University of Illinois Press.

WOODWARD, C. VANN. 1971. *Origins of the New South, 1877–1913.* Baton Rouge: Louisiana State University Press.

GREGORY MIXON

WATSON, JOHN B. (1878-1958)

John B. Watson was an important contributor to classical behaviorism, who paved the way for B. F. Skinner's radical or operant behaviorism, which has had a major impact on American educational systems.

A professor of psychology at Johns Hopkins University (1908–1920), Watson is often listed as one of the most influential psychologists of the twentieth century; his work is standard material in most introductory psychology and educational psychology texts. Yet his academic career was brief, lasting for only fourteen years, and his legacy has been hotly debated for nearly a century. Watson helped define the study of behavior, anticipated Skinner's emphasis on operant conditioning, and emphasized the importance of learning and environmental influences in human development. Watson's often harsh criticism of Sigmund Freud has been given credit for helping to disseminate principles of Freudian psychoanalysis. Watson is widely known for the Little Albert study and his "dozen healthy infants" quote.

Popularizing Behaviorism

John B. Watson is generally given credit for creating and popularizing the term *behaviorism* with the publication of his seminal 1913 article "Psychology as the Behaviorist Views It." In the article, Watson argued that psychology had failed in its quest to become a natural science, largely due to a focus on consciousness and other unseen phenomena. Rather than study these unverifiable ideas, Watson urged the careful scientific study of observable behavior. His view of behaviorism was a reaction to introspection, where each researcher served as his or her own research subject, and the study of consciousness by Freud and others, which Watson believed to be highly subjective and unscientific.

In response to introspection, Watson and other early behaviorists believed that controlled laboratory studies were the most effective way to study learning. With this approach, manipulation of the learner's environment was the key to fostering development. This approach stands in contrast to techniques that placed the emphasis for learning in the mind of the learner. The 1913 article is often given credit for the founding of behaviorism, but it had a minor impact after its publication. His popular 1919 psychology text is probably more responsible for introducing behaviorist principles to a generation of future scholars of learning. In this way, Watson prepared psychologists and educators for the highly influential work of Skinner and other radical behaviorists in subsequent decades.

The Little Albert Study

In 1920 Watson and an assistant, Rosalie Rayner, published one of the most famous research studies of the past century. Watson attempted to condition a severe emotional response in Little Albert, a nine-month-old child. Watson determined that white, furry objects, such as a rat, a rabbit, and cotton, did not produce any negative reaction in the baby. But by pairing together a neutral stimulus (white, furry animals and objects) with an unconditioned stimulus (a very loud noise) that elicited an unconditioned response (fear), Watson was able to create a new stimulus-response link: When Albert saw white, furry objects, this conditioned stimulus produced a conditioned response of fear. This study is generally presented as a seminal work that provided evidence that even complex behaviors, such as emotions, could be learned through manipulation of one's environment. As such, it became a standard bearer for behaviorist approaches to learning and is still widely cited in the early twenty-first century.

The "Dozen Healthy Infants"

To a behaviorist, manipulation of the environment is the critical mechanism for learning (e.g., the Little Albert study). To illustrate this point, Watson wrote in 1930, "Give me a dozen healthy infants, well-formed, and my own specified world to bring them up in and I'll guarantee to take any one at random and train him to become any type of specialist I might select—doctor, lawyer, artist—regardless of his talents, penchants, tendencies, abilities, vocations and race of his ancestors" (p. 104). This quote routinely appears in introductory texts in education and psychology and is used to illustrate the radical environmental views of behaviorists.

But that sentence is only the first part of the quote. In that same statement, Watson subsequently wrote, "I am going beyond my facts and I admit it, but so have the advocates of the contrary and they have been doing so for many thousands of years" (p. 104). This second sentence is rarely quoted with the first sentence. In taking this quote out of context, authors have presented Watson and classical behaviorism as having an extreme perspective on the importance of environment. However, Watson was reacting to the work of other psychologists and educators who believed that heredity was solely responsible for human development and learning. Early behaviorists accented the role of environment, but their views were probably not as radical and extreme as they are often presented.

Life after the University

Following a personal scandal in 1920, Watson resigned his position at Johns Hopkins and entered advertising, where he achieved some degree of success. He also published popular accounts of behaviorism after leaving his university position. His book *Psychological Care of the Infant and Child* (1928) was very popular, advocating a rather detached approach to parenting, with few displays of affection such as kissing and hugging of children. Given Watson's relatively short academic career, his lasting contributions in the areas of learning, psychological methods, and behaviorism are remarkable.

See also: EDUCATIONAL PSYCHOLOGY.

BIBLIOGRAPHY

COHEN, DAVID. 1979. *J. B. Watson, the Founder of Behaviourism: A Biography.* London: Routledge and Kegan Paul.

TODD, JAMES T., and MORRIS, EDWARD K., eds. 1994. *Modern Perspectives on John B. Watson and Classical Behaviorism.* Westport, CT: Greenwood.

WATSON, JOHN B. 1913. "Psychology as the Behaviorist Views It." *Psychological Review* 20:158–177.

WATSON, JOHN B. 1919. *Psychology from the Standpoint of a Behaviorist.* Philadelphia: Lippincott.

WATSON, JOHN B. 1930. *Behaviorism,* revised edition. Chicago: University of Chicago Press.

WATSON, JOHN B., and RAYNER, ROSALIE. 1920. "Conditioned Emotional Responses." *Journal of Experimental Psychology* 3:1–14.

JONATHAN A. PLUCKER

WEBSTER, NOAH (1758–1843)

The first person to write a dictionary of American English and permanently alter the spelling of American English, Noah Webster through his spelling book taught millions of American children to read for the first half-century of the republic and millions more to spell for the following half-century.

Born a farmer's son in what is now West Hartford, Connecticut, Webster attended Yale College from 1774 to 1778, during the Revolutionary War. After graduating, he taught at Connecticut district schools before studying for the bar. The dismal conditions of these schools, combined with his patriotism and a search for self-identity, inspired him to compose three schoolbooks that, he believed, would unify the new nation through speaking and writing a common language. (Previously, almost all American schoolbooks had been reprints of imported British ones.) Part one of Webster's *A Grammatical Institute of the English Language,* a spelling book, was printed in 1783; part two, a grammar, in 1784; part three, a reader (a compilation of essays and poetry for children who could already read), in 1785. Webster then left on an eighteen-month tour south to promote his books and register them for state copyright, in the absence of national copyright legislation. In 1787 he revised the *Grammatical Institute,* retitling his speller the *American Spelling Book* and his reader *An American Selection of Lessons.*

He began editing periodicals in New York: the *American Magazine* for one year (1788–1789) and the pro-federalist *American Minerva* (1793–1798). Between the two came his marriage to Rebecca Greenleaf in 1789, the publication of various collections of essays, and an introduction to his reader, the *Little Reader's Assistant* (1790). In 1798 he retreated from politics and periodicals to New Haven and helped open a private school there.

After publishing a commercially unsuccessful history of epidemics, Webster began writing schoolbooks with renewed vigor, issuing the first three volumes of *Elements of Useful Knowledge* (1802–1806). He had obtained national copyright protection for his speller in 1790, when the first national copyright law was passed, a law that granted protection for fourteen-year periods. However, the income from his speller, for which he negotiated a penny a copy in 1804 (the date of his first copyright renewal), could not support his large family, and in 1812 he moved to Amherst, Massachusetts, to economize. He was instrumental there in founding Amherst Academy, now Amherst College. In 1816 Webster sold the entire rights to the *American Spelling Book* for its third copyright period, 1818 to 1832, to Hudson and Company of Hartford, Connecticut, in order to work solely on his major dictionary. In 1824, with his son William to aid him, he voyaged to Europe to complete it. Titled *An American Dictionary of the English Language,* it was published in New York in 1828. A year later, Webster produced the final revision of his speller, the *Elementary Spelling Book,* in conjunction with Aaron Ely, a New York educator. From then until his death in 1843 Webster issued several other schoolbooks and a bowdlerized edition of the Bible. The latter was the fruit of a conversion experience to fundamentalist Christianity in 1807.

Webster's Innovations

One of Webster's most important and lasting contributions to American English was to change, for the better, the spellings of certain groups of words from their British spelling. He used the principle of uniformity to justify his alterations, arguing that words that were alike, such as nouns and their derivatives, should be spelled alike. He therefore transformed words such as *honour* to *honor* (compare *honorific*), *musick* to *music* (compare *musical*)—the latter a change now adopted by the British—*defence* to *defense* (compare *defensive*) and *centre* to *center*. This last alteration actually violated his own principle— compare *central*—but brought *centre* and congruent words into conformity with numerous other words ending *-er*. Webster also respelled many anomalous British spellings, writing *gaol* as *jail,* and *plough* as *plow.* Earlier, in works such as the *Little Reader's Assistant,* Webster had gone much further with his reforms, with spellings such as *yung* and *nabor.* However, these had evoked so much ridicule that he soon abandoned them. His ability to introduce his major classes of spelling reform into his spellers and dictionaries was crucial to their success, as they became imprinted on the minds of each new generation.

Webster's second major contribution to American education was in the field of lexicography. Indeed, the word *Webster* is still virtually synonymous with *dictionary.* Although Webster issued a small stopgap dictionary, his *Compendious Dictionary,* in 1806, his masterpiece was his *An American Dictionary of the English Language* of 1828, a two-volume work of more than 70,000 entries and the first truly American dictionary. In it, Webster eliminated words that were not useful to Americans, such as words associated with coats of arms, and included those unique to the United States, like *squash* and *skunk.*

Webster was not equally successful in all aspects of his dictionary. By modern standards, his etymologies are flawed. His conversion to fundamentalist Christianity had led him to believe in one original language as the progenitor of all the rest, and his etymologies were compromised by his efforts to fit all words into this framework. On the other hand, he brought a new approach to definitions, which were more accurate, comprehensive, and logically organized than in any previous dictionary. His orthography has become standard American orthography. His indication of pronunciations by the use of diacritical marks was also innovative; lexicographers still use similar markings in the early twenty-first century.

Perfecting the Spelling Book for Reading Instruction

Important as Webster's lexicographical work was, his contributions to the spelling book tradition were even more significant. His spellers enjoyed vastly greater popularity than any other of his works. His original speller, the first part of the *Institute* (1783), sold out its first edition of 5,000 copies within a few months. By 1804 more than a million copies of its revision, the *American Spelling Book* of 1787, had

been printed, most of them in Hartford and Boston. From 1804 to 1818 Webster's account books document the sales of licenses of another 3,223,000 copies. Between 1818 and 1832, the third copyright period, an estimated 3 million copies were printed. Even higher numbers are documented for Webster's completely revamped version, the *Elementary Spelling Book* of 1829, which he published in response to what he perceived as the slipping sales of the *American Spelling Book* under Hudson and Company. Between 1829, the *Elementary's* first publication, and 1843, the year of Webster's death, almost 3,868,000 copies were licensed for sale. Over all its editions, a conservative estimate puts the total sales of the speller at 70 million.

The national popularity and huge sales of Webster's spelling books can only be understood if it is appreciated that they were books designed primarily to teach children to read, and only secondarily to spell, through the alphabet method of reading instruction. The underlying assumption of all spelling books was that "reading" (defined as oral, not silent, reading) was a matter of pronouncing words, spelled aloud syllable by syllable, and that once a word was pronounced correctly, comprehension would follow. Webster's contribution to the spelling book tradition was to indicate how words should be pronounced. He introduced a system of numerical superscripts to indicate vowel pronunciation and altered the syllabification of words to their present format (*si-ster* now became *sis ter*). In so doing, he improved significantly on his model and rival, *A New Guide to the English Tongue* (1740) by the British Thomas Dilworth. In his final revision, the *Elementary* of 1829, Webster replaced the superscripts with diacritical marks very similar to those he had used in his *American Dictionary* a year earlier—another innovation.

Other Works

A fourth contribution to education by Webster was to originate works that others would improve upon. He had a very large view of American education: He attempted to influence school content, "beginning with children & ending with men" (Monaghan, p. 69) who would progress from the Webster spelling book through other subjects up to the Webster dictionaries. Webster's grammar of 1784 was swiftly superseded by Lindley Murray's grammar, and his revised reader, *An American Selection,* was also overtaken, first by Caleb Bingham's *American Preceptor* and later by Murray's *English Reader.* (The latter would appear in some 350 editions by 1840.) Webster's school dictionaries, his four-volume *Elements of Useful Knowledge* (1802, 1804, 1806, 1812), his *Biography, for the Use of Schools* (1830), his *History of the United States* (1832), and his *Manual of Useful Studies* (1839) introduced many topics that would later evolve into school staples: geography and history of the United States and elsewhere and (in a primitive form in the fourth volume of the *Elements*) biology.

The "First" American Author

Webster was innovative in a fifth arena: he was the earliest American author to make a living from his own publications. He saw as a young man that there was money to be made from a schoolbook and sought protection for his first spelling book even before it was in print and before any state had yet passed laws protecting intellectual property. Webster has become known as the "father of copyright," and indeed he remained active in promoting copyright protection throughout his life. He might with more justice be termed the "father of royalties," as he was one of the first to exact payment from his publishers according to the number of books they printed or that he licensed to them.

Webster's ability to live from the proceeds of the spelling book was aided by another factor: his extraordinary promotion of his own books. He was the first, but certainly not the last, American author to involve himself deeply in the publishing and promotional aspects of his books. His activities prefigure almost all aspects of modern publishing. His first concern, particularly for part one of the *Institute* and later for the *Elementary Spelling Book,* was with the quality of the printed product. He monitored every printer himself, first across New England and then in the middle and southern states. He fussed over every internal detail of the product in an effort to make all his editions uniform across publishers: the spelling, the paper, the standing type. He revised and corrected each edition unceasingly.

His second concern was with promotion. No aspect of it escaped him. As was common practice at the time, he sought recommendations. (Both Benjamin Franklin and George Washington turned him down.) He went on promotional tours, as he did for the Institute in 1785. He gave lectures that brought him to the public's attention; he advertised the series and, when possible, planted "notices" (equivalent to press releases) in local newspapers; he donated his books to colleges and schools; he even gave portions of his proceeds to worthy causes. He was originally his own best agent, and used paid agents only late in his life. Above all, Webster kept an eye out for competitors and did not hesitate to launch stinging attacks, often in newspapers, on his rivals. In much of this, for better or worse, he foreshadowed modern practice.

The view of reading instruction incorporated in Webster's spellers—as systematic, sequential, letter-based, and learned by rote—would not be challenged until the 1820s. The charge brought against all spelling books hinged on the meaninglessness to the child of much of the spelling book's content. Reformers deplored the long lists of syllabified words that children had to encounter before they met sustained reading passages. By the late 1830s the success of the new-style readers, those like the *Eclectic* series originally authored by William Holmes McGuffey, were rendering spelling books obsolete as reading instructional texts.

Yet the sales of Webster's *Elementary Spelling Book,* now dubbed affectionately the "blue-back speller" or just "ole blue-back," continued to increase. By 1859, according to Appleton and Company of New York, the firm was printing the speller at the rate of a million and one-half copies per year. For the blue-back speller still had an educational role to play: It lived on for the rest of the century as a spelling instructional text and as the favorite arbiter at spelling bees in and out of school.

See also: CURRICULUM, SCHOOL; READING, *subentry on* TEACHING OF; SPELLING, TEACHING OF.

BIBLIOGRAPHY

MONAGHAN, E. JENNIFER. 1983. *A Common Heritage: Noah Webster's Blue-Back Speller.* Hamden, CT: Archon Books.

ROLLINS, RICHARD M. 1980. *The Long Journey of Noah Webster.* Philadelphia: University of Pennsylvania Press.

ROLLINS, RICHARD M., ed. 1989. *The Autobiographies of Noah Webster: From the Letters and Essays, Memoir, and Diary.* Columbia: University of South Carolina Press.

SKEEL, EMILY ELLSWORTH FORD. 1971. *A Bibliography of the Writings of Noah Webster* (1958), ed. Edwin H. Carpenter Jr. New York: New York Public Library and Arno.

WARFEL, HARRY R., ed. 1953. *The Letters of Noah Webster.* New York: Library.

WARFEL, HARRY R. 1966. *Noah Webster: Schoolmaster to America.* New York: Octagon.

WEBSTER, NOAH. 1783. *A Grammatical Institute of the English Language . . . , Part I.* Hartford, CT: Hudson and Goodwin.

WEBSTER, NOAH. 1787a. *An American Selection of Lessons in Reading and Speaking, Calculated to Improve the Minds and Refine the Taste of Youth . . . ,* 3rd edition. Philadelphia: Young and M'Cullough.

WEBSTER, NOAH. 1787b. *The American Spelling Book Containing, an Easy Standard of Pronunciation. Being the First Part of a Grammatical Institute of the English Language.* Philadelphia: Young and M'Cullough.

WEBSTER, NOAH. 1790. *The Little Reader's Assistant . . . .* Hartford, CT: Elisha Babcock.

Webster, Noah, to Samuel L. Mitchell, June 29, 1807.

WEBSTER, NOAH. 1828. *An American Dictionary of the English Language . . . ,* 2 vols. New York: S[herman] Converse.

WEBSTER, NOAH. 1829. *The Elementary Spelling Book; Being an Improvement on the American Spelling Book.* Middletown, CT: Niles.

E. JENNIFER MONAGHAN

WELFARE REFORM

EFFECTS ON FAMILIES AND CHILDREN
  Catherine Dunn Shiffman
MOVING MOTHERS FROM WELFARE TO WORK
  Pearl Sims
  Bill Tharp

EFFECTS ON FAMILIES AND CHILDREN

In 1996 the Personal Responsibility and Work Opportunity Reconciliation Act (PRWORA) brought sweeping changes to the welfare system in the United States. This federal law was designed to move adults quickly and permanently into the workforce, promote family stability, and allocate greater flexibility to states in designing public-assistance programs. Though welfare reform primarily targets the behaviors of adults, children are indirectly affected by the reorganization of family roles and responsibilities, and by the shifts in resources associated with new employment. Research regarding the effects of welfare reform on families and children is preliminary, but nonetheless illuminates areas that warrant further study and has implications for children's ability to succeed in school.

Summary of Welfare Reform

The American welfare system is a diverse array of state programs that emphasize the promotion of family stability, the provision of time-limited cash assistance, and the movement of recipients into full employment. Under PRWORA, several existing federal welfare programs were eliminated, including the entitlement programs Aid to Families with Dependent Children (AFDC), Job Opportunities and Basic Skills Training (JOBS), and Emergency Assistance (EA). In their place, PRWORA created Temporary Assistance for Needy Families (TANF), which provides block grants to the states to provide cash assistance to families, and which supports other state programs consistent with the welfare law. PRWORA also made various changes to other government benefits designed for low-income families. The affected programs provided benefits for child care, health care, food stamps, individuals with disabilities, child-support enforcement, and child welfare. In addition, under PRWORA most immigrants are denied welfare-related benefits.

In general, TANF rules move more low-income adults into the workforce by: (1) requiring current recipients to participate in employment or training-related activities; (2) imposing a five-year lifetime limit on cash assistance; (3) terminating benefits if rules are violated; and, (4) reducing the number of families exempt from work requirements. Of particular impact to young children, federal TANF guidelines limit work exemptions to parents with children under one year of age. Eighteen states require a mother to resume work when her child is six months old or less. Welfare caseloads dropped dramatically from a record high of 14.4 million in 1994 to 5.3 million in 2001.

Along with these changes, government support for child care increased substantially to address the needs of low-income parents entering the workforce. PRWORA consolidated federal funding for child care under the Child Care and Development Fund (CCDF), and federal and state funding under CCDF rose from $2.8 billion in 1995 to $8 billion in 2000. Nonetheless many eligible families are not receiving subsidies.

PRWORA also altered several long-standing federal welfare programs. Significant changes were made to Medicaid, Food Stamps, and Supplemental Security Income. Historically, Medicaid provided health care coverage to families eligible for welfare assistance. PRWORA extended this coverage to children and their parents for up to one year after leaving welfare. For children whose family income exceeded the Medicaid limit, Congress created a special program, the State Children's Health Insurance Plan (SCHIP), to serve their needs. Second, PRO-WRA made eligibility for Food Stamps more restrictive. Program participation dropped significantly (and out of proportion to these changes in eligibility). Third, PRWORA tightened eligibility for Supplemental Security Income (SSI), the program that provides financial assistance to low-income individuals who have a disability. By changing the definition of child disability, roughly 100,000 children were no longer eligible for this government benefit.

Economic Picture for Low-Income Children and Families

While national statistics point to an improved economic picture for low-income families, mitigating factors temper an overly optimistic assessment of welfare reform. The employment rate of current and former adult welfare recipients increased by 33 percent between 1996 and 1999; however, this increase coincided with a period of unprecedented economic prosperity. Similarly, while the percentage of children living in poverty dropped to 16.2 percent, the lowest percentage since 1978, many families did not substantially improve their living standard.

Definitive conclusions about the relationship of welfare reform to family and child well-being are problematic for at least three reasons. First, welfare programs vary across states and communities in their programmatic emphases and in the types of support available. Second, these programs target adult behaviors and measure success in terms of economic indicators, rather than employing a more multidimensional assessment of family and child well-being. Third, much of the existing research is based on samples drawn from experimental welfare programs that predate the 1996 law.

Welfare Reform and Changes in Parenting Practices

Research to date has found limited effects of welfare reform on parenting, with the exception of changes in how mothers select nonparental care for their children. Parents in welfare-to-work programs with increased resources tend to place children in higher quality child care and after-school programs. Not surprisingly, as mothers move into full-time employment they tend to use formal child care, such as centers and family-based home care, rather than informal arrangements.

Much remains unknown, however, about the effects of welfare-to-work programs on the less tangible aspects of parenting. The Growing Up in Poverty Project found few changes in parenting practices three years after researchers began following families in PRWORA welfare-to-work programs. Slight declines in child-development activities and an increase in television use were detected among families in welfare-to-work programs, when compared to unemployed households.

Welfare Reform and Child Outcomes

The evidence collected thus far does not point to dramatic changes in children's well-being associated with welfare-to-work programs. Detected impacts tend to be found in terms of a child's behavioral and emotional adjustment, and to a lesser extent in cognitive development. Programmatic emphases, family characteristics, family circumstances, and a child's developmental stage influence the effect of welfare on children.

In general, children tend to fare better when family income improves, irrespective of specific programmatic emphases. Studies that compared job-training programs with work-first programs have not found patterns of difference in child outcomes in three domains: behavioral/emotional adjustment, cognitive development, and health and safety.

Family circumstances and characteristics can influence the relationship between welfare reform and child well-being. Children whose families received welfare for less time tended to fare worse under welfare-to-work requirements than children of long-term recipients in some studies. Maternal depression in combination with welfare-to-work requirements may be associated with declines in academic achievement, and with increased emotional and behavioral problems, among school-age children.

Many researchers and policymakers predicted that young children would be most adversely affected by parental employment. Findings thus far are mixed, however, suggesting that the influence of welfare-to-work on outcomes for young children is likely mediated by other factors, particularly the type and quality of nonparental care. Two studies of welfare-to-work that predate PRWORA found minimal impacts on young children. One of these studies showed that outcomes tended to be favorable in terms of cognitive development and unfavorable in terms of health and safety outcomes. Related findings on behavioral and emotional adjustment were mixed. A third study of families receiving TANF found that low-performing children placed in child-care centers showed greater gains in learning and school readiness than those children in home-based care. Further increases in cognitive development were found among children in higher-quality child-care centers.

There is some evidence that welfare-to-work programs are associated with cognitive, behavioral, and emotional changes among school-age children and among adolescents in particular. Detected effects are small but troubling. Adolescents whose parents are engaged in the welfare-to-work transition may be more likely to exhibit behavioral problems—such as school suspension or expulsion—and declines in school performance such as more frequent use of special educational services and grade repetition. Research suggests that adolescents in families who recently left welfare are more likely to be employed—and working longer hours—than youth of current welfare recipients. Long work hours may be detrimental to academic achievement. The influence of welfare-to-work programs on adolescents may be uneven. For example, youth with younger siblings have exhibited more behavior problems and lower school performance than those without younger brothers and sisters.

Conclusion

Government welfare programs underwent a substantial transformation in the 1990s. The influence of these changes on family and child outcomes is only beginning to be understood. Early evidence suggests that changes in family and child outcomes associated with welfare reform are due to the interaction of programmatic, family, and contextual factors.

See also: POVERTY AND EDUCATION.

BIBLIOGRAPHY

AHLUWALIA, SURJEET K.; MCGRODER, SHARON M.; ZASLOW, MARTHA J.; and HAIR, ELIZABETH C. 2001. *Symptoms of Depression Among Welfare Recipients: A Concern for Two Generations.* Washington, DC: Child Trends.

BROOKS, JENNIFER L.; HAIR, ELIZABETH C.; and ZASLOW, MARTHA J. 2001. *Welfare Reform's Impact on Adolescents: Early Warning Signs.* Washington, DC: Child Trends.

BROWN, BRETT. 2001. *Teens, Jobs, and Welfare: Implications for Social Policy.* Washington, DC: Child Trends.

CHASE-LANSDALE, P. LINDSAY, and PITTMAN, LAURA D. 2002. "Welfare Reform and Parenting: Reasonable Expectations." *The Future of Children: Children and Welfare Reform* 12(1):167–179.

CHILD TRENDS. 2002. *The Unfinished Business of Welfare Reform: Improving Prospects for Poor Children and Youth.* Washington, DC: Child Trends.

FULLER, BRUCE; KAGAN, SHARON L.; CASPARY, GRETCHEN L.; and GAUTHIER, CHRISTIANE A. 2002. "Welfare Reform and Child Care Options for Low-Income Families." *The Future of Children: Children and Welfare Reform* 12(1):97–119.

GENNETIAN, LISA A., et al. 2002. *How Welfare and Work Policies for Parents Affect Adolescents: A Synthesis of Research.* New York: Manpower Demonstration Research Corporation.

GREENBERG, MARK H.; LEVIN-EPSTEIN, JODIE; HUTSON, RUTLEDGE Q.; OOMS, THEODORA J.; SCHUMACHER, RACHEL; TURETSKY, VICKI; and ENGSTROM, DAVID M. 2002. "The 1996 Welfare Law: Key Elements and Reauthorization Issues Affecting Children." *The Future of Children: Children and Welfare Reform* 12(1):25–27.

GROWING UP IN POVERTY PROJECT. 2002. *New Lives for Poor Families? Mothers and Young Children Move through Welfare Reform: The Growing Up in Poverty Project—Wave 2 Findings, California, Connecticut, and Florida: Executive Summary.* Berkeley, CA: Growing Up in Poverty Project.

HUSTON, ALETHA C. 2002. "Reforms and Child Development." *The Future of Children: Children and Welfare Reform* 12(1):59–77.

TOUT, KATHRYN; SCARPA, JULIET; and ZASLOW, MARTHA J. 2002. *Children of Current and Former Welfare Recipients: Similarly at Risk.* Washington, DC: Child Trends.

U.S. DEPARTMENT OF HEALTH AND HUMAN SERVICES. 2000. *Temporary Assistance for Needy Families (TANF) Program: Third Annual Report to Congress.* Washington, DC: U.S. Department of Health and Human Services, Administration for Children and Families, Office of Planning, Research and Evaluation.

U.S. DEPARTMENT OF HEALTH AND HUMAN SERVICES. 2002. *Temporary Assistance for Needy Families (TANF) Program: Fourth Annual Report to Congress.* Washington, DC: U.S. Department of Health and Human Services, Administration for Children and Families, Office of Planning, Research and Evaluation.

ZASLOW, MARTHA J.; MOORE, KRISTIN A.; BROOKS, JENNIFER L.; MORRIS, PAMELA A.; TOUT, KATHRYN; REDD, ZAKIA A.; and EMIG, CAROL A. 2002. "Experimental Studies of Welfare Reform and Children." *The Future of Children: Children and Welfare Reform* 12(1):79–95.

INTERNET RESOURCE

HAMILTON, GAYLE; FREEDMAN, STEPHEN; and MC-GRODER, SHARON M. 2000. "Do Mandatory Welfare-to-Work Programs Affect the Well-Being of Children? A Synthesis of Child Research Conducted as Part of the National Evaluation of Welfare-to-Work Strategies." New York: Manpower Demonstration Research Corporation. <www.mdrc.org/Reports2000/NEWWS-CS/NEWWS-ChildSyn.htm>.

CATHERINE DUNN SHIFFMAN

MOVING MOTHERS FROM WELFARE TO WORK

Welfare policy at the start of the twenty-first century is the result of many changes in the nature of assistance to the economically disadvantaged throughout the history of this nation. Before 1900 the federal government played a minimal role in the alleviation of poverty. During this period, assistance to the poor was given through religious organizations and private philanthropic societies in the form of in-kind benefits such as clothes, shelter, and food. This assistance was often predicated on some type of work done in return on the part of the recipient, thus allowing for the recipient to retain a sense of pride and responsibility in "working" for the assistance given. Around the turn of the century, the plight of America's poor was just beginning to catch the attention of commentators such as Jacob Riis (1890) and Jane Addams (1902), who chronicled the conditions of urban housing tenements in New York and Chicago. Still, the government was a relatively small part of the American welfare structure at this time. As indicated by Carl Chelf (1992), in the years prior to the Great Depression, only about 12 percent of the assistance provided in the nation's fifteen largest cities came from public sources. Nevertheless, the idea that the federal government had a role in ameliorating the conditions of poverty was beginning to creep into the American consciousness.

In 1909 the first significant recognition of the problem of poverty by the federal government occurred when President Theodore Roosevelt invited 200 experts to the White House Conference on the Care of Dependent Children, which was essentially a brainstorming session on how best to devise programmatic solutions to assist widows and impoverished children. Two primary movements arose out of this conference—one to provide mothers' pensions and one to establish a federal children's bureau. The mothers' pension movement was primarily manifested at the state level, and by 1919 such pensions were available in thirty-nine states. The movement to establish a federal children's bureau culminated in the passage of federal legislation in 1912 that created the U.S. Children's Bureau, which provided federal grants to states that funded maternal and child health services. Federal involvement on this front was further institutionalized with the passage of the Sheppard-Towner Act of 1921, which supported the implementation of the first direct federal expenditures for child welfare.

The national economic collapse experienced during the Great Depression created the impetus for a much greater federal involvement in social welfare. In the face of unemployment rates of more than 20 percent that negatively affected the ranks of the middle and even the upper class, President Franklin D. Roosevelt created the Committee on Economic Security. This committee provided the momentum for the passage of the Social Security Act of 1935, which had two primary components: The first was an employment-based social insurance system based upon the contributions of employees and employers and the second provided assistance to economically disadvantaged mothers that was noncontributory in nature. This latter program, known as Aid to Families with Dependent Children (AFDC), would form the foundation of the welfare state well into the 1990s.

In the years after World War II America's urban centers began to deindustralize, as advances in mass-produced housing construction and the development of the national highway system facilitated the movement of industry and population to peripheral suburban areas. This movement was skewed by income and race. Those that moved outward tended to be largely more affluent and Caucasian, while those that remained within the urban core were largely economically disadvantaged minorities that faced declining opportunities for employment near their residences. These changes in the "structure of opportunity" resulted in highly concentrated populations of disadvantaged people within the nation's inner cities. As a result, the number of AFDC recipients increased 17 percent between 1950 and 1960. According to the U.S. Bureau of the Census, by 1960, more than 22 percent of the nation's population continued to live at incomes below the poverty line.

The persistence of poverty in America was addressed through federal initiatives in the 1960s, including John F. Kennedy's "War on Poverty" and Lyndon B. Johnson's "Great Society." Perhaps the most significant result of these efforts was the passage of the Economic Opportunity Act of 1964, which created the Office of Economic Opportunity (OEO). The OEO operated through a huge network of "neighborhood service centers" that facilitated the allocation of benefits to the community. The effect of the Economic Opportunity Act was profound. Between 1960 and 1970 the number of AFDC recipients increased by 107 percent and the national poverty rate declined to just under 13 percent.

From Welfare to Work: Federal and State Programs

The first federal effort to connect employment to welfare receipt was embodied in the Workforce Incentives Program, which was part of the AFDC law between 1967 and 1989. Under this program, states were required to register through their employment services any AFDC recipients with no preschool children. Of 1.2 million AFDC recipients in 1986, only 130,000 "worked" their way out of welfare, most

without the assistance of the program. An attempt at addressing these shortcomings was represented in the Family Support Act of 1988 (FSA), which created the Job Opportunities and Basic Skill (JOBS) Program. The JOBS program required any woman whose youngest child was three or over to participate in activities intended to promote self-sufficiency. Although FSA was a significant improvement over past efforts in that it provided for job training, childcare, and transitional assistance, states had difficulty meeting the 40 percent match requirement for the JOBS program. As a result, states were exempting more than half of the adult caseload in 1992, with some states reaching a 70 to 80 percent exemption rate. Overall, only about 7 percent of the adult caseload participated in the JOBS program in 1992.

The Personal Responsibility and Work Opportunity Reconciliation Act (PRWORA) of 1996 effectively ended the federal direct cash benefit to disadvantaged parents by reverting to funding awarded in the form of block grants to states. This policy gave states wide latitude in expending this funding, although several parameters were established. First, PRWORA placed a sixty-month lifetime limit on the receipt of benefits. States were allowed, however, to allow for a time limit exemption for up to twenty percent of the caseload. Second, PRWORA limited consecutive receipt of benefits to twenty-four months, after which recipients would have to reapply to continue participation in the program. Third, recipients were required to work as soon as they were determined to be "job-ready." Thus, PWORA re-established welfare policy as a means of providing short-term assistance as recipients worked towards employment.

The implementation of this latest permutation of welfare policy was a response to a wave of efforts at welfare reform at the state level, as more than forty states had been granted waivers to impose major changes in their welfare systems between 1993 and 1996. The passage of PRWORA only accelerated this tendency. Within the framework of PRWORA, the imposition of time limits at the state level was an important component of these changes. As of 2000, the enforcement of time limits had resulted in the loss of benefits for approximately 60,000 families nationwide.

The Impact of Welfare Reform

According to statistics published by the U.S. Department of Health and Human Services and Economic

Policy Institute in 2001, all of these sweeping changes in federal and state welfare policy resulted in a 56 percent reduction in caseload between 1993 and 2000—from more than five million families (5.5 percent of the population) to just over two million families (2.1 percent of the population). In fiscal year 1994, only 8 percent of TANF adults were employed while receiving assistance compared to 28 percent in fiscal year 1999.

However, it is important to note that the PR-WORA was implemented during the one of the strongest economic cycles in history. Researchers have found that at least 40 percent of the fall in caseloads may be attributable to the growth in the economy, rather than to changes in welfare policies. As unemployment ticked upwards in 2000 and 2001, caseloads again began to rise. Food stamp caseloads jumped by nearly 600,000 from September to October 2001—a 3 percent increase—and the majority of states saw increases in welfare caseloads during the latter part of 2001. Welfare caseloads became increasingly concentrated in America's cities. As of 1999, nearly 60 percent of all welfare cases were in 89 large urban counties, and ten urban counties accounted for almost one-third of all U.S. welfare cases.

Analysis of the poverty data regarding those moving from welfare to work indicates that although the poverty rate has declined overall, it has increased among working families, particularly those headed by single mothers. For those families that were already poor, poverty deepened between 1995 and 1999. The poverty rate among people in these families, after government benefits and taxes are taken into account, was 19.4 percent in 1999, nearly the same level as in 1995, when it stood at 19.2 percent. The census data also show that in 1999, the incomes of working single-mother families that were poor fell below the poverty line by an average of $1,505 for each person in these families. The number of working single-mother families that were poor climbed considerably between 1995 and 1999 and was larger in 1999 than at any other time in the 1993 to1999 period. These data indicate that while welfare reform policies resulted in the employment of more single mothers, an unintended consequence of this public policy has been that working-poor families headed by single mothers have grown poorer.

Work supports were also implemented in the welfare to work reform efforts. The major areas of support focused on childcare, health care, the EITC,

food stamps, and housing. The total federal dollars available for childcare nearly doubled from the early 1990s to the start of the twenty-first century and new regulations allowed states to use TANF monies for childcare expenditures. However, in 1999 only 12 percent of eligible families received assistance through the Child Care and Development Fund and Head Start served less than half of eligible children. Furthermore, despite increased federal funding on childcare over the 1990s, wages for childcare workers stagnated, resulting in recruitment and retention problems among child care workers.

As families transition to work, the costs of health care and housing costs become major concerns. Some employers do not offer affordable health benefits to the dependents of the employee. A parent in a family of three earning more than $7,992 (59 percent of the poverty guideline) is not eligible for Medicaid coverage. Former welfare recipients experience levels of health hardships similar to those of welfare families, and higher than those of poor families overall. In addition, the welfare reform legislation did not recognize the large role of housing in the budgets of poor families. A recent report concluded that "families are experiencing high rates of housing hardships: among parents who recently left welfare, 28 percent report being unable to pay housing or utility bills" (Wright, Gould, and Schill, p. 46).

See also: PARENTING; POVERTY AND EDUCATION.

BIBLIOGRAPHY

ADDAMS, JANE. 1902. "The Housing Problem in Chicago." *Annual of the American Academy of Political and Social Science* 20:97–107.

ADMINISTRATION FOR CHILDREN AND FAMILIES, AND OFFICE OF PLANNING RESEARCH AND EVALUATION. 2000. *Temporary Assistance for Needy Families (TANF) Program: Third Annual Report to Congress.* Washington, DC: U.S. Department of Health and Human Services.

BANE, MARY J., and ELLWOOD, DAVID T. 1994. *Welfare Realities: From Rhetoric to Reform.* Cambridge, MA: Harvard University Press.

BLOOM, DAN, and MICHALOPOLOUS, CHARLES. 2001. *How Welfare and Work Policies Affect Employment and Income: A Synthesis of Research.* New York: Manpower Demonstration Research Corporation.

BOUSHEY, HEATHER, and GUNDERSEN, BETHNEY. 2001. *Just Barely Making It: Hardships Experienced after Welfare.* Washington, DC: Economic Policy Institute.

BOUSHEY, HEATHER; GUNDERSEN, BETHNEY; BROCHT, CHAUNA; and BERNSTEIN, JARED. 2001. *Hardships in America: The Real Story of Working Families.* Washington, DC: Economic Policy Institute.

BRAUNER, SARAH, and LOPREST, PAMELA. 1999. *Where Are They Now? What States' Studies of People Who Left Welfare Tell Us.* Washington, DC: The Urban Institute.

BROOKINGS INSTITUTION. 1999. *The State of Caseloads in America's Cities: 1999.* Washington, DC: Brookings Institution, Center on Urban and Metropolitan Policy.

CHELF, CARL P. 1992. *Controversial Issues in Social Welfare Policy.* Newbury Park, CA: Sage.

KATZ, BRUCE, and ALLEN, KATHERINE. 2001. "Cities Matter: Shifting the Focus of Welfare Reform." *Brookings Review* 19:30–33.

KNIESNER, THOMAS, and ZILAK, JAMES. 1998. *The Effects of Recent Tax Reform on Labor Supply.* Washington, DC: AEI Press.

LOPREST, PAMELA. 1999. *How Families that Left Welfare Are Doing: A National Picture.* Washington, DC: Urban Institute.

PARROTT, SHARON. 1998. *Welfare Recipients Who Find Jobs: What Do We Know About Employment and Earnings?* Washington, DC: Center on Budget and Policy Priorities.

PORTER, KATHRYN H., and DUPREE, ALLEN. 2001. *Poverty Trends for Families Headed by Working Single Mothers: 1993 to 1999.* Washington, DC: Center on Budget and Policy Priorities.

RIIS, JACOB. 1890. *How the Other Half Lives: Studies among the Tenements of New York.* New York. Scribners.

STRAWN, JULIE; GREENBERG, MARK; and SAVNER, STEVE. 2001. *Improving Employment Outcomes Under TANF.* Washington, DC: Center for Law and Social Policy.

U.S. BUREAU OF THE CENSUS. 1995. Current Population Reports, P60-194.

WRIGHT, DAVID J.; GOULD, ELLEN INGRID; and SCHILL, MICHAEL H. 2001. *Community Development Corporations and Welfare Reform: Linkages, Roles, and Impacts.* Albany, NY: Rockefeller Institute Press.

INTERNET RESOURCES

ADMINISTRATION FOR CHILDREN AND FAMILIES. 2001. "Temporary Assistance for Needy Families (TANF), 1960–1999." <www.acf.dhhs.gov/news/stats/6097rf.htm>.

CHILDREN'S DEFENSE FUND. 2000. "Welfare to What? How Are Children and Families Faring After Three Years of the Welfare Law?" <www.childrensdefense.org/fair-start-welfaretowhat_2000.htm>.

MANPOWER DEMONSTRATION RESEARCH CORPORATION. 2001. "Poverty Trends for Families Headed by Working Single Mothers, 1993 to 1999." <www.cbpp.org/8-16-01wel.pdf>.

SHERMAN, ALOC, et al. 1998. *Welfare to What: Early Finding on Family Hardship and Well-Being.* Washington, DC: Children's Defense Fund. <www.childrensdefense.org/pdf/wlfwhat.pdf>.

PEARL SIMS
BILL THARP

WESTERN EUROPE

Western Europe is a concept of rather recent origins, reflecting the post–World War II split between those European countries that fell under Soviet domination and much of the rest of the continent. With the collapse of the Soviet Union, the concept may become obsolete. Contemporary western Europe includes France, Spain, Portugal, Italy, Germany, Austria, Switzerland, the Low Countries (Belgium, Luxembourg, and the Netherlands), Scandinavia, Britain, and certain small states such as Liechtenstein. Almost all of the countries of the European Union (EU) are in western Europe, although certain countries such as Norway and Switzerland have chosen not to be a part of the EU. Greece, on the other hand, has joined the EU but is rarely considered to be part of western Europe.

At varying levels, western European countries are intent on giving a European dimension to their education systems. However, the concept of western Europe and a European identity is constantly transforming because many countries from central and eastern Europe hope to join the EU in the coming years and are also committed to a European dimension in education.

Educational Roots

The European educational tradition traces its roots directly to the establishment of universities toward the end of the Middle Ages. These universities generally emphasized special fields of knowledge, such as law, medicine, philosophy, and theology. Although the primary beneficiaries of medieval schooling were clergymen, separate schools were established where children of merchants and masters, and even females, could develop literacy skills.

In the fourteenth and fifteenth centuries, the intellectuals engaged in a struggle to incorporate classical humanistic studies into the curriculum, known generally as the *liberal arts.* Secondary schools emerged at this time, serving the rising middle class and providing university preparation as well as a liberal arts curriculum. At the time of the Reformation, primary schools were established, which were separate from the universities and secondary schools, both in terms of the pupils they served and the programs of studies they provided. Consequently, a basic dualistic educational structure emerged, reflecting the highly stratified social structure in Europe: universities and higher schools served elites, while primary schools served the masses.

By the seventeenth century, classical ideals and religious loyalties gave way to educational efforts in the name of nationalism and vernacular languages began to prevail over Greek and Latin. Many thinkers saw the advantages of popular education to address national concerns, regardless of gender or class.

There was some variation as to the structure of the state-run education systems in different European countries. Germany created different educational tracks, which provided separate schools for future leaders of the state and for the common people. Its system tended to become the model for other countries that were establishing their own state systems. Following the French Revolution in 1789, France moved toward universal, popular education, where citizenship was to be emphasized over religious values.

By the nineteenth century, Germany achieved nearly universal literacy within the dualist system, due in part to compulsory schooling. In contrast to Germany and France, education in England was not nationalized until the twentieth century and has historically been one of the most decentralized systems in Europe. In fact, England did not create a Ministry of Education until 1944.

Even though the state gained control over the educational enterprise in all the countries, it recognized the importance of the private sector. The major issue in the struggle between church and state was not so much school sponsorship, but school control. In some areas, where there are strong religious cleavages, such as the Netherlands and Belgium, the state has continued to rely on the church to sponsor most of its schools. Consequently, more than 70 percent of the children in the Netherlands and 45 percent in Belgium attend private schools. In more homogeneous populations, such as Norway and Sweden, the state has monopolized schooling to such an extent that less than 3 percent of the children attend private schools. In contrast to areas such as the United States, which maintain a strong separation of church and state, all European states continue to provide substantial financial and regulatory support for private schooling. The level of state support is usually correlated with the level of state control. Private schools that receive support equivalent to public schools are usually under tight state control, while schools that receive less support have more autonomy. Another feature of state regulation concerns private school teachers, who must usually be certified in the same manner as public school teachers and whose salaries are usually defined by the state.

Reform in the Twentieth Century

During the twentieth century, the major school reform issue was social justice, as advocates of change stressed the need to achieve greater participation of all young people in schooling in order to prepare them to participate more fully in the economy of the state.

By the 1950s, all western European countries had adopted compulsory education requirements, and children were required to begin school from as early as age five in England to as late as age seven in the Scandinavian countries. School quickly became mandatory for seven or eight years in age-graded schools, although the length of mandatory schooling has increased in most countries. Compulsory education continues until age fourteen in Italy; age fifteen in Austria, Greece, and Portugal; and age sixteen in most other countries. In countries such as Germany and Belgium, students are required to stay in school on a part-time basis until the age of eighteen. The age requirements of compulsory schooling continue to be important, for it is in the state's interest that all citizens acquire a thorough basic education, though it is also important that the age when students leave school coincide more or less with the age when they enter the workforce.

As schooling became universal and the age requirement was extended, some structural reforms were necessary. The major cultural symbol of educational reform in western Europe has been some form of comprehensive school structure that can provide a common schooling experience. At the primary school level, Norway and Sweden adopted a common school even prior to the turn of the twentieth century. France mandated a common primary school in the 1930s, and just before the end of World War II, Great Britain joined most western European countries by adopting a policy of common primary schooling. Germany did not realize common primary schooling until democratization policies were adopted after World War II. By this time all western Europe maintained universal primary schools lasting from four to six years.

Once universal primary schooling was accomplished, the focus of school reform shifted to the secondary level. Sweden led the way in 1949 when it adopted a plan for a universal common nine-year school. Sweden was followed by other countries, such as Italy, Norway, and France, while other western European countries engaged in comprehensive school reforms with varying degrees of success. The German-speaking countries, for example, have been reluctant to move away from the dualistic tradition. Toward the end of the twentieth century, conservatives called the comprehensive school agenda into question, although in some countries the liberal reform agenda continued to take priority.

During the twentieth century, the curriculum debate, which had previously focused on the struggle between religious instruction and a study of the classics, was no longer relevant in societies that were becoming more interested in scientific and practical training. Questioning the classical curriculum was initially due to the humanist realism philosophies that emphasized the importance of experience and practice in education. However, with the advent of the Industrial Revolution, schools recognized the need for a more expansive curriculum. In 1974, Norway, for example, adopted eight branches in its upper secondary school structure: general education, manual and industrial studies, arts and crafts, fishing and maritime studies, sports, clerical and commercial studies, domestic arts and sciences, and social and health studies.

Some countries, such as Norway, have chosen to harmonize general studies and vocational studies by emphasizing the practical aspects of general studies and making vocational studies more academic and theoretical. What this means is that progress has been made in bringing the two worlds together by requiring that the vocational studies programs look more like the general studies programs. This trend has been accompanied by a substantial increase in enrollments of students planning on attending higher education.

All European countries offer vocational training in addition to the general curriculum. French students, for example, can opt for one of the vocational or technical tracks at around age fourteen or fifteen. Two major vocational education models exist. West Germany developed a dual-system model in the 1950s and 1960s, requiring upper secondary students to attend formal school for two half days or one full day and to be under supervision in the work environment for the rest of the week. In contrast, the French model places young people in formal schooling full-time until the end of compulsory attendance, when they may become full-time vocational students. The major distinction in the two models is that German youth are exposed to the work world at a much earlier age. In some countries, such as Norway, researchers and policymakers have structured their system so that a full range of options is available. In all systems, it is difficult for students to return to a university track once they move to vocational and technical training. As can be expected, countries have developed systems of orientation to deal with tracking issues.

Another debate that carried into the twentieth century from past centuries is one concerning the role of the central government in education. Contrary to previous efforts at the time of the Reformation and the French Revolution that favored an exclusively state-controlled school, the post–World War II movement has been toward decentralization of control from the state to local school authorities. Both private and state schools tend to be centralized in terms of state funding, but decentralized in the administration and management of schools. This enterprise has the aim of making schools more autonomous and democratic by encouraging parental and community involvement. This trend is especially evident in Denmark, England, Italy, Scotland, and

Spain and can even be found in countries where education has been historically quite centralized, such as France and Sweden.

Toward the end of the twentieth century, the different political forces in Europe began moving away from an emphasis on social justice and toward individual choice and economic advantage. The social-democrat position had attempted to be more inclusive of the needs of disadvantaged groups, including women, immigrants, and the poor, stressing cultural imperatives. In contrast, conservative efforts of the 1980s and early 1990s focused more on market-oriented policies, emphasizing school choice, privatization, and other economic imperatives. In the United Kingdom, the Netherlands, and Sweden, for example, the issue of choice has driven reform discourse into the twenty-first century. Conservative governments have tried to reverse past trends, and their reforms might be seen partly as an attempt to address discontent among parents, particularly among the middle classes, who have been dissatisfied with what they deem declining standards of state-provided education. In the United Kingdom in 1981, the Conservatives introduced an *assisted place scheme,* providing a state subsidy to poorer parents whose children were previously less able to gain entry to private schools.

Of course, the market-oriented trend was not identical across Europe. Furthermore, some may argue that there has not been a significant change in education due to the ideological differences of different governments. Nevertheless, European education systems at the end of the twentieth century experienced a general movement toward further decentralization and deregulation of state control.

Contemporary Reform Trends

With the creation and opening up of the European Union, educational systems are tending to become more alike. This tendency has been in process at least since the establishment of the Council of Europe in 1949 and of the European Community in 1967. In education, policymakers have thus far stressed the value of each nation's historical development by maintaining the linguistic and cultural diversity of individual European countries. Nevertheless, the Council of Europe is interested in developing a European dimension to education. The goal is not to abolish national differences in favor of a European identity, but to strive for unity in diversity. One way the Council of Europe has attempted to create a pan-

European identity is by organizing teachers' conferences that focus on how to avoid national stereotyping and bias in curricula and textbooks. Educational reforms in the twenty-first century illustrate a move away from discovering how to be Dutch or English, and instead learning how to think of oneself as European.

In primary and secondary education, language has been one of the most important issues. As there are eleven different official languages in the European Union, most European schools have decided to teach more languages and to begin teaching them as early as possible—usually in primary school. Moreover, because many European schools are decentralized and some do not even have a central curriculum, language training is one of the ways to bring the European dimension into the curriculum. Such is the case in the Netherlands, where students must prepare for the foreign language and culture component of their exams. Language instruction in all EU countries must be developed for participation in academic exchanges in other countries, which will also contribute to creating a European identity.

These exchanges are an important part of the European dimension agenda in education, and they occur at all levels, from primary school to higher education and teacher and vocational training. The European Union project SOCRATES is useful in improving the quality of language training and school partnerships at the primary and secondary level with the LINGUA and COMENIUS programs (subsets of SOCRATES). Involving both EU and non-EU countries (about 30 total), SOCRATES promotes the buildup of European knowledge and a better response to the major challenges facing the contemporary world. To achieve these goals, it utilizes student exchange, cooperative projects, European networks, and research studies.

At the higher-education level, all national systems have grown massively in terms of student numbers, institutions, faculties, and courses. While university reforms in the twentieth century were few, limited in scope, and rarely applied, fundamental changes are beginning to occur in the early twenty-first century. The most far-reaching reform agenda is related to the Bologna Declaration of 1999, signed by twenty-nine European countries. The declaration aims to establish, by 2010, a common framework of readable and comparable university degrees, including both undergraduate and postgraduate levels. This framework will be relevant to the labor market, will have compatible credit systems, and will ensure a European dimension. In Italy, for example, the new higher-education system has a first cycle that lasts three years and leads to an undergraduate degree, a second cycle that lasts two years and leads to a postgraduate degree, and a final three-year program resulting in a doctorate. Within these general constraints, the universities are given great autonomy in terms of programs and administration.

Another major innovation is the development of a European Credit Transfer System (ECTS), meant to enhance cooperation between universities. It is embryonic and completely voluntary, but suggests the development of a process for determining curricular transparencies and equivalencies of grades, course credits, and degrees. ECTS enables students to receive credit in their home university or to transfer permanently to the host institution or to a third institution, mainly by generating transcripts that translate the different educational systems into an internationally recognized document.

Student exchange has also become a major policy issue. ERASMUS is an exchange project under SOCRATES that allows university students to participate in exchanges in universities throughout the European Union and receive credit at their home university. The creation of the ECTS renders such an exchange possible for students who may not have the time or finances to take courses that will not count towards their degree. This cooperation between universities does not necessarily mean that they will become identical, but it does suggest the importance of transparency, as well as trust that other universities are equal in quality to one's own. This trust must also be extended to a mutual recognition of diplomas at all levels of the education system, which puts pressure on the various countries to maintain acceptable standards.

One of the difficulties that has arisen regarding exchanges is that they often must be reciprocal, and people may thus be discouraged from taking part in an exchange in countries with less widely spoken languages, such as Dutch or Danish. While many people study English, French, or German and could fathom spending a year in a university where one of these languages is spoken, students may hesitate to study in a country where they are not proficient in the language. One solution at the university level is to offer some courses in a more widely spoken language. Such is the case at the University of Amsterdam, where 25 percent of the classes are taught in English. Another solution at the primary and secondary levels is to create bilingual programs, especially in the border regions of a country.

Future Challenges

Some of the immediate challenges for Europe at the beginning of the twenty-first century include those surrounding educational mobility. Educational exchanges are sometimes not possible financially. Although in principle students can freely occupy available places in member states with identical fees and financial aid, grants from the home country are not always available for studies abroad, an issue that has arisen in the Netherlands. Furthermore, language skills will need to be further valued and developed if exchanges are to be reciprocally appreciated and practiced between the countries of the European Union and possibly with other countries on the European continent and elsewhere. Europeans will need to make special efforts to improve language skills in order to encourage the maximum success of exchange projects.

In addition to developing students' language skills, schools are also facing the task of dealing with societal and economic demand for people who are technology and information literate. The schools themselves must learn to cope with an ever-changing world, where people have to learn how to adapt rather than to learn a stable and firm body of knowledge. Schools need to remain current so that they can help students respond to contemporary exigencies.

At the higher-education level, open distance-learning universities exist in countries such as Britain, Spain, and Portugal to help students adapt to change by way of professional and technological training. These universities need to continue to be developed to accommodate people in the workforce who would like to update their skills, or students from other countries who do not have access to adequate universities, but who cannot necessarily live abroad or reside on a university campus for extended periods of time.

A higher-education issue that EU members must address more systematically involves greater compliance in the recognition of diplomas and certification between countries. Some countries, such as the Netherlands, have even suggested the granting of double degrees between the national institution and an associated institution. University overcrowding and high unemployment throughout Europe are not simplifying the dilemma, and there is a concern that the costly expansion of the university may lower the quality of education and lead to the devaluation of degrees.

These issues need to be considered throughout Europe, because the greatest challenge for many countries, perhaps to even a greater extent for the smaller countries, is to preserve national differences in the creation of a European unity. As various countries from central and eastern Europe plan to become part of the European Union, and borders are fading on a global level, recognizing and respecting institutional differences may be key to the success in efforts to establish unity in diversity.

See also: CURRICULUM, INTERNATIONAL; DISTANCE LEARNING IN HIGHER EDUCATION; INTERNATIONAL EDUCATION.

BIBLIOGRAPHY

BEATTIE, NICHOLAS. 1985. *Professional Parents: Parent Participation in Four Western European Countries.* Brighton, Eng.: Falmer Press.

BROCK, COLIN, and TULASIEWICZ, WITOLD, eds. 2000. *Education in a Single Europe.* London: Routledge.

COUNCIL OF EUROPE PUBLISHING. 2000. *Strategies for Educational Reform: from Concept to Realization.* Strasbourg, France: Council of Europe Publishing.

DALIN, PER, and RUST, VAL D. 1996. *Towards Schooling for the Twenty-First Century.* London: Cassell.

PECK, BRYAN T. 1998. *Issues in European Education.* Commack, NY: Nova Science.

POWER, EDWARD J. 1991. *A Legacy of Learning: A History of Western Education.* Albany: State University of New York Press.

VAL D. RUST
TRACI WELLS

WHITEHEAD, ALFRED NORTH (1861–1947)

One of the twentieth century's most original metaphysicians and a major figure in mathematical logic, Alfred North Whitehead was also an important social and educational philosopher. Born in England, he was educated at Trinity College, Cambridge, where he also taught mathematics from 1884 until 1910. He then moved to London, where he was professor of applied mathematics at the University of London until 1924. Receiving an invitation to join the philosophy department at Harvard University, Whitehead came to the United States and taught at Harvard until 1937. He remained in Cambridge, Massachusetts, for the rest of his life.

While Whitehead's metaphysical and logical writings merit his inclusion in any pantheon of twentieth-century philosophers, his work in social and educational philosophy is marked by singular qualities of imagination, profound analysis, and personal commitment. His thought resembles much in the philosophy of John Dewey (1859–1952). In the philosophy of higher education, where Dewey wrote very little, Whitehead is probably the most important figure since John Henry Cardinal Newman (1801–1890).

The Nature of Education

"Education is the acquisition of the art of the utilisation of knowledge." This simple sentence from Whitehead's introductory essay in his *Aims of Education* (1929, p. 4), epitomizes one of his central themes: Education cannot be dissected from practice. Whitehead's synthesis of knowledge and application contrasts sharply with educational theories that recommend mental training exclusively. His general philosophical position, which he called "the philosophy of organism," insists upon the ultimate reality of things in relation, changing in time, and arranged in terms of systems of varying complexity, especially living things, including living minds. Whitehead rejected the theory of mind that maintains it is a kind of tool, or dead instrument, needing honing and sharpening. Nor is it a kind of repository for "inert" ideas, stored up in neatly categorized bundles. It is an organic element of an indissoluble mind/body unit, in continuous relationship with the living environment, both social and natural. Whitehead's philosophy of organism, sometimes called "process philosophy," stands in continuity with his educational thought, both as a general theoretical backdrop for this educational position and as the primary application of his fundamental educational themes.

Educational Development and the Rhythm of Growth

Whitehead's general concept of the nature and aims of education has as its psychological corollary a conception of the rhythm of education that connects him with developmental educators such as Jean-Jacques Rousseau (1712–1778). For Whitehead, education is a temporal, growth-oriented process, in which both student and subject matter move progressively. The concept of rhythm suggests an aesthetic dimension to the process, one analogous to music. Growth then is a part of physical and mental development, with a strong element of style understood as a central driving motif. There are three fundamental stages in this process, which Whitehead called the stage of romance, the stage of precision, and the stage of generalization.

Romance is the first moment in the educational experience. All rich educational experiences begin with an immediate emotional involvement on the part of the learner. The primary acquisition of knowledge involves freshness, enthusiasm, and enjoyment of learning. The natural ferment of the living mind leads it to fix on those objects that strike it pre-reflectively as important for the fulfilling of some felt need on the part of the learner. All early learning experiences are of this kind and a curriculum ought to include appeals to the spirit of inquiry with which all children are natively endowed. The stage of precision concerns "exactness of formulation" (Whitehead 1929, p. 18), rather than the immediacy and breadth of relations involved in the romantic phase. Precision is discipline in the various languages and grammars of discrete subject matters, particularly science and technical subjects, including logic and spoken languages. It is the scholastic phase with which most students and teachers are familiar in organized schools and curricula. In isolation from the romantic impetus of education, precision can be barren, cold, and unfulfilling, and useless in the personal development of children. An educational system excessively dominated by the ideal of precision reverses the myth of Genesis: "In the Garden of Eden Adam saw the animals before he named them: in the traditional system, children named the animals before they saw them" (Whitehead 1925, p. 285). But precision is nevertheless a necessary element in a rich learning experience, and can neither substitute for romance, nor yield its place to romance. Generalization, the last rhythmic element of the learning process, is the incorporation of romance and preci-

sion into some general context of serviceable ideas and classifications. It is the moment of educational completeness and fruition, in which general ideas or, one may say, a philosophical outlook, both integrate the feelings and thoughts of the earlier moments of growth, and prepare the way for fresh experiences of excitement and romance, signaling a new beginning to the educational process.

It is important to realize that these three rhythmic moments of the educational process characterize all stages of development, although each is typically associated with one period of growth. So, romance, precision, and generalization characterize the rich educational experience of a young child, the adolescent, and the adult, although the romantic period is more closely associated with infancy and young childhood, the stage of precision with adolescence, and generalization with young and mature adulthood. Education is not uniquely oriented to some future moment, but holds the present in an attitude of almost religious awe. It is "holy ground" (Whitehead 1929, p. 3), and each moment in a person's education ought to include all three rhythmical elements. Similarly, the subjects contained in a comprehensive curriculum need to comprise all three stages, at whatever point they are introduced to the student. Thus the young child can be introduced to language acquisition by a deft combination of appeal to the child's emotional involvement, its need for exactitude in detail, and the philosophical consideration of broad generalizations.

Universities and Professional Training

The pragmatic and progressive aims of education, accompanied by Whitehead's rhythmic developmentalism, have ramifying effects throughout the lifelong educational process, but nowhere more tellingly than in their application to university teaching and research. Whitehead was a university professor throughout his life, and for a time, dean of the Faculty of Science at the University of London. Personal experience makes his analysis of higher studies pointed and relevant. Strikingly, Whitehead chose the modern business school as representative of modern directions in university theory and practice. As a Harvard philosopher, he was in an excellent position to comment on this particular innovation in higher education, since Harvard University was the first school in the United States to have a graduate program in business administration. The novelty of the business school should not be overestimated, since the wedding of theory and practice has been an unspoken motif of higher education since the foundation of the university in the Middle Ages. What has happened is that business has joined the ranks of the learned professions, no longer exclusively comprising theology, law, and medicine. The business school shows that universities are not merely devoted to postsecondary instruction, nor are they merely research institutions. They are both, and the active presence of young learners and mature scholars is necessary to their organic health. "The justification for a university is that it preserves the connection between knowledge and the zest of life, by uniting the young and the old in the imaginative consideration of learning" (Whitehead 1929, p. 93). This community of young and old is a further extension of the organic nature of learning. It makes the university analogous to other living associations, such as the family. The place of imagination in university life illustrates Whitehead's insistence on the aesthetic element in education. Universities are not merely institutions of analytic and intellectual skills, but of their imaginative integration into life. There is a creative element to all university activity (and not merely to the fine arts), a creativity necessary to the survival of life in a world of adventurous change. "Knowledge does not keep any better than fish" (Whitehead 1929, p. 98) and, while universities have a calling to preserve the great cultural achievements of the past, this conservatism must not be allowed to degenerate into a passive and unreflective commitment to inert ideas. "The task of a University is the creation of the future" (Whitehead 1938, p. 233). Ironically perhaps, the modern university, even one containing a business school, should not be managed like a business organization. The necessary freedom and risk, so important to the inventive scholar, requires a polity "beyond all regulation" (Whitehead 1929, p. 99).

Civilization, as Whitehead expresses it in his 1933 book, *Adventures of Ideas* (pp. 309–381), is constituted by five fundamental ideals, namely, beauty, truth, art, adventure, and peace. These five capture the aims, the rhythm, and the living, zestful and ordered progress of education and its institutional forms. They constitute a rich meaning of the term *creativity*, the ultimate driving source and goal of Whitehead's educational theory and program.

See also: PHILOSOPHY OF EDUCATION.

BIBLIOGRAPHY

BRUMBAUGH, ROBERT S. 1982. *Whitehead, Process Philosophy, and Education.* Albany: State University of New York Press.

DUNKEL, HAROLD B. 1965. *Whitehead on Education.* Columbus: Ohio State University Press.

JOHNSON, ALLISON H. 1958. *Whitehead's Philosophy of Civilization.* Boston: Beacon.

LEVI, ALBERT W. 1937. "The Problem of Higher Education: Whitehead and Hutchins." *Harvard Educational Review* 7:451–465.

WHITEHEAD, ALFRED NORTH. 1925. *Science and the Modern World.* New York: Macmillan.

WHITEHEAD, ALFRED NORTH. 1929. *The Aims of Education and Other Essays.* New York: Macmillan.

WHITEHEAD, ALFRED NORTH. 1933. *Adventures of Ideas.* New York: Macmillan.

WHITEHEAD, ALFRED NORTH. 1938. *Modes of Thought.* New York: Macmillan.

ROBERT J. MULVANEY

WHITE HOUSE FELLOWS

Every year, the White House Fellows program offers a small number of America's most promising young leaders an opportunity to participate in government at the highest levels. The White House Fellows program is one of the most prestigious and selective fellowship programs for leadership development and public service in the country. White House Fellows are selected by the President's Commission on White House Fellowships, a nonpartisan commission of thirty to forty leading American citizens representing a range of backgrounds and professions. All commission members are appointed by the president; many are former White House Fellows.

Selection Process

Any citizen of the United States who believes that he or she has leadership qualities, the ability to function effectively at the highest levels of government, and a commitment to serve the country may apply for the White House Fellowship program. The competition is extraordinarily keen with 500 to 800 applicants to fill only eleven to nineteen positions each year. There are no age restrictions for admittance to the program, but most Fellows are in their early thirties. Applications must be submitted by February 1 for the fellowship year beginning September 1 and running till the end of August the following year. Candidates may be nominated by universities, colleges, professional associations, or other groups, but the majority of candidates apply on their own initiative.

A screening committee of the President's Commission reads and rates the applications, referring about 100 of the most impressive applicants to ten regional panels for further screening. Applicants are evaluated on the basis of their professional and academic accomplishments, as well as on their potential for growth as leaders. The regional panels designate regional finalists, interview them, and recommend national finalists to the President's Commission. All finalists must undergo background checks to ensure that they qualify for the security clearances necessary to work in the White House. After further interviews over a period of several days, the President's Commission makes its choices known to the president, who then appoints the White House Fellows. The new class of White House Fellows is announced every year in early June.

Job Assignments

White House Fellows perform various functions for their respective principles in the executive branch of the federal government. The commission staff determines each Fellow's job assignment in consultation with the government officials for whom they will be working. Fellows may work as assistants to the vice president, cabinet officers, agency heads, and other top-ranking government officials. Often, Fellows serve as troubleshooters, working on whatever problem requires immediate attention in the highest ranks of their agencies and departments. They may also prepare reports, write speeches, help draft legislation, chair meetings, and conduct briefings. Fellows are paid a salary at federal pay grade GS-14/Step 3 (about $80,000 in 2001) and are not allowed to receive compensation from any other source during their fellowship year.

Educational Program

Despite their services to the government, many White House Fellows argue that the immediate benefits of the program flow mainly in their direction. First, their job experience gives them a unique opportunity for understanding the operations of one government department or agency, including the

style and methods of top decision makers. In addition, the president's commission operates an education program that provides Fellows with an understanding of areas of government outside of those to which they have been assigned, as well as a knowledge of the major issues and problems with which the government must cope. In this way, the education program supplements job experience.

In a typical year's education series, White House Fellows meet off-the-record with cabinet secretaries, Supreme Court justices, members of Congress, military leaders, and foreign heads of state. Fellows may also meet with governors, mayors, sociologists, urban planners, scientists, representatives of interest groups, foreign service officers, foreign policymakers, fiscal experts, business and labor leaders, and commentators from the press and academic circles. White House Fellows are also offered the opportunity to travel to major American cities, foreign countries, and military bases to explore government and policy in action. These activities help Fellows develop an increased understanding of the challenges facing American society and a greater sensitivity to the role of the federal government in dealing with these challenges.

History

The White House Fellows program was established in October 1964 by President Lyndon B. Johnson for the purpose of enabling the U.S. government to benefit from the services of the large numbers of bright, able, and talented citizens not ordinarily seeking careers in government. The program was a result of the concern expressed by John W. Gardner, then president of the Carnegie Corporation, and shared by President Johnson that the contributions of such citizens were not directly benefiting the government and the nation except in times of national crisis, such as during a war. During its first years, the White House Fellows program was supported entirely by private grant funds. Major support was provided by the Carnegie Corporation and the Ford Foundation, and David Rockefeller made a sizable personal donation to the commission. Gradually, however, the costs of the program have shifted to the federal government.

Since 1964 many former White House Fellows have made significant marks in various fields. Former Fellows of note include Doris Kearns Goodwin (1967–1968 Fellow), who became a Pulitzer Prize-winning author, historian, and television commentator; Henry Cisneros (1971–1972 Fellow), who became mayor of San Antonio, Texas, and secretary of Housing and Urban Development during the Clinton administration; Colin Powell (1972–1973 Fellow), who became a general in the U.S. Army, chairman of the Joint Chiefs of Staff, and secretary of state during the administration of George W. Bush; Wesley Clark (1975–1976 Fellow), who became a general in the U.S. Army and supreme allied commander, Europe; William Roper (1982–1983 Fellow), who became dean of the University of North Carolina School of Public Health and director of the Centers for Disease Control and Prevention (CDC); Elaine L. Chao (1983–1984 Fellow), who became president and chief executive officer of the United Way of America and director of the Peace Corps; and Paul Gigot (1986–1987 Fellow), who became a columnist and editor for the *Wall Street Journal*.

INTERNET RESOURCE

WHITE HOUSE FELLOWS PROGRAM. 2002. <www.whitehouse.gov/fellows>.

STEPHEN P. STRICKLAND
Revised by
JUDITH J. CULLIGAN

WOMEN'S STUDIES

Women's studies is an interdisciplinary field of inquiry that arose in the early 1970s. Within thirty years, it developed into a recognized discipline with undergraduate majors, masters and doctorates programs, university departments and programs, a scholarly literature of books and journals, and professional associations. The origins of women's studies are multiple, the scope and nature of the inquiry extensive, and its relationships to other campus and community organizations related to women and gender diverse.

Origins, Offerings, and Organization

The first courses in women's studies were taught at Cornell University and San Diego State University in 1969. They were undergraduate offerings, team taught, and provided overviews of the issues that arose out of the women's liberation movement.

The landscape of higher education changed dramatically in the 1960s as larger numbers of women

and minorities entered the professorate and the number and size of institutions grew. Many of the women who entered the academy in the next decade had been influenced by the women's movement and undertook research on women. Thus, scholarship on women grew in the existing disciplines and was designated as feminist scholarship. However, many of the questions that arose fell outside the bounds of disciplines as they were defined then. The field of women's studies emerged as the site for investigating these questions, forging new subject matter, employing multiple research methodologies, and experimenting with pedagogies that took into account gender differences in learning styles. Women's studies refers to the campus administrative unit and concentration of courses covering this material on women.

Women's studies grew rapidly in the 1970s, so that by the end of the decade, the National Women's Studies Association counted some 200 programs offering undergraduate minors and majors. A typical major consisted of an introductory course, courses on women selected from cooperating departments, and a capstone seminar. Many included internships that enabled students to experience first hand the issues community women encountered. The introductory course covered some aspects of women's history, an examination of quantitative research on women's status, selected reading of literary works by women, and attention to issues largely absent from the overall curriculum. These issues centered on the oppression of women, sexual assault, questions of marriage and family, the professional advancement of women, pay equity, and representations of women in media, among other topics. Courses offered by departments—The Psychology of Women, for example—constituted the majority of courses for the major. Some programs and departments were able to offer special topics courses (i.e., Images of Girls in Literature) or additional core courses (i.e., Feminist Methods, Feminist Theories). Most programs attempted to offer a research seminar as a capstone course, enabling majors and minors to come together for research and reflection.

As programs became departments and as departments grew, the course offerings of the major changed to reflect the emergent scholarship. Courses on identities and differences among women, courses with a global focus, courses that linked with other new fields (cultural studies, American studies, popular culture, media studies, ethnic studies, gay and lesbian studies, queer studies) all emerged in the 1980s and 1990s. The most significant shifts in course offerings at the undergraduate level occurred in the 1990s as the study of gender and of race were added to the study of women.

Feminist scholarship on women grappled with the question of gender, that is, of the relationships among men and women, masculinity and femininity, and social power. Research revealed that new information and interpretations about women forced a reframing of what was known about men and masculinities at any given time or place. Advocates of research on gender argued that the expanded focus enabled scholars to see the sex/gender system holistically. Other scholars and many activists argued that a focus on gender buried a concern with the inequalities women still suffered in society and therefore did not advance an agenda of social change. By 2000 women's studies programs numbered nearly 800; most had added a concern with gender to their teaching and research missions while retaining a focus on women's inequality.

Equally important to the origins and offerings of women's studies through its short history has been the question of identities, particularly those that are race based. While the initial scholarship focused on the ways in which *all* women had suffered injustices, research as well as experience quickly revealed the obvious fact that there were substantial differences *among* women that bore investigation. African-American women and lesbian women advocated greater attention to the ways in which being female was interwoven with other identities, demonstrating that each combination was reflected and refracted in the social world in a distinct way. Developing the conceptual tools as well as the methods to investigate these multiple manifestations of *woman* became the focus of scholarship.

Just as the undergraduate subject matter of women's studies became more complex over time, the relationship of programs and departments to other campus units diversified. There are two primary sets of relationships, one with campus women's centers and the other with graduate schools. On most campuses, either a women's studies program, usually housed in academic affairs, or a women's center, usually housed within a division of student affairs, came first. The unit that was created first was seen by the campus community as *the place* for women's issues to be handled and efforts to establish additional units to deal with the multifaceted needs of women students, faculty, and staff often had to compete for resources. Because their origins are distinct, their administrative homes different, their missions discrete, and occasionally their audiences separate, the relationships between women's studies and women's centers vary from campus to campus.

Graduate programs, arising in the 1980s, were structured much like undergraduate programs, with core requirements, courses selected from other departments, and an emphasis on either research or practicum to prepare students for careers. The Ph.D. in women's studies emerged in the 1990s. In the United States, M.A. and Ph.D. programs tended to be organized around issue clusters and offered students opportunities to enter the professorate as well as to assume research positions in government, corporate, and non-profit sectors. In Europe, Japan, Latin America, and the United Kingdom, undergraduate degrees in women's studies were less common and graduate research degrees more frequent.

Intellectual Contours

Women's studies scholarship is in its most basic form an epistemological endeavor. It asks teachers, students, and researchers to develop a reflective critical consciousness whose goal is not only to inform, but also to transform what one knows and how one knows it. To accomplish this goal, it uses a wide variety of methodological approaches and investigates questions at the center of women's lives, questions that have not been central to formal knowledge systems. This innovativeness raises a series of intellectual debates. For some, these debates are a sign of vigor, for others a quagmire. The central topics for debate include the meaning of interdisciplinarity, the relevance of feminist scholarship, the relationship of scholarship to activism, and the utility of various feminist theories.

Women's studies claims to be an interdisciplinary discipline. For some, *interdisciplinary* refers to the fact that the questions and methods used in teaching and research are drawn from two or more of the traditional disciplines, whether by one person or a team. For others, *interdisciplinary* is more specifically defined as the intersection of questions and methods that are used in combination to arrive at new knowledge. For those who see interdisciplinarity in this way, it is not additive but transformative: the methods employed to investigate a subject come from the question that is asked and the question derives from the goals of the researcher or teacher.

Thus, interdisciplinary women's studies scholars use methods and approach questions in distinct combinations, often viewed as nontraditional. This approach requires that scholars balance the breadth of the tools and queries they utilize with the need for depth in analysis.

For those outside the field, the most commonly asked question is *why women's studies?* The question is asked from a least two different standpoints. In the 1970s, colleagues in other disciplines frequently claimed that women's studies was unnecessary. They claimed that any of the questions pursued in women's studies could be handled by the extant disciplines. Women's studies scholars countered that such questions had not been—and were unlikely to be—addressed without a separate site for the production of knowledge about women. The subject matter of women's studies is distinctive: it places women and gender at the center and analyzes practices, contexts, and ideologies from that standpoint.

Given the institutional successes of women's studies, the *why women's studies* question has taken a second form. At least three decades after the founding of this field of study, the claim is made that the questions of discrimination and agency that are foundational to the field are now resolved and therefore irrelevant. Some argue that the questions of the twenty-first century are issue-based, not identity-based, and that questions of women and gender are now included in all such issues, making their separate study unnecessary. Women's studies scholars counter that the inclusion of conversations about women cannot be ongoing without the continuing infusion of new knowledge that derives from specialization.

It is generally agreed among feminist scholars that the impetus for women's studies arose in the activism of the women's movement in the late 1960s. Once faculty and students began investigating the conditions and representations of women's lives as subjects of academic study, however, activism's role became problematic. The issues are formulated in a variety of ways. Some investigators believe that research outcomes should always be of social value. Thus, psychologists who investigate sexual assault often encourage the use of their work in policy and legal projects. Other scholars take the position that all knowledge is ultimately socially useful but that research and teaching on any subject is an end in and of itself. For example, a philosopher who writes in the area of feminism might argue that the critical

thinking skills students develop benefit an informed citizen over the course of a lifetime.

The evolution of scholarship on women and gender in yet other fields, particularly the humanities, has become so specialized that it has developed language, theory, and traditions that are difficult for casual readers to comprehend. These scholars may claim that social activism—the engagement with cultural and political organizations and their activities—is separate from formal study and should be pursued according to individual inclinations. Thus, debates continue: Should an internship in an activist organization be a required part of a major? Should information in women's studies classes explore the links to activism? Should departmental structures support activist endeavors? Given the origins of women's studies in political activism and the continued inequalities in society and culture based on gender, these questions are likely to remain at the center of debates in the field.

A final debate centers on the choice of theories to explain women's positions in the gender systems of societies and cultures. This is perhaps the most controversial of all the debates. Much of the work in women's studies in the 1970s grew out of the social sciences, particularly history, cultural anthropology, sociology, and psychology. These scholars infused theoretical paradigms already in play—liberalism, Marxism, socialism, and psychoanalytic approaches, among others—and revised them to include women. Joined by colleagues in literature and art history, the first generation of feminist scholars engaged in the recovery of texts by, and information about, women, finding patterns in their discoveries that offered new explanations for women's exclusion as well as agency.

By the late 1980s developments in philosophy, literature, and other interdisciplinary fields—cultural studies, queer studies, media studies, studies of popular culture, studies of sexualities—came to prominence in women's studies. These approaches focused more on the representations of women in texts (written and visual as well as spoken) and less on empirical investigations. Known as post-structuralism, post-modernism, and critical theory, they emphasized the fluid and temporal nature of interpretations of women and gender, making the meaning and use of theory both more complex and more contested.

The place of theory was further complicated by the development of a global perspective in women's studies. Beginning with the first of the United Nations Decade for Women meetings in Mexico City in 1975, followed by meetings in Copenhagen in 1980, Nairobi in 1985, and Beijing in 1995, feminist scholars increasingly conducted research around the globe, and scholars from every country investigated women's issues. The introduction of material on women globally called into question Western-based theories of sex and gender.

For scholars who came from the empirical tradition, theory conveyed a broad range of endeavors aimed at identifying patterns that would yield explanations over time and space. For scholars who worked within the humanities paradigms, theory meant critical theory, the investigation of texts and their meanings. For policy makers who looked to women's studies scholarship to identify women's material conditions, theory had a utilitarian focus. For those in the natural sciences who followed traditions of experimentation, feminist theory often appeared as an unlikely tool. And the work of global scholars, working out of yet other intellectual traditions, further contributed to theoretical debates. However, the evolution of these various debates about what constitutes theory had, by the twenty-first century, encouraged many scholars to examine the interstices and find linkages.

See also: ACADEMIC DISCIPLINES; ACADEMIC MAJOR, THE; MULTICULTURALISM IN HIGHER EDUCATION.

BIBLIOGRAPHY

ALLEN, CAROLYN, and HOWARD, JUDITH A. 2000. *Provoking Feminisms.* Chicago: University of Chicago Press.

BOXER, MARILYN J. 1998. *When Women Ask Questions: Creating Women's Studies in America.* Baltimore, MD: Johns Hopkins University Press.

MAHER, FRANCES A., and TETREAULT, MARY KAY THOMPSON. 2001. *The Feminist Classroom: Dynamics of Gender, Race, and Privilege.* Lanham, MD: Rowman and Littlefield.

MOI, TORIL. 1999. *What Is a Woman? And Other Essays.* New York: Oxford University Press.

YOUNG, IRIS MARION. 2000. *Inclusion and Democracy.* New York: Oxford University Press.

JEAN FOX O'BARR

WOODSON, CARTER GODWIN (1875–1950)

Teacher, scholar, publisher and administrator, Carter Godwin Woodson articulated ideas that are antecedents to the discipline of black studies; however, he is best known as the "father of black history."

Woodson was born in New Canton, Buckingham County, Virginia, to former slaves Ann Eliza (Riddle) and James Woodson. The oldest of nine children, Woodson labored on his father's farm and in the coal mines of West Virginia. Attending elementary school only a few months per year, Woodson was mostly self-taught. At age nineteen he enrolled in the Frederick Douglass High School in Huntington, West Virginia, where he excelled and completed the four-year curriculum in under two years.

Education and Early Career

Woodson attended Berea College in Kentucky for two years, until the institution closed its doors to blacks. Woodson took courses at the University of Chicago, returning to Berea (when blacks were readmitted) to complete his bachelor's degree in literature in 1903. Securing a position as general superintendent of education in Manila, the Philippines, for the United States Bureau of Insular Affairs, Woodson taught English, health, and agriculture. He resigned for health reasons in 1907, and traveled to Asia, North Africa, and Europe.

Woodson applied for graduate study at the University of Chicago; however, school officials would not recognize his Berea degree. This situation forced Woodson to earn a bachelor's degree from the University of Chicago, which he received in 1907. His master's thesis, completed in 1908, examined French diplomatic relations with Germany in the eighteenth century. Woodson then enrolled in the doctoral program at Harvard University. After completing coursework, he sought employment in Washington, D.C., so that he might have access to the Library of Congress. While teaching courses in American history, French, Spanish, and English at local Washington, D.C., high schools, Woodson researched and completed his doctoral dissertation on secession, entitled "The Disruption in Virginia," in 1912. At the time, he was the first African American of slave ancestry and the second African American, after W. E. B. Du Bois, to receive a doctorate from Harvard.

Woodson's desire to move into the academic world met with frustration. He failed to get his dissertation published and discovered that his professional options were limited. Committed to writing black history, he published another manuscript, *The Education of the Negro Prior to 1861* (1915). Quickly tiring of academic politics, he sought other avenues to advance his passion for the scientific study of blacks and black history.

The Association for the Study of Negro Life and History

In 1915 Woodson, with associates Dr. George C. Hall, James E. Stamps, William B. Hartgrave, and Alexander L. Jackson, met at a downtown Chicago YMCA to establish the Association for the Study of Negro Life and History (ASNLH), later changed to the Association for the Study of African-American Life and History. Founded as a historical society devoted to the research of black America, the organization was meant to be ideologically and politically independent. There were three organizational tiers within ASNLH: branch members who paid dues; professional historians who conducted research; and a publication department. In 1916 the association established a quarterly, the *Journal of Negro History*.

Woodson evolved a philosophy about black history: He wanted to free black history from white intellectual bias and present blacks as active participants in history. Additionally, he wanted both black and white people to be exposed to the contributions of blacks. He believed that black history should be a part of the school curriculum. Finally, Woodson saw value in James Robinson's "new" history that asserted that history could serve social change. His passion became obsession as he worked to protect and promote the ASNLH. He never married, and friends and supporters noted that Woodson worked day and night for his association.

Financing ASNLH proved difficult as member dues were never sufficient. Woodson raised funds from white corporate philanthropists; however, frequent disagreements and accusations of "radicalism" forced him to compromise his beliefs and declare his loyalty to American capitalism.

Struggling to support the organization and himself, Woodson accepted a position as principal at the Armstrong Manual Training School in Washington, D.C., in 1918. From there he moved on to become the dean of the School of Liberal Arts at Howard University. Clashing with Howard president J. Stanley Durkee, Woodson left after two years to become dean at West Virginia Collegiate Institute.

After 1922, Woodson was finally able to work full-time for ASNLH, conduct research, and publish prolifically. The spread of Pan-Africanism, Garveyism, and the emergent Renaissance cultural movement were indications of heightened racial consciousness among African Americans. This climate provided support for "race men." Woodson founded Associated Publishers, Incorporated, in 1921 to produce books endorsed by the association. By 1925 the *Journal of Negro History* had published ten monographs and many articles. Woodson expanded his public presence by writing articles for mass consumption, including many newspaper editorials and regular contributions in the Garvey organization's *Negro World*.

In 1926 Woodson and his association made their indelible imprint on America and the world. He began the celebration of Negro History Week—a special commemoration of the birthdays of Frederick Douglass, Booker T. Washington, and Abraham Lincoln. Additionally it would celebrate the achievements of blacks throughout history. In 1976 this celebration was expanded to the widely celebrated Black History Month.

In 1933 Woodson published his most celebrated work, *The Mis-Education of the Negro*. This penetrating work critiqued the established school curriculum as grounded in racism and Eurocentric thought. Such education, he believed, could only result in the colonial subordination of African people in America. The often quoted passage, "When you control a man's thinking, you do not have to worry about his actions. . . . He will find his proper place and will stay in it" (p. viii) points to Woodson's assessment of the deleterious effect of existing schooling on the black psyche. Educated blacks would dissociate themselves from the majority of their race, and black people could never achieve unity and racial advancement with this type of education.

Concerned that the *Journal of Negro History* only reached a limited audience, Woodson established the *Negro History Bulletin* in 1937. Aimed at schools and young people, the *Bulletin* cost very little and used accessible language. Woodson's commitment to make black history accessible to elementary and secondary school students led him to write books for school children, which were often accompanied by study guides, chapter questions, and recommended projects.

Throughout the 1940s, the widely respected Woodson worked to popularize black history, maintain the ASNHL, and continue publication efforts. He was honored with the prestigious Spingarn Medal from the National Association for the Advancement of Colored People along with several honorary degrees. The U.S. Postal Service honored him with a memorial stamp in February 1984.

See also: MULTICULTURAL EDUCATION.

BIBLIOGRAPHY

GOGGIN, JACQUELINE. 1993. *Carter G. Woodson: A Life in Black History.* Baton Rouge: Louisiana State University Press.

HINES, DARLENE C. 1986. "Carter G. Woodson, White Philanthropy and Negro Historiography." *The History Teacher* 19:405–425.

WOODSON, CARTER G. 1915. *The Education of the Negro prior to 1861.* New York: Putnam.

WOODSON, CARTER G. 1998. *The Mis-Education of the Negro.* (1933). Trenton, NJ: Africa World Press.

WOODSON, CARTER G. 1971. *The African Background Outlined.* (1936). New York: Negro Universities Press.

WILLIAM H. WATKINS

WORK AND TRAINING PROGRAMS IN SCHOOLS

See: VOCATIONAL AND TECHNICAL EDUCATION.

WRITING, TEACHING OF

Writing pedagogy has been shaped by an array of influences over the years, including social and demographic change, insights derived from research, and grassroots movements among teachers. Recognizing that writing assumes many guises and serves varied purposes, teachers and researchers continue to chart the challenge of preparing diverse students to meet the literate demands of private, academic, and civic life.

History

Written composition became a concern for American high schools in the late nineteenth century. At the time, elementary schools did not teach composition; rather, writing instruction meant teaching students to form letters, to spell words, and to have legible (if not beautiful) handwriting. The high schools, however, focused on preparing an elite group of males for universities, a task that would increasingly demand attention to writing. In 1873 Harvard University initiated a writing requirement as part of its admissions process, asking each candidate to produce a composition about a literary work. Other colleges soon followed with similar requirements, and high schools began to prepare students to fulfill these expectations. Further guidance was provided by the illustrious "Committee of Ten," chaired by Harvard president Charles W. Eliot and charged with formulating parameters for secondary curriculum nationwide. In its final report, the group made the then-revolutionary claim that one purpose of English was "to enable the pupil . . . to give expression to thoughts of his own" (p. 86). And so began the teaching of composition in the nation's schools.

Writing continued to have a place in the secondary curriculum throughout the twentieth century. Students were commonly assigned essays in the forms of description, narration, exposition, or argument, following rhetorical traditions dating back to the late nineteenth century. If teachers followed contemporary textbooks, they taught lessons on the ideal written product, focusing on words, sentences, and paragraphs as component parts, and emphasizing usage and style. Student essays were graded on the basis of how well they approximated these forms and conventions.

Stimulated by the 1966 Dartmouth conference, which brought together leading British and American specialists in the teaching of English, major pedagogic and empirical shifts marked the late 1960s and early 1970s. Active research programs studying writing in the schools followed in both countries, and new ideas were introduced from abroad. The consequences were twofold. First, leading literacy educators argued that assigning and grading writing was not enough, suggesting that students should be supported through an elaborated process of generating ideas, reflection, planning, composing, and revising. Second, U.S. educational leaders began to argue for the teaching of writing in these ways at the very start of schooling, maintaining that learning to write could help students learn to read, and vice versa.

Founded in 1974, the National Writing Project (NWP) quickly emerged as a major professional development movement in the United States. Building from the work of exemplary classroom teachers, the NWP has continued to influence writing curriculum, instruction, and evaluation internationally. By 1985 the U.S. federal government funded a research center devoted to the study of written language; attention turned to how writing develops across the lifespan, the influences of varied school and out-of-school experiences on learning to write, and how these lived experiences intersect with learning to write in school.

Issues and Trends in School-Based Writing Instruction

As educators have recognized that writing is judged effective where it is appropriate to audience, purpose, and occasion, innovative classrooms have come to provide practice in addressing a range of rhetorical contexts and composing challenges. This focus on the contexts in which writing occurs has been accompanied by an equally intensified interest in the diverse profiles of individual writers—what they bring to particular composing events, and how teachers can effectively support and monitor their growth over time. While these concerns have been reflected in university-based research and emerging theoretic conceptions of the writing process, pedagogic innovations have been primarily formulated by teachers themselves, most notably through the work of the NWP.

A hallmark of these teaching innovations has been an abiding concern with the nature of students' composing processes, and with how teachers across the grade levels might more effectively gear instruction to individual needs, backgrounds, and interests. Process-oriented instructional approaches have become common, with teachers providing opportunities to brainstorm ideas, complete initial rough drafts, receive peer and teacher feedback, and revise and proofread. Ideally, such approaches acknowledge that writers in the world beyond school do not follow a prescribed series of steps. Acknowledging the social aspect of the writing process, many teachers have also provided paper and electronic publication opportunities. Recognizing that discrete grammar instruction does not reliably enhance student writing, teachers have increasingly addressed matters of correctness and style as students polish their own drafts.

Guided by theory, research, and insights from their own work with students, teachers have also formulated instructional approaches that acknowledge the developmental trajectories of writers of various ages. Although teachers continue to guide young children toward the standard forms, many are encouraging students to explore sound-letter correspondences through their own "invented spellings," drawing on research that explores these approximations as important developmental building-blocks. Later, as students move through secondary language arts classes, teachers provide assignments similarly informed by an awareness of students' emerging abilities, as thematic instructional units offer opportunities to build from basic writing tasks to more sophisticated challenges that ask students to synthesize and critique information gleaned from divergent sources.

The Writing-to-Learn and Writing-Across-the-Curriculum movements have fostered interest in activities that encourage writing as a tool for exploration and learning in all fields of study. Students may be asked to generate hypotheses or reflect on issues in journals and during spontaneous writing, while more formal writing assignments provide opportunities to learn the discourse conventions of particular disciplines. Especially in middle schools, interdisciplinary teams are creating promising venues for language-arts teachers to assist subject-area colleagues in integrating writing activities across the curriculum.

Given this interest in writing as a process and as a tool for learning, some have worried that teachers may be paying insufficient attention to the quality of students' written products. This focus on the quality of completed writing has infused recent policy debates, and both national and state-level efforts have introduced standards for writing and testing programs. Because writing varies considerably across tasks and contexts, developing valid standardized tests that reliably measure achievement and growth is an enterprise fraught with challenge. Although the most credible tests include actual writing samples, the cost of rating such exams has led some to advocate the use of machine-scored tests assessing students' knowledge of vocabulary and grammar; because students' scores on such tests often correlate well with scores on actual writing, argue some, they offer an affordable and efficient alternative. Because tests tend to drive curricula, teachers and literacy scholars worry that such assessments may encourage teaching practices predicated on an insufficient model of proficiency in writing—one that privileges discrete skills over an ability to negotiate the demands of writing for real purposes and audiences. As literacy educators argue the need to ground instruction in a broader conception of writing achievement, test-makers continue to work toward assessment strategies that better encompass the range and complexity of the kinds of writing people do in their lives beyond school. During the 1990s the National Council of Teachers of English convened the New Standards project, a group of literacy educators charged with formulating approaches to portfolio assessment that might serve both classroom-level and larger-scale purposes. The cost and complexity of such endeavors have relegated portfolios primarily to the levels of schools and classrooms, where they continue to provide evidence of students' processes, products, and growth over time.

As writing pedagogy enters a new millennium, several issues present enduring challenges for educators. Large-scale writing assessments have continued to reveal comparatively lower levels of achievement among linguistic minority students; in the mid-1990s, for instance, National Assessment of Educational Progress (NAEP) data suggested that European-American students were achieving at a higher level on most of the assessed writing tasks than students from other ethnic groups.

The technological revolution has considerably changed the views of what might be deemed minimal writing and literacy skills. Computers provide new kinds of support for writers as they generate and organize written text and also, through electronic mail and the World Wide Web, have introduced what Melanie Sperling and Sarah Warshauer Freedman (2001) call "a new textual component to human relationships." Amidst widespread conjecture concerning the long-term consequences of these new technologies, researchers continue to explore students' and teachers' experiences with such tools. The implications are many—in terms of expanding our definitions of the writing process, and our conceptions of the relationships among writers, readers, and the texts they create and encounter.

Negotiating this and the many other issues before them demands much of teachers' time and focus, even as most continue to see well over a hundred students each day and to juggle multiple responsibilities. These new approaches to teaching writing are considerably more energy intensive than the decontextualized drills of earlier times, but in most quarters, teachers' workloads have not been adjusted accordingly.

Research

During the 1970s cognitive studies by John Hayes and Linda Flower (1980) provided insight into the recursive nature of writing. This work charted the various subprocesses that writers negotiate in the service of fulfilling goals and solving rhetorical problems. That is, writers plan what they wish to say, translate those plans into writing, and evaluate and revise their work. Researchers found that these subprocesses do not follow a fixed sequential pattern; rather, writers move recursively among these various activities (pausing in the midst of composing, for instance, to revise or to pursue additional planning).

Teaching innovations related to this research have been informed by continuing interest in the nature of students' composing processes, and in how teachers across the grade levels might more effectively gear instruction to support the processes of diverse writers. Process-oriented instructional approaches have become common, with teachers providing opportunities to brainstorm ideas, complete initial rough drafts, receive peer and teacher feedback, revise, proofread, and pursue paper and electronic publication opportunities. As teachers experimented with new classroom practices that supported writers through such elaborated composing sequences, researchers began to compare the effectiveness of varied kinds of process-based instruction on writing improvement. George Hillocks's meta-analysis of these studies (1986) revealed that the approaches leading to the most significant gains in student writing provided students with clear and specific objectives, and opportunities to work together to solve particular writing problems.

Research on the nature and development of spelling knowledge and skills, especially among preschoolers and primary grade students, has been conducted on primarily white, middle-class, monolingual youngsters. This work has revealed that students' spellings follow a developmental trajectory, with their initial errors providing much information about how they understand the system of English writing (information that can guide teachers' efforts to help their students to acquire standard forms).

Focusing on a similar student population base, research on the teaching of grammar has suggested that such instruction has little effect where it remains divorced from students' actual writing; however, teaching that links grammar to students' genuine communicative needs as they attempt to write for real readers does appear to benefit students' writing and learning.

Finally, researchers have found important links among the activities of writing, speaking, and reading. These links are related to the finding that writing is primarily a process of making meaning, enacted in social, cultural, and material contexts. Thus, especially given the diversity of our student population, it is critical that teachers understand the ways students make meaning outside of school and that teachers know how to help students use what they bring as a resource for what they learn inside the classroom.

See also: JOURNALISM, TEACHING OF; LANGUAGE ARTS, TEACHING OF; LITERACY, *subentry on* WRITING AND COMPOSITION; READING, *subentry on* TEACHING OF; SPELLING, TEACHING OF.

BIBLIOGRAPHY

APPLEBEE, ARTHUR; LANGER, JUDITH; MULLIS, INA; LATHAM, ANDREW; and GENTILE, CLAUDIA. 1994. *NAEP 1992 Writing Report Card.* Report No. 23-W01. Washington, DC: Office of Educational Research and Improvement, U.S. Department of Education.

COMMITTEE OF TEN OF THE NATIONAL EDUCATION ASSOCIATION. 1894. *Report of the Committee of Ten on Secondary School Studies, With the Reports of the Conferences Arranged by the Committee.* New York: American Book Company.

FREEDMAN, SARAH WARSHAUER, and DAIUTE, COLLETTE. 2001. "Instructional Methods and Learning Activities in Teaching Writing." In *Advances in Research in Teaching,* Vol. 8, ed. Jere Brophy. Oxford: JAI Press, Elsevier Science.

HAYES, JOHN R., and FLOWER, LINDA. 1980. "Identifying the Organization of Writing Processes." In *Cognitive Processes in Writing,* ed. Jere Brophy. Hillsdale, NJ: Erlbaum.

HILLOCKS, GEORGE. 1986. *Research on Written Composition: New Directions for Teaching.* Urbana, IL: ERIC Clearinghouse on Reading and Communication Skills.

HODGES, RICHARD E. 1991. "The Conventions of Writing." In *Handbook of Research on Teaching the English Language Arts,* ed. James Flood, Julie M. Jensen, Diane Lapp, and James R. Squire. New York: Macmillan.

PURVES, ALAN. 1992. "Reflections on Research and Assessment in Written Composition." *Research in the Teaching of English* 26(1):108–122.

READ, CHARLES. 1971. "Pre-School Children's Knowledge of English Phonology." *Harvard Educational Review* 41(1):1–34.

SPERLING, MELANIE, and FREEDMAN, SARAH WARSHAUER. 2001. "Research on Writing." *Handbook of Research on Teaching,* 4th edition, ed. Virginia Richardson. New York: American Educational Research Association.

SARAH WARSHAUER FREEDMAN
ANNE DiPARDO

Y

YALE UNIVERSITY

Yale University, a private institution, is situated in New Haven, Connecticut. Its library of more than 10 million volumes is the second largest university library and third largest library system in the United States. The Yale Center for British Art (1977) holds the largest collection of British art and illustrated books outside the United Kingdom. Yale College provides a liberal arts education in which undergraduate students explore a variety of fields and obtain a wide cultural background. The Graduate School of Arts and Sciences and the ten professional schools—architecture, art, divinity, drama, forestry and environmental studies, law, management, medicine, music, and nursing—award master's, doctoral, and professional degrees.

Historian Franklin Dexter chronicles that in 1701 ten Connecticut ministers obtained a colony charter "to Erect a Collegiate School" whose mission was to instruct youth in the arts and sciences and fit them "for Publick employment both in Church & Civil State" (pp. 20–21). In 1716 the college was moved from Saybrook to New Haven, and in 1718 when Elihu Yale, an Englishman with New Haven ties, donated books and saleable goods the college was named after him. The early curriculum consisted of traditional liberal arts studies and strict Congregational instruction, and most graduates became ministers. By the 1770s the students were entering other fields and actively supported the American revolutionary cause. In 1802 President Timothy Dwight (1795–1817) advanced the sciences by appointing Benjamin Silliman the first science professor in America.

Over the next half century Silliman developed the arts and sciences, establishing a medical school in 1810, the first university art gallery in 1832, and the first American graduate school and scientific school in 1846. In 1852 the engineering school and the bachelor of philosophy degrees were instituted, and science instruction was consolidated into the Sheffield Scientific School in 1861. Graduate education was formalized in America when Yale awarded the first doctor of philosophy degrees in 1861. In 1876 Yale awarded the first American doctorate to an African American, physics student Edward Bouchet. The college continued to maintain its liberal arts tradition as affirmed in its 1828 *Report on the Course of Instruction,* a landmark document in nineteenth-century education.

In the 1820s the divinity and law schools were established, and by mid-century Yale was the largest U.S. college. The first university art school, Yale's first coeducational school, was founded in 1869. In the 1870s, the Peabody Museum opened to exhibit the first dinosaur bones and fossils collected by Professor Othniel C. Marsh on Western expeditions. The college became Yale University in 1888, and women were admitted to the graduate school in 1892. In 1900, Gifford Pinchot established the oldest continuously operating forestry school in America.

American college sports and traditions were largely developed at Yale, beginning with rowing in 1843. Yale's greatest sports contributions have been in the invention of American football by Walter Camp, and in developing the sports of swimming, baseball, basketball, golf, and boxing.

Yale's distinguished professors, such as Josiah Willard Gibbs, Irving Fisher, and William Graham Sumner, earned international reputations in the late nineteenth and early twentieth century. In the first quarter of the twentieth century Yale made further advances in the education of women, admitting them to the schools of medicine in 1916 and law in 1919, and establishing the first academic nursing school in 1923. President James Rowland Angell's administration (1921–1937) was marked by extensive development of the graduate and professional schools as well as the college. Gifts of John W. Sterling and the Harkness family enabled Yale to reform its educational system, rebuild its campus, and broaden its educational mission. One of the most significant features, the undergraduate residential college system, was instituted in 1933. The twelve colleges are separate entities designed to give the students of a sense of belonging to and participating in smaller groups. In the 1950s, President A. Whitney Griswold (1950–1963) strengthened the liberal arts educational mission of Yale and modernized its architectural appearance. Under President Kingman Brewster (1963–1977), Yale became more democratic and diverse, and women were admitted to Yale College in 1969. The School of Management was established in 1973. As New Haven's largest employer, Yale, under president Richard C. Levin (1993–), is strongly committed to working with the city in developing mutually beneficial educational, cultural, and economic projects.

See also: HIGHER EDUCATION IN THE UNITED STATES, *subentry on* HISTORICAL DEVELOPMENT; RESEARCH UNIVERSITIES.

BIBLIOGRAPHY

DEXTER, FRANKLIN BOWDITCH, ed. 1916. *Documentary History of Yale University, under the Original Charter of the Collegiate School of Connecticut, 1701–1745.* New Haven, CT: Yale University Press.

KELLEY, BROOKS MATHER. 1974. *Yale: A History.* New Haven, CT: Yale University Press.

PIERSON, GEORGE W. 1952. *Yale: An Educational History 1871–1921.* New Haven, CT: Yale University Press.

PIERSON, GEORGE W. 1955. *Yale: The University College 1921–1937.* New Haven, CT: Yale University Press.

PIERSON, GEORGE W. 1979. *Yale: A Short History.* New Haven, CT: Yale University Press.

Reports on the Course of Instruction in Yale College; By a Committee of the Corporation and the Academic Faculty. 1828. New Haven, CT: H. Howe.

INTERNET RESOURCE

YALE UNIVERSITY. 2002. "Factsheet: Some Facts and Statistics about Yale University." 2002. <www.yale.edu/oir/factsheet.html>.

JUDITH ANN SCHIFF

YEAR-ROUND EDUCATION

A concept designed to minimize three-month summer learning losses, year-round education (YRE) maximizes the use of public facilities by dividing the school attendance days into rotating instruction and vacation segments. Students are enrolled in formal learning programs over a twelve-month year, keeping school buildings open at least 240 days.

Intersessions—the equivalent of summer schools—are offered each vacation block. They can be full or partial days, located on campus or cooperatively based in the community. Voluntary intermittent intersessions overcome the nine-month wait for remediation in difficult classes, while creating acceleration, enrichment, and interest specializations for all students throughout the year. They are especially of value for those who lack stimulating out-of-school activities.

Districts often promote this modification of the calendar as a *multiple-vacation plan* featuring shorter segments for both studies and vacations, in contrast with the *single-vacation plan,* which offers one longer instructional period followed by an extensive vacation. The brief but more numerous breaks, which can be one to six weeks in duration, appeal to many families. Six weeks is accepted as the maximum to be classified as YRE unless an individualized format purposely provides for special furloughs.

Educator visionaries go beyond this basic concept. They do not view YRE as a calendar configuration for space, achievement, or enrichment, but rather as part of the transformation toward a philosophy of lifelong continuous learning. They believe that schools and universities, like hospitals, are helping institutions, and therefore should offer planned and spontaneous learning opportunities through combinations of on- and off-campus studies, home computers, and distance instruction 365 days per year.

Related to this perception, supportive community advocates state there is no rationale for utilizing expensive facilities only one-fourth (e.g, 6 hours) or one-third (8) of the hours of the day, one-half (180) of the days of the year, and three-fourths (9) of the months of the year; no other public or private institutions consider such patterns. Therefore, districts and cities together should create community schools where infants through senior citizens may share an array of services as in child care, library, electronic, theater, and arts centers, vocational enhancement, health clinics, social services, and parks and recreation programs.

Traditionally, there are four reasons for implementing such year-round education designs: (1) to improve student achievement; (2) to increase building capacity; (3) to reduce capital expenses; and (4) to accommodate special-needs youth. Innovators add the following eight criteria:

- promotion of continuous progress: Billy can learn about bugs in July
- employment realities: not all can take summer vacations
- lifestyle diversities: many prefer varied vacations
- curriculum facilities: reduced enrollment provides space for expanded offerings
- improvement catalyst: nongraded individualized programs can create success
- community enhancement: year-round swimming pools, Bible schools, and traffic reduction
- people considerations: especially offering varied support and opportunities for the less affluent
- personal choice: the option of twelve- or nine-month patterns

Adopting YRE does require strong philosophical convictions and plans to make the school better. Combining the four traditional and eight nontraditional categories creates a powerful agenda for year-round education.

Track Plans

In implementing year-round programs, a *track* is related to the calendar, not ability. In a single-track program all students and teachers follow the same instructional blocks, intersession offerings, and vacation periods. For example, in a 45-15 plan, all students and teachers learn together for forty-five days, and then vacation or attend intersession for the next fifteen days. They return for three more forty-five day blocks of instruction, each followed by fifteen days of vacation. State-required and common holiday periods are preserved. Single-track plans do not increase space or save money, but they do promote continuous learning, especially when combined with intersession programs.

Multiple-track adoptions follow the same calendar configurations, but offer three, four, or five tracks to increase building capacity. Using the 45-15 rotation illustration, a school constructed for 600 can enroll 800 students by placing 200 students in each of four tracks (A, B, C, D). When A, B, and C are in school (600 students), D (200) is on vacation. When D returns, A goes on vacation.

Dual track creates two schools-within-a-school; families choose whether to remain on a nine-month calendar (School X), or participate in a twelve-month pattern (School Y). Flexible-track plans allow some students to change groups when rotations are scheduled, or enroll in studies during intersessions, to meet the required attendance days while creating a special-need calendar. Personalized-track programs individualize curriculum and instruction through nongraded teams of teachers, allowing families, students, and teachers to self-select their own vacation periods. The school ensures a balance of student and staff attendance to maintain a twelve-month program.

There are more than thirty possible calendar configurations, with more being invented as communities seek to meet their own unique environments. Multiple plans can create a 50, 33, or 25 percent increase in capacity; the fewer the tracks, the greater the enrollment, as illustrated by a sampling of patterns, each of which can also be implemented as a single track:

A four-track design of forty-five days in school, fifteen days on vacation; a middle school of 1200 can house 1600 through four rotating tracks (A, B, C, D) of 400 each, with only three groups in attendance at one time. Four hundred of 1200 creates 33 percent increase in capacity; in enrollment figures, 400 of 1600 equates to a 25 percent gain in student numbers.

A four-track plan of 60 days in school, 20 days away; three 60-day blocks equal 180 days, while three 20-day blocks provide 60 days of vacation and intersession programs. Four tracks (A, B, C, D) create the same space figures as in the 45-15; the primary differences are the length of the periods, and the three versus four room change cycles.

Concept 6

A three-track calendar dividing the year into six blocks of approximately 41 days is termed *Concept 6*. Students attend two consecutive eight-week periods, followed by an eight-week vacation. For Concept 6, most states allow 163 days of attendance rather than 180 by increasing the number of minutes per day. A high school built for 1600 can house 2400. Three tracks (A, B, C) each enroll 800 students. While A and B are in school, C is on vacation. When C returns, A vacations. Thus 800 of 1600 is a 50 percent increase in building capacity; 800 of 2400 is a 33 percent enrollment gain. Modified Concept 6 is the same except there are twelve four-week blocks. A student rotates eight weeks in and four weeks out of school. An elementary facility built for 600 can house 900 (300 each in A, B, C) by rotating the three groups.

A five-track calendar stipulates that students attend school for 60 days and have vacation for 15 days. Three such rotations equal 180 days in school, but with only 45 days off, providing 15 days to use as desired for additional vacation time. If space is an issue, a school constructed for 400 can house only 500 students; with five groups (A, B, C, D, E), 100 of 400 equals 25 percent increase in capacity, while 100 of 500 increases the enrollment figure by 20 percent.

Personalized Year

A completely individualized calendar, personalized year's curriculum is continuous and self-directed. Students and teachers may be away any length of time—two days or even a year. Upon returning, they continue from where they were at their last attendance. This plan can function as a single or multiple track program by assuring a balance of staff and students.

Other Calendars

Other possible calendars among the more than thirty include Concept 8, 25-5, 30-10, 90-30, Flexible All-Year, and the Orchard Plan. Such modified configurations are not new, as YRE dates from 1904 in Indiana. Many successful programs existed prior to World War II. Reinvented in the 1960s, year-round education has witnessed steady growth. By the turn of the twenty-first century, more than 2 million youths were enrolled in over 3000 schools in forty-four states and Washington D.C., four Canadian provinces, and four Pacific Islands.

In considering the adoption of a continuous learning model, there are more than sixty basics that must be addressed. Each is easy to resolve with creative thinking, commitment, and visitations, for numerous districts have offered modified calendars for twenty to thirty years. All the perceived dilemmas—costs, community acceptance, teacher union contracts, and other realistic factors—can be resolved, but even more, arranged to enhance the learning climate. There are students who never attended a nine-month school, for when they enrolled in kindergarten, year-round was offered at all grade levels. They graduated from a year-round high school after spending their K–12 years in a twelve-month calendar pattern.

Major Obstacles

The major obstacle in the adoption of year-round education is tradition. When first proposed, 30 percent of the community are strongly in favor, 40 percent are undecided, and 30 percent are strongly opposed. The ideal is to begin on a voluntary basis for the 30 percent who are ready; they usually will be joined by half of the middle group. If YRE must be mandated for space reasons, the key is to convince the 40 percent group that it is the best solution. Critics cite numerous objections:

- Possible separation of families (elementary student on twelve-month and high school student on nine-month calendar)
- Employment of parents during the traditional school year (that may require vacation in the summer)
- Child care issues
- Family lifestyles preference
- Disruption of summer recreation and camp programs
- Changing rooms in multiple track calendars
- High school social and athletic schedules
- Student employment and family events
- Assemblies at the school

Arguments in Favor

Those who oppose YRE overlook numerous factors: (1) construction workers in cold states can best vacation in January and February; (2) the single-parent hotel housekeeper may best vacation in November; (3) the snow-ski family living in warm climates may want winter vacation in the mountains; and (4) children from low-income families and those who are low achieving can benefit from food service, caring, and twelve-month assistance from concerned staff. More than fifty percent of the population in the United States either cannot or should not take a summer vacation because of employment issues or other activities or family factors; in addition, many prefer three or four shorter seasonal vacations.

Wherever year-round education has been implemented, it has been successful. Every program that began and then closed was the result of political reasons (new board, new superintendent, parents' desire for uniformity of calendar), or unusual circumstances. No district ever discontinued YRE from lack of success. More than thirty evaluation studies have verified that students in continuous programs do as well as or better than matched pairs of nine-month students in every category of school achievement and personal growth. Surveys of satisfaction, including doctoral dissertations that document interviews of parents and teachers, have verified that the overwhelming majority of those who have participated in YRE like it, and would vote to continue the concept. Surprising to many are the number of sport, music, and drama championships earned by schools on rotating school calendars.

See also: COMMUNITY EDUCATION; ELEMENTARY EDUCATION, *subentries on* CURRENT TRENDS, HISTORY OF; SCHOOL FACILITIES, *subentry on* MAINTENANCE AND MODERNIZATION OF; SECONDARY EDUCATION, *subentries on* CURRENT TRENDS, HISTORY OF; SUMMER ENRICHMENT PROGRAMS; SUMMER SCHOOL.

BIBLIOGRAPHY

BALLINGER, CHARLES. 1990. *Year-Round Education: Learning More for Less.* Washington DC: National School Boards Association.

BINGLE, JAMES, and GLINES, DON. 2002. *NAYRE: A Historical Perspective.* San Diego, CA: National Association for Year-Round Education.

CORDI, TERESA, et al. 2001. *From Teacher to Teacher: A Look at Year-Round Education.* San Diego, CA: National Association for Year-Round Education.

FOGARTY, ROBIN, ed. 1996. *Year-Round Education: A Collection of Articles.* Arlington Heights, IL: IRI Skylight Publishing.

GLINES, DON. 1995. *Year-Round Education: History, Philosophy, Future.* San Diego, CA: National Association for Year-Round Education.

GLINES, DON. 2000. *Reflecting Year-Round Education: Traditions and Innovations.* San Diego, CA: National Association for Year-Round Education.

HAWKINS, SANDY. 1992. *From Parent to Parent: A Look at Year-Round Education.* San Diego, CA: National Association for Year-Round Education.

KNEESE, CAROLYN. 2000. *Year-Round Learning: A Research Synthesis on Achievement.* San Diego, CA: National Association for Year-Round Education.

LEPZINSKI, CINDY. 2000. *YRE Intersession Handbook.* San Diego, CA: National Association for Year-Round Education.

MUSSATTI, DAVID, and GLINES, DON. 2002. *Year-Round Education: Paths to Resources.* San Diego, CA: National Association for Year-Round Education.

NATIONAL ASSOCIATION FOR YEAR-ROUND EDUCATION. 2000. *YRE: Frequently Asked Questions.* San Diego, CA: National Association for Year-Round Education.

NATIONAL EDUCATION COMMISSION ON TIME AND LEARNING. 1994. *Prisoners of Time.* Washington DC: U.S. Government Printing Office.

SHIELDS, CAROLYN, and OBERG, STEPHEN. 2000. *Year-Round Schooling: Promises and Pitfalls.* Lanham, MD: Scarecrow Press/Technomic Books.

SPECK, MARSHA. 2000. *Handbook for Implementing High School Year-Round Education,* 2nd edition. San Diego, CA: National Association for Year-Round Education.

STENVALL, MARILYN. 1997. *A Checklist for Success: Implementing Year-Round Education.* San Diego, CA: National Association for Year-Round Education.

DON GLINES

YOUNG, ELLA FLAGG (1845–1918)

Superintendent of the Chicago schools from 1909 through 1915 and elected president of the National

Education Association (NEA) in 1910, Ella Flagg Young attempted widespread reform in an increasingly industrialized and diverse America. During her teens, Young enrolled in a normal school in Chicago, and after graduation began teaching, receiving a series of rapid promotions eventually leading to her appointment as assistant superintendent. During her fifties, she completed her doctoral studies in the newly created education program at the University of Chicago where she wrote her dissertation under philosopher and educator John Dewey's direction and later served as a popular faculty member. When the Chicago school board could not agree on a new superintendent in 1909, they chose Young, an experienced insider, making her the first woman superintendent of a large-city school system in the country. A year later, the membership of the NEA elected her as its first woman president. Eventually Young resigned as superintendent in 1915 after a tumultuous relationship with several board members. She died in 1918 during the great influenza pandemic.

During her long and distinguished career, Young led the Chicago schools through a period of dramatic change in which industrialization rapidly dominated the economy and diverse new populations arrived. She responded to these and many other challenges by instituting a range of reforms. To ensure the quality and welfare of the system's teachers, she created school governing bodies in which all teachers and administrators discussed curriculum and logistical matters, insisting that work time be reserved for this purpose. She encouraged the formation of study groups where educators considered educational theory, and designed screening programs for students entering the city normal school. She decentralized many administrative functions, delegating greater authority to school-level, rather than central office, staff. She endeavored to change the principalship from a position of rigid accounting and paperwork to one requiring a deep knowledge of curriculum and pedagogy. She added deans to schools to help counsel students. With her leadership, the Chicago schools also added sex hygiene programs, among the first to be offered in schools anywhere.

Beyond her administrative service, Young published works on a variety of topics including peace, literature, manual training, and ethics. Perhaps her most enduring work is *Isolation in the Schools* (1900), where she analyzed the relationships between schools and an industrial society, and suggest-

ed that a rigidly compartmentalized educational system alienated students who then failed to find their studies personally meaningful. Essentially, she contended that schools had adopted the mechanization of industry and that the rigid differentiation of work functions robbed people of their humanity and intelligence. In schools, this differentiation appeared in such forms as schools and classes divided by student age, and also as clock-driven courses with artificially neat content divisions. She argued that both students and teachers found their capacity for independent thought diminished by a system that made little provision for it. She claimed that much as a new class of supervisors had emerged in industry to drive the increasingly hierarchical structure, new classes of administrators had arrived in schools. These administrators, she explained, were determined to make all school-related decisions of substance for those positioned below them. This reduced students and teachers to mere operatives in a larger mechanical system. She explained that an inherent problem with this system was its lack of reciprocity—that school administrators were unwilling to endure the same demands for uniformity and obedience as students and teachers. Compounding matters, she argued, administrators higher in the hierarchy became more insulated from the primary work of schools, and as such they understood less about it. This effectively isolated them and kept them from making wise decisions.

In stark contrast with other prominent school administrators of her day, Young maintained that teachers, and in turn students, needed much more power in running schools. Only when people could make significant decisions for themselves and with each other could they tap their natural intelligence and begin to develop it fully. This meant teachers and students must have the freedom and power to create and execute their own ideas. Young argued that this responsibility would attract the most talented and qualified individuals while repelling those more inclined toward rote, prescriptive, and punitive systems. To foster the deliberative process that would build school communities, she maintained that schools needed to provide time and space for teachers to engage in the intellectual, legislative, and logistical functions of running their schools. In the pages of *Isolation,* Young detailed this difficult but liberating vision of schools as democratic institutions. Her years of service to the Chicago schools informed the volume along with a lifetime of disciplined study of philosophy, schooling, and society. Both her writing and leadership, then, demonstrated a remarkable balance of theory and practice.

Finally, as a gifted leader during the era of women's suffrage, Young worked closely with women's organizations and provided important leadership for their causes. Suffragists regarded Young as an exemplary leader whose successes reflected well on all women. Many women, especially teachers, propelled her into a variety of leadership positions. When Young encountered opposition, they comforted her and sometimes staged rallies of support for her efforts. Young reciprocated by continually championing the causes held dear by organized women's groups. She also sought to lead in a manner compatible with her beliefs: She involved those around her in making critically important decisions; she structured time and opportunities so that her constituents could discuss and carry out their plans; and she engaged in her work with a spirit of community-building. Though this manner of leadership often proved difficult and time-consuming, she sought it as a matter of course. As a result, her relationships with organized women and the general public were intense, mutual, and ongoing. The strong support she engendered was critical to the success of many of the daring programs she established. Clearly, Young was as much a part of the women's movement as she was a national symbol of its finest successes.

See also: SUPERINTENDENT OF LARGE-CITY SCHOOL SYSTEMS; URBAN EDUCATION.

BIBLIOGRAPHY

DONATELLI, ROSEMARY V. 1971. "The Contributions of Ella Flagg Young to the Educational Enterprise." Ph.D diss., University of Chicago.

MCMANIS, JOHN T. 1916. *Ella Flagg Young and a Half-Century of the Chicago Public Schools.* Chicago: McClurg.

SMITH, JOAN K. 1979. *Ella Flagg Young: Portrait of a Leader.* Ames, IA: Educational Studies Press.

YOUNG, ELLA FLAGG. 1900. *Isolation in the Schools.* Chicago: University of Chicago Press.

YOUNG, ELLA FLAGG. 1902. *Ethics in the School.* Chicago: University of Chicago Press.

YOUNG, ELLA FLAGG. 1902. *Some Types of Modern Educational Theory.* Chicago: University of Chicago Press.

YOUNG, ELLA FLAGG. 1903. *Scientific Method in Education.* Chicago: University of Chicago Press.

JACKIE M. BLOUNT

YOUTH DEMOGRAPHIC TRENDS

The United States has a complex and rapidly changing population and is fortunate in having analytical tools such as the U.S. Census, which is compiled each decade, and the Current Population Survey, which is compiled every year. Thomas Jefferson directed the first census in 1790, implementing the Constitution's provision that each state add or lose seats in the U.S. House of Representatives based on changes in their population—the major reason why the census has such a powerful political and economic impact. The first census showed that 95 percent of Americans lived on farms or in rural areas. In the early twenty-first century, more than half of the U.S. population lives in the suburbs (which were unknown in Jefferson's time), a quarter are in large cities, and a quarter live in small towns and rural areas. Every census since 1790 has seen a change in the racial categories being profiled, from Jefferson's "free males, free females, slaves, and others," which included "mulattos," to the current complex mélange of races, ethnic groups, and national origins. However, through the end of the twentieth century, the census has always forced people to select only one racial category, creating a good deal of confusion. The first time people could admit that they were of mixed racial ancestry was in Census 2000.

General Population Trends

In 1900, the average American was only twenty-one years of age, while in 2000 the average age was thirty-seven. The average person lived for only forty-seven years in 1900, while in 2000 the average U.S. citizen lived to be nearly seventy-eight—a life expectancy increase of nearly two-thirds in only a century. Much of this increase has come from the elimination of childhood diseases through vaccination, safe drinking water, and public health measures. In 2000, about seven babies in 1,000 died in the United States; while in New York City in 1900, for every baby born, another baby died. (In 1861 in London, Charles Dickens reported that half the funerals were for children under ten.)

In the twenty-first century, most Americans are living longer, though the average white female in the United States (and in the world) currently has only 1.7 children over her lifetime, not enough to replace the population, which requires 2.1 children—enough to replace one's mother and father (the .1 covers infant mortality). Almost all developed nations have fertility rates below replacement levels, signaling both rapid aging and population declines. (In 2030 there will be only two workers per retiree in the United States, while in Italy there will be only seven-tenths of a worker per retiree—meaning more retirees than workers.) The United States has an advantage over other developed countries due to its large and growing population of immigrants and minorities. Young families from these groups have much higher fertility rates than the older white population, keeping the U.S. population more youthful. While the average white female in the United States gives birth to 1.7 children over her lifetime, the average black female gives birth to 2.6 children and the average Hispanic female gives birth to 3.0 children (as of 2000), a situation referred to as *differential fertility*.

World Population

In the early twenty-first century, the human species consists of about 6.1 billion people, with 95 percent of the population growth occurring in developing nations. Throughout the world, women are having fewer babies, but in the developing nations the decline may be from six to four babies per female, still enough for population growth. In 2100, the human species will stabilize at 11 billion people, and most humans will have aged out of the childbearing years. The developed nations of Europe, Asia, and the Americas will account for less than 2 percent of the world's population in 2100. Those born in 2000 will have a good chance of being there, if life expectancy continues to increase throughout the world. Characteristics of the split between rich and poor in 2100 are not predictable, but will likely define the human species.

American Demographics

There is a demographic principle that states that nothing is equally distributed across the nation—not race, not age, not wealth, not religion, not jobs. For example, Census 2000 put the U.S. population at 281 million, but California has 33 million people and Wyoming has only half a million. This means that the difference between the biggest and smallest state in terms of population is increasing. Additionally,

more than half of the 281 million live in only ten states (California, Texas, New York, Florida, Illinois, Pennsylvania, Ohio, Michigan, New Jersey, and Georgia), and a third live in only nine metropolitan areas (New York, Los Angeles, Chicago, the District of Columbia, San Francisco, Philadelphia, Boston, Detroit, and Dallas). Hispanics are the fastest growing minority, yet 90 percent live in only ten states. Only 5 percent of Utah's people are over age sixty-five; while 18 percent of Floridians are over age sixty-five. Such statistics mean that federal policies will be increasingly difficult to apply identically in each state, and state policies will be increasingly difficult to apply equitably in each county.

These differences are often studiously ignored. For example, the Department of Education's main compendium, *Conditions of Education, 2001,* contains more than 300 tables and graphs, but not a single one presents data using state or county comparisons. However, nonfederal educational publications (and the U.S. Census) are full of state education comparisons, which are essential to understanding the nation.

An Aging America

It is true that America is a rapidly aging society—young people have steadily declined as a percentage of all Americans. In the early twenty-first century, less than a quarter of U.S. households have a child of public school age (five to eighteen). At the upper end, there are 34.5 million Americans over age sixty-five, and the 72 million baby boomers born between 1946 and 1964 are between thirty-eight and fifty-six years of age, poised to create the biggest increase in retirees in history, beginning in 2011 and ending in 2028, although many are retiring before and after age 65, a trend that will continue. However, sixty-five no longer signals the onset of severe physical decline, which now happens mainly in the seventies, suggesting that baby boomers will not retire and remain retired permanently as has been the pattern. About a quarter of the baby boom generation will live past age eighty-five. Their retirement experience may include part-time work, starting a small business, a little travel, time with family, gardening, golf, volunteering—in other words, they plan to give nothing up in their "senior" years. However, there are severe implications for schools if this population of 70 million voters decides that support for public schools is not in their self-interest.

Family Changes

Children are being brought up in very different family patterns compared to a few decades ago—23 percent of all children live only with their mothers, a figure that rises to 51 percent for African-American children. The biggest change is from a preponderance of divorced mothers to an equal number of never-married single mothers and divorced mothers. Four percent of children live with just their father, and 3 million children are being raised by their grandparents, with no parents present. About 75 percent of preschool children have working mothers, making quality day care a major component of the education agenda. In addition, the Census Bureau's definition of *family* and *parent* was not appropriate for the number of children being raised by two parents of the same sex, in a gay or lesbian relationship. Census 2000 figures also indicated a small decline in the number of children being raised by single mothers and a larger decline in single mothers with two or more children.

The Role of Race

Ethnic diversity in the United States is also increasing, and one surprise in the Census 2000 numbers was the rapid increase in the number of Hispanics to 35 million, surpassing the number of African Americans (34.7 million). However, of the 7 million people of mixed race, 2 million indicated that they were black and some other race. It is not entirely clear how such people should be counted—if they are counted as black only, the total number of African Americans would jump to almost 37 million, but then what would happen to their other racial composition? Hispanics are not a race but an *ethnic group,* which is extremely difficult to define, so that all Hispanics are forced to choose at least one race on the census form. While most chose white in 2000, there were 3 million black Hispanics in the nation. There are, in fact, no physical qualities that define Hispanics, not even language—15 percent of California's Hispanics do not speak Spanish. If to these are added American Indian/Eskimos (2.4 million, plus 300,000 mixed Indian/Hispanics) and Asians (almost 11 million), minorities are about 30 percent of the U.S. population, and almost 40 percent of those under eighteen are minorities.

Census projections for 2050 show that 50 percent of Americans will be members of minority groups, though the term will be meaningless if minorities are half the total. Minorities are also not distributed evenly—Hispanics and Asians will account for 61 percent of U.S. population growth between 1995 and 2025 (44 percent Hispanic and 17 percent Asian), but California alone will add 12 million Hispanics and 6 million Asians, while Texas and Florida will add 8 million more Hispanics. Seventy percent of the U.S. Hispanic population now live in California, Texas, New York, and Florida, a situation that will exist for the foreseeable future. There is good news regarding minority access to the middle class, particularly involving major increases in suburban black residents. While not perfect, suburban residency is a good indicator of middle class status. Similar successes can be found in other minority groups. Although Hispanics are not doing as well as African-Americans in getting into college in the early twenty-first century, they are starting small businesses and buying homes at a rapid rate, while Asians are doing well in both college admission and small business ownership.

There is also some confusion in the area of defining one's ancestry. In a Census 2000 supplement, 20 million Americans said that their ethnic ancestry was "American" or "United States." Increasing intermarriage, and increasing years between the arrival in America of one's ancestors and the present day, will probably increase the number of people who will report their race as "American."

Sources of Change

There are four major factors that change the U.S. population: (1) There are almost 4 million births per year; (2) There are about half as many deaths (2.3 million) as births; (3) There are about one million immigrants coming to the United States each year; and (4) 43 million Americans change their residence each year, the highest figure by far of any nation. Transience is strongly related to crime (it is easier to steal from, hurt, or kill strangers) and presents numerous difficulties for health care and education, as both health care professionals and educators can do a better job if they can get to know their patients and students over an extended period of time. If a child attends two or three schools in a year, they are less likely to make friends, get to know teachers and the school, and be loyal school members. Certainly the forces of cohesion have a difficult time against these forces of instability.

Educational Demographics

Most striking about the U.S. educational system is its complexity, with many different routes to get where one is going. (In France, great pride is taken in the fact that at 10 A.M. on Wednesday every child in the fourth form is studying the predicate nominative.) Americans can return to acquire a high school diploma at age twenty-five, or even at fifty, an impossible task in most centralized nations. This flexibility is necessary because of the country's diverse population. Rather than a ministry of education, U.S. public schools are governed by 15,000 locally elected school committees, as well as a chief state school officer for each state and a state legislative structure. The federal government provides only about 11 percent of all public school expenditures, but represents far more than 11 percent of influence on educational decisions. Federal programs concentrate in areas difficult for state and local governments to fund, such as antipoverty programs like Head Start and Title I, programs for children with disabilities, school transportation and construction funds for schools and colleges, and student scholarship support at the college level.

There are also demographic implications in where the 80,000 U.S. public schools are located—19,000 in central cities, 22,000 in suburbia, and 39,000 in small towns and sparsely populated rural areas. Every one of the 3,100 U.S. counties provides schools, whether they have six people per square mile or 1,500. Just as the citizens of Wyoming have more "pull" with their senators (only a half million people) than do California residents (33 million people, but only two senators), it is also true that wealthy districts can spend more per pupil than poor ones, and a dense school district will have more taxpayers per square mile than one with only six people per square mile. In many states, such as Kentucky, low-density, high-poverty rural districts have sued the state on the grounds that there is no way they can provide the same level of investment in every child that wealthy suburban districts can. These economic inequities in household income and tax revenues have resulted in unequal investments in education. There will always be income differences in any society, but American rhetoric suggests that every child should enter kindergarten at the same starting line as all others. The media focus on big-city school systems, where poverty is concentrated, and on large school systems in the suburbs. In these systems, superintendents often last no more than three years, whereas in rural systems a superintendent usually lasts for more than a decade and teachers know who

their students will be a year before they actually arrive in their classroom.

There is, in general, little national media interest in rural issues, even though rural and small town populations are a quarter of the U.S. total, and these areas contain the largest number of the nation's schools. In these 80,000 schools there are 47 million students—24 million of them in 52,000 elementary schools, 8 million in 134,500 middle schools, and 12.6 million in 15,900 high schools. There are 2.8 million teachers (1.7 million elementary school teachers and 1.1 million middle and secondary school teachers), who are paid approximately $40,600 each. There are 9.7 million computers in schools, but only 60 percent of U.S. classrooms have a computer in them. The evidence on the computer's utility in improving student subject-matter knowledge, as judged by scores on so-called high-stakes tests, is, thus far, mixed. In addition to the nation's 2.8 million teachers, there are 2.6 million salaried nonteachers working in U.S. schools as well, including janitors, cafeteria workers, nurses, guidance counselors, administrators, curriculum specialists, bus drivers, librarians, secretaries, and others.

School Successes

Several major accomplishments of American schools have been mostly ignored by the media. First, there has been a major increase in American adults who possess a bachelor's degree—from 20 percent in 1990 to 25 percent in 1999, probably the largest increase in any nine-year period in the nation's history. There are, however, large differences between states, ranging from West Virginia's 14 percent to Maryland's 41 percent. Second, the rate of high school graduation for African Americans has become virtually the same as that of whites, and in access to higher education the gap between blacks and whites has been narrowing rapidly. The only severe gap left is in college graduation rates, with blacks graduating at about half the rate of whites. In that there is such a direct relationship between educational level and personal income, there should be a concerted effort to increase college graduation rates among African Americans. Hispanics are graduating from high school only about half the time, about where blacks were in 1982. High school graduation rates must be increased for Hispanics before their college-going rates can improve.

Third, a massive effort to provide a computer for every school in the nation has been very successful, especially compared with other developed countries. However, the evidence of the impact of the more than nine million computers in U.S. schools on student learning is far from clear, due largely to a shortage of subject-specific software that could help teachers teach specific subjects more creatively and more efficiently. Countries with virtually no computers in schools still outscore the United States by a large margin on international comparison tests, such as the Third International Mathematics and Science Study (TIMMS).

Although many observers have projected a massive increase in high school enrollments in the next decade, the data do not support such a notion. (see Figure 1). What matters, however, is the variation in high school graduation rates, ranging from a 61 percent increase in Nevada to Wyoming's 23 percent decline. The states vary enormously in the number of nineteen-year-olds that graduate from high school and are admitted to college, with 55 to 60 percent of students graduating and going to college in North Dakota, Massachusetts, New Jersey, Iowa, and South Dakota (all very stable populations), but only 25 to 30 percent doing so in Alaska, Nevada, Florida, Georgia, and Texas, the six most transient states, and those with the six highest crime rates. These differences in state performance of the major task in education—high school graduation and college admission—are far greater than any international comparisons of the U.S. educational system with other nations, according to data from the Mortenson Institute. It seems clear that parental level of education and household income are strong predictors of success in these areas.

The Issue of Poverty

The U.S. poverty rate among children is 18 percent, the highest in the developed nations. The media generally presents pictures of poor black children in the United States, although the largest number of poor children are white (8.9 million of the 14 million poor children in 1999 were white, 4.2 million were black, and 3.9 million were Hispanic.) However, only 19 percent of all white children were poor, while 37 percent of black children were poor. It is no longer true that race is a universally handicapping condition—more than 25 percent of black households have a higher income than the white average. But poverty is a universal handicap. While efforts to eliminate racial segregation have been mostly effective, this has not led to increased economic equality, and the dif-

ference between the richest tenth of society and the poorest tenth continues to increase. The goal to "leave no child behind" is unreachable without equal investments in each child's education, starting with preschool.

See also: MULTICULTURAL EDUCATION; POPULATION AND EDUCATION; POVERTY AND EDUCATION; RACE, ETHNICITY, AND CULTURE.

BIBLIOGRAPHY

ANNIE E. CASEY FOUNDATION 2000. *Kids Count.* Baltimore: Annie E. Casey Foundation.

BRACEY, GERALD, and RESNICK, MICHAEL. 1998. *Raising the Bar: A School Board Primer on Student Achievement.* Alexandria, VA: National School Boards Association.

EDUCATION WEEK. 2001. *A Better Balance: Quality Counts,* 5th edition. Washington, DC: Education Week.

FEDERAL INTERAGENCY FORUM ON CHILD AND FAMILY STATISTICS. 2001. *America's Children: Key National Indicators of Well-Being.* Washington, DC: Federal Interagency Forum on Child and Family Statistics.

HODGKINSON, HAROLD. 1999. "Census 2000 Is Coming!" *Education Week* 19(5):34, 48.

HODGKINSON, HAROLD. 2000. *Secondary Schools in a New Millennium.* Reston, VA: National Association of Secondary School Principals.

MARTIN, PHILIP, and MIDGLEY, ELIZABETH. 1999. "Immigration to the United States." *Population Bulletin* 54(2):1–44.

MORTENSON INSTITUTE. 2001. *Postsecondary Education Opportunity.* Oskaloosa, IA: Mortenson Institute.

NATIONAL CENTER FOR EDUCATION STATISTICS. 1996. *Racial and Ethnic Classifications Used by Public Schools.* Washington, DC: National Center for Education Statistics.

NATIONAL CENTER FOR EDUCATION STATISTICS. 2001. *The Condition of Education, 2001.* Washington, DC: National Center for Education Statistics.

O'NEILL, BRIAN, and BALK, DEBORAH. 2001. "World Population Futures." *Population Bulletin* 56(3):3–40.

U.S. CENSUS BUREAU. 2000. *Statistical Abstract of the United States.* Washington, DC: U.S. Census Bureau.

FIGURE 1

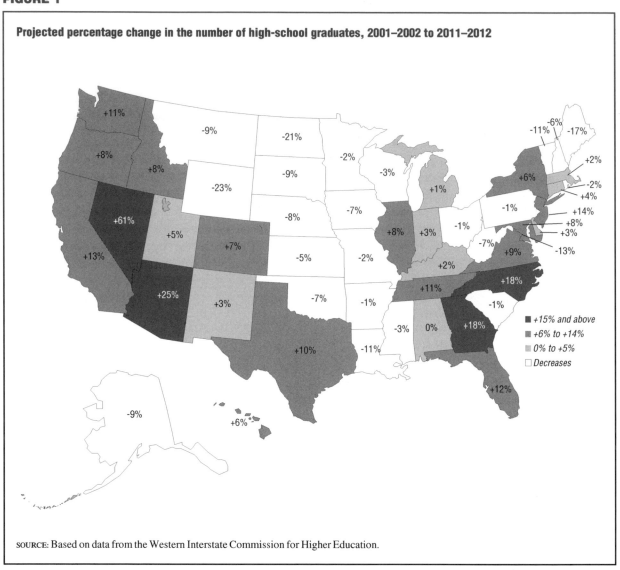

Projected percentage change in the number of high-school graduates, 2001–2002 to 2011–2012

SOURCE: Based on data from the Western Interstate Commission for Higher Education.

WELNER, ALISON. 2002. "The Census Report." *American Demographics,* January (special issue).

HAROLD HODGKINSON

YOUTH DEVELOPMENT PROGRAMS

Youth development programs seek to improve the lives of children and adolescents by meeting their basic physical, developmental, and social needs and by helping them to build the competencies needed to become successful adults. Examples of youth development programs include community service, mentoring programs, and neighborhood youth centers.

It is unclear exactly how many youth development programs are operating in the United States in the early twenty-first century. In 1998 the Internal Revenue Service identified more than 5,700 nonprofit organizations—almost 3 percent of all charitable agencies—that focused their primary services on youth development. In addition, countless other organizations offer youth development activities within a different primary focus. Examples include youth groups within religious organizations and after-school activities offered by public elementary schools.

The purpose of this entry is to provide an overview of youth development programs. It is organized in the following manner. First, a brief history of services for children and youth is presented. Second, the current framework for youth development programs, including school-based youth development efforts, is discussed. Next, issues regarding access to youth development programs and findings from evaluations of youth development efforts are presented. Finally, several issues regarding implementation of youth development programs and future research directions are discussed.

Historical Development of Youth Development Programs

The concept of childhood as a unique and crucial stage of human development is a relatively recent idea. Until the mid-1800s, children were viewed as miniature adults who, without strict guidance from their families, would follow their natural inclination toward aggression, stubbornness, sinfulness, and idleness to their doom. Not surprisingly, the earliest programs and services for children who were poor, orphaned, delinquent, or mentally ill focused heavily on helping them avoid their natural inclination toward vice and sought to help them gain useful occupation. Apprenticeships were arranged for older children, while younger children were cared for in almshouses where their health, morals, and education would be improved with the overall goal of ensuring future self-sufficiency.

Beginning in the mid-1800s, numerous factors combined to influence a transformation in the view of children and childhood and subsequently in services for children. Writings of the English philosopher John Locke (1632–1704) and American transcendentalists fostered the view of children as pure and good human beings who learn from experience and, as a result, are corrupted only by the influence of society. The nineteenth-century English naturalist Charles Darwin's theory of evolution—specifically its premise of environmental influence on behavior and development—contributed to the growing belief that, with appropriate nurturing, children could be molded into successful adults. As a result, childhood began to be viewed as a particularly critical point in human development. Friedrich Froebel (1782–1852), the German educator and founder of the kindergarten movement, encouraged this viewpoint and contended that children required special preparation for adulthood, as well as opportunities

for recreation and play. The publication of American psychologist and educator G. Stanley Hall's seminal work *Adolescence* in 1904 expanded this notion to older children and served to further cement such views.

This shift led to significant changes in services for children and adolescents. Institutions specifically designed to nurture the needs of children replaced apprenticeships and almshouses. Although the earliest institutions for children date to the mid-1700s, the movement to remove children from almshouses did not gain broad support until the nineteenth century. In 1861 Ohio passed the first state statute calling for the mandatory removal of all children from county almshouses, and by 1890 about 600 institutions—mostly owned and operated privately by religious and ethnic groups—were serving indigent children. Institutional child care during this period tended to take an undemocratic and antifamily approach characterized by discipline, training, and rehabilitation. These institutions operated with minimal oversight and mass care, rather than individualized attention, was the norm. Support for institutional child care waned for several reasons including increased economic uncertainty; the inability to build institutions at a rate sufficient to meet the needs of a growing number of orphaned, dependent, and delinquent children; the rise of public education; and the reduction in apprenticeship and legal indenture opportunities.

Child-care institutions were quickly replaced by a movement to place needy children with families. Led by the New York Children's Aid Society and its founder, the Reverend Charles Loring Brace, this movement focused on helping delinquent and needy children from New York City's poorest classes by transplanting them to a more healthful environment. Under Brace's direction, thousands of children were transported on *orphan trains* from New York City slums to live with farm families in the expanding West. Although they were subsidized by the city and the state, Brace's orphan trains failed to live up to his ideals. The families with whom the children lived often took advantage of their labor and failed to provide them with even the basic necessities and education. Poor families resented having their children sent so far away, and eventually the western states complained about what they perceived to be the dumping of thousands of delinquent and needy children each year. The economic shift from an agrarian society to an industrial society reduced the need for child labor on farms and further doomed this movement. Brace's conviction that family life was best for children and youth, however, continues to influence services for children to this day.

The first half of the twentieth century brought growing interest in the problem of juvenile delinquency. Investigation done by Dr. William Healy's Juvenile Psychopathic Institute led to the realization that the problem of delinquent children was not limited to the poorest classes. Further, delinquency was increasingly viewed as resulting from numerous factors, with the most prevalent being the lack of parental discipline resulting from the loss of one or both parents. Concurrently, it was becoming increasingly clear that efforts to punish offending youth did not deter future criminal action and that many of the youth who left institutions often returned. As a result, interest shifted to finding ways to treat troubled youth, rather than merely punish them, and led to the creation of the juvenile court system, which separated juvenile and adult offenders and focused on rehabilitation and cure. The first juvenile court law was enacted in Illinois in 1899, and by 1919 all but three states had established similar legislation.

Exploration into the causes of delinquency continued well into 1900s. Particularly influential were Richard Cloward and Lloyd Ohlin, who in a 1960 book advanced the opinion that young people turned to delinquency out of frustration with the lack of opportunity available to them. Opportunity theory suggested that providing at-risk youth with increased opportunity—particularly for economic success—could serve to prevent delinquency. As a result, services for children began to focus for the first time on the prevention of youth problems. One early such effort was the Mobilization for Youth Program, funded by the National Institute of Mental Health, which offered a comprehensive array of services including employment bureaus, training programs, education programs, antidiscrimination activities, and neighborhood service centers. Despite the mixed results of this program and others like it, the interest in prevention set the stage for the youth development efforts of the early twenty-first century.

Youth Development Programs in the Early Twenty-First Century

In the early twenty-first century, youth development programs take a more positive or strengths-based approach to prevention. Rather than trying to keep teens from engaging in risky behaviors, youth devel-

opment programs focus on helping them grow into happy, healthy adults. This approach mandates a conceptual shift from thinking that "youth problems are the principal barrier to youth development to thinking that youth development serves as the most effective strategy for the prevention of youth problems" (Pittman and Fleming, p. 3). Although professionals and researchers have yet to agree on a single definition of youth development, they have identified a set of principles common to most youth development programmatic efforts.

First, youth development efforts focus on meeting needs and developing competencies for *all* youth, not just for those engaged in problem behaviors or perceived to be at risk for doing so. The youth development model assumes that because all youth must pass through a specific developmental process to become successful adults, all youth are at risk for problems.

Second, youth development replaces the deficit-based focus of public-health prevention models with a strength-based approach that focuses on meeting needs and building competencies, rather than solving problems and providing treatment. The needs that must be met and the competencies that must be built to ensure the transition to successful adulthood are outlined in Table 1.

Third, unlike the public-health prevention model's focus on individual behavior, youth development assumes that "the way to improve the lives of young people is to improve the communities in which they live" (Jarvis, Shear, and Hughes, p. 721). Thus, community-level variables, rather than individual-level variables, are targeted for intervention and play a key role in youth development initiatives. Youth development's focus on community-level interventions influences how youth development initiatives are structured and implemented. Specifically, youth development programs focus on the "creation of a supportive community for children and families" and mandates that community-wide support and participation must be objectives "not only within an initiative's institutional collaboration structure, but also between a community's institutions and those citizens who live within it" (O'Brien, Pittman, and Cahill, p. 8). In 1994 Karen J. Pittman and Shepherd Zeldin further maintained that the establishment of youth development as a policy goal "must become incorporated into public institutions of education, employment, training, juvenile justice and health services to be successful" (p. 15).

Finally, the youth development approach requires the active participation of youth in the planning, delivery, and evaluation of services. The notion of involving youth as partners, rather than simply as clients, is unique to the youth development approach and is deeply rooted in empowerment theory, which focuses on the process of individuals' gaining power in order to improve their life circumstances. These points are summarized in Table 2.

Youth Development Programs and Education

Schools are viewed as a critical component of community-based youth development efforts. Of particular interest are efforts to provide youth development activities in school buildings during nonschool hours. Such activities range from educational enrichment, career exploration and development, and social and recreational opportunities. Four basic models of school-based youth development programs have been identified.

The Beacons model was established in New York City in 1991 and implemented as part of a comprehensive antidrug strategy. The model is based on the premise that youth development and academic achievement are strengthened when parents and community residents are involved in schools and when gaps between the home and the school are minimized. School-based community centers were opened to create safe places for youth and families in poor neighborhoods beset with drugs and violence. In addition to keeping school buildings open sixteen hours a day, seven days a week, 365 days a year, the Beacons model strived to create an environment within each school that promoted youth development and resiliency.

The Bridges to Success model, a school-based youth development model developed by the United Way of Central Indiana, began in Indianapolis in 1991. This model seeks to increase the educational success of students by improving the ability of schools to meet the noneducational needs of students and their families through a partnership between educators and the local human and community-service delivery systems. Activities, including educational enrichment, career development, arts and culture, life skills, counseling, case management, health and mental health services, and recreation, seek to establish schools as lifelong learning centers and focal points within their communities.

TABLE 1

Critical components of youth development

Meeting Needs	Building Competencies
Young people have basic needs critical to survival and healthy development. These needs are: • Safety and structure • Belonging and membership • Self-worth and an ability to contribute • Independence and control over one's life • Competence and mastery • Self-awareness	To succeed as adults, youth must acquire adequate attitudes, behaviors, and skills in the following areas: • Cognitive and creative competence: broad base of knowledge; ability to appreciate and participate in creative expression; good oral and written language skills; problem-solving and analytical skills, ability to learn, and an interest in learning and achieving • Personal and social competence: intrapersonal skills (understanding of self), interpersonal skills, and judgment skills • Health and physical competence: good current health, plus evidence of appropriate knowledge, attitudes, and behaviors that will ensure future health • Vocational competence: broad understanding of vocational and avocational options and of the steps needed to act on choices; adequate preparation for chosen career; understanding of value and function of work (and leisure) • Citizenship competence: understanding of nation's and community's history and values; understanding of pluralism and ability to function in a heterogeneous society; the desire to be involved in efforts that contribute to nation and community

SOURCE: Adapted from Pittman, Karen J., and Cahill, W. E. 1991. *A New Vision: Promoting Youth Development.* Washington, DC: Center for Youth Development and Policy Research, Academy for Educational Development.

Developed by the Children's Aid Society of New York City and initially implemented in New York City's Washington Heights neighborhood in 1989, the Community Schools model seeks to provide a myriad of health and social services within a public school setting. Operating fifteen hours a day, six days a week year-round, community school activities include medical, dental, and mental health service; recreation; supplemental education; parent education; family life education; and summer programs. This model is based on the premise that children's educational outcomes cannot be separated from that

TABLE 2

Comparison between traditional youth services and youth development programs

Traditional Youth Program Paradigm	Youth Development Program Paradigm
Adolescent problems, such as teen pregnancy, substance abuse, and violence, are viewed as unique and unrelated.	Adolescent problems, such as teen pregnancy, substance abuse, and violence, are viewed as interrelated and rooted in similar causes.
Service providers develop specialties in particular problem areas and offer services independently.	Programs and services are developed through collaboration between providers, community members, and youth.
Services and programs are focused on correcting deficits.	Services and programs are focused on enhancing the potential for healthy youth development.
Youth have access to services if they are identified as having a problem or at risk of a problem.	All youth have access to services and programs aimed at helping them to avoid problems.
Adolescents are viewed as clients.	Adolescents are viewed as partners in planning and treatment.
Providing services to adolescents is viewed as a way to improve the community (by reducing problem behaviors and delinquency).	Improving the community is viewed as a way to nurture and support adolescents, thereby improving their lives.

SOURCE: Courtesy of author.

of their families and other community residents. As a result, the model seeks to transform schools into institutions that house a comprehensive array of services, provide a focal point for community life, and ultimately strengthen the entire community.

The fourth model, the West Philadelphia Improvement Corps, a program initiated at the University of Pennsylvania in 1985, features university-assisted schools. The underlying strategy of this model is to create a partnership between a school and a university that strengthens both institutions and produces positive outcomes for youth, university faculty and students, and the greater community. Specific programmatic activities include the development of enrichment activities, school-based health and social services, and community service projects. This model stresses community participation in program design and planning.

Private and public funders are expected to continue their push for school-based youth development efforts. Unlike programs offered in other community settings (such as churches and social-service agencies), school-based programs are viewed as being able to reach many youth and eliminating or reducing issues related to disparities in access.

Access to Youth Development Programs

A handful of studies have identified major discrepancies in access to youth development programs. In general, these studies have found that white or suburban youth have greater access to youth development activities than do their minority, urban, or rural counterparts. In addition, access to youth development programs also appears to be positively correlated with family income level.

In 1982 Judith Erickson found that members of youth organizations were more likely to come from families whose fathers were better educated or whose incomes were higher. Fred Newmann and Robert Rutter found in 1986 that private Catholic and alternative public schools were more likely to include community-service programs in their curriculum than regular public schools. Furthermore, larger schools and those with a larger minority population were also more likely to stress community service than smaller schools or those with predominantly white students.

In their 1985 examination of library distribution within communities, Mark Testa and Edward Lawlor found a link between family income and library availability. Specifically, they found that in Chicago neighborhoods where the median family income was below $25,000, the average number of children per public library was twice the average number of children per library in neighborhoods with a median family income above $25,000. Similarly, more than twice as much money was spent per child on the libraries in more affluent communities as compared to communities with lower family incomes.

Julia Littell and Joan Wynn further explored this issue in a 1989 study that compared the youth development opportunities available for middle-school-aged youth (eleven- to fourteen-year-olds) in two Chicago communities that differed strikingly on numerous socioeconomic factors including educational attainment, occupational status, employment rates, median age, and racial composition. One community, given the pseudonym "Innerville" by the authors, was a low-income African-American community on Chicago's west side. The other community, which the authors called "Greenwood," was an affluent suburban municipality with predominantly white residents. They found stark differences in the number of community resources available for youth in these two communities. For every 1,000 youth aged eleven to fourteen, the inner-city community had 9.4 nonreligious organizations providing activities or facilities for youth, compared to 24.4 such organizations in the suburban community. In an average week, children in the inner-city community had access to 22.8 activities (per 1,000 youth aged eleven to fourteen), compared to 70.6 activities in the suburban community. In an average week, children in the inner-city community had access to 12.8 youth development activities offered through the public school (per 1,000 sixth through eighth graders), compared to 20.9 such activities for the suburban youth. Similarly, inner-city youth had access to 2.2 public-park programs (per 1,000 youth aged eleven to fourteen), compared to 18.2 public-park programs for youth living in the suburb. Finally, the urban youth had access to about 9.4 facilities each week (per 1,000 youth aged eleven to fourteen), whereas the suburban youth could access 42.4 facilities.

Evaluation of Youth Development Programs

The effectiveness of youth development programs remains somewhat unsubstantiated because of the dearth of comprehensive, rigorous evaluations. In their 1999 review of more than sixty evaluation studies of youth-serving programs, Jodie Roth and colleagues were able to identify only six that used rigorous research designs. Findings from such studies, however, are generally promising.

As reported in 1995, an eight-site evaluation of the Big Brothers Big Sisters of America program found that after eighteen months youth who participated in the program were less likely to start using illegal drugs or to initiate alcohol use; were less likely to report hitting someone during the previous twelve months; earned moderately higher grades; skipped half as many days at school; skipped fewer classes; felt more competent about doing their schoolwork; and reported better relationships with peers and parents than the control group. No differences were found between the two groups in the number of times they stole or damaged property, were sent to the principal's office, engaged in risky behaviors, fought, cheated on a test, or used tobacco. There were no statistically significant gains in self-concept or in the number of social and cultural activities in which the youth participated.

As outlined in a 1994 report, a longitudinal study of the Quantum Opportunities Program, a multiservice youth development program operating in five states, identified several long-term positive effects of participation. Compared to the control group, program participants had significant increases in academic skills and educational expectations; were more likely to have graduated from high school or received their GED; were more likely to attend a postsecondary school; were less likely to have been in trouble with the police within the previous twelve months; and had fewer children. Additionally, 22 percent more participants received honors or awards during the previous twelve months and 30 percent more were involved in community service within six months of finishing the program. No differences were found in grades or knowledge about contraceptives and AIDS.

A 1997 evaluation of an effort to promote interracial, interethnic, and intercultural harmony among youth found that the treatment group (which numbered 244) had significant improvements in reported school attendance and race relations and significant decreases in drug and alcohol use in the previous month compared to the control group (which numbered 471). Program participants also tended to report higher self-esteem, less drug and alcohol use for the previous year, and greater control of aggressive behavior.

An evaluation of the ADEPT Program, a comprehensive after-school program focusing on building positive self-esteem and providing homework assistance and activities for social and emotional growth, found that the program did not have any measurable effects on personality variables, such as self-esteem, risk-taking behavior, depression, and in-class behavior. Further, there was no positive program effect on standardized test scores. There was, however, a statistically significant improvement in average standardized test scores for students who received the self-esteem-building curriculum.

A two-year, longitudinal study of ten after-school programs offering alternative supports to improve educational achievement found that, two years following program completion, program youth received significantly higher grades than comparison group students in mathematics, science, social studies, reading and composition. Further, program participants showed greater improvement in their reported effort in science and social studies. The students who participated in the program for two or more years held significantly more positive attitudes about themselves and school; felt safer during the after-school hours; knew more people in college; had higher educational expectations; and liked school more than nonparticipants.

A three-year longitudinal study of the South Baltimore Youth Center featuring multiple comparison groups found that the program had a significant impact on participants. The amount of self-reported alcohol consumption increased significantly less than the comparison group for youth who participated in the program's social activities such as mentoring, tutoring, and job training. Further, the self-reported amount of drug use decreased significantly for the program youth during the study. The amount of self-reported delinquent behavior, both minor and serious, decreased significantly for the program youth. There were no differences, however, in the pro-social behavior of either group.

Issues Regarding Youth Development Programs

The required level of community-wide collaboration, the basic tenants of the youth development approach, and limited evaluation efforts are all barriers to widespread implementation of youth development programming.

Community-wide collaboration. The high level of community-wide collaboration required for successful youth development efforts has been identified by many researchers as posing a significant barrier to successful adoption of this approach. Previous research has documented that collaboration is often the element that distinguishes between successful youth development initiatives and those that fail. Both Marian W. Edelman, in 1987, and R. Jenkins, in 1989, concluded that targeting critical needs with proven programs is secondary to establishing broad community support in ensuring the long-term success of youth development interventions.

While both practitioners and researchers agree that community-wide collaboration is critical for youth development efforts to be successful, they concede that garnering such support is often difficult. Specific barriers to community-wide support include the lack of clarity regarding the concept of youth development and outcomes associated with it, the lack of clear leadership in many youth development efforts, and the wide range of values and perspectives that participants bring to the collaboration. Until such barriers to collaboration can be meaning-

fully addressed through research and practice, youth development initiatives will continue to prove to be difficult to implement and to maintain.

Conflict with youth development philosophy. Several studies have found that the basic tenants of the youth development approach prove troublesome for many participants in youth development initiatives. Faced with many pressing community needs, collaborators may have difficulty prioritizing prevention over treatment, and, as a result, it is often more difficult to mobilize parents, community leaders, policymakers, and service providers around promoting overall health or wellness than attacking a specific problem or crisis. Joan Wynn and her colleagues also noted the challenge of shifting institutional attention from "day-to-day survival and maintenance toward a more 'future' orientation" (Wynn, Costello, Halpern, and Richman, p. 48).

In addition, collaborators frequently have different viewpoints regarding another hallmark of the youth development approach: the involvement of youth and families in planning and policy development. One reason for this challenge is the lack of a theoretical framework that practitioners may use to guide collaborative efforts. However, work by N. Andrew Peterson and colleagues may begin to fill this gap. In a 1996 report, the National Clearinghouse on Families and Youth contended that while many youth-serving agencies believe in client participation, putting that belief into practice to the extent required by youth development is often a challenge for many community organizations.

Finally, researchers have hypothesized that embracing youth development may be particularly difficult for social service agencies, whose philosophies, programs, and funding are likely to be deeply rooted in the traditional youth services paradigm. In 1995 Joan Wynn and her colleagues contended that such a paradigm is often too narrow to accept the broader youth development perspective, and, as a result, many of these agencies find it particularly difficult to institute the fundamental changes needed to embrace youth development. Funding streams that favor treatment and intervention over prevention may further discourage agencies from shifting services to the youth development paradigm.

Limited evaluation efforts. The lack of rigorous evaluation efforts has also limited more widespread adoption of the youth development approach. In its 1992 review of evaluation of youth-serving programs, the Carnegie Council on Adolescent Development identified several reasons for the lack of evaluative effort. First, they found that many agencies failed to allocate appropriate resources for outcome evaluation. Second, they found that many existing evaluations had weak evaluation designs and as a result their findings were unclear at best. Third, the staff of youth development programs were often resistant to participating in evaluation efforts. Finally, the council found that no clear, universally agreed-upon outcome measures for youth development programs had been identified. The council, however, felt that improving the state of youth development evaluation was critical to expanded implementation.

See also: CLUBS; COMMUNITY EDUCATION; NEIGHBORHOODS; URBAN EDUCATION; YOUTH ORGANIZATIONS.

BIBLIOGRAPHY

ABBOTT, GRACE. 1938. *The Child and the State.* Chicago: University of Chicago Press.

AXINN, JUNE, and LEVIN, HERMAN. 1992. *Social Welfare: A History of the American Response to Need.* White Plains, NY: Longman.

BAKER, KEITH; POLLACK, MARCUS; and KOHN, IMRE. 1995. "Violence Prevention through Informal Socialization: An Evaluation of the South Baltimore Youth Center." *Studies on Crime and Crime Prevention* 4:61–85.

BARTON, WILLIAM H.; WATKINS, MARIE; and JARJOURA, ROGER. 1997. "Youth and Communities: Toward Comprehensive Strategies for Youth Development." *Social Work* 42:483–493.

BOGENSCHNEIDER, KAREN. 1996. "An Ecological Risk/Protective Theory for Building Prevention Programs, Policies, and Community Capacity to Support Youth." *Family Relations* 45:127–137.

BRACE, CHARLES LORING. 1880. *The Dangerous Classes in New York.* New York: Wynkoop and Hallenbeck.

CARNEGIE COUNCIL ON ADOLESCENT DEVELOPMENT. 1989. *Turning Points: Preparing American Youth for the Twenty-First Century.* Washington, DC: Carnegie Council on Adolescent Development.

CARNEGIE COUNCIL ON ADOLESCENT DEVELOPMENT. 1992. *A Matter of Time: Risk and Opportunity in the Out-of-School Hours.* Washington, DC: Carnegie Council on Adolescent Development.

CARNEGIE COUNCIL ON ADOLESCENT DEVELOPMENT. 1996. *Great Transitions: Preparing Adolescents for a New Century,* abridged edition. New York: Carnegie Council on Adolescent Development.

CLOWARD, RICHARD A., and OHLIN, LLOYD. 1960. *Delinquency and Opportunity: A Theory of Delinquent Gangs.* New York: Free Press.

DEWITT WALLACE–READER'S DIGEST FUND. 2001. *Supporting Young People's Positive Development during the Nonschool Hours: An Overview of the Extended-Service Schools Initiative.* New York: Dewitt Wallace–Reader's Digest Fund.

DRYFOOS, JOY G. 1990. *Adolescents at Risk: Prevalence and Prevention.* New York: Oxford University Press.

EDELMAN, MARIAN W. 1987. *Families in Peril: An Agenda for Social Change.* Cambridge, MA: Harvard University Press.

ERICKSON, JUDITH B. 1982. *A Profile of Community Youth Organization Members, 1980.* Boys Town, NE: Boys Town Center for the Study of Youth Development.

FROEBEL, FRIEDRICH W. A. 1899. *Education by Development.* New York: Appleton.

GUTIERREZ, LORRAINE M. 1990. "Working with Women of Color: An Empowerment Perspective." *Social Work* 35: 149–153.

HAHN, ANDREW; LEAVITT, TOM; and AARON, PAUL. 1994. *Evaluation of the Quantum Opportunities Program. Did the Program Work? A Report on the Post-secondary Outcomes and Cost-Effectiveness of the QOP Program (1989–1993).* Waltham, MA: Center for Human Resources, Heller Graduate School, Brandeis University.

HALL, G. STANLEY. 1904. *Adolescence: Its Psychology and Its Relation to Physiology, Anthropology, Sociology, Sex, Crime, Religion, and Education.* New York: Appleton.

JARVIS, SARA V.; SHEAR, LIZ; and HUGHES, DELLA M. 1997. "Community Youth Development: Learning the New Story." *Child Welfare* 76:719–741.

JENKINS, R. 1989. *Youth at Risk.* Washington, DC: Youth Policy Institute.

KAHNE, JOSEPH; NAGAOKA, JENNY; BROWN, ANDREA; O'BRIEN, JAMES; QUINN, THERESE; and

THIEDE, KEITH. 2001. "Assessing After-School Programs as Contexts for Youth Development." *Youth and Society* 32:421–446.

LERNER, RICHARD M. 1985. *America's Youth in Crisis: Challenges and Choices for Programs and Policies.* Thousand Oaks, CA: Sage.

LITTELL, JULIA, and WYNN, JOAN. 1989. *The Availability and Use of Community Resources for Young Adolescents in an Inner-City and a Suburban Community.* Chicago: Chapin Hall Center for Children, University of Chicago.

LoSCIUTO, LEONARD, and FREEMAN, MARK A. 1997. "An Outcome Evaluation of the Woodrock Youth Development Project." *Journal of Early Adolescence* 17:51–67.

MILLSTEIN, SUSAN G.; PETERSEN, ANNE C.; and NIGHTENGALE, ELENA O., eds. 1993. *Promoting the Health of Adolescents: New Directions for the Twenty-First Century.* New York: Oxford University Press.

NATIONAL CLEARINGHOUSE ON FAMILIES AND YOUTH. 1996. *Reconnecting Youth and Community: A Youth Development Approach.* Washington, DC: U.S. Department of Health and Human Services.

NATIONAL CLEARINGHOUSE ON FAMILIES AND YOUTH. 1997. *Understanding Youth Development: Promoting Positive Pathways of Growth.* Washington, DC: U.S. Department of Health and Human Services.

NATIONAL CLEARINGHOUSE ON FAMILIES AND YOUTH. 1999. "FYSB Demonstration Projects Focus on Youth Development." *FYSB Update,* April. Washington, DC: U.S. Department of Health and Human Services, Administration for Children and Families, Administration on Children, Youth and Families, Family and Youth Services Bureau.

NEWMANN, FRED M., and RUTTER, ROBERT A. 1986. "A Profile of High School Community Service Programs." *Educational Leadership* 43:65–71.

O'BRIEN, RAYMOND; PITTMAN, KAREN J.; and CAHILL, MICHELE. 1992. *Building Supportive Communities for Youth: Local Approaches to Enhancing Community Youth Services and Supports.* Washington, DC: Center for Youth Development and Policy Research, Academy for Educational Development.

PETERSON, N. ANDREW, and SPEER, PAUL. 2000. "Linking Organizational Characteristics to Psychological Empowerment: Contextual Issues in Empowerment Theory." *Administration in Social Work* 24(4):39–58.

PITTMAN, KAREN J. 1991. *Promoting Youth Development: Strengthening the Role of Youth-Serving and Community Organizations.* Washington, DC: Center for Youth Development and Policy Research, Academy for Educational Development.

PITTMAN, KAREN J. 1992. *Defining the Fourth R: Promoting Youth Development through Building Relationships.* Washington, DC: Center for Youth Development and Policy Research, Academy for Educational Development.

PITTMAN, KAREN J., and CAHILL, MICHELE. 1992. *Pushing the Boundaries of Education: The Implications of a Youth Development Approach to Education Policies, Structures, and Collaborations.* Washington, DC: Center for Youth Development and Policy Research, Academy for Educational Development.

PITTMAN, KAREN J., and FLEMING, W. E. 1991. *A New Vision: Promoting Youth Development.* Washington, DC: Center for Youth Development and Policy Research, Academy for Educational Development.

PITTMAN, KAREN J., and WRIGHT, MARLENE. 1991. *Bridging the Gap: A Rationale for Enhancing the Role of Community Organizations Promoting Youth Development.* Washington, DC: Center for Youth Development and Policy Research, Academy for Educational Development.

PITTMAN, KAREN J., and ZELDIN, SHEPHERD. 1994. "From Deterrence to Development: Putting Programs for Young African-American Males in Perspective." In *Nurturing Young Black Males: Challenges to Agencies, Programs, and Social Policy,* ed. Ronald B. Mincy. Washington, DC: Urban Institute.

ROTH, JODIE; BROOKS-GUNN, JEANNE; MURRAY, LAWRENCE; and FOSTER, WILLIAM. 1998. "Health Promotion and Youth Development: Synthesis of Current Program Evaluations." *Journal of Research on Adolescence* 8:423–459.

ROTH, JODIE; MURRAY, LAWRENCE F.; BROOKS-GUNN, JEANNE; and FOSTER, WILLIAM. 1999. "Youth Development Programs." In *America's Disconnected Youth,* ed. Douglas J. Besharov. Washington, DC: Child Welfare League of America.

SWIFT, MARSHALL S., and HEALEY, KATHRYN N. 1986. "Translating Research into Practice." In *A Decade of Progress in Primary Prevention*, ed. Marc Kessler and Stephen E. Goldston. Hanover, MA: University Press of New England.

TAPPER, DONNA; KLEINMAN, PAULA; and NAKASHIAN, MARY. 1997. "An Interagency Collaboration Strategy for Linking Social and Criminal Justice Services." *Social Work in Education* 19:176–188.

TESTA, MARK, and LAWLOR, EDWARD. 1985. *The State of the Child, 1985.* Chicago: Chapin Hall Center for Children, University of Chicago.

TIERNEY, JOSEPH P.; GROSSMAN, JEAN BALDWIN; and RESCH, NANCY L. 1995. *Making a Difference: An Impact Study of Big Brothers/Big Sisters.* Philadelphia: Public/Private Ventures.

TRATTNER, WALTER I. 1994. *From Poor Law to Welfare State: A History of Social Welfare in America.* New York: Free Press.

U.S. INTERNAL REVENUE SERVICE. 1998. *Form 990 Return Transaction File.* Washington, DC: U.S. Internal Revenue Service.

WENTWORTH, KEITH. 1982. "Positive Youth Development: Prevention as a Process of Positive Community Change." *Journal of Primary Prevention* 2:240–243.

WYNN, JOAN; COSTELLO, JOAN; HALPERN, ROBERT; and RICHMAN, HAROLD. 1994. *Children, Families, and Communities: A New Approach to Social Services.* Chicago: Chapin Hall Center for Children, University of Chicago.

WYNN, JOAN R.; MERRY, SHEILA M.; and BERG, PATRICIA G. 1995. *Children, Families, and Communities: Early Lessons from a New Approach to Social Services.* Washington, DC: American Youth Policy Forum of the Institute for Educational Leadership, Education and Human Services Consortium.

WYNN, JOAN; RICHMAN, HAROLD; RUBINSTEIN, ROBERT A.; and LITTELL, JULIA. 1987. *Communities and Adolescents: An Exploration of Reciprocal Supports.* Chicago: Chapin Hall Center for Children, University of Chicago.

INTERNET RESOURCE

NATIONAL YOUTH DEVELOPMENT INFORMATION CENTER. 1999. "Definitions of Youth Development and Related Terms." <www.nydic.org/devdef.html>.

DONNA VAN ALST
N. ANDREW PETERSON

YOUTH ORGANIZATIONS

AMERICAN FIELD SERVICE

The American Field Service (AFS) is a nonprofit volunteer-based educational organization concerned

2718 YOUTH ORGANIZATIONS: BIG BROTHERS BIG SISTERS OF AMERICA

with promoting understanding among people throughout the world. Its purposes are to involve high school students, young adults, and teachers in the family, community, and school life of other nations.

Program

Each year the AFS sends more than 10,000 students, young adults, and teachers to a foreign country through one of its several international exchange programs. Through its Americans Abroad Program, the AFS annually provides opportunities for approximately 1,700 American high school juniors and seniors to live and study in one of forty-four foreign countries for a year, a semester, or a summer. Each year, the AFS also brings approximately 2,500 high school students from more than fifty countries to the United States to live for one year or one semester with an American family and attend the local high school. High school graduates can participate in the AFS Community Service Program, which sends men and women for four months to a year to one of twenty countries to perform volunteer work. Community Service volunteers may work with street children, orphans, or people with disabilities. Volunteers may also tutor children in local schools or participate in community development and environmental programs.

Through its Global Educators Program, the AFS sends American teachers, counselors, and educational administrators to Argentina, China, Indonesia, Mexico, South Africa, Spain, Thailand, and several other countries. Exchange educators live with host families and teach in local schools for one month or one semester. The AFS also brings teachers from other countries to live and teach in the United States for a semester or a year.

AFS programs are administered in cooperation with volunteer organizations throughout the world and with the help of local volunteer chapters in the U.S. communities where students are placed. Participating students and teachers must pay their own program fees. The AFS helps by offering more than $1 million each year in financial aid and scholarships through the Awards for Excellence Merit Scholarship, the AFS World Citizen Scholarship, the Stephen Galatti Scholarships, and other AFS scholarship and financial aid programs.

Organization

The AFS is controlled by fifty international trustee members, who meet annually to review policies, guide the development of programs, and elect a board of directors, which conducts the organization's business throughout the year. In most foreign countries participating in AFS programs, a small paid staff coordinates the work of volunteers and serves as liaison with international headquarters. In some counties, a private citizen, a binational center director, or a cultural assistant on the U.S. embassy staff handles the representation procedures.

Membership

In the United States there are approximately 3,000 chapters that represent the AFS program in every high school in which an overseas student is placed. These schools are eligible to nominate candidates for the AFS Americans Abroad Program. Each chapter assumes financial responsibility for an overseas student; many chapters also raise funds to assist needy Americans Abroad students.

History

In 1914 Americans residing in Paris, France, organized the AFS as a volunteer ambulance service to assist French hospitals in the evacuation of the wounded from the French war front. Additional volunteers formed both ambulance and trucking units under the command of the French armies. After World War I the remaining funds were used to operate a postgraduate scholarship program for the exchange of American and French students. During World War II the AFS provided ambulance drivers for the French forces and later for the British forces in the Middle East. Units also served in Italy, France, Germany, and on the India–Burma front. The international scholarship exchange program began in 1947 when fifty-two students came from ten countries to the United States for one year. Since then, nearly 290,000 students have participated in AFS exchange programs.

INTERNET RESOURCE

AMERICAN FIELD SERVICE. 2002. <www.afs.org>.

ARTHUR HOWE JR.
Revised by
JUDITH J. CULLIGAN

BIG BROTHERS BIG SISTERS OF AMERICA

Big Brothers Big Sisters of America is a social service organization that provides guidance for young boys and girls who lack normal parental and family relationships. Big Brothers Big Sisters of America is committed to the principle that every boy and girl needs adult companionship, and it encourages mature, responsible men and women to offer friendship and counsel to boys and girls who have been deprived of such support from their fathers, mothers, and other adult family members.

Program

Big Brothers Big Sisters of America serves member agencies in the United States and Canada. It enlists dedicated men and women from all walks of life to help guide, instruct, and influence young girls and boys from economically and educationally disadvantaged backgrounds. Adult volunteers (called "Bigs") dedicate themselves to developing positive social and educational attitudes in young boys and girls. As a result of their assignments to Big Brothers Big Sisters, boys and girls have shown marked improvement in schoolwork and decreases in juvenile behavioral problems. According to the organization's national office, children involved in the program have developed more positive attitudes toward school, achieved higher grades and better attendance records, strengthened their relationships with family members and peers, and demonstrated higher levels of self-confidence and trust. Boys and girls in the program were also less likely to become drug and alcohol abusers.

Although there is no structured educational program, all men and women who volunteer as Big Brothers or Big Sisters are concerned with helping boys and girls learn the best ways of relating to society. Many Big Brothers Big Sisters agencies have a High School Bigs program in which mature teenagers can serve as mentors and role models for at-risk elementary and middle school children. In some communities, agencies work with local police departments to provide early intervention for first-time juvenile offenders by matching them with a Big Sister or Big Brother. In most instances, referrals to Big Brother agencies come from local schools.

Big Brothers Big Sisters staff carefully screen prospective volunteers, then match them to children with whom they can form a useful, harmonious, and long-lasting relationship. Adult volunteers undergo orientation before meeting the child to whom they are matched. After the organization brings together the child and adult, the pair will meet regularly to go to movies and shows, visit museums and parks, attend sporting events, and engage in various other activities and outings. Bigs may also help children with schoolwork and talk to them about problems at home. Big Sisters and Big Brothers are free to spend as much money as they wish while with the child.

Organization

In some large metropolitan centers there may be several separate Big Brothers Big Sisters agencies that help match children and adults. Most smaller communities have only one such agency. A large national board determines program policies and standards for all Big Brothers Big Sisters agencies. A small paid staff at the national headquarters organizes regional professional staff conferences, council meetings, and an annual meeting at which all agencies are represented. Each local agency has its own board of directors. Many of the local agencies receive a portion of their support from local United Way appeals; much of the work is financed by contributions from foundations, private donors, and corporate partners.

Big Brothers Big Sisters of America is affiliated with Big Brothers Big Sisters International (BBBSI). Established in 1998, BBBSI promotes and supports the development of Big Brothers Big Sisters-type programs throughout the world by offering materials, funding, consultation, and professional training. Agencies have been established in many countries, including Australia, Poland, South Africa, Japan, and Israel.

Membership

The work of Big Brothers Big Sisters of America is carried out at the local agency level, where volunteers are interviewed and screened prior to being accepted as Big Brothers or Big Sisters. Boys and girls are also introduced to the program at the local agency level, where an adult and a young person are assigned as a team. No dues or fees are charged either to the adults or children. Most youths who take part in the program are between the ages of ten and fourteen. The majority are boys; about half are minorities. Most of the children come from low-income households and single-parent families, many of which have a history of substance abuse or domestic violence.

History

The Big Brother concept of one man working with one boy began in 1904 in New York City as a result of a clerk's interest in children's court. The clerk, who was concerned with the increasing rate of juvenile crime, spoke to a church men's club about the problem. As a result, each man in the club agreed to befriend a boy who had experienced behavioral problems. Later that year, an organization called Catholic Big Sisters was formed in New York; it was the first known Big Sisters program in the country. Although other similarly motivated groups joined the movement, Big Brothers of America was not officially organized until after World War II. The organization undertook a growth and development program that encouraged communities to form agencies. It sought highly skilled social workers to staff local agencies; launched a public information program; and initiated a research program to determine need, effectiveness, and value for the national organization and its local affiliates.

By 1970 there were 192 member agencies in the United States and Canada, with 175 other communities in the process of organizing agencies. In 1977 separate Big Brothers and Big Sisters organizations merged into Big Brothers Big Sisters of America and the national headquarters was established in Philadelphia, Pennsylvania. By 2001 the organization had over 500 affiliates in communities across North America.

BIBLIOGRAPHY

BEISWINGER, GEORGE L. 1985. *One to One: The Story of the Big Brothers Big Sisters Movement in America.* Philadelphia: Big Brothers Big Sisters of America.

FURANO, KATHRYN. 1993. *Big Brothers Big Sisters: A Study of Program Practices.* Philadelphia: Public/Private Ventures.

GREIF, RICHARD S. 1997. *Big Impact: Big Brothers Making a Difference.* Boston: New Hat.

INTERNET RESOURCE

BIG BROTHERS BIG SISTERS OF AMERICA. 2002. <www.bbbsa.org>.

RAYMOND J. HOFFMAN
Revised by
JUDITH J. CULLIGAN

B'NAI B'RITH YOUTH ORGANIZATION

The B'nai B'rith Youth Organization (BBYO) is an international organization whose purpose is to help young Jewish people achieve personal growth so that they may lead satisfying and socially useful lives in the Jewish community and in the larger community in which they live. The BBYO encourages its members to participate in a broad program of cultural, religious, community service, educational, human relations, athletic, and social activities.

Program

All BBYO activities are designed as learning experiences. The community-service program combines fund-raising and personal service. Each local chapter contributes to the International Service Fund. The money is used for leadership training activities within the BBYO and for such philanthropic organizations as the Leo N. Levi Memorial Hospital in Hot Springs, Arkansas; the B'nai B'rith Children's Home near Jerusalem in Israel; the Kennedy Center for the Performing Arts in Washington, D.C.; the United Nations Educational, Scientific and Cultural Organization (UNESCO); Cooperative for Assistance and Relief Everywhere (CARE); and many others. B'nai B'rith Youth Organization groups also participate in local Jewish Welfare Fund campaigns, local health drives, and other local community-service efforts. The BBYO operates two camps for members: the B'nai B'rith Perlman Camp in Starlight, Pennsylvania, and the B'nai B'rith Beber Camp in Mukwonago, Wisconsin. In addition, the BBYO sponsors summer exchange programs for members to study and work in Israel, with Israeli teenagers traveling to the United States and other countries.

In the area of personal service, the BBYO sponsors the Adopt-a-Grandparent Program, in which youngsters provide companionship to the aged in or out of institutions. B'nai B'rith Youth Organization groups also entertain and help children in hospitals, homes, and other institutions. BBYO members read to the blind and help the physically and mentally handicapped. Further BBYO activities include tutoring underachievers, taking disadvantaged children to museums and recreational events, and collecting books for use in economically deprived areas.

The BBYO also sponsors various interfaith initiatives and runs the College Ambassador Alumni program and the Holocaust Expression Theatre. Religious services and holiday celebrations, as well as contests in athletics, drama, oratory, storytelling, creative writing, sermon writing, music, and visual arts are held at the chapter level. Local winners proceed through chapter and regional levels to the international finals held at Perlman or Berber Camp.

The BBYO publishes numerous pamphlets about Judaism for use by teenagers. The organization also publishes adviser newsletters, various program guides and other program aids, and newspapers called *Shofar* and *The Commish.*

Organization

The BBYO is a federation of three youth organizations: the Aleph Zadik Aleph (AZA) for high school boys, the B'nai B'rith Girls (BBG) for high school girls, and the B'nai B'rith Teen Connection for middle school boys and girls. Each local chapter has a volunteer adviser who is supervised by the professional staff of social group workers. Chapters are united into regions, each of which has a youth structure, an adult policymaking structure, and a professional staff structure. There are thirty-seven BBYO regions in North America, which report directly to the BBYO International Executive Board. The international office is responsible for setting standards and goals, budget and staffing, and publications. Most programs and activities are organized at the local level.

Membership

Because Jewish aspirations are emphasized, membership is open only to Jewish youths. Parents of BBYO members need not be affiliated with the larger B'nai B'rith organization. By 2000 the BBYO had more than 50,000 members in over 1,500 chapters throughout the world.

History

The B'nai B'rith youth movement originated in 1924 in Omaha, Nebraska, with a single chapter of sixteen boys who opposed the exclusive high school and college social fraternity system. Three other chapters were formed during the same year, and the four groups held their first convention in July 1924. In 1925 the youth organization received official sponsorship by the B'nai B'rith organization. The first chapter of B'nai B'rith Girls was founded in 1927 in San Francisco, California. In 1944 the two organizations merged and became the BBYO. The Teen Connection was established later to meet the needs of younger boys and girls.

INTERNET RESOURCE

B'NAI B'RITH YOUTH ORGANIZATION. 2002. <www.bbyo.org>.

MAX F. BAER
Revised by
JUDITH J. CULLIGAN

BOYS AND GIRLS CLUBS OF AMERICA

The Boys and Girls Clubs of America's tradition of service to the nation's youth began in 1860, when the first Boys Club was established in Hartford, Connecticut. Since then the organization has grown to serve millions of young people in thousands of Boys and Girls Clubs across the country.

The national organization—originally named Federated Boys Clubs, and later Boys Clubs of America—was founded in 1906 by the fifty-three local Boys Clubs in existence at that time. The purpose of the organization was to provide leadership and programs for member clubs, and to help establish new clubs in disadvantaged communities. In 1990 the name became Boys and Girls Clubs of America (B&GCA), reflecting an expanded mission of service to all young people who need the support, guidance, and character-development experiences the clubs provide.

In the closing years of the twentieth century, Boys and Girls Clubs of America experienced dramatic growth, chartering more than 1,000 new club locations. Many factors contributed to this successful outreach effort, among them the dedication of national volunteers—men and women whose experience and knowledge are drawn upon to advise and strengthen the organization. Strong partnerships with committed corporations and foundations also provide invaluable support, helping raise funds and awareness on behalf of Boys and Girls Clubs of America and local clubs.

B&GCA's efficient use of financial resources has won national recognition. In a 2000 "Philanthropy 400" report, *The Chronicle of Philanthropy* ranked B&GCA thirteenth among all nonprofit organizations, while placing B&GCA in the number one position among youth organizations for the seventh consecutive year. *Forbes, Fortune, Money, Newsweek,* and *U.S. News and World Report* have all ranked B&GCA among the top charitable organizations in America, based on cost-effective use of donor dollars. *SmartMoney* magazine ranked B&GCA as one of the two top children's charities, and among the top ten of all nonprofit organizations, based on financial efficiency, strength of reputation, and program effectiveness.

Boys and Girls Clubs of America continues to maximize its human and financial resources to reach more young people and communities in need. At the beginning of the twenty-first century, an estimated 15 million American children live in poverty. Half live in urban areas, and many face serious obstacles to achieving productive futures, but all deserve the chance to achieve their full potential as productive, responsible, and caring citizens and leaders.

B&GCA's commitment to growth and quality is based on its concern for deserving youth, as well as the national interest: soon these boys and girls will become the mainstay of America's economy. Club programs and services promote and enhance the development of boys and girls by instilling a sense of competence, usefulness, and power. By aiding their development, all of society benefits.

B&GCA is especially committed to high-quality after-school programming. According to the U.S. Department of Justice, nearly half of all juvenile crimes occur on weekdays between 3 P.M. and 8 P.M. B&GCA's proven after-school programs not only keep children safe and out of trouble, they also provide a prime opportunity to increase learning. Young people in B&GCA's after-school programs show better achievement in math, reading, and other subjects.

Among the children in greatest need are those living in America's public housing developments. In 1986 fewer than forty clubs operated in public housing. By the end of the twentieth century, however, more than 400 public housing–based Boys and Girls Clubs served more than 150,000 youths. This number grows steadily, thanks to effective collaboration between clubs, schools, housing authorities, government agencies, and private funding sources.

B&GCA continues to break new ground, reaching out to at-risk youth in nontraditional ways. Boys and Girls Clubs work with young people in schools, homeless shelters, shopping malls, and on military bases and Native American lands.

Boys and Girls Clubs of America's mission is to inspire and enable all young people, especially those from disadvantaged circumstances, to realize their full potential as productive, responsible, and caring citizens. While America's youth face many difficult

challenges, Boys and Girls Clubs continue their tradition of offering proven solutions that work. Clubs have provided millions of girls and boys with daily character-development programs, firmly establishing a nationwide reputation as "The Positive Place for Kids."

CHERI TIERNAN

BOYS AND GIRLS STATES

Boys State and Girls States are educational programs aimed at teaching American high school students the duties, privileges, rights, and responsibilities of American citizenship. Boys State programs are funded and organized by the American Legion; Girls State programs are funded and organized by the American Legion Auxiliary. The program provides teenagers with hands-on experience in government by enabling them to participate in the practical functioning of fictional "states."

Program

The content and method of Boys State and Girls State programs vary from state to state, but all adhere to the basic goal of teaching about government from the city to the state level. Most state programs last for one week, but some run for as many as fourteen days. Enrollments also vary, with as few as 25 to as many as 1,500 participants in a single "state." Most state programs are held at a college campus or other educational institution.

Participants in Girls State and Boys State programs become citizens of a mythical fifty-first state. As such, they help plan and execute all the main functions of the state, guided by the basic laws and procedures of the actual state where the program is being held. The practical and nonpartisan program is designed to teach students how government actually works in a democratic society.

On arrival, each boy or girl is assigned to a "city," where he or she joins other "citizens" in establishing a city government. They begin by electing a mayor and other city officials, including perhaps a city administrator, city council members, judges and district attorneys, and a sheriff. The newly established city government then enacts and enforces ordinances to govern the city. In larger Boys State and Girls State programs, cities may be organized into counties, which establish county governments. Participants in larger programs may also set up banks, post offices, schools, clinics, and even stores.

At the beginning of the program, each participating student is appointed to an imaginary political party. Most Boys State and Girls State programs include two parties (e.g., Tories and Whigs, Nationalists and Federalists). The two parties are not modeled after the real Republican and Democratic parties, but are meant to teach participants how political parties function and how a two-party system of government works. Party members develop their own party platforms, highlighting issues the participants think are important. Citizens of each party nominate members to be candidates for various city and county offices. They also hold caucuses and political conventions to nominate party members for state office, after which candidates run campaigns and statewide elections are held. Some states even hold inaugural ceremonies after elections, where the new "governor" and other officials take an oath of office.

Elected officials then form state governments and name various appointive officials, including perhaps an attorney general, a secretary of state, and a state treasurer. State officials also establish a supreme court and lower courts, where citizen attorneys defend and prosecute lawbreakers. In addition, citizens elect state representatives and senators and form a functioning legislature.

Each Boys State and Girls State also includes "journalists," who interview candidates and public officials, report on events within the city and state, and write editorials. The state paper is edited, printed, and published by the student participants themselves, with the goal of teaching the importance and function of a free press in a democratic society. In most states, a newspaper will be published each morning with the news of the preceding day. A summary journal may be published at the end of the program.

During the program, participants also engage in seminars where they discuss subjects pertaining to government, law, and politics. Real public officials and professional leaders often present special lectures about government and citizenship. Student participants are further guided by volunteer adult counselors, most of whom are actual attorneys, judges, teachers, law enforcement officials, and civil servants.

Every year, outstanding "citizens" from the Boys State and Girls State programs around the country are chosen to participate in the Boys Nation and Girls Nation programs in Washington, D.C. In these programs, run by the national American Legion and American Legion Auxiliary organizations, students take on the roles of "senators," representing their state within a fictional federal government.

Membership

The majority of participants in Boys State and Girls State programs are high school juniors or seniors who have been sponsored by an American Legion post or auxiliary unit. Students interested in taking part in a Boys State or Girls State program must apply to their local legion post. Application procedures and selection criteria vary from state to state, but in most cases, applications are reviewed by a board of legion members who select the best candidates. The board may require applicants to undergo an interview before final appointment. In general, the legion is looking for candidates with above average academic records, demonstrated leadership abilities, and high moral character. Applicants must also show an interest in government, current events, and public service.

Financial support for Boys State and Girls State programs comes from the budgets of the American Legion and American Legion Auxiliary national organizations, as well as the state and local legion and auxiliary units. Additional funding is provided by local businesses and other civic and nonprofit organizations. Student participants pay no fees.

History

The American Legion Department of Illinois conducted the first Boys State program in 1935 at the Illinois State Fairgrounds in Springfield, Illinois. Two Illinois Legionnaires, Hayes Kennedy and Harold Card, initiated the program to counter the influence of the Young Pioneer Camps being promoted by the Communist Party during the 1930s. The Legion Auxiliary of the District of Columbia initiated the first Girls State program in 1938. The first Boys Nation, then called Boys Forum of National Government, was held in 1946. The first Girls Nation was held the following year. By 2000 Boys State and Girls State programs were held annually in every American state except Hawaii.

INTERNET RESOURCES

AMERICAN LEGION. 2002. <www.legion.org>.

AMERICAN LEGION AUXILIARY. 2002. <www.legion-aux.org>.

JAMES C. WATKINS
Revised by
JUDITH J. CULLIGAN

BOY SCOUTS OF AMERICA

The Boy Scouts of America (BSA) provides educational programs for boys and young men that can be delivered through local organizations. The aims of the BSA programs are to develop character, citizenship, and fitness among its members. The Scout promise (oath) and scout laws identify the specific virtues the BSA wishes boys to pursue. Those virtues are honesty, loyalty, helpfulness, friendliness, courteousness, kindness, obedience, optimism, courage, thriftiness, cleanliness, and reverence.

The BSA programs attempt to achieve the stated aims and develop the identified virtues through several methods. First, adult scout leaders are meant to serve as role models who guide members through an advancement system. Second, scouts select activities in their small groups, and each member is expected to take on and share leadership roles. Third, as members demonstrate that they have attained skills through mastering and completing specific challenges set forth in the manuals, scouts earn awards, badges, and advancements to the next level of scouting. Community service and outdoor activities are central features of the programs.

History

At the beginning of the twentieth century there was a general consensus, both in the United States and Europe, that boys needed educational and recreational activities beyond those provided by schools. In 1910 William Boyce, a publisher from Chicago, incorporated the BSA, after meeting with Robert Baden-Powell, the British author of *Scouting for Boys.* On incorporation in the United States, the Young Men's Christian Association (YMCA) undertook to support the formation and maintenance of Boy Scout programs by community organizations. The Sons of Daniel Boone, founded by Daniel Beard, merged with the BSA and Beard became the first national scout commissioner. Ernest Seton, who had founded the Woodcraft Indians, became the first volunteer national chief scout. The U.S. Congress chartered the BSA in 1916. Membership grew rapidly to approximately 850,000 boys by 1930.

Legal Status and Governance

Although the BSA holds a congressional charter, the U.S. Supreme Court has affirmed that the BSA is a private organization that can restrict membership. The BSA has chosen to exclude atheists and homosexuals from both membership and volunteer positions. The exclusionary policy has been highly controversial.

Local community and religious organizations sponsor troops led by adult volunteers. The national executive board, made up of volunteers representing local councils, sets guidelines and approves materials and content of leader training and scouting programs. The executive board elects the chief executive who is responsible for operating the BSA. There are several thousand paid employees who administer the organization. Throughout the United States there are 300 local councils organized into twenty-eight areas in four regions.

Membership

Boy Scouts may be seven through twenty years of age. The initial programs, which are family and home based, are Tiger Cubs for first graders (seven years old), Cub Scouts for second through fifth graders (eight through ten years old), and Webelos Scouts for fourth and fifth graders preparing to be Boy Scouts. Boys in the initial programs attend meetings in dens comprising about eight to ten boys, and the dens are organized into packs. Boy Scouts, who are eleven through seventeen years old, are organized into patrols of five to eight boys who are part of larger troops. Varsity Scouts are fourteen through seventeen years of age. Venturer Scouts are boys or girls from fourteen through twenty years old. Approximately four percent of Boy Scouts earn the Eagle Scout rank, the highest advancement in Boy Scouting, which is obtained by accomplishing specific requirements and badges. In the year 2000 there were approximately one million active scout members and half a million adult volunteers in 52,582 troops.

Publications

The BSA publishes the magazines *Boys' Life* and *Scouting.* Handbooks are published for boys and leaders at each level of Boy Scouts. Pamphlets, training manuals, and guidebooks provide information for members, parents, and leaders.

Influence and Significance

Few independent external evaluations of the BSA are available. However, several small studies point to benefits of participation, such as a positive sense of self, leadership skills, work habits, and a sense of responsibility to the community through participating in the Boy Scouts.

BIBLIOGRAPHY

HOYT, KENNETH. 1978. *Exploring Division Boy Scouts of America, Girl Scouts of the U.S.A., and Career Education.* Rockville, MD: Educational Resource Information Center.

KLEINFELD, JUDITH, and SHINKWIN, ANNE. 1983. *Getting Prepared: Nonformal Education in Boy Scouts.* Rockville, MD: Educational Resource Information Center.

INTERNET RESOURCE

BOY SCOUTS OF AMERICA. 2002. <www.scouting.org>.

LEE SHUMOW

CAMP FIRE USA

Camp Fire USA is a national youth organization that offers leisure-time education and recreation programs to all girls and boys from preschool through twelfth grade. The aim of the organization is to assist girls and boys in preparing for adult life through gradually more complex experiences.

Program

Camp Fire USA's programs are designed to be youth-centered and fun but with serious learning goals, such as fostering tolerance, building friendships and relationships with adults, developing a sense of family and community, and providing service to others in need. Unlike many youth organizations, Camp Fire programs do not segregate boys and girls. All clubs and activities are coeducational. The four program levels of Camp Fire USA are: Starflight for boys and girls from kindergarten through second grade, Adventure for children in third through fifth grades, Discovery for children in sixth through eighth grades, and Horizon for boys and girls in ninth through twelfth grades. Each year some 200 Camp Fire members are named Wohelos, the organization's highest honor.

Most Camp Fire clubs include eight to twenty members who meet at least once a week after school, in the evenings, or on weekends. Each club is lead by one or more adult volunteers. At meetings members may play games, sing and dance, learn crafts, and explore nature. Camp Fire clubs also visit interesting and educational places and take camping trips. Older members engage in community-service activities, such as visiting homes for senior citizens, serving food at a homeless shelter, or tutoring younger children.

Camp Fire USA sponsors special self-reliance and community-service classes. These include I'm Safe and Sure, to teach children in kindergarten and first grade about home safety and family responsibility; Count on Me Kids, to teach children in kindergarten through second grade about alcohol and drug prevention; I Can Do It! to teach second and third graders about safety and nutrition; I'm Peer-Proof, to teach fourth through sixth graders how to build friendships and resist negative peer pressure; I'm Taking Care, to teach fifth and sixth graders how to care for younger children; and A Gift of Giving, to teach kindergarten through sixth-grade children to identify community needs and get involved in worthwhile community-service projects.

Camp Fire clubs are actively involved in teen leadership development. Every two years Camp Fire USA organizes a Youth Leadership Forum, during which hundreds of Horizon members gather to discuss issues of importance to society. In 2001 the forum addressed violence and how to combat it. Camp Fire teenagers also spend time exploring career possibilities.

Organization

Camp Fire programs are carried out by 120 Camp Fire USA councils serving over 650,000 boys and girls annually in forty states and the District of Columbia. Each council oversees the work of numerous local clubs. Camp Fire USA has a national executive director and policymaking body called the National Council. Representatives from the regional councils serve on the National Council.

Membership

Camp Fire USA accepts members without regard to race, gender, socioeconomic status, disability, sexual orientation, or religious affiliation. Most boys and girls who participate in Camp Fire programs are between the ages of five and eighteen. They are guided by adult volunteers and are sponsored by individuals and by civic, religious, fraternal, educational, and other organizations. Financial support is derived from membership in the United Way, private and corporate donations, the sale of official merchandise, program fees, and membership dues. The organization also raises funds though its annual fundraiser, the Camp Fire candy sale.

History

Camp Fire Girls was founded in 1910 by Luther Gulick, a medical doctor, and his wife, Charlotte. It was the first nonsectarian organization for girls in the United States. The organization began including boys in 1975 and changed its name to Camp Fire Boys and Girls to emphasize the coeducational nature of the programs. The organization changed its name to Camp Fire, Inc., in 1984. By 2001 boys accounted for 46 percent of Camp Fire membership.

In 1999 the organization adopted a new mission statement: "Camp Fire builds caring, confidant youth, and future leaders." In 2001 the organization changed its name to Camp Fire USA and launched a major image-awareness campaign, which included television, radio, and magazine spots designed to educate the public about the value and mission of Camp Fire programs.

BIBLIOGRAPHY

ALLEN, MARTHA; BUCKLER, HELEN; FIEDLER, MARY; and SCHAUMBURG, RON, eds. 1980. *Wo-He-Lo: The Camp Fire History.* Kansas City, MO: Camp Fire, Inc.

INTERNET RESOURCE

CAMP FIRE USA. 2002. <www.campfireusa.org>.

ROSEMARY KORNFELD
Revised by
JUDITH J. CULLIGAN

DISTRIBUTIVE EDUCATION CLUBS OF AMERICA

Distributive Education Clubs of America (DECA) is a youth organization for American and Canadian high school and college students interested in business, marketing, management, and entrepreneurship. The major goals of the organization are to prepare students for careers in business and market-

ing; to develop the leadership abilities, self-confidence, and citizenship of DECA members; to engender an understanding of the free enterprise system; and to foster in its members a healthy competitive spirit, high standards of business ethics, and proper social and business etiquette. DECA works in cooperation with high school and college marketing and business education programs.

Program

DECA programs are designed to create interest in all phases of marketing management and distribution study and to provide avenues of expression for individual talent. DECA programs offer members the chance to learn about marketing and international business, become involved in commerce, and develop leadership, competitive, and interpersonal skills. Chapter programs, which are always classroom centered, usually include the cooperation of the local business community; most national programs are run in partnership with national and international corporations. Such partnerships offer DECA members the chance for practical application of the skills and concepts they learned in the classroom. In addition DECA's partnerships with business afford members the opportunity to meet professional businesspeople, giving budding young entrepreneurs and marketers a head start in forming the networks of associates they will need for a successful career in business. Operation Holiday Help, for example, is a popular DECA program through which students who want to work during the holiday season are offered opportunities for on-the-job training and an introduction to local businesses.

DECA sponsors a variety of leadership development and competitive events programs, including the Creative Marketing Project, the E-Commerce Business Plan Event, the Free Enterprise Event, and the Civic Consciousness Project. DECA also sponsors numerous creative marketing projects, through which members study and survey the economic development of their communities. Many local, state, and international businesses employ DECA members because of their interest in and related study of that particular business. DECA contributes to the employability of its members by encouraging and conducting competitive activities in such areas as advertising, sales, job interviews, public speaking, public relations, online advertising design, marketing studies, and management decision-making.

DECA sponsors numerous marketing-related meetings, seminars, workshops, and conferences. State and regional DECA Leadership Conferences are held every fall, leading up to the annual International Career Development Conference. A popular Apparel and Accessories International Marketing and Finance Mini-Conference is held every year in New York City. An annual Sports and Entertainment Marketing Conference focuses on such activities as advertising, promotions, and niche groups. DECA's State Officer Leadership Institute, held each summer in Washington, D.C., teaches DECA state officers how to successfully fulfill their responsibilities.

DECA encourages high school students to stay in school and continue their education at postsecondary institutions by offering scholarships and awards to exceptional and needy DECA members. DECA presents more than $125,000 each year to winners in competitive events and awards more than $250,000 annually in scholarships. DECA's most important recognition program is the National Marketing Education Honor Award, given to outstanding high-school-senior business students and DECA leaders.

The association's national publications include *DECA Dimensions,* the official membership magazine featuring business and association news, as well as articles about job skills, leadership, and citizenship; the bimonthly *Advisor,* which offers instructional materials and tips to teachers of business and marketing; the annual *DECA Guide,* which contains guidelines concerning DECA's competitive events programs; and the *DECA Images Catalog,* which features DECA products and curriculum materials.

Organization

Local chapters are usually organized within a high school as part of the school's business and marketing program, with the business and marketing teacher-coordinator serving as chapter adviser. All chapters within a state belong to a state association under the leadership of the state DECA adviser. Each state association elects its own student advisers. Student delegates elected by each state in turn elect their own national leaders.

The national organization, composed of state associations, has a national executive director and a board of directors made up of state supervisors of distributive education and an appointed representative of the U.S. Department of Education.

The national DECA organization includes a Collegiate Division of DECA, which was formed in 1970. DECA is also affiliated with Delta Epsilon Chi, an international organization for college students preparing for careers in business, marketing, and management.

Membership

Any high school or college student with an interest in business, marketing, and entrepreneurship is eligible to become a DECA member. In 2001 there were over 180,000 DECA student members and faculty advisers in secondary and postsecondary schools in all fifty states, U.S. territories, and Canada.

INTERNET RESOURCE

DISTRIBUTIVE EDUCATION CLUBS OF AMERICA. 2002. <www.deca.org>.

HARRY A. APPLEGATE
Revised by
JUDITH J. CULLIGAN

FOUR-H PROGRAMS

Four-H is a youth organization dedicated to fostering better family living, community progress, social understanding, and civic responsibility. It sponsors projects in agriculture, homemaking, personal improvement, community service, and good citizenship.

Program

The earliest 4-H programs were tightly focused on agriculture and other rural concerns. Since then, however, the 4-H has evolved into a nationwide organization operating under the auspices of the U.S. Department of Agriculture (USDA), Cooperative Extension Service. It has chapters in urban and suburban as well as rural counties and has redefined its mission from improving agricultural production to developing the character and skills of young people in a variety of different ways.

Four-H activities are administered through the county extension agencies in the states, and students may join through their schools. The program offers meetings, camps, workshops, and social activities, but the core of the program is the 4-H project. Members are expected to tackle projects from one or more of eight categories: citizenship and civic education, communications and the expressive arts, consumer and family sciences, environmental education and earth science, healthy lifestyle education, personal development and leadership, plants and animals, and science and technology. Projects are designed to allow the participant to "learn by doing," in accordance with the 4-H slogan.

Organization and Support

Approximately 6.8 million young people are members of 4-H clubs nationwide. Leadership is provided by the USDA, and the program is administered through county extension agents. Council groups at the state, district, and county level provide planning and guidance. Individual clubs are led by adult volunteers, many of whom were themselves 4-H club members during their youth. Meetings are usually held in the home of the club leader, in community centers, or in schools. The local clubs draft their own programs, in accordance with the general organizational standards set by the USDA.

There are no dues for membership in the 4-H. The bulk of the program's funding comes from the government, but civic groups, local businesses, and other organizations often donate to 4-H groups at the local level. In addition, local clubs may hold fund-raising activities for a particular project.

Membership

Any boy or girl age nine to nineteen is welcome to join the 4-H, regardless of race or creed. Interested young persons can join a club through their school or by contacting the county extension office in their area. There are no dues. The early clubs allocated projects according to the gender attitudes of their time, assigning boys to farm and livestock projects and girls to domestic skills, such as canning, baking, and sewing. Today, however, this has changed: all projects are open to any member, with no distinction made between boys and girls.

History

At the start of the twentieth century, rural America was still the cornerstone of the nation's economy, but times were clearly changing. Young people were moving to the cities, while older people were holding tenaciously to outmoded farming techniques, so that many of the family farms were in danger of failing. In the Midwest, local civic leaders and educators responded to these problems by looking for ways to make agriculture attractive to young people, while also making improved farming techniques more available to established farmers. Out of this original grassroots movement, the 4-H clubs were born.

The early clubs were based on the idea that education, especially agricultural education, was best accomplished through hands-on experience. This principle has remained a core concept in 4-H. Much of the organization's early success came from the effective use of members as demonstrators of new farming technology. For example, to spread the word about improved seed corn strains, contests were held in which the young person who achieved the best crop would win a prize. Project-based contests were, and continue to be, held at a countywide level, and they have widened to include competitions in such diverse activities as livestock breeding, conservation, and personal development.

By 1914 4-H had become a truly national movement, and the Smith-Lever Act, passed by Congress in that year, forged a formal link between the local clubs and the County Extension Service of the USDA. With the passage of this act, the local groups became eligible for federal funds. To help foster a national identity, the leadership of the movement adopted an official emblem, a three-leaf clover with a capital H on each leaf, denoting *Head, Heart,* and *Hands* to express the organization's emphasis on personal development through action. The fourth H was added soon after; at first it stood for *Hustle* but was quickly changed to *Health*. The 4-H philosophy is summed up in the official pledge:

I pledge . . .

My Head to clearer thinking,

My Heart to greater loyalty,

My Hands to larger service,

and my Health to better living

For my club, my community, my country, and my world.

INTERNET RESOURCE

U.S. Department of Agriculture. 2002. <http://national4-hheadquarters.gov>.

Frances C. Dickson

Revised by

Nancy E. Gratton

FUTURE BUSINESS LEADERS OF AMERICA–PHI BETA LAMBDA

Future Business Leaders of America–Phi Beta Lambda (FBLA-PBL) is a nonprofit 501 (c)(3) educational association of students preparing for careers in business and business-related fields. The association has four divisions: FBLA for high school students; FBLA Middle Level for junior high, middle school and intermediate school students; PBL for postsecondary students; and the Professional Alumni Division for business people, educators, and parents who support the goals of the association.

FBLA-PBL is headquartered in Reston, Virginia, and organized on local, state, and national levels. Business teachers/advisers and advisory councils (including school officials, business people, and community representatives) guide local chapters, while state advisers and committee members coordinate chapter activities for the national organization. FBLA-PBL, Inc. is funded by membership dues, conference fees, corporate contributions, and grants.

Dr. Hamden L. Forkner, head of the Commercial Education Department of the Teachers College of Columbia University, developed the FBLA concept in 1937. In the fall of 1940, the National Council for Business Education accepted official sponsorship of FBLA, and on February 3, 1942, the first high school chapter was chartered in Johnson City, Tennessee. In 1958 the first Phi Beta Lambda chapter was chartered in Iowa. The Professional Division (originally the Alumni Division) began in 1979; as of 2001 the latest group to join FBLA (in 1994) was the FBLA Middle Level, for students in grades five through nine.

The board of directors is comprised of local and state educators, business leaders, and the membership division presidents. The board sets policy and employs a president/CEO, who directs a national staff program and association programs. The association's national center is an 11,600 square foot building, which was completed in 1991. The 1.6-acre site it occupies was purchased through a grant from the Conrad Hilton Foundation.

Membership

Total membership, including students and advisers, approaches a quarter million members. The high school level has more than 215,000 members, while Phi Beta Lambda (postsecondary level) reaches over 10,000 college students. The newest group, FBLA Middle Level, is showing remarkable growth with 8,000 student members, and is also developing member interest for the high school level.

Conferences, Seminars, and Publications

Each year the best and brightest of FBLA and PBL convene at the National Leadership Conference to compete in leadership events, share their successes, and learn new ideas about shaping their career future. These four-day sessions are considered the pinnacle of the FBLA-PBL experience, especially for those running for national office.

FBLA-PBL also sponsors conferences and seminars for members and advisers, which are designed to enhance experience initially developed on the local and state level. The Institute for Leaders is a four-day seminar focused on leadership experience for state and local chapter officers, members, and advisers. Participants build lifetime leadership and career skills in tracks focusing on entrepreneurship, communication, and FBLA-PBL leadership. The institute is held in conjunction with the National Leadership Conference. Each fall, new leaders and advisers from chapters across the nation gather for National Fall Leadership Conferences, which are regional conferences designed to guide and motivate their success for the year. This includes workshops, seminars, and a plenary session, as well as the benefit of networking among their peers.

FBLA-PBL publications bring fresh ideas, new directions, and network building news to members and advisers. They are published three times each year (except *Tomorrow's Business Leader*, which is produced quarterly). *Tomorrow's Business Leader* is circulated to FBLA and FBLA Middle Level students; *Adviser Hotline* to high school teachers; *Middle Level Advisers' Hotline* to Middle Level teachers; and *PBL Business Leader* to PBL members and advisers. The Professional Division receives *The Professional Edge*. A new electronic publication, *PBL E-line* is distributed to PBL advisers by e-mail three times per year, with additional publication as needed.

FBLA-PBL is officially endorsed by the American Management Association, the Association for Career and Technical Education, the Career College Association, the March of Dimes, the National Association of Parliamentarians, the National Association of Secondary School Principals, the National Business Education Association, the National Management Association, and the U.S. Department of Education.

BETTY PENZNER

FUTURE SCIENTISTS AND ENGINEERS OF AMERICA

Future Scientists and Engineers of America (FSEA) is a national nonprofit organization of elementary, middle, and secondary school science clubs. The FSEA aims to identify, motivate, and inspire young girls and boys who have the potential to become scientists, engineers, and science teachers and give them the opportunity to experience science and technology through challenging, interesting, and fun science projects.

Program

FSEA clubs are organized to give students an opportunity to meet and benefit from sharing scientific interests and abilities. Each club is a scientific community in miniature and is free to develop a program most suited to the interests and needs of its members. FSEA projects are designed to stimulate interest in mathematics, science, engineering, and technology and to train students in techniques of innovation and creativity, problem solving, and trial and error to achieve a stated objective. Most projects are hands-on and team oriented; projects can take anywhere from several hours to an entire semester to complete. Club members can design their own projects or they can use an FSEA-designed project. The national FSEA office provides materials and directions for almost fifty projects for different age levels.

Some projects are simple, such as the Model Airplane, where teams of two students learn about aerodynamics by building and testing a rubber-band-powered model airplane; and the Marble Slide, by which students experiment with potential and kinetic energy by rolling marbles down different types of inclines. Other projects are more advanced, including the Earthquake Tower, where teams of two students learn about drafting and engineering by designing and building a thirty-inch wooden tower that can withstand a simulated earthquake; and the Land Yacht, where teams build a vehicle that will move as far and fast as possible in the wind produced by a fan.

The national FSEA office conducts workshops for science teachers, parents, and sponsors who want to organize a science club in their local school or want training in how to help students successfully complete advanced FSEA projects. The FSEA also issues an extensive list of volunteer science and technology experts who can answer questions and help students complete difficult projects.

Organization

FSEA clubs are organized in elementary, middle, and high schools that have agreed to sponsor the club as a sanctioned school activity. As such the school provides a room for club meetings and for storage of materials, as well as a teacher to lead the club. Clubs usually consists of about twenty-five members and can include students from several grade levels. Elementary school clubs start in the fourth grade. Most FSEA clubs also include parent advisers and volunteer mentors. Ideally, mentors will be professional or retired engineers or scientists, or college students majoring in the sciences. Local clubs are organized into regions, headed by a volunteer regional director. The FSEA national headquarters has a small staff that helps new clubs get started, provides training for advisers and mentors, designs new science projects, and ships project materials and manuals to local clubs.

Membership

FSEA membership is open to all boys and girls from the fourth through twelfth grade who are interested in science and technology. Membership dues are $5 per year, with the parents, school, or private sponsors contributing an additional $60 per student each year to pay for program materials. That fee covers costs for up to five projects for each student each year. Many clubs organize fund-raisers, such as bake sales or car washes, to help pay program fees.

History

The FSEA was founded in 1989 by George Westrom, a rocket scientist and science educator. In 2001 there were FSEA clubs in hundreds of schools across the United States.

INTERNET RESOURCE

FUTURE SCIENTISTS AND ENGINEERS OF AMERICA. 2002. <www.fsea.org>.

DOROTHY K. CULBERT
Revised by
JUDITH J. CULLIGAN

GIRL SCOUTS OF THE USA

The Girl Scouts of the USA (GSUSA) describes itself as an "informal educational organization dedicated solely to girls." GSUSA seeks to help girls to develop character and skills, which will help them to succeed throughout their lives. The GSUSA program, promise, and law are all designed to promote the four main goals of the organization. First, GSUSA strives to help girls to develop their full potential. Girls gain competencies through participating in activities and are expected to develop positive self-esteem as a result. Second, GSUSA fosters the development of social skills, including understanding and respect for one another and for individual differences. Third, GSUSA aims to promote sound decision-making skills and the ability to enact decisions based on values, ethics, ideals, and convictions. Fourth, GSUSA encourages Girl Scouts to use their talents and work cooperatively with others to improve their communities and society.

The Girl Scout programs involve participation in a variety of activities. Individual girls and troops choose activities based on the interests and needs of members. Activities are focused in the following areas: (1) arts; (2) environment; (3) global awareness; (4) health and fitness; (5) literacy; (6) mentoring; and (7) science and technology. Badges are earned to recognize skills and knowledge that girls have gained through participation in a set of activities. Girl Scout camps are available throughout the country, and girls are encouraged to attend the camps in order to develop skills and accomplish goals in the camp setting.

History

Juliette Low founded the Girl Scouts of America (GSA) in 1912 to expose girls to outdoor experiences and to involve them in community service. Initially she modeled the Girl Scouts on the British Girl Guides. The first group of eighteen Girl Scouts met in Savannah, Georgia. GSA was incorporated as a national organization in 1915 and grew and diversified rapidly to a membership of 137,000 girls by 1926. Since its inception, Girl Scouts has sought to be inclusive. African Americans, Native Americans, and girls with disabilities were members as early as the 1920s. Girl Scouts changed programs and activities to meet the needs of girls and to adapt to historical circumstances throughout the twentieth century. The GSUSA was reincorporated under a congressional charter in 1950.

Legal Status and Governance

GSUSA is a nonprofit organization governed by the National Board of Directors. The national president provides leadership for the National Board. A national executive director leads the national staff. Most (99%) of the 915,000 adults who work for the Girls Scouts are volunteers. There are approximately 300 local Girl Scout councils throughout the United States. Girls join local troops of which there are 233,000. The local troops are led by volunteer leaders who receive training through their local councils.

Membership

Girl Scouts are organized into small groups that meet with leaders who have been trained to facilitate the programs. Girls between the ages of five and seventeen may join Girl Scouts at any time. Girls join at the appropriate age level and are not required to have been a member at previous levels. Levels include Daisies (five years old or kindergartners), Brownies (six and seven years old), Juniors (eight through eleven years old), Cadettes (eleven through fourteen years old), and Senior Girl Scouts (fourteen through seventeen years old).

Publications

GSUSA publishes numerous books, reports, and pamphlets. Books for use by leaders and scouts are available. The Research Institute of GSUSA sponsors and publishes research on the needs and development of girls.

Influence and Significance

The GSUSA conducted an extensive evaluation in 1997. Girls, their parents, and adult volunteers reported that scouting had made positive contributions to their development. In another study, Louis Harris and Associates interviewed a sample of women listed in *Who's Who of American Women* and found that 64 percent had participated in Girl Scouts compared with 42 percent of a random sample of adult women in the United States. Respondents identified contributions that belonging to Girl Scouts had made to their development.

INTERNET RESOURCE

GIRL SCOUTS OF THE USA. 2002. <www.girlscouts.org>.

LEE SHUMOW

HOSTELLING INTERNATIONAL– AMERICAN YOUTH HOSTELS

Hostelling International–American Youth Hostels (HI–AYH) is a nonprofit organization that emphasizes the values of simple and inexpensive travel and offers reasonable overnight accommodations in the United States, Canada, Mexico, and parts of Asia, Africa, Europe, and South America. The major educational aims of HI–AYH are to help people of all ages gain greater understanding of the world and other people through outdoor activity and educational travel and to develop fit, self-reliant, and well-informed citizens.

Program

HI–AYA offers inexpensive accommodations to travelers from around the world. Hostels may be located in urban high-rises with hundreds of beds or in small rural houses with fewer than twenty beds. Some hostels are located in preserved historic buildings. Most hostels have cafeterias or self-service kitchens; many also offer recreational facilities, meeting rooms, swimming pools, laundry facilities, libraries, and bicycle rental services. In 2001 overnight hostel rates ranged from $8 in rural areas to $24 in large cities such as New York City and San Francisco, California.

When travelers stay at HI–AYH hostels, the organization offers them the chance to meet and interact with other travelers and with people from the community where the hostel is located. HI–AYH programs help broaden a traveler's understanding of an American or foreign community by providing a rich intercultural experience. Programs are offered to groups and individuals and are variously designed for children, teenagers, adults, and senior citizens. At many hostels special activities and programs are designed for people with disabilities and for disadvantaged youths.

Each summer HI–AYH plans and sponsors numerous hostelling trips through the United States, Canada, Mexico, Europe, Israel, Japan, the Caribbean, and other areas. The trips, which are priced low enough to offer planned travel to people with limited financial means, range from one week to eight weeks. Hostelling International also offers educational and cultural tours in cities where hostels are located. Tours are conducted by local volunteer guides, who share inside information about their cities and neighborhoods, describe local history and customs, and offer tips about the most interesting places to visit and the best places to find good affordable meals.

The organization's Teach-In Program provides hostel guests and local school children and community members the opportunity to learn about one another's countries, customs, languages, and societies. The Cultural Kitchen program offers teenagers the chance to meet and talk with travelers from around the world. Participants stay overnight at a hostel and work in the hostel's kitchen to prepare and share an evening meal. Travelers to New England can participate in the Passport to Adventure Program, which focuses on geography, diversity awareness, and environmental education. The Discover Your World Program in southern California teaches interpersonal skills and intercultural understanding to economically and educationally disadvantaged youths from the Los Angeles area. Participants stay overnight at a Los Angeles hostel, meet with international travelers, and visit local museums and historical sites.

HI–AYH issues periodic *Hostelling International Guides* to sites around the world. The organization also publishes numerous newsletters, brochures, and bulletins to help people plan their trips. In addition, HI–AYH offers online travel resource centers, which are continually updated and include links, maps, advice about transportation and attractions, visa and customs laws, and other information.

Organization

HI–AYH operates a network of 125 hostels throughout the United States. The national organization comprises thirty-four associate councils, which function as local offices and provide visitors with special programs, events, and activities. Several HI–AYH council offices operate Travel Centers, where members can purchase train and bus passes, airline tickets, tickets to local attractions, backpacks, sleeping bags, and other travel necessities.

HI–AYH is headed by an executive director and a national board made up of representatives from the thirty-four associate councils. HI–AYH is affiliated with the International Youth Hostel Federation (IYHF), a network with nearly 4,500 hostels in more than 70 countries.

Membership

Membership in HI–AYH is open to people of all ages. A member must purchase a hostel pass, which is valid for use in all hostels throughout the world. Membership is free for people under 18 years of age. Adults pay from $15 to $25 annually, depending on their age. People can also purchase lifetime memberships for $250. The organization's operating income comes from program and memberships fees, accommodation payments, private contributions, sales of publications, and partnerships with businesses involved in the travel industry.

History

The youth hostel idea was first conceived in 1909 in Germany by an elementary school teacher Richard Schirrman. Eleven national associations were represented at the first International Youth Hostel Conference, which was held in Amsterdam in 1932. In the United States, AYH was founded in 1934 by two school teachers, Monroe and Isabel Smith, who started the first American hostel in Northfield, Massachusetts. From its beginning, AYH has been a completely integrated movement. Hostels have been established on farms and in schools, camps, lodges, students' houses, and community centers; they are open to people of any age, nationality, income level, or religious affiliation. The first American urban hostel was opened in May 1965 in Philadelphia, Pennsylvania, at Fairmont Park, when the city turned over the famous colonial Chamounix mansion to a local group for use as a metropolitan youth hostel.

INTERNET RESOURCE

HOSTELLING INTERNATIONAL–AMERICAN YOUTH HOSTELS. 2002. <www.hiayh.org>.

SAM SHAYON
Revised by
JUDITH J. CULLIGAN

NATIONAL FORENSIC LEAGUE

The National Forensic League (NFL) is a nonpartisan, nonprofit educational honor society founded in 1925 by Bruno E. Jacob at Ripon College, Wisconsin. Its purpose is to encourage and motivate high school students to participate in and become proficient in the speech arts: debate, public speaking, and oral interpretation of literature.

Since its founding, NFL has enrolled more than 1 million members in all fifty states, U.S. posses-sions, and several foreign countries. At the start of the twenty-first century more than 2,600 high schools, 93,000 high school students, and 3,500 high school teachers were active members.

Any public or private high school is eligible to become affiliated with NFL upon payment of dues and with the permission of the school's principal. High school students enrolled in an NFL member school who rank scholastically in the top two-thirds of their class and who have earned twenty-five NFL points may apply for NFL membership by paying a onetime fee. Students earn points by participating in interscholastic speech and debate contests, student congresses, or community speaking. NFL encourages improvement of student speech skills by awarding NFL points and granting degrees based upon points earned. These degrees are: Degree of Merit (25 points), Honor (75 points), Excellence (150 points), Distinction (250 points), Special Distinction (500 points), Superior Distinction (750 points), and Outstanding Distinction (1,000 points).

The NFL believes that contests are one of the most effective educational devices. The National Speech Tournament has been held continuously since 1931 (except during World War II). Contests are held in the following areas:

- policy debate
- value debate
- legislative debate
- U.S. topic extemporaneous speaking
- foreign topic extemporaneous speaking
- original oratory
- interpretation of dramatic literature
- interpretation of humorous literature
- duo interpretation
- commentary
- impromptu speaking
- prose reading
- poetry reading
- expository speaking
- storytelling

More than $100,000 in college scholarships is awarded to the winning students at each national tournament. Qualification for the national finals is earned by placement in one of the 103 district tournaments, conducted in all parts of the nation.

A nine-member executive council governs the league. Four councilors, who are active high school coaches and teachers, are elected every two years by the membership. Each elected councilor serves a four-year term. The ninth councilor is a high school administrator, who is elected every two years by the other councilors. The NFL president and vice president must be councilors and are elected by the council every two years.

The National Student Congress, first established in 1938, has met continuously since 1952. Students are elected from 103 district congresses to serve in the national congress. Student legislators author bills and resolutions, learn to use parliamentary procedure, conduct hearings and committee meetings, engage in floor debate, and vote on proposed legislation. During congress week, eighteen preliminary chambers elect members to eight semifinal chambers, which in turn name twenty-four senators and twenty-four representatives to a final congress. A scholarship is awarded to the superior legislator in each house of the final congress.

The NFL publishes its monthly magazine, *Rostrum,* during the school year, which features news of the league, educational articles to improve student skills, and teaching materials for coaches. The National Forensic Library contains more than fifty videos of the nation's finest high school and college speech educators, each teaching their specialty. These tapes are free to member schools.

NFL was founded with the motto: "Training Youth for Leadership." NFL alumni are found in the business community, the professions, academic institutions, government, communications, and the arts. Prominent NFL alumni include President Lyndon B. Johnson, Vice President Hubert H. Humphrey, many senators and representatives, Supreme Court justice Stephen Breyer, the scholar Lawrence Tribe, college presidents David Boren and John Sexton, television personality Oprah Winfrey, and CSPAN founder Brian Lamb.

JAMES M. COPELAND

NATIONAL FUTURE FARMERS OF AMERICA ORGANIZATION

Future Farmers of America (FFA), officially called the National FFA Organization, is an educational organization for high school and college students who are interested in agriculture. The National FFA Organization works in conjunction with the National FFA Foundation, a not-for-profit organization that seeks partnerships with corporations, foundations, and government agencies to help provide funding for FFA programs. The FFA's main objective is to develop in its members qualities of leadership, character, scholarship, cooperation, and citizenship through agricultural education. The FFA is an integral part of many high school agriculture programs. The organization operates in cooperation with the Office of Vocational and Adult Education in the U.S. Department of Education, as well as with state and local boards for vocational and agricultural education.

Program

The FFA offers a variety of programs designed to supplement schoolwork by encouraging the practical application of classroom instruction in agricultural science. Many FFA programs also offer information and incentives for students wishing to pursue a career in agriculture. Local FFA chapters sponsor educational tours, agriculture workshops, and on-the-job training. Local chapters also organize recreational activities and hold their own award ceremonies and fund-raisers. The National FFA Organization helps local chapters by supplying program guidance and materials, by offering scholarships and awards, and by sponsoring an annual FFA week, an annual national convention, and agriscience fairs with activities at the local, state, and national level. In addition, the national organization sponsors numerous conferences and workshops covering many agriculture-related topics, and publishes a quarterly student magazine called *New Horizons,* a monthly member newsletter called *Update,* and *Making A Difference,* a bimonthly magazine for FFA chapter advisers.

The FFA's many programs include the New Century Farmer Program, which helps young people become aware of new opportunities in twenty-first century agriculture. New Century farmers are sent on traveling seminars to meet with and learn from innovative professional farmers and agriculture educators around the country. FFA Global Programs send members to foreign countries where they can learn the value, traditions, and role of agriculture in other cultures.

Because the majority of FFA members hope to pursue careers related to agriculture, the FFA sponsors numerous career development events at the chapter, state, and national level. These events help members explore the hundreds of career options available in the modern agriculture industry, from agronomy to food technology, forestry, floriculture, agricultural communications, and environmental and natural resources management. The FFA also provides information, incentives, and financial aid to members who wish to become college and high school teachers of agriculture.

Another career development program, Supervised Agricultural Experience (SAE), offers members an opportunity for hands-on application of the agricultural skills and principles they learned in the classroom. A student involved in SAE may be placed in an agriculture-related job or may start his or her own agriculture-related business under the guidance of an adult mentor.

In 1984 the National FFA Collegiate Scholarship program was established to counter a trend toward rising costs and declining enrollment in agricultural colleges. Each year, the National FFA Organization awards more than $1 million in scholarships to hundreds of FFA members. Many FFA scholarships are sponsored by local businesses and national corporations.

Among the numerous awards offered by FFA are the H. O. Sargent Award, which recognizes FFA members who have actively supported cultural diversity in agriculture. The award is named in honor of H. O. Sargent (1875–1936), an agricultural educator who worked to establish an organization similar to FFA for African-American students.

The National FFA Organization also presents three annual Honorary American FFA degrees for exceptional adult teachers and other individuals who have demonstrated support for agricultural education. The annual VIP awards and distinguished service citations are given to individuals, agencies, and organizations that have made a continued contribution to agricultural education over a long period of time.

FFA star medals are awarded to outstanding FFA members of differing age and grade levels. Star Discovery medals for seventh and eighth graders and Star Greenhand medals for exceptional first-year members are awarded at the chapter level. Star Farmer, Star Agribusiness, and Star Agriscience medals are given to outstanding members involved in SAE programs; these awards are given at the chapter, state, and national level. State-level star awards include a $200 prize. National-level star awards include prizes of $1,000 to $2,000.

Organization

Local FFA chapters are usually organized at a high school, with the school's agriculture and science teachers serving as chapter advisers. All chapters within a state belong to the state FFA association, which is headed by an adviser and executive secretary.

The National FFA Organization is governed by a board of directors and a board of student officers. The elected officers of the adult board include a president, four vice presidents representing different regions in the United States, and a secretary. The board of directors also includes several members of the Office of Vocational and Adult Education in the U.S. Department of Education. Student officers are elected each year by the national convention delegates. State associations and local chapters elect their own officers annually.

The National FFA Foundation is administered by a board of trustees representing the businesses, industries, organizations, and individuals who have agreed to sponsor FFA activities. The foundation board also includes representatives from state FFA associations, vocational agriculture teachers, and members of the Vocational and Adult Education Division of the U.S. Department of Education.

Membership

Any boy or girl aged twelve to twenty-one who is enrolled in an agriculture course or program is eligible to become a member of FFA. The FFA also includes honorary and alumni members.

History

The FFA was organized in 1928 and was chartered by the U.S. Congress in 1950. In 1965 a similar organization for African-Americans called the New Farmers of America merged with the FFA. Women were accepted as national FFA members for the first time in 1969, although some chapters had accepted women members much earlier. In 1988 the organization changed its name from Future Farmers of America to the National FFA Organization. In 2001 the FFA had approximately 457,000 active members in more than 7,300 urban, suburban, and rural high school chapters located in all fifty states, the Virgin Islands, Puerto Rico, and Guam.

INTERNET RESOURCE

NATIONAL FFA ORGANIZATION. 2002. <www.ffa.org>.

A. DANIEL REUWEE
Revised by
JUDITH J. CULLIGAN

QUILL AND SCROLL

The Quill and Scroll Society is a high school honor society devoted to fostering interest and excellence in the field of journalism. It has member chapters in all fifty states and in forty-four countries around the world, serving more than 14,000 students.

Program

Quill and Scroll fulfills its mission in a variety of ways. It administers the Edward J. Neil Memorial Scholarships, granted annually to ten seniors who have demonstrated excellence in high school journalism, and the Lester G. Benz Memorial Scholarship, granted to a high school journalism faculty or yearbook adviser who desires to further his or her education with journalism courses at the college level.

The organization also sponsors contests, open to high school student members. The International Writing, Photo Contest awards a prize to the winning student submissions in eight categories of journalism, including editorial writing, feature writing, and photojournalism. The Yearbook Excellence Contest awards a prize to the participating high school that is judged to have produced the best yearbook.

Quill and Scroll also offers a news media evaluation service to participating high schools, in which the school's newspaper and other media are given a detailed critique along with suggestions for improvement. In addition, the society publishes *Quill and Scroll* magazine, which features articles on the journalism profession.

Seeking to advance the cause of good journalism to as broad a public as possible, Quill and Scroll also awards prizes to nonmember schools and individuals who have, in the opinion of the national committee, made singularly important contributions to the profession.

Organization

Quill and Scroll is governed by a board of trustees, the Quill and Scroll Corporation. The board is re-sponsible for administrating the affairs of the national society. The Quill and Scroll Foundation administers the scholarship program and conducts research in high school journalism.

Local chapters operate autonomously, when it comes to planning local activities, under the leadership of a faculty adviser drawn from the journalism or English department. Participation in most of the nationally sponsored contests and activities requires an application form filed with the society's headquarters.

Membership

High schools must apply for a charter from the national organization before they can open an official chapter of Quill and Scroll. Individual membership can only be achieved through a local school chapter. Faculty members of a chartered school who teach journalism courses or who advise the school newspaper or yearbook automatically become society members. Prospective student members must be in their junior year, must be in the upper 30 percent of their class, and must work on one or more of the school's publications. In addition they must secure the recommendation of their publication's faculty adviser. Applications for membership must be approved by the secretary-treasurer of the national society.

Members do not pay dues but are obligated to pay an initiation fee. On initiation, the new member receives a gold badge bearing the society insignia and is issued a membership card. In addition he or she receives a year's subscription to *Quill and Scroll* magazine.

History

The Quill and Scroll Society was founded in 1926 by a group of educators at the University of Iowa, led by George H. Gallup, best known for his groundbreaking work in public polling (the Gallup Poll). At the time of its inception, the Quill and Scroll was intended to foster interest and excellence in the field of journalism. From these beginnings in Iowa, the Quill and Scroll Society has spread to schools throughout the country and overseas.

INTERNET RESOURCE

QUILL AND SCROLL SOCIETY. 2002. <www.uiowa.edu/~quill-sc>.

LESTER G. BENZ
Revised by
NANCY E. GRATTON

SKILLSUSA–VICA

SkillsUSA–VICA is a national organization serving high school and college students (and their instructors) who are preparing for careers in technical, skilled, and service occupations, including health occupations. SkillsUSA–VICA has 250,000 members annually, organized into nearly 13,000 chapters and fifty-four state and territorial associations.

SkillsUSA–VICA was founded in 1965 as the Vocational Industrial Clubs of America (VICA). It is a nonprofit educational organization, incorporated in the District of Columbia. The association changed its name to SkillsUSA–VICA on July 4, 1999. It is governed by a board of directors elected from the corporation's members.

SkillsUSA–VICA, Inc. members of the corporation are not to be confused with the student and instructor members of the organization known as SkillsUSA–VICA. Corporate members are those persons designated by the state boards of vocational education to be responsible for trade and industrial education, technical education, and health occupations education in each state, territory, or possession of the United States where secondary and/or postsecondary state associations have been chartered by the corporation.

Five corporate members, one from each SkillsUSA–VICA region, are elected to serve staggered three-year terms as the board of directors. The board, in turn, elects its own officers. In addition to the corporate members elected to the board, there are four ex-officio members: the vice president of the Trade and Industrial Division of the Association for Career and Technical Education; the chair of the State Association Directors Association; the chair of the Youth Development Foundation of SkillsUSA–VICA (the fundraising arm of the organization); and the chair-elect of the Youth Development Foundation. In addition, the bylaws allow a total of four business and/or organized labor representatives on the board and a representative from the National Association of State Directors of Vocational Technical Education Consortium (NASDVTEc).

The board of directors is responsible for directing and managing the affairs, funds, and property of the corporation. The board sets policies in accordance with its certificate of incorporation, its bylaws, and the laws of the District of Columbia. The board administers the national student organization, which is composed of the chartered state associations; hires an executive director; and oversees the operation of the organization. In all national matters, state associations are subordinate to the board of directors.

An effectively-run SkillsUSA–VICA chapter prepares America's high-performance workers in public career and technical programs. It provides quality education experiences for students in leadership, teamwork, citizenship, and character development, and it builds and reinforces self-confidence, positive work attitudes, and communications skills. It emphasizes total quality at work, including high ethical standards, superior work skills, lifelong education, and pride in the dignity of work. SkillsUSA–VICA also promotes understanding of the free enterprise system and involvement in community service.

More than 13,000 teachers and school administrators serve as professional SkillsUSA–VICA members and instructors. More than 1,000 business, industry, and labor sponsors actively support SkillsUSA–VICA at the national level through financial aid, in-kind contributions, and involvement of their people in SkillsUSA–VICA activities. Many more work directly with state associations and local chapters.

SkillsUSA–VICA programs include local, state, and national competitions in which students demonstrate occupational and leadership skills. At the annual national-level SkillsUSA Championships, more than 4,000 students compete in seventy-two occupational and leadership skill areas, and each year new areas are added. SkillsUSA–VICA programs also help to establish industry standards for job-skill training in the lab and classroom.

SkillsUSA–VICA's Total Quality Curriculum program emphasizes the competencies and essential basic workplace skills identified by employers and the U.S. Secretary of Labor's Commission on Achieving Necessary Skills (SCANS) and in subsequent national voluntary skill standards. The Professional Development Program guides students through eighty-four employability skills lessons. These include goal setting, career planning, and community service.

Publications of the organization include *Sharp,* a newsletter for the postsecondary and secondary student members; the *Professional,* a newsletter for teachers and administrator members of the organization; and *Partners in Quality,* a newsletter specifically for the organization's business and industry partners and supporters.

INTERNET RESOURCE

SKILLSUSA–VICA. 2002. <http://skillsusa.org>.

THOMAS W. HOLDSWORTH
JANE A. DESHONG JONES

YOUNG MEN'S CHRISTIAN ASSOCIATION

The Young Men's Christian Association, often called the YMCA or simply the Y, is an international membership organization concerned with the physical, educational, social, and religious needs of young men, women, and boys. The YMCA stresses the Christian code of conduct, ecumenism, and community responsibility, but the organization is open to people of all religious faiths.

Program

The major programs of the YMCA are conducted through classes and club activities. Program offerings vary from city to city, depending on local needs. Most YMCAs offer a variety of programs addressing adult education (including technical and vocational courses), athletics (especially swimming), health and fitness, child care, community development, arts and humanities, family support, and teen leadership. Club activities for children and teenagers include Hi-Y, Youth and Government, Model United Nations, Black Achievers and Minority Achievers, and the Earth Service Corps. These groups emphasize the development of individual initiatives and leadership qualities. In YMCA urban action efforts throughout the United States, members have undertaken projects for the needy. As one of the six founding organizations of the United Service Organizations (USO), the YMCA also provides welfare, recreational, and religious programs for members of the American armed forces.

YMCA buildings have gymnasiums, swimming pools, and rooms for classes and club activities; many YMCAs also have residence facilities. In addition, the YMCA operates summer-camp and day-camp programs and facilities around the country.

Organization

Each local YMCA is an autonomous corporation with its own board of directors and staff and is responsible to its community and the distinctive needs of the people who live there. Each YMCA is also a part of the national organization as a member-affiliate of the National Council of YMCAs, the legislative and policymaking national body. The National Council in turn is a member of the World Alliance, the YMCA international body.

Membership

Membership in the YMCA is open to all men, women, and children, regardless of religious affiliation, race, age, ability, or income. In 2000 approximately 970 corporate YMCAs operated almost 1,500 branches, units, and camps in the United States; the organization served over 17 million Americans, making the YMCA one of the country's largest not-for-profit community-service organizations. Financial support for local associations is derived from program fees, membership dues, community chests, foundation grants, charitable contributions, sustaining memberships, and corporate sponsors. YMCAs have also been established in more than 120 countries around the world, providing service to over 30 million people.

History

The YMCA was founded in 1844 in London by George Williams, a clerk in a dry-goods firm. The first meeting room was located in a coffeehouse. The American YMCA was established in 1851 in Boston by Thomas V. Sullivan, a retired sea captain. The following year YMCAs were formed in New York City and Buffalo, New York; Worcester and Springfield, Massachusetts; Portsmouth and Concord, New Hampshire; New London and Hartford, Connecticut; Detroit, Michigan; Baltimore, Maryland; Washington, D.C.; and New Orleans, Louisiana. By 1860 there were more than 200 YMCAs with more than 25,000 members in the United States.

Most early YMCAs were open only to men, although a few accepted women members, often unofficially. Some YMCAs were established to serve particular ethnic or immigrant groups. The first YMCA for African Americans was established in Washington, D.C., in 1853 by Anthony Bowen, a freed slave. Beginning in 1875, YMCAs were founded in San Francisco, California, to serve the city's large Chinese population. Thomas Wakeman, a Dakota Sioux, started the first YMCA for Native Americans in 1879 in Flandreau, South Dakota.

Early YMCA leaders were concerned with addressing the difficulties and temptations facing young men arriving in the cities, far from the stabilizing influence of home and family, during the American Civil War and the Industrial Revolution. In the United States revival meetings were the outstanding programs offered, and the associations sent out the first street workers to preach on street corners and around the wharves. They also sent out "gospel wagons" to distribute Christian tracts and Bibles and give sermons in city neighborhoods.

Delegates from fifteen associations met in New York City in 1861 and formed the United States Christian Commission, the first volunteer agency for spiritual and physical aid to American armed forces. During World War I the American YMCA provided religious services, recreational materials, entertainment programs, and canteens in home ports, on the front lines, and in cities overseas.

During World War II, the YMCA, as part of its United Service Organization affiliation, worked with the armed services throughout the world. In the postwar years the international associations undertook service to displaced persons by providing athletics programs, summer schools, entertainment, and children's camps. The YMCA also helped with the repatriation and resettlement of refugees from Europe.

By the end of the war most YMCAs were accepting women and girls as members and had began establishing centers in suburbs and outside of major urban areas. During the 1960s and 1970s, urban unrest in America and a lack of funding caused a decline in YMCA membership and many YMCAs reduced program offerings or closed entirely. The organization managed to rebuild in the 1980s and 1990s by seeking new sources of funding, by renovating many older YMCA buildings and constructing new ones, and by changing its focus to include intensive community outreach, job training, drug abuse prevention, mentoring programs, youth development and leadership training, family support and services, and aid for senior citizens. In 2001 the YMCA celebrated its first 150 years in America.

BIBLIOGRAPHY

HINDING, ANDREA. 1988. *Proud Heritage: A History in Pictures of the YMCA in the United States.* Chicago: National Council of the YMCA of the USA.

MACLEOD, DAVID I. 1983. *Building Character in the American Boy: The Boy Scouts, the YMCA, and Their Forerunners, 1870–1920.* Madison: University of Wisconsin Press.

MJAGKIJ, NINA. 1994. *Light in the Darkness: African Americans and the YMCA, 1852–1946.* Lexington: University of Kentucky Press.

MJAGKIJ, NINA, and SPRATT, MARGARET, eds. 1997. *Men and Women Adrift: The YMCA and the YWCA in the City.* New York: New York University Press.

INTERNET RESOURCE

YOUNG MEN'S CHRISTIAN ASSOCIATION. 2002. <www.ymca.com>.

JOE A. PISARRO
Revised by
JUDITH J. CULLIGAN

YOUNG MEN'S HEBREW ASSOCIATION AND YOUNG WOMEN'S HEBREW ASSOCIATION

The Young Men's Hebrew Association and the Young Women's Hebrew Association (YM–YWHA or often simply "Y") are part of an organization called the Jewish Community Centers Association of North America (JCCA). Jewish community centers are established by residents of a city with a large Jewish population to provide leisure and educational activities for their members. The aim is to strengthen Jewish family life, foster Jewish living in a democratic society, and provide shared experiences for all age groups.

Program

Center programs are multifaceted, flexible, professionally directed, and designed to meet the needs of the community where the center is located. Program activities stimulate personality development, leadership, participation in community affairs, and each member's sense of his or her Jewish identity. Extensive programs for health and physical education, camping, and outdoor recreation afford the opportunity for acquiring new skills and developing friendships. Many Jewish community centers also offer courses in music, arts and crafts, dance, drama, literature, and Jewish studies, in addition to lectures, concerts, art exhibits, theatrical performances, poetry and fiction readings, and cultural festivals.

The JCCA provides to local centers a variety of program materials dealing with all aspects of community center work, and it organizes and conducts regional and national conferences, institutes, seminars, competitions, and intercenter activities. The JCCA also recruits, orients, and places staff in Jewish community centers and oversees scholarship programs for their continued training.

Jewish community centers throughout the United States and Canada offer day care and early childhood educational services for Jewish children ages three to six. Jewish community centers also offer programs for Jewish senior citizens, permitting elderly men and women the chance to socialize, become involved with their community, and stay mentally and physically fit.

The JCCA and YM–YWHA chapters also offer Jewish athletes a chance to train and compete at local, national, and international sporting events through their sponsorships of Macabbi USA and Macabbi Canada. Every year approximately 6,000 young Jewish athletes compete at JCCA Macabbi Games. The best athletes compete at the World Macabbi Games, a two-week international competition held every four years in Israel. In 2001 Macabbi USA sent 360 athletes representing thirty-nine states to Israel to compete in the world games.

The JCCA and YM–YWHA work in cooperation with twenty-two resident camps throughout the United States and one in Ontario, Canada. Most camps offer day, short-term, and long-term camping programs where young people can learn swimming, canoeing, horseback riding, archery, and other outdoor activities. Many camp programs also include cultural and creative activities, such as jewelry making, wood sculpting, pottery, dance, and theater. Some resident camps organize family camping events. In addition, many local Jewish community centers run their own day-camp programs.

Through the Jewish Welfare Board Chaplain's Council, the JCCA serves the religious and social needs of Jewish military personnel and their families. Regional consultants and national United Service Organizations (USO) staff provide services to stateside USO clubs and councils and to small, isolated Jewish communities serving Jews in nearby military installations.

Organization and Membership

The JCCA includes 275 affiliated community centers in thirty-nine states, the District of Columbia, and ten Canadian cities. The JCCA is also affiliated with a Jewish community center in Hong Kong. Together, the JCCA-affiliated centers have a membership of more than 1 million people. Most centers and Ys make membership available to anyone in the community, regardless of religious affiliation. Financial support is derived from membership dues, course and programs fees, fund-raisers, corporate sponsorship, and foundation and private donations.

History

The first Young Men's Hebrew Association (YMHA) was founded in 1854 in Baltimore, Maryland, to provide services and support for Jewish immigrants. By 1884 approximately seventy such agencies had been organized. They served as libraries, settlement houses, cultural centers, and helped new Jewish immigrants adapt to life in America by offering instruction in the English language and the American way of life. In 1913 the National Council of Young Men's Hebrew and Kindred Associations (YMH&KA) was formed to unite the disparate YMHAs into a national association. The national Jewish Welfare Board (JWB) was founded in 1917 to meet the religious needs and improve the morale of Jewish men in the armed forces. In 1921 the YMH&KA merged with the JWB, making the JWB the national association for Jewish community centers and YM–YWHAs. During the 1950s and 1960s many Jewish-Americans moved to the suburbs, and new community centers were established to serve the needs of this more affluent community. The centers began to expand their services to include day camps, travel camps, performing arts, day-care centers, sports programs, adult education, and services for senior citizens.

During the 1970s and 1980s, pride in Israel flourished in the American Jewish community, and many young people became interested in their Jewish roots. In response, Jewish community centers began to sponsor cultural events related to Jewish heritage and history, including Jewish film festivals and celebrations for Hanukkah, Israeli Independence Day, and other Jewish holidays. Many Jewish community centers also organized trips to Israel. The Jewish Welfare Board changed its name to the Jewish Community Centers Association of North America in 1995.

BIBLIOGRAPHY

KAUFMAN, DAVID. 1998. *Shul with a Pool: The "Synagogue-Center" in American Jewish History.* Waltham, MA: Brandeis University Press.

RABINOWITZ, BENJAMIN. 1948. *The Young Men's Hebrew Associations, 1854–1913.* New York: National Jewish Welfare Board.

INTERNET RESOURCE

JEWISH COMMUNITY CENTERS ASSOCIATION OF NORTH AMERICA. 2002. <www.jcca.org>.

BERNARD POSTAL
Revised by
JUDITH J. CULLIGAN

YOUNG WOMEN'S CHRISTIAN ASSOCIATION

The Young Women's Christian Association (YWCA) is a membership organization with a local, national, and international program aimed at helping all women and girls achieve their full potential in a society where justice and peace prevail. The YWCA stresses improving the quality of education with special emphasis on preparing girls to perform their multiple roles in society, providing opportunities for girls and women to continue their education, supplementing the academic work of high school and college students with involvement in community affairs, exploring the problems and needs of women and students in urban settings, and motivating dropouts to return to school or prepare for gainful employment. The YWCA is also actively involved in promoting nonviolence and tolerance throughout the United States and the world.

Program

The YWCA of the U.S.A. offers numerous education programs designed to meet the needs of the community where the YWCA is located. Literacy, tutoring, English as a second language (ESL), and General Education Development (GED) classes are popular in many areas. Many YWCAs also offer welfare-to-work programs to help unemployed women learn to support themselves. YWCA's job training, job placement, and career counseling services enable thousands of women who are out of work to improve their employability and find meaningful jobs. The organization helps working mothers by offering quality child-care services. In 2001 more than 750,000 children participated in YWCA day-care and after-school programs, making the YWCA the largest nonprofit child-care provider in the United States.

Approximately 200 of America's YWCAs provide housing services for women and children; services include emergency shelter, transient housing, and transitional housing. The YWCA will also help needy women find permanent housing.

The YWCA's teen development programs include the YWCA/PepsiCo Girls Leadership Program for economically and educationally disadvantaged teenage girls. In 1997 the YWCA launched its Tech-GYRLS program, in which girls ages nine to thirteen can explore computers and other new technologies under the guidance of technology professionals.

The organization's health care and fitness initiatives include sports and exercise programs, breast and cervical cancer screenings and referrals, breast cancer support groups, and courses on sexually transmitted diseases, prenatal care, self-defense, and substance abuse prevention. Further programs and services address crisis intervention, violence prevention, and family counseling. Many YWCAs also offer a program called Adolescent Pregnancy Prevention Evaluation for teenage girls.

In its ongoing effort to combat violence, the YWCA of the U.S.A. annually designates the third week in October as Week Without Violence. This observance promotes awareness and alternatives to domestic violence, gun violence, ethnic violence, hate crimes, and violence in the media. In addition, since 1992 the YWCA of the U.S.A. has recognized April 30 as National Day of Commitment to Eliminate Racism.

Organization

The World YWCA provides a channel for the sharing of resources and the exchange of experience among its affiliated associations in 100 countries, including the United States. The World YWCA also works for international understanding, for improved social and economic conditions, and for basic human rights for all people. In times of emergency, the World YWCA undertakes and sponsors international humanitarian, welfare, and relief work, irrespective of religious, social, political, national, or racial differences. The World YWCA includes in its membership all women and girls who wish to participate.

The YWCA of the U.S.A. is composed of three types of member associations: community YWCAs, registered and accredited state and regional YWCAs, and student YWCAs. In 2001 there were 312 YWCA affiliates across all fifty states. Each local association governs itself and adopts a constitution in keeping with the requirements of affiliation with the national organization and the needs of the community it serves.

The YWCA of the U.S.A. is headed by a president and a chief executive officer. A twenty-five-member national board of directors works with the president and CEO. The national board unites the autonomous member associations into an effective organization for furthering the YWCA mission. The board also plans the annual YWCA convention for the development of a national program and acts as a link between local YWCAs and the World YWCA. The board is assisted in its work by one national student council representative. Through its placement services and training programs, the national YWCA helps secure professional staffs for the local affiliates.

Membership

Membership in the YWCA is open to any girl or woman twelve years of age or older from any economic, racial, occupational, religious, or cultural group. College women may join a campus-based student YWCA. Membership privileges are transferable from one YWCA facility to any other in the country. All dues-paying members seventeen years or older have voting privileges. Boys and men may become YWCA associates and take part in coeducational activities, especially in recreation, education, discussion, and community projects. In 2001 there were approximately 2 million members in the YWCA of the U.S.A. The World YWCA served over 25 million women worldwide.

Local YWCAs derive most of their financial support from the United Way, membership dues, and program fees. The national organization derives its funding from the local YWCAs, earnings on investments, and gifts from individuals, foundations, and corporations.

History

The organization that became known as the Young Women's Christian Association began as a movement that gradually organized into a full-fledged association. The North London Home for women, also called the General Female Training Institute,

founded in London, England, in 1855, is generally recognized as the first YWCA. London's Prayer Union for Women and Girls was organized around the same time. By 1859 these two organizations had merged under the name of Young Women's Christian Association. In 1858 a similar organization called the Ladies' Christian Association was founded in New York City. In 1866 a women's group in Boston, Massachusetts, began using the name Young Women's Christian Association. Such organizations proved popular in the United States, and soon YWCAs were established in other communities around the country. By 1875 there were twenty-eight YWCAs in the United States. The first YWCA branch for African-American women was opened in Dayton, Ohio, in 1889. The following year, the first YWCA for Native American women was established in Chilocco, Oklahoma. By 1900 there were 106 American YWCAs. Realizing the need for centralized administration, the local associations formed the National Board of the YWCA in 1907.

Since the early 1900s the YWCA has pioneered the fight against racial discrimination and segregation in the United States. The first interracial conference in the South was held at a YWCA facility in Louisville, Kentucky, in 1915. In 1936 the first coeducational interracial collegiate seminar was held at a YWCA in Raleigh, North Carolina. During World War II the YWCA gave aid and comfort to Japanese-American residents being held in relocation centers, and the YWCA helped resettled Japanese women and families after the war. In 1946 the YWCA adopted a groundbreaking interracial charter to protest racial injustice. In 1960 the cafeteria of the Atlanta YWCA became the first desegregated public dining establishment in the city.

The YWCA was also a pioneer in offering sex education in its health programs as early as 1906; the organization continues this effort by offering educational programs and services addressing such issues as sexual harassment, sexually transmitted diseases, acquaintance rape, adolescent pregnancy prevention, and birth control.

BIBLIOGRAPHY

BOYD, NANCY. 1986. *Emissaries: The Overseas Work of the American YWCA 1895–1970.* New York: Women's Press.

MJAGKIJ, NINA, and SPRATT, MARGARET, eds. 1997. *Men and Women Adrift: The YMCA and the*

YWCA in the City. New York: New York University Press.

Seymour-Jones, Carole. 1994. *Journey of Faith: The History of the World YWCA 1945–1994.* London: Allison and Busby.

INTERNET RESOURCE

Young Women's Christian Association. 2002. <www.ywca.org>.

Edith M. Lerrigo
Revised by
Judith J. Culligan

Z

ZACHARIAS, JERROLD
(1905–1986)

Experimental physicist at the Massachusetts Institute of Technology, Jerrold R. Zacharias directed the Physical Sciences Study Committee curriculum development project and other science education reform efforts. Born in Jacksonville, Florida, Zacharias earned his A.B. in 1926, A.M. in 1927, and Ph.D. in 1933, all in physics, from Columbia University. He held a teaching position at Hunter College in New York City until 1940 when he was appointed as a staff member of the Radiation Lab at MIT. In 1946 he became a professor at MIT, and directed the Laboratory for Nuclear Science and Engineering there until 1956. Subsequently at MIT he held the ranks of institute professor and institute professor emeritus. He served on the President's Science Advisory Committee from 1952 to 1964. For his scientific, engineering, and educational work Zacharias received numerous honors, including election to the National Academy of Sciences and the American Academy of Arts and Sciences, the President's Certificate of Merit, and the National Science Teachers Association Citation for Distinguished Service to Science Education. Zacharias's educational projects are best understood as an extension of his earlier scientific and governmental work.

Career as a Physicist

As a member of Nobel Prize winner Isidore Isaac Rabi's laboratory at Columbia University during the 1930s, Zacharias participated in early molecular beam magnetic resonance experiments and in the successful measurement of magnetic and electric quadrupole movements of molecular nuclei. During World War II, he contributed to the development of radar defense systems at MIT and of nuclear weapons at Los Alamos. After the war, under his direction the MIT Laboratory for Nuclear Science and Engineering achieved several breakthroughs in atomic beam research, including the development of a cesium atomic beam clock. The commercial feasibility of the cesium atomic clock led to the definition in 1967 of the atomic second and the subsequent adoption of atomic time as a laboratory standard and as a frequency source in aircraft navigation systems.

From the late 1940s to the mid-1950s Zacharias directed important national defense studies, from which he recalled concerns he had heard from military sources about the advantage that the Soviets gained from superior education. In 1956 Zacharias conceived a project to create a series of instructional films to promote the teaching and learning of physics in pre-collegiate education. This idea soon grew into the curriculum development project for which he became known, the Physical Sciences Study Committee (PSSC).

Physical Sciences Study Committee

Zacharias's sharing of his idea with an associate who directed the fledgling National Science Foundation (NSF) led to a formal proposal of the plan and initial funding. For the project, Zacharias first recruited from within his circle of physicists and other scientists. The realization that the "problem" of science education reform required a solution grander than a film series, and the promise of NSF and other funding, made possible the expansion of the breadth of the project to include plans for developing four textbooks and a series of dozens of monographs, as well as the participation of scientists from around the United States. The PSSC held its first meeting in September 1956, and by the end of the following summer the first textbook was drafted. During the fall of 1957 eight schools were piloting materials.

Within a few months of the successful Soviet launch of *Sputnik I* on October 4, 1957, and *Sputnik II* on November 3 of the same year, the blame for the second place status of the United States in the space race fell squarely on the public schools. For PSSC, this meant a virtual guarantee of funding not only from NSF, but also from the Ford Foundation and the Alfred P. Sloan Foundation. During 1958 PSSC established a film studio, conducted an eight-week summer development workshop, and held five training institutes for teachers. During the 1958 though 1959 academic year, 250 schools piloted PSSC materials and a summer institute was held for teachers. Five hundred schools employed the materials in 1959–1960. In the fall of 1960 a finalized PSSC course was implemented in schools throughout the United States.

In September 1959 Zacharias participated in the Woods Hole Conference that defined the structure-of-the-discipline concept that dominated curriculum reform in the years ahead. The hallmark of these curricula was expressed by Harvard psychologist Jerome Bruner in a sentiment that Zacharias often reiterated: the intellectual work of a research scientist and of an elementary school pupil are essentially identical. Thus, students would best learn subject matter—and be better prepared potentially to contribute to the military and space races—by mastering the structure of academic disciplines as defined by research specialists. PSSC became a model for academic specialists in other disciplines as they developed and implemented specialized academic curricula across the land.

Zacharias's intent for PSSC was to foster a scientific mindset that embraced observation, evidence, and basis for belief, while exposing students to state-of-the-art scientific knowledge. In the development stage, PSSC materials benefited from feedback that emerged from piloting. When implemented in its final form, however, the PSSC course expected fidelity from teachers; PSSC and other NSF curriculum projects were designed as "teacher-proof" packages to assure that all students would learn then-current scientific knowledge. Participants in the NSF projects generally valorize those efforts as models of educational reform, while researchers point to the failure of the projects to conduct systematic evalua-

tions and of the movement to achieve its stated goals.

The Physical Sciences Study Committee was the most prominent but only the first of many education reform activities that Zacharias spearheaded under the auspices of Educational Services, Incorporated, a nonprofit organization that emerged from the PSSC project. During the 1960s, the Elementary Science Study developed science curricula and instructional materials for use in schools in the United States. During the late 1960s the African Primary Science Program and the African Mathematics Program developed teaching materials and conducted teacher training for African educational systems. At MIT Zacharias participated in efforts to improve undergraduate physics curricula and proposed reforms for medical education. During the 1970s he took on the issue of standardized testing, which he criticized for stifling student's independent thinking and curiosity in science. Zacharias referred to standardized tests as "the Gestapo of educational systems" (1973, p. 43). He continued, "Uniformity and rigidity require enforcement, so I have chosen a most denigrating title for the enforcement agency. Its hallmark is arbitrariness, secrecy, intolerance, and cruelty." Apparently, Zacharias never reconciled his dissatisfaction over the curricular homogeneity that standardized tests enforced with the top-down curriculum implementation model that characterized PSSC.

See also: SCIENCE EDUCATION; SCIENCE LEARNING, *subentries on* EXPLANATION AND ARGUMENTATION, KNOWLEDGE ORGANIZATION AND UNDERSTANDING, STANDARDS, TOOLS.

BIBIOGRAPHY

GOLDSTEIN, JACK S. 1992. *A Different Sort of Time: The Life of Jerrold R. Zacharias, Scientist, Engineer, Educator.* Cambridge, MA: MIT Press.

RAMSEY, NORMAN F. 1995. "Jerrold P. Zacharias, January 23, 1905–July 16, 1986." In *Biographical Memoirs 68,* ed. National Academy of Sciences of the United States of America. Washington, DC: National Academy Press, pp. 435–449.

TURNER, DAVID. 1984. "Reform and the Physics Curriculum in Britain and the United States." *Comparative Education Review* 28:444–453.

ZACHARIAS, JERROLD R. 1957. "Today's Science—Tomorrow's Promise." *Technology Review* 59:501–503, 550.

ZACHARIAS, JERROLD R., and WHITE, STEPHEN. 1964. "The Requirements for Major Curriculum Revision." In *New Curricula,* ed. Robert W. Heath. New York: Harper and Row.

ZACHARIAS, JERROLD R. 1975. "The Trouble with IQ Tests." *National Elementary School Principal* 54:23–29.

ZACHARIAS, JERROLD R. 1975. "Testing in the Schools: A Help or a Hindrance?" *Prospects* 5:33–43.

WILLIAM G. WRAGA

ZIRBES, LAURA (1884–1967)

Laura Zirbes was a leader in elementary education and reading instruction. A professor at the Ohio State University, Zirbes founded its elementary laboratory school and was a strong practitioner and promoter of the Progressive education philosophy.

Zirbes taught elementary school in Cleveland from 1903 to 1919, then worked at the experimental Lincoln School at Teachers College from 1920 until 1926. She received her doctoral degree from Columbia University in 1928. From 1928 until her retirement in 1954 she taught at Ohio State, then conducted workshops and summer sessions until 1964, sixty-one years of teaching in all.

During those sixty-one years Zirbes encountered most of the important issues affecting education in the United States throughout the twentieth century. In Cleveland she taught a class of fifty-six fourth graders, children of immigrants. At Columbia she listened to Edward L. Thorndike, John Dewey, and William Bagley discuss the value of testing, and heard Bagley debate with William Heard Kilpatrick about Kilpatrick's Project Method. She coauthored articles with William S. Gray but turned down his offer to help write the famous Scott-Foresman basal reading series because she disagreed with the philosophy of basal readers. Zirbes's dissertation made her one of the nation's experts on teaching children to read but she never considered herself a reading expert because she did not believe in isolating one subject from other subjects. She founded the laboratory school at the Ohio State University to study the best ways of teaching; the school continued, under her influence, for over thirty years.

The central issue in Zirbes's work was the question, "How do children learn?" She believed they learned best when their interest was high. That was not a unique observation; others such as Franklin Bobbitt argued that teachers should stimulate children's interest in the subject that the teacher planned to teach, while the teacher remained in complete control and dispensed the knowledge. But Zirbes took the child-centered approach that the teacher should find out the child's needs and interests, and then develop units of study around those needs and interests. Yet Zirbes supported the child-centered approach only if the teacher had a firm understanding of the skills and concepts she wanted the children to learn, and carefully guided her class in that direction. Zirbes was not a laissez-faire progressive who let students do what they pleased.

The next step in learning, according to Zirbes, was to provide good learning experiences that would enlarge children's understanding and their vocabulary. Zirbes believed that the *child,* not the teacher, would make the connections between the new experience and what he or she already knew, following the way it happens in real life, for young and old. When the teacher provided a well-designed experience it would happen the same way in school.

Once a colleague asked Zirbes, "How old must children be before you can teach them generalizations?" Zirbes replied, with wry humor, "Eighty, at least." Then she explained: "You do not teach generalizations. You teach *people* to generalize" (1959, p. 226).

Zirbes believed that several other elements contribute to learning. First, the lesson should be meaningful to the child, and second, learning should be intrinsically motivating. It is better to build on children's interests and to demonstrate that material is relevant to them than it is to force learning. What if, for example, a child is taught reading through *extrinsic* motivation—the child may indeed learn to read, but he may also learn an unintended second lesson: that he hates to read!

The final two key elements of learning, for Zirbes, were that the lesson should stimulate thinking and should be integrated with other subjects. Zirbes wanted students to make observations, to draw inferences, and to learn to think inductively, in science class and in other subjects too. Learning was science with a lowercase "s." Zirbes considered science part of life, part of learning in all subjects, and a way of thinking. She saw science as Dewey saw it: the exciting probing of the unknown in all fields.

Zirbes's teaching philosophy touched upon another great debate of her time, whether educators should teach the arts or focus more on science. In the 1920s Zirbes shared the belief of her times that scientific methods could and would lead to the improvement, indeed to the perfection, of education and of mankind. Though that hope was severely tested by the Depression, she continued to test her classroom practices scientifically throughout her career. At the same time, Zirbes valued the fine arts. She was an amateur painter and an avid art collector; she sang and played the organ. She insisted that a sound education should include art, music, and physical education, integrated with the other subjects. She valued both science and art as part of the vast world of knowledge to be explored and enjoyed.

A related debate was: Is teaching science or art? Zirbes saw that good teaching was both. Child development was a science, which all teachers must study and understand. Applying that knowledge in classrooms was an art. There should be no fixed rules about how to teach; no one method would apply to all situations. The science of child development showed that children learned in different ways and at different rates, but choosing the right teaching method was an art.

As Zirbes neared retirement, her developmentalist approach to education came under attack from critics like Arthur Bestor, who charged schools with neglecting their basic duty of teaching children to think through rigorous training in the academic subjects. Zirbes responded by asking, how do we teach children to be creative? How do we teach them to adjust in an age of expanding knowledge and unprecedented change? The answer came in her best book, *Spurs to Creative Teaching* (1959). She said teachers must become creative and realize that conditions in the classroom can either facilitate or block students from becoming creative. All students, not just the gifted, can benefit from an environment in which teachers are open to new possibilities and not argumentative about change. A teacher who just goes through the motions and is bound to his manual is little better than an organ-grinder "who makes his rounds, grinding out his ready-made tunes in sequence, over and over, without really making music or getting much out of it" (p. 41). The creative teacher, then, is not only more of a professional, but finds the profession more rewarding.

See also: CURRICULUM, SCHOOL; ELEMENTARY EDUCATION, *subentry on* HISTORY OF; LEARNING; PROGRESSIVE EDUCATION; READING, *subentry on* TEACHING OF.

BIBLIOGRAPHY

CAVANAUGH, MARY P. 1994. *A History of Holistic Literacy: Five Major Educators.* Westport, CN: Praeger.

MOORE, DAVID. 1986. "Laura Zirbes and Progressive Reading Instruction." *The Elementary School Journal* 86:663–671.

REID, TONY. 1991. "Laura Zirbes: Forerunner of Restructuring." *Childhood Education* 68:98–102.

REID, TONY. 1993. "Towards Creative Teaching: The Life and Career of Laura Zirbes, 1884–1967." Ph.D. diss, University of South Carolina. Abstract in *Dissertation Abstracts International* 51:05A.

ZIRBES, LAURA. Papers. ACEI Archives, University of Maryland.

ZIRBES, LAURA. 1928. *Comparative Studies of Current Practice in Reading; With Techniques for the Improvement of Teaching.* Contributions to Education, no. 316. New York: Bureau of Publications, Teachers College, Columbia University.

ZIRBES, LAURA. 1959. *Spurs to Creative Teaching.* New York: G. P. Putnam's.

ZIRBES, LAURA. 1961. *Guidelines to Developmental Teaching: A Booklet for Use in the Education of Elementary Teachers.* Columbus: Bureau of Educational Research and Service, Ohio State University.

TONY REID